The New York Times
Chronicle of American Life

The 1940s

Decade of Triumph and Trouble

ALSO BY CABELL PHILLIPS

Dateline: Washington (Ed.)
The Truman Presidency
From the Crash to the Blitz: 1929–1939

The New York Times
Chronicle of American Life

The 1940s

Decade of Triumph and Trouble

By Cabell Phillips

Macmillan Publishing Co., Inc.
New York
Collier Macmillan Publishers
London

Macmillan Publishing Co., Inc.
866 Third Avenue, New York, N.Y. 10022
Collier-Macmillan Canada Ltd.

First Printing 1975

Printed in the United States of America

Library of Congress Cataloging in Publication Data

Phillips, Cabell B   H
   The 1940s: decade of triumph and trouble.

   Includes bibliographical references.
   1. United States—History—1933-1945. 2. United
States—History—1945-1953. I. Title.
E806.P5   973.917   74-17466
ISBN 0-02-596100-4

*For Stephanie and Nicole
and Eliot—to whom all of this
will seem very ancient history indeed.*

Contents

Foreword

THE YEARS FROM 1940 TO 1950 embraced a decade of transition that will forever be marked in history. It was the period in which the United States was thrust from its isolationist moorings to assume the pivotal responsibilities of world leadership. It was the period in which vast new frontiers of science and technology were breached for the first time. It was a period in which ancient barriers of racial and social distinction began to crumble and the ordinary citizen began to gain a new sense of his status and individuality. And it was a period marked by radical innovations in the economic and political structure of this nation and many other nations as well. The catalyst of the transition was two wars occurring in close sequence, one hot the other cold. Together, they changed the face of the world.

This book is a selective chronicle of life in the United States during the decade of the forties. The narrative is set against the background of the two wars rather than embracing them in detail. For my concern is less with the events of military and diplomatic history than with the impact these events had on the way people lived and behaved.

In the introduction to the earlier volume in this series, *From the Crash to the Blitz: 1929–1939,* I described it as "a journalistic *reprise*" rather than formal social history, saying that scholars of great eminence had drawn the last scholarly deductions and conclusions from the subject already. "I have sought, rather," I added, "to describe the thirties in the round and to recreate the sense of involvement and propinquity that so many of that generation experienced in the midst of those stirring times."

And so it is with this book. My aim has been to set the important happenings of the forties in the context of contemporary human experience—to tell what it was like to be there at the time.

My principal source of information has been the files of *The New York Times,* which is incomparably the best extant record not only of the events which I wrote but also of the setting and relationships in which they occurred. I have drawn heavily also on such contemporaneous periodicals as *Time, Newsweek, The Saturday Evening Post, Harper's, The New Republic,* etc.; on many published histories, biographies and memoirs, and on government reports and documents almost without number. In many instances I have been greatly assisted by interviews with persons who were directly involved in the events recorded here. All of which has served to refine and amplify my own recollections and impressions, for as a Washington reporter during most of those years I had a fairly close-up seat from which to observe much of what went on.

The New York Times, with which I was associated for almost thirty years, has been a most generous and sympathetic sponsor in this enterprise. My gratitude is unstinted. My thanks go also to Bruce Carrick, of Macmillan, for his editorial judgment and patience, and to Ms. Trudy Steinfeld for her genius as copy editor on the final manuscript. As before, my wife Syble has supplied the protein, the vitamins, the tender-loving-care, and an occasional exasperated prod that has kept this operation operable.

CABELL PHILLIPS
Hilton Head Island, S.C.
July 1974

Acknowledgments

THE AUTHOR WISHES TO THANK the following individuals and organizations for their kind permission to reprint material in this book:

Howard G. Bruenn, M.D., and American College of Physicians for a selection from Dr. Bruenn's article, "Clinical Notes on the Illness and Death of President Franklin D. Roosevelt," which appeared on pages 579–591 of *Annals of Internal Medicine,* vol. 72, no. 4, 1970.

Simon & Schuster, Inc. for *Men and Atoms* by William L. Laurence, © 1946, 1959 by William L. Laurence.

Time, Inc. for two passages from *Memoirs* by Harry S. Truman, copyright © 1955 by Time, Inc. Reprinted by permission.

Harper & Row, Publishers, Inc., for a passage from Leslie R. Groves' *Now It Can Be Told,* published by Harper & Row, Inc.

Alfred A. Knopf, Inc., for a passage from *Hiroshima* by John Hersey. Copyright 1946 and renewed 1974 by John Hersey. Reprinted by permission.

The New York Times
Chronicle of American Life

The 1940s

Decade of Triumph and Trouble

1

The Way It Was

I

TAKE A LONG BACKWARD LOOK at your world of 1940. You may find it hard to believe some of the things you will see.

If you were past your teens and of even a moderately thoughtful turn of mind your greatest preoccupation was with the war which had just broken out in Europe. *Could* we, or *should* we, stay out of it? This dilemma haunted the American conscience that year like a national neurosis, a choice between alternatives that seemed equally freighted with danger and guilt.

For five years and more you had watched the blight of fascism expand in Germany and Italy until now it cast its ugly shadow across all of Central Europe, withering freedom and democratic institutions wherever it fell. In the summer of 1939 Nazi Germany had swallowed up Austria and Czechoslovakia in two swift, bloodless gulps. In September it had smashed Poland under a rain of fire and steel, unveiling to an incredulous world the overpowering technique of the blitzkrieg. Its unexpected partner in this venture was the Soviet Union which, until that moment, had been regarded as a counterforce to the spread of Fascist power.

France and Great Britain, the great bastions of democracy in Europe, flung furious words of challenge at the aggressors, but without effect. They had been weakened not only by years of economic depression but by a misreading of—among other things—the implications of the Nazi revolution in Germany. After the failure of diplomatic maneuver—"appeasement" was the popular word for it at the time—to save republican Czechoslovakia from extinction, they declared war on Germany in defense of Poland. But their help was too little and too late. Warsaw fell in less than a month—on September 27—and the Germans and the Russians divided up the spoils without let or hindrance from Poland's allies.

Now came the period of the "phony war"—the "sitzkrieg"—a winter hiatus extending over into 1940, in which the Nazi's Adolf Hitler plotted

3

his further strategy, in which Russia went off on its own to invade Finland (and to get embarrassingly trapped in the subarctic terrain), and in which Britain and France bent in panic to the task of rearming and building their defenses. This period of relative calm induced a desperate hope that Hitler had satisfied his appetite in the West and that any further covetousness would lead him eastward toward the Balkans and the Ukraine, the historic direction of German imperial ambitions.

But the calm was deceptive and the hopes it induced were fatuous. Early in April, with scarcely a premonitory feint, Nazi armor swept into Denmark and Norway, crushing their defenses like so many sand castles. A month later the triumphant Wehrmacht pointed south and west toward the Low Countries. "Soldiers of the Western Front," an ecstatic Fuehrer proclaimed in Berlin on the night of May 9, "the hour for you has now come. The fight beginning today decides the fate of the German nation for the next thousand years!"

To a world aghast this came not as a hollow boast. The mighty Nazi war machine with its clanking panzer columns devouring the landscape and clouds of warplanes spitting bombs and machine gun bullets from the skies seemed very nearly invincible. And now it was clear that Hitler's ambitions lay not to the east but to the west; that his goals were not merely geographical but political as well.

The Netherlands and Belgium were overwhelmed in three weeks. French and British troops had been rushed into the Flanders campaign but they were no match for the highly mechanized Wehrmacht and its vastly superior air cover. As the Nazi spearhead pressed on into France in mid-May, a major segment of the allied force, some 350,000 men, were isolated and pressed into a pocket on the Channel coast, subjected around the clock to murderous artillery and air attacks. On May 30 they began one of the most heroic and tragic maneuvers in military history: the evacuation from Dunkirk across the Channel to England.

Meanwhile, Nazi armor turned and raced toward Paris, outflanking the famed Maginot Line of static border defenses on which France rested its hopes of salvation. Invaders began pouring into the city on June 13 and two weeks later France had been knocked out of the war. Now it was up to Great Britain alone to face the tide of Nazi aggression. Winston Churchill, assuming the role of Prime Minister in mid-May, said he could offer to British people no panaceas other than "blood, toil, tears, and sweat." And these would be abundantly required of them as the Battle of Britain opened in August with massive, day-after-day air raids on British cities and shipping. At year's end the overall toll of 15 months of war was reckoned at four million dead, wounded, and missing and 3.5 million tons of shipping destroyed. Britain alone counted over 14,000 civilian dead and 20,000 wounded from three months of German air attacks. But the British were holding, however tenuously, and beginning to strike back. It was, said Churchill, "their finest hour."

That, in bare bones, was the state of the war in Europe as one perceived it in 1940. For most Americans it was a grim and frightening outlook. Brute force and tyranny rode triumphant across the world's stage (China was a theater of war, too, remember) and freedom was in ignominious retreat. The evidence confronted you daily in black newspaper headlines, in the somber broadcasts of on-the-scene radio reporters like Edward R. Murrow and William L. Shirer, in the chilling realism of the newsreels. Could Britain alone, with her fleet intact but woefully wanting in air power and weaponry of every sort, stand up indefinitely against the Fascist tide? Many people in that anxious year doubted it. And the corollary of their despair was the realization that if Britain did fall America would stand isolated in a hostile, totalitarian world. Maybe, some said, this was the inexorable swing of history's pendulum and the epoch of democratic freedom was over.

Could we, or *should* we, stand free of such a conflict? The question had moral connotations, true, but for most people it was essentially pragmatic. Where did our national interest, our best chance for survival, lie? Was it in resolute, inflexible neutrality that depended on the historic impregnability of our ocean barriers on the simple preposterousness of the idea that any nation would dare attack us? Or did it lie in forestalling the enemy before he could strike, in joining forces with Britain to destroy fascism before it destroyed democracy?

That was the great, the overriding dilemma of 1940 and it split the country down the middle.

II

The country was predominantly isolationist as 1940 began, reflecting a cynical reappraisal of the motives and stratagems that had led us into the First World War, and disillusionment over its political consequences. For a decade there had grown up a hardening attitude toward Europe's endemic power struggles, its chronic inability to put its house in order, which was sharpened by resentment over the failure of most of those nations to repay their war debts. Many Americans, moreover, had started out in life with an ingrained suspicion of most foreigners, Europeans especially—of their morals, their ideologies, their "stuck-up ways"—and a belief that they were ready to outsmart us at every turn. For all such reasons (and many more) there was a popular consensus in the land, that, at all costs, we should avoid involvement in the quarrels and intrigues of other nations. We had burned our fingers once, trying to pull

Europe's chestnuts out of the fire: Never again. Furthermore, the United States was big enough, strong enough, and smart enough to go its own way and could best stay out of trouble by strictly minding its own business.

This conviction deepened as war clouds piled higher on Europe's horizon during the late thirties. The old slogan, "No Foreign Entanglements," gave way to a passionate insistence upon "No Foreign Wars." As late as September 1939, when the first hammer blows of Nazi aggression were being struck on the Polish frontier, a Roper public opinion poll showed that 67 percent of Americans favored staying out of the war under any circumstances and treating both sides impartially in the matter of selling supplies and munitions. The remainder favored varying degrees of assistance "short of war" for the Allies alone, with only 2.5 percent advocating immediate military intervention in their behalf. (The polls showed an even more pronounced aversion to involvement in the war in Asia, where Japan was overrunning China. In this conflict, remote both ethnically and geographically, the Chinese had our sympathy and best wishes, but little else.)

In its varied guises, isolationism was a political doctrine as well as a cult, and it profoundly influenced the course of national affairs. On the one hand, most of the liberal community and the clergy embraced it because it comported with their pacifist convictions. It had the support of many prominent political leaders, such as Senators Arthur H. Vandenberg of Michigan, William E. Borah of Idaho, Hiram W. Johnson of California, and Burton K. Wheeler of Montana, as well as scores of outstanding businessmen, college presidents, editors, and writers. Colonel Charles A. Lindbergh, the reigning folk hero of the day, shed his traditional aloofness to make speeches warning of the futility of trying to oppose the onward rush of nazism, which he seemed to hold in high regard as the wave of the future. "We have to face the fact," he said in a nationwide broadcast in mid-June, "that before we could take effective action [in behalf of Britain and France] the German armies may have brought all Europe under their control. In that case Europe will be dominated by the strongest military nation the world has even known, controlling a population far larger than our own."

On the other hand, isolationism was an inviting platform for the expounders of more shortsighted and demagogic appeals. It was used to fan the flames of bigotry and chauvinism that flourish naturally at the American grassroots, and as a club to belabor President Franklin D. Roosevelt and his "liberal-internationalist" New Deal. Father Charles E. Coughlin, the Detroit "radio priest"; the Reverend Gerald L. K. Smith, heir to the late Huey Long's "Share the Wealth" crusade; and similar popular spellbinders of the day drew tens of thousands to their public rallies and numbered their radio audiences in the tens of millions as they harangued against the "evil, hidden forces" attempting to "drag America into war." The powerful Hearst and McCormick-Patterson newspaper combines, among others, thundered in a similar vein almost daily in their news and editorial columns. And farther out on the fringe of respectability there rose the clamor of such patently subversive groups as the Christian Front, the Silver Shirts, the German-American Bund, and others like them to whom isolationism was a shield to be used for an eventual Fascist take-over in America.

The preponderance of isolationist sentiment, in Congress and throughout the country generally, forced an uneasy ambivalence on the Roosevelt Administration as it faced the worsening realities of the world crisis. Roosevelt was no hot-eyed warmonger, as some of his enemies attempted to depict him. He hoped as desperately as they that the United States could avoid being sucked into the war. But he foresaw with a great deal more clarity than they, first, what the consequences to this country would be of an unchecked Nazi victory in Europe, and second, that our best, long-run hope of survival lay not in blind neutrality-at-all-costs but in doing everything within our power to avert the catastrophe of Hitler's subjugation of Britain.

There were limits on what it was within our power to do. The Neutrality Act of 1935, with its subsequent extensions and amendments, put a severe halter on the President's options. Its most pertinent prohibition in 1940 was that it forbade the shipment in American bottoms of war material to any belligerent in a declared war. They could be had on a cash and carry basis only. Another prohibition (under different legislation) forbade credits to any nation in default of its debts from the First World War. These prohibitions were meaningless to the Germans, since they had no merchant shipping to speak of that could penetrate the British blockade. Moreover, they had abundant sources in Europe. For the British, however, these barriers foreshadowed slow strangulation. Her production and raw material resources were limited, her merchant fleet was suffering a fearful toll from Nazi submarines and bombers, and her supply of gold—the only currency for cash and carry—was diminishing fast. Typical of the impediments imposed by law was the fact that during the early months of the year, airplanes which she was buying in the United States as fast as they could be turned out were flown from the factories to the little town of Houlton in the far northeast corner of Maine, and there dragged by mules or trucks across the border into Canada, and then flown by Royal Air Force pilots to Halifax for transshipment to the war zone.

Roosevelt's hand was also being stayed during these months by the realities of domestic politics. Nineteen-forty was an election year and marked the end of his second term. While he resolutely refused right up

7

to the time of the Democratic national convention to say whether he planned to run for a third term, he had to protect his party and its ultimate candidate against charges of "interventionism" and "warmonger-ing," the two favorite epithets of the more radical isolationists. There was no question, moreover, that the overwhelming majority of the American people did want to stay out of the war, and as a politician and a leader he had to respect that sentiment. But by early summer—coincident with the downfall of Belgium and France—the public's adamancy on that issue began to soften: They were coming around to the belief that we should give the British all the help we could "short of war"—food, munitions, weapons—even at some risk of involvement in the fighting. This trend was documented in a series of Gallup polls during the year. While those favoring an immediate and outright declaration of war against Germany never scored as high as 10 percent, those favoring "all help short of war" for Britain went from 36 percent in May to 60 percent in December. The American people were coming to realize that, like it or not, they had a big stake in the outcome of Europe's war.

Roosevelt, as President and as candidate (he did, of course, opt for a third term), played adroitly upon this shifting public sentiment, pushing as far as he dared in the direction of intervention yet holding back from any overt act or promise. It seems probable that from the time Hitler launched his spring offensive against Denmark and Norway Roosevelt foresaw the inevitability of this country's ultimate involvement as a belli-gerent. But he was determined to put off the evil day as long as he could—for humanitarian reasons no less than political ones. If he moved impulsively he ran the grave risk of alienating his political support, in Congress (already shaky enough) as well as in public opinion.

By the autumn of 1940, while an historic political campaign at home offered but feeble diversion from news about the Battle of Britain, the line separating measures that were short of war from those that were acts of war grew taut and narrow. But Candidate Roosevelt (like his Republican opponent Wendell Willkie) felt obliged to reassure American fathers and mothers as he traveled across the hustings: "I have said this before, and I will say it again and again: Your boys will not be sent to fight in any foreign war."

Isolationism did not die in 1940 but it lost a great deal of its emo-tional and political punch. As the year ended, the national consensus had shifted from intransigent neutralism to an elastic nonbelligerence which, for all its mutation still focused on the hope that somehow peace could be maintained. But that hope was diminished as the rampant Japanese aligned themselves with the Berlin-Rome Axis, as the Soviet Union con-summated its conquest of Finland and the Baltic States, as Italy turned covetously toward Egypt and Greece, as Nazi warplanes rained death and destruction unremittingly on London and other English cities. The question, *could* we, or *should* we, stay out of the European conflict continued at year's end to be the great American dilemma.

III

Concern with the war did not, however, monopolize the whole spectrum of one's life in 1940. There were other things to worry about, wonder about, complain about, to enjoy, to covet, and to eschew.

The grinding experience of economic depression and social upheaval which marked the decade of the thirties still dominated the life attitudes of most citizens. The sting of poverty, either as reality or as threat, would never be erased from their minds. Their faith in many of the verities with which they had grown up—in the rewards of thrift, in the incorruptibility of laissez-faire capitalism, in the wisdom and virtue of Great Men—had been badly shaken, and new anchorages were still to be found. The New Deal had been an exhilarating experience for most, but its rewards seemed never to match its promise and its once brave banners were becoming faded and threadbare. No one in his right mind, of course, wanted to go back to the Old Way, but you were no longer confident that FDR had the only map to the New Way.

Anyway, the worst of the economic crunch seemed to be over: Business activity had been picking up steadily for a couple of years, the stock market was humming, jobs were becoming more plentiful, wages were slowly rising, and the labor unions were showing their muscle. There were still eight million unemployed in the cities, and the sharecroppers down South and the Dust Bowl refugees in the Great Plains were still having a hard time of it, but you had become a little callous about this sort of thing by 1940. Maybe this was the way it would have to be from here on out, and the government would have to continue indefinitely to "take up the slack" with its work projects and relief programs. That would be all right as long as you weren't a part of the slack.

The population was 131.6 million in 1940, up a scant seven percent over 1930. This was less than half the growth recorded in previous decades, and the experts said that the birthrate was leveling off permanently because we had become a predominantly (56 percent) urban society. They projected a total population of 156.5 million by 1970, missing the mark widely (we reached that level in 1955). It was still a country of magnificent distances and the fastest air schedule from New York to Los Angeles was 15 hours, given good weather all the way. But most travelers covered such distances by rail. Time had not the obsessive quality it has since acquired.

If economic conditions were better in 1940 than they had been a few years earlier, the country was still a long way from the affluent society of more recent times. The gross national product that year was $97.1 billion, the national debt $36.7 billion, and the cost of running the federal government was $9.1 billion. The Internal Revenue Service collected $1.5 billion in personal income taxes from 7.5 million persons. The tax rate was a modest 4.09 percent, the average tax bite was $102; only 48,000 taxpayers fell into the high-level, $25,000–$100,000 income bracket and only 52 declared incomes of over $1 million. Wages in manufacturing averaged 66¢ per hour and the average take-home pay of a factory worker was $25.20 a week. The median annual income of urban families was $1,463, and only 2.3 percent of those city families had incomes of $5,000 or more. Members of Congress, never noted for ignoring their official perquisites, did quite handsomely on salaries of $10,000 a year.

By extrapolation, to use the economist's language if not his impersonal method, these bare statistics on income can be refocused to reveal a possibly more meaningful picture of what life was like in 1940. A young, middle-class family with a college background which had not been set back too roughly by the Depression might, with luck, count on an income in the range of $200 to $300 a month. Rent, food, and other necessities would take about two-thirds of this and the balance could be stretched to afford, perhaps, the upkeep of an automobile (most probably bought second-hand), a weekly trip to the movies, two weeks at the beach in the summer, and a modest assortment of other amenities and luxuries. A haircut cost 50¢, a glass of beer was a dime, and most doctors charged a flat fee of $2 for office visits. A good winter suit would cost the husband about $40, shirts could be had for $2, and his wife could buy a dressy wool coat for under $50. Twelve to 15 dollars would just about fill up the weekly market basket for a family of four, with milk at 13¢ a quart, eggs 35¢ a dozen, bread 8¢ a loaf, butter 35¢ a pound, pork chops 33¢ a pound, and chuck roast at 29¢. Three dollars plus a quarter tip would provide dinner for two at many good restaurants.

There were, in those Spartan days, no frozen "TV dinners" to be slipped in the oven (nor any TVs, either), no prepackaged fruit juices, no garbage grinder under the kitchen sink, no laundromat in the apartment basement, and no home air conditioning beyond what could be achieved with a couple of electric fans. Even so, a family so situated was living fairly high on the hog in terms of the national average in 1940, but not conspicuously so in terms of their peer group in the urban, middle-class social complex.

IV

The political life of the country revolved in 1940, as it had for most of the previous decade, around the commanding figure of Franklin D. Roosevelt. He had aged somewhat since his dramatic emergence on the scene in 1932, but he still retained his unsinkable optimism and infectious self-confidence. People had long since ceased to pity him for the affliction (poliomyelitis) that had confined him permanently to a wheelchair, for his spirit had so manifestly conquered that disability as to make it seem of no account. So pervasive were his personality and his influence, so much a fixture in the shifting pattern of events, that he had become almost as much a national symbol as the Capitol dome or the Statue of Liberty.

He no longer enjoyed, of course, the uncritical adulation which was heaped upon him during his first term. He had acquired, in fact, a sizable and vocal opposition centering in the conservative ranks of Congress and the business world. At no time during the preceding five years did he have sustained support of more than a handful of the more influential newspapers of the country. Some of his detractors had worked themselves into a state of pathological bitterness over him and his New Deal. They depicted him as an unregenerate opportunist willing to betray his patrician heritage and the fundamentals of capitalist theology—things that were at the very heart of what they construed as "the American way of life"—in his lust for political power.

But Roosevelt, gaily, cockily indifferent to such blasts, turned their enmity to his own advantage. They were just the sort of enemies that a man of the people required, and this he indisputably was. To most Americans, even after nearly eight years in office, he was still the leader of their choice. Some of the magic had rubbed off, true; he had blundered here and there and sometimes had failed to deliver on his promises. But this weighed lightly against his many triumphs, real or imagined—lifting the nation's spirit out of the depths of despair, reopening the banks and protecting the people's wealth, creating work relief and farm subsidies and TVA, and bringing forth laws to protect a working man's right to belong to a union.

The Great Depression was more than a memory in 1940. It was an ordeal that wrenched dangerously at the economic vitals of the nation and shattered many articles of a person's faith. For a few millions it was still a grinding reality, and millions more still bore the scars and open wounds of their recent experiences. The Depression was deeply imprinted upon the common culture of that day—and as a corollary, so was the image of Roosevelt in the role of deliverer.

That image occupied the foreground of a mind's-eye panorama called the New Deal. Strictly construed, the New Deal was an instrument of politics and politicians, a matter of votes and issues and power. But by 1940 it had been on display for so long that it had acquired an apolitical context as well, a perceived existence only vaguely defined, that was a part of the ambience of everyday life. Whether you liked or disliked its implications, there it was—indelibly woven into the fabric of your consciousness. As you could not think of the church without the steeple, so you could not think of government without the New Deal.

Or the New Dealers. Their names and faces were a part of the mosaic. There was Harry Hopkins, the lanky, sardonic one-time relief adminstrator who had become FDR's closest adviser and a full-time resident of the White House. There was Henry A. Wallace, the shy, gifted, Iowa-born Secretary of Agriculture, whose left-wing philosophy was mixed with an inscrutable mysticism. There was Henry Morgenthau, the Secretary of the Treasury, and Fanny Perkins at Labor, and Harold Ickes at Interior, and the agile White House team of Tommy Corcoran and Ben Cohen, whose legal and intellectual legerdemain had for so long kept the conservative Right in a state near apoplexy. All had their separate identities, of course, but collectively they merged into the larger panorama of the New Deal.*

Such, then, was the political ingredient of the common culture that most Americans carried with them into the new decade of the forties. Regardless of one's tastes and convictions in matters of partisan politics, Roosevelt and the New Deal were durable fixtures of the national consciousness.

V

Where else can we look for clues to the quality of life in that far-off year of 1940? What besides war and politics engaged the popular interests and catered to the prevailing tastes of the day?

As good a sampling as any is afforded by a random journey through a typical issue of the *New York Times,* in this case the issue for Sunday, June 16. Skipping the big black headlines on the front page, we encounter this kind of miscellany in the inside columns:

The Metropolitan Museum of Art announced it had added 14 paintings by contemporary American artists to its permanent collection. Among the artists so honored were Junius Allen, Paul Lantz, A. S. Ballynson, and Doris Rosenthal . . . Harvard alumni leaders promised that, because of war tensions, they would refrain from their usual jabs of ridicule aimed at their fellow-alumnus, Franklin D. Roosevelt ('04), during the annual Class Day parade on Wednesday . . . Sixty members of Jehovah's Witnesses were given "protective custody" over the week-end in the local jail at Litchfield, Illinois, to shield them from the ire of a mob of townsmen (the visiting missionaries had refused to salute the flag when so ordered by the local American Legion Post) . . .

* Other members of the Cabinet in June 1940, were Cordell Hull, Secretary of State; Harry H. Woodring, Secretary of War; Charles Edison, Secretary of the Navy; Robert H. Jackson, Attorney General; and James A. Farley, Postmaster General. The Vice-President was John Nance Garner of Texas.

The city of Newark was set on Monday morning to inaugurate a food stamp plan to help relieve hunger among its 83,000 residents on WPA and relief rolls . . . Chairman Norman H. Davis of the American Red Cross announced that his agency had spent over $7.5 million so far during the year for shiploads of food, clothing, and medical supplies sent to the relief of war refugees in Western Europe, principally France . . . The University of Illinois announced plans to begin construction in the fall on one of the most powerful cyclotrons in the country, estimated to cost $31,500 . . . President Ernest M. Hopkins of Dartmouth College, in a commencement address, scored the current generation of college men for their unwillingness "to stand on their own feet or to listen to any voices except the echo of their own desires" . . . The Reverend Doctor Joseph R. Sizoo admonished his congregation at the Collegiate Reformed Church in New York that "The world will never be saved by the childish way of force but by mature ways of good will and understanding." In similar vein, the Reverend Doctor Norman Vincent Peale said the world must now abandon "nonspiritual human leadership and turn to God for guidance" . . . In the classified pages there were 13 columns of "Help Wanted" ads, over half of them for salesmen willing to sell on commission, and 17 columns under "Situations Wanted."

Along with the usual plethora of stories about weddings and engagements, the society pages on that Sunday were enlivened with such headlines as these: Colorful Throng Attends United Hunts at Roslyn . . . Parties for Debutantes and Sports Events Fill Calendar for Next Fortnight at Tuxedo . . . Fete Arranged for Polish Relief . . . Junior Riders from Four States to Participate in Fairfield Horse Show . . . Benefits Planned for Red Cross.

The drama section led off with a six column illustration of a scene from Pulitzer-prize-winning playwright Robert E. Sherwood's *There Shall Be No Night,* starring Alfred Lunt and Lynn Fontanne, one of the earliest contemporary war plays to stir Broadway. Other current hits prominently advertised that week included *Life With Father, The Man Who Came To Dinner, Separate Rooms, Hellzapoppin', Louisiana Purchase,* and *Tobacco Road* (then nearing the end of its record-making seven-year run). The biggest spectacle on the movie screens was Margaret Mitchell's panoramic Civil War romance *Gone With the Wind,* which had its premiere in January and was on the way to making cinema history. Other top-rated attractions which were available at the time included *Our Town,* with William Holden and Martha Scott; *The Mortal Storm,* with Margaret Sullavan and James Stewart; *The Doctor Takes A Wife,* with Loretta Young and Ray Milland; and *The Way Of All Flesh,* starring Akim Tamiroff.

The front page of the *Times Book Review* on that Sunday was devoted to an admiring discussion of a new socio-political novel, *World's End*, by that incorrigible old polemicist, Upton Sinclair. Well placed on the best seller list were: (fiction) *Stars On The Sea*, by F. Van Wyck Mason; *How Green Was My Valley*, by Richard Llewellyn; *King's Row*, by Henry Bellamon; *Night In Bombay*, by Louis Bromfield; and (general) *I Married Adventure*, by Osa Johnson; *American White Paper*, by Joseph Alsop and Robert Kintner; *Failure Of A Mission*, by Neville Henderson; and *How To Read a Book*, by Mortimer Adler.

In 30 pages of travel notes and advertising there was a conspicuous dearth of references to Europe, heavy emphasis on the allure of vacations nearer home—the Poconos, the Catskills, Maine, the White Mountains, the Jersey coast, the Great Lakes, White Sulphur Springs. The rates seemed inviting too: $6 a day, American plan, at the Asbury Carleton; $40 weekly at Atlantic City's Ambassador; as little as $25 weekly at less pretentious spas. For the sea-going vacationer, the Moore-McCormack Lines suggested, "There's variety in South America," and offered a 38-day cruise for $360 tourist, $480 first class. The Caribbean had scarcely been discovered by the travel industry in 1940, but Havana rated a high priority and one could enjoy a six-day cruise there for as little as $75.

In sports, Saturday had been a good day for New York baseball fans, according to the next day's paper. The Giants clobbered Pittsburgh, 12–1; the Yankees edged out St. Louis, 7–6; and the Brooklyn Dodgers, leading the National League, topped Cincinnati (eventual winner of the world series), 11–6. In St. Louis, Betty Jameson tumbled the women's national golf champion, Patty Berg, two-up in a seesaw 36-hole match to take the "trans-Mississippi" regional championship. Yale overpowered Princeton, 15–5, in the Ivy League polo circuit (whatever became of polo, by the way?), and world heavyweight champion Joe Louis was reported nearing the peak of training for his match later in the week with Art Godoy. (Louis knocked out the Chilean challenger in eight rounds.)

The *Times*' Index of Business Activity was reported to have "continued its advance in the week ending June 8, moving up to 98.8 from 95.7. It was 89.9 in the week ending June 10, 1939. All but one of the components made gains in the week. . . ." The stock market was reported also to be in a vigorous state, and President William McChesney Martin, Jr., of the New York Exchange, announced that his organization was "ready and equipped" to aid the government's arms policy.

The war aside (and it was not easy to put aside), 1940 was a year of hope rather than a year of fulfillment. Individually and collectively most people felt that the worst of the Depression was over, that the false idols and outworn dogmas that had led them into error were expunged, that with luck the nation could avoid the economic and social pitfalls of the past, and that the quality of life would continue to improve. With the return of hope there was a return of confidence; confidence not only in the future of the nation but in one's individual capacity to make his own way, to take risks, to make decisions. The fear of finding oneself without a job did not hold quite the terror that it had just a few years earlier; nor was the compulsion as strong to band together for social reform, for political solidarity, or for the other benefactions of tribal dependence. The difference was that in 1940 a person could feel that he had a chance, which was more than he felt in 1930—and that was quite a difference.

Such was the shape of 1940. Few had the prescience at the time to see it as a landmark year. But, historically, it was. It opened a decade of momentous events, of the unleashing of strange and powerful new forces in human affairs. The 1940s was a transitional decade leading directly into what men now call the Modern Era. How we in America made the transition is what this book is about.

2

Politics Not As Usual

NEXT TO THE WAR, the most absorbing preoccupation of 1940 was politics. No Presidential election is ever dull, but some are livelier than others. The 1940 contest between Franklin Roosevelt and Wendell Willkie was packed to the brim with drama, suspense, and historical significance, as well as a few good laughs. There has not been another quite like it in this century.

I

The political climate in the country as the year opened was about as cloudy and ambiguous as it can get. The Roosevelt New Deal, rounding out its eighth year front and center on the national stage, had lost much of its shine and all of its novelty. Most of its major reforms had been firmly cemented into place and, like them or not, everyone knew they were there to stay. They had not wrought the miracles promised of them—indeed, they had created some problems which had not existed before—but critics as well as advocates were more intent on making these innovations work, or softening their impact, than on scuttling them. The dispute was over how, and that rose at times to heights of bitterness that involved Democrats and Republicans equally.

Roosevelt had acquired almost as many enemies within the conservative wing of his own party as he had within the GOP, as far as his domestic program was concerned. The lines of allegiance held most firmly on foreign policy and attitude toward the war in Europe. Most Democratic leaders, and public opinion generally in the South and Northeast where the principal Democratic strength lay, adhered to a moderate isolationism that did not rule out material assistance to the hard-pressed democracies opposing dictatorships.

The most radical isolationist voices were Republican voices, most particularly those arising from the Midwestern and Western states. Their

shrill notes colored the whole tone of the Republican protest and gave
the entire party a strongly isolationist cast. Organizationally, the GOP
was still a shambles from the disastrous defeats it had suffered in 1932
and 1936, but it had made an encouraging comeback in the midterm
elections of 1938, improving its posture not only in Congress but in
governorships and state offices as well. Thus, the party's leaders viewed
1940 as a possible year of redemption. By tradition there had to be
a new face in the White House after a two-term tenure, and with all
the dissension tearing the Democrats apart there was at least the reasonable hope that the new face could be a Republican's. The question was,
whose?

There are substantial reasons for believing that, as 1940 opened,
Roosevelt had no firm intention of running for a third term; that he
sincerely looked forward to the role of an elder statesman still commanding a large endowment of public esteem and affection. And that he would
have had such an endowment there can be no doubt: His popularity
with the masses of the people, as opposed to their more articulate
political hierarchs, was largely undimmed. Not for him would there be
an eclipse and sullen withdrawal like Hoover's, nor a cruel rejection
like Wilson's. But, typical in a man of his vanity and insouciance,
Roosevelt had not brought up a likely successor. Late in the game he
entertained briefly the implausible notion of grooming Harry Hopkins,
the one-time relief administrator and now his most intimate White House
adviser, for the role. Later still, he refrained from setting up any
obstacles (or encouragements, either) to the ambitions of his Vice-
President, John Nance Garner, or his Postmaster General and chief
political tactician, Jim Farley, to vie for the succession. So, by indecision
and negation, and then by a studied concealment of his own intentions
right up to the time of the July nominating convention, Roosevelt added
a cloying enigma to the cloud of confusion that overhung the political
landscape. Juxtaposed on the same page of the *New York Times* for
June 30 that year was a story telling how Willkie had just captured
the Republican nomination, and another headed, "Will Roosevelt Run?
The Debate Is Renewed."

II

The Republican search for "a man who" was routine and relatively
uncomplicated—up until the last minute. Then it erupted into one of the
most dazzling dark horse melodramas in political history.

After half a century of virtually unchallenged dominance as the
majority party in the country, the GOP had fallen on hard times early
in the thirties and had never recovered. All its proud banners and
slogans, its ancient alliances between the rich, the business elite, and

the politically entrenched went into limbo with President Hoover after his defeat by Roosevelt in 1932, never to emerge in their former glory. The stock market crash and then the systematic debasement of the cult of Wall Street moneymen by the New Dealers sapped the party structure of its essential glue and caused its most influential masters to go into exile. After the debacle of 1936 it bore scant resemblance to a national organization, but resembled rather the Hebrew tribes in the Diaspora. The Republican Party was what Colonel Robert R. McCormick said it was in Illinois, and what Joseph N. Pew said it was in Pennsylvania, and what any number of surviving satraps said it was in their domain. The National Committee, with ex-candidate Alf M. Landon's campaign manager, John D. M. Hamilton, as chairman, survived—but ineffectually and on starvation rations.

The notion that 1940 might be a Republican year penetrated this pall of gloom with a ray of hope. Our political system seems never to run out of men with the ambition to be President, and one by one a clutch of them let their "availability" be known to their Republican colleagues that year. Among the earliest was a solemn, balding, vaguely arrogant, and inflexible conservative freshman Senator from Ohio, Robert A. Taft, son of former President William Howard Taft who, in his time, had done battle with an earlier Roosevelt, the redoubtable Teddy. Another was Arthur H. Vandenberg, a second-term Senator from Michigan with what appeared to be excellent Republican vote-getting potential: He was the only Republican Senator challenged in the 1934 midterm election to stand against the Democratic onslaught. Something of an unknown quantity at the outset was a third aspirant, Thomas E. Dewey, the trim, brisk, thirty-eight-year-old special prosecutor from New York who quickly had won a reputation as a gang buster. He had established good political credentials in 1938, however, when he came within an eyelash of unseating Democrat Herbert Lehman, Roosevelt's surrogate in the New York governorship, and he soon moved to the head of the line in the preconvention parade of 1940. An enigmatic figure in the procession that spring was former President Herbert Hoover, who had come out of his self-imposed exile a few years earlier grimly determined to rehabilitate himself in the history books and in the annals of the Republican Party. He never did proclaim his candidacy but he conspicuously positioned himself on a number of occasions where he thought the lightning might strike.

And, finally, there was Willkie, the big, handsome, amiable, and articulate public utility tycoon from New York who had led the fight against the New Deal's most cherished symbol—TVA, the Tennessee Valley Authority. He was most emphatically an unknown quantity, with no political credentials whatever—he had been a Democrat until 1936 when he cast his first Republican ballot for Landon—and the professionals wrote him off as a spoiler. They did, that is, up until a couple of weeks before the convention when they suddenly began to realize what kind of spoiler he really was.

Wendell Lewis Willkie was as American as a jug of apple cider; he might have walked right out of the pages of a Horatio Alger, Jr., novel as rewritten by Dale Carnegie. He was born in the little town of Elwood, Indiana, in 1892, one of five sons of third-generation German immigrants. His parents were moderately well-off by contemporary middle-class standards, practiced law together (his mother was the first woman admitted to the bar in Indiana), and had cultural and intellectual tastes somewhat beyond the norm for their small-town environment. A good bit of this rubbed off on the Willkie boys, along with parental insistence on industry and self-reliance, but they were typical of their generation in every respect—outgoing, exuberant, mischievous. Wendell, in fact, earned something of a reputation as a brilliant roughneck in his early years at the University of Indiana. One campus prank landed him overnight in jail during his sophomore year, and he was as notable as an antiestablishment activist as he was as a scholar. In a solidly Republican environment, he was a taunting undergraduate Populist who quoted William Jennings Bryan. In the heyday of the social monopoly of the Greek-letter societies, he led the antifraternity cabal on the Indiana campus. He relented in his senior year, however, to join the most prestigious fellowship at the University, Beta Theta Pi, and when he graduated from law school in 1915 he was at the head of his class and walked off with the three top scholastic prizes.

After two years in the Army during the First World War he entered law practice in Akron, Ohio, and established a reputation as a trial lawyer who was rough-and-tumble but who had a keen legal mind and an infinite capacity for making friends. He gravitated as naturally as a fish toward water into the periphery of local Democratic politics, turning down repeated urgings to run for office (including Congress) but attending the 1924 Democratic National Convention as a delegate. One of his Akron clients was the Northern Ohio Power and Light Company whose chief, Bernard C. Cobb, was so impressed by him that when the company was merged into the Commonwealth and Southern in 1929 and Cobb went to New York to become its president, Willkie went along as the $36,000-a-year general counsel. Three years later he succeeded Cobb as president of one of the largest, but also one of the most enlightened, utility combines in the East. (In that same year, 1932, he showed up at the Democratic National Convention in Chicago plugging for the nomination of Newton D. Baker over Roosevelt.)

Willkie began to gain national attention in 1935 as one of industry's most effective voices raised in protest against the New Deal's Public Utility Holding Company Act and its invasion of the power field, specifically TVA. When TVA announced its intention to distribute power in its area competitively with local private utilities, Willkie went roaring into combat, his company, Commonwealth and Southern, being the principal victim of such an arrangement. He demanded that if the government could not be forbidden to raid a private business in this fashion, that at the least it should buy out C & S rather than force it to compete at such a hopeless disadvantage. The Supreme Court knocked out his prime contention by upholding TVA's right to sell its surplus energy. The New Deal Administration then acknowledged the validity of his second contention and offered to buy C & S's distributive system for $55 million. Willkie indignantly turned it down, asking for $100 million. From beginning to end the conflict raged for two years in broad public view, coming to epitomize the basic struggle between the New Deal and Big Business. When, in February 1939, the government raised its ante to $80 million and C & S accepted, Wendell Willkie became a hero on the order of Jack the Giant Killer to the entire anti-New Deal public.

Willkie was a prolific public speaker and writer of articles for magazines and newspaper syndicates, and highly articulate in both media. He was educated in the humanities as well as in the law, had wit and imagination, a tremendous gift of empathy, and the knack of seeming to make a great deal of sense. There was nothing doctrinaire about his social and political philosophy. He belonged with the "rugged indi-vidualists" but not with the "economic royalists." He was one of the most effective foes the New Deal had, but he was no Roosevelt-hater. He had been a Republican since 1936, but he did not fit any conventional Republican mold. He could say, for example (as he often did): "Any man who is not something of a Socialist before he is forty has no heart; any man who is still a Socialist after forty has no head." And in the light of his long ordeal with the TVA, he could write an article for that bible of business orthodoxy, *Barron's:*

I was one of those who hoped the New Deal meant a truly liberal faith. Certainly no liberal movement ever had a greater opportunity or was ever given more wholehearted support by the people. But the present leaders seem to prefer to punish rather than to reform; to destroy the evil-doers even if the doers of good should also succumb. This lack of discrimination is no longer puzzling. It is apparent now that the purpose of the New Deal government was not to eliminate monopolistic control but merely to change its ownership.

Of the scores of troubled citizens who perceived in the image of this earnest, plain-spoken Hoosier an intimation of St. George the Deliverer, a few decided to do something about it. Here might be just the man, they told themselves, to offer a practical and constructive Republican alternative to the chaotic reign of Franklin Roosevelt's New Deal. It was not the professional pols who spoke thus but men of a broader political vision, with national rather than partisan fortunes in mind. Among the earliest to pose the question "Wendell, why don't you consider running for President?" was Russell Davenport, managing editor of *Fortune* magazine, at a small dinner party in his New York home in the summer of 1939. Willkie, at something of a loose end in his career since the divestiture of C & S responsibilities, answered neither "yes" nor "no" to Davenport but admitted the idea had attractions for him. A little later another friend, Charlton McVeagh, a one-time member of the House of Morgan and a whilom aide to John D. M. Hamilton in the 1936 Landon campaign, also put the question to him. Willkie told him: "Russ Davenport brought up the same thing not long ago. Why don't you two get together?" This MacVeagh did, bringing into the joint council Wall Street banker Frank Altschul, who had also dipped his toes into the political waters in 1936 as vice-chairman of the Republican finance committee.

Thus, by the fall of 1939 the triumvirate was formed that would propel a still skeptical Wendell Willkie on one of the briefest but most amazing political careers in American history. Davenport was responsible for projecting the Willkie image, for getting pieces by or about him into the newspapers and magazines, for arranging personal appearances by him before prestige audiences and on such popular radio shows as *Information Please*. The effort was highly successful: Willkie was first-class "copy." Altschul was responsible for raising a campaign chest and his familiarity with wealthy businessmen all over the country made the task relatively easy. MacVeagh's assignment was to lay the foundations for a national organization of "Willkie Clubs" and to stimulate a grassroots movement for their man. He had a wide acquaintance with Republican leaders in many parts of the country as a result of his labors in the 1936 campaign and he quietly nourished these relationships in Willkie's behalf. But he was careful not to become fenced in with the professional party machines. As it turned out, his most effective organizational gambit was to enlist the help of various utility trade associations in having officials of local power and light companies become the secret nucleus of "Willkie for President Clubs" in their communities. Several hundred of these popped into existence "spontaneously" over the next few months, dispensing Willkie buttons, banners, bumper stickers, and letters-to-the-editor in great profusion.

For as long as they could, the Davenport-Altschul-MacVeagh team worked in anonymity. When they set up their first headquarters it was in three small, unmarked suites on separate floors of the Old Murray Hill Hotel. They shunned press conferences and gave evasive answers to nosey questioners. Inevitably, others had to be admitted to the inner circle of this exciting crusade. Prominent among them were Bruce Barton, the advertising executive and member of Congress; Fred Smith, a prominent public relations consultant; Irita Van Doren, literary editor of the *Herald-Tribune* and a leading figure of the New York intellectual set, and a handful of other talented but nonprofessional kingmakers.

The emphasis throughout was for these managers and manipulators to remain in the background, to make the Willkie groundswell appear to be a spontaneous eruption of the popular will: They successfully floated such slogans as "The Commuters Counter-Revolution" that caught the people's fancy and their credence. Willkie himself was properly modest and enigmatic about his intentions, joshing away the idea that he could ever be a serious contender for the nomination. But by April he was conceding that, sure, he would run if it should just happen that the Republican convention wanted him.

At that time he was almost out of sight on the public opinion polls, running far behind Dewey, Taft, Vandenberg, Hoover, and the others. Then a pair of smart public relations coups—one contrived, the other spontaneous—gave his standing a sudden boost.

Davenport published in the April *Fortune* an article over Willkie's name entitled, "We, The People," which was a rousing summons to the American public to reject the archaic and stultifying partisanship of the past—of the New Deal especially—and to seek bold new remedies for the nation's afflictions. He called for a rapprochement between business and government, not on Republican terms, but on the terms of the common necessity and welfare. He called not for the abolition of New Deal domestic reforms and foreign policy, but for their implementation in an atmosphere free of suspicion and vindictiveness. It was a remarkable document that, while patently critical of the existing Democratic regime, gave scant comfort to Republican orthodoxy. Its tone was bluntly nonpartisan, its thrust plausibly optimistic. In an accompanying editorial, the editors of *Fortune* urged the Republican Party to nominate Wendell Willkie as its Presidential candidate.

One whose imagination was fired by the Willkie manifesto was Oren Root, Jr., a brilliant but politically inexperienced twenty-eight-year-old Wall Street lawyer. "I thought a lot of people must feel the way I did and ought to have some way to express themselves," he said later. At his own expense and on his own responsibility—he had never met Willkie or any of the Willkie inner circle—he had a few hundred copies of a condensed version of "We, The People" printed and mailed out, using the Princeton and Yale yearbooks for 1924 as his mailing list. Accompanying the article was a letter from Root urging the recipients to get behind a "Willkie for President" drive. The response was so great that within 10 days Root had to run a small ad in the "Public Notices" column of the *Herald-Tribune* pleading, "Help Oren Root, Jr., organize the peoples' demand for Willkie. Send Root a contribution to 15

Broad Street, New York." Several hundred did. By the end of April the astonished young tyro had been deluged with some 200,000 requests from all over the country for copies of the petition, had taken a leave of absence from his law firm, and had joined forces with Davenport at the now openly active Willkie campaign headquarters.

Throughout the month of May and on into June the Willkie bandwagon rolled merrily onward, gaining speed and converts as it went. The Willkie Clubs were beating the drums for their man in virtually every city and town in the country, showering letters and petitions on their newspapers, their Congressmen, and their local Republican bosses. Thousands of youngsters of high school and college age were caught up in the excitement, imparting an air of youthful exuberance to the performances. Buttons proclaiming "We Want Willkie" blossomed profusely on businessmen's lapels, even occasionally on workmen's overalls. Willkie's picture and his words turned up repeatedly in newspapers and magazines, and political commentators speculated knowingly on his probable impact on the Republican convention. Some of these persisted in writing him off as a public relations phenomenon, a "30-day wonder," who had entered no primaries, gained no state delegations of consequence. Stirring up a sudden frenzy of hero worship was one thing, they said, but translating it into solid votes at the convention was something else again. Politics just didn't work that way.

Such skeptical analyses seemed to be borne out by a Gallup poll published on June 12, just two weeks before the convention was to open. It showed Dewey far ahead in the rating with 52 percent and Willkie in fourth place with only 17 percent. But the significant statistic was that Willkie was the only man on the ladder who had gained steadily over the preceding four weeks. He was on the way up and Dewey was on the way down, and that trend was escalating faster than anyone knew.

The Willkie buildup has been described by experts as one of the classic achievements of modern publicity. But there was more to the feat than carnival and fanfare. Underpinning the popular image, and all but hidden from view, was a solid base of political bedrock. MacVeagh and Altschul (with a big assist from Root) had carried out their end of the bargain, which was to build a viable Willkie organization as efficiently as Davenport had manipulated the public relations keyboard. They sought out not only the recognized Republican chieftains but, more contacts in all the states where the Willkie strength showed promise. They sought out not only the recognized Republican chieftans but, more importantly, the big wheels of industry and finance who called the tune and paid the bills for the GOP in their state or region. To most of these, Willkie was their kind of man, whatever his political antecedents, and the likeliest challenger to take the measure of the hated FDR. Few of them would show up in the roster of voting delegates at the convention, but they often were in a position to dictate who those delegates would be and how they would behave when the balloting began. This fit well with the strategy of the Willkie managers. In order to preserve the fiction of a spontaneous groundswell, they were aiming less for first ballot commitments than for promises to switch to Willkie on succeeding ballots when and as called for.

The planning went even further, into control of the machinery of the convention itself. Early on, National Chairman John Hamilton had been recruited as a silent but active collaborator in the Willkie conspiracy. His chairman's role forced him to wear the mask of neutrality during the preconvention maneuvering, to treat all of the aspirants for the nomination impartially. But he gave all the undercover help he could to the Willkie team, buttressing their inexperience with his professional skill and insight, pinpointing weaknesses in their strategy as well as that of their foes. He helped to maneuver into the Willkie corner, where they would remain unseen until zero-hour, such key convention officials as young Governor Harold Stassen of Minnesota, the keynoter; Representative Joseph W. Martin of Massachusetts, the permanent chairman; and Samuel F. Pryor, Jr., national committeeman from Connecticut, chairman of arrangements, which put him in charge of seating and the issuance of floor badges and gallery tickets—a critically useful function at any convention.

All of these maneuvers were achieved with such finesse that, even as opening day arrived, Willkie appeared to many on-lookers as little more than a happy-go-lucky adventurer who had ambled onto the scene just for the hell of it. He arrived in Philadelphia that morning without any retinue of flacks or aides, stepping off the train accompanied only by Mrs. Willkie, whom he sent along to the hotel by taxi while he walked the distance chatting amiably with the platoon of reporters who were his only welcoming committee. While other leading candidates secluded themselves in deep strategy conferences in their hideaway headquarters, Willkie wandered about downtown Philadelphia like a strolling minstrel, greeting friends and strangers by the hundreds, dropping quotable remarks for the shadowing reporters, seeming surprised and flattered by the coveys of gaily uniformed "Willkiettes" (most of them imported from the stenographic ranks of Wall Street brokerage and law offices) passing out buttons and hatbands with his name on them along the crowded streets.

To an incredulous Arthur Krock, the leading political columnist for the *New York Times* whom he encountered in a hotel lobby late that night, he said he had done nothing about naming a floor manager to handle his affairs once the balloting started; in fact, he added disarmingly, nobody had told him such a functionary was necessary! Krock delivered a brief lecture to the unwary candidate on convention tactics, and jotted down in his notebook for future reference: "He seemed like a man who had set out on a mule to defeat a German panzer division, confident of his star, sure that he needed nothing more to rout the mechanized political forces against him. If it's an act, it's a good one." (It *must* have been an act. Governor Stassen had already promised Hamilton in confidence that, once his keynote speech was out of the way, he would step forth as Willkie's floor manager. It is unlikely that the candidate was ignorant of this.)[1]

III

The Republican convention, opening on June 24, proceeded according to ritual in the vast, gaily decorated Philadelphia Convention Hall, running through the dry routine of welcoming speeches, resolutions, and other formalities that always eat up the first two days at such affairs. But consternation was beginning to grow in some of the candidates' headquarters, most notably those of Dewey and Taft, ostensibly the top entries in the coming sweepstake. The Willkie whoop-la was getting on their nerves, inching them out of the limelight, nibbling at their confidence. Delegates from all over were finding their hotel mailboxes stuffed to overflowing two and three times a day with letters and telegrams and petitions from back home demanding that they pump for Willkie. The galleries in the convention hall, the restaurants and hotel lobbies downtown, were jammed with incorrigible young Willkie fans screaming "We Want Willkie" at the top of their lungs. The mood was infectious; the whole atmosphere of the city seemed keyed to the Willkie frenzy. And harassed agents from the Dewey and Taft camps brought back increasingly pessimistic reports from their scouting expeditions into state caucuses where they had gone to line up secondary support for their men. With ominous frequency even the most disciplined, machine-run delegations told them: "We'll wait and see how the ball bounces." On Wednesday night Dewey and Taft conferred secretly on combining forces to scotch the Willkie boom, but neither man was willing to take second place on the other's ticket, which was the gist of the proposal that each offered, and the scheme died aborning.

Wednesday and most of Thursday were taken up with the nominating speeches and their seconders. There were 13 candidates all told, including a clutch of favorite sons who entered the race for trading purposes only. Willkie's nominator was a young Congressman from Indiana, Charles A. Halleck, who almost missed the boat. When Indiana was reached in the first call of the states, Indiana "passed," signifying it had no candidate to offer—to the infinite dismay of convention chairman Joe Martin and several hundred Willkie enthusiasts on the floor. The reason was that over half the state's delegation was pledged to Taft and they did not want Willkie presented in the guise of a Hoosier favorite son. When the call of the states was completed Halleck gained the floor to give a rousing, fighting nominating speech for his man that sent the massed Willkie supporters in the galleries into new paroxysms.

The rest of the story of that historic week can be told best in a few columns of figures, as reproduced below. At the outset it was a three-man race, Dewey, Taft, and Willkie, in that order. The Dewey forces threw in everything they had on the first ballot, hoping to create a blitz effect. They didn't have enough and it didn't come off. They had considerably fewer votes, in fact—360—than the 400-plus they had boasted of in the preballoting lobby talk. (A simple majority of 501 was needed to clinch the nomination.) What was even worse, the Dewey men had no reserves; from here on their lead could only fade. Taft, like Willkie, held back some of his strength to see how much speed the frontrunner could show, planning to gain on him lap by lap until he or some of his backers threw in the towel. The rest of the field scarcely mattered except as they might yield up their strength to one of the three top contenders. Some nerve-wracking, split-second decisions were involved here, and it was not until the fifth ballot when Michigan decided, on what amounted to a toss of the coin, to throw Vandenberg's votes to Willkie instead of Taft that the verdict was sealed. The table below, with the also-rans excluded, tells the story.

CANDIDATES	BALLOTS				
	1st	*2nd*	*3rd*	*4th*	*5th*
Dewey	360	338	315	250	57
Taft	189	203	212	254	377
Willkie	105	171	259	306	429

When the sixth ballot was called, the stampede to Willkie was on. As state after state switched to the Willkie column, Ohio's Governor John Bricker, Taft's floor manager, moved to make the vote of the convention unanimous, and it was so ordered.

What a night it had been! Writing in the next day's *New York Times,* Arthur Krock described it as a "political miracle," the like of which had not occurred since the materialization from nowhere of Warren G. Harding at the Republican convention of 1920:

> In the light of all political experience Mr. Willkie's nomination was impossible. He has voted the Republican ticket for only four years and has been registered with the party for only one. His claims to this nomination were not submitted to any party primary or convention before this one met. . . . And not until the day before this convention met did Mr. Willkie form a professional political group to pilot his campaign.

To some observers who could hardly believe it before it exploded before their eyes, the nomination of Mr. Willkie seems to be a step in the revolution of ideas which has been sweeping the world.

Such a step in the revolution of ideas it may well have been, but it was no more than a step. Wendell Willkie reached the peak of his political orbit at 1:47 A.M. Friday, June 28, 1940, when, flushed with victory, he stepped forward to the convention rostrum for that first acclaim as the Republican candidate. But the price of victory included more ideological deadweight than he had bargained for. His course from there on was a disheartening downward spiral.[2]

IV

When the Gridiron Club gave its annual dinner in Washington in March 1940, the dominating feature of the decor was a huge replica of the Sphinx with the unmistakable face of Franklin D. Roosevelt wearing a rougish grin and the familiar uptilted cigarette holder. The symbolism was patent: When would this inscrutable deity resolve the third-term riddle? Reporters at White House press conferences had been laughingly condemned to "stand in the corner and wear a dunce cap" for putting the question directly. It had top priority as a subject of political speculation in the Capital all through the latter half of 1939 and on into midsummer of the following year. Even as the Democratic National Convention assembled in July, Roosevelt had said neither yea nor nay in public as to his intentions.

The record on when, where, and why Roosevelt reached the ultimate decision to seek a third term is as unclear to the researcher 30 years after the event as it was to the most privileged observers on the scene in 1940. Jim Farley records that the President said to him at Hyde Park in July 1939: "Of course, I will not run for a third term." He coupled this with a solemn demand that Farley keep the fact secret, saying: "I don't want you to pass this on to anyone, because it would make my role difficult if the decision were known prematurely." This was an essential precaution, for a lame duck President is immediately shorn of a good part of his political influence, and at the time Roosevelt had not too much to spare.

He was less candid with his wife, Eleanor—he did not share many secrets with her in any event—but as late as the spring of 1940 she felt:

[there was] every evidence to believe that he did not want to run again. . . . It became clearly evident to me, from little things he said at different times, that he would really like to be in Hyde Park, and that the role of elder statesman appealed to him. There were innumerable things that all his life he had meant to do—write on naval subjects, go through his papers, letters and so on. He had the library at Hyde Park and had even agreed on a job which he would take on leaving the White House. As I remember, he was to write a longish editorial or article at stated intervals for one of the large New York magazines. . . .

On the other hand, many believed—and still believe—that Roosevelt had nurtured third-term ambitions almost from the time of his second election. Among the Roosevelt haters there was a firm conviction that he meant to be a dictator for life and that the destruction of the third-term barrier was a calculated step in this strategy. A less prejudiced and more prevalent view was that he wanted a third term to consolidate the New Deal and to complete the remaking of the Democratic Party in the New Deal's image. Thomas G. ("Tommy the Cork") Corcoran, who was a key figure in the "third-term cabal," insists that the decision grew out of the residual animus left over from Roosevelt's frustrated effort to "pack" the Supreme Court in 1937 and to "purge" certain Democratic conservatives in the 1938 midterm elections. "He damn well was not going to entrust the fate of the country and the party to men like Walter George and Harry Byrd, even if he had to spend another four years in the White House to thwart them," Corcoran has said.

Still others, like Warren Moscow, a competent on-the-scene observer and historian of these events in 1940, relate his determination to the onset of hostilities in Europe:

Looking backward, it seems most probable that Roosevelt decided to be his own successor when the general war in Europe first loomed as inevitable. This was in the spring of 1939 when Hitler, scrapping the six-months-old Munich Pact, marched his armies into the remainder of Czechoslovakia, which the Munich dismemberment had left defenseless. . . . It is almost impossible to conceive that the President, as the months went on, contemplated turning over his world leadership in the battle against Hitler that following year.

In this writer's view, the most reasonable synthesis of all this conflicting but circumstantial testimony is that Roosevelt was being pulled in opposite directions by two strong but wholly contradictory impulses, and that, like any other mortal, he simply couldn't make up his mind. So he dawdled, dissembled, argued with himself, grew testy and irritable (as many have observed) until he was shocked into a decision by a crisis. Most probably, considering the sequence of events, that shock was delivered by Hitler's march into the Scandinavian countries in April, which revealed incontestably to the President both the reach of Hitler's aims and the impotence of the Allies' resistance. Almost single-handedly, Roosevelt himself had fashioned the program of "all aid short of war" to Britain and France, battling isolationist opposition in both the Democratic and Republican parties. Now, he was convinced, it was more urgent than ever not only to maintain and increase that aid abroad but also to strengthen the sinews of democracy here at home. There was no one he could trust to carry out what he had begun, so he would do it himself.

If such was, indeed, the circumstance of timing of Roosevelt's decision to stand for a third term, he disclosed his plans to no one, including the intimates of the White House circle. There was a certain validity in his silence up to this point to avoid the effects of the lame duck blight, and validity beyond that point in avoiding an angry public wrangle over the morality of flouting the third-term tradition. A side effect, however, as Farley bitterly reminded him later, was that he made it impossible for anyone else to bid seriously for the nomination. Both Farley and Vice-President John Nance Garner, traditionalists to the brims of their hats, had allowed their names to be entered in a few state primaries as far back as February, since, as they said, the President had not pre-empted the field.* As Roosevelt well knew, these stalwarts of his administration were the spiritual leaders of a determined "no third term" bloc on Capitol Hill that had many allies in the conservative ranks of the Democratic Party, but they remained discreetly quiet about it in public. With beguiling amiability he raised no objections to their ventures, but he offered them no encouragement nor any enlightenment on his own plans.

In the guessing game that went on in the press and inside the administration as well, speculation centered from time to time on the prospects of Secretary of State Cordell Hull, of Federal Security Administrator Paul V. McNutt, of Federal Loan Administrator Jesse H. Jones, of Senator Burton K. Wheeler, and a handful of others. In public, Roosevelt maintained a smiling and noncommittal impartiality toward all of them. In private, as Farley and others have since recorded, he gave the impression of having weighed each and, regretfully, found him wanting.

Meanwhile, a pro-third-term drive was gathering speed in other quarters, and the President was as careful not to impede it as he was not to discourage its opponents. Its principal impetus came from such hard core New Dealers in and around the White House as Hopkins, Corcoran, Ickes, David K. Niles, and Leon Henderson; from organized labor; from some of the more powerful Democratic big city bosses such as Mayor Ed Kelly of Chicago, Frank Hague of Jersey City, and

---

* Both asserted privately that their candidacies were no more than a token protest against violation of the third-term principle. This altruistic disclaimer on Farley's part, at least, is open to doubt. He truly believed that if Roosevelt stepped aside, he, Farley, could win the presidential nomination, or at least the vice-presidential slot on someone else's ticket. Writing about it some years later he said: "Had it not been for the man many have credited me with putting in the White House, I might have been Vice-President or even President." (James A. Farley, *Jim Farley's Story,* Whittlesy House, 1948, p. 151.)

Ed Flynn of the Bronx; and from a small cadre of New Deal Senators and Congressmen. They were motivated by the certainty that any visible Democratic alternative to Roosevelt—Farley, Garner, Jones, or who-ever—would yield to conservative pressure to slow down or even to dismantle the New Deal, and also, perhaps, to revert to isolationism in foreign affairs. Such a candidate, moreover, would have a fight on his hands against almost any Republican opponent—that fellow Willkie was looking like more of a menace every day—whereas, they believed, Roosevelt would be a shoo-in against any challenger the other side could put up.

Self-interest is a powerful motivator whether it be philosophical or material. In this case it was both: The New Dealers wanted to protect the New Deal and the politicians wanted to protect their perquisites and organizations. With or without sanction from Roosevelt—the question is still unanswered 30 years later—they pooled their energies and talents to assure him the nomination for a third term. With most of the convention machinery under their control, they clearly had the muscle to do it. As a Tammany leader told reporters a few days before the convention opened: "We're for Roosevelt for a fourth term. The third term is all wrapped up." [3]

V

The twenty-eighth quadrennial convention of the Democratic Party opened at noon on Monday, July 15, 1940, in the echoing vastness of the old Chicago Stadium. Reporting the scene in the next morning's edition of the *New York Times* under a headline reading, "Democrats Glum Facing Inevitable," Anne O'Hare McCormick wrote:

This is not a happy convention. It is extraordinarily well organized. Arrangements for the delegates and the press are much better than they were at Philadelphia [where the Republicans had met a fortnight earlier]. The stadium in its bright colors looks very alive and gay. But it is not gay. The materials for whooping it up in the superior Democratic fashion are all present. All that is lacking is the spirit.

The spirit was still missing five days later when the proceedings were adjourned. Few conventions in the party's history had been more ravaged by dissension, resentment, and anger than this one. And few had been so cynically manipulated—steamrollered—to achieve a predetermined result.

The initial goal of the White House clique was to dispense with the formality of balloting and have Roosevelt, who was technically not a candidate, nominated by acclamation. This was something that had never happened at a major party convention. If it could be pulled off, it would remove much of the sting from the third-term controversy and it would also reburnish the President's somewhat tarnished political halo.

In the process, of course, such candidates as Farley and Garner and those representing the party's anti-New Deal wing would be ignominiously brushed aside.

Such a script calls for a smoke-filled room, and sure enough there was one—the original. It was suite 308–309 in the Blackstone Hotel where, just 20 years earlier, the materialization of Warren Gamaliel Harding had been wrought by a group of Merlins. By ironic accident or by design, this was the suite assigned to Harry Hopkins, who had come to Chicago as the personal but, he stubbornly maintained, unofficial representative of the President. He was accompanied by Senator James F. Byrnes, a stout Southern New Dealer, by Corcoran, Henderson, Niles, and a small group of others representing the third-term cabal in and around the White House. Farley, the party chairman and titular boss of the convention, was headquartered in the Stevens Hotel (later to be known as the Conrad Hilton) across the street, but few reporters or delegates were beating a path to his door. He was completely overshadowed by Hopkins and his crew, and out of touch with the real nerve center of the convention, the White House. In fact the only direct telephone link between the White House and Chicago that week terminated in Harry Hopkins' bathroom, the one place where privacy could be assured.

By the time the convention got down to business on Monday it was clear to even the most innocent what the outcome would be: Roosevelt for a third term. The New Dealers and the big state delegations were in undisputed control, not only of the convention floor but of the galleries—and the public address system. Anger and resentment swept through the convention hall and the hotel lobbies as the delegates came to realize that they had been summoned merely to ratify a predetermined decision. Even those who were prepared to go along with breaking the two-term precedent were, in many cases, miffed over the heavy-handed tactics being used, but there was little they could do about it. Farley and Garner firmly refused all overtures from Hopkins' men to withdraw and let the nomination go through uncontested in a shimmering display of harmony and unanimity. They were determined to force a roll call, not with any hope of upsetting the Roosevelt bandwagon, but as a last ditch rally of the anti-third-term forces.

Their strategy worked up to a point. Two overt efforts to stampede the convention into naming Roosevelt by acclamation were frustrated. On Monday night, Chicago's Mayor Kelly, as host of the convention, converted his traditional speech of welcome into a rousing paean for Roosevelt and a demand that the convention "in this hour of peril" draft him for four more years. The galleries, packed with Kelly henchmen, roared their approval, but the delegates seemed not to hear. They were unmoved.

The following night, Senator Alben Barkley of Kentucky closed his keynote speech by reading a message from the President saying he had no wish to be a candidate and releasing all the delegates pledged to him. This was a carefully calculated ploy. On its face it was an act of renunciation: Roosevelt wanted it known he was not actively seeking the nomination. When one turned it over, however, it could be seen as an invitation to a draft. The concluding paragraph as Barkley read it said: "He wishes in all earnestness and sincerity to make it clear that all the delegates to this convention are free to vote for any candidate."

Any candidate? That could mean Roosevelt as well as anybody else . . .

This was the second cue for a spontaneous lift-off. Suddenly every microphone in the hall went dead, the noise level fell to a low rumble. Then a single, bellowing voice filled the void, coming from loudspeakers everywhere: "Illinois wants Roosevelt! . . . New York wants Roosevelt! . . . Iowa wants Roosevelt! . . . America wants Roosevelt! . . . and so on for the better part of an hour as the convention proceedings dissolved in consternation and confusion. The voice was that of Thomas F. Garry, superintendent of Chicago sewers, who, at Mayor Kelly's bidding, had contrived to capture the public address system circuitry in a hidden room in the basement and to monopolize it. But the "voice from the sewer" generated more turmoil and resentment than it did enthusiasm. When Garry was finally ousted from his post and a semblance of order was restored it was past midnight. The delegates roared their assent to a recess until noon and the "spontaneous draft" died a second time and for good.

The third-termers had overreached themselves in these two abortive sallies, but the strength of their basic strategy was not seriously affected. If they could not contrive a choice by acclamation for Roosevelt, they still had the votes for an overwhelming first ballot nomination.

As the call of the states began on Wednesday, the President's name was formally put in nomination by Senator Lister Hill of Alabama, accompanied by the traditional whoop-la from the galleries and demonstrators on the floor. The names of Farley, Garner, and Senator Millard Tydings of Maryland were also presented, but unmistakably as gestures of a hopeless defiance. State after state, as their names were called in alphabetical order, let it be known that their commitment was to Roosevelt.

The roll call for the first ballot was begun at 9:30 that evening. When it was over an hour and 10 minutes later, Roosevelt had a top-heavy victory of 947 votes, with 149—a majority of them Farley's—distributed among the other contenders. As the result was announced, Farley, his always genial countenance unmarked by the anguish he felt, marched to the microphone on the platform. In a brief speech notable for its generosity and good sportsmanship—everyone knew that his relations with the President had long been strained—he moved that the vote be made unanimous. There were a few cries of "No, No," above the general roar of assent, and chairman Barkley gaveled the motion through. It was not a draft in the true sense of that term, but it was the next best thing.

Inescapably, there was a strong residue of unhappiness among the delegates over this breach of the third-term tradition, and resentment over the manner of its contrivance. For many, these emotions turned to sheer outrage as the selection of a candidate for Vice-President progressed. To have had some hand in this choice might have assuaged their injured feelings: It had been the liveliest topic of speculation among them in their caucuses and gossip sessions. Most of the interest centered around William Bankhead of Alabama, the conservative Speaker of the House of Representatives, and around Paul McNutt and Jesse Jones. (Garner had long since stated that he would not run.) But by Thursday morning the word had filtered down from the Hopkins headquarters that the choice had been made for them—in Washington. Roosevelt's one and only preference was for Henry Aagard Wallace, his Secretary of Agriculture.

In the view of most, Wallace had performed admirably in dealing with the agricultural crisis, which actually had antedated the economic depression. But he was also identified as one of the most radical New Dealers in his social philosophy, and as a person he was diffident, withdrawn, and rather hard to know—not the sort that other politicians or masses of voters would be likely to cotton up to. To most of the delegates his selection seemed not only inept but inexcusably arbitrary as well. Having kept their emotions pretty well bottled up during the first three days of the convention, they now let the cork fly with a bang. Their fulminations had already been anticipated by Hopkins and Byrnes in their Blackstone redoubt. They notified the President that a dangerous revolt was brewing. He was adamant in his choice, but he consented to have Mrs. Roosevelt fly out for an impromptu address to the convention —not as an advocate but for the calming effect her presence would have. The First Lady's reception at the Stadium on Thursday evening was respectful and affectionate, but her emollient soothed only briefly. Again, Hopkins, hunched over his bathroom telephone, entreated the President to give the convention some leeway in the Vice-Presidential choice, to concede at least one alternative to Wallace. Roosevelt's unyielding answer was that it was Wallace, or else—the "else" being that he would dispatch to the convention a message that lay prepared on his desk declining his own nomination for President.

Later that night the ballot was taken. As Hopkins and his men sweated out the tally, quite uncertain how well their lines were holding,

Wallace inched slowly ahead to the magical 551 votes needed for a majority and on beyond to a fairly respectable margin of 626. Bankhead's total was 329. This would not have been an unusual spread in an "open" convention. But this was not an open convention; the votes for Bankhead were a quite accurate measure of the resentment which that fact had engendered. The result was announced amid an uproar of cheers equally mixed with boos. So ugly was the mood, indeed, that the dismayed and crestfallen Wallace was persuaded by the convention managers to stay away from the rostrum and to forego the acceptance speech which he had prepared. Roosevelt's acceptance, delivered by radio from his desk in the White House Oval Room, was received without untoward incident.

From first bell to last, the Democratic Convention of 1940 had been an eye-gouging, knee-in-the-groin brawl. When it was over, the party was more grievously split than it had been since 1928. The solid South, which long had held a balance of power with the big city states of the North and Midwest, had been shunted into a secondary role. Scores of influential party "regulars"—Chairman Jim Farley (who resigned his post) among them—had become disenchanted and rebellious. To all appearances, Roosevelt had turned the Democratic Party inside-out to make it into the New Deal Party. To thousands of the faithful, this was intolerable, and no considerations of national policy or of war and peace could, in the first bitter flash of comprehension, assuage their anger.

Or so it seemed at the time. . . .[4]

VI

Postmortems of election campaigns have an almost ritual sameness about them. In the splendid clarity of hindsight it is always obvious that the winner did everything right while the loser did everything wrong. The difference in 1940 was that one did not have to wait for the revelation of hindsight: Willkie's mistakes became apparent almost from the beginning and piled up with glaring persistence right to the end. Roosevelt, by and large, simply let Willkie stumble along to his own undoing. It couldn't have happened to a nicer fellow, as the victor himself, in so many words, was to concede after it was over.

In the recriminations that followed, Willkie was faulted by the GOP leadership less for having squandered a golden opportunity than for being a spoiler who got in the way of others who might have won. It just went to prove, they said, that amateurs should keep out of politics and leave it to the professionals. They were right, up to a point: Savvy and technique were conspicuously lacking in the Willkie operation. A more important ingredient of failure, however, was the very refusal of the professionals to let Willkie be his own man, to let him swing along in that freewheeling style of his that already had captivated so large a share of the public fancy. But that style, and the rhetoric that went with it—heretically New Deal-ish, it often seemed—just did not comport with Republican orthodoxy. So the Old Guard pros undertook to make the amiable big Hoosier over in their own buttoned-down likeness. Willkie, too naive to know better, let them try, and the resultant image was a mishmash.

That, of course, is not the whole story of the Democrats' five-million-vote margin on Election Day. The old Roosevelt magic was still at work in the American bloodstream, if not quite as potent as it once had been. A sense of national crisis, engendered by the war in Europe, was creeping across the landscape, giving new pertinence to the old adage about swapping horses in the middle of the stream. And as President, Roosevelt was able to hold the center of the stage, relegating his opposition to the wings; to act out and dramatize his role of leadership while Willkie could only read his lines and make distracting noises off-stage.

The odds always run heavily with an incumbent in such a contest. All things considered, it is probable that Willkie could not have won against Roosevelt in any event. But he might have made a better showing in the voting score, and the vitality he pumped into the tired arteries of the Republican Party might have lasted longer had he not sacrificed his identity and his sense of purpose during the campaign.

Symptomatic of the dichotomy that was to plague his effort throughout were two basic choices made for him by the party regulars before the convention adjourned. His designated running mate was Charles L. McNary of Oregon, the Minority Leader of the Senate. McNary was an isolationist and a conservative—conservative with an important distinction. Coming from the conservation-conscious Northwest he was a devout advocate of TVA and similar regional power developments. Willkie had made his reputation fighting TVA but he condoned most of the other social and economic reforms of the New Deal—which McNary had made *his* reputation by fighting. Similarly, Representative Joseph W. Martin of Massachusetts, Minority Leader of the House, was picked to supersede John D. M. Hamilton in the critical post of national chairman and, therefore, campaign manager. Martin's record as an isolationist and political conservative was, if anything, more pronounced than McNary's. These two choices, presented to Willkie as faits accomplis, gave "balance" to the ticket geographically (one of the dogmas in the politician's handbook), but the principal purpose was to appease and reassure the GOP hard-liners in their dismay over the maverick who had emerged as their unwelcome champion. And its public effect was to dampen the exciting, innovative quality of the Willkie candidacy.

Following the convention, Willkie repaired first to Colorado Springs, Colorado, and then to Rushville, Indiana, near his hometown of Elwood, to rest up and to plan his campaign strategy. The excitement and novelty of his swift rise to the political summit had lodged him firmly on Cloud Nine; he could scarcely contain his ebullience and the surges of his inexhaustible energy. He was impatient of details and skull practice; he wanted the ball to be snapped so he could go charging down the field. This mood of happy chaos pervaded his growing entourage of advisers and aides. His campaign organization mushroomed into a haphazard, uncoordinated structure of eager amateurs, dedicated veterans of the original Willkie movement, and a few hard-eyed and skeptical professionals from the regular party organization. It was an unstable mix with a built-in potential for conflicts and embarrassing gaffes in public. A distinguished Republican committeeman in the East who wrote the candidate a warm offer of his services in the campaign got back a form letter advising that he could best help the cause "by joining your local Willkie For President Club."

Willkie made his formal acceptance speech to a throng of some 20,000 friends, neighbors, and visitors from afar gathered in a grove outside Elwood on a broiling hot day in mid-August. As the testament of a political Independent, it staked out some impressively high ground— so high that it caused immediate grumblings from his party's Old Guard. Its tone was liberal and guardedly interventionist. He categorically endorsed very nearly the whole catalogue of New Deal reforms in respect to business regulation, collective bargaining, and social welfare. He also said that he agreed with the President that we should extend all necessary material aid to Great Britain, and that we should assemble and arm a sufficient military force at home to provide against any contingency. (The Selective Service Act, supported by Roosevelt and opposed by many Republicans, was then pending in Congress.)

But then he went on to score the New Deal for its failure to reap the benefits of its innovations and for blindly smothering the sparks of recovery. Its policy of "deliberate scarcity," he said, should be replaced by a policy of "unlimited productivity." He uttered what was to become a slogan of his campaign: "Only the strong can be free, and only the productive can be strong," adding that the New Deal's suppression of free enterprise was hampering the return of jobs and prosperity. And to balance off his endorsement of the Administration's foreign policy, he condemned the President for having "dabbled in inflammatory statements and manufactured panics" and for having "unscrupulously encouraged other countries to hope for more help than we are able to give." In a rousing peroration, he summoned one and all to join him in a "crusade" to fulfill "the destiny of America."

In aim, content, and structure, this was possibly the best speech Willkie made in his entire campaign, although it read a good deal better than it sounded to the millions who heard it on the radio. His style was always inhibited by the strictures of a prepared text. It was the speech of an Independent, which at heart Willkie was, and not the speech of a card-carrying Republican, which he was not; and his Republican mentors went to work on him forthwith to correct the deficiency. At the other extreme, Norman Thomas, perennial Socialist candidate for President, observed that Willkie had "agreed with Mr. Roosevelt's entire program and said that it was leading to disaster." On the whole, however, the press comment was favorable and the campaign seemed to be off to an auspicious start.

The favorable auspices did not last long. Willkie set off on his first major swing around the country early in September aboard a 12-car train which the 50-odd reporters along promptly dubbed "the squirrel cage." This seemed to reflect accurately the general air of confusion, indecisiveness, and schedule foul-ups which prevailed. The route meandered through the Middle West and the Mountain States to the West Coast and back over a period of about two weeks. An early disaster was that the candidate lost his voice. Disdaining use of the public address system set up for him, he attempted by sheer lung power to make himself heard at the farthest edge of whatever assemblage was before him, either at a railroad siding or in a ball park. Within the first 48 hours he was reduced to a croak. A throat specialist was quickly recruited and became a permanent part of the entourage, and the PA system was reinstalled, but Willkie's voice never fully recovered during the remainder of the campaign.

The candidate drove himself (as well as his aides and the accompanying press corps) at a killing pace. He averaged about 10 speeches a day—sometimes the total reached 15—from the back platform of his railroad car and at scheduled stops that called for a motorcade and a major address. Impressively large audiences turned out to hear him wherever he went—30,000 at Tulsa, 15,000 at Albuquerque, 30,000 at San Diego, 75,000 at Los Angeles, and so on. He devoured speech material like a hungry lion attacking a carcass. An on-board speech-writing team headed by Davenport was never able to keep up with the demand nor to maintain a schedule of topics. Willkie used the texts they prepared merely as a springboard for ad-libbing, often roaming far afield to subject matter they were holding back for a different occasion, and even more grievously, clouding over or contradicting a position he had taken earlier. "If Mr. Willkie has weaknesses as a campaigner," the *Times'* James A. Hagerty reported from the candidate's train, "it is because he insists on doing too much and is inclined to scatter his fire. His speeches during a day would furnish headlines for half a dozen newspaper stories if they were not overshadowed by his more important speech at night."

The fine nonpartisan stance which Willkie had struck at Rushville was soon eroded by his own volatile frustrations and by the prodding of his more conservative Republican campaign managers. He had tried and failed to goad Roosevelt into some kind of debate. The President studiously ignored him. Willkie hacked away with increasing vehemence at the New Deal's failure to end unemployment and to promote business recovery, but it seemed to make no great impact on his listeners. The fact, as most people were aware, was that war industry was beginning to boom and the new jobs were opening up at the rate of almost half a million a month. Willkie had no soundly thought-out alternative to the New Deal, and that was plain.

He bore down anew on the third-term issue, passing beyond the "indispensable man" thesis to proclaim that if Roosevelt were reelected the country would have a dictatorship in another four years. That seemed to be a straw man, too.

He went even more deeply overboard on foreign policy, virtually turning his back on the endorsement he had accorded Roosevelt earlier. With a stridency that ill-became the image of temperate good judgment which he hitherto had projected, he denounced the President for deviousness, insincerity, and other assorted evils in confronting the war threat from Europe. Like the most ardent isolationist, he demanded time and again to know what "secret deals" Roosevelt had entered into that would entrap the nation in war. Time and again he asked "Does anybody in this audience think Roosevelt is sincerely trying to keep us out of war?" When the deal to swap overage destroyers to Britain in exchange for naval bases in the Caribbean was announced midway in the campaign, Willkie first expressed his approval of it (as had, indeed, that high oracle of radical isolationism, the *Chicago Tribune*) but later denounced it as "the most dictatorial and arbitrary act of any President in the history of the United States." In an incredible lapse into irresponsibility, he charged that during the Munich crisis a year earlier Roosevelt had "telephoned Hitler and Mussolini and urged them to sell Czechoslovakia down the river." That was such an egregious blunder (there had been a dozen other of lesser caliber) that his press secretary had to call in the reporters and admit that the candidate's zeal had simply carried him out on a nonexistent limb.

Willkie drew large audiences wherever he spoke and, usually, dense crowds along the route of his motorcades in the cities. But reporters soon detected a significant phenomenon in the crowd reactions. Downtown in the shopping and financial districts—white-collar territory—they responded to his genial grin and waving arms with cheers and shouts of encouragement. But in the blue-collar country around the stockyards and the factory gates the response was sullen, often hostile.

"He had a frosty time of it in Detroit and other Michigan cities last week," the *Times* reported in mid-October. "His audiences were small and labor was noticeably absent. In city after city—Toledo, Cleveland, Pittsburgh—the business districts were friendly, the factory districts hostile and booing. Mr. Willkie seemed tired and discouraged."

And in city after city, too, the hostility took an overt turn: Hecklers began pelting him with tomatoes, eggs, and a variety of other missiles with such frequency that the *Times* (in the interest of journalistic accuracy, perhaps) began running a daily box score of hits and misses.

The Willkie campaign was running down-hill. To thousands of on-lookers, the gallant crusader who had stormed the ramparts of conventional Republicanism at Philadelphia in the summer seemed to have turned into an old-fashioned Republican stooge by autumn. He looked and sounded more and more like what Harold Ickes had called him: "the barefoot boy from Wall Street." None of the issues which he had first proclaimed and then so lamely revised, altered, and hedged on, seemed to have ignited any fires at the grassroots. The dissatisfied Democrats and the switch-vote Independents on whose support his success depended had become disenchanted, and turned away. Turner Catledge, after a swing through the states west of the Mississippi, reported on this trend in the *Times* just a fortnight before the election, concluding:

If the fight against Mr. Roosevelt's succession to a third term is getting anywhere, it is not overwhelmingly apparent in the western part of the country. The participants in the anti-third-term cause are [the same people who] have long since been identified with opposition to Mr. Roosevelt. . . .

There is a question among Mr. Willkie's supporters whether he has gotten the most out of the issues at hand. A criticism often heard is that he has spread himself too thin, attempted to answer too many questions, and passed up opportunities to develop a major issue or a trend.

The very nature of his own campaign has complicated rather than simplified the campaign itself.

To such reports as these Roosevelt gave a knowing, I-told-you-so nod and a pleased smile. His own strategy was clear and uncomplicated. In his acceptance speech to the Chicago convention he had said: "I shall not have the time or the inclination to engage in purely political debate, but I shall never be loath to call the attention of the nation to deliberate or unwitting falsification of fact which are sometimes made by political candidates." In pursuit of that lofty, just barely supercilious, aim, he busied himself with the weighty responsibilities of the Presidency and, until the last two weeks before the election, eschewed all the overt trappings of electioneering.

His covert politicking was something else again. Inevitably, anything a President seeking reelection does has a bearing on his candidacy, for his roles are inseparable and interreacting. With his finely tuned political sensors, Roosevelt utilized this phenomenon with great skill. His leadership of the nation during the four months from July to November was conscientious and constructive, and it poured dividends into his politician's drawing account.

One of his earliest gambits was to strengthen his Cabinet by the appointment of two outstanding Republicans to posts of prime importance. Henry L. Stimson, who had served in the Cabinets of Presidents Taft and Hoover, was named Secretary of War. Colonel Frank Knox, the Chicago publisher who had been Landon's running mate in 1936, was appointed Secretary of the Navy. This came close to being a coalition "war" Cabinet that was bound to blunt Republican isolationist attacks on Roosevelt's handling of defense and foreign affairs. Its timing —two weeks before the Republican convention met—left that party's leaders sputtering with impotent rage. But from the standpoint of merit and ability, no one could find fault with either appointment.

The sense of international crisis built steadily through the summer and fall, the Battle of Britain having begun with devastating fury on August 11, and there stood FDR with the levers of power and authority in his hands. Congress remained in almost continuous session up to Election Day with Roosevelt exercising his leadership to secure enactment of the first peacetime draft in the nation's history; to gain authority to call up the National Guard; to pile up record-breaking appropriations for national defense ($17 billion worth in the year 1940 alone), and to consummate the swap of 50 overage destroyers to Britain (which did not require Congressional approval). His actions in office and his comments on the state of the world and on such burning questions as defense production and the buildup of the Army and Navy regularly overshadowed news from the political front. And he found it increasingly expedient as the weeks wore on to sally out of Washington on one- and two-day inspection trips to arsenals, navy yards, army cantonments, airplane factories, and the like as a boost to the nation's morale. It was always carefully explained that the President could not afford to venture more than 12 hours distant from the Capital and that such visitations were strictly nonpolitical in character. But he managed nevertheless to gain maximum visibility and personal contact with the public, and under the most favorable auspices, on these little goodwill junkets.

Late in October he said the time had come to set the record straight on "the systematic falsification of facts" that had been spread by his political opposition. On the twenty-third he set out aboard a campaign train of his own bedecked with flags and bunting, replete with staff aides and speech writers and carrying a full complement of reporters and photographers. His route carried him by broken stages up through New England as far as Boston, across New York, Pennsylvania, and Ohio as far westward as Cleveland. These were the critical states which, coupled with the dependable South, he needed to assure victory; the farm states and the West he left to the ministrations of Henry Wallace and certain members of his Cabinet.

Roosevelt stressed two principal themes in the major speeches he gave on this trip. The first was the progress which had been made on defense production, using facts and figures which refuted Willkie's increasingly bitter criticisms that the country was falling dangerously behind. The other was the laggardness of Willkie's Republican colleagues in Congress to support the defense program as enthusiastically as their candidate did. The purpose here was to highlight the sharp philosophical and political cleavages within the GOP and to raise doubts about Willkie's ability to lead. Roosevelt showed, for example, that a majority of Republicans in both houses of Congress had voted against the Selective Service Act, although Willkie had publicly endorsed it.

Roosevelt's style as a stump speaker was masterful. He established immediate empathy with his audience, never patronized, impressed with his command of language and knowledge, never descended to anger or vituperation. His most skillful oratorical thrusts were often couched in gentle, sophisticated ridicule. One of the most memorable of such ploys occurred in the speech he gave at Madison Square Garden early on this final campaign tour. Three Republicans who had most consistently opposed him on defense measures were Speaker Joe Martin, now Willkie's campaign manager; Representative Bruce Barton, who was now Willkie's candidate for Senator from New York; and Representative Hamilton Fish of New York, an outspoken isolationist who was ranking minority member of the House Military Affairs Committee. Roosevelt used this trio as representative of Republican obstructionism in general, citing their names repeatedly in the sing-song cadence of a nursery rhyme— "Martin, Barton, and Fish." By the second or third repetition, the delighted audience seized the phrase as their own, picking it up as Roosevelt pronounced the first syllable of "Martin" and shouting back in unison— "Barton and Fish!" It sent the hall into gales of laughter and applause. Roosevelt used the gimmick in one or two other speeches with identical results, but even where his text did not include such a cue the chant sometimes erupted spontaneously from the crowd as though prompted by an invisible cheerleader. "Martin, Barton, and Fish" injected a note of merriment into the closing days of the campaign, but needless to say it was not universally shared. Robert Sherwood quotes Willkie as saying later, "When I heard the President hang the isolationist votes of Martin, Barton, and Fish on me and get away with it, I knew I was licked." [5]

VII

Election Day was Tuesday, November 5. Roosevelt received 27,243,466 votes, 55 percent of the total; Willkie's share was 22,304,755, or 45 percent. The margin was much wider in electoral votes. Roosevelt carried 38 states with 449 votes in the electoral college, while Willkie carried 10 with a total of 82 electoral votes. Maine and Vermont went safely into the Republican column, and Indiana and Michigan joined by paper-thin margins that took days to calculate. The only consistent regional pattern of Republican majorities was in the five farm states—North Dakota, South Dakota, Iowa, Nebraska, Kansas—and neighboring Colorado. Republicans gained three new seats in the Senate but gave up eight in the House to Democrats.

It was not a close election, yet Willkie made a substantial showing considering the handicaps under which he labored. He rolled up the largest total of Republican votes ever recorded up to that time, which included, according to some estimates, as many as six million cast by citizens who had not previously voted the Republican ticket—first-timers, Democrats, Independents. This was the "new blood" of which the badly battered GOP stood in such desperate need, but the party regulars refused to recognize the contribution he had made.

The fear of war was the dominant concern of most voters, and Willkie was doubly handicapped on this score. Roosevelt, with his aura of experience and popularity, was in command; his known faults represented a lesser gamble than the unknown virtues of his challenger. Moreover, Willkie could not escape the isolationist coloration of his party—indeed, he invited it toward the end—at a time when isolationist sentiment was rapidly fading.

Finally, he could not shake off the shadow of his past as a "Wall Street lawyer" for the utilities. His professed and genuine liberalism remained suspect to millions in the white-collar and blue-collar middle class. Even the eleventh-hour endorsement he received from John L. Lewis of the mine workers union failed to break the solid resistance of organized labor to his candidacy.

Warren Moscow has observed: "There is no convenient place in the American political system for either ex-Presidents or ex-nominees for the Presidency." The fading away of the latter has been particularly pronounced, although their status as titular leader of the defeated party is supposed to endure for at least the next four years. Wendell Willkie's role in this respect was an extraordinary one. In spite of his defeat and the personal misadventures which he encountered—and even walked into—during the campaign, he inspired thousands of his followers with an enduring new political faith and zeal. His apotheosis closely resembled that of Adlai Stevenson, the defeated Democratic candidate of a little more than a decade later.

Following a period of seclusion in the Florida sun, Willkie emerged prepared to throw off the alien political influences which he had allowed to obscure his star and to blur his own clear sense of purpose. The world was full of danger, and he had the right, and the obligation to do what he could, in his own way, to avert it. The great imperative of the moment, as he saw it, was to give all possible help to Britain to stave off an Axis victory. Roosevelt was the undisputed leader of the nation for the next four years, and this, too, was Roosevelt's goal. So he would get behind Roosevelt with all the power and influence he possessed.

Roosevelt warmly welcomed his new ally. The rapport which speedily developed between these once-hostile adversaries, each a man of great pride and forcefulness, was unique in the political annals of the country. In January 1941, Willkie went to England as the President's emissary in order to see the war at firsthand and to meet Churchill and the other allied leaders. On his return he took a leading, and possibly decisive, role in the public debate over the lend-lease bill which was designed to increase vastly the flow of war goods overseas. By this time, Willkie's break with the isolationist wing of the Republican Party was complete and irrevocable, a break marked by extreme acrimony on the part of the GOP old guard, who had never trusted him in the first place. The *Chicago Tribune* denounced him as "a Republican Quisling" for his testimony in support of lend-lease before a committee of Congress. Later, Willkie made a fact-finding trip around the world for Roosevelt with the rank of Ambassador, and Warren Moscow records that throughout 1941 and during much of 1942 he was a frequent secret visitor to the White House for consultation with the President on a wide range of foreign and domestic affairs.

Willkie aspired to seek the Republican nomination again in 1944. By this time the animosity toward him within the ranks of the party regulars was so intense that his prospects looked minimal. Moreover, Dewey, who had been elected Governor of New York in 1942, also had well-laid designs on the same prize. The two met head-on in the Wisconsin primary in April. Willkie was decisively beaten and he dropped out of the race. For a spell there was intense speculation that the Democrats would offer Willkie the vice-presidential spot on their own ticket, or at least a Cabinet post, but nothing came of it. In September he suffered the first of a series of heart attacks, he entered the Lenox Hill Hospital in New York and died there on October 8. For a brief time, America had responded enthusiastically to Willkie's clear, strong voice —for its strength came not from any power he had gained, but from the ideals he expressed.

3

Day of Infamy*

I

In the predawn hours of Sunday, December 7, 1941, the U.S.S. *Condor,* a stubby little minesweeper, was on routine patrol through the choppy and faintly luminescent waters of the Pacific a mile and a half off the mouth of Pearl Harbor in the Hawaiians. The waning moon hung low on the western horizon, obscured most of the time by a broken overcast. Ensign R. C. McCloy, who was the officer of the deck for the midwatch, took one casual glance at the ship's clock on the bridge and made a mental note that his relief was due up in 10 minutes—at four o'clock.

As the *Condor* plowed along at an unworried seven knots, Ensign McCloy spotted a faint splash of white on the dark sea about 50 yards ahead off the port bow. At first he thought it was a bit of foam riding the crest of a wave. But it seemed to have a purposefulness and direction about it, and it didn't disappear as foam should have done. He swung his binoculars to his eyes and studied it a minute. Then he passed them over to his helmsman, Quartermaster 2/C. R. C. Uttrick, and asked him what he made of it.

"That's a periscope, sir, and there aren't supposed to be any subs in this area," Uttrick said.

Ensign McCloy seized the glasses and took another look. The white shadow had crossed the water toward the harbor entrance. There was no doubt in his mind about it now. It was the wake of a periscope, and even if it were one of his own—as he thought it probably was at the moment—it had no business being where it was.

* This account of the Pearl Harbor attack and its immediate aftermath is adapted from an article by the author which appeared in the *New York Times Magazine* for Sunday, December 2, 1951, marking the tenth anniversary of the event. It is based principally on the thirty-nine-volume report of the *Joint Committee on the Pearl Harbor Attack* (77th Congress, First Session, July 1946).

Two miles away at that moment, cruising at 15 knots on routine channel entrance patrol, was the destroyer *Ward*. At 4:05 A.M. the *Ward*'s deck officer observed a blinker signal from the *Condor*, "Have sighted submerged submarine on westerly course."

General quarters rang through the whole ship and the sleepy crew of the *Ward* stumbled to battle stations. On the bridge, the order was given for full speed to the *Condor*'s side. Additional data on course and speed of the strange submarine were procured and the *Ward* began to maneuver through elaborate search patterns. Although the search continued, the general quarters alert was relaxed at 4:58 A.M.

One hour later, as sunrise lighted the skies overhead, the *Ward* spotted "a strange object" in the water two miles off the starboard bow. Closing the distance under full steam, Commander William Outerbridge, the skipper, who had again been routed out of his bunk by an excited watch officer, identified it as the conning tower of a "baby" submarine— not an American type.

At 100 yards the *Ward* fired two salvos from her forward gun. The second scored a direct hit on the conning tower, which immediately plunged from view. As she passed over the spot, the *Ward* dropped a depth charge and a moment later saw a huge, black oil bubble break the surface.

At 6:54 A.M., Honolulu time, the *Ward* radioed the commandant of the Fourteenth Naval District, Pearl Harbor: "We have attacked, fired upon, and dropped depth charges on a submarine operating in defensive sea areas."

The United States had won the first preliminary skirmish—but only that—in the as yet unrevealed war with Japan.

There is a five-and-a-half-hour time differential between Washington and Honolulu. At almost the precise moment that the *Condor* spotted the Japanese baby sub, cryptanalysts 5,000 miles away in the Navy Department in Washington finished deciphering an intercepted radio message from the Foreign Office in Tokyo to its Ambassador in the United States, Admiral Kichisaburo Nomura.

This was the fourteenth—and critical—part of a long diplomatic dispatch in which the Imperial Government was to turn down the urgent request of the United States for peaceful mediation between the two countries in the Pacific. The first 13 parts (decipherable because the United States had long since broken Japan's most secret code) had been intercepted the day before. These had been the subject of troubled study by President Roosevelt; Secretary of State Hull; Secretary of the Navy Knox; General Marshall, the Chief of Staff; Harry Hopkins; and a handful of others late into Saturday night. It was obvious that the Japanese were on the brink of a massive breach of peace, but precisely where and when the blow would fall none of our officials could tell. The fourteenth part, which had not been transmitted from Tokyo until after midnight, was believed to contain the key to the ominous puzzle, and was therefore awaited with trepidation.

At 9:30 on Sunday morning a courier left the Navy Department with a transcript of the fourteenth part. He delivered one copy at the office of Secretary of State Hull, who had already come down from his apartment at the Wardman Park Hotel, and took another across the street to the White House. Captain John R. Beardall, a naval aide, delivered it to the President in his bedroom at 10 o'clock.

As the President read the concluding sentence, "The Japanese Government regrets to have to notify hereby the American Government . . . it cannot but consider that it is impossible to reach an agreement," he shook his head and said, "It looks as though the Japs are going to break off negotiations."

Meanwhile, Secretaries Hull, Knox, and Stimson were threshing over the implications of the message in Mr. Hull's office at the State Department. All available evidence pointed to a Japanese thrust at Indochina, and they were considering the steps to be taken by this country in that event. While they were talking, two other intercepts arrived from the Navy Department. They were in "purple" code and marked "Urgent —Very Important."

They instructed Ambassador Nomura to deliver the 14-part message to the Secretary of State precisely at one o'clock that day and, after deciphering Part 14, "to destroy at once the remaining cipher machine and all machine codes. Dispose in like manner also secret documents."

This added a sinister and portentous imminence to whatever it was that was about to happen. After satisfying themselves that the President had also received copies of the two latest messages, the conferees separated at 11:15 A.M. Mr. Knox went to his office in the Navy Building and Mr. Stimson to his home on Woodley Road, a couple of miles away, for lunch.

Bright sunlight streamed through the windows of the old State Department Building as the three Secretaries broke up their conference. But at Latitude 26 degrees North, Longitude 158 degrees West, 275 miles north of the island of Oahu, six carriers of the Pearl Harbor Striking Force under the command of Admiral Chuichi Nagumo rendezvoused just as the first gray hints of dawn touched the horizon.

This was the terminus of a 4,000-mile voyage that had begun from an obscure anchorage in the Kurile Islands on November 16, and which had been completed in total invisibility to the eyes of the rest of the world. The Japanese force was made up, in addition to the six carriers, of two battleships, two cruisers, and two destroyers, with a compliment of more than 15,000 men.

On board the flagship *Agaki,* the "Z" flag, which had flown at the Battle of Tsushima in 1905, was flown beneath the scarlet emblem of the Rising Sun. All hands who could be spared were called to the flight decks for a final, fanatical dedication to the task that was about to begin. In each pilot's hand was placed a mimeographed chart of Pearl Harbor, with ship positions and other target data corrected up to the last 24 hours.

"Zero" was set for six o'clock, and the first wave of planes roared in the air amid frenzied shouts of "Banzai! Banzai!" from those on deck. Ninety "Kates" loaded with bombs and torpedoes, 50 "Val" dive bombers, and 50 "Zeke" fighters circled into formation, climbed over the cloud cover to 9,000 feet, and in the sparkling early-morning sunlight streaked southward toward Hawaii.

A lowly seaman, Kuramoto, tried to preserve for posterity the rapture of the moment by writing down these words:

. . . and now our Eagles were moving into a great formation. Our 10 years and more of intensive training would now bear fruit. At this thought a thousand emotions filled our hearts as, close to tears, we watched this magnificent sight. One and all, in our hearts, we sent our pleas to the gods, and putting our hands together, we prayed.

While Kuramoto and his friends were praying for the safe return of their "Eagles," General Marshall in Washington hurried to the War Department from his quarters across the Potomac at Fort Myer. He had been out for his usual horseback ride that morning. In response to an urgent message he reached his office at precisely 11:15.

Impassively, he read the full text of the 14-part Japanese message— he was not among those who had seen it the night before. But when he came to the two supplements, the "one o'clock" and the code-destruction messages, his granite features showed unaccustomed alarm.

"This certainly means that something is going to happen at one o'clock today," he said to the aides grouped about him. "When they specify the day, that's significant enough, but when they specify the hour . . . Get Admiral [Harold R.] Stark [Chief of Naval Operations] on the phone for me right away."

In a tensely brief conversation, Marshall and Stark agreed on a warning message to be sent immediately to all Army and Navy commanders throughout the Pacific. Other general warnings had been sent before, the latest on November 27. But this was to have a superseding note of urgency. The general scribbled it out in longhand:

The Japanese are presenting at 1 P.M., E.S.T., today, what amounts to an ultimatum. Also, they are under orders to destroy their code machines immediately. Just what significance the hour set may have we do not know, but be on the alert accordingly.

At 11:50 General Marshall handed the message to his communications officer, Colonel Edward F. French, who put it in code and hurried it in person to the Army's Communications center. There he found that radio contact with Honolulu was temporarily suspended. On a hasty decision he turned it over to Western Union. The hours was 12:02 P.M. Western Union received it in San Francisco 15 minutes later and gave it to RCA for radio transmission. RCA-Honolulu stamped the message "In" at 1:03 P.M. (7:33 A.M., their time).

There was no teletype connection with Fort Shafter, headquarters of Lieutenant General Walter C. Short, the commanding general in Hawaii, so RCA handed the Washington message to one of its motorcycle messengers for delivery.

In an exploit that should surely compete for fame with the "Message to Garcia" of an earlier decade, RCA's swift courier was interrupted on his rounds by the first wave of Japanese bombs and strafing fire to rake Pearl Harbor that morning.

General Marshall and Admiral Stark, feeling they had done all they could in view of the remaining uncertainties of the emergency, reported their action to Secretary Knox at his office in the Navy Department. He advised them, in turn, that he had learned from Secretary Hull only a moment before that the Japanese Ambassadors, Nomura and Kurusu, had telephoned the State Department at noon asking for an appointment with the Secretary for the fateful hour of one o'clock.

Noon in Washington was 6:30 in Honolulu, the hour of sunrise. Sunday, December 7, for the few who were abroad at that hour, promised to be an uncommonly lovely day. The sky was a brilliant blue. Here and there a fleecy bit of cloud drifted in the gentle trade wind. The verdant slopes of Mount Tantalus and Mount Olympus glistened with dew.

At their berths in Pearl Harbor, tied up two-by-two, lay 94 combat and auxiliary ships of the Pacific Fleet, including 8 battleships, 29 destroyers, and 5 submarines.

Many of their crews were on weekend shore leave, for the Navy was operating under the relaxed strictures of a peacetime "Condition 3." None of the main batteries was manned. The plotting rooms were shut down, ammunition for the few machine and antiaircraft guns, which had skeleton crews that morning, was stored in locked compartments for which only the deck officers had the keys.

At Wheeler, Hickam, and Ewa Airfields the 192 usable combat planes of the Army and Marine Air arms were tied down wing-to-wing in precise, tidy rows on the aprons. Air reconnaissance at dawn was confined to three Navy Catalinas covering a narrow sector extending only 200 miles northwesterly. The Army's primitive radar equipment was being used on a training basis only and none of its antiaircraft emplacements had ammunition on hand.

No premonitions troubled the waning slumbers of Pearl Harbor at sun-up on that Sunday in 1941. Such pertinent activity as there was at that hour was centered largely in only two widely separated spots.

At a remote radar station two Army privates trying to learn the intricacies of this new long-range detection gadget picked up a large and unexpected "blip" on their scope at 7:02 A.M. They calculated its bearing at almost due north and its distance at 132 miles. They tracked it in fascinated and growing apprehension for 18 minutes. At 7:20 they called the Information Center at Hickam Field on their field telephones to report their puzzling discovery. A passing flight lieutenant who happened to receive the call told the men, "Forget it." It probably was a flight of our own planes, he said.

Almost simultaneously, Navy Lieutenant Harold Kaminsky, watch officer at the Pearl Harbor Submarine Base, was handed the radio message from the destroyer *Ward* announcing her successful attack on the strange submarine. The *Ward* had filed her message at 6:54 A.M., but for some reason it did not get to Lieutenant Kaminsky's hands until 18 minutes later, at 7:12. This was the first intimation ashore of the submarine hunt that the *Condor* had initiated three hours earlier.

At that improbable hour, telephone switchboards on the base were manned by 10-thumbed yeomen. It was 7:20 before Lieutenant Kaminsky was able to get through to the staff duty officer, Commander Vincent R. Murphy, who had just risen and was shaving in his quarters. Excitedly, Commander Murphy gave Lieutenant Kaminsky a list of key officers to call and told him to order the ready destroyer, *Monaghan,* to pursue the search. He finished dressing and went to his office on the double.

When he got there he found that Lieutenant Kaminsky had been unable to get a call through to the base commander, Admiral Husband E. Kimmel. Commander Murphy took over the switchboard himself. As the admiral uttered a sleepy "Hello," there was a shattering blast as the first Japanese bomb exploded on the seaplane ramp 200 yards away. It was 7:55 and the "Day of Infamy" had begun.

Now there was bedlam outside: the deep-throated whine of planes roaring past at tree-top level, the irregular thunder of bursting bombs and torpedoes, the chatter of strafing machine guns. One could glimpse the scarlet "meatball" insignia on the wing-tips as the planes whipped past.

Commander Murphy ran down the hall to the communciations room and dictated a top-priority radio message to the Commander in

Chief of the Asiatic Fleet and to the Chief of Naval Operations in Washington:

JAPANESE ATTACKING PEARL HARBOR—THIS IS NO DRILL.

Washington at that moment was as calm and untroubled, outside the tight little periphery of the White House, as Honolulu had been two or three minutes earlier. Here, too, it was a clear, bright day with a touch of winter crispness in the air.

Readers of the *Washington Post* were apprised over their morning coffee that the Japanese were ominously massing their forces in the Far East, that King Leopold III of the Belgians had been married, that Soviet Ambassador Maxim Litvinov was due to arrive at National Airport at 9:40 A.M. The society columns noted that Mrs. Evalyn Walsh Maclean would entertain at Friendship that evening for her daughter and new son-in-law, Senator Robert R. Reynolds of North Carolina. And sports fans were notified that the kickoff in the Redskins-Philadelphia Eagles game was set for 2:00 P.M. at Griffith Stadium.

As one o'clock approached, Secretary Hull was sitting in his office with Green Hackworth and Joseph W. Ballantine, two of his closest aides, discussing just what he should say to the two Japanese emissaries when they arrived. They were interrupted by a telephone call from Admiral Nomura asking that the appointment be postponed 45 minutes because of difficulties they were having in decoding their instructions from Tokyo. This was agreed to.

Across the street at the White House, President Roosevelt and Harry Hopkins were lunching together in the Oval Room, discussing, as Mr. Hopkins recalled later, "things far removed from war." At the Navy Department, a few blocks away on Constitution Avenue, Secretary Knox and Admiral Stark were together in the latter's office discussing things not far removed from war.

At 1:50 a communications officer burst unceremoniously into the room and thrust into Admiral Stark's hand Commander Murphy's startling message from Hawaii: "Japanese attacking Pearl Harbor—this is no drill."

Secretary Knox exclaimed: "My God, this can't be true! They must mean the Philippines."

A moment's reflection convinced him that so wide an error was highly improbable. He hurried to his own office, picked up his White House telephone and read the message to the President. With shock and anger in his voice, President Roosevelt, too, conceded the probable accuracy of the message; he asked the Navy to rush whatever confirmation it could.

That was just the unexpected kind of thing the Japanese were capable of doing, he said turning to Harry Hopkins; at the very moment they were discussing peace in the Pacific they were plotting to undermine it. Mr. Roosevelt dialed the code number for the State Department on his private phone.

Mr. Hull had just been informed of the arrival of Ambassadors Nomura and Kurusu in the diplomatic waiting room outside his office when the call from the President came through at 2:05. After the first stunning impact of the news, Mr. Hull recalled later, he thought he would dismiss the Japanese envoys without a hearing. On second thought, he decided to see them on the remote possibility that the report was inaccurate.

His famed Tennessee anger was at white heat but under rigid control when the two smiling, morning-coated Ambassadors bowed stiffly before his desk at 2:20 P.M. He greeted them coldly and did not ask them to be seated. He flipped perfunctorily through the first couple of pages of the document—the now-familiar 14-part message—that they handed him.

Then in a voice vibrant with restraint and indignation he said:

In all my conversations with you during the last nine months, I have never uttered one word of untruth. This is borne out absolutely by the record.

In all my 50 years of public service I have never seen a document that was more crowded with infamous falsehoods and distortions—infamous falsehoods and distortions on a scale so huge that I never imagined until today that any government on this planet was capable of uttering them.

Nomura sucked in his breath as if he were about to speak. With a peremptory gesture of his hand, Mr. Hull waved him and Ambassador Kurusu out of his offices.

By the time this tableau was completed a few minutes before 2:30 Washington time, Pearl Harbor was already a shambles. The first phase of the attack, which had swept in at 7:55 and lasted for about 30 minutes, had wrought 90 percent of all the damage and casualties to be inflicted that day.

Twice the attackers withdrew briefly to regroup and then roared back over the flaming, panic-stricken target.

At 9:45, just two hours after the first bomb had been dropped, it was all over. Seaman Kuramoto's Eagles winged back to their nest, 29 short of their original number.

Behind them they left a scene of chaos unmatched on American soil in all history. Dense columns of black smoke boiled high into the sunlit sky. Flames from oil and gasoline tanks shot into the air, spread out over the waters, turned buildings and trees and human bodies to cinders.

Of the eight battleships in the harbor that morning—the backbone of the Pacific Fleet—four were sunk or capsized. The remaining four, as well as three destroyers, three cruisers, and four auxiliary vessels, were heavily damaged and burning.

One hundred and eighty-eight planes were destroyed on the ground, and most of the hangers and repair facilities demolished.

Human casualties were 2,403 dead and 1,178 wounded.

Seldom in all the annals of warfare had one force won so complete and devastating a victory over another is so short a time.

The aftermath of terror did not begin to lift from the island of Oahu for another 24 hours. Governor Joseph B. Poindexter instituted a state of emergency almost as the last Japanese planes disappeared to the north. The Red Cross set up emergency medical and feeding facilities before noon. Civil defense forces were mobilized, and families living on the base were evacuated to homes, schools, and churches in outlying districts.

Rumors of new attacks, of paratroop landings, of wholesale sabotage by Japanese residents of the island spread panic in ever-recurring waves through the civilian population. The Japanese consulate in Honolulu was raided while its members were in the act of burning their papers.

On orders from President Roosevelt martial law was declared throughout the Territory of Hawaii at 4:30 that afternoon.

The American public got its first news of the disaster while the attack was still in progress. A good part of that public, at least in Washington, had its mind on anything but war that inviting Sunday afternoon. It was a day to load up the family automobile for a jaunt into the country, to get in what might be the last round of golf before winter set in, or to see the Redskins play their last home game of the season, which is what 27,102 persons did.

At 2:35 P.M. Louise Hachmeister, White House switchboard superintendent, rang up the three press associations and put them on a simultaneous conference hook-up with Steve Early, the President's press secretary.

"All on?" she asked. "AP? UP? INS? Here's Mr. Early."

"This is Steve Early at the White House," came a familiar but strained voice over the wire. "At 7:55 A.M., Hawaiian time, the Japanese bombed Pearl Harbor. The attacks are continuing and . . . no, I don't know how many are dead."

"Flash" bells on news tickers all the way across the country began to jangle. Radio programs were interrupted by excited announcers who blurted out the first bulletins.

Throughout Washington telephone facilities were swamped by the curious and the alarmed and by harassed government and military officials trying to round up their staffs.

The loudspeaker at Griffith Stadium called off the names of one admiral, general, and Cabinet officer after another, instructing them: "Please get in touch with your office at once."

Within an hour a crowd of several thousand had congregated silently on the sidewalks in front of the White House. Another thousand, strangely unbelligerent, tied up traffic in front of the Japanese Embassy on Massachusetts Avenue. As they watched, two carloads of FBI men dashed up to establish a guard over the premises—a service which the Japanese had thoughtfully already provided for themselves through the Burns Detective Agency.

The Cabinet "Big Three"—the Secretaries of State, War, and Navy —were summoned to the White House at three o'clock, after which there ensued a string of emergency orders designed to protect the internal security of the country. The FBI was ordered to pick up all Japanese aliens. The Army and Navy were ordered to throw armed guards around all military installations and government buildings. The Treasury impounded $131 million of Japanese assets in this country. The Navy clamped censorship on all outgoing cables. Private planes were grounded and radio amateurs were silenced.

At 8:30 President Roosevelt met with his full Cabinet for nearly an hour.

At 9:30 he summoned the legislative leaders from both parties, making one ostentatious omission—Representative Hamilton Fish, the New York Republican, who had been the loudest in his cries of "warmonger." The President told them he would want to address a joint session of Congress the next day.

At 11:30 P.M. the Oval Room was cleared. The President said he would take no more calls nor see any other visitors. With Harry Hopkins pacing moodily behind his chair and Grace Tully sitting across the desk with open notebook and with poised pencil, he began to dictate the simple message he would deliver to Congress at 12:30 P.M. on Monday:

Yesterday, December 7, 1941—a date which will live in infamy—the United States of America was suddenly and deliberately attacked by naval and air forces of the Empire of Japan. . . .

II

Pearl Harbor was the worst military disaster in this nation's history. It was also a part of one of the boldest, most perfectly executed offensive operations in all military history.

The blow at Pearl fell with the swift finality of an executioner's sword. Almost simultaneously, moreover, other blows were struck at key points thousands of miles distant in the Pacific—Guam, Wake, the Philippines, and British naval installations at Singapore and Hong Kong. Oil storage tanks were still exploding at Pearl Harbor on the other side of the international date line when the first flight of Japanese dive bombers roared in from the China Sea over Clark Field, the principal U.S. air base on the island of Luzon in the Philippines. Row upon row of glistening bombers and fighter planes were neatly tied down along the runways. When the invaders roared away a couple of hours later, more than half the planes in General Douglas MacArthur's Far Eastern Command had been destroyed like targets in a shooting gallery, and the complex of shops and hangars at Clark Field was enveloped in flames. The islands of Guam and Wake were attacked within the same 24-hour span, and a day later the back of the British Asiatic Fleet was broken with the sinking of two of its newest and mightiest ships, *Repulse* and *Prince of Wales,* in air attacks off Singapore.

The dive bombers over Luzon were soon followed by paratroopers and by tens of thousands of Japanese infantry landed from naval transports. They easily overrode the defending forces made up of American infantry plus large numbers of undertrained and poorly equipped Filipinos, and pushed toward Manila, the capital. The small American Far Eastern Naval Command under Admiral Thomas Hart, and the surviving remnants of the Army Air Force under Major General Lewis Brererton, had previously been dispersed to safe havens in Borneo. Without effective naval or air protection, and with no prospect of help from the outside, MacArthur's position quickly became hopeless. By Christmas he had abandoned Manila and withdrawn with what troops he had left to fortifications on the Bataan peninsula to carry on for a few more weeks a courageous but futile holding operation.*

In less than a month, the incredible Japanese had all but obliterated American and British power throughout the Pacific.

American strategy, with its eye fixed on Europe, had been slow to recognize the full implications of Japanese expansionism in the Far East. There were compelling economic and demographic impulses behind that urge to spread out. In little more than a single generation, the Island

---

* American combat strength in the Far Eastern Command in December 1941, was approximately as follows: Army, 30,000 U. S. troops, 100,000 Filipino; Air Force, 35 B-17 heavy bombers, 81 P-40 fighter-pursuit planes, about 50 other aircraft of older vintage; Navy one heavy cruiser, one light cruiser, 13 destroyers (mostly World War I vintage), 29 submarines. Plans were underway to strengthen substantially both the ground and air forces early in the year. Several shiploads of military supplies were en route to Manila when the Japanese struck and never reached their destination. The first 12 of 50 new B-17s destined to be flown out to Brererton's command by the end of the year landed for a scheduled fueling stop at Pearl Harbor on Sunday, December 7, while the Japanese attack was underway.

Empire had caught up with the Industrial Revolution, emerging from feudalism to become the most progressive economy in the Orient. With a land area (for Japan proper) roughly that of California's but with a population 10 times as great (72 million) she coveted not only more living space on the nearby land mass of China, but also the raw materials and markets that China and the rest of Asia afforded. Wherever she looked, however, her path seemed to be blocked by the diplomatic and commercial influences of the British, French, Dutch, and Americans, who had gotten there first. The "open door" policy which Western powers had imposed on the region at the turn of the century seemed to be barred by a sign reading "Whites Only." This grated harshly on the sensibilities of the growing class of nationalists who were coming to power in Japan in the decades following the First World War.

When diplomacy failed to relieve the pressures the Japanese turned to conquest. In 1932, after a nearly bloodless coup, they converted Manchuria into the puppet state of Manchukuo, a colonial dependency. In 1935 they attempted by the same strategy to annex the five northern provinces of China, but met stiffened resistance from forces led by Chiang Kai-shek, the Chinese nationalist leader. Two years later this conflict spread into open warfare with massive commitments of Japanese land, air, and sea forces. The Chinese were badly outmatched in everything except raw manpower, and the invaders inched inexorably southward. American sympathies, both governmental and public, ran heavily toward the Chinese: We had cultural and sentimental ties with their country running back almost a century, plus an economic stake on the order of $250 million. Since the conflict was never graced with a formal declaration of war, the strictures of our Neutrality Law did not apply. We made extensive loans to the Chinese government for the purchase of munitions and supplies, but continued to ship needed raw materials (though no munitions) to the Japanese under the terms of a 10-year-old trade treaty. United States (as well as British) military garrisons and naval patrols, admitted under earlier treaties with China, remained at their stations in the face of the oncoming Japanese tide. In December 1937, Japanese planes bombed and strafed the U. S. gunboat *Panay* on patrol in the Yangtze River, resulting in heavy damage and casualties.

For most Americans the *Panay* incident provided their first awareness that this country might have a direct stake in the Far Eastern conflict. But by and large they regarded it as a diplomats' war to be fought with verbal and legalistic weapons: A shooting involvement in that far-off part of the world was simply unthinkable. And indeed the diplomats in Washington and Tokyo were strenuously engaged, the Japanese insisting that their program for a Greater East Asia was essentially benign and economic, the Americans protesting that it was aggression in defiance of treaty obligations and inimical to American interests. Thus, as the tempo of the land war in China stepped up, so did the severity of the diplomatic war. In January 1940, after due notice, this country terminated its long-standing trade treaty with Japan, which severely limited both our exports to and our imports from that country, a traffic upon which the Japanese war economy was heavily dependent. In September of that year, when Japan announced it was joining Germany and Italy in an anticommintern pact aimed at Russia, but intended primarily to intimidate Britain and the United States, we retaliated by putting an embargo on shipments of steel and scrap iron to Japan. This was a severe tightening of the economic noose we had previously put about her neck.

In spite of such obstacles, the Japanese conquerors had bombed and fought all the way to Hong Kong and beyond. In July 1941, their forces occupied French Indochina and were aiming their next thrust at Thailand, or possibly the Netherlands East Indies farther south. Crisis signals flashed frantically in Washington (and in London, too, where the British, pinned to the wall by Hitler, had little strength to spare for the Far East but much to lose there). In August President Roosevelt ordered a freeze on all Japanese assets in the United States, clapped an embargo on the shipment of vital aviation fuel for Japan's air force, and dispatched his sternest note to date to Tokyo, warning that any further aggression (meaning against Thailand in particular) would compel the United States "to take immediately any and all steps necessary to safeguard the legitimate rights and interests" of this government and its nationals in the area. This was tough medicine, indeed, and it brought the boil to a head.

As we now know, this passage of events created almost as much alarm and consternation in Tokyo as it did in Washington. The Greater East Asia propaganda and the successes of the campaign against China had generated intense patriotic fervor among a large proportion of the Japanese people. It had greatly advanced the cause of the militant nationalists in the government and eroded correspondingly the influence of the conservatives grouped around the unwarlike Emperor Hirohito. The embargoes and other obstacles which the United States had thrown across their path of conquest had already cut deeply into their strategy; now it appeared that the strategy might be derailed completely. Within the war party of the Imperial Cabinet the alternatives were clear: either persuade the United States to relent or make war upon her. Others argued that a military solution was foredoomed. The controversy raged for weeks within the Cabinet. It was finally resolved in mid-October: The conservative government led by Prince Fumimaro Konoye fell and General Hideki Tojo, Minister of War and leader of the war party, was installed as Prime Minister.

As far back as September Tojo and the High Military Command had worked out a tentative plan and timetable for the launching of the attack against the United States around the end of October, its triggering contingent upon the outcome of whatever diplomatic negotiations might meanwhile intervene. Upon taking office as Prime Minister, one of his first acts was to activate the secret September war plan. To further this he sent Saburu Kurusu as his special envoy to the United States to work with Ambassador Kichisaburo Nomura in a final effort to talk the Americans into making some concession. They understood that if, within the prescribed time limit—moved from late October to late November—the desired results had not been achieved, the war button would be pressed.

The punctilious, inscrutably bland diplomats never knew until later —much later—that every proposal and insinuation they placed before Secretary of State Cordell Hull in their many visits with him during late October and November had been anticipated and prejudged by that wily official before the visitors arrived at his office. Months before, U.S. intelligence had broken Japan's most secret diplomatic codes. Daily, voluminous transcripts of these "Magic" intercepts of communications between the Foreign Ministry in Tokyo and its representatives in Washington and elsewhere around the world were regularly studied by Hull, the President, and a tight circle of other high government officials.

On November 20 the two ambassadors brought to Hull what he knew to be Japan's final proposal for resolving its differences with the United States in East Asia. In turgid diplomatese it set forth these conditions: that the United States supply Japan with the oil she needed, unfreeze her assets, resume regular commercial relations, and desist from giving aid and comfort to China and Indochina. Hull, forewarned, was able to read this inflammatory document without a flicker of emotion crossing his craggy features. He informed his visitors that their proposals would receive consideration and courteously bowed them out the door. His subsequent burst of outrage is nowhere recorded. In his memoirs he merely observes, "The commitments we should have to make were virtually a surrender . . . and acceptance of the role of silent partner aiding and abetting Japan in her effort to create a Japanese hegemony over the western Pacific and eastern Asia."

For the next two weeks newspapers bristled with ominous reports of the worsening state of Japanese-American relations. But only a handful of top government officials in Washington and a few other capitals (the British, Australians, and Dutch were being informed on a "need to know" basis) knew how desperate the situation had really become.

In effect, the Japanese note of November 20 was an ultimatum. Hull was forewarned by "Magic" that this was their last negotiating offer; that if it were rejected there would be a resort to force. Even the deadline of this decision was known. An intercepted message to Nomura from Tokyo on the twenty-second advised him:

It is awfully hard for us to consider changing the date we set in my #736. Stick to your fixed policy and do your very best to bring about the solution we desire. There are reasons beyond your ability to guess why we wanted to settle Japanese-American relations by the 25th. But if you can finish your conversations with the Americans, if the signing can be completed by the 29th . . . we have decided to wait until that date. This time we mean it, that the deadline absolutely cannot be changed. After that things are automatically going to happen. . . .

What "things"? Washington wanted desperately to know, but "Magic" and other intelligence sources supplied only inconclusive answers. It was learned on the twenty-fifth that an expeditionary force of from 40 to 50 Japanese troop ships was progressing south from Shanghai, presumably toward Indochina. And it was learned two days later—on the twenty-seventh—that a large naval air task force which had been assembled in the Kuriles to the north had steamed away during the night to a "destination unknown" (which turned out to be Pearl Harbor). These were clear signs that Japan was preparing a war strike *somewhere,* and American commanders throughout the Pacific were put on the most urgent "war alert" they had received to date. It read as follows:

Top Secret.
This dispatch is to be considered a war warning. Negotiations with Japan looking toward stabilization of conditions in the Pacific have ceased and an aggressive move by Japan is expected in the next few days. The number and equipment of Japanese troops and the organization of naval task forces indicate an amphibian expedition against either the Philippines, Thai, or Kra Peninsula or possibly Borneo. Exercise an appropriate defensive deployment preparatory to carrying out the tasks assigned to WPL 46. . . .

Neither this nor prior alerts included Hawaii among the probable targets, but the instructions were meant to be as applicable there as at Guam or the Philippines.

On November 26 Hull delivered to the Japanese ambassadors the official United States response to their note of the twentieth. Its preparation had consumed days of the most intense deliberation. The Army and the Navy wanted to buy time by making modest concessions to the Japanese demands in order to build up American defensive capabilities, particularly in the Philippines. Hull agreed with them. They were argued down by others (including the British and Dutch ambassadors, who were brought in on the discussions) who contended the Japanese would construe this as a sign of weakness and only increase their belligerence. Roosevelt agreed that nothing was to be gained by dabbling with semantics and token concessions; that the only safe posture was one of firmness. Hence, the American response on November 26 was about as categorical and arbitrary as the Japanese demand of November 20: It proposed a non-aggression pact among all the Pacific powers, resumption of normal trade relations, and agreement by Japan to give up her territorial gains and renounce any future conquests in China and Indochina. It was wholly negative to Japan's inflated aspirations.

The American note was handed to the Japanese diplomats by Secretary Hull at five o'clock in the afternoon. They took the news stoically and departed. The hinge of fate had snapped shut. Hull called Stimson on the telephone and said, "I have washed my hands of it and it is now in the hands of you and Knox, the Army and the Navy." It was also in the hands of Admiral Nagumo, whose Task Force 1 was a day out of Hitikapu Bay, steaming eastward toward a secret rendezvous 250 miles off the island Oahu.[1]

III

No national disaster ever struck the United States with such swift and stunning force as the attack on Pearl Harbor. For a whole generation of Americans, that instant of personal awareness would remain imprinted for a lifetime upon their memory like an indelible snapshot, vivid and undiminished. It had come like a bolt out of the blue on a placid Sunday afternoon—*"The Japs have bombed Pearl Harbor!"* They heard it over the loudspeakers while watching a football game, while listening idly to the radio, walking home from church, in a breathless call over the telephone. Everyone has his own story of how he first got the news, each a little more bizarre than the last. The general reaction was one of disbelief, then of shock, then of anger mixed with humiliation. And inevitably there came the outcry to know how such a thing could have happened, and who was to blame.

Those questions urgently needed answering. Within days a Presidential Commission headed by Supreme Court Justice Owen J. Roberts had begun the monumental task. Over the next five weeks the Commission held 29 closed-door sessions in Washington and Hawaii, examined 127 witnesses from the highest brass to the lowliest enlisted man, and compiled over 5,000 pages of testimony and exhibits. The report was submitted to the President on January 23, 1942, and at his direction released to the public the next day.

The Roberts Commission painted an appalling picture of complacency and divided authority between Army and Navy commands at Pearl Harbor, and of failure to react appropriately to the war warnings sent them from Washington. The President, the Secretaries of State, War, and Navy, and the two service chiefs were absolved of blame. Washington, the report said in effect, had done all that could be expected of it in detecting and interpreting the Japanese threat, but in Hawaii a barrier of ancient protocol and interservice rivalry prevented the Army from knowing or caring what the Navy did about the warnings, and vice versa. The chief burden of guilt was placed upon the two military commanders on the scene, Admiral Husband E. Kimmel and Lieutenant General Walter C. Short. (The President had by this time relieved them of command.) Both were officially charged with dereliction of duty. In its summary the report said:

> Had orders issued by the Chief of Staff and the Chief of Naval Operations on November 27, 1941, been complied with, the aircraft warning system of the Army should have been operating; the distant reconnaisance of the Navy and the in-shore patrol of the Army should have been maintained; the anti-aircraft battalions of the Army and similar shore batteries of the Navy, as well as additional anti-aircraft artillery located on vessels of the Fleet in Pearl Harbor, should have been manned and supplied with ammunition, and a high state of readiness of aircraft should have been in effect.

> None of these conditions was in fact inaugurated or maintained for the reason that the responsible commanders failed to consult and cooperate as to necessary actions based upon the warnings and to adopt measures enjoined by the orders given them by the chiefs of the Army and Navy commands in Washington. . . .

> In the light of the warnings and directions to take appropriate action, transmitted to both commanders between November 27 and December 7, and the obligations under the system of coordination then in effect for joint cooperative action on their part, it was a dereliction of duty on the part of each of them not to consult and confer with the other respecting the meaning and intent of the warnings and the appropriate measures of defense required by the imminence of hostilities.

For most people the Roberts report confirmed the suppositions they already had formed about the cause of the disaster, and it satisfied their need for a scapegoat. There were instant demands that Kimmel and Short be court-martialed. (They were not.) Others were less than satisfied that the Commission had dug out all the answers, and some hinted that it had contrived to "whitewash" the President and the responsible members of his Cabinet. Isolationists were particularly bitter, for their cause had now been wiped out utterly: Representative Hamilton Fish postulated that the Japanese attack had succeeded because Roosevelt had weakened the Navy by the swap of destroyers to Britain, and the *Chicago Tribune* asserted that the President had *encouraged* the attack as a means of getting the nation into the war.

Strong sentiment developed in Congress for a more sweeping congressional investigation of the affair. The temptation was quickly dissipated, however, by the onrushing imperatives of actually waging war and by the tide of patriotic fervor sweeping across the country. But the idea did not wither; instead, it fattened on the political nourishment of die-hard isolationism and Republican frustration over the seeming indestructibility of the Roosevelt mystique (which was strong enough to carry him to a fourth term in 1944). Hard on the heels of VJ-Day, the Joint Congressional Committee to Investigate Pearl Harbor was authorized. It began work in November 1945, ran through 75 days of hearings, accumulated 39 printed volumes of testimony and exhibits, and released its report in July 1946. The study revealed a vast amount of detail that hitherto had been concealed under wartime security regulations. But, in respect to pinpointing responsibility for the disaster, it did not stray substantially from the earlier findings of the Roberts Commission. Two Republican members, Senators Homer Ferguson of Michigan and Owen Brewster of Maine, filed a minority report accusing Roosevelt of contributory negligence in failure to enforce the needed cooperation between the Army and Navy. But no one cared very much any more. The war was over, Roosevelt was dead, and the nation's attention was focused on an untried successor in the White House as he wrestled with the problems of peace and reconversion.*

In retrospect, it seems perfectly true, as his detractors so strongly maintained, that Roosevelt "wanted" to get the United States into the war weeks and even months before the issue came to a head at Pearl Harbor. But the word "wanted" should not be applied in any context of willfulness, short-sightedness, or irresponsibility. The reason was that he foresaw so

---

* The question: "Who was responsible for Pearl Harbor?" has never been resolved to everyone's satisfaction. Quite aside from partisan political motivations, some historians and other qualified students continue to feel, many years after the event, that President Roosevelt, the members of his Cabinet, and the high command of the Army and Navy shared more of the blame than was attributed to them by either the Roberts or the congressional investigations. Among these is Hanson W. Baldwin, the distinguished military editor of the *Times* for almost 40 years, who, in a letter to the author in September 1969, had this, among other things, to say:

I have little respect for the Roberts Commission investigation; it was superficial and political and did what it was intended to do—focus the blame, not entirely fairly, on the two commanders involved. The congressional investigation was very thorough as to the marshalling of facts, but it had the inevitable political dichotomy which nearly all such investigations produce.

I would bear down a little more heavily on the President, a little less on Admiral Stark [Chief of Naval Operations]. Stark, after all, did make clear to Kimmel his belief that war was coming. Roosevelt, however, took the political actions that led to war, made war inevitable, but kept proclaiming we wouldn't go to war. But Roosevelt's own personal assessment, and that of his intimates, was that war was coming. And everybody from top to bottom, General Marshall particularly, underestimated the Japs and thought they would strike at Southeast Asia, and not Hawaii.

But Kimmel and Short were the commanders on the scene; they should have been better prepared. I feel sorry for both men. They were not complacent commanders; they did stir up some things and tried, by their lights and in accordance with their information, to get ready for war. But there was the prevailing impression, "It can't happen here," and they let themselves be swayed by it.

clearly that without direct United States intervention Britain would fall and take with her the whole structure of democratic society as the West had come to know it.

This concern became particularly acute, and raised a particularly agonizing dilemma, with the southward spread of Japanese aggression during 1941. Japan's alliance with the Rome-Berlin Axis was of less importance militarily at the moment than it was politically—ideologically. Japan sought to impose the same kind of hegemony in East Asia that Hitler sought to impose in continental Europe. If totalitarianism succeeded in both Europe and Asia, then almost certainly it would converge in time upon the Western Hemisphere. At the least, the United States would then be isolated in a hostile world and at the worst be subjected to direct military aggression from both the east and the west.

Yet, the intensity of isolationist-pacifist feeling in the country, and in Congress particularly, made it politically impossible for the President to contrive a direct intervention short of some major and overt provocation —a provocation so gross as to constitute a clear and present danger to the national security. During the summer a routine order by the Army making overseas caps a standard item of military wear drew an hysterical blast from some isolationist quarters that another American Expeditionary Force was being secretly readied. In October a bill to extend the draft law squeaked through the House of Representatives by one—repeat: *one*— vote.

In Roosevelt's view, the Japanese thrust toward Indochina, Thailand, Hong Kong, and the Netherlands East Indies (to say nothing of the Philippines) was almost as great a threat to the United States as Germany's assault upon England and France. If the Japanese conquest were not halted at the outset it would pick off these virtually undefended targets one by one, and then press inexorably toward Australia and possibly toward India with its New Order in East Asia. But could we go to war with Japan, 5,000 miles away on the other side of the world, to defend such places as Indochina, the Kra Peninsula, the Burma Road, the island of Borneo, or British interests in Singapore and Hong Kong—places that most Americans could not even locate on a map, and about which they cared less? As Roosevelt well knew, we could not without waging a fierce and possibly losing political battle here at home.

As events moved toward a climax in the Far East during the late months of 1941, the President was subjected to insistent pressure from the British, the Dutch, the Australians, and the Chinese to take decisive action. They knew, and Roosevelt knew, that only the United States could keep the dam from bursting. Prime Minister Churchill told him at one point that the British would rather have an American declaration of war and no supplies for six months than double the quantity of supplies and no declaration. Roosevelt replied: "I may never declare war; I may make war. If I were to ask Congress to declare war, they might argue about it for three months."

The Pearl Harbor attack resolved this dilemma.[2]

IV

Monday, December 8, was cold and blustery in Washington; a bleak day to match the spirit of its people. The sense of anger and mortification over the disaster of the day before was almost universal. The routine of business was all but suspended in most commercial establishments and government offices as people went about repeating over and over the by now well-known facts and the latest rumors and speculations. The newspapers had fed extras into the street throughout the night and all the radio stations had stayed continuously on the air. Hundreds of people continued to congregate aimlessly and silently in Lafayette Square, across the street from the White House (the sidewalk before the high iron fence had been blocked off by the Secret Service), and well before noon a couple of thousand had gathered in the windswept plaza before the Capitol, anticipating the President's arrival there. Knots of Marines, bayonets on their rifles, stood sentry duty at all the entrances and elsewhere about the great, domed building. Downtown, there were more uniforms on the street than one could remember in nearly two decades, and the recruiting offices suddenly found themselves swamped with long lines of young men wanting to volunteer. A skeleton force of Civil Defense workers was scurrying about the city locating air raid shelters, appointing block captains, and laying in supplies of sand and shovels and bandaids.

Here and there on the streets one spotted an Oriental wearing a conspicuous, hand-lettered card on his lapel reading, "Chinese, not Jap." It was known that the police and the FBI were rounding up Japanese nationals right and left, yanking them off trains and buses and out of their homes, curio shops, and restaurants. For laughs (and there were not many that day) some derived ironic amusement from reports of the food crisis at the heavily guarded Japanese Embassy out on Massachusetts Avenue. The emergency had tripled the handsome sandstone building's normal live-in population of about a dozen. That morning an Embassy official had telephoned an order for over $200 worth of food to avert incipient famine. When the grocer's driver arrived he demanded cash on delivery. Offered a check, he bluntly turned it down. "Your funds have been impounded and your check's no good," he said and drove away with his cargo intact.

"Serves the little yellow bastards right," people said with a grim chuckle.

In that morning's *Times* Arthur Krock had written:

The circumstances of the Japanese attack on Pearl Harbor were such that national unity was an instant consequence. You could almost hear it click into place in Washington today. Congress, as interpreted by leaders and individual members, made a national front that grew in length and depth as fast as its members heard of the President's announcement. . . .

That fact was well documented as Roosevelt, on the arm of his son James, who was in Marine uniform, entered the House chamber a few minutes before 12:30 to address the joint session of Congress. This was a moment of crisis as sensitive as any the nation had ever known, and the awareness of its gravity showed clearly in the faces of the members and those in the packed galleries above them. There were no partisan holdouts in the respectful applause that greeted the President as he climbed painfully to the rostrum. He paused for an instant to look up at Mrs. Woodrow Wilson, widow of the last wartime President, who sat with Mrs. Roosevelt in the gallery before him, to scan the faces of the assembled justices and members of the diplomatic corps who occupied the front row of seats on the floor. Then in tones as solemn and moving as the rendering of a high mass he began to read:

Yesterday, December 7, 1941—a date which will live in infamy—the United States of America was suddenly and deliberately attacked by naval and air forces of the Empire of Japan.

The United States was at peace with that nation, and, at the solicitation of Japan, was still in conversation with its government and its Emperor looking toward the maintenance of peace in the Pacific. . . .

The attack yesterday on the Hawaiian Islands has caused severe damage to American naval and military forces. Very many American lives have been lost. In addition, American ships have been reported torpedoed on the high seas between San Francisco and Honolulu.

Yesterday the Japanese government also launched an attack against Malaya.

Last night Japanese forces attacked Hong Kong.

Last night Japanese forces attacked Guam.

Last night Japanese forces attacked the Philippine Islands.

Last night the Japanese attacked Wake Island.

This morning the Japanese attacked Midway Island.

Japan has, therefore, undertaken a surprise offensive extending throughout the Pacific area. The facts of yesterday speak for themselves. The people of the United States have already formed their opinions and well understand the implications to the very safety and life of their nation. . . .

I believe I interpret the will of the Congress and the people when I assert that we will not only defend ourselves to the uttermost, but will make very certain that this form of treachery shall never endanger us again.

Hostilities exist. There is no blinking at the fact that our people, our territory, and our interests are in grave danger.

With confidence in our armed forces—with the unbounded determination of our people—we will gain the inevitable triumph—so help us God.

I ask that the Congress declare that since the unprovoked and dastardly attack by Japan on Sunday, December 7, a state of war has existed between the United States and the Japanese Empire.

It took less than 10 minutes for the President to deliver his historic message. As he concluded and looked up, his hands gripping the edge of the lectern, the air of solemnity in the great chamber was shattered by thunderous shouts and hand-clapping. No one had wanted war, but now that war had come—the gauntlet flung back at the challenger—there was a sudden release, like floodgates bursting open, of the pent-up fears, angers, and frustrations of many hours and weeks. Now there was a mighty consensus of national purpose and destiny. The President's words were broadcast across the nation and wherever people could get to a radio, millions of ordinary citizens exulted in his call to arms. A roundup of editorial opinion the next day showed scarcely a dissent amid the vast chorus of acclaim. And Hamilton Fish, the most strident voice of isolationism in the land, promptly proclaimed: "If there is a call for troops, I expect to offer my services in a combat division."

Within an hour, and with no debate, Congress had done the President's bidding by approving a declaration of war against Japan. The vote in the Senate was 82 to 0; in the House, 388 to 1.* The Joint Resolution was signed by the President at the White House at 4:10 that afternoon. The next day Germany and Italy joined their Axis partner by declaring war on the United States, and on Thursday, December 11, the United States returned the dubious compliment. Now we were in it all the way, against powerful enemies strung out around the globe, and there could be no turning back. Playwright Robert Sherwood, walking past the White House late that night, was reminded by his companion that the windows were darkened and the gate lights out.

"I wonder how long it will be before that light gets turned on again," the friend remarked.

"I don't know," Sherwood replied, "but until it does, the lights will stay turned off all over the world."

The light did not go on again for three and a half years.[3]

* The dissenter was Representative Jeanette Rankin of Montana, a motherly woman deeply devoted to peace who had also voted against war with the Kaiser's Germany in 1917. Her lone stand in 1941 caused her deep anguish and when she left the House floor she hid in a telephone booth to escape reporters' questioning. Still emotionally shaken but staunch in her conviction, she voted "present" rather than yea or nay to the war declarations against Germany and Italy that followed two days later. "It has been a terrible week for Mrs. Rankin and she showed the strain," a sympathetic *Times* reporter noted.

V

As the United States plunged into war in December 1941, the state of the world and the nation was, in capsule, approximately as follows:

The fighting in Europe, after almost two years of unbroken Axis triumphs, had taken a turn for the better. Hitler, finding the British Isles virtually impregnable, had relaxed somewhat the intensity of his daily air assaults but increased the almost intolerable pressure of his sea blockade. Aerial and submarine attacks threatened to sever Britain's vital lifeline to her dominions and to the United States, but enough supplies were getting through to enable her to mount retaliatory air attacks against Germany and to slowly strengthen her position in the Mediterranean. During the spring, Hitler had sent his Wehrmacht slashing through the Balkans and to a linkup with the Italians in a crushing pincers movement against Greece. At about the same time combined Axis forces had swept through North Africa and driven the British into Egypt. There was little the British could do about Greece, but with the help of the Free French forces they launched a preemptive campaign in Syria and Iraq in the early summer to keep the Near East out of German hands. And in November, the Imperial Army of the Nile, heavily reinforced with American planes, tanks, and guns, broke out of its Egyptian bondage with a determined counter-offensive aimed at retaking Libya and (in time) all of North Africa.

Overshadowing other events on the continent, however, was Hitler's surprise attack in June on his reluctant ally, Soviet Russia. Scarcely bothering to formulate a pretext (ultimate destruction of the Communist citadel had been a part of his strategy from the beginning) he suddenly and simultaneously struck half a dozen points along Russia's western frontier with overpowering masses of infantry, armor, and aircraft. The Russians were caught flat-footed and unprepared: The dilemma of the defenders of Leningrad, for example, was as acute as that to be experienced a few months later by American commanders at Pearl Harbor and Manila.* Through the summer and fall the mighty Nazi war machine rolled onward, overrunning the buffer states, conquering the Ukraine, smashing through the defenses of Kiev and Odessa. By November the Wehrmacht was pounding at the gates of Moscow and Leningrad and had swept far eastward to Rostow, threatening the Caucasus. The Russians fought tenaciously, but were forced back along the whole thousand-mile front.

And then help came, first in the shape of tanks and planes from Britain and the United States, and second and most important in the shape

* Many astonishing parallels are to be found in Harrison E. Salisbury's excellent account of the siege of Leningrad, *The 900 Days* (Harper and Row, 1969).

of a devastating Russian winter—providentially early that year. The Nazi advance bogged down and halted in the limitless snow and ice. The Russians seized the offensive and Hitler had to tell his worried people at Christmas that the campaign was suspended for the winter and that German lines were "reforming"—many miles to the west, as it turned out.

The United States entered the war with a relatively modest military force but one that had begun to grow, and would continue to grow, prodigiously. The Army, organized around 29 regular and 4 armored divisions, numbered approximately 1.6 million officers and men, up about two and one-half times over the 1940 level and heading toward a then-current goal of 3 million. Its Air Force numbered 167,000 men and approximately 3,000 combat planes, the mainstays of which were the recently developed B-17 heavy bomber ("Flying Fortress") and P-40 fighter. The Navy, just recently launched on a "two ocean" expansion program, numbered 344 capital ships of varying age and effectiveness that included 17 battleships, 6 carriers, 208 heavy cruisers and destroyers, and 113 submarines—with approximately an equal tonnage in all categories either under construction or authorized.

During the two years that were coming to a close in December 1941, Congress had authorized the unheard-of sum of $74.4 billion for defense production—ships, planes, tanks, guns, and the tools, machinery, and raw materials needed to convert the nation's industrial plant into "the arsenal of democracy." The pace of that conversion drew a lot of political fire in the beginning—for or against, depending upon the protestor's bias—but with the grim reality of war it surged rapidly forward. To control and direct this great convulsion in the nation's economy, to achieve a tolerable balance between guns and butter, a score of civilian war agencies had been set up. By the time of Pearl Harbor this bustling new bureaucracy, numbering over 100,000 persons, had already become a prominent feature of the national landscape. This phenomenon will be discussed in more detail in later chapters.

Legislatively and administratively it had been a notable year. The Seventy-seventh Congress, first session, sat continuously for 365 days, from January 3, 1941, to January 2, 1942. A major achievement of its early months was enactment of the lend-lease law, with total first-year appropriations of $7 billion. This made it possible for the government to expand enormously the flow of food and war supplies to its embattled friends abroad and to ignore the earlier strictures of cash on delivery. The Russians were cut in for a share shortly after the Nazi invasion of their country in June.

In the spring of 1942 the President declared an "unlimited national emergency" that greatly strengthened his ability to act decisively without permission from Congress—and, incidentally, to inch the nation closer to the brink of hostilities. In retaliation for the undeclared sea war on American shipping in transit to England, he ordered the seizure of all Axis vessels in American ports and instituted naval patrols far off shore throughout a so-called "defensive zone"; later, these patrols were directed to "shoot first" when challenged. In March he negotiated with Iceland to assume responsibility for its defense in exchange for air bases from which to fly protective cover over the North Atlantic sea routes to Britain, and he made a similar arrangement with Greenland a few months later. In November Congress amended the Neutrality Act to permit arming of mechant vessels (one had been sunk and several attacked on the high seas), and narrowly approved an 18-month extension of the draft law.

The year had also been marked by intense labor unrest and many strikes that threatened to slow down production for defense. In several critical instances the Army or Navy was directed to take over strikebound plants while union contracts were being negotiated. Stiff antistrike legislation by Congress was averted late in the year with the creation by the President of new mediation machinery, and after the Pearl Harbor attack labor and industry got together on a pledge of no strikes and no lockouts that greatly reduced tensions. Unemployment had all but evaporated by this time; the WPA, CCC, and similar Depression relief agencies were on the way out, and the typical factory worker saw his weekly wage go up during the year from $25.20 to $29.58.

The events of this memorable year were laced together with some memorable rhetoric. In his annual message to Congress on January 6, Roosevelt enunciated the Four Freedoms which he said must stand as the moral foundation of whatever role the nation might have to play in world affairs. For people "everywhere in the world," he called for "freedom of speech and expression . . . freedom for every person to worship God in his own way . . . freedom from want . . . [and] freedom from fear [to the end] that no nation anywhere will be in a position to commit an act of physical aggression against any neighbor."

Here was the seminal concept for a new world society not unlike that of which Woodrow Wilson had dreamed more than 20 years earlier. Its maturing was rapid. In August Roosevelt met with Prime Minister Churchill in a secret rendezvous at sea off the coast of Newfoundland. From this historic encounter there emerged what came to be known as The Atlantic Charter, and from this there evolved the United Nations Organization.

Late in December Churchill paid his first state visit to the United States. Arriving on the afternoon of the twenty-second he spent five days as a guest at the White House while he and the President and important members of their staffs worked out problems of military collaboration and priorities. To millions of Americans he was already a figure of legend;

the stocky frame, the grumpily cherubic features, the poetic imagery of his speech had become familiar to them through the press and radio. Now that he was here in the flesh, their enchantment with him soared. His principal public appearance, and the burden of his message to the American people, was reserved for a scheduled address to a joint session of Congress on the day after Christmas that impressed even the most skeptical with the sincerity of his faith in ultimate victory over fascism. His reception in the chamber packed with legislators and diplomats was extraordinarily warm and enthusiastic.

But it is probable that he reached a great many more ordinary citizens with an impromptu performance on Christmas Eve. On the south lawn of the White House late that afternoon a crush of 20,000 men, women, and children had gathered around a towering, graceful fir for the traditional lighting of the nation's Christmas tree. As the red-coated Marine Band played and massed choirs sang carols, there came the distant boom of the sunset gun from Fort Myers across the river, and the President and his guest stepped out on the White House south portico. With appropriate ceremony, Mr. Roosevelt pressed the button that caused the tree to spring alive in brilliant spangles of color. Then he introduced the beaming figure at his elbow and stepped aside. Churchill's face was barely visible through the thicket of microphones on the lectern but there was no mistaking the voice—strong, deep, mellow with sentiment and spontaneity:

I spend this anniversary and festival far from my country, far from my family, yet I cannot truthfully say that I feel far from home. Whether it be the ties of blood on my mother's side, or the friendships I have developed here over many years of active life, or the commanding sentiment of comradeship in the common cause of great peoples who speak the same language, who kneel at the same altars, and, to a very large extent, pursue the same ideals, I cannot feel myself a stranger here in the center and at the summit of the United States. I feel a sense of unity and fraternal association which, added to the kindliness of your welcome, convinces me that I have a right to sit at your fireside and share your Christmas joys.

He talked on for a minute or two about the shared agonies of war and the shared hopes for peace, and concluded with a simple benediction: "And so on, in God's mercy, a happy Christmas to you all."

It was not great oratory as such things are reckoned, but it was moving and full of warmth and gratitude and friendliness, and it made the historic bond between Britain and America seem more than ever a personal kinship.

Such, then, was the mood and manner of our entry into the Second World War. The flash point came at Pearl Harbor, but in retrospect we know that a long, twisting fuse led to the powder keg that probably would have detonated anyway, in time, with or without that particular Day of

Infamy. Most Americans clung desperately to the hope that we could go on living our separate life in a world becoming ever more compressed, crowded, and competitive. But it was not to be. History was inexorably fashioning a new world order, and it required that we take our place in the lineup.[4]

4

Mobilization

THE DISABLING TRAUMA of Pearl Harbor caused the welfare of the nation, in President Roosevelt's words, to be taken out of the hands of "old Dr. New Deal" and transferred to those of "his partner, Dr. Win-the-War."

This corny little metaphor expressed quite well the change in the public's mood and attitude which occurred between 1940 and 1942. The impetus for social reform and economic tinkering had about spent itself, anyway. Its place had been taken by a growing concern for national defense, whether by isolation from conflict or by arming to control it. And even the isolationist alternative was fading as the chilling evidence of what a Nazi victory in Europe would mean to American security continued to pile up. This was documented in dozens of public opinion polls, in the increasing willingness with which Congress passed legislation that inched ever closer to the brink of war, in the growing awareness of quite ordinary citizens that involvement sooner or later was probably inevitable, whatever we did.

Step by step the nation moved toward a state of mobilization. The pace was laggard and uncertain at times but it quickened as the hour of crisis approached, and by December 1941, at least the framework of a regimented wartime society was in place.

I

One of the earliest and most unambiguous elements in that structure was military conscription, the first peacetime draft in the nation's history. On December 16, 1940, newspapers all across the country carried prominently on their front pages a notice similar to this one in the *New York Times:*

REGISTRATION

If you are a man who has reached his 21st birthday but has not reached his 36th birthday, you must register today for selective service.

If you have no valid reason for failing to do so you are liable to arrest, and if convicted you may be sentenced to as much as five years in prison and fined $10,000.

You are to register between 7 A.M. and 9 P.M. at the nearest school in the election district in which you live or where you are staying if you are from out of town. If you have used your best efforts to locate your registration place and cannot find it, inquire at the police station nearest where you are staying.

Not many young men required this warning to inform them of the obligation that faced them on Wednesday, October 16. The advent of Registration Day had been heralded for weeks by an intensive publicity campaign that ranged from bleak flyers thumbtacked to post office walls to flamboyant outdoor billboards, from skits by radio comics to solemn exhortations from the pulpit.

From before dawn to long after dark on "R-Day" long queues of registrants—there were 16,316,908 all told—filed through countless schools, firehouses, police stations, and church basements in every community in the nation, giving essential information about themselves to volunteer enumerators. Smartly tailored executives and dungareed truck drivers; Fords and Rockefellers along with WPA workers and skid-row bums; black field hands and slum dwellers; tongue-tied immigrants, ex-convicts, homosexuals, illiterates, scholars, and even a scattering of conscientious objectors—all made the scene that day in an historic muster.

It was a surprisingly trouble-free occasion considering the intensity of antiwar feeling that existed in many quarters. The most serious incidents, apparently, were occasional fist fights, mainly over who was ahead of whom in the waiting line. The organized protests were few and generally peaceful: About 2,000 New Yorkers belonging to the War Resisters League, the Youth Committee Against War, and similar organizations picketed some of the principal registration centers but seemed to attract more derisive hoots than converts. The mood of the men in the line, the *Times* reported, "seemed to be one of philosophical resignation, and in lesser degree an obvious eagerness for military training."

In New York, a small group of divinity students at Union Theological Seminary proclaimed their refusal to register on grounds of conscience (eight were later sentenced to a year and a day in jail), and in Florida scores of eligible Seminole Indian braves disappeared into the fastness of the Everglades without signing up, attesting that their "nation" had never acknowledged the sovereignty of the paleface invaders in the first place. In Bloomington, Indiana, Socialist presidential candidate Norman Thomas told students at the state university that if elected he would work for repeal of the Selective Service law. He described Registration Day as "a day of mourning for the death of the American way of life." Franklin D. Roosevelt, Jr., en route to the same campus to make a campaign speech for his father, popped unexpectedly into an Indianapolis firehouse to register, giving his occupation as "unemployed." As he turned to leave, a voice in the crowd which had quickly gathered called out: "Tell your old man we're all behind him out here."

And so it went across the country that day as "the flower of the nation's manhood" (so described, inevitably, by countless orators and editorial writers) was converted into an anonymous pool of manpower for compulsory service to the state. This was mobilization of the kind everyone could feel and understand. The draft was not new: It had been employed in the First World War and, with modifications, in other wars previous to that.* The difference this time was that the draft had been invoked while the nation was still at peace and hoped (with some misgivings) to remain at peace. Peacetime conscription had many ominous implications, not the least of which was that it was a familiar tool of militarists and dictators, that it was a contradiction of the democratic ethos.

These were the attitudes which had to be combatted when the selective service bill went before Congress on June 20, 1940. It was not an administration measure, its sponsors being Senator Edward Burke of Nebraska and Representative James Wadsworth of New York, but the administration gave it quiet support. Only the month before, President Roosevelt had sought (and would soon again) authority to call up the National Guard and the organized reserves for active duty. He felt that this was as far as he could go at the moment in the direction of military mobilization without raising the cry of "warmonger" and "interventionist" from the pacifist-isolationist bloc. He thus welcomed the initiative of the two legislators, neither of whom had been notable among his supporters in the past.

Predictably, the controversy over so revolutionary a measure was heated and often emotional, spilling over from the halls of Congress into the press and pulpit, and enlisting particularly the anguished concern of organized mothers. The Senate devoted two full weeks to debate on the bill during late July and August, and the House another week, both before galleries full of agitated and sometimes noisy spectators. But events abroad did as much as logic and oratory to ensure enactment. The fall of France and the British retreat from Dunkirk that summer shocked millions of Americans into a new awareness of the shaky foundations upon which their hopes for peace rested. Between mid-June and mid-August a major

* A detailed blueprint and table of organization, with a skeletal staff in Washington and each state capital, was already in existence for the administration of a selective service law when and if enacted. This was a principal component of a master mobilization plan prepared years earlier and kept constantly up to date by the War Department. For details (some of which were modified in the 1940 legislation) see "M Day and After," by Cabell Phillips and J. D. Ratcliff, *Reader's Digest*, August, 1939, pp. 23-27.

public opinion poll on the question of compulsory military service shifted from an enigmatic 50-50 to an emphatic 65 percent favoring such legislation. The Senate passed the bill on August 28 by a vote of 58 to 31; the House followed suit a week later, 263 to 149. As passed, the act contained three significant limitations: Terms of service were one year, the number to be inducted could not exceed 900,000 in any year, and service for inductees outside the Western Hemisphere was prohibited. President Roosevelt gratefully signed the bill on September 16 and decreed that registration should take place one month later.

It is worth remembering that these events took place during an acrimonious political campaign in which Roosevelt himself was the principal issue. His presumption in seeking a third term was offensive to traditionalists of both parties, and was trumpeted by many partisans as a devious prelude to establishing a dictatorship. To the isolationists, he was secretly plotting to get the United States into the European war, and to a large body of nonisolationists—including Wendell Willkie—he was dragging his feet on the defense buildup. It probably is true (as Roosevelt surmised) that, had he taken the lead in demanding peacetime conscription, the political consequences—up to the time of the unforeseen collapse of France, at least—would have been disastrous. As it turned out, however, this painful wrench of the democratic tradition was achieved without lasting scars and bitterness. In fact, the federalizing of the National Guard and reserves occurred at about the same time without serious hitch, and voluntary enlistments climbed during the autumn to record peacetime levels.

The Selective Service Administration, one of the first big increments to what was to become a vastly swollen wartime bureaucracy, was headed during its first year by Clarence A. Dykstra, the scholarly and urbane president of the University of Wisconsin. His deputy and ultimate successor was a muscular, square-framed professional soldier with a wiry brush of reddish-gray hair and the voice of a drill sergeant, Lieutenant Colonel Lewis B. Hershey—who survived an unbroken tenure in the job until his forced retirement (with four stars and an aura of good-natured contentiousness) in February 1970. Procedures were worked out for the administration of the draft law, including the assignment of a number to each registrant within his home district, and a network of 6,175 local draft boards was set up, staffed largely by volunteers. Each board was supplied with, among other things, cartons of a terse, peremptory missive that, over the next 30 years at least, would play more havoc with the lives of millions of American men than any letter most of them would ever receive:

"The President of the United States

"To—

"Greeting

"You are hereby ordered to report for induction into the armed forces of the United States . . ."

The first drawing in this great national lottery was set for Tuesday, October 29, an occasion marked by appropriate pomp and fanfare. The scene was the blue and gold Departmental Auditorium on Constitution Avenue, with the resplendent Marine Corps Band providing the musical accompaniment. The seats were filled with spectators, the press tables crowded, and microphones for the radio networks bristled at vantage points here and there. At noon, with a flourish and ruffle from the band, the President appeared on the flag-draped stage accompanied by Secretary of War Stimson. Other members of the Cabinet, Congressional leaders and a contingent of veterans of the world war crowded before the backdrop.

At front center an enormous glass bowl rested on a mahogany table. The same bowl had been used for the identical purpose in 1917. In it were 9,000 bright blue capsules, each containing a numbered slip of paper running from one to 9,000. These were serial numbers duplicated in most instances from draft board to draft board, with about 2,800 added as a safety margin. The order in which they were removed from the bowl would prescribe the order in which each holder of that number would be called up for induction. A polished ladle, carved from a beam in Philadelphia's Independence Hall, lay alongside the bowl so that the capsules could be stirred up periodically, in token of the fairness of the proceedings.

The preliminaries were brief. The National Anthem was played, there was an invocation, and the President and Dykstra each made a short address. Then Secretary Stimson stepped forward to the table, was elaborately blindfolded (with a swatch of upholstery snipped from a chair used by the signers of the Declaration of Independence), put his hand into the bowl, and drew out the first capsule. He handed it to the President. Roosevelt extracted the bit of paper, looked at it closely, and then read slowly into the battery of microphones arrayed before him, "one–five–eight." Thus, holders of serial number 158—there were 6,175 of them—had the unique if not exactly enviable distinction of being put at the head of the line for the first peacetime draft in American history. How many of them were actually called up subsequently for induction and made it into uniform is not recorded.

After a few more ceremonial withdrawals from the bowl, the chore was turned over to the staff of the Selective Service Administration. It was dawn of the next day before the last capsule was drawn and its number recorded. The radio networks stayed with the proceedings to the end, for all across the country tens of thousands of anxious youths and their parents were tuned in to follow the tracings of this finger of fate. So, incidentally, were the "numbers" writers in a thousand grubby little gambling dens catering to the nickel and dime trade. And at the Rockingham race track outside New Orleans there was a sudden stampede to get down bets, in the fifth race on a filly named Ungin, who bore the magic number in the program: 158. Ungin rewarded the hunch by paying off at $13.20.

The first call-up of draftees was set for late November, but relatively few had to be chosen. Volunteer enlistments were more than meeting the Navy's needs and the Army was hard pressed, in spite of a crash expansion program, to provide barracks and tents for all the recruits clamoring to get in. The regular Army stood at approximately 375,000 at the time, plus an increment of about 100,000 from the National Guard. New trainees would be added at the rate of 20,000 to 50,000 a month to reach a projected level of 1.4 million by the summer of 1941. Never before had the nation mobilized so large a fighting force while still at peace.[1]

II

As previously noted, Congress had appropriated lavishly for national defense in the two years preceding the Pearl Harbor attack: $64 billion for ships, planes, and guns, plus $7 billion for the first year's operation of lend-lease, plus $3 billion in increased lending authority for the Reconstruction Finance Corporation to be used primarily for the expansion of defense industries. This enormous input sent the national economy on a dizzying upward spiral. The gross national product went from $88.6 billion in 1939 to $198.7 billion in 1945. Unemployment virtually vanished, prices and wages rose, and the threat of runaway inflation—the memory of $4 steaks and $25 shoes from the days of the First World War was still fresh for many—hung like a cloud on the economic horizon. Moreover, there were by the beginning of 1941 clear signs of incipient industrial chaos as manufacturers and producers attempted to sandwich defense orders into the booming demand for civilian goods. Many were reluctant to sacrifice a sure thing to gamble on the uncertainties of military procurement, to retool and convert their factories and to allocate steel and scarce metals to turn out guns and airplane engines instead of automobiles and vacuum cleaners. For a time, cantankerous old Henry Ford, a devout isolationist and Anglophobe, refused to accept war orders offered by a British purchasing mission.

This was no way to run an "arsenal of democracy," nor even to build up the military defenses of the homeland; the nation had to mobilize its resources as well as its manpower. The business of defense had to be given top priority without completely destroying business as usual; the urgency for guns weighed against the urgency for butter. This would involve some very difficult and touchy maneuvering, with technological as well as political overtones.

In the files of the War Department there was a comprehensive Industrial Mobilization Plan—the so-called M-Day Plan—based upon the experiences of the War Industries Board of the First World War. Bernard M. Baruch, a true Renaissance man—capitalist, philosopher, patron of the arts, all-purpose elder statesman—had been director of WIB and had helped guide the steady evolution and updating of the M-Day Plan. In theory, it was available for immediate use and implementation when war struck: an instant mobilization of the nation's industrial and manpower resources under one vastly powerful administrator to be named by the President.

But the plan had a number of deficiencies, some of them fundamental. It was predicated on the existence of an actual state of war, with all the psychological impetus such a crisis would bring—patriotism, fervor, self-sacrifice, political unity. It was not geared to a state of peace, however tenuous, when those same psychological factors might well work in reverse. It was also predicated on a simplistic economic structure that had become outmoded by the rapid advance of technology, corporate gigantism, the complexities of labor-management relationships, and other factors that made the concept of effective administration by a superagency and an "industrial czar" highly dubious. And, finally, it put control of the wartime industrial complex in the hands of a potential oligarchy of businessmen, generals, and admirals operating beyond the effective reach of the civilian Commander-in-Chief. The President would thus be deprived of—or at least greatly limited in—his ability to direct overall defense strategy and foreign economic policy, or to accommodate the war's impact to the essential needs of the civilian population.

Baruch, less secure in his role of "adviser to Presidents" with Roosevelt than he had been with Wilson, Coolidge, and Hoover, pressed the M-Day plan on the President early in 1940, and even prepared an alternative version that attempted to meet some of Roosevelt's principal objections. This retained, however, the concept of the superagency and the "czar," which Baruch considered indispensable. But FDR, being FDR, would not countenance any arrangement that diluted his own power to run the mobilization show or to direct the defense buildup. Moreover, he sensed the acute political hazards in this tense election year of invoking a full-scale mobilization plan that his enemies could so easily turn against him. He reasoned, in fact, that this or any similar step he took that required legislative sanction might easily, in the prevailing political climate, backfire with the imposition of new restrictions designed to tie his hands. He rejected Baruch's advice for an expedient of his own devising.

In 1939 Congress had passed the Government Reorganization Act which, among other things, gave the President wide authority to reorganize and enlarge his Executive Office. This included an inconspicuous provision for the creation, in the event of the declaration of a national emergency, of "such office for emergency management as the President shall determine." As he signed the reorganization act, Mr. Roosevelt also issued a proclamation declaring the existence of a "limited national emergency." On May 25, 1940, he invoked his emergency powers for the first time with an executive order creating the Office of Emergency Management (OEM) as the newest addition to the White House table of organization. Three days later, using a statute left over from the First World War, he reactivated the National Defense Advisory Committee (NDAC) and placed its operations under OEM. Here were the beginnings of what was to become a huge wartime bureaucracy.

The NDAC was purely an advisory body of seven members representing as many broad bands of the industrial spectrum. They could conduct studies, make recommendations, and interpret the needs of the Army-Navy Munitions Board to suppliers and manufacturers, but they could not order anyone to do anything. The OEM sat above the NDAC like a holding company and provided a channel to the President for such exercise of executive power or moral pressure as might be decided upon. For all its impressive facade, NDAC was a paper tiger with a limited life expectancy, but it cast a prophetic shadow of what industrial mobilization would one day look like, and of some of the men who would run it.

Its Division of Industrial Production was headed by William S. Knudsen, the doughty production wizard of General Motors. Edward R. Stettinius, the handsome but only moderately talented inheritor of a fortune in United States Steel, was in charge of the Division of Industrial Materials. Sidney Hillman, a wizened Lithuanian immigrant who had been president of the Amalgamated Clothing Workers Union since 1915, was chief of the Division of Employment (manpower). The Division of Transportation was under the direction of Ralph Budd, a leading manufacturer of railroad equipment. Leon Henderson, an outspoken economics freethinker who had been making waves in Washington since the early days of NRA, was in charge of the Division of Price Stabilization. And, just off to the side as Coordinator of Defense Purchasing, was the dour, no-nonsense chief executive of Sears, Roebuck, Donald M. Nelson. In time, most of these same functions and functionaries of the NDAC (which would itself disappear in an administrative reshuffle) would emerge as powerful separate entities in a vastly enlarged OEM constellation.

This setup was impressive on paper but largely ineffectual in practice. During the summer and fall of 1940, there was little correlation between the ambitious production goals proclaimed by the administration for new airplanes, tanks, guns, and munitions and what actually came off the production lines. Wendell Willkie, in fact, made this the principal thrust of his campaign to win the Presidency. Roosevelt, for his part, was unwilling to run what he believed to be the graver political risks of a severe clampdown on the "business as usual" mentality that prevailed throughout much of the industrial community. But with the election safely and decisively won, with the sense of crisis deepening as the Battle of Britain grew in intensity, the President moved to make industrial mobilization a reality.

In January 1941, the NDAC was shelved and its usable parts salvaged to become the nuclei of a new set of administrative satellites orbiting around the Office of Emergency Management. The first and most important of these was the Office of Production Management (OPM), created by executive order on January 7. To some, the OPM bore a resemblance to the "superagency" advocated by Baruch, Willkie, and others, but the resemblance was more apparent than real. Instead of being headed by an all-powerful "czar," it was headed by a troika of coequals: Knudsen, Director General; Hillman, Associate Director General; and the Secretaries of War and Navy acting together in an unaccustomed administrative embrace as a third, but untitled, associate director general. Knudsen, obviously, was responsible for the managerial side of the production cycle, Hillman for the manpower side, and the service secretaries for the consumption side. Of course, the man in the driver's seat who held the reins of this improbable hitch was, therefore, none other than FDR.

"Why don't you want a single, responsible head?" a reporter asked the President when OPM was announced.

"I have a single, responsible head," the President shot back. "His name is Knudsen and Hillman."

"That's two heads."

"No, that's one head. If you are in trouble, would you rather come to one law firm, or two?"

"I don't think that's comparable," the reporter insisted doggedly.

"Just the same thing exactly," the President told him with a mischievous grin, pleased with his elaborate non sequitur. "Wait until you run into trouble."

OPM had more than advisory powers: It could at least influence (though not control) the issuance or withholding of contracts by the Army-Navy Munitions Board, the Maritime Commission, and the other purveyors of defense orders. Its principal statutory muscle derived (after March) from the Lend-Lease Act, which strengthened its hand in the enforcement of priorities, both in production and in the allocation of raw materials. Up to a point, suppliers could be made to toe the line. Thus, a metals fabricator could be told to turn out so many shell casings before he made any more toasters or kitchen utensils if he wanted to continue to get sheet steel, and an auto maker could be pressured without too much difficulty into converting a part of his output to tanks and airplane engines. These were halfway measures at best; their success was impeded by indifferent cooperation on the part of many producers, by the recalcitrance of labor unions which wanted a bigger share of defense profits diverted to wages, and by administrative confusion inherent in the troika set-up.

With war a reality after Pearl Harbor, halfway measures would not do. In January 1942, OPM was succeeded by a new agency with a wider bite and more teeth, the War Production Board (WPB). The troika was dissolved: Knudsen put on a uniform with two stars on his shoulder to become the Army's top production expert, Hillman went back to his union duties (briefly), and the military presence in the person of the two service secretaries was demoted to second-rank status as the new agency took over direction of the contracting operations of the Army-Navy Munitions Board. Donald M. Nelson was designated as the one-man boss of the operation, under the general purview of OEM and thus of the President.

The first War Powers Act, which Congress passed within a fortnight after the blow at Pearl Harbor, conferred extraordinary powers on the President to manage the nation's industrial plant, from raw material to finished product. He was empowered to allocate materials, to establish priorities, to ration supplies and output, to tell a producer what he could and could not produce and, in extremis, to commandeer his plant if he didn't go along. The President delegated most of these powers to Nelson, and the flood of directives that began to flow from his office had, implicitly at least, the force of law. By and large, free enterprise was put on ice for the duration and bureaucracy took charge. How this operated to produce the "arsenal of democracy" will be examined more fully in a later chapter.[2]

III

The companion to WPB in the mobilization diagram—its bureaucratic sibling, in a sense—was the Office of Price Administration. OPA was to the man in the street (and his wife in the kitchen) what OPM-WPB was to the industrial tycoon, although there was some overlapping in jurisdictions. It, too, evolved as a spin-off from NDAC in the spring of 1941 with the initial designation of Office of Price Administration and Civilian Supply (OPACS). Its basic purpose was to try to maintain a stabilized civilian economy amid the industrial turbulence created by OPM; to keep prices in line and to regulate the flow of consumer goods through the wickets of defense requirements.

OPA was born in strife and lived in turmoil. It was given a very nearly impossible job and, at the outset at least, few of the tools to do it with. Stabilizing a war-boom economy means putting a halter on all its principal elements—the supply of goods, the price at which they are sold, the volume of purchasing power—all of which, like a team of fractious horses, interact one upon the other. As the Bureau of the Budget defined the problem in a memorandum to the president:

Bold and concerted action is required. Inflation cannot be stopped as long as wage increases, as well as Government expenditures, create additional purchasing power. Wage increases cannot be stopped as long as prices rise. The price rise cannot be stopped unless part of the rapidly increasing purchasing power is absorbed by fiscal measures. Fiscal measures cannot be effective as long as businessmen, wage earners, and farmers can make up for taxes by increasing their income. Only simultaneous action on all fronts can stop the inflationary spiral.

When OPACS was created by executive order in April 1941, it was, in effect, a junior partner of OPM. It had no powers of its own to channel the "residual supply" of materials and commodities not needed for defense into the civilian sector, and none beyond the talents of verbal suasion to control prices. Baruch and others urged the President to establish by ukase a general ceiling across the board on all prices, rents, wages, interest rates, etc. Roosevelt, instead, yielded to political pressures for a less drastic approach: He was already under heavy partisan fire for allegedly attempting to use the defense emergency to further entrench the New Deal. It was not until mid-summer, when inflation was threatening to get wholly out of hand, that he asked a sullen Congress for statutory authority to make OPACS' price controls stick. And it was not until January 1942, that the authority was granted, considerably watered down by the exclusion of farm products (which meant most foods) from price regulation, and the absence of any controls over wages.

From the outset, the whole price control mechanism was an administrative and political shambles. That it held together at all during its early months, and survived to become in time one of the most effective instruments of wartime mobilization, was due very largely to the aggressive, hardboiled New Dealer whom Roosevelt picked to run it, Leon Henderson.

People said of Leon Henderson that he looked like an ambulant laundry bag, that he had the truculent manner and the social graces of a saloon keeper. He was powerfully built, standing nearly six feet tall, with a majestically bulging waistline, an untidy black pompadour, and swarthy facial features invariably accented by a big cigar clamped in the corner of his mouth; and he was perpetually seized by restless energy and vocal discontent. He emerged on the New Deal scene in 1934 when, as economist for the Russell Sage Foundation, he turned up in Washington one day with a delegation that had come to argue about consumer policies with the National Recovery Administration director Hugh Johnson. The irascible Johnson, who could brook no criticism of NRA, quickly boiled over at Henderson's irreverent heckling. "If you're so damn good," he barked, "why don't you go to work here?"

"I'm game," Henderson said and hung up his hat.

Henderson was born poor in Millville, New Jersey in 1895. He entered Swarthmore College on an athletic scholarship and worked the rest of his way there to a degree and to two years of graduate study at the University of Pennsylvania with a variety of odd jobs. He planned initially to study journalism but became so fascinated with a required freshman semester in economics that he made it his major and compiled a brilliant scholastic record in that subject. For the next dozen years he taught economics and held a number of consultant jobs with, among others, Gifford Pinchot, the crusading liberal Governor of Pennsylvania. At the time he showed up in Washington he was director of consumer research for the Sage Foundation, traveling about the country to expose loan shark practices and to lobby for model small-loan legislation.

In the volatile climate of NRA, Henderson soon filtered to the top as director of research and planning, with a special bent for demanding a fair shake for the consumer under the industrial codes. His blunt, free-swinging style gave extra clout to his intellectual talents: He was a hard man to refute or argue down. This gave him solid footing with the upper hierarchy of the New Deal but won him mortal enemies among the conservatives of Congress and the business world. Within a year he had become a permanent fixture of the New Deal and one of the liveliest and most provocative figures on the Washington scene (Georgia's hard-bitten Representative Gene Cox suspected him of being a communist, and a Washington society reporter observed that "Mr. Henderson seems to dance sidesaddle"). After the demise of NRA he progressed through a number of other top-level assignments and was a member of the Securities and Exchange Commission in 1940 when Roosevelt picked him to head the Division of Price Stabilization in the original NDAC. When OPACS was created a year later, Henderson was the obvious choice as director.

The President's fight to gain legislative sanctions for mandatory price controls was a bitter one that lasted through the summer and fall of 1941. The steady escalation of defense production was beginning to create scarcities of some consumer goods, with consequent grumbling from the public. Prices were rising rapidly in the face of the government's limited ability to hold them down, and workers were demanding matching wage increases and striking when they were not promptly forthcoming. To all these domestic aggravations were added, of course, deepening tensions over the steadily worsening international situation.

The legislative hangup over strengthening price control authority had multiple roots. Conservatives in general opposed any governmental restraint on "the free play of the market"; any tampering with the sacred formula of supply and demand. Such efforts, they suspected, could well be a New Deal plot to "Sovietize" the American economy under the cloak of an emergency. The organized farm bloc, with its powerful allies in Congress, held out against any effective control on farm prices as discriminatory and destructive of the American agricultural system. Organized labor held out as adamantly against any wage controls which were not matched by across-the-board price controls and by stiff limitations on corporate profits.

Henderson was up to his eyebrows in this fight to get a workable price control law out of Congress. At the same time, he was in a running feud with Knudsen at OPM over production priorities that would produce a more meaningful balance in the "residual supplies" available for civilian consumption. Inevitably, there grew up a barbed ideological polarization between the two agencies. OPM, largely staffed by dollar-a-year men from industry, was business-oriented and imbued with the prevailing business attitude that the defense program could somehow be accommodated to the existing way of doing things. They resisted large-scale plant conversions or expansions for fear that it would leave them a few months or a year later with costly excess capacity on their hands. OPA, with almost as much sprawl as OPM, was staffed largely by people from the universities and New Deal agencies and was emphatically consumer-oriented. In the public mind, OPM and OPA seemed to have staked out opposite ends of the politicoeconomic spectrum. Henderson shared with Knudsen (on an imperfectly defined ratio) the power of ordering production priorities, and he fumed no less over the poor yield of guns for OPM then the poor yield of butter for OPA. It was the "business as usual" mentality that set New Dealer Henderson's blood pressure soaring.

The issue came to a head in August. Six months earlier, Knudsen had gotten voluntary agreement from his former colleagues in the auto industry to cut back civilian production by 20 percent. This, in theory, would mean a corresponding stepping up in the output of tanks and airplanes while reducing the drain on the residual supply of steel, already in short supply, for critical civilian needs. But the promised cutback never materialized. Detroit was enjoying the greatest auto boom since 1929 and turned out 88 percent more passenger cars in August 1941 than it had in the same month of the year before. Henderson exploded. Using his own somewhat dubious priority powers he ordered an immediate cutback of 50 percent in auto production and decreed that it should be sustained through the new model year which was just beginning. The auto makers were outraged. So was Knudsen, who complained that Henderson was invading his jurisdiction. Their dispute was laid on the President's desk where a compromise substantially favorable to Henderson was worked out.

Characteristically, FDR applied a poultice to the breach by creating another new agency, Supply Priorities and Allocation Board (SPAB), to sit as a mediator above OPM and OPA but only slightly diminishing the authority of the two warring administrators. SPAB was soon superseded, however, in a more fundamental shake-up—the same one that transformed OPM into WPB: the declaration of war on the Axis. OPA, too, won a new mandate and new muscle, though less than what Henderson and others considered necessary.

Early in January, Congress passed the Emergency Price Control Act of 1942, over which it had been dawdling since summer. In many respects, it already was obsolete in terms of the rapid pace of inflation. It gave the OPA administrator power to impose price ceilings on almost the whole range of consumer goods with one glaring exception—agricultural products, which meant most foods, a tribute to the tenacity of the congressional farm bloc. He was also empowered to order rent controls in areas heavily congested by defense industries and, to a limited extent, to ration items in short supply. Rationing was applied almost immediately to gasoline and automobile tires, where shortages already had become critical. Rent controls went promptly into effect in a score of communities where the housing crunch was most severe.

Price controls, however, were applied sparingly on a selective basis. This proved to be an enormously complex task, one which never had been attempted before and for which there were no precedents nor any backlog of experience. Determining which items, out of thousands in the consumer-goods category, should be put under a price ceiling, and adapting these to varying quality standards and regional trade patterns, presented almost insuperable difficulties. A partial solution was achieved in April with the promulgation of a General Maximum Price Regulation. This stipulated that the price of every item on a merchant's shelves or in his warehouse (excepting foods, of course) should be frozen at whatever price they sold for at retail in the preceding month, March.

There was a lusty outcry against this, coming mainly from businessmen and their sympathetic spokesmen in Congress. Not only were such stringencies uncalled for in the existing state of the emergency, they argued, but the wholesale application of price controls threatened the existence of many business enterprises, and in the end would result in diminishing the overall supply of goods. The OPA, which had set up an extensive field organization that included over 5,000 local price and rationing boards, was overwhelmed with complaints, adjudications, and mountains of paper work. Its people were adrift in an administrative wilderness where experimentation and improvisation had to take the place of rules and precedents, where legal authority was vague and popular support was, at the best, dubious. Their task was made no easier by the exuberant cooperation of many housewives, labor union members, and others who constituted themselves as unofficial vigilantes to spy on businessmen whom they suspected of cheating on the price ceilings.

Meanwhile, the cost of living continued to creep inexorably upward in spite of OPA's fevered exertions. Henderson was repeatedly put on the carpet by congressional inquisitors demanding that he justify OPA's existence. He argued back that until they agreed to put the price of food, the biggest item in most consumers' budgets, under the ceiling, the battle against inflation could not be won. Uncontrolled wages were also a factor, he admitted, but lying outside his jurisdiction. These rationalizations made little impression on a Congress bedeviled by constituent pressures, and with midterm elections coming up in November, Henderson and the OPA served as an excellent target against which to vent a whole catalogue of frustrations.

In the great welter of his wartime preoccupations, President Roosevelt often neglected the principal battle on the home front, that against inflation. Confronted by the steady rise in living costs, however—the index of the Bureau of Labor Statistics (BLS) showed a stubborn increase of 2.6 points between May and October 1942—and Henderson's impatient prodding, he at last came to grips with the problem. In September, he sent a new stabilization bill to Congress with the firm warning that if it failed to act by October 1, "I shall accept the responsibility, and I will act." Faced with this ultimatum, Congress did as it was bidden.

The Stabilization Act of 1942 was passed on October 2. It greatly broadened OPA's statutory authority to enforce consumer price controls, placed all foodstuffs except fresh fruits and vegetables under its mandate, and gave it virtually a free hand to impose rationing restrictions as it deemed necessary. At the same time, the War Labor Board was given added authority to hold wages in check.

Finally, the whole anti-inflation campaign was given fresh impetus and status through the creation of an overriding Office of Economic Stabilization (OES). To head up this superagency, the President induced James F. Byrnes, an incisive, tough-minded former Senator from South Carolina, to step down from the Supreme Court, to which he had been appointed only months before. Byrnes, a liberal Southern Democrat, commanded great respect among his former colleagues in Congress, which was the principal reason Roosevelt chose him to head OES. From that time on the anti-inflation campaign won a more respectful, though never complacent, following.

A casualty of the changeover, however, was Leon Henderson. In his single-minded determination to get a workable system of price controls, he had built up an impressive list of enemies on Capitol Hill and in the business community. As a part of the price exacted for bowing to the President's ultimatum, Congress demanded Henderson's head. Henderson, himself, was not wholly averse to such a sacrifice. He had suffered some disenchantment over FDR's on-again-off-again support of OPA, and his own exertions had brought him close to the point of physical exhaustion. At the end of December he resigned, feeling that his efforts were largely vindicated by the Stabilization Act. He was succeeded briefly by Prentiss M. Brown, a former Senator from Michigan, and later by Chester Bowles, a wealthy advertising man who had been state OPA administrator for Connecticut. Sharing much of Henderson's bluntness and zeal, Bowles piloted OPA through its most productive, but never tranquil, years until the end of the war.

The Stabilization Act and the prestige of OES gave OPA a new lease on life. Beginning early in 1943 rent controls were extended nationwide. The former system of general price ceilings was replaced for many commodities, notably foods, by forthright dollars-and-cents ceilings. As regular monthly intervals OPA decreed, area by area, what the local ceiling price would be for a loaf of bread, a can of peaches, a pound of steak, and scores of other consumer commodities, and those prices were posted in plain view of the customer. Keeping these price schedules up to date and consonant with local conditions of supply and demand was an enormous one. The responsibility fell mainly on the local OPA offices, who maintained a constant check not only on their local market conditions, but through their enforcement officers, on observance of the pricing regulations. The agency now had full authority to take a violator to court.

At the same time, rationing was expanded to cover not only gasoline, tires, and fuel oil, but sugar, coffee, meats, butter, and a variety of processed foods. This was an even bigger administrative undertaking than price controls, and called for thousands of volunteers to staff local rationing boards.

Simply stated, each person over 16 in the civilian population was limited in the quantity of those goods he could buy each month. To buy them he had to present, in addition to cash, the requisite number of ration stamps, a new kind of currency in American experience. To procure your supply of stamps you applied periodically to the nearest ration board, usually set up in a school house. Stamps were of two kinds: Red for meats, butter, and fats; blue for processed foods and certain other commodities. They were issued in booklets, six months' supply at a time, and the stamps were coded to indicate their "point value" and their period of validity. Point values fluctuated from time to time depending on supply and other factors: A pound of beef roast might cost you three red points one week and only one point a week later. Point values as dictated by local

OPA officials were regularly posted in the stores and were carried in their advertisements.

To prevent hoarding, stamps with a given code letter were valid for only a stated period of time, usually a month. Thus, if you didn't spend all your "D" stamps for red meat in June, you could not double up for a feast in July. (The accepted means of beating the chronic meat shortage in most cities was to patronize a restaurant, provided you did not arrive on a "meatless day"—which most establishments were obliged to observe periodically because they had run out of *their* red stamps— and were content to wait in block-long lines that often queued up at the better places before the dinner hour.)

Rationing was an incredibly cumbersome operation; some three billion less-than-inch-square bits of gummed paper changed hands each month, passing up the line from consumer to retailer to jobber to whole-saler who, in turn, had to "cash" them with the producer (who had to account to OPA) in order to replenish the shelves. Dealers' inventories had to be checked periodically to see that they were not getting more than their allotted share of choice items. Now and then one would be barred from further trading in some rationed commodity because he was "over-drawn" at the ration bank. And local ration boards were in constant con-flict with aggrieved householders who had lost their ration books or needed more generous treatment to avoid severe family disasters of hunger and cold, or were demanding to know why the Smiths couldn't have as much gasoline as the Joneses. Unquestionably, rationing was the most common social irritant to afflict the home front during the war, and it fostered a kind of low-caliber lawlessness even in the very best circles that was widely tolerated if not always condoned.

Rationing and price controls were unknown in the First World War as far as the consumer was concerned. In the years from 1917 to 1920 his cost of living had shot up by 51.7 percent. From 1941 to 1946 the in-crease was 34.1 percent, a marked improvement but still a sizable bite out of the consumer's pocketbook. But in the years of OPA's maximum effectiveness, 1942 to 1945, the rise was a tolerable nine percent. For all the headaches it caused and endured, OPA was manifestly worth the price.[3]

IV

Mobilizing manpower for the defense program was more of a political problem than an economic one. A truly rigorous ordering of the nation's work force, such as was in vogue in the dictatorships and to a lesser degree even in Britain, would have inflamed the consciences of both American workingmen and American liberals, those principal bas-tions of the New Deal's political strength. The Roosevelt administration was unwilling on both practical and ideological grounds to antagonize them in such a fashion. Actually, during the war years the country did not at any time face an overall manpower shortage, but minor and localized crises erupted with such frequent and occasionally startling effect as to suggest that the home front might not be able to back up the military. The result was a succession of alarms and dire prophesies, of demands for stringent legislation (particularly to outlaw strikes), and of official compromises and accommodations to find the path of least resistance through the obstacles to a workable national manpower policy.

On and off throughout the early years of the decade reports of turmoil and discord on the labor front played in harsh counterpoint to the news of sacrifice and heroism from far-flung military fronts. Plane production in the Boeing plant in Seattle was held up for lack of enough skilled metalworkers. Tanks were slow coming off the Chrysler production lines in Michigan because of absenteeism among the workers. Meadville, Pennsylvania, the "zipper capital of the world," became a virtual ghost town because of the flight of its work force to the higher-priced labor markets of Detroit and Cleveland. Production of batteries for the Army Signal Corps, concentrated in a few factories in Ohio, came to a weeks-long standstill because of a jurisdictional squabble between competing unions. Among other similar actions, the government was forced to seize an airplane plant in California and a shipbuilding plant in New Jersey to break an illegal strike in one case and to force an employer to abide by an arbitration ruling in the other. Miners in the Appalachian coal fields went out on strike and caused steel mills in Pittsburgh and Birmingham to bank their furnaces.

Quite aside from such glaring instances of chaos on the national scene one could encounter in his everyday experience seemingly incontrovertible evidence that the country was in a manpower squeeze. The mechanics who fixed your car or repaired your furnace or wired your house had gone into the Army or off to a better-paying job in a defense plant. The few doctors remaining in the neighborhood no longer had time for house calls. Male teachers disappeared from the schools; restaurants switched to cafeteria service; hotel bellboys were bent with age and sore feet; and women bus drivers became commonplace. The "help wanted" columns in the newspapers bulged with seductive job offers, and industrial recruiters scoured the countryside for talent.

But the manpower problem looked more serious than it really was. Its worst manifestations—and in some cases they were acute—were usually localized either as to particular skills or as to place: Huge defense installations were often built "in the middle of nowhere" without regard to the availability of a labor supply. Overall, the manpower supply was plentiful. The civilian labor force remained fairly constant at between 53 million and 55 million. The inroads made upon it by the military draft were quickly filled from the ranks of the unemployed (which dropped from nine million in 1940 to less than one million by the end of 1942), by some five million women who entered the labor market for the first time, and by a stretching of the average work-week from 37.3 hours to 45.3 hours. The six-day work-week became common in business as well as in the manufacturing trades after 1942.

However, the manpower side of the rapidly escalating defense program could not be left entirely to chance and patriotism. No one could foresee at the time of Pearl Harbor what the future demand would be. As price and production controls were fastened on producers and as government sought to check the upward spiral of inflation, there was an intensified demand for comparable controls on labor, mainly in respect to the unchecked use of its principal economic weapon, the strike. After 1940, capitalizing on the legislative gains it had made a few years earlier under the New Deal, organized labor suddenly found itself possessed of more power than it had ever known. Not only was it in a favorable position, with demand running high, but it was spurred on to greater tests of strength by the intense competition for primacy within its own divided ranks between the old-line American Federation of Labor and the upstart Congress of Industrial Organizations. Nineteen forty-one, with defense production just beginning to swing into high gear, was a near record year in the annals of labor-management strife. There were over 3,500 strikes that year causing the loss of approximately 23 million man-days of work. Production schedules in scores of defense plants were disrupted and popular indignation, particularly in Congress, ran high against the strikers. For the first time serious proposals were advanced for a national service law that would be a counterpart for the civilian population of the selective service law—mandatory registration of all able-bodied adults below the age of 65 and their assignment to jobs under government orders.

Roosevelt sought in a number of ways to appease this mood and also bring more coherence into the manpower picture. The United States Employment Service, with branches in every large community in the land, was designated as the vehicle for assessing national manpower needs and for getting workers to where they were most needed—on a wholly voluntary basis. Hillman's function as the labor boss of OPM was a nebulous one of coordinating manpower supply and demand between the competing segments of the economy and of attempting through exhortation to avoid labor-management strife. Where exhortation failed (and Hillman's efforts were largely ineffective), cases went before the National Defense Mediation Board (NDMB), which was created in mid-1941 to settle amicably deadlocks over collective bargaining. The Board had an equal number of members representing labor, management, and the public, and it relied upon sweet reasonableness and the power of public opinion to enforce its findings.

The NDMB came to grief and its inevitable doom in less than a year, however. In November 1941, it collided head-on with the rocky intransigence of John L. Lewis of the United Mine Workers of America. He had called some 200,000 coal diggers out of the pits all across the country to enforce his demand for a union shop in the handful of "captive" mines owned by the great steel companies. The Mediation Board voted solidly against Lewis except for the three CIO members of the six-man labor panel who backed up their negative by resigning—in person and organizationally in behalf of the entire CIO. Thus stripped of an important segment of its labor support, the NDMB collapsed.

John Llewellyn Lewis strode across the labor scene of the 1940s like a truculent Paul Bunyan, daring Presidents, Congress, and the courts to put him in chains. A bear of a man with an imposing crest of hair and fearsome mein, he was part evangelist, part philosopher, and part rogue. He had gone into the mines as a boy of twelve and risen by the time he was forty (in 1920) to the presidency of the mine workers union, a vital component of the American Federation of Labor. Combining shrewdness with violence, he built the UMW into one of the most powerful monopolies in the land, won measurable benefits for his impoverished constituency, and emerged in the era of the New Deal "liberation" as labor's most feared and powerful spokesman.

In 1935 he broke with the AFL over the issue of industrial versus craft unionism and set up a competing federation, Congress of Industrial Organizations, with the UMW at its core. Nourished by New Deal legislation which vastly strengthened the organizational drive of the unions, there followed seven years of bitter and often bloody contention as the two halves of "the house of labor" fought either between themselves to dominate the premises, or separately against the antiunion citadels of industry. No period in history since the 1860s had witnessed such civil strife.

Not a man to share honors willingly with another, Lewis had been a grudging supporter of FDR during the early years of the New Deal. His Mine Workers treasury contributed $500,000 to the Democratic campaign in 1936 on the mine czar's assumption that he had thereby bought himself a seat at FDR's council table. He was mistaken. Thereafter, Lewis turned progressively more hostile toward the administration (he supported Willkie in the 1940 election but was unable to persuade many in the rank and file of labor to follow his lead), flouting its overtures for peace and cooperation, and castigating it when it refused to take his side in some major dispute. In one such instance Roosevelt had privately condemned both parties with an offhand "a plague on both your houses," remark which found its way into the newspapers. Lewis thundered back a few days later in his typically bombastic fashion: "It ill behooves one who has supped at labor's table . . . to curse with equal fervor and fine impartiality both labor and its adversaries when they become locked in deadly embrace." The coal strike in the autumn of 1941 that brought the National Defense Mediation Board down was neither the first nor the last with which the redoubtable John L. harassed the government during the prewar and war years.

The scuttling of the Mediation Board in November 1941, almost brought the festering labor question to a head. This had been the heart of the government's temperate manpower policy and now it lay in ruins. The newspapers boiled with indignation over the administration's failure to "crack down" on the unions, and into the congressional hoppers poured some 30 bills designed to outlaw strikes or otherwise restrain labor's freedom of action. Sentiment for enactment of a national service law soared to the point where the President and his Secretary of Labor doubted that they could prevail against it.

But that crisis suddenly dissolved in the shock waves of the greater crisis, the December 7 attack on Pearl Harbor. Within two weeks, a large delegation of leaders from industry and organized labor was assembled in Washington where, under the compelling impetus of the national emergency, they hammered out a pledge of no strikes, no lockouts for the duration of the war.

The pledge was a valuable testament of the national will but it alone could not be counted to resolve the inescapable frictions of a volatile war economy. It simply papered over some of the principal causes of labor-management conflict. The pledge carried no stipulations, for example, as to whether or how wages were to be standardized nor how the thorny question of the open shop versus the union or closed shop would be settled. To handle such flammable controversies, the NDMB was replaced early the following January by a new War Labor Board (WLB) with wide powers not only to mediate but, where necessary, to impose its own rulings on wages and working conditions when collective bargaining became deadlocked.

To surmount the principal barriers to mutual accord, the WLB evolved two generally successful compromises. The pressure to hold down wages was being applied as assiduously by the Office of Price Administration as by employers. OPA argued strenuously that wage levels should be frozen at their January 1941, levels as a barrier against inflation. But the labor unions protested that the cost of living had increased approximately 15 percent between that date and mid-1942 and demanded that the rise be offset by a general increase in the wage level. The WLB solution (first adduced in a case involving the "little steel" companies) was to grant increases of up to 15 percent where existing rates had not kept pace with the rise in living costs since January 1941. The Board also made generous concessions respecting incentive and overtime pay and various fringe benefits in contract negotiations. A good deal of flexibility was condoned in the application of these standards, but in the main a relatively tight lid was kept on wages for the duration of the war.

The Board's other most notable compromise hewed a path around the stubborn obstacle of the union shop, an arrangement under which all employees in a given plant are required to become members of the dominant union in that plant—craft or industrial as the case might be. This was a device for which the unions, still in the stage of demanding recognition, had fought most bitterly over the previous several years. It had been opposed with equal determination by most employers, who had amassed a preponderance of public and political opinion on their side. Since the late thirties this had caused more unrest on the labor front than any other single issue.

Almost the first order of business confronting the new WLB, therefore, was whether, as a matter of policy, it should include the union shop among the enforceable conditions of its dispute-settling function. After weeks of internal debate, and a strong indication of Presidential preference ("I don't think the government should force anyone to join or not join a union"), the decision was made in the negative. It agreed, instead, on the novel "maintenance of membership" doctrine which required only that those who were members of a union at the time a contract was negotiated must maintain their memberships as a condition of employment. This did not fully satisfy either labor or management but it succeeded in taking a great deal of the punch out of their belligerence. This pattern, too, remained substantially in force to the end of the war.

Along with the WLB, a War Manpower Commission (WMC) was established with the prescribed function of overseeing and directing the flow of the civilian work force into channels where it was most needed. Its principal operative arm was the United States Employment Service, which had a semiautonomous status within the WMC and was largely self-operative. Aside from this, the new agency was relatively ineffectual, lacking any control over the principal consumer of manpower, the Selective Service Administration, or even over the major defense contractors supplying goods for the military. Had stiff manpower controls ever been invoked, as in a national service law, the WMC would have been the obvious vehicle for their enforcement. But by the time the industrial manpower pinch began to get serious in late 1944, the war began simultaneously to wind down, with a consequent lessening in demands both for fresh soldiers and for the weapons and materiel to support them. Official concern switched, indeed, to what to do with the surplus manpower once the war was ended.

As a group, labor suffered less from wartime regimentation than any other segment of the economy. Workers were free to accept or turn down a job, or to switch jobs, at their pleasure. They were free to strike, in spite of the no-strike pledge and the ministrations of the WLB, and they did so, but with markedly less frequency and disruption to defense production than in 1941. (John L. Lewis, in defiance of the WLB, again called his men out of the coal mines in 1943, posing a serious threat to the entire defense production program. The rift was settled—uneasily— by government seizure of the mines.) While *basic* wage levels held reasonably firm under WLB surveillance, most workers' pay envelopes swelled moderately but consistently throughout the war years under the nourishment of overtime and other differentials. Thus, average weekly earnings in manufacturing, which were $25.20 in 1940, jumped to $36.65 in 1942 under the impetus of the "little steel" formula, and climbed to $47.08 in 1944. That was a gain of about two-thirds over the five-year span as against an increase of about one-fifth in the cost of living. White collar workers fared less well on this economic seesaw. And in spite of the restrictions on union shop contracts, union membership gained steadily over the period, from 8.9 million in 1940 to 14.6 million in 1944.

Labor, or more properly the "labor bosses," were under almost constant attack from conservative management and political sources throughout the period, much of it inspired by military procurement officials who could not understand why there should not be the same spit-and-polish discipline on the production line as on the firing line. Lewis, Philip Murray of the Steel Workers, and Walter Reuther of the Auto Workers, among others, were regularly depicted as ogres lusting for power at the expense of the nation's security. But the spirit of patriotism ran just as high for the men in overalls as it did for those in blue serge suits, and in the long-run the "arsenal of democracy" managed to reach its quota.[4]

V

Information is a critical commodity in wartime which is put under manipulative control by government. When it is of tactical or strategic concern to the military we call it intelligence. When it affects the public psychology we call it propaganda. Each has a dual field of applicability: behind the enemy's lines and behind our own. In the one case, we want to find out what he is up to and prevent his knowing what we are up to. In the other, we want to destroy his morale—his will to fight— and build up our own.

In the pursuit of these objectives there is inevitably a good deal of tampering with what the civilian population is permitted to know and to say about his nation's war efforts. During the Second World War we in the United States were constantly being cautioned to "Button Your Lip!" or exhorted by such patriotic slogans as "America at War Needs You at Work!" Our overseas mail was read by censors; the news we got (as it related to the war, at least) was filtered through a watchful bureaucracy, and our attitudes about the righteousness of our cause and the valor of our allies were the object of skillful manipulation.

These meddlesome impositions were endured with varying degrees of tolerance.

Censorship became an instant necessity when the first bomb dropped on Pearl Harbor (though it can well be argued that it was a necessity some weeks *before* that). There was no governmental machinery for such an operation but the Army and the Navy leaped into the breach in an effort to conceal from the enemy the extent of the damage done to the fleet and to put a clamp on all communications going to the outside world from Hawaii. It was two months before the American public was fully informed of the devastating success of the Japanese raid.

One of the first fruits of the War Powers Act, whipped through Congress in the heat of the catastrophe, was the creation on December 19, 1941, of the Office of Censorship. As its head, President Roosevelt summoned one of the most respected newsmen in the country, Byron Price, General Manager of the Associated Press. In the First World War, censorship and the dissemination of official information had been combined under a single head, George Creel, a prominent writer and editor. Wisely this time, the decision was made to separate the two functions. There is a natural antipathy between the two which, when coupled, erodes the effectiveness and credibility of each.

As Director of Censorship Price was authorized, "in his absolute discretion," to censor all communications entering or leaving the United States by whatever medium: first, to prevent the transmission of information of value to the enemy, and second, to procure from abroad information of intelligence value to the United States. Scores of censorship offices were set up at ports and other cities throughout the country to monitor international cables, telephone and radio communications, and mountains of printed matter and personal correspondence passing over the borders by mail. A familiar experience for many during the war years was to receive a letter from abroad which had been slit open and resealed with a bit of tape saying "Opened by Censor," and to find inside a missive from which a few words, sentences, or even entire paragraphs had been neatly scissored out. It may have offended one's sense of privacy, but it also brought the reality of war a little closer to home.

In January 1942 (after Price had held extensive consultations with the publishing and radio industries), censorship was extended to the domestic news media in order to prevent the publication of information which might be of use to the enemy.

The genius of this arrangement was that news censorship was to be voluntary rather than mandatory. The natural instinct of the reporter or editor to scoop the opposition or to browbeat important news out of a government official, and let someone else worry about national security, was effectively subdued by an "honor system." The Director of Censorship laid down certain guidelines defining types of information which should be published only on release or confirmation by appropriate government authority—the movement and location of troops and fortifications, the identification and movement of vessels carrying troops and cargoes, ship sinkings and enemy sabotage, the disposition and characteristics of our fighter planes, certain details of the defense production program, even long-range weather forecasts.

Editors were asked, on their own responsibility, to forego publishing stories of this nature until and unless they were officially authorized by the government. In borderline cases where legitimate doubt existed as to whether a piece of information was privileged, the Office of Censorship maintained a round-the-clock clearance desk which an editor could telephone to get a yes or no. News from the fighting fronts was censored at the source by the theater commanders.

Price prescribed a code of ethics for his operation which, by its observance, won the general confidence of newsmen. Only material clearly endangering national security was censorable; bans applied uniformly without favoritism; expressions of editorial opinion were not censorable, nor were the statements of public officials; censors were forbidden to vouch for the truth of accuracy of any item submitted to them; and so on. Where pertinent information already known to the press was being held up for security reasons in a government agency, the Office of Censorship often sought to expedite its release. In some instances the press was advised confidentially in advance of a pending development on the understanding that nothing would be said about it until the wraps were off. Thus, many Washington newsmen were told that President Roosevelt was making an important trip "somewhere out of the country" early in January 1943. Without this precaution, his prolonged absence from the White House would have been noted and become the subject of excited and possibly injurious speculation. It was not until nearly two weeks later that they—and the world—learned that he had flown to Casablanca for a conference with Churchill and de Gaulle.

Sometimes the censors, in the line of duty, were put uncomfortably on the spot. When the former French liner *Normandie* (renamed the *Lafayette*) burned and sank at her dock in New York in February 1942, a spectacle witnessed by thousands, the Office of Censorship enforced a 24-hour hold-down lest the success of this supposed act of sabotage become known to the enemy. (It was later ruled an accident.) And when man's first atomic bomb was exploded in the New Mexico desert in

May 1945, sending a booming shock wave felt 100 miles away, the Office of Censorship was obliged to "confirm" that an enormous ammunition dump had blown up.

On the whole, the Office of Censorship operated efficiently, relatively painlessly, and free of controversy throughout the war years. It was less in the public eye than its sister agency, the Office of War Information (OWI), and consequently a less inviting target for the critics. There were no major breaches of its voluntary codes nor, so far as is known today, any catastrophic leakages of security information through its blue-pencil defense.

An article in *Collier's* magazine in June 1944, opened with this provocative observation:

> After you spend a day with Mr. Elmer Davis and his Office of War Information you have several convictions, the clearest of which is you are glad you don't have his job. You've started at eight in the morning pondering on last night's cables from Chungking to Capetown and the latest bellyaches from Seattle to Teheran. . . . In general, it is a typical day in that, no matter what happens, someone is sure to blame it on OWI.

OWI, as its name suggests, was the affirmative side of the government's bifurcated wartime information program. It dealt in both straight news and propaganda, a notoriously incompatible mix that kept it in a state of trauma throughout most of its existence. However, it faced a job that had to be done and did it in such a fashion that its flamboyant miscalculations often concealed its solid, more pedestrian accomplishments. This was an inevitable burden of the assignment, yet the two men responsible for carrying it out did so without any loss of personal stature.

Davis, the head man of OWI from its inception, was a soft-spoken, utterly unflappable, and mildly iconoclastic Hoosier who had established over two decades a solid reputation for integrity as a journalist both in print (the *New York Times*) and on radio. Robert E. Sherwood, a Pulitzer-prize-winning playwright and author with a more volatile disposition than Davis and with more pronounced political leanings (he was an intimate of the New Deal circle in Washington), was chief of the Overseas Branch—the propaganda tail that in time came to wag the OWI dog.

Together, these two juggled the hot potato of what the public at home and abroad should know and should believe about America's role in the war. Their mission was but a pale imitation of Dr. Goebbel's Ministry of Propaganda and Enlightenment, but even the barest resemblances were enough to excite suspicions here at home. With all their genius and acumen, Davis and Sherwood could not keep the OWI out of hot water for long. That was, perhaps, its natural habitat.

Government information policies in a democracy are by nature chaotic. On the one hand, there is the public's right to know what is going on, abetted and intensified by the press. On the other, there is the bureaucrat's natural disposition to reveal what suits his purpose or his vanity and to obscure or conceal the rest. In this always-seething conflict of interests, partisan politics often intrudes to stir things up still more. In a crisis situation such as that which developed with the approach, and then the onset, of war in the early forties, the handling of government information (which often embraced the most important news of the day) degenerated into a sort of battle royal. It resulted from a host of voracious reporters mixing it up with a host of government officials, many of the latter new to the game and eager because of pride, ego, zealousness, and often bureaucratic jealousy either to get into print or to keep out of it.

An early effort to bring some order into this scramble was the creation of a Division of Information in the Office for Emergency Management. Here was to be the central, coordinated news source for all the emergency war agencies (Army and Navy excluded), but it lacked authority to make its rules stick. On parallel and often converging tracks there grew up an Office of Government Reports (OGR), and Office of Facts and Figures (OFF), and an Office of the Coordinator of Information, the last being concerned exclusively with news for foreign rather than domestic consumption. Inevitably, the more cooks there were, the worse the broth tasted. Nowhere along the line was there a clear-cut news and information policy nor the authority to back up such a policy had one been devised. It provided a carnival setting for "the Battle of Washington," which engaged the public's attention only slightly less than did the battles abroad.

In March 1942, a special White House task force advised the President as follows:

> Much information released daily is still of the "agency glorification" type and is not designed to implement an overall war information policy. There is competition in obtaining funds, in building staffs, and preempting special fields of information. Conflicts in press releases have been numerous, as for example, the contradictory statements recently issued on the rubber situation. Coordination between domestic and foreign information programs has been weak. Finally, there has been too much reliance placed on "making the press" as opposed to the development of information programs designed to stimulate citizen understanding of the war effort. . . .

Acting largely on this group's recommendations, the President issued an executive order on June 11 creating the Office of War Information and designating Davis as its head. The new agency was given explicit powers for overseeing the news and information output of all civilian government departments and bureaus and of devising through use of the press, radio, motion pictures, and other information media, programs "to facilitate the development of an informed and intelligent understanding, at home and abroad, of the status and the progress of the war effort and of the war policies, activities and aims of the government." To this end, OWI was to take over the functions of the other specialized agencies in the field. The OES Information Division, the OFF, and the OGR disappeared into the Domestic Branch of the OWI, and the Office of the Coordinator of Information's Foreign Information Service, of which Sherwood was the director, became OWI's Overseas Branch.*

Davis set out on the laudable premise that the people should know the truth and that the truth would make them free; that his function was simply to facilitate the fullest and most rapid dissemination of information at the government's disposal consistent with the requirements of national security. OWI would leave propaganda and morale building to others. The theory was excellent but it was difficult to prove.

OWI's Domestic News Branch was the nerve center of its varied and far-flung operations. Daily it pulled together from scores of government agencies the facts, figures, and policy pronouncements concerning their operations, their boastful claims, and their reluctant admissions of failure, synthesized them as accurately as it could and made the results (a deluge of mimeographed "handouts") available to the press and radio. A major exception to this treatment was war news from the fighting fronts: The military handled its own communiques. Also excepted as a general practice was routine news from the regular government departments —Agriculture, Treasury, etc.—which had no direct bearing on the war.

The task was a formidable one. The wartime government was a labyrinth of fiefdoms large and small, each with its own esoteric function and its sense of mission and self-importance, and each subject to the whims and crotchets of individual chieftains. Most had their own public relations staffs to whom they looked for a favorable projection of their personal and corporate image on the public consciousness. The interposition of the OWI seemed to threaten these prerogatives and to invite end-runs around its authority—an exercise in which the press corps was ever ready to collaborate.

A more troublesome obstacle was the poorly defined one of national security: What information could legitimately be withheld on the grounds

* The Office of the Coordinator of Information, which had been set up in 1941 to deal mainly with foreign intelligence, was headed by Colonel William L. ("Wild Bill") Donovan. After the amputation described above, the agency moved under military control to become the Office of Strategic Services, noted for its exploits behind enemy lines during the war. OSS was assigned the responsibility for "black propaganda"—that which is designedly false and disruptive—while OWI dispensed a blend of "white" and "gray."

that its disclosure would aid the enemy? Beyond a few obvious categories, hard definitions were elusive and nearly always vexatious. Some things the OWI could not divulge at all, such as the specifications and delivery rates of certain weapons and aircraft. Some facts it could admit only after an awkward period of silence, such as the sinking offshore of a tanker or freighter by Nazi submarines. And some things it could talk about only with gingerly circumspection, such as shifts in war strategy or the manifest deficiencies of an allied or neutral power. OWI constantly had to face the challenge that it was engaged in covering up a disaster or blunder, or that it was using good news to balance off the bad.

Against such odds, however, the Domestic News Branch managed during its brief existence to give a reasonably full, coherent, and believable day-by-day account of America at war. Newsmen were generally inclined to forgive its sins and to commend its efforts to lead a virtuous life.

In addition to its news function, the OWI was charged with fostering "an informed and intelligent understanding" among the citizenry of the "aims and policies" of their wartime government. In spite of Davis's rejection of the term, this was a thinly disguised propaganda operation. Its purpose was not only to explain to the people what their civilian obligations were but to win their assent and cooperation in doing the unpleasant things required of them. This meant persuading them of the righteousness of their nation's cause and the promise of its ultimate glowing triumph; of the patriotic necessity of giving their all to their civilian jobs ("the boys on Bataan don't work a 40-hour week"); of faith in the wisdom of OPA, WPD, OCD, WLB, and, inferentially at least, FDR; of the virtue and valor of putting up with scarce housing, overcrowded transportation, and the denial of many luxuries and essential commodities.

There were scores of one-shot and longer-ranged campaigns aimed at the supposed soft spots in the civilian morale, carried on through the newspapers and magazines, the radio, movies, pamphlets, posters, bill-boards, and every other channel of communication. This required the talents of a small army of writers, artists, publicity and advertising specialists, psychologists, and sociologists. Such a volatile collection of temperaments was not destined to live at peace, either with one another or with their scornful colleagues in the News Branch. Their noisy contentions added to the growing din of "the Battle of Washington." Fifteen writers, some of them the possessors of well-known by-lines, staged an angry walkout in the spring of 1943, accusing the OWI of attempting "to soft-soap the American public." And the mission on which they were engaged—domestic propaganda—was clearly one to excite the suspicions of conservative and orthodox opinion.

The Overseas Branch under Sherwood did all the things the Domestic Branch did but with a special flair and license all its own. With outposts scattered literally all around the globe (there were approximately 8,400 people on its payroll by VE-Day), OWI was the preeminent American mouthpiece to a world at war; an official huckster-evangelist charged with making "the American way" seem both palatable and indispensable—to the English bank clerk no less than to the Malay coolie. It was the principal disseminator of hard news, not only from the United States but—for many locales where other sources were deficient—from the war fronts and the allied capitals, as well.

Not infrequently the news might be tailored to fit some important propaganda line being locally advanced, for propaganda was a more readily acknowledged function of the Overseas Branch than of the Domestic. The purpose was not only to promote the cause of the United States and the Allies in the war, but also to counteract virulent enemy propaganda emanating from the Axis.

Radio was one of the most powerful weapons in this "war of words," and the OWI manned scores of transmitters strategically located in Europe and Asia as well as more than a dozen powerful shortwave stations spotted along the Atlantic and Pacific coasts of the United States. Here the "Voice of America" was born: It was a name destined to become familiar in a hundred languages and dialects—and to remain so without a break from February 1942, to the present.*

Additionally, millions of posters, leaflets, booklets, and magazines —even comic books—poured off the OWI production line, written in many tongues and for every educational level in the hope of arousing the understanding, the sympathy, the admiration, or the self-interest of foreign populations. One of the most ambitious undertakings—or perhaps it was only the most conspicuous—was a monthly picture magazine, *Victory,* done in the lavish style and format of *Life* and *Look.* With 12 separate language editions per issue, it was aimed at an influential upper-class readership abroad and designed to persuade them of America's military, industrial, and political prowess.

It was said of the OWI that it was the most vulnerable wartime agency in Washington and the safest to raise hell with. This was pretty well borne out by the record.

Its mission was a delicate and a sensitive one. In a free society any governmental agency with the power to control the flow and quality of information to the people is automatically suspect. For years prior to the war there had been a growing clamor against "New Deal press

---

* The Voice of America has persisted through war, peace, and political vicissitude to broadcast daily the news and opinions of the United States to the farthest corners of the world. It is currently lodged in the U.S. Information Agency, which is itself a lineal descendant of OWI.

agentry" as practiced by the regular government departments, a charge that was greatly overblown but which made good political fuel and good newspaper copy. Now the practice was being openly sanctioned by the creation of OWI for the purpose, as some liked to put it, of "spoon-feeding the American people and telling them what to think." There was just enough truth in this to keep Davis and his men constantly on the defensive.

This natural animus was intensified by a nagging assortment of war-caused anxieties. The war was going against us in 1942 and much of 1943. Our forces in the Pacific had suffered cruelly at the hands of the Japanese; now, after a long and humiliating period of enforced inaction, General MacArthur was beginning his costly counteroffensive from bases in Australia. Triumphant Axis armor had swept over nearly all of Central Europe, the Balkans, and North Africa virtually without hindrance until the first American expeditionary force splashed ashore on the coast of French Morocco in November 1942—there to meet a dubious Vichy ally as well as determined Nazi firepower. In the coastal water and sea-lanes of the North Atlantic, enemy submarines and surface raiders were taking a fearful toll of American shipping, as testified by gloating Nazi propaganda and by the mute, oil-stained evidence that frequently washed onto the beaches from Florida to Nova Scotia.

The rumor mills ground constantly, fed by an eyewitness here, a bit of gossip or inside information there, sending sporadic shivers of alarm through the countryside. Not only was it said that disasters on the battle-fronts were being painted as victories, but frightening tales abounded that OWI was hushing-up bad news on the home front—of enemy agents sneaking across the borders or dropping from the skies, of terrifying acts of sabotage, of subversives infiltrating government bureaus and labor unions and army camps, of production hang-ups and structural failures plagueing the aircraft and munitions factories, of poison pellets dropped into a city reservoir.

How much of all this are we *really* being told, people asked? And how much is being held back, glossed over, deliberately distorted?

The target of their distrust, naturally, was the OWI. In truth, the OWI was giving them all the facts, or very nearly all of them, the good along with the bad, subject only occasionally to some overriding considerations of timing and juxtaposition. As believable as Elmer Davis was in his frequent reiterations of this truth, he could never completely eradicate the notion that OWI was somehow hoodwinking a gullible public.

Nowhere was this antipathy toward OWI more eagerly exploited than in Congress. Republicans in general and the growing body of anti-Roosevelt Democrats found it a handy weapon with which to belabor the administration without risking direct interference with the war effort.

With no popular constituency of its own to defend it, OWI was an inviting target for any political huntsman who wanted to take a pot shot at the White House without seeming to aim that way. The impulse was strong in mid-1942 with the biennial congressional elections coming up in November; it was stronger still in 1943 as the suspicion grew that Roosevelt might seek a fourth term the next year. Much of the pent-up frustrations with the course of the war, with the noisy infighting between the civilian defense agencies, and with the government's indulgent handling of defense-crippling labor disputes could be vented by blasting the OWI as the propaganda arm of the Democratic-New Deal establishment.

"We don't need a Goebbels or a Virginio Gayda in this country," Representative Joe Starnes thundered on the floor of the House one day in 1943 in a typical outburst against Elmer Davis and all his works. "I think it's an insult to the intelligence of the American people to have foisted upon them the kind of propaganda being put out by the OWI. They are trying to tell us, like we were six-year-olds, why we are at war."

Some of the many domestic "educational" campaigns backfired with painful results. An OWI effort to explain the dangers of and cures for wartime inflation stirred the wrath of conservatives who complained that the program was an exercise in "New Deal economic theories." Davis, embarrassed to concede that there was some justification to the charge, recalled thousands of copies of a booklet, "Battle Stations for All," designed as a campaign manual for local leaders. The *Chicago Tribune* contributed to the uproar by denouncing OWI as a haven for communists and draft dodgers.

A short and laudatory biography of President Roosevelt, done in the simplified style of a juvenile cartoon booklet, created another uproar when it appeared in the spring of 1943. It was denounced by politicians as "a blatant example of fourth-term propaganda." Davis explained —futilely—that the booklet was meant exclusively for overseas distribution (it was printed in a dozen languages in addition to English) and that its purpose was not to solicit nonexistent votes among the peasantry of Greece and China but to build their confidence in America's war leadership. Similarly, issues of the slick magazine *Victory,* of a short volume of popular history called *A Handbook of the U.S.A.,* and of a pamphlet entitled *The Negro and the War,* were exhibited with horror in the halls of Congress and loudly condemned. Senator Taft demanded in a resolution that the OWI supply the Foreign Relations Committee regularly with samples of its propaganda output so that the Senate might learn if the agency was "playing European politics about which we know nothing."

Interestingly enough, the strongest defense of OWI came from its principal and most exacting clientele—the newsmen here at home who dealt and wrestled with it daily. Many in their news stories, editorials, and broadcasts endeavored to keep the record straight by crediting OWI with its virtues while deploring its faults. As the attacks were approaching a climax in June 1943, the national convention of the American Newspaper Guild, meeting in Boston, unanimously adopted a resolution declaring: "Elmer Davis as Director of the OWI is the strongest guarantee of a free press in wartime that the nation could have."

That was quite an endorsement, but it was of little avail. OWI's appropriation bill was up for consideration at the time. Its enemies in the House succeeded not only in slicing its funds virtually in half but in decreeing the abolishment of the entire Domestic Branch. (The Overseas Branch was spared, not because it was thought to be any less culpable, but because it wore an aura of belonging somewhere in the plan of wartime strategy.) The Senate was grudgingly more generous. It overrode the House's mandatory death sentence on the Domestic Branch but condemned it instead to starvation by granting it a niggardly $2.7 million out of a total appropriation of $24 million for the agency as a whole.

The end result was the same. The domestic operation, with some 2,000 employees and 46 field offices, was finished. Davis reluctantly closed it down except for a small headquarters cadre in Washington and concentrated for the remander of the war on OWI's activities overseas. But the political climate did not noticeably improve, even with the OWI forbidden to trespass on its native soil. Its enemies on Capitol Hill continued to snipe at it and its friends in the press continued to defend it. When the House approved a crippling cut in its funds in June 1945 (after the German surrender), a group of eight war correspondents, including such well-known stars as Quentin Reynolds and William L. Shirer, urged the Senate to make full restitution. "We have seen the OWI at work on the spot," they cabled from Europe, "and we know it is vital that that work should continue on an enlarged scale. Destroy the OWI and you leave the field to the enemies of democracy."

That vote of confidence by a group of reporters, men with a built-in skepticism toward any official meddling with the news, turned out to be a most fitting epitaph for OWI. On September 1, hard on the heels of VJ-Day, it was dissolved, along with a number of other emergency agencies, by executive order. The President, too, commended it for an "outstanding contribution to victory." There must have been more than flattery in these kudos, for OWI was destined for a slightly modified reincarnation after the war and the guarantee of a long and often tempestuous existence as the United States Information Service. Elmer Davis went on to even greater eminence than he had previously enjoyed as writer and commentator, and Robert Sherwood acquired new honors as author and playwright.[5]

VI

In broad outline, this was the shape of mobilization that changed the pattern of American life in the early forties. Some 50 to 60 emergency war agencies were, at one time or another, empowered to lay down rules and regulations affecting nearly every sector of the economy, from General Motors to the corner grocer. They were told what they could produce, buy, or sell, the prices they could charge, and the profits they could make. Their performance was dictated by a deluge of orders and printed forms—often confusing and contradictory—and policed by an army of bureaucrats and citizen-busybodies.

As an employee, your salary or wage rate was frozen, technically at least, so that the simplest way to get more money was not to argue with the boss but to change jobs, which for most was easily done. Even so, it was sometimes hard to spend all you made. After 1942, a new automobile or refrigerator or radio simply was not to be had. Furniture, appliances, clothing, and scores of other necessities, all under prescribed "ceiling prices," were scarce and often shoddy. You stood in long lines to get your books of red and blue ration stamps without which you could not buy tires and gasoline, or fuel for heating, or leather shoes, or meats, sugar, and many kinds of processed foods—and then stood in other lines hoping the supply of whatever it was you wanted would not run out before your turn came. Meanwhile, from billboard and radio you were constantly exhorted to put the money you couldn't—or shouldn't—spend into war bonds, to "Pay Your Taxes, Beat the Axis," to consider as you set out on a journey, "Is This Trip Necessary?" All in all, it was regimentation on a scale the nation had never experienced before, an abridgment of the cannons of capitalist do-as-you-please which you had always taken for granted.

In actuality, these restrictions were neither widely opposed nor heavily burdensome. The war brought an upsurge of national unity; the Axis enemy was easy to hate, and elemental good sense made it obvious that special exertion and sacrifice were needed for victory. Dissention came —and in unlimited volume—over *how* the restrictions were to be applied. Questions of efficacy and adequacy were debated as loudly as those of necessity and fairness. Spokesmen for industry were in constant conflict with military and government officials over how best to make the system work.

Greed and self-interest were not, of course, wholly submerged in altruistic fervor. Thousands of complaints were lodged against war contractors, manufacturers, and merchants, alleging sharp practices and price-gouging. Many were convicted for war frauds of one kind or another and hundreds of war contracts were "renegotiated" to recover millions of dollars in overcharges and excess profits. Rationing and price controls at the retail level met stubborn resistance not only from many merchants and businessmen but also from large numbers of their customers. The grocer who was "out" of your favorite brand of canned peas at the 22¢ ceiling price could often find one for you under the counter at an illicit 40¢. He lamented loudly—and with some justification—that the "squeeze" between his costs and the rigid price regulations threatened to put him out of business. Grumbling about the annoyances and inequities of the rationing system was universal. Much of the consuming public regarded it with the same grudging tolerance that, only a decade earlier, they had accorded prohibition: It was something to be got around if you could manage it without being caught. Hoarding and black marketing became spirited avocations in thousands of households of otherwise blameless rectitude.

But in spite of all the contention and the grumbling, wartime mobilization did not cut deeply into the soft flesh of the civilian population. Their sacrifices were supportable and far less onerous than those borne by their British allies. The reason lay principally in the undreamed-of productivity of the American economy: It proved capable of producing enough of everything, or almost everything, for both the fighting fronts and the home fronts. In five years of war its yearly output of munitions soared from $8.4 billion to $57.8 billion—from 10 percent to 40 percent of the gross national product—enough by the beginning of 1945 to supply almost half of all the armaments used on all the fighting fronts of the world. In the same period it also stepped up the production of consumer goods by 12 percent, not in the variety of plentitude that everyone could wish for, certainly, but sufficient to avert anything resembling the denial the British people experienced, where consumer production *declined* by 22 percent.

Meanwhile, everybody who stayed at home got a little richer than they had been before. Corporate profit after taxes climbed steadily and so did personal incomes, which almost doubled by 1946. With fewer things to buy, personal savings went up, too, at an unprecedented rate, leading to a great splurge when the wraps came off in 1946. It was, the armchair warriors and the stay-at-homes conceded a bit self-consciously, "a pretty good war if you don't get shot at." [6]

5

Enemies Within the Gates

THE FREER A SOCIETY is the more vulnerable it is to attack. The moral values which it espouses act to inhibit suspicion and to delay effective response until the provocation is formally delivered and signed for. Desirable as such restraints may be under most circumstances, they involve manifest dangers in time of crisis. When the Second World War struck we were no better prepared to protect our internal security than we were for military combat. Our intelligence resources were primitive and our legal safeguards against all except the most aggravated forms of subversion were inadequate and out-of-date. We had given little thought to dealing with spies, saboteurs, seditionists, and other enemies within the gates.

Such enemies there were, however, some already within the gates and others who were slipping in by stealth. Some were clumsy amateurs and adventurers, but some were right out of the pages of fiction: shrewd, fearless, professionally expert, and dedicated to their sinister missions. And those missions ran the gamut from stealing our military and diplomatic secrets and blowing up war plants to frothy schemes for setting up a Fascist dictatorship.

But with good luck, good police work, and a certain amount of improvisation (some of it inept) we managed to thwart most of their evil designs. At least as far as the public record discloses there is no evidence that enemy agents, for all their trying, succeeded in any important act of espionage or sabotage between Pearl Harbor and VJ-Day. There is one allowable exception, a major coup of foreign espionage which will be described later. But this was the act of a "friendly" government, an ally against the Axis, and we didn't find out about it until the war was over.

I

A severe case of war nerves seized the country in the weeks after Pearl Harbor. From the highest to the lowest, people were stunned by that unbelievable blow to the national pride, by the enormity of the loss that had been inflicted upon them. As they struggled back to reality it was with an obsessive hangover of fear that enemies still stalked unseen among them, that hostile eyes followed their movements, that somewhere out of sight and hearing other plots were being concocted against them.

So much pent-up anxiety required a target against which to vent itself, a culprit to atone for their's and the nation's humiliation. Inevitably, the finger of guilt pointed to the Japanese, in particular to the large colony of them concentrated in California and elsewhere along the Pacific coast.

Retribution was swift, violent—and blind. Within weeks these West Coast Japanese were officially proscribed *as a class,* much as Hitler had proscribed the Jews of Germany. Citizens and non-citizens alike—Nisei as well as Issei, 110,000 men, women, and children—were stripped of their constitutional rights, deprived of most of their property, and shipped off to imprisonment at internment centers far in the interior. Not a person of Japanese birth or ancestry was left within 200 miles of the coast.

Officially designated the Japanese Exclusion Program, it stands as one of the most shameful episodes in American history. Nowhere did we blunder more grievously in our effort to protect ourselves against the enemy within.

"When this war is over," said Milton Eisenhower (brother of the General) early in 1942, soon after taking over direction of the program, "I feel most deeply that we as Americans are going to regret the avoidable injustices of this unprecedented migration."

And Francis Biddle, the wartime Attorney General who did his best to block the program, noted bitterly in his memoirs 20 years later:

This mass evacuation illustrates the influence that a minority, uncurbed and substantially unopposed, can exercise. It shows, too, the power of suggestion which a mystic cliche like "military necessity" can exercise on human beings. Through lack of independent courage and faith in American reality, a superb opportunity was lost by the government in failing to assert the human decencies for which we were fighting.

How did this deplorable business come about?

In June 1940, Congress passed the Alien Registration Act in response to the nation's deepening concern about subversion, a concern that had been cultivated sedulously by isolationists and some committees of Congress. Each of some five million adult aliens in the country was thus required to register and be fingerprinted and to carry an official identification card with him at all times. When war was declared a year and a half later, some 900,000 of these—Germans, Italians, Japanese—automatically became "enemy aliens." This label, Attorney General Biddle pointed out, was a description of citizenship and not necessarily a judgment about loyalty.

Meanwhile, however, the FBI and the Immigration and Naturalization Service had been quietly combing through the registration records to spot the potentially disloyal and dangerous when and if war should come. When it did come—in fact, by nightfall of Pearl Harbor Sunday—the FBI began to round them up by the hundreds, herding them into jails and armories irrespective of background, residence, and economic status. Within two months some 10,000 "dangerous" enemy aliens had been impounded at Army stockades at Missoula, Montana, and Fort Lincoln, North Dakota. About half of them were Japanese, 3,500 were Germans, and 2,000 were Italians.

Their condition was not as hopeless as it seemed, however. A system of special parole boards was soon created to which the prisoners could appeal and present witnesses and testimony concerning the innocence of their intentions toward the United States. In the course of a year, a majority of the German and Italian internees were released, usually under some form of restriction as to movement and occupation. Evidence that they posed a threat to the national security was scant indeed for all but a few hundred. And in 1943 Italian aliens generally were, by Presidential proclamation, relieved of the stigma of "enemy": They were ordinary aliens again, just as they had been before the war. This amnesty was not merely an exercise in sentimentality and fair play, it was calculated to cut the ground from under the Italian dictator, Benito Mussolini, in the eyes of Italian expatriates worldwide.

The Japanese did not fare so well, especially in the West. In the immediate aftermath of Pearl Harbor, the coastal cities from San Diego to Puget Sound were in a state of near panic. Each was certain that it was the next target for an air attack or invasion. Tension was heightened by the imposition of blackouts, the hasty construction of air raid shelters, the rumbling of Army and National Guard convoys through the streets. Rumors spread with the speed of sound—of submarines and warships lurking off the coast, of mysterious radios and signal lights blinking seaward from isolated coves or mountain peaks, of secret caches of arms and explosives, of vast plots of sabotage and assassination. In the light of what had happened at Pearl Harbor, no rumor seemed too fantastic.

Inevitably, suspicion fastened like a steel magnet upon the hundreds of Japanese families who lived in and around those communities. In many cases they had been there for a generation or more, the wizened elders who had emigrated from Japan in the early decades of the century—the alien Issei—and their myriad offspring—the Nisei, United States citizens by right of birth, who had grown up in the ways of the West. But they had always lived on the social fringe of the Caucasian world, tolerated but never accepted, discriminated against openly and in covert ways. Under federal law, the aliens among them were debarred from acquiring citizenship, and under California law most were prevented from owning land. In spite of such obstacles, they managed to prosper. They were a shrewd, industrious, self-reliant people; they farmed, fished, managed small businesses, and a few sent their sons into the professions. Though the second-generation Nisei attended public schools and adopted the styles and manners of the white majority, the Japanese community remained a thing apart, set off by language, custom, and the indelible physiognomy of the Oriental. Even to their white neighbors they were an inscrutable race, never quite trusted and sometimes regarded with jealous contempt. Now they were feared and despised.

In cities like Los Angeles and San Francisco bands of hoodlums, many of them wearing American Legion caps, smashed windows in Japanese shops, tore up the nets and scuttled the boats of Japanese fishermen, overturned the trucks and destroyed growing crops of Japanese farmers. Stores and business houses hung signs on their doors saying, "Japs Keep Out." Many newspapers and civic organizations and some public officials added to the fury by branding everyone of Japanese ancestry as a potential enemy of the state.

"A viper is nonetheless a viper wherever the egg is hatched," the *Los Angeles Times* proclaimed in an editorial.

The California Attorney General, Earl Warren (later to become Governor and an outstandingly liberal Chief Justice of the United States) warned that the Nisei posed a greater threat to the national security than their alien parents: There were nearly twice as many of them and they were younger and more daring and agile than the Issei. To a congressional committee which had come out to investigate the state of national defense on the West Coast in February, Warren described as "ominous" the fact that, in over two months, no fifth-column activity of any kind had been traceable to the Japanese community. "It looks very much to me," he said, "as though it is a studied effort not to have any until the zero hour arrives."

Under such goading, public opinion was swiftly mobilized behind the idea of getting the Japanese away from the West Coast. In mid-February, the President, acting through the Justice Department, decreed that *all* enemy aliens of whatever nationality should be immediately excluded from approximately 100 "sensitive areas" adjacent to defense installations, docks and railway terminals, power plants, and the like along the entire West Coast. Where and how they went was, at first, the aliens' own responsibility. Hundreds of them picked up what possessions they could, locked their doors, and moved in with friends and relatives or migrated to towns in the interior and in nearby states where they knew no one.

To the more zealous patriots, this was only a half measure, and it created some unwanted side effects. Thousands of Orientals were still at large—and presumably up to no good—outside the prohibited zones; while at the same time hundreds of manifestly harmless German and Italian families were suffering needless distress. You couldn't see behind the mask of a Jap, it was argued, but Germans and Italians were different —"more like us." Who could believe that the aged parents of baseball hero Joe DiMaggio endangered anything in their little house on the San Francisco waterfront?

But no such sympathy was directed toward the Japanese. A clamor grew for their total exclusion from the coastal region, a demand given almost irresistible impetus by Lieutenant General J. L. DeWitt, chief of the Army's West Coast Defense Command, and backed up by the nearly unanimous insistence of the three states' delegations in Congress.

"The Japanese race is an enemy race," General DeWitt affirmed, "and while many second- and third-generation Japanese born on United States soil and possessed of United States citizenship have become 'Americanized,' the racial strains are undiluted." He could not guarantee the security of the region, the General said, by any means short of locking up everyone of Japanese birth and ancestry. American Legion posts, chambers of commerce, union locals, farmers' organizations, and many newspapers and radio stations seconded his move.

Only the President could authorize so drastic a stratagem, and the issue was quickly laid before him. In a heated Cabinet session Biddle opposed the wholesale exclusion as violating a basic assumption of Anglo-Saxon justice, by making membership in a class rather than individual dereliction the substance of guilt. Moreover, he said, while aliens might be interned at the whim of the government, there was no basis in civil law for interning citizens—Nisei—without upsetting the constitutional guarantee of due process. War Secretary Stimson argued just as heatedly that military necessity rather than legal niceties should be the paramount consideration, and he endorsed General DeWitt's dire warnings about a fifth-column uprising among the West Coast Japanese population.

The President heard the arguments out "with mild impatience," Biddle recalled later. "I do not think he was much concerned with the gravity or implications of the step. What must be done to defend the country must be done. He was never theoretical about things."

At all events, the President did come down on the side of the military. On February 19 he issued an executive order empowering the Secretary of War to establish, at his own discretion, military areas from which "any or all persons" could be excluded. Shortly thereafter the whole coastal area from the Mexican to the Canadian borders, extending some 200 miles inland, and including also an enclave in Arizona, was designated Military Area Number 1. The order directed all persons of Japanese origin to evacuate the area forthwith.

Several thousand fled voluntarily, but for the great majority this was impossible. They had no place to go, and as much hostility seemed to await them in the unknown regions to the east as it did where they were. The governors of neighboring states like Nevada and Colorado let it be known they would tolerate no Oriental migrants across their borders.

The War Department resolved that dilemma early in March by ordering the internment of all the Japanese then remaining in the prohibited zone. Initially, they were herded into temporary holding centers —stadiums, fair grounds, and tent colonies set up in open fields not far from the principal centers of population. Later, the great migration to the permanent internment camps began. Trainloads and busloads of frightened, resentful men, women, and children, weighted down with baggage and bundles, were carted across mountains and deserts to a form of imprisonment unique in American experience.

An official government report on the operation described the scene with surprising candor:

Then in June, with gathering momentum, the next phase of the forced migration got under way. At the former migratory labor camp doing duty near Sacramento as an assembly center, trains were loaded with men, women, children and babies and moved northward to unload their cargo near the little town of Tule Lake, California. Here the rough barracks of one of the first relocation centers were still under construction. Farmers from the rich Salinas Valley were transported to the Arizona desert. San Francisco businessmen were sent from the Tanforan race track to the bare, intermountain valleys of central Utah. From the fertile central valley of California to the sandy flats of eastern Colorado, from southern California to the plains of Wyoming, from the moist coastland of the Northwest to the sagebrush plains of southern Idaho, from the San Joaquin Valley to the woodlands of Arkansas, the trains moved during the spring, early summer and fall.

For the involuntary travelers, the break with the accustomed and usual was now complete. In the assembly centers behind fences and under guard by military police, the evacuees had suddenly found themselves, although looking out at familiar hills and highways, in a strange new world of social relationships. They were outcast but still in their own country. Now the world of human relations was matched by an equally strange physical world. It was clear, as the trains moved over the wastelands of the mountain states, that they were to be exiled in desert and wilderness.

There were nine of the so-called relocation centers, each accommodating around 10,000 persons, plus military security detachments and civilian administrative personnel of the hastily created War Relocation

Authority (WRA). The centers were about as bleak as the circumstance of their existence, their grim isolation, and the exigencies of a slapdash construction could combine to achieve. Bulldozers had scraped the area clean of every living thing, leaving piles of debris and ankle-deep dust. The housing consisted of row upon row of long, one-story barracks covered with tarpaper, interspersed at regular intervals with common latrines and bathhouses, common dining halls, and an occasional recreation and medical center. Some of the barracks were partitioned; a family of four, or two couples, was allotted a room about 20 by 20 feet. Others were consigned to open dormitories with no vestige of privacy. The sole furnishings provided, at least at the outset, were one army cot and blanket per inhabitant. Also at the outset, the standard menu was army rations, prepared army style, which made scant provision for Japanese dietary peculiarities or for such unmilitary necessities as warming a baby's bottle.

The inmates themselves, working out their own form of social organization, managed in time to alleviate some of the worst deficiencies of life in the compounds. They elected their own community leaders and organized work details (on which they could earn up to $19 a month) to perform the necessary functions of their communal life. There was no barbed wire, but a constant patrol of military police served all the necessary purposes of security. The temptation to escape was not overwhelming in any event. To most of the inmates the world beyond their compound was a hostile one in which no one with the telltale features of an Oriental could hide.

In the panic that attended their roundup and confinement, thousands of Japanese families saw the accumulated treasures of a lifetime scattered to the winds. They were preyed on by vandals, thieves, and swindlers with virtually no protection from the authorities. In countless cases an aged householder or shop owner would be approached by a white stranger and told that his possessions were going to be confiscated by the government and that he had better sell out while he had the chance. Many stripped their premises bare under such threats, receiving but a pittance for valued heirlooms, art objects, household furniture, and equipment of every kind. Fishermen, farmers, merchants, and businessmen by the hundreds were given time enough only to pack suitcases for their families before abandoning their properties. Many who entrusted their affairs to agents and caretakers were mercilessly fleeced. The official record of the War Relocation Authority is replete with such case histories of which the following (somewhat abridged) is typical:

Woodrow Wilson Higashi, a Nisei, owned a small but prosperous drugstore in Los Angeles. He was unable to dispose of his stock and fixtures before being taken to the holding center at the Santa Anita race track, preliminary to internment. He was visited there by one "Edwards," a white acquaintance, who said he could dispose of the store's fixtures and Mr. Higashi's seven-year-old automobile for approximately $500, and he also offered to store his friend's household goods and personal possessions. The offer was gratefully accepted, and "Edwards" requested and was given a power of attorney to handle Higashi's affairs. That was the last Higashi saw of "Edwards."

After a few weeks at Santa Anita, Higashi was transferred to the Granada relocation center in Colorado. In October 1943, after he had been interned for more than a year, he persuaded the WRA authorities to demand from "Edwards" an accounting of his stewardship. Months later, WRA reported that all of the property, including household and personal possessions, which had been placed in "Edwards'" care had simply vanished; that "Edwards" had no assets which could be attached to recover the value of the store fixtures and automobile, and that, furthermore, the Los Angeles district attorney was not inclined to bring any charges against "Edwards."

That was the way it was for Higashi, and that was the way it was for most of the internees who had anything to leave behind. There was no recourse. The government had made virtually no provision for protecting the abandoned property, and none whatever (at the time) for restitution. Individual losses varied from a few hundred dollars to many thousands of dollars and aggregated, according to an estimate by the Federal Reserve Bank at San Francisco, about $400 million. In 1948 Congress sought lamely to right some of the wrong that had been done by passing a Japanese-American Evacuee Claims Act. Over the succeeding 15 years some 30,000 individual claims were adjudicated on an average of 10 cents to the dollar: The total restitution was about $30 million, which included the considerable enrichment of a number of lawyers. But most of the internees had simply been wiped out financially—physical assets stolen or destroyed, insurance policies lapsed, homes and farms liquidated under foreclosure and tax delinquency—and there was nothing to do but start over again.

Late in 1943 many residents of the internment centers were encouraged to leave provided they could find employment and a livelihood somewhere in the interior, away from the prohibited zones. About 30,000 availed themselves of the opportunity, filtering out apprehensively to unknown places like Omaha and Kansas City and Chicago, and some 1,500 young Nisei opted to join the armed services.

Then, late in 1944, the whole Japanese relocation program began to collapse. In December the Supreme Court, in *ex parte Endo,* upheld the contention that Francis Biddle had made all along, that citizens—Nisei —could not indefinitely be denied the right of due process. Their internment was ruled unconstitutional. The Army thereupon lifted its exclusion orders affecting Military Area Number 1 (the fear of invasion had long since vanished) and the WRA began to dismantle its custodial operations.

Many of the internees faced the prospect of freedom with trepidation.

Internment had been a shield to which they had become accustomed, and they were dubious about the reception they would receive on the outside. But during the first six months of 1945 virtually the entire impounded population—now numbering about 70,000—moved out. A few went to join friends and relatives who had already migrated eastward; the majority returned to their former homes along the West Coast, to pick up the threads of their disrupted lives.

This dismal episode can never be expunged from the record books; it is a permanent blot on our democratic escutcheon. The best excuse that can be made for it is that faced by danger we reacted in panic.

The fault lay chiefly with the military, for it has since become evident that they grossly exaggerated the danger of Japanese subversion on the West Coast. General DeWitt's alarming disclosure about the amount of contraband—weapons, cameras, radios, etc.—seized from Japanese owners was highly deceptive. The "many guns and 60,000 rounds of ammunition" he reported uncovering during a single raid in January 1942, for example, turned out to be the stock-in-trade of a Japanese-owned sporting goods store. And the FBI concluded that virtually all of the hundreds of radios, cameras, and binoculars it confiscated were of the harmless consumer-goods variety and hardly adapted to the exacting specifications of the spy trade.

No evidence whatever has been turned up, indeed, that a Japanese fifth column ever existed either on the West Coast or in Hawaii after Pearl Harbor.[1]

II

Sedition is an elusive and tricky concept in American jurisprudence. A good working definition of it is that it is conduct which tends toward treason but falls short of it for want of an overt act. Sedition is essentially verbal. How far can one go in denouncing his government and its policies without committing an overt act that is punishable? The question immediately becomes entangled in the First—the "free speech"—Amendment to the Constitution. We have always had a sedition statute in the law books, but so loosely drawn as to defy interpretation. The language was somewhat stiffened in 1940 by defining sedition as language "deliberately designed" to overthrow the government or to cause disaffection in the armed forces. This was not much help in resolving the free speech dilemma, particularly for a libertarian Attorney General like Francis Biddle. But in time the issue was forced upon him.

In the two years leading up to our entry in the Second World War, and for several months after there was enough activity that *seemed* seditious to arouse the anger and the anxiety of a good many ordinary citizens. Operating at the fringe of the isolationist movement, and often enjoying its protective cover, there was a ferment of demagoguery that sometimes ap-proached nihilism. The doctrines espoused by these noisy advocates were as confused as their company: There were pacifists, Fascists, anarchists, pro-Germans, anti-Semites, anti-Communists, and religious and political fanatics in all ideological shapes and sizes. If there was a central theme to their preachments it was that the American political system had been seized by knaves and traitors, that the barn would have to be burned down to get rid of the rats. They organized "fronts" and crusades—some of them with military trappings, staged rallies and picket lines, and published scores of tracts, manifestoes, and newspapers.

It was obvious to the discerning that a good part of this furor was the work of cranks and psychopaths, but not all the participants could be dis-missed so easily. There were some among them with talent and learning, expert in the arts of propaganda and persuasion, well organized and fi-nanced. They could fill an arena with cheering adherents, ignite massive letter-to-the-editor campaigns across the country, or command congres-sional committees as a pulpit for their views. Crackpots and hardheads together, they were an unwelcome lot. In a nation being drawn inexorably toward war, they were sowing the seeds of discord. If there were to be an American fifth column, it would surely arise from their ranks.

There was no mystery about who these dissidents were and not much about what they were up to. Until the actual outbreak of war, they clamored for all the publicity they could get.

For almost five years, brown-shirted young Storm Troopers of the German-American Bund had been a familiar phenomenon in many cities of the East and the Middle West. Newspapers and magazines frequently carried pictures of them, arms upraised in the Nazi salute, marching in military array with the Swastika flying alongside the Stars and Stripes. They were mostly first- and second-generation German-Americans, fa-natically loyal to the Fatherland; but there were some non-Germans among them, drawn by the Bundist's two-fisted militarism and ethnic code. How many they were and how really sinister were their goals no one was quite sure. But as recently as 1939 their Fuehrer, Fritz Kuhn, had drawn a frenzied throng of 22,000 to a rally at Madison Square Garden to hear him extol Adolf Hitler as the modern counterpart of George Washington. Post-Pearl Harbor the Bund went underground but not out of business.

Equally familiar was Father Charles E. Coughlin, the famous "radio priest" of Royal Oak, Michigan, long a scourge of FDR and all his works. His political wings had been clipped by the Catholic hierarchy following his oratorical exertions in the 1936 election campaign, but around 1940 he had surfaced again. The newspaper he had established, *Social Justice,* with a circulation of 185,000 copies weekly, was his principal forum. His theology now had a sharp edge of deliberate anti-

Semitism and thinly veiled admiration for Fascist doctrines. Germany, he wrote in the spring of 1942, was the victim of a "sacred war" instigated years earlier "by the race of Jews" and the United States had been euchred into it by unscrupulous British banker-politicians at the behest of their Jewish masters. (That happened also to be a favorite postulate of Dr. Josef Goebbels, the Nazi Minister of Propaganda.) The Father's political congregation was nationwide in scope, running heavily to Irish Catholics with a built-in bias against the British and any American collaboration with them. He had swayed millions with his anti-New Deal invective during the thirties. How many was he reaching now?

Centered in Chicago was a militant feminist group. We, The Mothers Mobilize For America, Inc., which for sheer stridency outdid most of the other entries in the field. Its leadership came from the far right wing of isolationism and included such well-known crusaders for the cause as Mrs. Agnes Waters, Mrs. Lyrl Van Hyning, and Mrs. Elizabeth Dilling. Mrs. Dilling had acquired fame a few years earlier with the publication of *The Red Network,* in which she claimed to identify several hundred members of the Communist underground in the United States, including Eleanor Roosevelt, the President's wife. The main pitch of We, The Mothers was anti-Communist and anti-Semitic. America was preparing for war against the wrong enemy, they said: not fascism but the "world conspiracy of Godless communism." Among their many demands was the dispatch of troops to the Mexican border to head off an invasion by 200,000 "Communist Jews," which they said was imminent. In 1942 they began a campaign for the impeachment of President Roosevelt on the grounds that he had conspired with the Japanese to bring about the attack on Pearl Harbor.

It was often difficult to take We, The Mothers seriously, yet one could never be sure how deeply their divisive propaganda was penetrating. They were actively organized in many cities, could easily mobilize delegations several hundred strong for a "march" on Washington or a state capital, and produced a steady flow of leaflets and newsletters expounding their dogma.

The Reverend Gerald L. K. Smith, the flamboyant Southern evangelist who a few years before had helped Senator Huey Pierce Long make "Share the Wealth" a slogan of hope for tens of thousands of the gullible, had by 1940 converted his constituency into The Committee of One Million. Mixing supernationalism with old time religion in his house organ, *The Cross and the Sword,* he regularly denounced the President and his administration for being dupes of the Communists and for entering the war to advance Marxist aims of world revolution.

The same theory, with a distinctly Fascist overtone, was being advanced in somewhat more sophisticated fashion by Lawrence Dennis, a Harvard-educated New York publicist. Dennis was the proprietor of, among other things, the *Weekly Foreign Letter* which purported to give up-to-the-minute political intelligence on what was really happening abroad, most of it highly favorable to the Axis. And out on the West Coast, a pair of frankly Fascist advocates, Robert Noble and Ellis O. Jones, organized as The Friends of Progress, denounced the government for making war against Germany and Japan. MacArthur, they said, was a deserter who had abandoned his troops at Manila, and they thrust into the hands of young men lined up at the Los Angeles induction centers leaflets asserting, "Young man, your lowest aim in life is to be a good soldier."

William Dudley Pelly brought a particularly rich blend of pseudo-intellectualism and metaphysics to the cause. He was a small, intense man with iron gray hair and goatee and the hard, piercing eyes of a Nazi gauleiter—which, in fact, he rather fancied himself to be. In 50 years he had knocked about in a variety of occupations, including that of itinerant printer, fiction writer, and professional mystic. This latter talent, he claimed, was acquired in 1926 when he "died" and was restored to life after seven minutes. During his heavenly sojourn he established contact with an "oracle" who ever since had guided his every move and thought. Thus blessed, he established a politicoreligious cult with members scattered through the South and Middle West to whom he ministered through a series of lectures and periodicals. When Hitler first came to power in 1933, Pelley's oracle directed him to organize the Silver Shirt Legion and to prepare himself to become, in the style of Hitler, America's deliverer.

The Silver Shirts seem to have been more a product of Pelley's imagination than a secret army in being, but from about the mid-thirties on he waged a vigorous campaign to win converts to his exotic brand of Fascist theology. He adopted the slogan, "For Christ and the Constitution," for his crusade and trumpeted its doctrines in a surprisingly literate and well-printed little magazine, *The Galilean*. It was described on the cover as "the magazine of Aquarian Soulcraft" and as the official organ of "a national congregation of earnest men and women, each located by divine plan in his place throughout America, to aid in bringing about a fundamental remodeling of Gentile institutions—Religious, Economic, Political."

Through *The Galilean* as well as a profusion of news letters and leaflets emanating from his headquarters in Noblesville, Indiana, Pelley became a leader in the chorus of anti-democratic, pro-Nazi voices that rose in volume and shrillness as war approached and then broke out. The whole thing was a Jewish-Communist plot, he asserted, and even democracy was a Jewish invention, the antithesis of "the aristocratic principle in nature" which Hitler was reestablishing in Germany. In an article entitled, "The Coming World Axis," he foresaw the emergence of a new world order whose line of command would run from Berlin through Washington to Tokyo. In that happy day, he added, "the putrid corpse of Jewish democracy will be eliminated by cremation."

To most thinking Americans it was tempting to dismiss the Pelleys, the Bundists, and their kind as paranoids and crackpots, as inhabitants of the lunatic fringe who were more of a nuisance than a threat. But there was an undeniable pattern of evil in their demagoguery—a violent hatred for Jews, Communists, liberals, and anyone else who did not share their rigid orthodoxies; scornful denunciations of the government's political and military leadership with extravagant charges of deception and even treason; derision of democracy and praise for Fascist discipline. Much of what they said and wrote matched—even outmatched—the familiar diatribes of official Axis propaganda. They spoke through at least 100 different publications of one sort or another scattered across the country. Many were cheaply done and barely literate in style and content, but some were quite sophisticated. In the aggregate they reached several hundred thousand persons, inevitably including some in the armed forces. And several, like *The Galilean,* claimed to be the organs of an assortment of militant and militaristic "fronts" designed as assault forces that, on signal, would spring to arms to "save" America from its domestic enemies. All of which had the unmistakable tenor of the crackpot, but Hitler and his Brown Shirts had long been dismissed as crackpots, too.

The pressure on the government to take action against such apparent seditionists as these rose steadily during 1941 and became intense after Pearl Harbor. Attorney General Biddle, with his legal-libertarian convictions, was reluctant, remembering the excesses—wholesale arrest and deportations—which had been perpetrated in the name of national security by another wartime Attorney General a quarter of a century earlier, A. Mitchell Palmer. He dreaded the risk of such a move getting out of hand and becoming a witch hunt. But the pressure on him grew, from the press, from Congress, from the White House. With increasing frequency he would find on his desk a news clipping of some recent provocation and pinned to it a curt note in the President's hand: "What are you doing about this?"

The government's decision to prosecute was reached in the spring of 1942. The war was at its worst for the Allies at that time and the fear of spies and fifth columnists at its height. Assembling the case was a tedious and time-consuming operation that embraced a special squad of Justice Department lawyers and FBI agents. A first indictment was handed down by a grand jury in Washington in July of that year, a second in the following January, and a third in January 1944.

The two earlier indictments seemed too weak to withstand challenge on Constitutional grounds. The third had been tightened beyond the usual scope of the sedition statute by incorporating evidentiary links between the defendants and the Nazi Ministry of Propaganda. Included among the defendants were Pelley, Mrs. Dilling, Dennis, Noble, and Jones, who have been mentioned previously. Also included were five officials of the German-American Bund (not including Fuehrer Kuhn, who was already in jail on another charge), and a mixed bag of other oracles, prominent and obscure, from the Fascist fringe, bringing the total to 30.

Father Coughlin was not included for the reason that he was too hot to handle. His stature as a Catholic priest and a longtime political foe of the New Deal gave him a kind of immunity the government was reluctant to challenge. As a face-saving compromise, Biddle sent an emissary, a well-known Catholic government official, on a secret mission to Coughlin's superior, Archbishop Mooney of Detroit, begging him to re-impose a rule of silence on the rambunctious cleric. This the Archbishop promptly did. Coughlin suspended publication of *Social Justice* in May 1942, retired for good from the political arena, and the Department of Justice gratefully dropped him from its list of suspects. For somewhat similar but less compelling reasons, the Reverend Gerald L. K. Smith was also excluded.

After more than two years of preparation, The Great Sedition Trial (*U.S. vs McWilliams, et al.*) actually got under way on Monday, April 17, 1944. The scene was the U.S. District Court for the District of Columbia and a courtroom severely cramped by the large number of participants who had to be accommodated. There were 30 defendants with, at the outset, about 40 lawyers representing them, the prosecution staff of six, a delegation of some three dozen reporters and photographers, and such spectators as could be squeezed into the few remaining seats. Justice Edward C. Eicher, grave and dignified in his black robe, presided. The chief prosecutor was O. John Rogge, tall, moon-faced, and excitable, who had won fame a few years earlier by getting mail fraud convictions against some of Huey Long's political heirs. The defense battery boasted no chief or principal spokesman—an ominous omission, as it turned out—and most were court-appointed for clients who pled they could not afford regular attorneys' fees.

In spite of the long build-up, the event had about it a air of anti-climax. Since the first grand jury indictment a year and a half earlier, a silence had fallen upon the defendants, and, indeed, upon most of the homebred Fascists for whom they spoke. Eight of those now before the bar had meanwhile been jailed on state or federal charges involving some form of subversion: They were present "on loan" and lodged in the D.C. jail. Throughout the whole movement the brave banners were furled and the uniformed storm troopers disbanded, their strident tracts and newspapers and broadcasts long since abandoned. With American troops pounding on the offensive in both Europe and Asia, people were no longer excited about enemy propaganda and fifth columns. The seditionists might well, therefore, have been relegated to the back pages and ultimate obscurity for their grand reprise had they not contrived otherwise.

From the outset they made a bedlam of Judge Eicher's courtroom. On the first day, when her name was called to establish her presence as one of the several female defendants, Lois de Lafayette Washburne, a huge orchid pinned to her coat, rose in her seat, stretched out her arm in the Nazi salute and cried, "Lafayette we are here—to defend what you gave us, our freedom from tyranny!" She swung her handbag at a photographer in the courtroom—and then, at recess, agreeably posed for him outside while thumbing her nose at the courthouse.

As the empaneling of the jury began, the defense lawyers and their clients set up a noisy clamor of objections and challenges as each candidate was called. Often, pursuing a kind of legalistic charade, a single juror would be asked the same question by half a dozen different lawyers. One of the lawyers insisted that each defendant be allowed 10 peremptory challenges —a staggering total of 300—and consumed a full day, with assists from his colleagues, in arguing it before the bench. Another moved—and argued at length—for dismissal of the entire jury panel on the ground that, since they had been interviewed beforehand by the FBI, they were ipso facto, prejudiced. Still another demanded that the Bill of Rights be read to each juror in turn, and that he be quizzed on its meaning.

The judge endured these obviously disruptive tactics with steady patience and courtesy, ruling soberly on the most frivolous motions, most of the time negatively. But two full weeks passed before a jury was finally chosen, and the sedition trial had become antic copy in the nation's press.

It was obvious that the defense had settled upon a catch-as-catch-can strategy of disrupting and delaying the trial by whatever means came to hand—by protracted courtroom conferences among themselves, by repetitious objections and labored elucidations of obscure points of law, by deliberate harassment of the judge and the prosecution, and by laying snares for the commission of errors that might lead to a mistrial or reversal. Often the same would be disputed in detail by five or six lawyers in tandem. They argued noisily and at length that Attorney General Biddle, FBI Director Hoover, Justice Felix Frankfurter, War Mobilization Director Byrnes, Henry Ford, Charles A. Lindbergh, and a dozen other prominent personages be subpoenaed as witnesses; that the trial be postponed until after the war so that President Roosevelt and Adolf Hitler could testify. Each introduction by the prosecution of a bit of evidence or testimony was met by the cry, "Objection!", which then had to be disposed of tediously before proceedings could resume.

Rogge (whose name was often mispronounced as "rogue" by some of his tormentors) fumed in impotent frustration: In one angry gesture he managed to dislodge his spectacles, which shattered on the floor to unrestrained guffaws of those around the defense table. With visibly re-strained impatience Judge Eicher sought to impose a measure of discipline on the mischief-makers, but with minimal results. By mid-summer he had fined seven of the most troublesome lawyers and one of their clients for contempt of court, and had ordered one of the attorneys, James J. Laugh-lin, removed from the case. In retaliation, several of them turned up in court one day with large lapel buttons imprinted, ECC. To reporters they explained with malicious pleasure that the letters stood for "Eicher Con-tempt Club."

Rarely had there been such a spectacle of boisterous insubordination in a federal courtroom. But as it persisted for week after dreary week, through the summer and into the fall, the public and the press lost interest in it. Other events of greater concern were happening on the war fronts. Rogge estimated that at the pace things were going, it would be four months before the government could complete presenting its case, and defense spokesmen said they would need at least six months beyond that for their own.

"Everybody, including the four reporters still on the job, seems to be getting a bit 'stir crazy'," the *New York Times* reported late in October. "Judge Eicher seems wearier and thinner. And while the 20-odd defense attorneys try occasionally to get together on a united line of defense, they spend even more time sneering and swearing at each other because of the conflicting lines they take."

On the government's side at least, everyone realized that the case was hopelessly bogged down, and probably futile to boot. Certain Supreme Court decisions during that year's fall term had cast a strong suspicion that, even if a conviction could be obtained, it would not stand up on appeal. The whole proceeding had become a hollow mockery.

And then deliverance came, swiftly and tragically. Justice Eicher, strained beyond his endurance by the seven-month ordeal, suffered a heart attack and died on November 30. Briefly, Rogge and the Attorney General contemplated continuing the trial with another judge, but all their wisdom and counsel was against it. A week later they announced a nolle prosequei, and The Great Sedition Trial, after 102 days in court, the taking of three million words of argument and testimony, and the disposition of nearly 500 motions for error and directed verdict, was washed out as though it had never begun.

Such, undoubtedly, was the wisest conclusion of the matter. The government's case hung on the tenuous proposition of linking the de-fendants in a deliberate and conscious conspiracy with officials of Nazi Germany. It is doubtful that this could have been done to the satisfaction of the courts. Only scanty corroborative evidence has ever come from the quantities of Nazi documents seized after the war. Moreover, it was generally apparent by the time the case came to trial that homegrown fascism, such as the 30 defendants represented, had no appeal for any considerable body of Americans. In no other war had the citizens of this country been in more solid agreement on their aims and obligations and on who the common enemy was. The Bundists, the Silver Shirts, the Christian Mobilizers, and their numerous company found the market for their wares pretty well closed after December 7, 1941.

They were certainly guilty of seditious behavior, at least by nonlegal standards. They advocated disloyalty and defeatism and made slanderous attacks on the institutions of democracy and the integrity of the government. Some, including Pelley, Noble, Jones, and a half-dozen leaders of the Bund, were actually convicted under this or related statutes before the big trial came along. But any notion that they were linked in a monster conspiracy with Nazi Germany to pull down the government was absurd. The Great Sedition Trial was, as Attorney General Biddle himself characterized it later, "a farce." [2]

III

War is the ultimate extension of diplomacy, and espionage is the secret weapon of each. Beginning at least five years before our entrance into the Second World War we unwittingly harbored a variety of enemy spies in our midst—Japanese, German, Russian—to say nothing of those of friendly powers whose missions could hardly be described as hostile. Japanese spies laid out the meticulously detailed plans for the attack on Pearl Harbor. Nazi spies sought out the secrets of our military capabilities, probed for the soft spots in our morale, plotted the sabotage of vital industrial resources. Soviet spies, though not enemy agents in the technical sense—they were allies in the war against the Axis—aimed initially only at establishing a political beachhead for future exploitation, but subsequently turned to the theft of our most prized military secret, the atom bomb.

This, like the Japanese effort, was brilliantly—devastatingly—successful. The Nazis, on the other hand, were notoriously inept; we captured their agents by the dozens before they could do serious harm. But we will never know how much harm those we did *not* catch may have done. The long and bloody string of disasters to our Atlantic convoys, continuing well into 1944, undoubtedly were abetted by the work of spies secreted somewhere on shore.

Though we tended to scoff at the seditionists, the homegrown Fascists with their strident dogmas of hate, we did not scoff at spies and saboteurs. These were the real article, malevolent and unseen, and the thought of them induced, during the early war years at least, a panicky anxiety. Not only in California but elsewhere as well, jittery patriots reacted with alarm to the most trivially untoward or suspicious behavior by their neighbors or fellow workers. The Dies Committee and other congressional watchdogs sounded an endless tocsin to beware of traitors. The newspapers and magazines dramatized every shred of news that touched on the subject. John Roy Carlson's book, *Under Cover,* a tour through the underworld of subversion, went into 28 printings during its first year of publication, 1943. Again and again, President Roosevelt had to warn the citizenry not to take action on their own against suspected subversion but to report their suspicions as quickly as possible to the FBI. Between 1940 and 1943 the number of "defense matters" (of which espionage was one category) reported to the Bureau increased almost twentyfold, to more than 200,000. That this was a serious business and not just panic is evidenced by the fact that up to the end of 1945 102 enemy agents were convicted under the espionage statute or its equivalent under military law alone. Six were sentenced to death and hanged.*

When the decade of the forties opened, the United States had no organized intelligence system worthy of the name. The Army G-2, the Office of Naval Intelligence, and the State Department numbered their intelligence staffs in the dozens, their operating budgets in grudging thousands of dollars. Worse, there was no machinery for correlating their activities or their findings, a shortcoming to which Pearl Harbor stands as a flaming monument. Under-Secretary of State Dean Acheson told a congressional committee in 1945 that, up to the opening of the Second World War, his department's "technique of gathering information differed only by reason of the typewriter and the telegraph from the techniques which John Quincy Adams was using in St. Petersburg and Benjamin Franklin was using at Paris."

The same confusion that prevailed in respect to *positive* intelligence was present to a lesser degree in respect to *counterintelligence*—internal security against spies, saboteurs, and other subversive forces. As far back as 1936 President Roosevelt, stretching a point of law, set the FBI to watching and secretly reporting upon the activities of Communist, Fascist, and other radical dissidents among the civilian population. As the tensions of the oncoming war built up, the Army and Navy asserted their rights in this area, too, with consequent jealousies and confusion. How this jurisdic-

---

* There was only one prosecution for the elaborate espionage that paved the way for the attack on Pearl Harbor. Otto Kuehn, a German national who settled in Honolulu in 1939 and who was in the pay of the Japanese government as a spy, was tried by a military court and sentenced to 50 years imprisonment in December 1942. The other perpetrators, numbering an astonishing 200, all enjoyed diplomatic immunity as members of the staff of the Japanese consulate. They were briefly interned and then repatriated. Kuehn's sentence was commuted in 1948 and he was deported to Argentina.

tional quarrel was finally settled need not concern us here beyond the fact that in June 1939, almost on the eve of Hitler's initial smash into Poland, the President by executive order gave the FBI clear and unequivocal jurisdiction for counterintelligence on the home front.*

Fed by their newspapers on a heavy diet of the treachery and intrigue which the dictators had loosed in Europe, Americans were no longer so sure "it can't happen here." But with the FBI—nemesis of the gangster and the bank robber—on guard, any alien villains who attempted to breach our shores would certainly meet their match. Spies and saboteurs were now the business of the fabled G-Men, and most people breathed easier.

Such extravagant confidence was not wholly misplaced. In due course the FBI made its first big haul in a style that Ian Fleming or any other competent mystery writer might have envied. The script went approximately as follows.

One day in February 1940, a stolid, middle-aged man obviously of German origin stepped into the telephone booth of a New York hotel, gave the number of the local FBI office, and when the call was answered asked for the Special Agent in Charge by name. When that official came on the line the caller said: "This is Sebold. Where can we meet?"

Though they were strangers they were expecting one another, and a rendezvous was promptly arranged at an obscure side-street restaurant. In this and subsequent clandestine meetings between a secret operative of the Nazi intelligence network and agents of the FBI there began to unfold one of the most bizarre espionage adventures in American history.

William Sebold was a native of Germany who had served in the Kaiser's army in the First World War. For the next dozen years he floated about the world as a seaman, machinist, and engineer, settling at last in New York, where he became a naturalized American citizen in 1936. In February 1939, he made a visit home to Mulheim to see his aged mother, quite possibly for the last time, since Europe seemed to be descending into chaos. As he stepped from the boat at Hamburg he was accosted by a stranger who identified himself only as an agent of the Reich Foreign Ministry and told him cryptically, "You will wait until you hear from us in the near future."

In subsequent encounters over the next several weeks the stranger made it clear that Sebold had been marked as a candidate for Nazi

* Two years later the President set up the Office of the Coordinator of Information, with Colonel (later Major-General) William J. Donovan in charge. It had loosely defined powers for coordinating existing operations in the field of positive intelligence and of collecting information on its own. As previously noted, this soon evolved into the far more efficient Office of Strategic Services (OSS) and, after the war, into the Central Intelligence Agency (CIA). In the immediate post-Pearl Harbor reshuffle the FBI retained its exclusive jurisdiction not only for internal security but also for full-scale intelligence and counterintelligence operations throughout Latin America.

espionage work in the United States. So indelibly marked was he, indeed, that members of his family, in which a trace of Jewish blood had been detected, would otherwise be made to suffer. With great reluctance, Sebold said, he consented to the proposition since there was no acceptable alternative. He was then shipped off to a special training facility on the outskirts of Hamburg where for the next several months he was drilled in Nazi ideology and in the techniques of the spy trade, with special emphasis in the construction and operation of a shortwave radio, in microphotography, and the use of codes. He was given a new identity as Harry Sawyer, native-born American, with a complete set of identification papers including birth certificate and driving permit.

He must have impressed his tutors well for when he had finished his course and was ready to set out on his mission he was provided with detailed instructions about the sort of information he was expected to get on American defense activities, much of it reduced to slips of microfilm which he secreted in the back of his watch, and a list of other Nazi agents already established in New York with whom he was expected to make contact. He was to be their principal liaison with abwehr (counterintelligence) headquarters in Hamburg and his first assignment was to build and install a secret shortwave transmitter and receiver for the purpose. When Sebold went to the United States consulate in Cologne to get his passport, he cautiously tipped off an official there about his clandestine mission and said that he was eager to turn the tables on his Nazi tormentors if it could be arranged.

Thus it was what the FBI in New York was ready for his call when it came in early February 1940. The G-Men had already checked out Sebold's career here and abroad in great detail, and after days of quizzing and examining his credentials as a bona fide Nazi agent, they agreed to take him under their wing as a double agent. In greatest secrecy they helped him to establish residence, to open a modest office as a "consulting diesel engineer" in an office building on 42nd Street to be used as a cover, and, in the course of time, to make it easy for him to get the necessary shortwave radio equipment and install it at a hideaway near the village of Centerport, Long Island. They even supplied an expert operator from their own ranks, a Special Agent of the FBI who was clever enough to keep his true identity a secret from many of Sebold's conspiratorial colleagues for well over a year. On May 20 he turned in on the special frequency assigned to him by the abwehr in Hamburg and tapped out the message, "Arrived safe. Had pleasant trip," a code message meaning that Sebold's espionage apparatus was in working order and ready for business. That was the first of nearly 500 transmissions that would flash between those points during the next 16 months—at least half of them constituting an elaborately contrived international hoax.

It is a rule of the spy-catching business to get as many of your victims as possible into range before springing the trap. Typically, they are found not in an integrated network but in a cluster of cells, each wholly or partially insulated from, and probably ignorant of, the others. To pounce prematurely on the first inviting suspect is to send the others scattering out of reach. Accordingly, "Harry Sawyer," scrupulously observing the arcane rituals of the espionage brotherhood, made his presence known to the half-dozen fellow spies whose names he had been given in Hamburg. The circle would widen five- or tenfold in time under the constant and unsuspected gaze of the FBI.

The Number One man on Sebold's list was Frederick Joubert ("Fritz") Duquesne, whom he found in a modest one-room office marked "Air Terminals Company" at 120 Wall Street. A robust man in his early sixties with crisp hair and hard lines about the eyes and mouth, he was a 40-year veteran of the German secret service and—in the estimate of the FBI, at least—the "master spy" of the current Nazi network in New York.

Duquesne was a native of South Africa but had spent a good part of his early life in Germany and knocking about the world as a soldier of fortune. He became a naturalized American citizen in 1913 but appears to have spent the years of the First World War as a German spy in Central and South America, turning up in New York again in the early 1930s after Hitler came to power. He had a professional's competence in the black arts of his trade—deception, burglary of safes and file cabinets, the use of invisible inks and codes, secret methods of transmitting documents and photographs, explosives and incendiary devices—and had an intuitive sense of where vital information was to be obtained. He guardedly accepted "Sawyer" as a confederate, introduced him to a number of his fellow spies, and confided to him the nature of certain projects in which he was engaged. From time to time he gave the new man information which he had garnered to be radioed in code to headquarters in Hamburg.

Another early contact was with a thin-faced young Nazi zealot, Paul Fehse, whose trade and cover was that of a ship's cook but who, like Sebold and many others in the New York network, had been trained at the abwehr's spy school in Hamburg. Fehse had come to the United States in 1934, been naturalized in 1938, and established a good work record with several prominent shipping lines operating out of New York. Now, he headed what amounted to a "maritime division" of the local Nazi espionage establishment. He was associated with 10 or a dozen other German-born seamen working on American vessels whom he had recruited into the network. Familiar with the waterfront and the ways of the shipping industry, not only in New York but in other western hemisphere ports as well, they were able to amass much valuable information on the movement of war cargoes, on the arming of merchantmen, on harbor defenses, and similar data of vital concern to their masters in Germany.

Many of "Sawyer's" encounters with Fehse took place in the Yorkville section of the city in a small restaurant on East 85th Street, the Little Casino, which was owned by another member of the spy group, Richard Eichenlaub, and was one of the favorite gathering spots for many of the conspirators.

Inevitably, there was a Mata Hari, or a reasonable facsimile thereof, in Sebold's expanding network. She was Lilly Carola Stein, a comely and libidinous Viennese girl in her mid-twenties who, in spite of her half-Jewish parentage, and because of the susceptibilities of an abwehr officer who briefly fell in love with her, was trained in espionage and dispatched to the United States in 1939. Lilly had a good deal of style and charm and set as her goal a break into upper-class social circles in New York where, presumably, she could forage for information according to her fashion among the political and industrial elite. Her cover was a small, fashionable dress shop which her Nazi bosses subsidized quite generously for a time. She also counted among her assets an ongoing love affair with a socially prominent young American diplomat whom she had met in Austria.

Lilly, however, soon proved to be more winsome than wily. Her business venture failed, and so did her social and amorous adventures. Her utility to the network was reduced to that of a "mail drop" and local courier, and she became, indeed, something of a pest in her insistent demands for money. In one late message from Hamburg, Sebold was given instructions about payments being forwarded via secret courier for various members of the group. The concluding sentence in the message was, "Nothing for Lilly."

There were a score of others in the network whom Sebold came in time to know and to serve as the principal communications link with headquarters in Germany. They made their reports to him and he passed on to them instructions from abroad. Most were native Germans who had become naturalized citizens of the United States, but a few were American-born. Socially and educationally they were a mixed lot, blending unobtrusively into whatever occupational background they had adopted. Most worked in and around New York at menial trades that gave them a low profile and high mobility—seamen, carpenters, waiters, mechanics— but a few were lodged in white-collar and professional jobs that put them closer to the centers of power.

Herman Lang, for example, was an engineer who since 1929 had been employed by the firm which developed the Norden bombsight, famed in the early days of the war as the most accurate device of its sort in existence, prized as a "secret weapon." He disclosed all of its technical details—and many others—to the Nazis. Everett Minster Roeder was a designer and inventor of fire-control and other devices used by the Army and Navy on some of their newest weapons. Carl Reuper was an inspector at the Westinghouse Electric plant in Newark, New Jersey, which was loaded with equipment manufactured under a variety of defense contracts. Gustaf Wilhelm Kaercher was also a professional engineer who had been employed at one time by the Navy and later by major industrial firms. And Edmund Carl Heine, who had lived in the United States since 1920, had held important executive posts in the export branches of both the Ford and Chrysler motor companies. With these credentials he was able to secure a wealth of technical and production information in respect to the output of aircraft, tanks, and the most sophisticated new weapons, which he passed on through Sebold to Hamburg.

Virtually every contact that Sebold had with the other spies was shadowed by the FBI. They had taken the office next to his on 42nd Street and "bugged" it with every device then known for secret surveillance. Most importantly, an innocent looking mirror on his office wall was in actuality a "see-through" for a movie camera in the adjoining room. Trained on his desk, where both a calendar and a clock were in clear focus, the G-Men took thousands of feet of film as he and his callers sat and casually discussed their nefarious enterprises. Their conversations were taken down on tape simultaneously. Whatever Sebold received from them for transmission over his secret radio, the FBI scanned first. Genuinely sensitive information was screened out, but enough that was authentic—or had at least the appearance of authenticity—was passed to keep the recipients in Hamburg content and free of suspicion. In this way the ramifications of the network were fully exposed, not only as to who was involved but about the sources of their information and the means used to obtain it. This mammoth hoax continued for well over a year, one of the most elaborate examples of counterespionage ever contrived.

The trap was sprung late in June 1941. In the space of 24 hours the FBI rounded up 33 members of the conspiracy, most of them in and around New York City. Charged with violating both the espionage and the Foreign Agents Registration acts, 19 pleaded guilty on arraignment. All were jailed under $25,000 bond each. Their trial in U.S. District Court in Brooklyn began on September 3 and lasted until December 13. It was a spectacular proceeding, highlighted by the showing of many filmed sequences of the defendants openly discussing their spying exploits with Sebold. (Its dramatic impact was largely lost on the public, however. In the rush of events leading up to Pearl Harbor and the Nazi's smashing drive toward Moscow, the spy trial was relegated to the back pages of most newspapers.) All were found guilty (four of violating the registration act only, which carried a lesser penalty than the 30-year maximum for espionage) and received sentences varying from 18 months to 18 years in prison. Duquesne and Lang were the biggest losers, drawing 18 years each. Paul Fehse was one of several given 15 years, and Lilly Stein drew 10. William Sebold, the hero of the piece, dropped from view into a protective anonymity prearranged for him by a grateful FBI.

There was a sequel to the Sebold-Duquesne affair of equally dramatic proportions. Abwehr headquarters in Berlin had been almost unendurably humiliated by the blowing of their prize spy network in New York. In a determined effort to regain face, they mounted an ambitious scheme to sabotage key war industries and railroads in the United States and to loose as well a series of terror bombings. The objective was not only to slow down the production of airplanes and other weapons, giving the Nazis more time to consolidate their anticipated victories over Britain and Russia, but to impress upon the American people the awesome reach of Hitler's wrath. In this, too, they blundered.

In the predawn darkness of Saturday, June 13, 1942, the German submarine *Innsbruck* silently broke to the surface a mile off Long Island, stealthily cruised to within 50 yards of the shore just off Amagansett Point. A dense fog shrouded the coast and muffled all sound save the distant breaking of the surf. On the blacked-out deck of the U-boat sailors inflated a larger rubber raft, carefully placed two heavy wooden chests and a tightly packed seabag aboard, and set oars in the oar locks. Four men dressed in German Navy fatigues shook hands and whispered their goodbyes to the *Innsbruck*'s skipper, clambered aboard the bobbing raft, and were almost instantly lost to sight as they were rowed toward the shore.

These four were Team Number One of the abwehr's ambitious "Operation Pastorious." The leader was George John Dasch, a lean-faced, tense, and cynical man of thirty-nine with a few flecks of gray in his hair and bitterness in his heart: Life, he felt, had always cheated him. He had spent more than 15 years in the United States, working as a waiter in hotels and resorts from New York to San Francisco; had served a brief hitch as an enlisted man in the peacetime Army Air Corps; had married a Pennsylvania girl; and had completed all of the steps for becoming a naturalized citizen when, responding to his restless impulses, he returned to Germany early in 1939. He was shrewd and quick-witted, seemingly sound in his Nazi beliefs, and his extensive familiarity with American cities, customs, and speech made him a promising candidate for enlistment by the abwehr. His three colleagues were, more or less, similarly endowed. They were Peter Burger, Heinrich Heinck, and Richard Quirin. All had lived for varying periods in the United States and all, including Dasch, had proved to be apt pupils at the special school for saboteurs which they had attended in Berlin.

Their training included intensive laboratory and practical experiments in the compounding and use of explosives and incendiaries: how to construct a bomb that looked like a lump of coal or an innocent bit of trash; the most effective means of blowing a bridge, wrecking a train, crippling a factory production line, or knocking out an electrical generating system. Their principal predetermined targets in the United States were the main plants of the Aluminum Corporation of America, on which aircraft production was dependent; locks on the Ohio River below Pittsburgh; and the Chesapeake and Ohio and other main rail lines supplying coal from Pennsylvania and West Virginia to the industrial centers of the Northeast and Middle West. Thereafter, they were to follow their instinct to whatever targets of opportunity presented themselves, including random terror-bombings of railway stations, post offices, theaters, whatnot. Each man wore a money belt stuffed with several thousand dollars in legitimate United States currency, and the two team leaders had cash reserves of more than $50,000 each.

Operation Pastorious, if all went well, would be self-sustaining for two years, by which time—also if all went well—Hitler would rule triumphant over the western world. But George Dasch, frustrated most of his life, was less than certain that this would bring the rewards he coveted.

The landing party was dumped precariously on the dark beach at Amagansett by a rolling comber. They scurried out of the raft, lugging their boxes and duffle bags onto the dunes above the waterline, and said goodbye to the oarsmen, who headed back into the mist toward the submarine. Dasch looked about in the murk for a suitable burying place for the boxes, which contained their supply of tools and explosives, and the seabag in which their civilian clothes were packed and which would receive their cast-off Navy gear. As he did so he was horrified to see a few yards up the beach a swinging sphere of luminescence—unmistakably a flashlight in the hand of someone walking through the dense fog. He debated in a moment of cold panic the quickest way to dispose of the intruder, and then decided on a direct confrontation. He walked boldly into the circle of light and stood with his feet planted firmly apart. He saw that the man was wearing the service uniform of the Coast Guard.

"What's going on here?" the startled Coast Guardsman asked. "Who are you?"

"Coast Guard?" Dasch asked, as though he hoped he had guessed wrong.

"Yes, sir," the other replied, and then more firmly: "Who are you and what're you doing here?"

"We are fishermen from Southampton. We got lost and ran ashore here." Dasch felt his confidence returning as he explained their dilemma and said they planned to wait on the beach until sunrise. In the midst of these explanations Burger emerged out of the darkness dragging the heavy seabag, and asked Dasch in German what he should do with it.

"Shut up, you damn fool," Dasch shouted in English. "Everything is all right. Go back to the boys and stay with them."

Now the young Coast Guardsman was thoroughly alarmed. He demanded that Dasch go with him to the Coast Guard station a half-mile up the beach. Dasch demurred, then became abusive.

"Look," he said, "you don't know what this is all about, and you don't want to know. Get me? Take a good look at me; look me in the eyes. You've never seen me before, have you?"

"No, sir," the other answered, his voice breaking nervously.

"All right, here's some money." Dasch pulled a number of bills from his pocket and pressed them into the other's hand. "There's about $300 there. Have a good time and forget all about this."

The younger man hesitated for a moment in indecision, then turned and ran up the beach. Dasch stood where he was for a moment to let his heart stop pounding, then went to where Burger and the others were waiting tensely behind a sand dune. "I had him buffaloed," he told them reassuringly, and commanded them to get on with the work of burying their boxes and changing into street clothes. It was still an hour before sunrise when the four stumbled up off the beach, found the tracks of the Long Island Railroad, followed them to the Amagansett station and took a train into New York. They arrived in the city about breakfast time Saturday morning and then, according to their original plan, split into pairs and went to separate hotels, Dasch and Burger to the Governor Clinton, Quirin and Heinck to the Martinique.

While Pastorious Team Number One was getting itself acclimated —rather uneasily as it turned out—to life in New York, Team Number Two was making its way cautiously aboard another U-boat toward the coast of Florida. The leader of this four-man squad was Edward Kerling, a strapping, handsome young German in his early thirties who had been a card-carrying Nazi since his teens. Even during some 10 years of residence in the United States he had faithfully sent his party dues back home each month. While here he had worked principally as chauffeur and butler for a number of well-to-do families in New York and Connecticut, and had acquired and disposed of a wife and an assortment of mistresses. He made no effort to become naturalized, and when he went home to Germany early in 1940 it was for the purpose of doing whatever he could to aid the Fatherland and his Fuehrer.

His teammates were Herman Neubauer and Werner Thiel, both also in their thirties, and Herbert Haupt, a brash youngster of twenty-two. They, too, had spent much time in the United States, and Haupt, though born in Germany, was an American citizen by virtue of his father's naturalization. He had been brought up in Chicago, where his family still lived, and returned to Germany only a year before almost by accident: It happened to be the terminus of a seafaring adventure that had carried him halfway around the world via the Orient. Like other members of Operation Pastorious, the Kerling group had gone through the sabotage school near Berlin, and came equipped with supplies and money; they were to link up with Dasch's team once both had safely landed on American soil.

That second landing was uneventful. The U-boat bearing Kerling and his mates crept close to the beach just off Ponte Vedra in the dark morning hours of Wednesday, June 17. They came ashore undetected, buried their gear, and took a bus about 25 miles north to Jacksonville. A few days later they paired off and separated, Kerling and Thiel going by train to New York and Haupt and Neubauer going to Chicago. Plans for a rendezvous of all eight members of the party had been worked out but were held in abeyance for the time being.

Operation Pastorious was already in deep trouble, however.

First, back at Amagansett on that previous dark Saturday morning, Seaman 2/C. John C. Cullen, USCG, who had stumbled on Dasch and his partners, rushed back to his station to report his alarming discovery. The officer in charge organized a patrol and went immediately to the scene. The beach was deserted but there was a telltale odor of diesel fumes in the moist air, and when daylight came they discovered the cache of explosives and discarded German Navy fatigues which Dasch and his men had left behind. The implication of what had happened was clear: Cullen had come upon a landing party of Nazi agents who now had disappeared inland. By noon the Coast Guard had turned over all its evidence and information to the FBI office in New York, who mounted a hurried and fruitless manhunt in the area.

Second, George Dasch, pacing restlessly in his room at the Governor Clinton Hotel that same afternoon, reached a momentous decision. He was going to defect, expose the whole plan of Operation Pastorious to the American authorities and reap—he was certain of this—the acclaim and rewards of a hero. Cautiously that evening he felt out Burger's attitude toward the mission, remembering that his rather slow-witted, complaisant colleague had previously had a bad run-in with the Gestapo back in Germany for which he still bore a grudge. When he was satisfied that Burger would be amenable, he disclosed his plan and won Burger's promise of cooperation. The next afternoon—Sunday—he telephoned the local FBI office, identified himself as Franz Daniel Pastorious, and told the mystified agent who answered his call to notify Washington that he, Pastorious, had a message of supreme importance which he would impart only to Director J. Edgar Hoover in person, and that he would appear in Washington for that purpose later in the week.

"Another nut!" the young G-Man mumbled to himself as he hung up the phone. But the next day he learned of the startling happenings at Amagansett. Maybe the two events were connected! He excitedly added his bit of intelligence to the file and Washington was warned to be on the alert for Pastorious.

Meanwhile, Dasch was moving cautiously. He had to be certain, first, not to alarm Quirin and Heinck about what he was up to, and second, that Team Number Two had made a safe landing. Satisfied, he took the train to Washington on Thursday, registered at the Mayflower Hotel, and on Friday morning telephoned the FBI. Within minutes a pair of agents appeared at his room and escorted him to headquarters in the Justice Department building. There, over the next two days, he poured out everything he knew about Operation Pastorious. It took a week of intensive surveillance for the FBI to locate the remaining seven members of the mission and to identify the many persons with whom they had made contact. And to his increasing dismay, Dasch discovered that he was being regarded by his around-the-clock custodians less as a hero than as a probable accessory in crime.

On Friday, June 27—barely two weeks after the first of the eight Nazi saboteurs waded ashore on that dark Long Island beach—the FBI, with appropriate fanfare, announced their apprehension and arrest. Only the barest details of the case were disclosed, however, and none at all about the manner in which its secrecy had been blown: Let the abwehr have *that* to worry about, too.

The decision was quickly made that the trial should be military rather than civilian. It was a wartime offense with which the prisoners were charged, and available civilian penalties, with their legalistic loopholes, seemed not commensurate with the gravity of the crime.* The trial was held before a military commission sitting in a converted meeting room in the Department of Justice, and the proceedings were conducted in almost total secrecy—to the intense and vocal displeasure of the press. The only publicly visible aspect of the affair was the daily procession of the prisoners in two black military police vans accompanied by several jeep-loads of heavily armed MPs and a motorcycle police escort, from the D.C. jail to the Department of Justice building, where huge iron gates shut out the reporters, photographers, and curious passers-by.

The trial began with unusual dispatch on July 8 and ran to July 29, with two days out for an extraordinary appeal by the court-appointed defense to a special term of the Supreme Court, which was denied. On August 3 the verdict was announced: all eight, including George John Dasch and Peter Burger, guilty as charged and sentenced to death. Four days later, the President announced that the sentences for Dasch and Burger, who had testified for the prosecution, was commuted to 30 years imprisonment. The following day, August 8, the remaining six—Haupt,

---

* This decision was considerably more complex than is indicated here. The military commission was novel if not unique, and it was authorized under a hastily drafted executive order of the President. The Supreme Court, in ruling on the habeas corpus plea of the defendants, used highly ambiguous, doubt-laden language in rejecting the appeal. Readers who may be interested in pursuing this legalistic phantom are directed to Attorney General Francis Biddle's memoir, *In Brief Authority* (Doubleday, 1962), chapter 21, or the legal literature surrounding *U.S. vs Quirin et al.*

Heinck, Thiel, Quirin, Kerling, and Neubauer—were electrocuted at the D.C. jail.

Thus ended ingloriously Operation Pastorious. But there is a footnote to the story.

Herbert Haupt, an indiscreet young braggart, could not resist the temptation, once he was back home in Chicago, of boasting about his secret identity to his family and a few intimate friends. In consequence, his mother and father, an aunt and uncle, and a third couple, fully cognizant of what he was up to and giving him aid and shelter, were tried for treason and condemned to death. On appeal, the charges against the women were dropped and the sentences of two of the men were reduced to five years imprisonment, but Hans Haupt, the father, received a life term. Four persons in and around New York who had fraternized with some of the other saboteurs but whose involvement in their conspiracy was marginal were tried on lesser charges and given prison sentences varying from 18 months to 5 years. Finally, Dasch and Burger had their 30-year sentences commuted by President Truman in 1948. They were deported to Germany, to what fate the record saith not.[3]

IV

The record of those years up to 1945 is enlivened by at least a dozen other spy dramas in which the Nazis were the villains and the G-Men incontestably the heroes. In spite of such conspicuous and costly early failures as those of the Sebold and Dasch-Kerling rings, the masterminds of the abwehr must be credited at least with the virtue of never-say-die.

There was, for example, the American-born Kurt Frederick Ludwig who, when his Nazi superior, Captain Ulrich von der Osten, was run down by a taxi in Times Square one day in March 1941, ignored his friend's plight but grabbed the secret-packed briefcase he was carrying and ran off into the crowd, thereby putting the FBI hot on his trail. By the time he was arrested nearly six months later (at the end of a frantic dash all the way across the continent), he had led the G-Men to eight accomplices in a ring that for a year had supplied the Germans with a quantity of valuable information on the American defense program.

There was Grace Buchanan-Dineen, an attractive, well-born French-Canadian, who was recruited into the Nazi espionage service while visiting Germany early in 1941 and who later established a base of operations in Detroit with a small circle of confederates. There was Gerhard Wilhelm Kunze, long a ringleader of the German-American Bund. And there was a bogus Russian Count, Anastase Vonsiatsky, and half a dozen fellow conspirators who appear never to have gotten beyond the conspiratorial stage in their spying before the FBI nabbed them. Among them also was Velvalee Dickinson, the quaint, fusty doll-fancier whose ambiguous letters to a correspondent in Buenos Aires about the damage and repair of dolls turned out to be coded information on the refurbishing of United States warships which was passed on by an Argentinian "mail drop" to officials of the Imperial Japanese Navy.

And quite late in the game indeed—November 1944, when the Nazis on their home soil were feeling the crunch of the Allied pincers—the abwehr dispatched another sabotage team via submarine to American shores. They were William Colepaugh and Erich Gimpel, trained and equipped for their hazardous mission as George Dasch and his crew had been. And like that earlier expedition, one of the members—Colepaugh— also took fright and went voluntarily with his story to the FBI. A military commission likewise condemned them to death but their sentences were commuted to life imprisonment.

In general, the courts dealt sternly with such subversives. There was little public sentiment for leniency for spies in wartime, and not even the abrupt execution of the six Nazi saboteurs caused more than a ripple of humanitarian protest. Of the 92 found guilty of espionage in civilian trials over the whole 1940–1945 period, at least 10 drew the maximum sentence of 30 years, more than a score were imprisoned for upwards of 20 years, and most of the remainder received sentences of 5 to 10 years. By the end of 1944 the incidence of such cases had dropped almost to the vanishing point, and Director Hoover of the FBI seemed quite justified in his boast that the nation's internal security had not been seriously endangered by any foreign-directed acts of espionage or sabotage.

That was almost true, but not quite. What neither Mr. Hoover nor anyone else in public life knew at the time was that, from late 1943 onward, a handful of Russian spies had penetrated the most tightly guarded sanctum of our entire defense establishment, the Manhattan Engineer District (MED), the organizational cover for the atom bomb project. The full story of that incredible episode—one that dangerously tilted the international balance of power—belongs properly to a later narrative, since it did not come to light until 1950. But it is pertinent here to sketch in some elements of the drama that were being played out invisibly during the war years.

The protagonist in the piece was a shy, withdrawn, and probably psychopathic young German scientist with British citizenship, Klaus Emil Fuchs. Reared in a cultured socialist family, he became an ardent Communist during his years at the University of Leipzig, from which he graduated with honors in physics. His Marxist proclivities made him an enemy of the Nazis and he fled the country for his life in 1933. He went to England, continued his studies at the University of Bristol, became a naturalized British citizen in 1939, and in 1941 was one of the earliest scientist recruits for the fledgling British atomic energy program, centered at Harwell. He avoided any open connection with communism during this period, but once he was installed at the atomic laboratory he sought out an agent of the Russian secret police, the NKVD as it was then called, and offered—on wholly idealistic grounds, he insisted later—to furnish them all the information he could on this revolutionary scientific breakthrough.

By 1943 the quiet, unassuming Klaus Fuchs was regarded by his superiors at "Tube Alloy," the British equivalent of the American MED, as one of their most brilliant specialists. Late that year he was dispatched to the United States with a small team of other scientists to work cooperatively with American and Canadian counterparts on the development of the A-bomb at the supersecret Los Alamos complex in the New Mexico desert. During his brief stay in New York City after his arrival, following detailed instructions given him by his Russian "control" in London (he was to go to a certain subway stop on the East Side upon a given day and hour, carrying a white tennis ball in his hand as a recognition signal), Fuchs made contact with a furtive, uncommunicative man he was to know thereafter only as "Raymond," who was to be his sole link in this country with the Soviet intelligence apparatus.

"Raymond" was Harry Gold, a chemist with bland, nondescript features who had joined the Communist espionage underground in his home city of Philadelphia in 1936. He was one of the most trusted agents of a small network now under the control of Anatoli Yakovlev, a Soviet vice-consul in New York. Gold knew Yakovlev only as "John." Their periodic meetings were surrounded by all the secretive abracadabra that is so familiar to students of spy fiction—cautious encounters on dark, deserted street corners or in obscure neighborhood taverns; cryptic messages left behind loose bricks or conveyed by cabalistic chalk marks on a lamp post; information and instructions folded into a newspaper and casually exchanged on a subway or park bench without a flicker of personal recognition—the whole cloak-and-dagger bit.

Another of Gold's contacts was Julius Rosenberg, also an active member of the Communist underground. Rosenberg's espionage operations were in the field of electronics rather than atomic energy, and so are of only collateral concern to us here. His wife Ethel, however, had a brother, David Greenglass, a machinist who was in the Army with the rank of Technical Sergeant. When David, after an elaborate security clearance that ignored or failed to discover his Communist background, was assigned to the MED at Los Alamos in July 1944, the Rosenbergs, at Gold's insistence, prevailed upon him to join them as a spy.

Between 1944 and the end of 1946 there were a dozen clandestine meetings between Gold and Fuchs and between Gold and Greenglass, always separately—the two atomic workers were unaware of each other's existence—and always of the briefest duration possible for the transaction of their business. These meetings occurred either in Santa Fe (convenient to Los Alamos) or in New York, and invariably were surrounded with all the furtiveness requisite to their hazardous nature. At each of these encounters Fuchs delivered to Gold a bundle of papers containing intimate scientific details of the progress being made on the development of the atomic bomb. As one of the ranking scientists in the MED hierarchy, Fuchs had access to a great deal of information beyond his own compartmented activity, which had to do principally with the refining of uranium-235, the explosive "heart" of the bomb. Greenglass's less-frequent contributions had to do with the mechanical structure of the bomb. The machine shop where he worked turned out many of the unique, highly complex components of the device. He turned over to Gold a number of sketches and descriptions of these parts, including the vital triggering mechanism. All of this Gold faithfully delivered to Yaklovev and Yaklovev as faithfully delivered to the Soviet Union.

The payoff came in September 1949. The Soviets shocked a world already hag-ridden by fear of the cold war by exploding their own atomic bomb. Western scientists had confidently been predicting that the American-British monopoly on the secrets of the atom were safe for at least five years. The Soviets could only have made such a giant technological leap forward with help from inside the guarded portals of Los Alamos and Harwell. But how . . . and who . . . ?

Dr. Fuchs had gone back to England at the beginning of 1946 and Sergeant Greenglass, demobilized, had returned to his old civilian job as a machinist in Brooklyn. Each of them must have read with some uneasiness in the fall of 1945 the newspaper stories about the breaking of an important Communist spy ring in Canada brought about through the defection of a Russian embassy code clerk, Igor Gouzenko. The implications were that atomic espionage was involved. Then, a few months later, they must have been more badly shaken by the arrest in England of Dr. Allan Nunn May, like Fuchs a top-rated nuclear physicist, who had worked mainly in Canada but had had frequent contact with units of the MED. May confessed in open court that he had passed atomic secrets to the Soviet Union. But the trail of the atom spies, none seeming to point in the direction of the United States, grew cold after that.

On January 1, 1947, control of the atomic energy program in this country passed from the Army and the Manhattan Engineer District to the civilian-run Atomic Energy Commission. Simultaneously, G-2, the Army intelligence branch, turned over to the FBI its relevant files and responsibilities for security in the MED (it had exclusive and jealously guarded jurisdiction up to that time). There was no pressing need at the time for a retrospective combing through the wartime records of the agency. But when the alarm bell signalling Russia's stunning triumph sounded more than two years later, there was a burst of investigative activity to discover how and by whom the secret of the bomb had been revealed.

The deeper the G-Men probed the more apparent it became that any leak of such magnitude must have been the work of a non-American who was close to the center of things. Had there been a counterpart of Canada's Allan Nunn May at Los Alamos? The British and Canadians had been responsible for the security clearance of all their people on the project and G-2 had accepted them without question. The FBI advised British security forces of their conviction and asked their help.

At London headquarters of MI5 a scent was already warming up, and it hovered improbably but persistently about the person who was now the second in scientific command at the great Harwell atomic facility, Dr. Klaus Emil Fuchs. Among the clues that reinforced the suspicions against him was the discovery in Nazi documents captured after the war of a Gestapo dossier detailing his strong Communist attachments. Trading whisps of information back and forth, MI5 and the FBI came almost simultaneously to the conclusion that Fuchs was their man.

Fuchs made a full and detailed confession of his espionage career in January 1950, and was sentenced to 14 years in prison, the maximum penalty under British law. He could not identify his Soviet contact in the United States beyond giving a physical description of the man he knew only as "Raymond." On this slender bit of evidence, however, the FBI was able to put the finger on Harry Gold a few months later, and were led by him to David Greenglass and the two Rosenbergs. Gold and Greenglass confessed and were sentenced to 30 years each. The Rosenbergs pleaded innocent, but after a long trial and emotion-packed public controversy were sentenced to death and executed.* So was disclosed and brought to final solution the nation's greatest wartime spy mystery, nearly eight years after its inception.[4]

---

* The question of the Rosenbergs' guilt continues, almost a quarter of a century later, to be disputed in some quarters where it is characterized as a gross miscarriage of justice.

6

Arsenal of Democracy

IN JANUARY 1940, we were two years away from the biggest, costliest, most destructive war of all time. Our "ready" military force consisted of a regular Army of about 300,000 men and a regular Navy of about 200,000, exclusive of militia and reserves. The manpower to put 12 million bodies into uniform, as we would do before the shooting stopped some six years later, was abundant and then some. But the weapons for them to fight with and the equipment to support them was woefully inadequate or, in some categories, nonexistent. Thousands of draftees during this and the following year had to use broomsticks to learn the manual of arms, and many a young airman got his first taste of flying in a World War I "Jenny."

I

Ever since the twenties the Army (and to a lesser extent, the Navy) had been starved for both manpower and materiel. This was the gloomy portrait of the Army at the end of 1939 as depicted a little later by George C. Marshall, the Chief of Staff:

Within the United States we had no field army. There existed the mere framework of about 3½ square divisions approximately 50 percent complete as to personnel and scattered among a number of Army posts. There was such a shortage of motor transportation that divisional training was impracticable. . . . As an army we were ineffective. Our equipment, modern at the conclusion of the World War, was in a large measure obsolete. In fact, during the post war period continuous paring of appropriations had reduced the Army virtually to the status of that of a third rate power. . . .

Of course we won the war, we and our allies. But it was not just valor and manpower and superior strategy and God's will. As much as, and perhaps more than, all of these the reason was the prodigious outpouring of the American economy. The "arsenal of democracy" smothered the Axis under a deluge of guns, bullets, airplanes, ships, and lethal scientific wonders the magnitude of which we, ourselves, could not at first contemplate. But such incontestably was the case. We simply had more of everything—raw materials, productive capacity, technical resources—than anybody else, and we managed somehow (there's the wonder!) to focus it on the unitary objective of winning the war.

A few statistics will illustrate the immensity of that achievement. During roughly the five years from 1940 through 1944 our gross national product (the sum of all goods and services produced) went up 125 percent, from an annual rate of $88.6 billion to $198.7 billion. The share of this that went into war production—guns, planes, ships, etc., for ourselves and our partners under lend-lease—rose from 2 percent to 40 percent, and we managed at the same time to keep civilian production *quantitatively* at about the same level it had been in 1939 (fewer durables, more non-durables). All told, the United States poured $183.1 billion into munitions production between 1940 and the end of 1945. That is a sum approximately equal to the aggregate spending of all the belligerents in the First World War.

We turned out fewer than 6,000 airplanes of all kinds in 1939 at a cost of $279.4 million. In 1944 the number of aircraft plants had doubled and their combined output was 96,369 planes, practically all of them combat types, at a total cost of $167 billion. In 1939 the aluminum industry consisted of a single company with an annual output of 300 million pounds, most of it going into pots, pans, and home appliances. In 1944 there were more than a dozen producers and fabricators in the field with a total ingot output of 2.3 billion pounds, all of it going into airplanes and other munitions. Steel production increased 85 percent during those years; copper, 70 percent; coal, 55 percent; and the output of synthetic rubber, which in 1940 was little more than a laboratory curiosity in this country (but not in Germany!) went from approximately zero to 900,000 tons. (In rubber we skirted close to the dilemma defined in Ben Franklin's *Poor Richard*—"For want of a nail . . . the kingdom was lost"—for want of enough tires for our almost totally motorized army we might have lost the war. There was a period when it looked like a near thing!) From our enormously expanded shipbuilding facilities the Navy got 1,200 new combat vessels and 64,546 assorted landing craft, and the Maritime Commission received over 53 million deadweight tons of new cargo shipping.

As the free world's armorer we produced, almost from a standing start, 12 million rifles, carbines, and machine guns; 47 million tons of artillery ammunition; and 3.5 million military vehicles from jeeps to tanks. Along with this outpouring of weaponry came many striking battlefield innovations: the shaped charge and armor-piercing shell, the incredibly versatile bazooka, the recoilless rifle, the proximity fuse, and automatic fire and bombing control devices employing radar and primitive computers. And of course there was the "ultimate weapon," the atomic bomb, but that fits properly into another context.

A year before Pearl Harbor, President Roosevelt had summoned the nation to become "the arsenal of democracy." That we did. At the war's end the United States was supplying 70 percent of all the munitions being flung against the Axis on all the war fronts of the world. It was a miracle of production such as had never been wrought before. Its achievement involved nature's bounty (resources), human ingenuity (technology), and large applications of sweat and table-pounding (administration). Great sectors of the free American economy were virtually nationalized in the process, put into a straightjacket of bureaucratic regulation and control. To a greater extent than ever before—or since—the business of the country was run from Washington during the war years.[1]

II

The President's "arsenal of democracy" speech was given in the form of a fireside chat on the evening of December 29, 1940. It was one of his most important utterances, the boldest challenge yet to the resistant forces of isolationism, which was a diminishing but still potent influence in American public opinion. Essentially, the speech was a tactical prelude to the introduction some days later of the revolutionary lend-lease bill, which Congress would enact in March 1941. Lend-lease was, of course, the instrument through which the "arsenal" would reach its maximum effectiveness. In grave but confident tones, the President said that our own defenses were being pressed "with the greatest urgency" (a considerable overstatement at the time), but that the needs of Britain and the other free nations must be integrated with that effort. He went on:

The experience of the past two years has proven beyond doubt that no nation can appease the Nazis. No man can tame a tiger into a kitten by stroking it. There can be no reasoning with an incendiary bomb. . . .

Thinking in terms of today and tomorrow . . . there is far less chance of the United States getting into war if we do all that we can now to support the nations now defending themselves against attack by the Axis than if we acquiesce in their defeat, submit tamely to an Axis victory, and wait our turn to be the object of attack. . . .

We must be the great arsenal of democracy. . . . No dictator, no combination of dictators, will weaken that determination. . . .

The President's speech met with general acclaim throughout the country except among the hardcore isolationists. Its effect was to speed passage of the lend-lease bill, which went through Congress in March with majorities of almost two-to-one followed by a special appropriation of $7 billion. Concurrently, the President shook up his faltering defense production bureaucracy, but with little more than short-run effect. Congress had appropriated unstintingly to create and equip a million-man army, to double the output of warplanes and other munitions. The total for the two years up to the declaration of war in December would reach a respectable $68 billion. But procurement seemed always to fall short of expectations: Actual spending in 1941 was only a shade over $18 billion. Charges of "bungling" and "inefficiency" were aimed at the Administration in growing volume, led in many instances by a prestigious new Senate watchdog committee headed by the outspoken junior Senator from Missouri, Harry S. Truman.

We have already seen how the defense production program haltingly evolved through such early phases as the National Defense Advisory Commission (NDAC), the Office of Production Management (OPM), and the Supply Priorities and Allocation Board (SPAB), culminating a few weeks after Pearl Harbor in the War Production Board (WPB). This evolution was a difficult one beset by many obstacles. There was the political one: Roosevelt's hesitancy to arouse the wrath of the isolationists and his other political enemies by imposing rigorous mandatory controls on industry so long as he could not invoke a full wartime emergency. There was the stubborn resistance of many industrialists to giving more than token support to a defense production drive in which their participation was largely voluntary. Their civilian market was booming in 1940–1941 as it had not done since 1929; they were not eager to interfere with this bonanza by converting to the dubious and probably short-term benefits of munitions making. And, finally there were mountainous administrative problems: ineptness and inexperience in trying to make a peacetime economy act like a wartime economy; the lack of firm production goals and objectives and of the administrative muscle to make even tentative goals truly meaningful. This was intensified by the incessant warring between the armed services, who were the consumers in this process, and the civilian bureaucrats, who ran the production end. As long as the Army and the Navy each had virtually unchecked authority to place munitions orders when, where, and in such volume as they chose, piling them one upon the other in helter-skelter fashion, there was little prospect of effecting a coherent, long-range production program—one that, for example, would take account of such national priorities as requirements under lend-lease or such critical shortages as those in machine tools and magnesium. This conflict, in which the men in uniform nearly always had the upper hand through propaganda, roared on well into the war years.

From the very outset Roosevelt had been under pressure to put the defense production program under an all-powerful "czar," someone who could "knock heads together" and "get results." Late in 1941 the Truman Committee added its powerful voice to this demand: The whole production program was being vitiated, they said, by inept direction and internal squabbles within the three-headed OPM–SPAB complex. And when war became a reality, when the emphasis shifted suddenly and decisively from *defense* production to *war* production, the President himself was won over. Early in January 1942, he reached over the head of William Knudsen, titular head of OPM, and summoned Donald Nelson, OPM's chief of procurement, to the White House.

"I'm tired of the way this production thing has been muddled," Roosevelt said. "How would you like to take over the job?"

"I will if I can boss it," Nelson replied.

"You can write your own ticket," the President answered, "and I'll sign it."

During the next 24 hours Nelson and John Lord O'Brian, the OPM general counsel, closeted themselves in an act of legal-literary creation. Their opus was issued almost verbatim on January 16 as Executive Order No. 9024. It called into being a War Production Board in whose chairman was vested all of the President's emergency wartime powers over industry, production, raw materials, factories, machine tools, rationing, priorities, and any other resource or device required to produce the implements of war. The "board," composed of key cabinet members, was purely advisory; the undisputed boss in this setup, the czar, was the chairman, and the military services were expressly directed to conduct their munitions business through him. Next only to the President, the chairman of the WPB held in his hands more power than any other official in government. Nelson was designated as chairman.[2]

III

In wartime Washington, a city heavily populated by temperamental extroverts, by real and aspiring big shots, Donald Marr Nelson was something of an anomaly. Fifty-six years old, he was large-framed, a bit on the pudgy side, with thinning hair and spectacles, and with the bland, untroubled countenance, as one observer put it, "of a Middle Western Buddha." He moved through the sweaty and agitated milieu of the wartime Capital with a kind of surefooted detachment, confident but never overbearing, patient sometimes to the point of complacency, rarely raising his voice or his profile, but seemingly always on a direct course from a carefully chosen premise to a logical conclusion. He habitually addressed everyone democratically as "Sir," but having established that deferential relationship he expressed his opinions to or about them with simple, unvarnished candor. "No," he would say to an aide at the conclusion of a labored exegesis on some administrative problem, "your plan doesn't hold together. I won't buy it." Once, at a cocktail party, after enduring a half-hour monologue by one of the more fluent economic theoreticians of the day, an admiring friend of the young professor said to him: "Jimmy is quite a brilliant fellow, don't you think?"

"No, sir," Nelson replied evenly, "I think he is fuzzy."

Nelson was a card-carrying big businessman (a breed that was somewhat in disrepute in Washington even during their wartime ascendency), in private life the $70,000-a-year executive vice-president of Sears, Roebuck and Company. (His government salary when he resigned from Sears to take the chairmanship of WPB was $15,000.) But he was no ideologue of either the right or the left, a disciple of the dogmas of neither the Chamber of Commerce nor the New Deal. He was a realist rather than an idealist and looked upon his various assignments, including that at WPB, as a job to be done rather than a goal to be won. He came to be an unabashed admirer of FDR as a wartime President, and he formed a close personal and working relationship with Leon Henderson, the aggressively New Deal-ish price administrator, but in spite of such apostasy he remained to most of the business community "our man in Washington." When he talked turkey to them, as he often had to do in his low-keyed way, he not only spoke their language as a native but knew the intricacies of their ingrained thought processes.

Nelson was born in 1888 in Hannibal, Missouri. His upbringing involved few of the vicissitudes of two more famous villagers of an earlier generation, Tom Sawyer and Huck Finn. His boyhood was quite circumspect, and he went on to the University of Missouri and was graduated with a B.S. degree in chemistry in 1911. He planned to take a Ph.D. degree and become a teacher in the same subject, and in order to earn money for it, took a summer job that year in the newly established testing laboratory of Sears, Roebuck at Chicago. He never got his Ph.D. and he never left Sears. Two years later he gave up his scientific career by moving out of the laboratory into the merchandising end of the business. And there he stayed, moving up steadily in the executive hierarchy to become vice-president in charge of merchandising in 1930 and executive vice-president and chairman of the executive committee in 1939.

Nelson was no stranger to Washington. He had served in several important capacities as a dollar-a-year man with NRA between 1933 and 1935. Later he helped the government set working standards in the textile industry under the new wage-hour law. In 1940 the President again "borrowed" him from Sears to be coordinator of purchasing for the National Defense Advisory Committee, and he stayed on in the same capacity when NDAC was transformed into OPM. In the summer of 1941, feeling he had had enough of Washington and discouraged over the unrelieved turmoil into which OPM had gotten itself, he tried to quit and go back to Chicago. Roosevelt blithely talked him out of it and a few months later, when the decision was reached to create WPB as a "superagency" for war production, Nelson was the first choice to head it.

It was a good choice in respect both to temperament and experience. Nelson had demonstrated his capacity to navigate coolly the roily political seas of Washington, to get things done with a minimum of friction and backlash. And his new job was not greatly different in essentials from what he had been doing for years at Sears, Roebuck. There each year he had to find out from all the department heads how much of each of the 100,000 items in the great mail order catalogue and the chain stores were going to be needed, and then see to it that the goods were bought at the best price available and were on hand when the orders came in. Sears had to buy annually around $750 million worth of merchandise, which often involved complex scheduling of production and, in some cases, plant conversion. This required an intimate knowledge of the industrial resources of the country, and it is quite possible that no one knew more about them than Nelson.

Testifying before the Truman Committee shortly after his appointment as WPB chairman in January 1942, Nelson said he had all the authority he needed, and that if the production job wasn't done, it would be nobody's fault but his own.

"And are you ready to be the goat?" one of the Senators said.

"Yes, sir," Nelson replied, "I'm ready to be the goat because I think the country expects it of me. I recognize this, too, sir—I have everything to lose and nothing to gain doing this job."

Some of his associates came to feel in time that Nelson was lacking in toughness and aggressiveness. His insistence in listening to all sides of a controversy, and then seeking a compromise solution based on the lowest common denominator of dissent, frequently resulted, they said, in delays and half-measures. Thus, he never fully exercised the authority he had to make the military services conform to the overall priorities of the production program.

For his part, Nelson did not have it in him to be a dictator; it was not his style and he would have been at a loss if he had assayed such a role. Moreover, he had learned from his previous experience that in government there can seldom be a straight line to an objective: The way is beset by too many countervailing interests and prerogatives. Whatever his shortcomings as an executive, however, the fact remains that his way of doing things won him, in the end, far more plaudits than blame. Even the hypercritical Truman Committee was often to be observed eating from his hand.[3]

IV

There was, indeed, quite a similarity between Nelson's old job at Sears, Roebuck and his new job at WPB, except that the latter was vastly greater in magnitude and it was considerably less manageable. On the one hand, he had to compile a "shopping list" of what was needed to win the war and to keep the civilian economy afloat. On the other hand, he had to compile an inventory of the nation's raw materials and industrial resources and figure out how to plug the gaps where the shortages were—or where they were likely to occur. Then the shopping list had to be fitted to the inventory in such a way that the "customers" would get what they needed when they needed it.

This was the toughest part of the job, for most of the customers had urgent, triple-plated priorities for their individual needs: The fate of the nation could be shown to depend on instant delivery. For example, the Navy wanted pursuit planes, the Army wanted bombers. There wasn't enough aluminum (at first) to fill both orders. Who was to get how many of which? The infantry wanted rifles and machine guns in infinite quantity at the same time that the artillery wanted howitzers and antiaircraft guns. Again, who was to get how many of which? Or, how much steel capacity could be taken away from building warships and tanks and diverted to rails and locomotives to meet a critical transportation shortage—or even to build a few urgently needed new steel mills? And how deeply could we afford to dig into our dwindling stockpiles of manganese, copper, and crude rubber to meet the critical needs of the British? Such examples can do no more than suggest the enormous complexities involved in the slogan "all-out production for war."

It would be tedious and pointless to attempt to analyze in detail WPB's table of organization and its infinite procedural constraints. It quickly became the biggest of the wartime Washington bureaucracies, a multilayered conglomerate headquartered in the new Social Security building on Independence Avenue and spilling over into a cluster of dreary "tempos" defacing the adjacent mall (the last of these eyesores was not removed until the summer of 1970). Its Washington work force rose to a peak of around 20,000 by the end of 1942, and a total of another 4,000 to 5,000 were in the field offices in every important city in the country. Its daily paper consumption—orders, directives, reports, bulletins, memos—was said to equal the pressrun of a fair-sized metropolitan newspaper. Many a businessman complained that any profits accruing to him out of war contracts was eaten up by the voracious demands of the paper work that went along with it.

The key to WPB's administrative mechanism was a large group of Industry Branches, each representing a major component of the total industrial complex—automobiles, steel, aluminum, copper, chemicals, construction, mining, transportation, fuels, and so on in bewildering variety. Each was staffed by experts and technicians within the field, including many topflight company executives on loan to the government at a dollar a year. They were responsible for knowing everything there was to be known about their respective industries: the potentials and

Wendell Willkie arrives in Philadelphia for the GOP Convention, June 1940, surrounded by supporters and with his Headquarters "under his hat." (UPI)

Oren Root, Jr. (left), Chairman of the Associated Willkie Clubs of America, and Wendell Willkie participating in a campaign broadcast. (UPI)

German, Japanese, and Italian officials toast the next Axis pact in Tokyo, October 1940. Right to left: German agent Heinrich Stahmer; German Ambassador Eugen Ott; Italian Ambassador Indelli; Foreign Minister Matsuoka; Minister Without Portfolio Naoki Hoshino; General Hideki Tojo; behind microphone, Toshio Shihatori. (UPI)

Franklin D. Roosevelt inspects construction in the yards of the New York Shipbuilding Corporation during his campaign for reelection. (UPI)

Roosevelt and British Prime Minister Winston Churchill meet at sea aboard the U.S.S. Augusta *off Newfoundland, August 1941. (UPI)*

Japanese Ambassador Nomura, left, and Special Envoy Kurusu arriving at the State Department to see Secretary of State Cordell Hull on December 1, 1941, shortly before the attack on Pearl Harbor. (UPI)

President Roosevelt signs the declaration of war against Germany, December 11, 1941. The declaration of war against Italy was signed one minute later. Senator Tom Connally times the occasion. (UPI)

December 7, 1941, Pearl Harbor. A dense black cloud of smoke marks the burning battleship U.S.S. Arizona. *Black spots in the sky indicate exploding U.S. anti-aircraft guns. (UPI)*

President Roosevelt speaking before the start of lottery drawing for wartime selective service. (UPI)

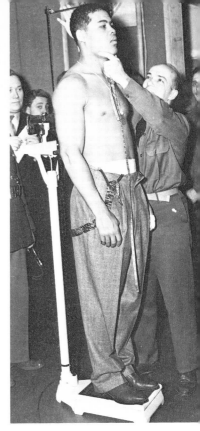

Joe Louis being measured during his physical examination at Governor's Island, January 1942, before final induction into the army. (UPI)

Japanese Americans in Los Angeles preparing to be shipped to one of the government internment camps inland, April 1942. (UPI)

Japanese relocation center at Minidoka, Idaho. (UPI)

Roosevelt's war cabinet, December 1941. Clockwise around the table: Harry Hopkins in the foreground (light suit), Lend-Lease Administrator; Frances Perkins, Secretary of Labor; Philip B. Fleming, Federal Works Administrator; Vice President Henry A. Wallace; Fiorello LaGuardia, Civil Defense Administrator; Paul M. McNutt, Federal Security Administrator; Jesse Jones, Secretary of Commerce and Federal Loan Administrator; Harold L. Ickes, Secretary of the Interior; Postmaster General Frank C. Walker; Henry L. Stimson, Secretary of War; Cordell Hull, Secretary of State; Roosevelt; Henry Morgenthau, Secretary of the Treasury; Attorney General Francis Biddle; Frank Knox, Secretary of the Navy; and Claude R. Wickard, Secretary of Agriculture. (UPI)

Churchill meeting with Roosevelt in Washington, D.C., May 1943. (UPI)

(ABOVE) *Under the American flag and the German Swastika, the German American League of Los Angeles celebrates German Day in a pre-war meeting. (UPI) (LEFT) William Dudley Pelley testifying before the Dies Committee, February 1940, about the activities of his pro-German organization, the Silver Shirt Legion. (Wide World Photos) (BELOW) Fourth from left, J. Edgar Hoover, Director of the F.B.I., attending the 1943 trial of the eight Nazi saboteurs who had sneaked into the United States by submarine the year before. At left foreground is Attorney General Francis Biddle. (Wide World Photos)*

New York Mayor Fiorello LaGuardia speaking at a defend America rally at Madison Square Garden, December 1941. The rally was sponsored by the CIO to stress labor's willingness to cooperate in the victory program. (UPI)

The Curtiss-Wright plant in Buffalo, New York, during wartime production of Commando military transport planes, the largest twin-engined airliners of the time. The plant received the Army-Navy "E" award for efficient production. (UPI)

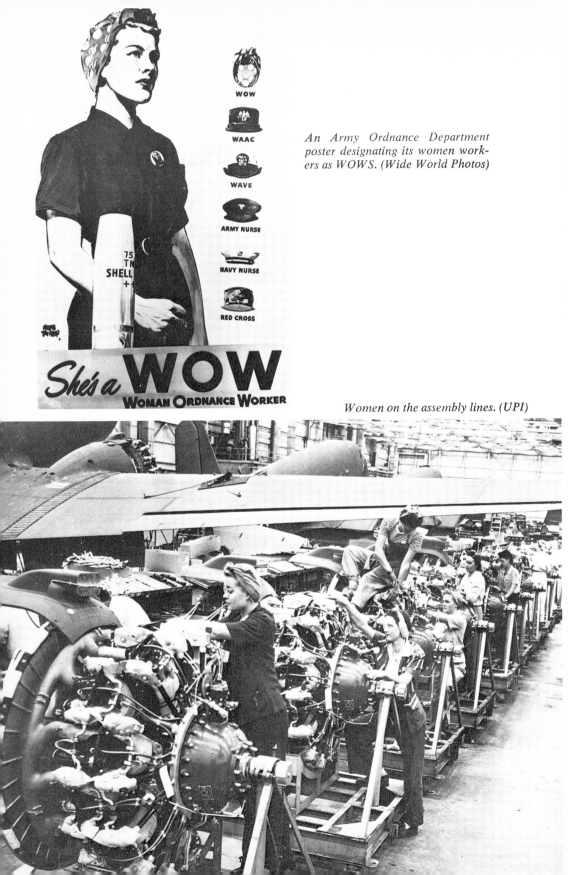

An Army Ordnance Department poster designating its women workers as WOWS. (Wide World Photos)

Women on the assembly lines. (UPI)

First meeting of the War Production Board, January 20, 1942. Left to right, seated: Leon Henderson of the O.P.A., James V. Forrestal, Jesse Jones of the Federal Loan Administration, Secretary of the Navy Frank Knox, Chairman Donald M. Nelson, Vice President Henry A. Wallace, Under Secretary of War Robert P. Patterson, William S. Knudsen of the O.P.M. Standing: Executive Secretary to the Board Herbert Emmerich and General Counsel of the Board John Lord O'Brian. (Wide World Photo)

Testifying before the Senate Defense Investigating Committee in March 1942, Leon Henderson of the Office of Price Administration uses charts to show the effects of consumption on the nation's supply of rubber. (Wide World Photo)

Secretary of the Interior Harold Ickes (left) and Mayor LaGuardia with a horse-drawn carriage when Ickes arrived in New York in May 1942 to make a speech. The carriage emphasized the need for gas rationing. (UPI)

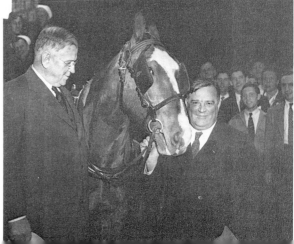

A shopper checking the point value table against her ration coupon booklet. (UPI)

The prairie prepares for war. In Dundee, Illinois, a poster and "vegetable man" bring home the message, while a housewife signs a pledge to avoid food waste. (Wide World Photo)

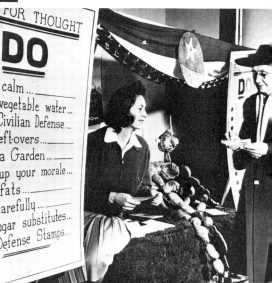

Shoppers in New York City lining up to buy not-so-perishable smoked meats, March 1943. (UPI)

Roosevelt and Churchill meet in Casablanca with Gen. Henri Giraud and Gen. Charles de Gaulle, French leaders in North Africa, during ten-day meeting of Allied chiefs to discuss war strategy, January 1943. (UPI)

Generalissimo Chiang Kai-shek, Roosevelt, and Churchill at the Cairo Conference, December 1943. (UPI)

Bob Hope and his troupe entertain wounded men, evacuated from Saipan, during their tour through New Caledonia in 1944. (UPI)

Actor James Stewart, who was a colonel in the Army Air Force, was one of many Hollywood figures involved in the war. (UPI)

Edward R. Murrow and William L. Shirer. (UPI)

Members of the British, Russian, and American delegations to the international security talks pose in the garden at Dumbarton Oaks, August 1944. (UPI)

Gen. Dwight D. Eisenhower in June 1944, talking to paratroopers about to fly across the English Channel. (UPI)

Omaha Beach, Normandy, during the Allied invasion June 6, 1944—"the longest day." (UPI)

Roosevelt delivers his fourth inaugural speech, January 1945, from the south portico of the White House. On his left his son, Col. James Roosevelt. (UPI)

Marshal Josef Stalin, Roosevelt, and Churchill dining at Livadia Palace during the Crimea Conference. Secretary of State Edward R. Stettinius raises his glass; Foreign Commissar Molotov is at right. (UPI)

Roosevelt arriving at Yalta in February 1945. This photo, showing the President's deteriorated state of health remained classified for six years. (UPI)

capacity of every plant, their current schedules, commitments, inventories. This data was fed steadily up the line to WPB divisions having to do overall with materials, supplies, allocations, production, and procurement. Through other channels the needs of the Army-Navy Maritime Commission, lend-lease claimants, and the civilian economy were funneled in, the needs of one weighed against the needs of others and also against the availability of supplies and of production capacity. Once the individual orders were approved—for so many airplane engines of a certain design, say, or the materials to build a new explosives plant—they were accorded a priority rating that might or might not put them ahead of other orders already in the pipeline, and the chosen producer or producers were given a comparable priority for drawing on the available supplies of steel and other necessary commodities.

The foregoing is, of course, a vast oversimplification of WPB's modus operandi: The system was under almost constant stress and criticism and was subject to frequent breakdowns, patchups, and overhauls. It does serve to illustrate, however, the sweeping power that WPB exerted over the nation's economy. It decided who could and could not have access to the output of steel and copper and rubber and gasoline and a score of other critical commodities. It prohibited the manufacture of automobiles, refrigerators, metal caskets, electric fans, household hardware, metal coathangers, and some 300 other items deemed not essential to the war effort. It could force a manufacturer to convert his plant to war production or to expand into a new plant built at government expense. And it could force a recalcitrant businessman to accept war orders under pain of punishment. In practice these coercive measures were rarely invoked since they violated Nelson's reliance on persuasion and cooperation.

The WPB did relinquish control—to its endless sorrow, it turned out—in the actual placing of the orders and in the follow-up that saw the goods come off the end of the production line. Nelson deliberately delegated this function, at least in respect to military goods, to the military services themselves. His reasoning was that the required precision in specifications and inspection of most such items was beyond the capacity of nontechnical civilians. He was motivated also by the fact that the Army and Navy adamantly insisted upon this prerogative—and a good deal more besides.

The military, and the top Army brass in particular, never resigned itself to the fact that a misguided political fate had put control of war production in the untried and incompetent hands of civilians; that the man in uniform could be challenged at any level or upon any grounds as to how much and what kinds of munitions were needed to win a war. Such concepts as that war production depended upon a viable civilian economy, or that a continuing balance had to be maintained in the variety and quantity of munitions output, or that shortages of materials and resources had to be anticipated and adjusted to—such ideas, it seemed, either were foreign to the military mind or were trivia to be dissolved in rhetoric and procrastination.

During the first six months of 1942 Congress had appropriated a stupendous $100 billion for armaments and war shipping, more than half of it earmarked for the Army and its Air Corps. Unlike peacetime appropriations, which were narrowly itemized, these were lump sum bequests, blank checks to the individual services. (Another $60 billion was added before the year ended.) Within the same six months, the whole $100 billion had been committed in signed contracts; war orders were being ground out as from a sausage mill in a volume that was bigger than the total output of the whole American economy in any previous year. The contracting agency, operating virtually independently of the WPB, was the Army-Navy Munitions Board (ANMB), which also exercised a free hand in the assignment of priorities to its orders. As the war contracts continued to pile up in a chaotic and indigestible mass on the door step of the munitions makers, the whole priorities system quickly went to pot. From an original set of ratings designated simply as A, B, and C, the ANMB grew impatient of A ratings and went on to AA, AAA, and even beyond. Thus an ordinary priority for, let's say, spare parts for Britain's Royal Air Force or new mining machinery to increase coal production in Pennsylvania came to have little more value than a hunting license in the scramble for scarce materials and factory space. In consequence, by mid-1942 the entire war production program was thrown dangerously out of balance and Nelson and his men were shuddering under a rising tide of criticism.

In late summer Nelson won from the President authority for another reorganization in WPB and a redefinition of its authority to make the military toe the civilian line. The grant had some ambiguities built into it, as Roosevelt was wont to allow when confronted by a conflict among the hierarchs of his administration (the Secretaries of the War and Navy Departments as well as the prestigious Joint Chiefs of Staff were solidly aligned against Nelson on this score). At all events, in seeking to bring the ANMB into the WPB corral, Nelson gained the transfer of ANMB's civilian chairman, Ferdinand Eberstadt, to the top level of his own staff as deputy chairman in charge of material allocations. Eberstadt was a brilliant, crisply decisive Wall-Streeter who had made a fortune in the stock market during the Depression, when most investors were being wrung dry. He was also a close friend of two other prominent Wall-Streeters in the Administration, Robert Patterson and James Forrestal, who were Under Secretaries respectively of the Army and the Navy and deeply involved in the struggle for supremacy over the WPB.

Eberstadt did not change his loyalties when he changed jobs. For a time, the renovated WPB, with very effective assistance from the new deputy chairman, seemed to be surmounting its difficulties. The internal stresses lessened, the friction with the military lost some of its stridency, and the production curve moved a little more decisively upward. But the man in uniform, and Eberstadt with them, were far from satisfied. They calculated that the gains being registered were achieved at their sacrifice, that with the big offensive push of the war lying just ahead they needed now more than ever their own undisputed hand on the industrial throttle. That could only be done by dislodging Nelson. To achieve that goal they concocted a plot that could have been set just as appropriately in the steaming barrios of a banana republic as in the urbane steel and concrete surgeries of Washington.

Almost from the inception of WPB the Army had been sniping at it, either through subtle derogation before congressional committees or in the leakage of critical comments to the press. From time to time stories appeared in the papers attributed to anonymous "Army sources" noting that production of one or another item of munitions was dangerously short, that military strategy was being impeded, even that lives were being needlessly lost, because WPB had failed to come up with the necessary weapons and supplies. The tempo of such "leaks" increased markedly in the late months of 1942. During December, as American forces were hammering their way across North Africa, a particularly alarming story blossomed on this grapevine: Anonymous but "high" Army sources revealed that bombing operations were having to be curtailed because of a shortage of high-octane aviation gasoline. Nelson responded that this simply was not true and produced figures to sustain his point, but the denial, as usual, never quite caught up with the allegation. Roosevelt, highly susceptible to this sort of propaganda, peppered Nelson and his other defense ministers with memos attached to clippings of such stories, asking tersely, "What about this?"

Meanwhile, the President's confidence in Nelson was being eroded in a more direct fashion by the Secretaries of War and Navy and by his old political ally, James F. Byrnes, whom he had recently called from the Supreme Court to head a new superagency, the Office of Economic Stabilization. While the overall production curve was rising satisfactorily under Nelson's guidance, they contended in private talks with the President that there still were too many gaps in the munitions pipeline, too much waste of resources going into the production of civilian goods, and too much bickering and confusion in WPB to secure maximum results. What they urged upon the President was that he "promote" Nelson up and out of WPB, that he call the aging Bernard Baruch back into service as titular chairman, and that Eberstadt be made first deputy chairman and the operating head of the agency. In time, the President was persuaded; he checked the matter out with Baruch and set a date for a "confrontation" in his office with Nelson and his accusers.

There was a new rash of newspaper speculation at about this time that Nelson was on the way out, but Nelson himself could get no con· firmation of the rumors. He was put off a couple of times when he tried to make an appointment to see the President in person. And then one night in mid-February it all came clear as he was awakened at his apartment by a telephone call from one of his subordinates. This trusted aide had dug out the details of the whole conspiracy. Nelson was to be summoned to a meeting at the White House at two o'clock on the following afternoon and told that he was being replaced by the Baruch-Eberstadt combine, that Baruch was little more than a figurehead in the switch, and that the real power would go to Eberstadt, who was the chief architect of the coup. Thus Nelson faced not only being personally demeaned by his arch-rival but also the wreckage of his entire campaign to keep the production program out of the clutches of the military.

Behind his conciliatory facade Nelson had a streak of toughness that could be tapped when the occasion warranted. He was not going to take this affront lying down. He was at his desk early that morning, and a little detective work convinced him that the story he had gotten the night before was true. In fact, his secretary had innocently placed on his desk the summons to his own execution—a telephone memo that he was expected at the White House at two o'clock that afternoon, the reason unstated. He tried first to make an earlier appointment to see the President in private. No luck; the President was "tied up all day." But he did get a call through to a friendly and knowledgeable White House aide, to whom he explained his dilemma.

"Look, Don," the friend told him, "in a situation like this the Boss likes to see a man take things in his own hands. Eberstadt is at the bottom of this, and you ought to know it. You do something about Eberstadt and the odds are that the President will invite you over for a nice, cozy chat— just the two of you."

The advice suited Nelson's mood exactly. He got Eberstadt on the telephone and said bluntly that he wanted his resignation immediately— orally; the exchange of formaliites, if any, could come later. He then called in his public relations man, dictated a press release stating tersely that he had that morning requested and received Mr. Eberstadt's resignation, and directed that the story be released at once. It was "bulletined" on the wire service news tickers before noon (reaching a startled FDR within minutes) and was splashed in black headlines in afternoon newspapers all across the country. For days this bit of mayhem in the higher bureaucracy made choice copy for a host of columnists and editorial writers, generally depicting Nelson as a hero.

The two o'clock meeting in the President's office was scratched. Instead, Nelson was invited over for a private chat late that same afternoon. He recalled later that he found Roosevelt in an amiable, if not exuberant mood, willing to listen and to ask questions about WPB's problems. He said he agreed fully with Nelson's thesis that war production should be in civilian hands. But, the President added:

I wish the job could be accomplished without these head-on collisions. I believe there are ways of maneuvering so that [they] can be avoided. It is my experience with businessmen in government that they always get into these battles, not alone with one another but with the heads of other government agencies. They don't know how to administer these things as well as the politicians do. . . .

But I am satisfied with the way the job is going and I should like to see it continue. But see if you can't keep the head-on collisions down some.

The full details of this most celebrated coup on the Washington war front were many days in reaching the public. The newspapers reported the affair initially as the outcome of a personal power struggle between Eberstadt and another WPB deputy of equal rank, Charles E. Wilson,* with Nelson in the role of umpire tipping the scales in Wilson's favor. This was true, but it was only a subplot in the larger design: It was Nelson's neck, not Wilson's, which was on the chopping block that day, and Eberstadt who unexpectedly got decapitated.

As the victor, Nelson won a few new medals, including a guarded but significant commendation from the Truman Committee, which, after hearing the disputants on both sides, reported to the Senate: "The competition of the Army, Navy and Maritime Commission for scarce materials, facilities, and manpower, with little or no restraint, created a chaotic condition and cost us much production. . . . The Committee regards the centering of authority with attendant responsibility as a long step toward elimination of one of the worst organizational faults of the war setup."

From this point onward, the WPB ran a somewhat more stable course. It was never free of controversy, conflict, and the clash of opinions and personalities, but its administrative and procedural structure had become essentially fixed, and production for both military and basic civilian needs soared to unexpected heights. By the middle of 1944, when the Allies had swung aggressively onto the offensive in both Europe and the Pacific, it was possible actually to cut back on some munitions items and to begin to think seriously about the problems of postwar reconversion.

---

* An official of General Electric, he is not to be confused with another Charles E. Wilson, of General Motors, who came to public prominence a decade later as Secretary of Defense in the first Eisenhower administration. Newsmen often distinguish between them by calling one "Electric Charley" and the other "Engine Charley."

Donald Nelson remained at the helm until July of that year, when Roosevelt asked him to go to China to help Ambassador Patrick J. Hurley put Chiang Kai-shek's economic house in order (an urgent but, as it proved, hopeless task). Nelson laid down his WPB chairmanship with full honors, in spite of some current gossip that he had been "kicked upstairs," and was succeeded by the man whom he had proposed for the post, Julius Krug, one of his long-time deputies.* [4]

V

While WPB occupied the big tent during the superspectacular called "all-out production for war," there were a number of supporting attractions along the midway that won a great deal of attention on their own. An outstanding one had to do with rubber, which for many months qualified as Subsidiary Crisis Number One.

Suddenly we discovered that rubber was just as important as guns and airplanes in waging a war, and that we were about to run out of it. It was not only a military crisis but one that hit the noncombatant civilian in a particularly sensitive spot: the use of his private automobile, delivery truck, farm tractor. The first gasoline rationing in the spring of 1942 was invoked less to conserve gasoline than to conserve tires. You were solemnly warned that when those wore out you were not going to get any more. But a "miracle of production" was indubitably wrought. In the space of two years we built from the ground up a totally new, billion-dollar, synthetic rubber industry that quickly outran the most extravagant expectations for it. By mid-1944 we and our allies were getting all the military rubber we needed and there was even some left over for the family auto.

In the past, automobile tires and other rubber products for general use had been made almost entirely from natural rubber, about 90 percent of which was imported from Malaysia and elsewhere in the Far East. In normal prewar years we consumed something less than 500,000 tons of this crude latex annually. As early as 1939 Congress took rather casual note of the fact that, for safety's sake, we should build a stockpile of some hard-to-get strategic materials, including crude rubber. Nothing very much was done about it, however, and at the end of 1941 our total rubber stockpile in both government and private hands amounted to about 540,000 tons, equivalent to less than a year's needs in the face of a rapidly accelerating consumption rate.

Meanwhile, some (but not much) thought was being given to the

* Nelson completed his China mission in May 1945. He settled in Los Angeles with his third wife, who had been his secretary in the WPB, and became president of the Society of Independent Motion Picture Producers. He died in Los Angeles at age seventy on September 29, 1959.

question of synthetics as a substitute for crude, just in case something happened to interfere with our normal sources of supply in Asia. We were aware that Germany and, to a lesser extent, Russia, had developed synthetic industries that supplied most of their enormously expanded needs. However, we had done little more than experiment in this field. DuPont and several of the major tire makers had produced an interesting variety of test-tube rubbers for specialized industrial uses and had even tried them out in auto tires. But the results in the latter case did not seem promising. Not only were there technical "bugs" in the formulas, but the production cost was so high in comparison to tires made with natural rubber as to make the process a poor business risk. Even so, officials of the NDAC and their successors in OPM began to worry about the matter and to press for action. In the summer of 1940 a Rubber Reserve Corporation was set up as a subsidiary of the Reconstruction Finance Corporation (RFC), both to handle the stockpiling problem and to do something about synthetics. Jesse Jones, the RFC chairman, appraising the scene with the coldly calculating eye of the successful banker (which he was in private life), was reluctantly persuaded a year later to risk government loans of $5 million to get four pilot projects going. Another year would be required to build the plants, whose combined output was estimated at 40,000 tons of synthetic annually.

That was the approximate shape of the rubber situation when the blow fell at Pearl Harbor. Immediately there was a frenzied effort to build up the stockpile of crude, and we did manage to bring in over 200,000 tons before the fall of Singapore sealed off the Asian sources for good in April 1942. Simultaneously, Rubber Reserve and the WPB looked about frantically for ways to vastly and speedily increase the output of synthetic. As the military and civilian experts put their heads together the need suddenly became astronomic. Our new army was a motorized army and it required millions of medium- and heavy-duty tires to roll on. There was a half-ton of rubber in every Flying Fortress that came off the production line, more than a ton in each medium and heavy tank, and some 50 tons in each destroyer or large cargo ship. And the needs of our British allies, if less in volume than our own, were no less urgent. Discounting supplies for the civilian sector entirely, our military needs for the 18 months between July 1942, and the end of 1943 were projected as 842,000 tons. This was some 200,000 tons more than we could lay our hands on unless the deficit could be made up from synthetic, which at the time—mid-1942—seemed a highly dubious prospect.

The prospect was dubious for several reasons.

Rubber Reserve had upped its goals for synthetic manufacturing capacity immediately after Pearl Harbor from a modest 40,000 tons annually to a projected level of 700,000 tons by 1944. But coming even close to such a target seemed a fantasy. In March 1942, only one new production unit, a Goodrich plant, was in full operation, with a capacity of 2,500 tons a year. In the rest of the field there was near chaos in disputes over processes, formulas, patent rights, manufacturing techniques, and even over the availability of steel and other materials with which to build the new plants. Industrialists and technicians fought among themselves and with officials of the government and Congress as to whether neoprene was superior to buna-s and Ameripol, and over the relative merits of grain alcohol, petroleum, molasses, city garbage, or the juice of the wild guayule plant as a basic raw material. It was a subject about which nobody knew much but about which a great many insisted they had all the answers, proclaiming them loudly and insistently. Rarely have basement inventors and crackpot theorists had such a field day.

An added complication arose in the form of international cartels. By most reckonings, a chemical substance called butadiene was the most practical first stage in creating synthetic rubber out of petroleum, natural gas, coal, grain alcohol, whatnot: a mysterious business of juggling hydrocarbon molecules. The only key to the secret in the United States was held by Standard Oil Company, but it was not a free agent in the matter. A dozen years earlier, Standard had entered into a binding cartel arrangement with the great German international chemical and manufacturing trust, I. G. Farben, involving a whole catalogue of industrial patents and processes, including butadiene and its end product, buna-s rubber. In substance, Standard and I. G. Farben agreed between themselves who was to have exclusive rights to which and divided the world markets accordingly: Farben, for example, would stay out of the petroleum field in the Western Hemisphere, and Standard would stay out of it in Germany and certain parts of Europe.

A quite minor (at the time) clause in this agreement left the buna-s process exclusively in Farben's hands. Beginning in the mid-thirties as the Nazi juggernaut began to roll, Farben developed a highly efficient synthetic rubber industry in Germany, making the resurgent Wehrmacht virtually independent of the far-off sources of natural rubber. In response to growing interest here in synthetics, Standard asked Farben late in 1939 for permission to develop the process in the United States, but the request was declined, in Farben's words, "for reasons of military expediency."

And there the matter stood for the next three years. As American officials groped their way through the unfamiliar thickets of the synthetic rubber jungle they were denied access to the most successful trail yet blazed. Standard claimed that its hands were tied by the code of international legal and business ethics. The bonds were not loosened until March 1942—four months into the war with Germany—when they were attacked by the trust-busting U.S. Assistant Attorney General, Thurmond

Arnold.* Under a consent decree obtained in the federal courts, Standard relinquished its buna-s patents to all comers. Thereafter, these became virtually the standard for synthetic rubber production in the United States.

Another complication in the muddle over synthetic rubber had its roots in domestic politics. It had been determined that butadiene could be extracted just as easily from grain alcohol as from crude petroleum—with this exception: The product derived from alcohol cost about 25¢ a pound as against half that cost for the petroleum-based product. This, however, was of small concern to the powerful farm bloc in Congress. They envisioned millions of bushels of corn being converted into alcohol and thence into rubber tires to the immense enrichment of the American farmer. Nelson and the rubber experts at WPB were willing to go part of the way with this plan, but not all the way; technical as well as cost factors were involved. But this did not satisfy the farm bloc, nor did it satisfy the big oil lobby. For weeks during the spring and summer of 1942 the debate raged in and out of the newspapers and especially on Capitol Hill, where one committee after the other insisted on holding public hearings on the question and asserting its own expertise. Somehow, even the House Committee on Coinage got into the act. At the peak of the din, farm leaders in both houses managed to push through a bill establishing and funding a wholly new synthetic rubber program to operate independently of WPB and committed to the exclusive use of grain alcohol. The President tartly vetoed it.

At this point things had reached such an impasse that President Roosevelt called in his reliable old troubleshooter, Bernard Baruch, and asked him to find a way of unsnarling the rubber tangle. A month later, in September 1942, the Baruch Committee laid its voluminous report on the President's desk. It used the bluntest kind of language to sound a warning and to lay out a crash program of action, thus:

We find the existing situation to be so dangerous that unless corrective measures are taken immediately this country will face both a military and civilian collapse. The naked facts [as to the visible supplies during the succeeding year-and-a-half] present a warning that dare not be ignored. . . .

We are faced with certainties as to demand; with grave insecurity as to supply. Therefore this committee conceives its first duty to be the maintenance of a rubber reserve that will keep our armed forces fighting and our essential civilian wheels turning. This can best be done by "bulling through" the present gigantic synthetic program and by safeguarding jealously every ounce of rubber in the country. . . .

The committee laid out its plan for "bulling through" in greater

---

* Around a dozen similar cases were brought during the war years to break up international cartels over such items as magnesium, nitrates, a variety of explosives, and pharmaceuticals. The subject is treated at length in Joseph Borkin's, *Germany's Master Plan* (Duell, Sloane and Pearce, 1943).

detail. In essence, its recommendations cut through all the conflicting arguments and rationalizations and called for concentration of effort on two or three leading processes, including buna-s from both grain and petroleum, and the immediate construction of 50 new refining and fabrication plants at an estimated cost of $750 million. Control of the program was to be withdrawn from the half-dozen agencies currently involved and centered in WPB under a "czar" responsible only to the chairman. (The rubber "czar" whom Nelson promptly named was William Jeffers, president of the Union Pacific Railroad.) Finally, the committee recommended direct rationing of tires as well as of gasoline, and a continuing drive to collect scrap.

The Baruch report, which the President approved in toto, cleared not only the air but also the way for some fast administrative action. Whatever was needed in dollars, steel, manpower, and materials to get new plants completed and additional ones underway was forthcoming. Before winter set in there were more than a score of sites across the country where massive steel columns and weirdly contorted tangles of pipe and other paraphernalia of an entirely new industry rose suddenly out of the landscape. In the final quarter of that year 8,000 tons of synthetic rubber were produced; in the final quarter of 1943 the total was 121,500 tons, and in the final quarter of the next year, 210,500 tons. Total output 1943–1944, approximately one million tons. An authentic "miracle of production" had licked the rubber problem.

It is worth recording that this wartime innovation has had a profound and lasting effect on the rubber industry as a whole. Alone or in compounds with natural rubber, synthetics have made possible an enormous proliferation in the variety and characteristics of rubber products used every day in the home and in industry. In 1969, according to the Rubber Manufacturers Association, 77 percent of all the rubber used—over two million long tons—was synthetic, produced substantially in accordance with the wartime formulas.[5]

VI

Scarcely less miraculous than the story of rubber was the prodigious outpouring of aircraft during the war years. It was a feat measured in superlatives, not only in the statistics of output and performance capability but in the application of technical and managerial talent of the sort we sometimes boastfully describe as "American business know-how." If that factor had to be evoked at times under governmental pressure, it nevertheless materialized with sufficient vigor to get the job done. It was, in fact, an indispensable ingredient. A cluster of about a dozen principal producers, highly competitive and using what amounted to handcraft methods to turn out about $280 million worth of planes in 1939, was transformed in less than five years into an integrated mass-production colossus with over two million employees and a total output for the year valued at nearly $17 billion. Business know-how and cooperation were indisputably a part of the formula.

In May 1940, when the President first said we needed 50,000 planes for our defense, many people, including those in the military and in industry, thought he was talking through his hat. He may well have been doing just that. In all the years since the Wright brothers first launched their motorized box-kite at Kitty Hawk, this country had produced not more than 75,000 airplanes of every kind and description. As an industrial entity, aviation was only about a dozen years old: The first scheduled commercial airlines, for example, did not begin to take hold until 1929. But from the mid-thirties on the industry began a spectacular rise. Air travel increased markedly year by year, the Army and the Navy initiated a modest buildup in their air arms, and in 1938 Britain and France, beginning to feel the hot breath of the Fascist dragon on their necks, started placing substantial orders with American plane manufacturers. Output doubled between 1935 and 1937 from 1,586 planes of all types to 3,200, and it had almost doubled again by 1939, when the total reached 5,856. Significantly, about one-third of that year's production was for military planes, most of them on foreign order. The total inventory of our Army and Navy air arms at the beginning of 1940, when President Roosevelt called for a buildup to 50,000 planes, was just under 5,000 planes of all types, many of them obsolete. No wonder people thought he was talking through his hat.

However visionary the President's goal may have been, his call set wheels in motion. The newly activated NDAC got together with the military and the leaders of the aircraft industry to explore the possibilities. After much wrangling and head-scratching they projected a program to April 1942, a span of less than two years, stretching those possibilities to the maximum—30,000 planes for the Army and Navy, 11,000 for Britain and France, and 2,000 for domestic and all other uses—a total of 43,000 that, in spite of its magnitude, fell short of the President's goal. Congress had appropriated $1.7 billion for U.S. military aircraft that year, and by mid-summer the Army and Navy had dumped nearly $900 million in new orders on the industry in one indigestible lump. But the gap between orders and deliveries was a long and torturous one. Total output of military planes for the year 1940 was just short of 3,000, of which a third were earmarked for Great Britain, leading Chief of Staff George C. Marshall to lodge a bitter complaint with Chairman Knudsen of the NDAC. Output for the following year, 1941, was destined for about an eightfold increase, but it was clear that even the shortened 43,000-plane goal set for April 1942, would be missed.

Obstacles to the achievement of that goal were many. The extensive plant expansion program, for which the RFC had put up close to $500 million (with more to come), was time-consuming and further hindered by growing shortages in steel and other structural materials. Skilled labor in quantities sufficient to meet a vastly increased work load was hard to get. The military services, never quite sure what kinds of planes they wanted the most of when, were constantly altering their orders and specifications. Critical shortages developed in machine tools, certain alloy metals, and particularly in aluminum. The total capacity of the one-company aluminum industry in 1940 was 400 million pounds annually, while the projected demand for aircraft construction alone through 1941 was in excess of one billion pounds. Finally, there was the complexity of the aircraft industry itself with which to contend. Essentially, in all but a few of the biggest companies, it was a piecework and assembly operation that depended upon a maze of independent suppliers for everything from engines and propellers and metal castings to electrical circuitry and hose clamps. Problems that affected any one of these myriad suppliers out on the periphery were likely to send traumas through the central nervous system of the industry as a whole.

In the early stages of the program no one apparently had given much thought to involving the automobile industry in any substantial way in aircraft production. But as the Low Countries and France were submerged in the Nazi tide and England began to reel under the murderous air raids of the luftwaffe, the determination to break some bottlenecks in the aircraft industry took on a new urgency. And where better to look for new potentials than to the auto makers? As Donald Nelson was to point out later, "It is quite possible that when the war started there were not more than three countries outside the United States whose entire war-making potent'al was greater than that of the American automobile industry." Detroit and its industrial satellites had an abundance of skills and experience adaptable to making airplanes and much of its plant and machinery was adaptable, too. The industry had already branched out tentatively into tanks, machine guns, and some other munitions items. It seemed natural for it to branch out into aircraft.

One to whom it seemed both natural and feasible was Walter Reuther, the dynamic young president of the United Auto Workers union. Late in December 1940, he came to Washington with a plan by which, he claimed, Detroit could begin within six months to turn out 500 warplanes a day without seriously curtailing the production of passenger cars. In great detail and with impressive technical documentation he showed that the automobile industry, busy as it was, was currently using only 50 percent of its productive capacity, that its production lines were easily convertible to making airplane engines as well as automobile engines, that its body plants could stamp out airplane wings and fuselages as well as auto fenders and sedan tops, that skilled labor for these operations was plentiful and willing—and much more in like vein. In fact, he argued, the transformation could go beyond aircraft production to a host of other munitions at any time that the nation—and the auto industry—was willing to forego the luxury of new passenger cars. To make this transformation possible he proposed that the entire industry, shelving its several corporate rivalries for the duration of the emergency, be brought under a specially created automotive production authority equally representative of government, management, and labor, with government sitting at the head of the table.

Reuther's plan got a full hearing and created intense interest—and controversy. It was the boldest and most imaginative proposal yet for truly mobilizing a major segment of industry. Liberals in the administration and much of the press greeted it enthusiastically. But not so the spokesmen for industry and their dollar-a-year adjutants in the defense establishment. They called it "radical," "vague," "unworkable," and "putting labor in the driver's seat," which was, as they saw it, its most fearsome aspect. And in the Olympian view of President Charles E. Wilson of General Motors, any such scheme "to divide the responsibility for management would be to destroy the very foundations upon which America's unparalleled record of industrial accomplishment is built."

Predictably, perhaps, the Reuther plan lost out. But it stimulated a fresh flurry of activity within NDAC and OPM to draw the auto makers more closely into the defense production effort. On several occasions in 1941 Chairman Knudsen took his onetime colleagues from Detroit on "shopping expeditions" through the vast munitions market, asking them to look over the displays, particularly the aircraft items, and see which ones they could and were willing to make. (This appealed to some cynics at the time as proving the theory that "wars are won by patriotism plus eight percent.") There were many takers on a selective basis and the pressure in a good many smaller bottlenecks in the aircraft factories in particular soon eased off. But the industry's gaze remained riveted on its booming civilian market. It was willing to go into big scale defense production whenever the government would build a new plant and buy new machines for the purpose, but it wanted no interruption to the exhilarating cash-register ring of its regular production lines. Each of the big three as well as scores of major suppliers had taken on some munitions business as a sideline by mid-1941—Chrysler was manufacturing tanks, Ford was erecting its mammouth Willow Run plant to build bombers, Packard was turning out Rolls-Royce engines for the RAF—but at the same time Chevrolets and Dodges and Mercuries and Cadillacs were rolling off the production lines in a volume not matched since the halcyon days of 1929.

It should be recalled that it was at this point—August 1941—that OPA Administrator Leon Henderson reached in exasperation over the head of his boss, Chairman Knudsen of the OPM, to impose a 25 percent cutback on the auto makers by limiting their allocations of steel. It was a gesture of defiance against the "business as usual" attitude of so many businessmen at that time, but largely an ineffectual one. A poll by *Fortune* magazine had recently shown that some 75 percent of business management was convinced the Roosevelt administration was using the emergency wherever it could as a pretext "for pushing still further the more radical social and economic aims of the New Deal." It was in this light that the outraged auto magnates interpreted Henderson's cutback order, and they managed to have most of its teeth pulled.

Coincident to all this, meanwhile, aircraft output continued to lag behind successively enlarged production targets. The total for all of 1941 was 23,240 planes, and up to December 7 of that year not a single new plant authorized to be built since June 1940, had come into production.

The impact of Pearl Harbor jolted loose a good many stuck gears, including those that were impeding aircraft production. On January 6, in his first war message to Congress, President Roosevelt laid out a new urgent priority for warplanes—60,000 for 1942 and 125,000 for 1943, with new emphasis on heavy bombers. At almost the same time, OPM and Knudsen were replaced by WPB and Nelson, a combination, as we have seen, with considerable more clout. WPB's first official edict was a "stop" order on the production of all passenger cars and light trucks after February 1. The auto industry now had no choice but to join hands with the aircraft industry—under legal duress if necessary—and it chose to join hands. Moreover, it quickly lost its distaste for the union. Representatives of the two camps began to mingle and visit one another's factories, to swap ideas and engineering lore, to come together on a common objective, which was to produce the maximum number of warplanes in the shortest possible time.

The auto makers had more to contribute than machines and factory floor space. They introduced the assembly line, showing that huge airframes could be put on a conveyor belt and bolted and riveted together by new mechanized processes that saved both time and the skilled labor. They brought to the aircraft makers a wholly new understanding of standardization and interchangeability of parts, and hundreds of techniques and manufacturing shortcuts that had been standard practice in the auto plants for years but were unknown in the handcraft-oriented aircraft industry. These were the secrets of mass production which had made the American automobile industry one of the marvels of modern technology, and its influence soon began to show up in a steadily rising production curve of bombers, fighters, and pursuit planes. The auto makers pooled and shared this knowledge not only with one another but with the primary aircraft manufacturers as well. They formed an Automotive Council for War

Production which included a dozen specialized trade and technical organizations in engineering, metallurgy, parts and equipment manufacturing, and tool and die design as a clearing house for information and a first aid station for a manufacturer in distress. A producer suddenly caught short for want of a process or a supply of components could usually get quick relief by picking up his telephone and calling the association's headquarters. Corporate rivalries and secrecy were largely forgotten in the process.

By the summer of 1942 all of the auto makers were heavily involved in the aircraft business. Only one was turning out a complete plane, from airframe to engine to flyaway, in its own plant: Ford concentrated on the B-24 "Liberator" heavy bomber under license from Consolidated, and also made engines under license from Pratt and Whitney. The others made engines and/or airframes and various components, and most of the larger units such as General Motors, Chrysler, and Hudson also maintained huge assembly operations. Thus, the Allison Division of GM became one of the largest producers of airplane engines during the war. Pratt and Whitney engines were turned out not only by Ford but by Buick and Nash-Kelvinator, and Wright engines by Dodge and Studebaker. Also coming off the auto makers' production lines were final assemblies of Boeing B-17s, Martin B-26s, North American B-25s, Republic P-37s, Douglas C-54s, and many other types whose names became familiar in the sky battles over Europe and Asia. By the war's end, the automobile industry had become a very big partner indeed of the aircraft industry, accounting for about half of all the engines and almost a third of all the airframe weight produced from mid-1940 to mid-1945.

The aircraft makers for their part, after an initial hesitancy (they suspected the Detroit octopus of offering them an embrace of death), accepted the intrusion upon their preserve pragmatically. They numbered about a dozen major companies. Their own resources had been stretched close to the limit, which clearly was not enough, and there were more orders to be filled and profits to be made than they alone could cope with. They adopted as rapidly as they could the techniques of mass production and the other innovations the auto makers offered them, and they expanded inland (they were heavily concentrated along the West Coast) to places like Tulsa and Omaha and Kansas City and Marietta, Georgia, to be nearer their new sources of supply and more abundant labor markets. And, like the auto industry, they also discovered the uses of cooperation. They organized the Aircraft War Production Council (AWPC), pooled their knowledge and experience, and began to act toward one another more like friendly neighbors than jealous squatters.

In fact, lending and borrowing "over the back fence" became one of the most conspicuous minor features of the wartime aircraft industry. The practice was frequent, informal, and often non-contractual, thus obviating many delays and bottlenecks. One typical example: North American had a group of B-25s all ready for delivery save for the installation of a fuel tank valve that was temporarily tied up by a labor dispute at the supplier's plant. A check through the AWPC showed that Douglas had a small surplus of the valves. A telephone call from North American to Douglas got the valves on their way that day and a new flight of B-25s off the ground a couple of days later. Similarly, when Douglas unexpectedly ran out of cotter pins it borrowed a thousand from Vultee, when Vultee ran out of a very special lock nut it got them from Lockheed, when Lockheed was caught short on a particular kind of aluminum sheet, a phone call brought relief from North American, and so on in infinite variations. Moreover, there was little exclusivity any more as to designs and trade names. Boeing's B-17 "Flying Fortress" was also made by Douglas and Lockheed, and its B-29 "Superfortress" by Bell and Martin; Consolidated's "Liberator" was also made by Douglas and North American in addition to Ford; the Grumman "Wildcat" and "Avenger" were also made by General Motors; the Vought "Corsair" was also made by Brewster and the Goodyear Tire and Rubber Company; and so on many times over.

It would be fatuous to assume that all the kinks and headaches of the aircraft program were washed away in this new spirit of harmony and go-ahead. As previously noted, clashes and controversies between the civilian bureaucracy, the military, and industry continued to erupt and to get in the way of progress. Nevertheless, the aircraft program "turned the corner" in quite decisive fashion in 1942, and by June of the following year was producing at the munificent rate of 7,000 planes a month—so munificent, in fact, the officials charged with taking the long view of things began to worry about *overproduction*. The total for 1943 was 85,898 military planes of all types, and for the peak year of 1944 the total was 96,318, a better-than-thirty-fold leap from the first year of the defense buildup, 1940. Moreover, we were making progressively better planes—bigger, faster, farther-ranging, more deadly in accuracy and fire power. The B-17, for example, the first successful four-engine bomber and the workhorse of the Air Force, underwent many modifications that increased its speed from 230 to 300 miles per hour and its combat range from 1,000 to 1,500 miles. It evolved before the end of the war into the B-29, which was nearly twice as big and had one-third greater speed and range. Fighters and fighter-bombers such as the P-38 "Lightning," P-47 "Thunderbolt," and P-51 "Mustang" were steadily upgraded until, in the closing months of the war, they were beginning to push the sound barrier at speeds close to 500 miles per hour and pressing toward the stratosphere at altitudes around 40,000 feet—dimensions which were quite incomprehensible to awestruck earthlings.

By the end of 1943 it was clear that the "miracle of production" had wrought its wonders in the aircraft industry. So much so, indeed, that the propagandists in the OWI were authorized for the first time to publicize actual production figures for the scare effect those awesome totals would have on the enemy.[6]

VII

The impact of science on warfare was never more emphatic than in the Second World War. We mobilized the talents and energies of thousands of our scientists to produce not only an impressive array of weapons and related gadgetry but, in one cosmic coup, to propel mankind into the nuclear age. Both the bazooka and the A-bomb came out of the "arsenal of democracy."

Splitting the atom was not an American discovery nor was the theory concerning the enormous release of energy to be achieved thereby. The Germans were ahead of us on this. But the technique of putting these together in controllable fashion to produce either megatons of destruction or megawatts of usable power was essentially an American achievement. Moreover, it was a wartime achievement aimed primarily at producing the most lethal bomb possible. The moral and philosophic questions about it did not arise until later.

What even the most literate citizen (outside a tiny elite of physicists) knew about atomic energy prior to August 5, 1945, could probably be compressed into a rather spongy paragraph. Over the preceding decade there had been occasional stories in the newspapers and magazines predicting, usually in the breathless rhetoric of the Sunday supplements, that a vast new world "in the heart of the atom" was about to be opened up for human exploitation. In an age of recurring wonders such far out intelligence as this did not cut very deeply into the public consciousness. Neither was there much concern outside the academic community that a group of refugee scientists such as Albert Einstein, Leo Szilard, Enrico Fermi, and others were busily exploring the secrets of the atom in their laboratories at Columbia, Princeton, and the University of Chicago.

For the same reason, probably, President Roosevelt was less than electrified to receive a letter from Professor Einstein in October 1939, stating that the conquest of the atom was imminent and urging that the government take the initiative in bringing this about. "This new phenomenon," the great mathematician wrote, "would also lead to the construction of bombs, and it is conceivable—though much less certain— that extremely powerful bombs of a new type may thus be constructed." He suggested that if the United States did not take the lead in this matter the Nazis almost certainly would. The President turned the Einstein letter over to an aide, casually suggesting that "We ought to do something about this," and apparently forgot about it for the next two years.

Something was done about it, though it was the barest minimum. A

Uranium Committee was formed with representatives from the Bureau of Standards, and the Army and Navy, and a grant of $6,000 was given Professor Fermi to advance his experiments in inducing a chain reaction in the breakdown of the uranium atom. A year later, with the creation of the National Defense Research Committee (and later the Office of Scientific Research and Development) under Dr. Vannevar Bush, things began to look up: The Uranium Committee was absorbed and the work on atomic fission was accorded the highest priority and a respectable budget. So much progress was being made by 1941, in fact, that the project was put on a classified—secret—status to prevent leakage of information about it to potential enemies, meaning Germany.

The atomic age can be said to have been born—not with a bang but with an insistent mechanical purring—on the afternoon of December 2, 1942, a year almost to the day after Pearl Harbor. The place was a squash court in Stagg Stadium at the University of Chicago, and the circumstance was the ultimate success of Fermi's long pursuit of a chain reaction. As he deftly manipulated the cadmium rods in his awkward-looking graphite pile, instruments told him that the transmutation of uranium atoms into a new form of matter (plutonium), plus a dividend of free energy, was taking place at a sustained, controlled rate. This historic moment has been described from eyewitness accounts as follows:

> The crucial experiment that made the atom bomb possible and marks the official beginning of the atomic age was performed on December 2, 1942. . . . On that day scientists learned after many months of anxious labors in great secrecy that just one atom of uranium split will release the energy to split two other atoms, the two atoms splitting four, and so on in a geometrical progression. That meant that an atomic explosion would take place in a self-perpetuating reaction, in the manner of a chain of firecrackers.
>
> On that historic day they completed the first atomic furnace (also known as a "pile" or a nuclear reactor), fashioned of bricks of uranium and graphite, in which they ignited the first atomic fire on earth. . . . In effect that first fire was also the first atomic explosion except that it was on a small scale and could be kept under control. Or so they had hoped. . . .
>
> The great moment came when Fermi ordered his assistant, George Weil, to pull out the last control rod "another foot." All the other controls had been pulled out previously.
>
> "This is going to do it," Fermi told Dr. [Arthur H.] Compton, who was standing beside him on the balcony overlooking the furnace.
>
> Four tense minutes passed. The neutron counters began to click louder and louder, faster and faster. Fermi, who was doing fast calculations on a slide rule as his eyes darted from one dial to another, suddenly closed the rule with a click. He looked calm and detached, a captain bringing his ship into port.
>
> "The reaction is self-sustaining," Fermi said amid the violent clicking of the neutron counters. His face, tense and tired, broke into a broad smile.

For twenty-eight minutes the atomic fire was allowed to burn. Then Fermi gave the signal and it was stopped abruptly. Man had released the energy of the atom's nucleus and had also proven that he could control it at will. . . .*

There were less than a dozen witnesses to this historic accouchement, each so bound by security that he could not convey his excitement and amazement even to his own wife. When the deed had been done someone in the laboratory broke out a bottle of Chianti and they solemnly drank a toast from paper cups welcoming the advent of a new age of man.

The saga of the A-bomb is by now a familiar chapter of folklore and does not require retelling here except in highlight. With Fermi's dramatic breakthrough, a bomb of unprecedented destructive force became a high but distant probability: "How distant was a crucial consideration if it was to be effective in shortening the war. In consequence, the project was awarded unmatchable priority for everything that was required in terms of manpower, money, and materials to win the race with time. In March 1943, it was given exclusive and exalted status under the euphemistic designation, Manhattan Engineer District, and the Army was brought in to share technical and administrative control along with the Office of Scientific Research and Development. The two men in ultimate authority thus were Dr. Bush and Major General Leslie R. Groves of the Army Corps of Engineers.

Never had so vast and complicated an enterprise proceeded at such a breakneck pace and in such impenetrable secrecy. It is probable that fewer than 200 people knew all of what the MED was up to, and a Vice-President of the United States, for example, was not one of them. (Harry Truman was President for more than a week in April 1945, before he learned about the A-bomb.) Within two years, tens of thousands of people were at work on some aspect of the project, and three new small cities—Oak Ridge, Tennessee; Hanford, Washington; and Los Alamos, New Mexico—almost literally had burst out of the ground and had spawned mysterious acres of industrial plants. Hallmark of these communities were the 10-foot chain link fence, the military guards at portals and in roving jeeps, and the ubiquitous red and white signs: "Restricted." Work in these areas was so tightly compartmentalized that employees in one unit knew practically nothing about what went on in the unit next door, and nothing

* William L. Laurence, *Men and Atoms* (Simon and Schuster, 1959), pp. 68-70. Laurence, chief science writer for the *New York Times,* was picked by officials of the Manhattan Engineer District in the spring of 1945 as the lone member of the press to be initiated into the mysteries of the atomic project and to witness the first demonstrations of the A-bomb, at Alamagordo and Hiroshima. His were the first public announcements of this historic development, released to the press immediately after the blast at Hiroshima on August 5, 1945. *Men and Atoms* is one of several books he subsequently wrote on the subject.

whatever about the end use of their collective labors. Censorship forbade any discussion of nuclear physics in the newspapers and magazines except in the most abstract terms, and discouraged open speculation about what was going on in such places as Oak Ridge and Hanford. The inquisitive visitor had to be satisfied with such flippancies as, "We're making front ends of horses and sending them up to Washington for final assembly," and for all the hard facts he could get to the contrary, this just might be the case.

The crucial test came in July 1945. Out of the $2 billion worth of striving had come a single ugly black bomb weighing about 1,000 pounds. It was hoisted to the top of a 100-foot metal tower in a desolate and isolated section of the New Mexico desert, 35 miles away from the nearest human habitation. Scattered around "Point Zero" over a radius of 20 miles was a series of recording instruments and heavily barricaded command and observation posts. In the pre-dawn hours of Monday, July 16, amid tension that became literally unbearable for some of the few-score watchers on hand, a switch was thrown that would tell whether or not all this Herculean effort had been in vain, whether the bomb would be a success or a dud.

It was, of course, a success, if a major cataclysm can be so defined, and three weeks later, on August 5, a duplicate of the test bomb obliterated most of the Japanese city of Hiroshima and killed about 100,000 of its people. Nine days and one more bomb later Emperor Hirohito surrendered unconditionally and the Second World War was over.

In retrospect the A-bomb inevitably overshadows the wartime scientific scene. There was, of course, an immense range and volume of scientific activity wholly unrelated to the bomb. While most of it involved weaponry and refinements in the art of killing, some of it was benign and added to man's enjoyment of life—or at least his ability to cope with life.

Vannevar Bush, onetime president of the Massachusetts Institute of Technology, was director of the Carnegie Institution when President Roosevelt asked him to help organize and run the National Defense Research Committee in June 1940. The agency and the superseding Office of Scientific Research and Development, which Bush also headed, was able over the next few years to command the services of some 30,000 scientists and engineers, including the most illustrious names in those professions, and approximately half a billon dollars in government appropriation. It was money without strings; Bush and his associates could dig where they chose, to get answers to questions asked of them by the Army and Navy or questions the military had never thought to ask. The research load was distributed in thousands of separate contracts to university and industrial laboratories, including many in Canada and England. There was, in fact, a brisk international traffic in scientific ideas and techniques, for in many areas the British experience was superior to our own.

For the first time in history, Bush recorded a few years after the war, "the decision was made to recognize scientists as more than mere consultants to fighting men. . . . In the National Defense Research Committee and the Office of Scientific Research and Development, scientists became full and responsible partners for the first time in the conduct of war."

The fruits of this partnership were impressive. The scientists not only improved upon most of the existing weapons and other implements of war, they brought some new ones into being. Radar as a defensive weapon probably saved London and other English cities from annihilation by German bombs; as an offensive weapon aboard Allied bombers it brought Berlin and a score of other German cities close to destruction. Similiar devices for the detection of submarines wiped out Germany's underseas mastery in the Atlantic by 1944. The proximity fuse increased the accuracy of Allied artillery fire tenfold when first used in the Battle of the Bulge, and a kindred homing device in aerial bombs helped to sweep the Japanese fleet from the South Pacific.

Many such wartime innovations have survived usefully into the days of peace. Radar safely guides your airliner through storm and darkness in and out of the airport. DDT, which made the American GI the most louse-free soldier in the world, later helped to rid the land of flies, mosquitoes, and the boll weevil—to say nothing of song birds and some species of freshwater fish. Intensive work in the war years on the just-discovered sulfonamides helped to create a whole spectrum of antibiotics that have since become almost as common as aspirin. And the crude, bulky, electronic mechanisms that brought such devastating accuracy to antiaircraft fire after 1942 are revered today as the progenitors of the ever more marvelous computer. Contemporary technology owes much to the urgency of wartime research a generation ago.[7]

VIII

The "arsenal of democracy" was not a closed corporation accessible only to blue chip shareholders. While a few score Big Fellows unquestionably got the lion's share of defense orders—as of December 1942, the 100 largest corporations held 71 percent of the war contracts—several thousand smaller companies, those with a few dozen to a few hundred employees, were ultimately let in on the feast. Small southern textile plants by the hundreds got contracts for uniforms, parachutes, tarpaulins, blankets. Run-of-the-mill metalworks and machine shops found that they could turn out small parts for airplanes, tanks, guns, what not. A manufacturer of textile machinery switched profitably to making carriages for antitank guns. A maker of burial vaults converted to bomb casings, and a bed spring manu-facturer turned to making links for machine gun belts. The variants of such cases were infinite, although special legislation (the Smaller War Plants Act of 1942) and endless exertions by the WPB were necessary to win and to preserve a reasonably fair shake for the Little Fellows. In the end, some 40 percent of the total industrial output of the nation and well over 50 percent of its factory workers were involved in war production. Inevit-ably, the impact of this great concentration of effort was felt to some extent along every Main Street in America. The coveted "E" banner (the Army-Navy award for "excellence") was as likely to be seen flying from the staff of a one-chimney factory in a lonely prairie town as amid the steel forests of Pittsburgh and Detroit.

For most businessmen war production was a highly profitable enter-prise. In spite of an excess profits tax (enacted in 1942) with a maximum bite of 90 percent, corporate profits soared—from $5 billion in 1939 to $10.8 billion in 1944, dropping back to a still impressive $8.5 billion in 1945. The downturn from 1944 to 1945 was due in large measure to an aggressive campaign by the government to recover some of the over-charges and excessive gains which had slipped through during the frenetic early months of the production program. Through 1946 some 72,000 war contracts were "renegotiated" to recover approximately $7 billion in excess profits.

Some overambitious entrepreneurs were caught in actual fraud in efforts to swell their profit margins, cheating in their bookkeeping, cutting corners on quality and production standards, and otherwise. Most of such culprits were small-time operators whose larcenous inclinations probably would have prevailed in peace as well as war, but a few big fish were caught in the legal nets, among them Anaconda Wire and Copper, Bohn Aluminum and Brass, and Sullivan Dry Dock and Shipbuilding. A member of Congress, Representative James M. Curley of Massachusetts (Boston's flamboyant onetime Mayor) was imprisoned for mail fraud in connection with a scheme for peddling war contracts. The Department of Justice set up a special unit late in 1942 to track down and punish such cheats. At war's end convictions for war frauds had been obtained against 65 corpo-rations and 756 individuals, with prison terms and fines totaling over a million dollars assessed.

The American working man was as indispensable to victory as his son or brother in uniform, but he did his bit at considerably less in personal sacrifice and public acclaim. The great war boom banished the blight of unemployment, made first-time wage earners of several million women, and in spite of a wage freeze (that thawed regularly around the edges), produced a steadily rising level of take-home pay for just about everybody who was able and willing to work. Average weekly earnings in manufacturing, for example, almost doubled between 1939 and 1944, rising from $23.64 to $45.70 with some extra fringe benefits thrown in. The cost of living, meanwhile, rose by less than 15 percent, and since such luxuries as a new house or a new car were not to be had, there was an immense pool of savings left over—a record-setting $49.9 billion of it in 1944. The home-based warrior was beset by myriad inconveniences but not much danger.

If he was a member of a labor union, however, he was not safe from attack. In the Congress, in the councils of businessmen, in much of the press and middle-class public opinion, he was often pictured as a selfish, greedy fellow of dubious patriotism, more concerned about his own welfare and that of his union than of the nation. This was a grievous distortion, of course, but the working man, or more particularly his union leaders, were in part responsible. The union movement itself was in a state of upheaval due to rivalries among its major constituents—AFL vs CIO vs UMW vs the railway brotherhoods, etc.—and each was on a course of dynamic expansionism to prove its own muscle. In spite of the no-strike-no-lockout pledge to which the unions had subscribed with management immediately following Pearl Harbor, strikes did occur throughout the war years with at least the threat if not always the substance of a body blow to war production. There were 2,968 work stoppages in 1942 costing 4.1 million man-days; 3,752 in 1943 with 13.5 million man-days lost; and 4,950 in 1944 totaling 8.7 million man-days.

What gave these events a particularly ominous cast was the arrogance of some of the union leaders, in particular John L. Lewis, the pugnacious miners' chief. Embittered by what he conceived to be his political rejection by FDR after the 1936 election, Lewis seemed determined to match his own power against that of the Commander-in-Chief. On three occasions during 1943 and 1944 he struck the coal industry, vital to virtually every aspect of the war production, in an effort to break the so-called Little Steel Formula for stabilizing wages. The President exerted his emergency war powers by seizing the mines, but to no avail in the end. "You can't mine coal with bayonets," Lewis reminded him surlily, and the wage formula collapsed, at least as far as the mine workers were concerned. The steel workers, the rubber workers, the railway workers also essayed such confrontations with authority but with less climatic effect.

As noted earlier wartime manpower controls were relatively flexible and unoppressive. It is doubtful that the harsh, punitive legislation with which Congress frequently threatened labor—and which the administration successfully thwarted each time—would have achieved any lasting benefits. In the long run, as WPB boss Nelson himself conceded on numerous occasions, labor's contribution to the "arsenal of democracy" was no less substantial and no less willingly given than that of management. But, typically, no one thought of "E" banners for the working man.

Summing up, stupendous is not too extravagant an adjective to describe this country's war production record. From 1940 through 1945 the monthly rate of munitions output rose from $341 million to more than $5 billion, a fifteenfold increase. The total value of all the war goods produced was $183.1 billion. In terms of hardware that meant, among other things, 299,300 military airplanes, 72,100 naval ships of all kinds, 4,900 merchant ships, 86,300 tanks, 8.5 million rifles and carbines, and approximately 14 million tons of ammunition and bombs. American production accounted for about 40 percent of the entire world consumption of munitions during the critical war years of 1943–1944. We succeeded literally in producing both "guns and butter" in more than adequate amounts, for the civilian economy suffered no severe privations during all these years. Indeed, the dollar value of production for the private sector was greater in 1944 than it had been in 1939.

By the middle of 1944 the battle of war production had been won. With victory over the military enemy also in sight, Washington began seriously to ponder how to get down off the mountain we had so successfully climbed—how to get back down into the valleys of peace without a crashing descent. It was no small problem.[8]

7

War on the Home Front

I

"LOOK, LADY (MISTER OR KID OR WHOEVER) there's a war on. Remember?"

That phrase, uttered in infinite variations and on a sliding scale of irritability, was about the most common admonition tossed back and forth on the home front during the war years. It was used by tradesmen and store clerks to put a complaining customer in his place, by taxi drivers to silence a fare resentful over sitting four abreast on the springless back seat, by waitresses scornfully denying a request for an extra chip of butter or a refill of an empty coffee cup, by ticket agents in lieu of explaining why all the Pullman reservations on the overnight to Chicago had suddenly been cancelled—again, by ration board clerks disdaining a prayerful entreaty for just one new tire to get a grounded motor car rolling again, by housewives wearily justifying a fifth consecutive dinner menu based on fish . . . and many, many more in like discouraging vein.

"Dontcha know there's a war on?"

It was a taunt and not a question because obviously everybody did know there was a war on. And whatever lack there may have been in one's personal experience was made up for him many times over by his daily intake of news. A New York commuter riding to work on the warm, sunny morning of Tuesday, June 1, 1943, for example, unfolded his copy of the *Times* and was confronted by such confirming testimony as the following:

A four-column headline on the right-hand side of the page informed him "100 FORTRESSES BATTER NAPLES HARBOR: SARDINIA AND PANTELLERIA ALSO RAIDED: De GAULLE AND GIRAUD FORM 'CABINET'." This was balanced by a three-column head in the opposite corner proclaiming, "COAL MINERS RESUME STRIKE WITH CONFEREES DEADLOCKED: CONTRACT ENDED AT MIDNIGHT," and in the center of the page just above the fold another commanding headline advised him, "ALLIES TEST AIR OFFENSIVE

IN MAY ATTACKS ON RUHR." There was a "War News Summary" boxed at the bottom of the page—a daily feature—that provided such capsuled information on the fighting as that the air raid on Naples was the seventieth in succession and the heaviest to date; that the part of the French fleet which had fled to Alexandria after the fall of France had put itself at the disposal of General Giraud, military leader of the Free French; that the Russians reported shooting down 31 Nazi planes over Leningrad on Sunday; and that Chiang Kai-shek was claiming one of China's greatest victories over the Japanese in action southwest of Ichang.

But there was much war news closer to home. The previous day had been Memorial Day, and *Times'* reporters described not only the spectacular parade and other patriotic ceremonies which had taken place, but a kindred development that was becoming all too familiar: Thousands of stranded weekend vacationers were unable to get home because of jammed transportation lines. Few travelers dared use their precious gasoline rations for pleasure jaunts, so they piled into buses, trains, and airplanes (themselves operating on restricted schedules!) in unmanageable numbers. Of the throngs which poured into New York for the three-day holiday, a couple of thousand were observed still milling about at one major bus terminal shortly before midnight, content to get even standing room on a home-bound bus. Other thousands who had poured out of New York were reported marooned at way-stations in the Catskills and at New Jersey shore resorts. Any trip far from home that was not backed up by a government travel order was quite likely to degenerate into a nightmare before it was over.

On almost any page of his paper that day, or any other day, our commuter would find evidence that, yes, there was a war on. Beginning that day, Tuesday June 1, New York dairies would cut doorstep milk deliveries to every other day, on orders of the Office of Defense Transportation. Shipyard workers in Camden, New Jersey, filed a solemn complaint with the Navy charging their employer with a lack of patriotism in decreeing a three-day holiday over Memorial Day. Members of the Amalgamated Clothing Workers in New York formally denounced John L. Lewis, chief of the miners' union, for a similar lapse in calling his men out on strike. The OPA announced that the value of B and C gasoline ration coupons was being cut from three gallons to two and one-half gallons each in the northeastern states in a drive to save 30,000 barrels of fuel daily. Simultaneously, the president of the Automobile Club of New York fired off a protest to the OPA administrator in Washington protesting the "gestapo methods" of OPA investigators in "harassing" such innocent motorists as housewives out to do their shopping or taking the children to church. At San Quentin Prison in California, 500 convicts began the task of processing some eight million ration book applications from citizens on the outside to break an administrative logjam in the state's price and rationing board.

That morning there were only two and one-half columns of classified ads offering apartments or rooms for rent in all of New York City, but there were four and one-half pages of "help wanted" ads—many of them carrying a note of desperation, such as "Men, Come Out of Retirement," or "100% War Work Guaranteed." That note of desperation carried over into the display ads as well. The Brass Rail, a popular midtown restaurant and bar, adjured its loyal customers in this fashion: "If you miss familiar Brass Rail faces . . . If we sometimes fall short of the perfect service you have always enjoyed . . . Please remember that about one-third of our crew have gone—with our blessing—into the service of our country." A score of automobile dealers scrounged daily for salable used cars with such ads as this one by the firm of Murphy and Holzer at 39th Street and Tenth Avenue: "OPA Bans Pleasure Driving. Now is the time to sell your car while our prices are extremely high. Describe your car and we'll buy it over the phone." Macy's biggest ad that day raised a universally worrisome question in large black type, "ENEMY PLANES OVERHEAD?" and announced a week-long, three-times-a-day showing in its sixth-floor auditorium of a special Army film depicting air raid defenses in and around New York, admission free. And to show that everybody, but everybody, was straining to the utmost to win the war, Coty, the perfumer, took a full page in that day's *Times* to announce that its "worldwide organization is in the service of the United States and the United Nations," its particular contribution being facial makeup for camouflaged jungle fighters. Not a word about L'Aimant.

II

The quality of everyday life in the United States in wartime was a variable and highly subjective experience.

For many, depressants and discouragements intruded on every hand. These could be acutely personal and painful as when a son or a husband or a friend turned up on the casualty lists, or when it was known or even feared that he was headed for a combat zone. With upwards of 10 million men already in uniform, and more joining their ranks each day, few families were spared some awareness of this particular anxiety. Or, if one's concerns were broadly gauged, his anxiety might be more general and impersonal, focusing upon the degradation and futility of all wars, this one included. There were millions in this country to whom the First World War was still a vivid, firsthand experience; an orgy of destruction and suffering . . . to what purpose? The world had gained nothing, really, from the defeat of the Kaiser in 1917, and now it was performing the same danse macabre all over again. For some there was a weighty sense of national guilt because their government, by inaction, had doomed the League of Nations to impotence, and thus abetted the onset of the present war.

Many, on the other hand, escaped this burden of anxiety, either by temperament or the accidents of fate. To them the war and the climate of war was simply a reality of life to be accepted and adjusted to as one does to any other kind of hard time. Living through 10 years of the Great Depression had left them with a protective coating of fatalism, or of cynicism: What will be will be, and one can't worry it away. In some ways, on the other hand, the war crisis could be rationalized as a boon. For hundreds of thousands of blacks and poor whites scooped up in the draft, army food, army barracks, army health care were incomparably better than anything they had known before. For other hundreds of thousands of their people who did not go into uniform, the war meant jobs, good pay, probably the illusory excitement of migration to a distant city. At the least, this might mean breaking the bonds of a stifling class or economic heritage; at the best it could mean a handhold upward on the cultural ladder.

There was little argument about the *rightness* of the war and our participation in it. The Reverend Daniel Alfred Poling, editor of the widely respected *Christian Herald,* put the moral dilemma of many churchmen to rest when he wrote in July 1943:

War is not holy. War is the sum of man's inhumanity to man. But there are holy causes. Freedom is holy. Human personality, declared by Jesus to be the most sacred thing, is holy.

What, then, should we do when holy things are threatened by the war machine? . . .

Let the church have no blessing for war, but shame upon us as churchmen if we have no blessings for our sons and no blessings for our government who, in the presence of war, defend with their very lives our holy things.

Pacifism and isolationism subsided very quickly after Pearl Harbor, and no great effort of propaganda was necessary in the years that followed to keep the public temper in fighting trim. The Coughlins, the Nyes, the America Firsters, the Bundists fell silent less because of the sedition statutes than because nobody was listening. The Japs and the Nazis were easy to hate and it was almost impossible to make plausible excuses for them on either nationalist or ideological grounds.

The mood was quite different from that of 1917–1918. There were avowed pro-German and antiwar factions throughout the country in those years who, if they were not politically potent, were at least determinedly articulate. For the great majority of Americans, however, the First World War was a holy crusade "to make the world safe for democracy." It evoked in most a fervent patriotism that welled up continuously in cheers and tears as the parades went by and the bands played and the crowded troop trains chugged off to distant destinations. It was a time of rousing marching songs like "Over There," and lachrymose ballads such as "Just a Baby's Prayer at Twilight," and sentimental poetry about flag and country and the nobility of death on the battlefield. It was a time of innocence before we had learned that wars are made by "munitions kings" and scheming statesmen.

In the Second World War the slogans and bands were muted, the marching songs few and tinged with cynical levity. Patriotism was not lacking but it did not have to be worn on the sleeve to be believed. There were not many romantic illusions about that war: We had watched it develop with mounting horror for two years before we got into it. It was a bloody, brutal business that had to do with self-defense, and not some nonsense about the sanctity of Old Glory and mom's apple pie. It was not a war wholly devoid of glamor and heroism—no war ever is—but these qualities were moderated by a pragmatic realism that made parades and flag-waving and other visible affirmations of our martial purpose seem trite and contrived. Public morale was none the worse for the omission.

The national mood fluctuated inevitably according to the fortunes of war. During most of 1942 a bleakness overhung the military outlook as the Japanese rampaged across the Pacific and fascism scored almost unchecked triumphs in Europe and North Africa. The successful completion of the Solomon Islands campaign late that year, and the landing in North Africa, brought a great resurgence of hope; thereafter, most people doubted not that we would win the war sooner or later. This reflected a quite prevalent confidence both in our allies and in our own leadership. There was unstinting admiration for the British. About the French, most people felt they were more to be pitied than blamed. About the Russians there was a good deal of ambiguity in the public mind, but the doughty Reds were manifestly a big plus for our side as long as they stayed hitched. And the Chinese, it was assumed, would one day pull themselves together and throw the Jap invaders out.

Churchill had become an American folk hero by the end of 1942; de Gaulle, Stalin, and Chiang Kai-shek, being less well known, were accepted willingly on faith. President Roosevelt, even as he gave signs of standing for a fourth term—anathema to most politicians—still commanded wide popular support as the wartime leader, and so did General George Marshall, General Douglas MacArthur, and most of the military hierarchy. The war was an unwelcome burden upon the nation's spirit but most people accepted it as an inescapable responsibility to which they were committed. In the aims and conduct of the war, the country was as firmly united as it ever had been.[1]

III

The butt of most popular discontent was the great web of emergency war agencies whose spreading strands seemed to entangle just about every facet of one's life. By a perverse illogic, they were often blamed as the cause of the various shortages and other economic malfunctions they were supposed to correct. The angry, puzzled citizen could safely vent any of his war-born frustrations against these alphabetized bureaucracies without putting his loyalty in question, for they were political instruments run by civilians like himself and so were bereft of the protective coloration of military dress. If he thought the boys at the front weren't getting enough bombers or bullets, or he couldn't buy nails at his neighborhood hardware store, he could explain it all by damning the WPB. If the trains weren't running on time, the obvious culprit was the ODT. If the coal miners were out on strike, blame the WLB or the WMC as well as John L. Lewis. If his car was beached for lack of gas or his hunger unappeased for lack of a steak, blame the OPA. Such bitching was the common currency of conversation on the home front, the bond beyond theology and politics that made the nation one.

Poor OPA! It was the most visible, vulnerable target of the lot, and the most fulsomely abused. Its price controls and rationing confronted —and affronted—just about everyone almost daily. And such was the nature of its task that its weaknesses nearly always outshone its virtues. It was easy to demonstrate what a colossal nuisance it was but not so easy—and far less gratifying—to demonstrate its restraining effect on the cost of living.

Rationing was the biggest headache of all. It meant getting used to an entirely new system of currency without which the coin of the realm was valueless for the purchase of most foods and variety of other necessities. Obtaining and keeping track of one's allotment of certificates and ration stamps (usually they were distributed on a family basis) was trouble enough, but even worse was keeping up with their shifting values and expirations. Such OPA guidelines as the following (for the first week in June 1943) were published regularly in practically every newspaper, and the wary consumer had to know about them if he was not to be left behind in the scramble for goods.

GENERAL PROVISIONS—Blue Stamps in War Ration Book No. 2 are used for most canned goods and for dried peas, beans, lentils, and frozen commodities like fruit juice. The Red Stamps are used for meats, canned fish, butter, cheese, edible fats, and canned milk. You have to give up more points when buying scarce foods than when buying the same quantity of a more plentiful one. . . .

Red Stamps J, K, and L may be redeemed through June 20. Blue Stamps

G, H, and J are valid through June 7, and Blue Stamps K, L, and M are valid through July 7. Ration stamps are not valid if detached from their appropriate books. . . .

Each person has a Red Stamp quota of 16 points a week (meats, cheese, butter, etc.), allowing an average of approximately two pounds per week per person. Each person has 48 points in Blue Stamps (most processed foods) to expend between June 6 and July 2. You may buy most fresh vegetables without ration stamps. . . .

In Ration Book No. 1, Stamp No. 13 is good for five pounds of sugar through August 1; Stamp No. 24 is good for one pound of coffee through June 30; Stamp No. 17 is good for one pair of shoes until June 15. (Dealers may not accept shoe stamps unless detached from ration book in presence of dealer.)

Gasoline and Tires—All pleasure driving is banned for holders of A, B, and C ration books. All A coupons are valued at 3 gallons; B and C coupons are valued at 2½ gallons. Coupon 5 in A book is good for 3 gallons through July 21. Motorists must write license number and state on back of each coupon before offering it to dealer. . . . No coupons for new or recapped tires will be issued unless motorist carries inspection card showing that required tire inspections have been made.

No matter how scrupulously one threaded his way through the intricacies of the OPA regulations, cutting a corner here, cheating a bit there, he could not avoid disappointments and frustrations. The things he wanted most, it seemed, were always in short supply. He might stand for an hour at the butcher shop, hopefully clutching a handful of red stamps and dreaming of roast beef, only to find when he got to the head of the line that there was nothing left but mutton and veal. Clearly (though not always accurately) it was OPA's fault that he had to learn to put up with imitation chocolate that tasted like paraffin, "stretchers" that were supposed to make last night's coffee grounds reusable for breakfast, strange and unpalatable brands of cigarettes, tequila and rum in place of honest whiskey, soap that refused to lather, and sweeteners that didn't sweeten. For the housewives of America at least, the war on the home front was fought in the supermarket.

Travel was another of the vexing tribulations of civilian life. The sheer grit that it usually took to get from one city to another—or sometimes only from home to office and back again—gave added pertinency to the ODT's slogan, "Is This Trip Necessary?"

Railroads were, of course, the mass public carrier in the forties. The war taxed their facilities to the breaking point—and beyond. Old coaches, old locomotives, old railroaders were called out of retirement in a vain effort to meet the demand. Thousands of troops were constantly on the move between cantonments and training stations and ports of embarkation. Their movement took priority over other traffic, commandeering scarce equipment, knocking schedules askew, leaving extra-fare "Limiteds" and their parlor car customers forlornly parked on sidings for hours at a stretch. A scheduled dinner-to-breakfast businessman's journey from New York to Chicago could be expected to put him at his destination by lunchtime if he were lucky, by the following dinner hour if he were a little less so. If he were unluckier still (and often he was) he might find that his reservation for a Pullman berth was valueless, that the dining car was reduced to emergency rations, that the ventilating system was incapacitated and that one of the wheels above which he rode was quite certainly square. And at each end of his journey he would find the terminals jammed with other migrants like himself, wrestling baggage without the aid of Red Caps, queuing up at the ticket windows and the lunch counters and the toilets, or just waiting in silent misery for their vagrant trains to arrive.

Air travel was still something of a novelty and not much more dependable than the trains and the interstate buslines. Moreover, an air passenger on his own without a government travel order was liable to be "bumped" before takeoff if a claimant for his seat showed up with such credentials in hand. One might reconcile himself to such misfortune if the interloper was in uniform, but if he turned out to be a self-important bureaucrat in civvies, one's indignation was likely to explode. Captain Elliot Roosevelt, the President's son, unwittingly set off such a storm by shipping his dog, Blaze, across the country on a high-priority airline ticket. The most widely believed story was that a couple of homeward-bound GIs were "bumped" to make room for Blaze, but this seems to have been one of the countless exaggerations that were spun off by the incident.

At the end of any journey there was always the element of gambler's luck in finding a hotel room, reservations to the contrary notwithstanding. Desk clerks were easily overwhelmed by the sudden appearance of a clutch of exuberant young officers in town on a three-day pass, or by a peremptory demand from Washington to make way for an emergency session of the Nut and Bolt Manufacturers' War Council. In spite of the demand for rooms, some large hotels were obliged to shut off a few floors from time to time simply because they could not get the help to service them. In some cities, and this was particularly true in resorts like Miami and Santa Barbara, the military commandeered entire hotels for long periods, using them as rest and transient facilities and even as resident quarters for men stationed at nearby posts.

The "car pool" was a wartime invention to meet the difficulties of incity transportation. Car owners took turns ferrying their colleagues and neighbors to and from work, on shopping expeditions, to church, divvying up the cost in gas ration stamps among them. This had the added advantage of social melding—or unmelding perhaps—as the car-poolers got to know one another better. Friendships were quickly made and unmade in these wartime forced encounters. Most municipal transit systems —buses, streetcars, subways—had a hard time of it during the war. Little new equipment had been added during the Depression years, and what was left by 1942 was generally in a state of obsolescence and near-collapse. In Washington, D.C., trolley cars that had begun service in 1912, their windows proudly capped by a bit of stained glass, were still clanking up and down Pennsylvania Avenue when VJ-Day came.[2]

IV

One of the most pervasive impressions of city life on the home front was that of crowding, of the unremitting pressure of masses of people on the sidewalks, in the stores and cafes, at the movies and the bus stops, in one's office building or apartment house or suburban enclave. Where in God's name, one asked, did they all come from? Obviously, of course, the majority of them had been there all along but their numbers were suddenly swollen by a vast influx of mostly young people from the farms and small towns, drawn by the lure of wartime jobs and a chance to get in on the action.

A far more pertinent question was, "Where do they all live?" for the crowding created a housing shortage that was one of the most stubborn and exasperating afflictions of the war years.

The abundance of jobs of every description that began to mushroom in 1941 set in motion the greatest mass migration the country had ever seen. Workers by the tens of thousands were constantly on the move, drawn hither and yon to the teeming centers of government, military, and industrial activity. They were men, boys, women, and often whole families; blacks as well as whites; professional people, skilled artisans, common laborers; college graduates, high school dropouts, semi-illiterates. They poured into the cities in indigestible numbers, overwhelming existing housing facilities and spilling over into tent and trailer colonies or into the bleak, jerry-built war housing developments that erupted like blisters on the suburban landscape.

For many of the older ones this was a repeat performance. Ten years before during the Depression they had also "hit the road," driven by desperation. This time they were fat with money, or relatively so. But money in the pocket and a job in hand were not always enough to secure a decent place to live. Apartment and rooming houses seemed to have "No Vacancy" signs permanently affixed to their doorposts. Even the slum tenements were overflowing. Publicly operated War Housing Centers scrounged their communities for unused living space, urged householders as a patriotic duty to double up and rent their spare rooms to war workers. But often the best they could do was to add you to the waiting list. Success might come by bribing a landlord with an extra month's rent to

179

let you bypass his own waiting list, or to persuade some of his existing tenants to let you squeeze in with them.

Government girls in Washington—there were uncounted thousands of them—were said to be "living in layers" in the boarding houses of Foggy Bottom and around DuPont Circle. And it was rumored that entrepreneurs in some cities were renting sleeping space on a shift basis—daylight hours for the night workers.

A popular fable of the times went like this: A man walking along the waterfront saw another man struggling in the water and crying for help.

"What's your name?" the man on shore called out.

"Joe Smith," the other gasped feebly.

"Where do you live?"

"Two-ten Fifth Street," came the weakening reply.

The shoreside citizen turned and ran as fast as he could to 210 Fifth Street and knocked on the door.

"Joe Smith has just drowned and I want to rent his room," he blurted to the woman who answered.

"You're too late," she replied. "I just rented it to the man who pushed him in."

You could almost believe it really happened.

Outside the cities, the boomtowns were a familiar and depressing aspect of wartime living. Most typically they were located in the more sparsely populated regions on the periphery of a great war plant or military establishment that had suddenly, for reasons that were obscure to the layman, been "plunked down in the middle of nowhere." They were government-built in most instances, erected as quickly and cheaply as possible—row upon row of nearly identical one- and two-story barracks-like structures of plywood and plasterboard with paper-thin walls and with minimal appurtenances in the way of plumbing, heating, and kitchen equipment. Some were simple dormitories grouped around a central mess hall. Others were divided into cramped family units. The marks of the bulldozers were often visible where the raw earth had been turned to clear the site and lay out the unpaved streets, and sometimes the water and sewer lines had been left above ground. In the larger towns a primitive sort of business district might be included, with a few stores and taverns, a firehouse, a movie theater, possibly a school that could double as a church on Sundays.

The whole scene had the unreal and temporary aspect of a movie set, of a contrived and implacable bleakness. Yet such a town might be "home" to a few hundred or maybe several thousand families and single persons for a couple of years or more. If they possibly never learned to love it, they often did develop a kind of exigent community spirit and social structure. A bit of grass would be encouraged to grow here and there, flowers would appear in window boxes, a ball diamond or tennis court might result from communal effort, and there would be Saturday-night beer parties and love affairs and neighborhood feuds "just like back home."

Under the aegis of the National Housing Agency more than a thousand of these emergency war housing communities—some the size of small cities—sprang into existence across the nation during 1942 and 1943. At the peak of occupancy they cared for as many as 1.5 million persons. The boomtowns meant hard living for most of their residents ("Don't you know there's a war on?") but without them the pace of the war effort could not have been maintained.

V

To a great many older people, and to parents in particular, it seemed that the exigencies of wartime living imposed dangerous stresses on the nation's moral and social fabric. Old patterns of decorum and behavior collapsed under the "new freedom" that put wives and mothers on the factory production lines, that filled the pockets of high school and college-age youngsters for the first time with wages that were their very own, that sent thousands of young girls to jobs in distant cities and exposure to all the alleged perils thereof, and that, by the miracle of an even ill-fitting uniform transformed a downy-faced youth of eighteen into a man and a soldier overnight. The unity of the family was ruptured, parental control became redundant, and even the stay-at-home siblings in many cases seemed to react to the anything-goes psychology of the times. Moralists were certain (as they seem always to have been) that society as a whole, and the younger generation in particular, were being drawn hellward at an alarming rate.

There was, of course, some hard evidence on which their fears were fed. While the incidence of crime in general decreased markedly during the war years (many of the potential miscreants were otherwise employed in the service of their country), juvenile delinquency rose sharply all across the country, eliciting anguished warnings from the pulpit and from such public figures as New York's Mayor LaGuardia and the FBI's J. Edgar Hoover. Mr. Hoover reported in the summer of 1943, in fact, that juvenile arrests for that year were already 17 percent above the comparable figure for the previous year, and that the trend had been steadily upward since 1939. More alarming still was the fact that the arrest of girls had more than doubled in that period, the principal offense being prostitution and related misdeeds. And a New York City welfare official said that over 60 percent of the cases of venereal disease reported by local Army medical authorities had been contracted from girls under twenty-one years of age.

It was widely known that prostitution flourished mightily in all the

181

war centers, and with little hindrance from the authorities. The trade had the dubious status of an unpleasant wartime necessity. The military thoughtfully established "pro stations" here and there in the various tenderloins frequented by servicemen where one who thought he might have contracted a "dose" could go for free prophylactic treatment. It was speedy and usually efficacious and led to the comforting belief in GI circles that a simple case of gonorrhea was "no worse than a bad cold."

Whether in uniform or not, all sorts of allurements were cast in the path of the footloose younger generation during the war. Cheap bars, night clubs, "skin shows," taxi dance halls, and similar flesh pots proliferated wherever they congregated. In nearly every big town or city, and especially in the environs of an active military post, there was likely to be a garish cluster of such establishments locally known by some such opprobrious designation as "The Strip" or "Bug Town." Sleazy little walkup hotels were said to offer rooms either by the night or by the hour, no questions asked. White-helmeted young MPs were much in evidence in such areas and sometimes they teamed up with the local constabulary to break up brawls or to raid a particularly obnoxious joint. Often younger teenagers of the community were attracted by all the sound and glitter, chattering groups of prenubile bobbysoxers or perhaps a clutch of zoot-suited young toughs touring the streets looking for fun and trouble. They could get both in unhealthy doses.

Preachers and editorialists regularly deplored such scandalous goings-on upon their doorsteps, called for cleanups by the police or a drive to provide less noxious forms of recreation. Curfews were imposed in many communities in an effort to keep the under-eighteens off the streets at night, and local military authorities cooperated by putting some of the gamier districts off limits for men in uniform. Such palliatives never seemed to work for long. "C'est la guerre," the distressed oldsters said, looking heavenward in resignation.

Actually, there were many thriving alternatives to the bars and clip joints that offered a more wholesome outlet for the restlessness and bewilderment of the war generation. United Service Organizations (USO), started in 1941, spread a network of off-base hospitality and recreation centers all across the country where servicemen on the loose could congregate in a club-like atmosphere and even find dates for the Saturday-night dances. Canteens sprang up everywhere, run by churches and civic clubs and welfare organizations, to provide a sometimes more varied program than did the USO—free food and beer, parties, theater tickets, even invitations for dinner or a weekend with a private family. Celebrities, local or national, were often an added attraction for the awestruck GI at such affairs. He might find Jack Benny in a long white apron opening a bottle of beer for him at the New York Stage Door Canteen or Vice-President Truman banging out a ditty with actress Lauren Bacall perched atop his piano at the **Press Club** canteen in Washington. Needless to say, not all of the uprooted young people were snared by the honky-tonk culture of "The Strip."

Romance bloomed early and profusely all during the war years. Young people thrown suddenly together in strange and exotic surroundings, their emotions and longings sharpened by the poetic uncertainties of war, fell easily and repeatedly in love. Old taboos about class and status and family consent, even fidelity to yesterday's sweetheart, could be swept aside by the glamor and instant passions of such wartime fantasies. Such an affair could be hastened to fulfillment if the young hero in uniform faced assignment overseas. "Quickie" marriages by the thousands ensued, based as often as not on courtships measured in days and weeks, and followed as often as not by long and disillusioning separations.

What also followed, according to the statistical tables that measure such intimate matters, was a sharp increase in the birthrate and, a bit later, an equally sharp rise in the divorce rate. That index did not peak until 1946 (at more than double the 1940 rate)—after the young lovers had come together again and reassessed the quality of their devotion.

It is quite obvious, of course, that the war generation did not succumb to mass depravity, as so many of their elders feared. What did happen was a dizzying speedup in the normal pace of youthful alienation, in the inexorable evolution of the nation's mores and manners, in the widening of what has come to be called the "generation gap." Most of that younger generation survived the pitfalls of the war years to become in time responsible members of society and to worry about the pitfalls facing a generation younger than their own.

VI

The war brought fewer changes in what people on the home front did for amusement and recreation than might have been expected. The entertainment industry, depending heavily on 4-Fs for male talent, ground out plays, movies, and radio scripts in satisfying volume. Professional sports, similarly handicapped by the draft, suffered no loss of patronage at the ball parks and prize rings in spite of a plethora of overage contestants. Book and magazine publishers did a thriving business in the face of WPB orders sharply limiting their supply of paper. Where the war hit deepest was in the enjoyment of vacation resorts and those pastimes that were dependent upon the internal combustion engine and other modes of travel. Many hotels shut down "for the duration" and even golf clubs in the more distant suburbs were pinched for customers. *Time* magazine assessed the 1943 vacationer's outlook in these words:

Summer's onset trapped many a U.S. vacationist flat on his own front porch. The plain citizen was marooned at home with a well-stuffed wallet. He had plenty of easy-come money to be easy-going with, and not a thrilling thing to spend it on.

The gas and rubber shortage made a mockery of his shiny car, whitewall tires agleam, the top battened down. The hard-breathing railroads warned him off; they had all they could handle without the likes of him. If his muscles were still good enough for a bicycling trip, that meant he probably would be drafted before the summer was over.

The advice of the Chicago Chamber of Commerce is: If you can't go fishing, go to the Shedd Aquarium and look at the fish. . . . The Bronx Zoo expects the biggest attendance in its history. . . . Hotels at Lake George advertise, "Everything within easy walking distance. You don't need a car. . . ."

The shortage that hurt worst of all was time. For the nation was, officially at least, on a full six-day, 48-hour week, and absenteeism or frivolous requests for time off were likely to be met with stern looks from one's boss and fellow workers. This cut into one's attendance at the ball park or the race track and into his readiness for an after-dinner trip to the movies or the bowling alley. Even so, there was little that smacked of austerity in the recreational pursuits available on the home front. If the quality of the fare offered seemed often to be below par, the quantity was adequate.

The great war novels and the great war plays came mostly after the war was over. This artistic lag, however, did not inhibit the publishers and producers from running with what they had; least of all was the movie industry to be put off. Hollywood turned out instant war films —melodramas, thrillers, comedies—in case lots, along with some truly magnificent footage in newsreels and documentaries. Much of the latter has lasting historical value to this day and is preserved in a dozen major archives. Most of the rest was, to be generous about it, of an evanescent quality—good for a passable evening's entertainment, a singable tune, a few good laughs, and soon forgotten.

A random sampling of the popular screen fare on display in mid-1943, for example, turns out about as follows: Leading the list in frequency were the action stories giving a sometimes realistic and always romanticized depiction of some facet of the war. They had such titles as *Crash Dive, Sahara, Commandos Strike at Dawn, So Proudly We Hail* (heroic nurses on Bataan), *Action in the North Atlantic, Watch on the Rhine,* and, perhaps most memorable of the lot, *Guadalcanal Diary,* based on the current nonfiction best seller of the same name. A lighter side of war was reflected in a number of comedies and musicals such as *They Got Me Covered* (a Bob Hope-Dorothy Lamour romp), *The More the Merrier, When Johnny Comes Marching Home, Thank Your Lucky Stars, Star Spangled Rhythm,* and a superb Irving Berlin creation, *This Is the Army.*

Pictures without a war angle that were of more than passing interest that year included a Hollywood version of Ernest Hemingway's grim epic of the Spanish Civil War, *For Whom the Bell Tolls* (which Hemingway angrily denounced); *The Ox-Bow Incident, Tennessee Johnson, Madame Curie,* and such comedies and musicals as *The Meanest Man In Town* (with the indestructible Jack Benny), *A Lady Takes A Chance, The Sky's The Limit,* and *Coney Island* (starring Betty Grable, who, by an overwhelming GI consensus, was said to have the most beautiful legs in the world). In addition to all of which, of course, the filmmakers continued to spin out their familiar line of westerns, gangland thrillers, and other candidates for B-grade anonymity.

For a great many people in wartime the lure of the movies lay less in the dramatizations and gaudy musicals than in the candid realism of the newsreels with on-the-spot visual reporting of battle scenes, disasters at sea, bombing runs, and major news events from around a news-packed world—the contemporary equivalent of today's television. The *March of Time,* issued monthly by the publishers of *Time* and *Life* magazines, was a hybrid evolved from a crossing of the newsreel and the documentary which, for all its rather theatrical pretensions, was immensely popular. (There was also a radio version of it.) Most of the documentaries were produced under the aegis of the military services and the Office of War Information. While they contained a certain propaganda ingredient, most of them were highly informative and entertaining.

The legitimate theater scarcely existed beyond the confines of Broadway during the war years, mainly because of the hold-down on travel. While road shows all but disappeared and many provincial theaters shut down or converted to movies, there was a corollary gain in the establishment of resident acting companies in a number of cities. Some of these—Washington, Minneapolis, and Dallas, for example—took firm root and have continued to prosper at highly professional levels.

Lewis Nichols, the *Times* drama critic, summed up the year's offerings on Broadway in 1943 as, "not bad, not bad at all." But it had been a year of greater commercial than artistic success. Reviewing the season near the end of the year, he wrote:

. . . for 1943 saw a public that was anxious to go to the theater, a public such as the playhouses had not welcomed in a number of years. All during the heat of the summer, when normally the continuing plays should have been gasping for breath, audiences stood waiting at box offices in order to get tickets in advance. It was a public so anxious to attend the theater that for a time it would attend almost anything playing in a theater. Some of the managers took advantage of this and offered plays which, in normal years, would never have passed Bridgeport. But the new public gradually grew discriminating and cautious. For a number of months it was news when a bad show closed through lack of trade. Now the proprieties are reasserting themselves, and it is news no longer. But for the managers it was wonderful while it lasted. . . .

Broadway's output during this middle year of the war split roughly along the same varietal lines as did Hollywood's—a rash of poor-to-middling war dramas, some average-to-better comedies and musicals with a war setting, a number of productions unrelated to the war, and, crowning the list, a few entries in each category of outstanding and memorable merit.

One of the greatest of modern musicals, Richard Rodgers and Oscar Hammerstein's *Oklahoma!,* with its gay melodies and exuberant choreography, had its premier in April and ran on through the war years and to a number of later revivals. It was as foreign to the prevailing mood of 1943 as a Sunday-school picnic, its locale being the bucolic middle frontier around the turn of the century. But it enraptured the tens of thousands who stood in line for tickets year after year and the millions who picked up its lyrics from the radio and phonograph.*

Other "greats" which the critics acclaimed that year were *Carmen Jones,* a rollicking, jazzed-up spoof on Bizet's opera with an all-Negro cast; *Doughgirls,* a rowdy musical built around the housing shortage in wartime Washington; *Winged Victory,* a spectacular war drama with its cast drawn entirely from the Army Air Force; Thornton Wilder's *The Skin of Our Teeth,* which won the Pulitzer drama award for the year; and Sidney Kingsley's *The Patriots,* which harked back to the days of the Revolution. Among other notable offerings on Broadway during the 1943 season were *Something for the Boys, Kiss and Tell, One Touch of Venus, The Two Mrs. Carrolls, Tomorrow the World, The Rock,* and *The Eve of St. Mark.* Meanwhile, *Life with Father* rolled up its fifth successive year on the boards, and *Arsenic and Old Lace* its third, and such old standbys as *The Merry Widow* and *The Student Prince* were dusted off and brought back for brief revivals.

The runaway best seller in the bookstores during 1943 was Wendell Willkie's *One World.* It topped a million copies in hardcover before the year was out, and then went on to further heights in paperback. (It also, incidentally, virtually put an end to isolationism as a political force in the United States.) Close behind it was Ambassador Joseph E. Davies'

* When it was revived *again* in June 1969, Lewis Funke, reviewing it for the *Times,* admitted that the first stirring strains of the overture brought a lump to his throat:

It seemed only yesterday that [*Oklahoma!*] had opened on Broadway and revolutionized the American musical theater. But of course it was much more than only yesterday. It was 1943, and I wondered whether anyone ever again would dare come up with a fairytale such as this, as antiseptic and as simple. . . . It may very well survive not only its contemporaries but also much of what has come on since.

Mission to Moscow (published in the previous year), and war correspondent Richard Tregaskis' *Guadalcanal Diary.*

What is significant here is that all three were nonfiction: factual descriptions and analyses of the forces that were torturing the world rather than imaginative dramatizations. This was a trend that had been pushing steadily forward in the world of letters for several years, and it would continue into the future. The novel and the short story had not been banished by the war—far from it—but more and more the creative writer was being forced to share the stage with the reporter and the polemicist. Along with the popular hunger for fantasy and escape in time of deep trouble, there was a growing demand to know how the world had gotten into such a fix and what could be done, and was being done, to alleviate it.

The demand was met not only by a great outpouring of factual and dialectical books but by a marked shift of emphasis in the popular magazines such as *Saturday Evening Post, Collier's, Harper's,* and *McCall's.* Reportorial pieces with a war angle usually dominated their tables of contents, upsetting the old ratio that had so heavily favored fiction. The news and picture magazines naturally profited greatly from this trend. Current magazines acquired, in fact, a kind of premium value during the early years of the war. The limited supplies quickly sold out at the newstands with the result that particularly interesting issues were saved and traded, neighbor to neighbor.

The wartime fiction was, on the whole, definitely inferior to the nonfiction—or so it seems to one who was occupationally predisposed to that viewpoint. As previously noted here, the "great" war novels, requiring lengthy gestation, did not come along until near the end or after the war. The coming crop of young war writers either had not hit their stride or were otherwise engaged. It was 1945 when John Hersey, one of the earliest and best of that crop to flower, produced his Pulitzer-prize-winning *A Bell for Adano.* The war stories that did come out during the war—and the 1943 output is a fair sample—were mostly replays of familiar plots and themes with the characters in uniform and the locale shifted from, say, Gopher Prairie to Algiers or London. The majority of the most important novels of that year (as well as a few biographies and historical works) were written by established authors and drew little if any of their substance from the war.

Illustrating the range of popular, and not scholarly, taste in wartime reading on the home front, here are the titles chosen by the Book of the Month Club for its many thousands of subscribers during 1943: *Headhunting in the Solomon Islands,* by Caroline Mytinger; *Let the People Know,* by Norman Angell; *Guadalcanal Diary,* by Richard Tregaskis; *The Human Comedy,* by William Saroyan; *Colonel Effingham's Raid,* by Berry Fleming; *The Year of Decision: 1846,* by Bernard DeVoto; *The Fifth Seal,* by Mark Aldanov; *Winter's Tales,* by Isak Dinesen; *Combined*

Operations, by Hilary A. St. George Saunders; *Western Star,* by Stephen Vincent Benet; *U.S. Foreign Policy,* by Walter Lippmann; *Origins of the American Revolution,* by John C. Miller; *Thirty Seconds Over Tokyo,* by Captain Ted W. Lawson; *So Little Time,* by John P. Marquand; *Paris-Underground,* by Etta Shiber; *c/o Postmaster,* by Corporal Thomas St. George; *The Battle Is the Payoff,* by Ralph Ingersoll; and *Taps for Private Tussie,* by Jesse Stuart.

Among the major titles missing from that list are three Pulitzer choices for the year—Upton Sinclair's *Dragons' Teeth* (fiction), Esther Forbes' *Paul Revere and the World He Lived In* (history), and Samuel Eliot Morison's *Admiral of the Ocean Sea* (biography)—as well as such widely popular works of fiction as Lloyd C. Douglas's *The Robe,* Louis Bromfield's *Mrs. Parkington,* and Betty Smith's *A Tree Grows in Brooklyn.* Nor does it include a phenomenal holdover from the previous year that still held most of the reading public in a state of mirthful hysterics, *See Here, Private Hargrove,* by an authentic GI of the same name.

If you didn't read books or magazines—and even if you did—you *had* to listen to the radio. Everybody did, if not for fun and cultural uplift, then to get the news "every hour on the hour." On a summer's day when windows were open you could walk around the block and not miss a line when an important program was being broadcast. Radio had entered its "golden age" in the mid-thirties when, institutionally speaking, it was still in knee pants. By 1943 it had become a billion-dollar enterprise that was vital to the war front and the home front alike—an instant channel of military and diplomatic communication and the ubiquitous conveyor of news, entertainment, and solace to the multitude. (Television, it should be remembered, was still in the obstetrical wards of RCA and other developers.)

Commercial broadcasting was in the hands of three national networks —CBS, NBC, and Blue (later to become ABC)—and some 900 standard broadcast stations, and their output was heard on an estimated 60 million home and automobile receivers. In addition, the Armed Forces Radio Service transmitted many of the regular programs to just about every corner of the world where American GIs were sweating out the war.

Except for the news programs, what one heard on the radio in a typical war year like 1943 was pretty much what one had become accustomed to—or addicted to—in the years before the war. The show scripts were war-angled and the comics' gags had a GI twist, but beyond that nothing much had changed. Night after night in their appointed time slots there turned up such sturdy old crowd pleasers as *Amos and Andy, Fibber McGee and Molly, Vic and Sade, Lum n' Abner, The Lone Ranger, Charlie Chan, Charlie McCarthy,* Fred Allen, Jack Benny, Bob Hope, Bing Crosby, Kate Smith, Connie Boswell, and others of that rich vintage. All the Big Bands were there throbbing with swing: Guy Lombardo, Tommy Dorsey, Fred Waring, Andre Kostelanetz, and for slightly more highbrow tastes, NBC's Symphony of the Air, the New York Philharmonic, the Detroit Symphony, plus, on Saturday afternoons, live performances of the Metropolitan Opera Company. Quiz shows were great favorites, with *Information Please* heading the list, as were "think" shows such as *Town Meeting of the Air*. Sports broadcasts were among the most popular of all and the breathless, staccato deliveries of announcers like Ted Husing, Red Barber, and Clem McCarthy—"direct from the press box at Yankee Stadium" or "ringside" or "at Churchill Downs"— were as familiar as any voices on the air.

Radio never let you forget there was a war going on. One way or another, in jest or sober homily, that fact was woven into practically every program. Many of the big variety shows were, from time to time, broadcast directly from an Army camp with the cheers and wolf whistles of the GI audience loudly audible in the background. "Charlie McCarthy," the bumptious and irreverent ventriloquist's dummy who had clung to the top ratings for years, was made an "honorary" Sergeant in the Air Force and then heedlessly went on to accept an "honorary" commission in the Marines. When his duplicity was exposed he made a shambles of the resulting "court martial"—broadcast live from Stockton Field, California, with Colonel Jimmy Stewart in the role of the hapless prosecutor. War themes and slogans, diligently promoted by the OWI, found their way into nearly every major program, if not integrally as a part of the script, then as a "curtain speech," with the leading comic or singer stepping out of character to solemnly urge you to buy war bonds or to make a visit to your local Red Cross blood bank. The sponsors of the programs were specially solicitous in this respect. They spent millions of dollars plugging their virtually unobtainable products with such reminders as this one (repeated ad nauseum) by the American Tobacco Company:—"Lucky Strike GREEN . . . has gone to WAR!" So had most of the Lucky Strikes, whether in a green pack or white. (There is, indeed, "no biz like show biz.")

Whatever its virtues and faults as an entertainment medium, radio reached quick maturity and solid renown during the war years as a news medium. It had been improving its stance and cultivating its talent in this direction since the mid-thirties. In the crisis years of the early forties it was able to dislodge the newspapers as the public's preferred source of news. As one spectacular event after another erupted around the world, radio was the first to report it. As the news tempo accelerated, the networks and major stations matched its pace by extending the hours devoted to newscasts: By 1943 the average was on the order of one-quarter of total broadcast time, and many stations had adopted a standing policy of "news every hour on the hour."

Meanwhile, the networks had sent their own correspondents to the war fronts and to foreign capitals—first-rate reporters like Eric Sevareid, Edward R. Murrow, Richard Hottelet, Larry LeSueur—whose voices from far-off places like Australia, Burma, Algeria, London, or somewhere on the high seas came squawkily via shortwave into millions of living rooms each night.

Backing them up on the home front, and more often than not running with the ball themselves, was a growing company of commentators and news analysts whose job it was to put things end to end so that they made sense. Often they did not succeed, tripping over their vanity and prejudices, which is an occupational hazard not restricted to radio journalism. The scales were tolerably balanced, however, by others with a more professional and objective view of their mission. Good or bad, there were a dozen or more whose nightly roundups and assessments of the news carried the weight of gospel for their faithful followers, among them William L. Shirer, H. V. Kaltenborn, Lowell Thomas, Gabriel Heatter, Fulton Lewis, Raymond Gram Swing, and, preeminent in the field until he was tapped to head the OWI in the summer of 1942, Elmer Davis.

Taking it all together, the war imparted to radio's "golden age" a becoming platinum rinse. And just in time, because its junior sibling, television, was hovering just offstage waiting to move in and take over.

In the world of sports, manpower and logistics gave the entrepreneurs a hard time of it but otherwise they did quite well. Throughout 1943 the ball parks, the prize rings, and the racetracks drew record crowds and record gate receipts. The draft bit heavily into the talent rosters—some 1,000 professional baseball players went into uniform between 1941 and 1945—but there were enough athletes with dependents, flat feet, and other military disqualifications, or who were below or above the draft age, to flesh out the major schedules and attractions. The Brooklyn Dodgers, for example, fielded a team in 1943 with half a dozen oldsters past 40 in the lineup but managed to finish third in the National League. All the major league teams survived by somewhat the same stratagem, but many minor league teams—and the leagues with them—were obliged to give up. Similarly, some 300 colleges canceled their football schedules for 1943 because of the player drain, but most of the Big Ten and Ivy League teams survived in relatively good shape. Their good fortune was due in many instances to the influx of thousands of students under the Navy's V-12 training program which put many seasoned players back on the campus.

Joe Lewis, the reigning heavyweight champion, was a Sergeant in the Army, and most of the other qualified ring fighters were also in uniform. The promoters gamely made do with what they had, charging top prices and reaping a rich harvest in the process. Mike Jacobs, the New

York impresario, staged 22 ring shows during 1943 drawing over 320,000 customers and $1,136,000 at the box office. "The public paid uncomplainingly and asked for more," according to Dan Parker, sports editor of the *Daily Mirror*. "Could he help it if people would pay Tunny-Dempsey prices to see two Quaker elders having a go at it with pillows?" A feature match in San Francisco that year had to be called off when the doctors discovered at the weigh-in that one of the contestants had a glass eye.

The racetracks set the most dazzling pace of all, enjoying records at both the turnstiles and the parimutuel windows during each of the war years until, in January 1945, they were abruptly shut down by the Office of War Mobilization. Their regularly jam-packed parking lots, in the estimate of War Mobilizer James F. Byrnes, were prima facie evidence of mass violation of the gasoline and rubber conservation rules and also a probable factor in the high rate of absenteeism from war jobs. Whether Mr. Byrnes was right or wrong, there was no question but that the racing fever was running at a high pitch. In 1943, for example, the three New York tracks—Jamaica, Belmont Park, and Aqueduct—ran up two new season records of their own: combined attendance of 3.5 million and gross wagers of $285 million. The story was much the same in most of the other horse parks around the country.

Who won? Well, almost by force of habit, the New York Yankees won the 1943 World Series—their seventh championship in eight years—taking four out of five games from the St. Louis Cardinals. Most valuable player awards went that year to Stan Musial of the Cards and Spurgeon Chandler of the Yankees. Notre Dame was the top-rated collegiate football team for the year, winning 9 of its 10 games and rolling up 340 points to 63 for the opposition. Navy beat Army 13–0, and Georgia beat UCLA 9–0 in the Rose Bowl—played at Durham, North Carolina, because of a wartime ban on large assemblages on the West Coast. In professional football, the Chicago Bears (Sid Luckman et al.) trounced the championship Washington Redskins (Sammy Baugh et al.) 41–21. The fastest horse on the turf in 1943 was Count Fleet, the first three-year-old in history to sweep five major-stake races. Exhibition golf and tennis were quiescent that year since most of the major competitions had been suspended "for the duration." Similarly, boxing exhibitions were for kicks and money alone since the war had put a "freeze" on recognized titles.[3]

VII

Wartime energies which could not be drawn off by going into uniform or by holding down a defense job found an outlet in the varied programs of the Office of Civilian Defense. For a stay-at-home, it was the most convenient and visible way of doing your bit to win the war.

A familiar figure on the home front was the OCD air raid warden in his white helmet and armband and a bulky gas mask slung about his neck, who rapped on your door at night to inform you that a sliver of light was showing through your blackout curtains, who manned the sand piles and the first aid stations and the public air raid shelters during air raid drills, and who stood lonely nocturnal watches on rooftops ready to sound the alarm at the first approach of enemy planes. He was a neighbor, in all probability, and his wife might have signed on as a driver in an OCD motor pool or to help out one day a week in an OCD child care center for the children of working mothers, while his teenage youngsters did their patriotic stint as members of the OCD Junior Service Corps.

There were some eight to ten million OCD volunteers enrolled in a number of such home-defense programs, organized all the way down to the neighborhood and block level. Many were imbued, at the outset at least, with the uncompromising zeal of their chief, New York's Mayor Fiorello H. LaGuardia, whom the President had picked to head OCD. Characteristically, the irrepressible "Little Flower" had construed his mandate as guardian of the home front in the most imaginative and expansive terms, inviting the inevitable confusion and backlash. Some OCD "block captains" correspondingly envisioned themselves as neighborhood commissars.

The fortunate reality was that OCD was an overelaborate response to a false alarm. It was hastily put together in the spring of 1941, fashioned as a shield to avert the horrors to civilian life that were being enacted in Western Europe and in England. The Japanese attack on Pearl Harbor and the mounting virulence of Nazi submarine warfare in the coastal waters of the Atlantic made the OCD's mission seem even more imperative. Who could be sure in those first months of 1942 that our cities would not be shelled and bombed, or that fifth columnists would not spread fear and panic among our people?

The OCD's response was a feverish one to prepare mass evacuation and emergency feeding plans; to mount guards (armed only with flashlights and police whistles) at reservoirs and power stations; to enforce blackouts and dimouts, particularly in the most vulnerable coastal cities; to establish air raid shelters in downtown buildings, schools, and subways. A huge shelter was dug in the north lawn of the White House and thousands of homeowners followed OCD do-it-yourself instructions for converting a corner of their basement into shelters and stocking them with canned food, water, and medical supplies. Doctors and nurses and auxiliary police and fire fighters were recruited and trained and organized into standby cadres against the coming of another Day of Infamy. For a time at least, OCD offered challenge and excitement. It seemed to answer the almost universal urge of the noncombatant to get a piece of the action, however minor.

But of course that second Day of Infamy never came. A Japanese submarine lobbed a few shells harmlessly onto the California coast one night

in 1942, and there were innumerable air raid scares there and elsewhere—
Trenton, New Jersey, was seized in brief panic one day when edgy citizens
mistook the fire siren for a "red" air raid signal—but all such occurrences
were false alarms. Gradually it became clear that our enemies were too
heavily engaged elsewhere to send an invasion force across thousands of
miles of ocean to attack the North American continent.

The tensions that had supported OCD wound down, and some of its
"morale building" activities, in which Eleanor Roosevelt had taken a
keen interest (she was briefly a duly accredited assistant chairman) began
to draw ridicule and harsh criticism. In setting up the OCD appropriation
for 1943, Congress, in an ill-deserved and ungallant rebuke to the chagrined
First Lady, specifically forbade it to engage in "instruction in physical
fitness by dances, fan dancing, street shows, theatrical performances, or
other public entertainments." By mid-1944 OCD had withered in public
esteem, LaGuardia and Mrs. Roosevelt had withdrawn their leadership,
the air raid wardens had turned in their white helmets (or hung them nos-
talgically among their trophies), and the business of civilian defense had
been relegated to a small, caretaker bureaucracy.

Like travel insurance, OCD was invaluable while danger lurked—
every prudent person wanted it—but worthless once the end of the journey
was in sight.[4]

VIII

The quality of life on the home front displayed many hues. The color
of life was unmistakably khaki. It clothed more bodies than any other
shade, and symbolically it was the background tint against which most of
what was important in the world was happening. It was the color of war
in far-off places; it was the color of political tensions in Washington and
London and Moscow; it was the color of a nation's collective gripes over
myriad discomforts; and it was the color of the wayward destiny that overhung the lives of millions of young men and of their families and wives
and sweethearts. The steady, inexorable transmutation of civilians into
soldiers—or sailors or Marines—did more to disrupt the familiar contexts
of life on the home front than any other aspect of the war. At every level,
the draft was central to the khaki syndrome.

There were 10 million men in uniform in the summer of 1943, about
three-fourths of them in the Army. They were still piling in at the rate of
about 100,000 a month, draining out of the schools and offices and off
the farms. Around 2.5 million already had been dispatched to the war
zones overseas, and more were being shipped out as rapidly as they could
complete their 8 to 10 months of training and transport could be found
for them. Since the beginning of selective service in October 1940, some
31 million men between the ages of 18 and 45 had been registered

although actual call-ups seldom reached those above 35. Now, in 1943, there were no more mass registrations: a youngster was legally bound to report to his draft board as soon as he turned 18. Also, his chances of being inducted had risen. In the face of a 40 percent rejection rate for physical and mental disabilities and other deferable causes, many of the standards of acceptability had been lowered, and even fathers and family breadwinners in the higher age brackets were being denied dependency exemptions. Clearly now, those familiar recruiting posters that declared "Uncle Sam Wants YOU!" meant exactly what they said.

The visual impact of so many uniforms wherever one turned—on the downtown streets, on the trains and buses, in the hotel lobbies, the movies, the churches—induced a subtle psychological reaction, an unarticulated tension and awareness of crisis. Though the novelty of the experience had long since worn off, it was not something to which you easily became accustomed or insensitive. The insistent, subdued presence of khaki (or blue or olive drab)—the constant reminder that life and freedom and happiness throughout the world were in danger—almost became a sentient being in itself.

But this was not the feeling you got from the kids ("the kids," in the vernacular of the times, meaning any GI below the rank of Sergeant or petty officer but including Lieutenants, second and junior grade). Collectively, their mood and demeanor seemed not greatly different from what it had been when they were wearing gray flannels or dungarees. Perhaps the boisterous ones were a little more reflective and the reflective ones a little more boisterous, for their lives had but lately been wrenched about and compensating reaction was inevitable. But they bore in their faces and behavior no trace either of dread or of high and knightly mission. If there was a predominant characteristic about them it probably was one of pride and self-esteem, a faintly arrogant cockiness. Some, of course, never lost the bewildered glaze of the bumpkin with which the Lord had endowed them, and never would. But by and large, the typical GI Joe, having survived the humiliation of his first few weeks as a "jeep" or "yard bird" and being hollered at by contemptuous noncoms and surmounting the pangs of simple homesickness, came in due time to think of himself as a man among men. He was in good health, he had more muscles than he probably knew about, and the enforced neatness in his appearance—shoes shined, trousers pressed, jacket buttoned—gave him a sense of well-being he may never have known before. In spite of the mandatory bitching over the fate that had put him where he was, he was proud of his uniform, proud of his outfit, proud of his country. In some private corner of his mind he may even have thought a bit about *why* he was where he was; how he, one guy among millions, related to a world seized in conflict.

There were more blacks in uniform this time than ever before, and more of them with officers' insignia on their shoulders. Most were in the

Infantry, the other branches of the service managing by one dodge or another to maintain an almost inviolate all-white policy. Segregation by units was still the practice if not the rule, and black troops customarily got the grubbier, more menial assignments. Friction flared sporadically with harrowing implications, and the national conscience began to feel the first pinpricks of shame at such overt injustice and discrimination. The clue to this guilt feeling was often expressed in the embarrassed over-solicitousness with which some community institutions—churches, hospitality committees—tried to make the black soldiers who came their way "feel at home." One of a dozen symtomatic anecdotes which went the rounds told of a society dowager who informed the commanding officer of a nearby camp that she would be pleased to have "six lonely young soldiers, gentiles of course" as her weekend guests. When the group arrived, all blacks, she drew back from the front door and gasped, "There must be some mistake!"

"No, ma'm," the leader told her with a mischievous grin, "Colonel Ginsburg don't make no mistakes."

The ambivalence of the black's role in the war—"good enough to die for you but not good enough to sit at your table"—troubled the conscience of the home front with the annoying persistence of a pebble in the shoe. Of course, one *could* stop, take off his shoe, and remove the offending pebble, but it might make him miss his train. He would attend to it later, if it was still there. So with the race question: Something would *have* to be done about it once the war was over. . . .

A totally new phenomenon was women in the service and uniform of the country's fighting forces.* There were WACs for the Army, WAVES for the Navy, SPARs for the Coast Guard, and Women Marines who somehow missed, or avoided acquiring a handy nickname. There were also WASPs—Women Airforce Service Pilots—whose status was that of auxiliaries rather than bona fide members of the Army Air Force, but whose mission as noncombat fliers and whose snappy uniforms gave them a quite special elan.

Congress authorized the enlistment of women in the spring of 1942 after a spirited fight. The logic of the case was inescapable—thousands of able-bodied GIs were tied down to desk and service and even mechanical jobs which women could perform as well or better than they—but the idea that young females should be officially introduced into the rough and celibate domain of army camps and naval stations (the WAVES never did go to sea) was socially and morally intolerable to many legislators. Having acceded to the inevitable, however, they went on to set another precedent, the commissioning of Mrs. Oveta Culp Hobby of Texas as Colonel, U.S. Air

---

* In the First World War uniformed "Yeomanettes" served in a clerical capacity in some Navy offices, but as volunteers rather than on an enlistment basis.

Force, and Miss Mildred McAfee of Barnard College as Captain, U.S. Naval Reserve, as commanding officers respectively of the WAC and the WAVES.

Within a year there were approximately 100,000 women in uniform. Somehow, the couturières hired by the Navy's Bureau of Personnel and the Army's Quartermaster Corps never quite succeeded in combining feminine chic with the utilitarian specifications of government issue. In the dress and winter uniforms, at least, the dominant stylistic note seemed to be a tidy lumpiness that emphasized shoulders instead of bosoms, calves instead of thighs. The women endured a period of good-natured kidding as to whether their undies were also government issue, whether they could requisition a girdle as necessary equipment, and was it really a fact that they were issued contraceptives and taught how to disable a male with a knee to the groin. But like their masculine fellows-in-arms, they had pride in themselves and their service and impressed this fact on the home front. Their femininity gave a refreshing touch to the khaki montage.

At the center of the canvas always, however, was the draftee. He might be a lad just out of high school, a buttoned-down young businessman with a wife and maybe children, a hustler with a police record and a knack for getting out of jams—except for this one—or he might even be a celebrity whose face adorned billboards or the sports pages. That letter that said, "Greetings: You are hereby instructed . . . ," was thrust with studied impartiality into the mail slots of the humble and the haughty alike when their number came up. And in the drafty, inhospitable armory or ex-warehouse that was the local induction center, they were all reduced to a common denominator of un-persons as they stood around in shorts and socks to be quizzed, prodded, sampled, and evaluated like a shipment of livestock—which, in cold reality, they were. Or, in official Army jargon, "bodies."

There were 20 classifications into which they could be slotted when the day-long ordeal was over, from 1-A, "available for military service," to 4-F, "physically, mentally, or morally unfit for service." In between was a whole spectrum of deferrable alternatives ranging from conscientious objection, to employment in an essential civilian capacity, to hardship family dependency, but by mid-1943 the authorities were becoming ever more vigilant in narrowing these loopholes for the physically fit. The result was a succession of little human dramas often enacted in full view of the other bodies standing in line—the confession of embarrassing domestic secrets by a young family man, the angry insistence by another that a medically undiagnosible backache was both real and chronic, or, in occasional contrast, the tearful entreaty of a youngster to be let into the Army in spite of flat fleet or some other minor deformity. "Look," he might say in a panic of discouragement, "I played football all through high school. I can march or run or jump as well as any of these other guys." Not everyone by any means faced the draft with fear and loathing.

The 1-As usually had a 10-day grace period in which to tidy up their affairs, say their good-byes, and to make such psychological preparations as they could for the plunge into Army life. On the day appointed they turned up, 100 or so at a time, at their designated point of departure, each with suitcase or bundle and sometimes with a wife or parents in tow. In smaller communities where such departures were not everyday occurrences, the city fathers and the high school band might turn out, too, "to honor our sons going into the service of their country."

Whatever the setting, however, the mood was usually the same. There was a forced gaiety and some brittle horseplay back and forth among the men, and maybe some tears from those who had come to say farewell. Conversation ran out, and the standing and waiting induced fidgets. Then a deceptively solicitous Sergeant with papers in his hand showed up (to be on the safe side, at that time you addressed any man in uniform without bars on his shoulder as "Sergeant") and shepherded them aboard the waiting buses or train, destined for a far-off place euphemistically called a "replacement center"—Dix, Meade, Benning, Pendleton. Basic training, $50 a month, and Sergeants with forked tongues. . . .

This was it—at last. The home front was behind you, for the duration. The world of khaki was no longer a mirage, it was a reality. Some of the guys aboard were already singing what seemed like a proper theme song and you joined in. It was not much more than a jingle set to the tune of an ordinary bugle call, and it went like this:

> *You're in the Army now,*
> *You're not behind the plow;*
> *You son of a bitch, you'll never get rich,*
> *You're in the Army now.*

Dontcha know there's a war on?

No one in the privileged sanctuary of the home front had much trouble remembering. The feel of it, if not its sights and sounds, was everywhere in the quality and color of life.

8

The Grand Design

The state of the union message which President Roosevelt delivered at the opening session of the Seventy-seventh Congress in January 1941, was an uniquely important document. It marked a bold step out of the cloistered nationalism where we had sought shelter for more than a century, across the threshold of an affirmative and dynamic internationalism.

The main thrust of his speech was to give life to the concept of lend-lease, a program that would soon involve us directly in support of the war against the Axis, both in Asia and Europe. Such a step, formally taken and publicly proclaimed while we were still at peace, was unprecedented in our foreign relations.

But equally significant, and almost overshadowed by the dramatic impact of the lend-lease idea, was the peroration of that speech. In fewer than 100 words, Roosevelt enunciated a moral base not only for our immediate aid to the anti-Axis forces but for our intentions and aspirations in respect to the world at large when the war was ended. What he did, in essence, was to revive the theme of global unity with which Woodrow Wilson had split the country apart 20 years earlier, and which still flared as one of the most divisive issues in American political life. Standing upon the rostrum of the House of Representatives and facing a closely attentive assemblage of legislators, Cabinet officers, Ambassadors, and gallery spectators (including the widow of Woodrow Wilson), the President spoke somberly but with ringing conviction in the tone of his splendid voice:

In the future days which we seek to make secure, we look forward to a world founded upon four essential freedoms.

The first is freedom of speech and expression—everywhere in the world.

The second is freedom for every person to worship God in his own way —everywhere in the world.

The third is freedom from want—which, in world terms, means economic understandings which will secure to every nation everywhere a healthy peace-time life for its inhabitants.

The fourth is freedom from fear—which, translated into international terms, means a worldwide reduction in armaments to such a point and in such thorough fashion that no nation anywhere will be in a position to commit an act of physical aggression against any neighbor.

Until such a peace is possible, the President concluded, the American people had "unalterably set their faces" against the tyranny of the so-called new order (of the Axis powers), and adopted a policy of "all-inclusive national defense," support for those resisting aggression, and opposition to "a peace dictated by aggressors and supported by appeasers."

This could be read as no more than moral sermonizing, a forensic device that Roosevelt often employed to good effect. Aside from the lend-lease portion, he enlarged his ideas with no specifications as to how his goals were to be won: Indeed, he had not then formulated them in detail even in his own mind. But they contained the seeds of the "grand design" —an effective worldwide instrumentality for peace and justice—that would lie very close to his heart and command much of his energies for the remainder of his life.

II

The first two weeks of August 1941, were a period of puzzlement and deepening mystery in Washington. On Saturday, the third, the President cheerfully informed the press that he was going to "take some time off" for sailing and fishing, his favorite means of recreation. The next day he boarded the Presidential yacht, *Potomac,* at New London, Connecticut, with a small party that included Princess Martha of Norway and her two children. They were observed cruising idly in the waters around Martha's Vineyard and the next day they put into port at South Dartmouth, where the royal visitors came ashore. The *Potomac,* with FDR on the fantail in shirtsleeves and a floppy cloth hat that was his favorite seagoing costume, put out to sea again for, it was explained, "some serious fishing."

Thereafter the yacht and its passengers dropped from sight as precipitously as if they had been sent to the bottom by a torpedo. That eventuality was minimized, however, as occasional and uninformative radio reports were received over the next several days from the *Potomac,* "somewhere at sea," blithely intimating that the President was enjoying his vacation. And by what seemed to be more than mere happenstance, London noted the unexplained absence from view at about the same time of Prime Minister Churchill and some of his key military and ministerial aides. Thus, the *Times* reported in a front page dispatch on August 11:

For the second day, the Navy Department received no report today from the yacht *Potomac,* on which President Roosevelt set sail on a cruise a week ago. . . . The President continued to keep the Capitol in the dark as to his whereabouts and, up to the time when reports from the *Potomac* ceased altogether, only scanty information came through as to the activity of the party aboard. . . .

In Britain, mystery was deliberately maintained as to the whereabouts of Prime Minister Churchill and of Harry Hopkins, the lend-lease administrator, who are officially declared to be together. . . .

Rumors persist that the President transferred to an escorted cruiser to go to a rendezvous with Mr. Churchill soon after boarding the *Potomac* eight days ago.

The rumors were borne out with resounding emphasis four days later. As heralded by the *Times* in an eight-column streamer across the top of its front page on August 15—

ROOSEVELT, CHURCHILL DRAFT 8 PEACE AIMS, PLEDGING DESTRUCTION OF NAZI TYRANNY; JOINT STEPS BELIEVED CHARTED AT PARLEY

The two leaders had contrived their historic rendezvous with almost flawless secrecy: Fewer than a dozen members of the Cabinet and the White House staff knew what was afoot when the President set off on his "vacation" that Sunday in early August. Two nights later, however, after its deceptive maneuvers in the waters of Buzzards Bay, the *Potomac* pulled alongside the heavy destroyer *Augusta,* laying to a few miles off Cape Cod, and Roosevelt was hoisted aboard. On hand to welcome him were a dozen of his top aides, including the Army Chief of Staff, the Chief of Naval Operations, and Under Secretary of State Sumner Welles. With an extensive escort to protect against U-boat attack, the *Augusta* steamed northward and two nights later dropped anchor in a sheltered cove on the desolate coast of Newfoundland, near the little fishing village of Argentia. Out of the morning mists of the following day there loomed the huge bulk of H.M.S. *Prince of Wales,* Britain's newest and proudest battleship, bearing Prime Minister Churchill and his party, including a desperately seasick Harry Hopkins. (Hopkins had been on a special mission to Moscow and flew into London with little time to spare before making connections with the Churchill party. The transfer was so rushed that he forgot to pay his hotel bill and tips at Claridge's and had to radio Ambassador Winant asking him to attend to these amenities for him.)

Churchill and his group were welcomed aboard the *Augusta* with a minimum of pomp and ceremony, but with warm personal greetings all around. "At last we've gotten together," he said grasping Roosevelt's hand.

Roosevelt had sought this meeting for a number of reasons. For more than a year he and the Prime Minister (using the whimsical pesudonym, "Former Naval Person") had been communicating volubly via letter, cable, and transatlantic telephone. It now seemed desirable to put their relationship on a more intimately personal basis, a decision in which Churchill enthusiastically concurred. Another pressing consideration was that Russia had now come into the war as a full-scale belligerent, and her needs for munitions out of the lend-lease basket had to be incorporated along with those of Britain. Stalin had already begun to clamor for a ground assault against the Reich from the west to relieve the intolerable Nazi pressure on his own frontier. The question of how much of their limited capabilities the British and the Americans could afford to divert to the Soviets was clouded by speculation over whether that nation could survive much longer as a fighting force in the face of the punishing Nazi offensive.

Roosevelt was also deeply concerned over whether the British had, or soon might, enter into some secret agreements with the Russians involving postwar territorial arrangements. Such arrangements had long been a part of British imperial strategy, and Russia at the moment held disputed sovereignty over Finland, the Baltic States, and a large part of Poland as reward for her erstwhile collaboration with Hitler. If such secret deals had in fact been made, or were contemplated by the Anglo-Soviet Pact which the two nations had initialed in July, they would, Roosevelt feared, hopelessly complicate future peacemaking efforts. This was one of the roadblocks over which the League of Nations had stumbled 20 years earlier, and the President was determined to avoid, if he could, a repetition of that error.

In sounding out Churchill about their possible rendezvous at sea, Roosevelt alluded to such fears in quite explicit fashion. He then went on to say that he thought it would be important for the two of them to agree on a declaration of broad objectives that would "hold out hope for the enslaved peoples of the world" with the promise of a postwar world order based on principles of universal freedom and justice. Churchill responded with an emphatic disclaimer of any agreements about territories with the Russians, secret or otherwise, and gave cordial endorsement to the idea of a declaration of joint principles for preserving the peace. In fact, he sent along a draft statement which he offered as a working paper on the subject.

Several privileged eyewitnesses have described in fascinating detail this singular encounter at sea of two of the world's greatest potentates. The weather during their three days together was sparkling and crisp. Shoreward, the rugged coast of Newfoundland retreated in undulating ridges of forested greenery, suggesting a primeval isolation from the fervid concerns of statesmen and warriors. Seaward, the two formidable warships lay at anchor near one another in the quiet waters of Argentia Bay while farther out toward the horizon the shapes of other warships and occasional aircraft came and went on their ceaseless protective patrol. Launches plied back and forth between the *Augusta* and the *Prince of Wales* as first one ship and then the other acted as host for the varied business sessions and the more convivial dinner meetings. The mood among the whole company on these occasions was marked by cordiality and mutual respect, coupled with a sense of historical significance.

A highlight of these meetings—in an emotional sense at least—was a joint church service on Sunday morning on the deck of the *Prince of Wales*. An Anglican and an Episcopal chaplain conducted the service together from a chancel draped with the Union Jack and the Stars and Stripes. Crowded among the gun turrets and the warlike deck gear were hundreds of British Tars and American Bluejackets, and in the foreground the very cream of their two countries' political, military, and naval leadership. As all joined in such familiar old hymns as "Onward Christian Soldiers" and "For Those in Peril on the Sea," a few vagrant tears spilled down Churchill's cheek. As he, himself, recalled years later: "Every word seemed to stir the heart. It was a great hour to live. Nearly half those who sang were soon to die." (The *Prince of Wales* was sunk with heavy loss of life by Japanese war planes in the South China Sea in January 1942).

Quickly evident to those at Argentia was the growing bond of friendship between the two principals. Both Roosevelt and Churchill were men of immense pride, even of vanity, conscious of their statures and their responsibilities. Yet each was drawn by the other into a state of relaxed comradeship, of candor and mutual confidence, of occasional banter and leg-pulling. Their differences were many; each was stubborn, and each had a demanding constituency back home to whom he must answer; but they managed to find their way around obstacles without lasting abrasions.

Not the least of these obstacles arose from the fact that Churchill had come to this conference with a different set of priorities from Roosevelt. For one thing, he was most anxious to have the United States take a firmly belligerent stand against Japanese aggression in Southeast Asia, where Hong Kong and Indochina were being threatened. Britain was in no position now to defend its interests in that quarter alone, and he felt that some timely sabre-rattling by the Americans might dampen Japan's reckless ardor. The Prime Minister was also apprehensive about the potential drain Russia's demands for arms might put on his own country's needs from the American arsenal. He was more suspicious than Roosevelt about Stalin's integrity as an ally and about the staying power of the Red Army. Finally, he was eager not only to increase the volume of American armaments for Britain under lend-lease but to improve their delivery by greater use of American warships in convoy duty. As to the joint declaration on peace aims, it was fairly far down on Churchill's agenda, a worthy but not pressing lagniappe to the main business at hand.

Roosevelt's options in most of these matters were more limited than Churchill's. His government was technically still at peace; he could not cloak his actions in the guise of wartime emergencies. Neither could he ignore the realities of domestic politics, of the potent capacity of the isolationists and other opposition blocs to thwart or to reverse his purposes. He firmly resisted the Prime Minister's urging for a more visible and emphatic American posture against Japan. Secretary Hull seemed to be staving off a crisis there through the tedium of diplomacy, and a show of belligerency now might hasten rather than delay a climactic showdown. Roosevelt was more disposed than Churchill to take Stalin at his word and to divert more supplies to the Russians while striving to build up deliveries to England. He would not, however, risk sending American warships on convoy duty beyond Iceland, as the British urged him to do. What he was willing to do was to redouble production efforts to supply Britain's ever growing list of requirements for planes, tanks, and guns.

Even when, on their last day together, the two leaders got around to the final drafting of their joint declaration on peace aims, Roosevelt was more hindered by reservations than Churchill. The President's intention was that their historic meeting be climaxed by a ringing and enduring testament of their purpose to achieve a new world order of peace and justice. This had been Wilson's goal, and now it was his. But he was determined at the same time that it be a broad statement of principles, unburdened by details of method or precise objectives on which his critics might seize.

Churchill's initial draft had been worked over several times by Welles and others, and in its penultimate phase Roosevelt now insisted on some further changes. He was concerned, among other things, that no one should be able to read into it—as some of the isolationists were certain to do—intimations of any "secret commitments" that would lead the country into war. He was even more concerned that the document not be used to raise the cry that he was attempting to sneak the country into a revived League of Nations—which, in the broadest sense, *was* his ultimate purpose. One paragraph in the draft spoke of achieving the desired goals through "an effective international organization." The President balked at that. The phrase could too easily be translated as "League of Nations," he said, putting a possibly lethal weapon in the hands of the isolationists. Churchill observed testily that their statement of principles would be meaningless if there was no instrumentality for its fulfillment. Roosevelt agreed, but he insisted that the political realities of his situation had to be observed. It was his idea moreover, he said, that in the immediate aftermath of the war their two nations would act as global policemen to maintain the peace, and that some permanent and democratic arrangement not unlike the League would, at some later date, evolve out of that. In the end, the offensive phrase was reworded to read, ". . . pending the establishment of a wider and permanent system of general security"—

which, for all its ambiguity, came down to about the same thing as the original.

Churchill was irked at such semantic doodling, but he went along in good grace. He regarded the document as little more than a pious gesture in any event, a concession to his friend's earnest idealism. Roosevelt, for his part, felt that he had put more building blocks into his grand design at the same time that he had disarmed his enemies.

In its final form, the paper expressed the concepts if not the language that Roosevelt had enunciated in his "Four Freedoms" speech eight months earlier.* The two leaders initialed their joint declaration (later to be dignified with the title "Atlantic Charter") late on the afternoon of Monday, August 11, without pomp or ceremony. It was turned over to the *Augusta*'s radio operator for transmission to Washington and London and marked for simultaneous release by the two governments (10 A.M. Washington time) on Thursday, the fourteenth. Consisting of nine relatively brief paragraphs, its preamble read as follows:

> Joint Declaration of the President of the United States of America and the Prime Minister, Mr. Churchill, representing His Majesty's Government in the United Kingdom, being met together, deem it right to make known certain common principles in the national policies of their respective countries on which they base their hopes for a better future for the world.

Thereafter, in the somewhat turgid language of diplomacy, they set forth eight propositions upon which they had agreed. In substance, these asserted that they sought no territorial or other aggrandizement for their respective governments; upheld the right of self-determination by all peoples as to their form of political organization, and their right of equal access to the sources of world trade, raw materials, and the opportunities for social and economic advancement. "After the final destruction of Nazi tyranny," the statement continued, the signatories looked forward to the establishment of a secure peace for all men and unrestricted freedom of the seas. They called also for a general abandonment of the use of force and, "pending the establishment of a wider and permanent system of general security," for complete disarmament of those nations guilty of, or likely to commit, aggression.

As already noted, news of the Atlantic conference and of the charter, coming after more than a week of suspense and speculation, broke upon the world with high dramatic impact. It was proclaimed in blaring head-

---

* Churchill was later pleased to assume credit for the document, thus: "Considering all the tales of my reactionary, Old World outlook, and the pain this is said to have caused the President, I am glad it should be on record that the substance and spirit of what came to be called the 'Atlantic Charter' was in its first draft a British production cast in my own words." (Churchill, *The Grand Alliance,* Houghton Mifflin, 1951, p. 434.)

lines in the newspapers and in excited bulletins and commentaries on the radio. Public reaction was preponderantly favorable. To the man in the street the statement was just what it purported to be, an inspiring affirmation of democratic faith in opposition to the evils of totalitarianism. Many spoke hopefully of it as a "peace offensive," others as the *"Mein Kampf* of the democracies." The *Times,* in a lead editorial titled, "Rendezvous With Destiny," said: "In the play of would-be gods and self-elected giants, they [Roosevelt and Churchill] are figures representing the only two great powers left in the world that speak with human voices in the name of the people."

But the dissenters had their say, too. John T. Flynn, columnist and New York City chairman of America First, derided the declaration as "a cover-up statement," and demanded that, "they should be frank and tell the American people why they did meet and what they actually decided to do. What we would like to know is what Churchill demanded and what Roosevelt promised." This expressed the stubbornly held suspicion among isolationists that the President had bound the country to Britain's fate through "secret commitments." (As a matter of historical fact, there were none.) Others, like Socialist leader Norman Thomas, saw it as a devious approach to war-making "without consulting Congress." Senator David I. Walsh, powerful chairman of the Naval Affairs Committee, accused the President of exceeding his Constitutional prerogative as no President before him had done. And the *Chicago Tribune* saw in it further confirmation of its belief in Roosevelt's traitorous subservience to British ends by reminding its readers—again—that the President was the grandson of "that James Roosevelt . . . who was a Tory of New York during the Revolution and took the oath of allegiance to the British King."

These were not inconsiderable voices and Roosevelt gave heed to them. It was a part of his political genius that he knew when to keep his head down and when to put on a show. This was a time for caution. During the very days that he had been at Argentia, a bill to extend the military draft for an additional year had squeaked through a balky House of Representatives by a margin of one vote. So for the next several weeks after his return he played down the Charter and its implications, and warned his aides as well against extravagant public elucidations of it. He would let the fires of dissent sputter out for lack of fuel. Meanwhile, along with Churchill, he quietly encouraged Stalin, Chiang Kai-shek, and leaders of the British Dominions and the Polish government-in-exile to add their endorsements. He extended a similar but unsuccessful invitation to Pope Pius XII.

Roosevelt's pose of disinterest in the Charter during those weeks was, of course, deliberately deceptive. He had few doubts about its importance, as did most of those closest to him. His admiring friend Felix Frankfurter expressed better than most the consensus of many thoughtful persons on the subject. In a "Dear Frank" letter a few days after the President's return to Washington he wrote:

Not even constant misuse can rob some phrases of their noble meaning. Therefore regard for the truth compels me to say that somewhere in the Atlantic you *did* make history for the world. And like all truly great historic events, it wasn't what was said or done that defined the scope of the achievement. It's always the forces—the impalpable, the spiritual forces, the hopes, the purposes, the dreams and the endeavors—that are released that matter. . . . It was all grandly conceived and finely executed. The deed and the spirit and the invigoration of a common human fraternity in the hearts of men will endure. . . .

The Charter was, indeed, one of the important landmarks in modern history. Its text, adopted almost verbatim, became the common pledge of a 26-nation coalition soon to be brought together and calling itself the United Nations.

This transition was hastily engineered in the weeks immediately following American entry into the war. Churchill and members of his General Staff had flown to Washington a few days before Christmas for conference with their new ally on joint military strategy. He and Roosevelt also determined that there should now be a genuine "grand alliance" binding together all the nations formally at war with the Axis (including nine small Latin American governments which had nominally joined the fight immediately behind the United States). The Charter, they agreed, was the ideal basis for such an alliance. But the transition was not wholly trouble-free.

By sheer inadvertance, the framers of the Charter had omitted religious freedom from their catalogue of goals. This raised a storm, particularly in the United States, where it was interpreted by some as a sly device for gaining the assent of the officially atheistic Soviet Union. Roosevelt denied the implication and set about correcting the oversight. He then found that he had the unexpected problem of persuading the Russian Ambassador, Maxim Litvinov, that adherence to the Charter did not commit his nation to a reversal of its traditional antireligious policy. The phrase "religious freedom," Roosevelt carefully explained (with his tongue in his cheek?), should be taken in broad philosophic sense in which Thomas Jefferson used it, which meant freedom to have no religion at all, if that was one's preference. Such, at least, is the version of the affair as handed on by Harry Hopkins. In any event, Litvinov, skeptical but disarmed, withdrew his objection.

He would not, however, withdraw his objection to the rephrasing of a paragraph which would have admitted de Gaulle's French government-in-exile into the fraternity, since he now suspected all Frenchmen of being Nazi collaborators at heart. Churchill strongly opposed this omission, but lost. He lost also in the tug-of-war with Roosevelt over the status accorded Chiang Kai-shek's China in the arrangement.

Roosevelt felt that the major allies against the Axis should be set apart from the noncombatants within the coalition by the placing of their signatures ahead of the others, who would appear in alphabetical order. He included in the former group the United States, Great Britain, the Soviet Union—and China. Churchill contended heatedly that this was giving the wavering, inept Chiang regime more recognition than it deserved; that moreover it committed the other principals to give material and political support to an almost certain loser in a two-front war against the Japanese, on the one hand, and Communist insurrectionists, on the other. Roosevelt conceded the probable correctness of Churchill's estimate, but he held his ground for two main reasons. First, he envisioned China as a future base for American retaliatory strikes against Japan. Chiang had to be propped up at all costs to prevent the swift fulfillment of Japanese hegemony throughout the Far East. Second, the American people felt a strong sentimental attachment to China going back many generations. They would support any reasonable prospect of making China the preeminent Asian power in the postwar world, and would resent vigorously any apparent collusion to deny her that prospect. It might be many months, the President argued, before any sizable amount of war supplies could be diverted to Chiang's tattered armies, but meanwhile the proud Generalissimo should have the psychological lift of being numbered among the great power leaders.

Churchill grumbled his acquiescence. And so there came into being a pattern of international relationships that was to profoundly influence the future course of the United Nations—the dominance of the Big Four, with a foredoomed China among them.

The drafting of the declaration and the many corollary arrangements necessary for its promulgation were carried out at the White House during Christmas week, interspersed with marathon staff discussions on military affairs. Most of the loose ends had been tidied up by New Year's Eve except for an acceptable name for the coalition. The best anyone had come up with was "The Associated Nations," and all agreed that this was lacking both in punch and precision. Sometime during the night, Roosevelt had an inspiration. Promptly the next morning he had himself wheeled down the hall to his distinguished guest's bedroom. Churchill stepped pink and dripping out of his bath to answer the knock at his door. After an instant of amused embarrassment, the pajamaed President said, "Why don't we call it 'The United Nations'?" "Splendid!" the nude Prime Minister responded, and whipped off from his capacious memory a quatrain from Byron's *Childe Harold* in which the phrase felicitously occurs. (Hopkins, describing this rare historical tableau to friends, said Churchill denied any embarrassment over the encounter, asserting with grave ambiguity: "The Prime Minister of Great Britain has nothing to conceal from the President of the United States.")

That afternoon—January 1, 1942—in a brief ceremony in the President's oval office, the Declaration by The United Nations was formally signed by the President, by the Prime Minister, by Ambassador Litvinov, and by Ambassador T. V. Soong of the Republic of China, in that order— the Big Four. On the following day, at the State Department, representatives of 22 other governments formally at war with the Axis, including the British Dominions, affixed their signatures in strict alphabetical order: Australia, Belgium, Canada, Costa Rica, Cuba, Czechoslovakia, Dominican Republic, El Salvador, Greece, Guatemala, Haiti, Honduras, India, Luxembourg, Netherlands, New Zealand, Nicaragua, Norway, Panama, Poland, South Africa, and Yugoslavia.

The text of this "majestic document," as Churchill called it, was brief. It read as follows:

The Governments signatory hereto,

Having subscribed to a common program of purposes and principles embodied in the Joint Declaration of the President of the United States of America and the Prime Minister of the United Kingdom of Great Britain and Northern Ireland dated August 14, 1941, known as the Atlantic Charter;

Being convinced that complete victory over their enemies is essential to defend life, liberty, independence and religious freedom, and to preserve human rights and justice in their own lands as well as other lands, and that they are now engaged in a common struggle against savage and brutal forces seeking to subjugate the world, DECLARE:

(1) Each Government pledges itself to employ its full resources, military or economic, against those members of the Tripartite Pact and its adherents with which such government is at war.

(2) Each Government pledges itself to cooperate with the governments signatory hereto and not to make a separate armistice or peace with the enemies.

The foregoing declaration may be adhered to by other nations which are, or which may be, rendering material assistance and contributions in the struggle for victory over Hitlerism.

Done at Washington
January First, 1942

So the seed that was the Four Freedoms speech had, in a year almost to the day, become the living embryo of the United Nations. But the historic moment at which this transmutation occurred passed almost unnoticed in the tumult of other events. In this country, people were still reeling from the trauma of Pearl Harbor and being shocked anew almost daily by fresh and terrifying reminders of the kind of war they were in. The Japanese were raging virtually unchecked through the far Pacific. Wake Island had collapsed after a gallant defense on Christmas Eve, Hong

Kong the day following, and Manila, with MacArthur's battered forces trapped in flaming rubble, had fallen on January 2. Across the Atlantic Hitler's armies were snowbound on the Russian front, while Rommel and Montgomery held one another indecisively at bay in North Africa. And in the Atlantic itself, sometimes within sight of the American coast, disaster piled upon disaster as ships and crews were sent to the bottom by U-boats faster than replacements could be found for them.

But if the UN Declaration was heavily overshadowed in the news of the day, its historic significance did not go wholly unrecorded. The *Times* gave this appraisal of it in an editorial two days after the signing:

> The agreement . . . may prove to be as important a political document as any signed in human history. Its moral effect, both within the nations that signed it and within the aggressor nations against which it is directed, will be instantaneous. Its military effects should be felt in the very near future. . . .
>
> To many of the men who signed the pact . . . the grim thought must have come of how different the world would be if such an alliance, backed by such a determination to end aggression, could have been formed only half a dozen years ago. . . . For this new agreement is a real league of nations. . . .[1]

III

Once the UN Declaration was signed and unveiled to the world, the problems of peace and postwar arrangements were temporarily eclipsed by the more immediate problem of fighting and winning the war. During most of 1942 the prospect of victory—certainly of an early victory—were anything but bright. On the U.S. home front the machinery for all-out mobilization creaked and spun its wheels exasperatingly. It often seemed that the "arsenal of democracy" would never amount to much more than a clever slogan. In the Pacific theater American and British forces had, by summer, been sent in pell-mell retreat down through the South China Sea as far as New Guinea. Triumphant Japanese armies swarmed westward through Indochina and Burma to the Indian border. The tragic remnants of MacArthur's troops in the Philippines had finally succumbed to the siege of Bataan, and the General himself, in what seemed almost hopeless defiance, had reestablished his headquarters over 3000 miles away in Australia. Closer to home, the map makers colored all of continental Europe black from the Pyrenees eastward to Stalingrad and "the gates of Moscow," and northward from Greece to the Arctic shores of Scandinavia, to illustrate the enveloping scope of Nazi conquest. British defenders in North Africa had, late in the year, been thrown back some 200 miles inside the borders of Egypt by Rommel's devouring panzers.

Nineteen forty-two was the bleakest year of the war for the proudly proclaimed but inchoate United Nations, a year in which all the gains and glories of conquest seemed to go to their enemies. It was not until late in the year—November 8, precisely—when the first American invaders swarmed ashore in French North Africa, that Allied hopes revived that the tide could be turned in their favor. Once more, the question of how the postwar world was to be ordered began to have some relevance.

The first operational unit of the UN came into being during the spring of 1943. Under United States and British leadership, representatives of the by then 44 signatory nations met for two weeks in May at Hot Springs, Virginia, to consider means of feeding, clothing, sheltering, and otherwise ministering to the basic survival needs primarily of the millions of persons uprooted and devastated by the war, and also of the many more millions worldwide who historically had lived in the shadow of ignorance and starvation. This was in hopeful fulfillment of the UN promise to secure "freedom from want" and it materialized in time in the creation of the United Nations Relief and Rehabilitation Administration and of the Food and Agricultural Organization.

Meanwhile, however, political concerns within the top layer of the coalition were piling up in menacing complexity. Chiefly they were about Russia—that brooding, inscrutable giant of an ally guarding the eastern front who now had managed to pull herself together and to fight back against the invader. Beyond the immediate objective of defeating Hitler, what was Russia after? What were her political and territorial goals in postwar Europe—the Middle East? What spoils and concessions was she going to demand for her sacrifices when victors and vanquished should get together around the peace table? How closely did her ideas of a democratic world order comport with those of other western powers, the Americans and the British in particular? Even under the Czars, Russia had been a closed and enigmatic land. Since the Communist revolution it had walled itself in even more securely, its visage to the outside world hostile, suspicious, withdrawn. Stalin was virtually unknown to other world leaders, and emissaries such as Litvinov and Molotov whom he sent to their councils imparted little in the way of enlightenment or reassurance.

Now, in 1943, with allied power beginning to swing onto the offensive, it became imperative for Washington and London to get from Moscow some clearer answers, political as well as military.

Moscow felt precisely the same way about Washington and London, but wanted military answers almost exclusively. Since early 1942 she had been pressing her allies not only for greater supplies of weapons and armaments but for the opening of a second front—an invasion through France or the Low Countries aimed at the German heartland—to relieve the fearsome Nazi pressure on her own western frontier. Lend-lease supplies were going to Russia but in a relative dribble by the only feasible route, a long haul over the hump of Scandinavia to the Arctic port of Murmansk. A second front was even more difficult of fulfillment in the face of American efforts to build and equip a two-ocean fighting force of its own and to keep the vital pipeline to Britain full.

To Stalin such arguments were trifling: The way to beat the enemy was to confront him directly with massive assaults on both his eastern and western flanks. Only the Red Army, he insisted angrily to various western deputations which visited him in Moscow, was in toe-to-toe combat with the common enemy, and paying an enormous toll in lives and material for the privilege. British bombing raids on German industry had their value, he conceded, and the American invasion of North Africa might prove to be a useful diversion, but they were peripheral and far off the main target and left Russia bearing the brunt of the fighting and the dying. His British and American partners-in-arms agreed fully with him on the need for a second front but they could not agree with him on its timing. A first promise that such a campaign would be launched across the English Channel in the spring of 1943 was amended early that year and postponed to the fall in favor of a summer assault on Italy. And then it was deferred again to the summer of 1944. The Russian dictator was infuriated by such apparent equivocation and his conspiratorial mind seethed with suspicions that his Anglo-American allies were deliberately letting him down; that the democracies were plotting to let communism and fascism fight one another to extinction while they looked on from a safe distance.*

With this aura of deep distrust pervading the Kremlin there was little wonder that the various American and British emissaries—Churchill

---

* How pervasive and deep-seated—even paranoid—was Stalin's distrust of his western allies has since been documented by Nikita Khrushchev, who became Premier in 1955—two years after Stalin's death. A ranking member of the Politburo throughout the war years, Khrushchev shared as much of the dictator's confidence as he was willing to grant any of his subordinates, which was not much. Khrushchev reveals in his memoirs that, to the extent he could trust and tolerate any "class enemy," Stalin had a feeling of warmth and rapport toward Roosevelt and a grudging respect for Churchill, but that he never permitted these flickerings of personal emotion to intrude upon his dealings with them. All non-Communists (and even some Communists), in Stalin's view, were enemies of the "working class" and the Soviet nation, and this went for his Anglo-American partners-in-arms. Khrushchev, the great anti-Stalinist, reflects much of the same wartime bias a whole generation later, as evidenced in this passage from his book, published in 1970:

It is difficult to judge what the intentions of the Allies were toward the end of the war. I wouldn't exclude the possibility that they desired to put a still greater burden on the shoulders of the Soviet Union and to bleed us even more . . . to bleed us dry so that they could come in at the last stages and determine the fate of the world. They wanted to take advantage of the results of the war and impose their will not only on their enemy, Germany, but on their ally, the U.S.S.R. as well. I can easily imagine how this thought played a significant role in their thinking. (*Khrushchev Remembers,* translated and edited by Strobe Talbott, Little, Brown, 1970, pp. 223-224.)

Here lie the seeds of the cold war.

among them—who went there on coordinating and placatory missions during 1942 and 1943 came away bleakly pessimistic about Stalin's commitment to postwar settlements within the benign framework of the UN Declaration. It seemed clear that the Communist conception of territorial aggrandizement and of interference in the political affairs of smaller states was considerably more permissive than that of the western democracies. He was explicit about the onetime Baltic states, about Finland and about Poland: He considered their "prewar boundaries" to be those which had been fixed as of June 1941—the dividend from his brief pact with Hitler—and not subject to further negotiation. For centuries the path of plunderers into the Russian domain had lain across what was now Poland and the region of the Baltic coast. The Soviets believed they had now secured their vulnerable western frontier and were not of a mind to abandon it.

Stalin's adamancy in holding onto a large slice of Polish territory was the stickiest political nettle the British and the Americans had to handle. It was a particularly acute embarrassment for Roosevelt, with large Polish constituencies in such states as New York, Pennsylvania, Michigan, and Illinois. Churchill, for his part, was hung up on a 1939 treaty with Poland guaranteeing its borders and by his commitment to the Polish government-in-exile resident in London—which, of course, regarded the Russians as their nation's historic and most baleful enemy. The Polish question reached a climax in April 1943, when Stalin abruptly withdrew Soviet recognition from the democratically oriented London Poles and transferred it to a more subservient group of emigres based in Moscow. This was a contretemps of menacing proportions. Obviously, no UN guarantee of territorial integrity for smaller nations would be worth a zloty if it condoned the partitioning of Poland.

All these signs of Soviet disaffection created deep concern for Roosevelt. Not only might the course of the war itself be adversely affected—suppose the temperamental Stalin should pull out and make a separate peace with Hitler?—but the prospect of unity and cooperation on postwar problems was growing progressively dimmer. It was becoming ever more essential, he concluded, that he and Churchill sit down at the table with Stalin, get to know and understand one another's problems at first hand, and try to create an atmosphere of mutual confidence among themselves. He had sought on a number of occasions to entice Stalin into meeting him at some convenient point between their distant capitals, but Stalin had refused on the grounds that he could not risk a long journey or long absence from his command post. He had once agreed earlier in the year to fly to Fairbanks, Alaska, for such a summit meeting, but had then reneged in a fit of pique engendered by the dispute over Poland.

Now, in the summer of 1943, Roosevelt pressed again for a personal get-together of the three heads of state, at a time and place of Stalin's own choice. The Marshal at last agreed, stipulating Tehran, just over the Soviet border in Iran, during the late autumn. He also proposed that their meeting be preceded by a preparatory conference in Moscow of their respective foreign ministers. Churchill and Roosevelt seized the offer promptly, although the President was somewhat appalled at the distance Stalin was willing to have him travel—half way around the globe—but was unwilling to travel himself.

IV

The Moscow foreign ministers meeting—of Hull (who got there by taking his first air flight), Eden, and Molotov—went off as smoothly as a clambake. Held late in October 1943, it scored two major achievements. First, the Soviets were convinced at last that their two allies now meant business in promising to open a massive second front in the summer of 1944. This, by Soviet insistence, was the first item on the Moscow agenda; with that satisfactorily disposed of they were ready to go on to other matters. Thus, the second major achievement was adoption of a four-power declaration (with China concurring in absentia) promising, in the name of the United Nations, to prosecute the war to its victorious conclusion, to collaborate in the drawing and enforcement of peace terms, and to work together toward "establishing at the earliest practicable date a general international organization . . . for the maintenance of international peace and security."

In the context of the preexisting atmosphere of suspicion, the statement was a resounding affirmation of unity. Some loose ends inevitably were left dangling: Molotov coolly informed his colleagues that Russia's borders (meaning Poland principally) "are no more to be discussed than California's." Hull and Eden prudently decided to get up from the table while they were still ahead and to put off going for the whole jackpot until a later, more propitious time. All in all, their winnings were quite substantial. The Moscow declaration, for all its vagueness and ambiguities, brought Roosevelt's grand design a long step nearer fulfillment.

Other encouraging developments were also occurring nearer home. Judicious propagandizing by the White House and State Department during the spring and summer of 1943 had brought an impressive weight of public opinion behind the idea of a postwar organization for peace. Characteristically, the voters seemed to be far ahead of their elected lawmakers in this respect. A Gallup poll in May asking whether the United States should join with other nations after the war in an organization to preserve the peace, found only about one-third of the Senate saying "Yes" compared with 74 percent of the public at large. But the lawmakers were beginning to catch up, slowly. In September a freshman Congressman from Arkansas, J. William Fulbright, offered a simple, one-sentence, "sense of the Congress" resolution in the House affirming the desirability of United States participation in the "creation of appropriate international machinery with power adequate to establish and to maintain a joint and lasting peace among nations of the world." The resolution sailed through the House 360 to 29 and, after a more deliberate and deliberative journey, through the Senate 90 to 6. It was apparent that a quite substantial revolution in American thinking had taken place in only one year.

One of the awkward paradoxes of the Big Four relationship was that there was no enemy common to them all. Russia was not at war with Japan and this necessitated some cumbersome locutions in preparing the various communiques. Another was the anomalous role of China. Churchill and Stalin held Chiang Kai-shek's Kuomintang regime in very low esteem both as a military force in being and as a dependable political influence in postwar Asia. Roosevelt apparently was under no illusions as to China's deficiencies on the battlefield but he clung to the notion that she would be the indispensable pillar of a democratic reconstruction in the Far East. He was persistent in his insistence that, ostensibly at least, China be treated as a coequal in the four-power partnership. Consequently, his journey to Tehran to meet Stalin provided for a stopover in Cairo where he and Churchill would meet with Chiang.

The President slipped out of Washington as inconspicuously as possible on Armistice Day, 1943, and far down-river boarded the spanking new battleship *Iowa* for the Atlantic crossing. On board with him was a large official party that included Hopkins, Admiral William D. Leahy, Chief of Staff to the Commander-in-Chief, and the chiefs of the Army, Navy, and Air Force. It was a pleasant and busy and, briefly, a terrifying journey. Three days out during an assault exercise by the *Iowa* and her protective screen of destroyers, a live torpedo was accidentally discharged from one of the convoy vessels and aimed directly at the President's ship. By a quick maneuver, the *Iowa* pulled out of the danger zone but not before those on board, including the President and Hopkins, who were watching from the deck, experienced several minutes of fascinated anxiety.

Whatever secrecy surrounded Roosevelt's departure from Washington, it had been thoroughly punctured before he reached his destination. Some 40 American and British news correspondents were on hand to greet him at Cairo, loudly petitioning to be let in on the forthcoming deliberations about which they seemed to be well informed. Unquestionably, the Germans also knew all about this high-level assemblage, and with Luftwaffe bases within striking distance in Greece it must have been an inviting target. No incidents of the sort occurred, however.

The Cairo talks were almost wholly about military strategy to be employed against Japan. They were inconclusive and generally disappointing to all concerned. Each of the principals seemed to view the problem from a different focus. Chiang wanted help—a great deal of it—in a massive land war against the Japanese invaders of his homeland, including a large-scale assault from the Bay of Bengal across Burma and Indochina. Roosevelt was now committed to a sea war against Japan and climbing up the island chain for bases from which to launch air attacks against the enemy's home base. To the extent that Churchill wanted to be distracted at all by an intensification of the Asian campaign, his interest centered on the former imperial bastions at Hong Kong and the Malay Peninsula. But above all, the stubborn Britisher wanted nothing to interfere with concentrating the greatest allied power possible for the opening of a second front in Europe—Operation Overlord, which was now shaping up. There simply was not enough clout in the allied arsenal, he argued, to fight two major wars at the same time. First things first, he said, and Europe came first.

Roosevelt was pulled both ways by these conflicting imperatives, and in his characteristic fashion he wound up trying to cover both. He was fully in accord with Churchill about the priority of a second front against Hitler, but he gave Chiang glowing if largely indefinite promises about more armaments and a seaborne assault into Burma. Later, after the conference at Tehran, he would have to renege on the second half of that promise, but the Generalissimo left Cairo believing he had gotten most of what he came for. And his pride was satisfied—also transiently—that he was now a full-fledged member of the team.

The Roosevelt and Churchill parties—they numbered something more than 100—flew on to Tehran on Sunday, November 28. It was a long journey traversing the eastern Mediterranean and the Holy Land, country which Roosevelt had never seen before and upon which he now gazed with fascination from the window of his plane, the "Sacred Cow." In the Iranian capital he was first quartered in the American Embassy, which was a considerable distance away from the British and Russian Embassies. At Stalin's urgent invitation he moved into a villa in the Russian compound. The city was full of spies, the Marshal said, and he did not want his friend to risk "an unhappy incident" in traveling back and forth. The villa was full of spies, too, Mike Reilly, the President's Secret Service bodyguard discovered: Even the chambermaids and butlers were NKVD agents packing guns under their garments. The President was amused by this little irony but felt that there was a good augury in Stalin's hospitable gesture.

The meeting at Tehran was as important for the congenial mood it established as for the hard commitments asked and made. Military affairs had top priority during the four days of discussion, and they were fruitful. Stalin gave a firm promise that Russia would enter the war against Japan as soon as Hitler was destroyed, and the three leaders and their staffs coordinated their plans for the opening of a second European front through France during the coming summer. Political talk centered mainly on Poland and what was to be done with a defeated Germany. Roosevelt and Churchill probed in every direction to find a formula acceptable to Stalin for a division of Poland that would satisfy Russia's demand for security and still leave the Poles a reasonably satisfying homeland. They also sought a formula for dismembering and regionalizing the German nation in such a way as to neutralize forever its war-making potential without destroying its cultural and economic viability. Neither search was wholly successful—Stalin proved to be a tough and resourceful bargainer—and final solutions to both questions had to be put off to some future time.

But throughout, the deliberations were carried on with enough candor and plain talk, and with enough disposition for give-and-take at critical junctures, to generate a wholly new and refreshing sense of confidence among the three leaders. There was promise in this burgeoning camaraderie, Harry Hopkins felt, that problems left unsolved today could be approached with hope tomorrow. He said that Roosevelt was exultant over the outcome and convinced that Stalin was "getable" for concurrence in any reasonable course of joint action. And Churchill, writing years later of the final dinner at Tehran at which he was host, remembered: "I felt that there was a greater sense of solidarity and good comradeship than we had reached before in the Grand Alliance. . . . I went to bed tired out but content, feeling that nothing but good had been done."

Discussions of a United Nations organization to monitor the peace that now seemed so certain of achievement were largely desultory and intertwined with other political considerations. But progress here was also encouraging, enhanced by the general mood of amity and common purpose. The concept of the "Four Policemen" still dominated Roosevelt's thinking, and at one point he outlined his ideas privately to Stalin in considerable detail. Hopkins, in fact, retrieved a "doodle" which the President made on a scrap of paper during the conversation that illustrated his plan. On the left was a circle inscribed "the UN" which would include all the UN members, much as the present General Assembly does. In the center was another circle labeled "Executive Committee," to be composed of the Big Four with token representation from other UN nations selected on a regional basis. These two bodies, the President explained, would be consultative and advisory only. Enforcement powers to settle disputes and threats of aggression—the real muscle of the UN—were reserved for the Four Policemen, represented by a third circle on the right, the members being the United States, United Kingdom, Soviet Union, and China. (Robert Sherwood, Hopkins' biographer, says this "doodle" represents "the first crude outline of the UN structure" that Roosevelt prepared.)

It appears that Stalin was favorably impressed with this delineation and that he made some constructive comments and criticism about it. Significantly, neither he nor Roosevelt broached the really tough issues of the territorial integrity of such countries as Poland and the Baltic States, nor what would happen in the event one of the Four Policemen was caught off base as an aggressor or international lawbreaker. There were no communiques or aide memoires specifically formalizing whatever understandings may have been reached in this and other discussions about a future UN organization, but both Roosevelt and Churchill left Tehran feeling that the climate for cooperation in this sphere had been markedly improved. And when he arrived back in Washington a couple of weeks later, the President told the nation in a buoyant fireside chat:

> Britain, Russia, China, and the United States and their allies represent more than three-quarters of the total population of the earth. As long as these four nations with great military power stick together in determination to keep the peace, there will be no possibility of an aggressor nation arising to start another world war. . . . But at the same time we are agreed that if force is necessary to keep international peace, international force will be applied—for as long as it may be necessary.

Even as he delivered this glowing report Roosevelt's political enemies were beginning to ask what "secret deals" had been made at Tehran. These hostile speculations covered a wide and often implausible spectrum but focused chiefly on Poland's postwar boundaries. This was a highly volatile subject since the Red Army was already in control of some 78,000 square miles of Polish territory adjacent to the Russian border, as well as of the three Baltic states and of a slice of Finland. Now, in early 1944, it was pushing even farther westward against a weakening German resistance. The Polish government-in-exile, recognized by both the United States and the United Kingdom, was demanding loudly to know what concessions as to postwar boundaries the British and American leaders had made to Stalin, and these demands were echoed in certain influential political quarters in the United States. While no such deals had been irrevocably nailed down at Tehran, it appears to be true that Roosevelt in particular, and Churchill to a somewhat lesser extent, had leaned far over to accommodate themselves to Stalin's stubbornly held point of view. To have taken a hard line to the contrary might very well have been futile as well as destructive of other gains. So, instead of saying "no" on the territorial question, they said "maybe"—and hoped for the best.[2]

V

In the months following the Tehran meeting there was intense activity in the State Department and in the foreign ministries of London and Moscow as teams of specialists attempted to devise concrete proposals to flesh out the framework of such an international security organization as the one upon which their leaders had tentatively agreed. Drafts were shuttled back and forth for analysis and criticism in search of consensus. (One facet of the work, that having to do with international monetary affairs, took on a life of its own; the International Monetary Fund and the World Bank for International Settlements were to come into being outside the administrative framework of the UN.) In May 1944, plans were developed for a meeting in Washington at which the various proposals for a permanent UN organization would be laid on the table and threshed out. Thus, the historic Dumbarton Oaks Conference was convened on August 21.

To many the timing seemed inauspicious. The pace of the war, especially in Europe, was hastening to such an extent that it appeared that victory might overtake the peacemakers. In the early hours of June 6—D-Day—the first waves of American, British, and Canadian troops stormed ashore on the beaches of Normandy to open the long-awaited second front. Italy had long since collapsed as a belligerent and the German defenders of what remained of the southern wing of the Axis were being driven slowly but inexorably up the Italian boot. Rome fell to the Allied Fifth Army even as Eisenhower's flotilla of landing craft plowed across the English Channel toward France. For many weeks past, German cities had been pounded unremittingly by ever-larger fleets of American and British bombers. The eastern front was aflame as a resurgent Red Army pressed the enemy back along a 1,500 mile line stretching from the Black Sea to the Gulf of Finland. And in the Pacific American forces had seized the island of Saipan in the Marianas in mid-June and, in one of the most furious air-sea engagements of that war, destroyed over 300 Japanese planes and a dozen ships, including a carrier and several destroyers.

The shape of the ultimate outcome was becoming clearer by the week during the summer of 1944. And this raised for some a troublesome question: What kind of a peace would an international peace-keeping agency be expected to preside over, and to enforce? Was it wise for the United States to commit itself to such an undertaking without knowing what would be demanded of it, either in political or military terms? A tripartite European Advisory Commission was already bogged down over the terms to be imposed on a defeated Germany and over the treatment of the soon-to-be-liberated satellite states. Soviet leaders had not yielded an inch in their demands for territorial concessions in Poland and the Baltic states, and now they were negotiating one-sided "understandings" with Partisan leaders in Rumania and other Balkan countries toward whose borders a liberating Red Army was pressing. At the very least, it appeared that the Russians were carving out "spheres of influence" in Central Europe that would be offered as faits accomplis at the peace table. Maybe, it was argued in some quarters, the United States ought to put off promising to join an international security pact until it knew more about what obligations went with it.

Meanwhile, the country was becoming embroiled in a heated and divisive political campaign. Roosevelt had opted to run for a fourth term, which made the split in his own party even more inflamed than it had been. The Republicans had chosen as their candidate New York's Governor Thomas E. Dewey, moderate on both domestic and foreign policy but with a talent for leaning into the political winds from whatever direction they blew. At their national convention, the Republicans had adopted a foreign policy plank that, in the most eloquently ambiguous terms, could be construed either as a full-bodied or as a very weak endorsement of U.S. adherence to an international security organization. Democrats derided it and GOP internationalists like Willkie were infuriated by it. "They had better leave well enough alone," Senator Vandenberg told a reporter while the convention was in progress. "If they insist on opening it up on the floor they might get an out-and-out isolationist plank that would curl your hair." Early in his campaign, Candidate Dewey denounced the cardinal idea of Big Four dominance of the proposed organization as "the rankest kind of imperialism." This seemed to signal that the whole UN concept would be tossed into the arena to become a major campaign issue, with possibly fatal results. Through the intercession of Secretary Hull the candidate was persuaded to moderate his position and to cooperate in trying to keep the whole UN question out of partisan debate. This gambit was partially successful, but dissent and suspicion continued to bubble audibly just below the political surface. It made a puzzling distraction in counterpoint for the visiting delegations who had assembled at Dumbarton Oaks.

Dumbarton Oaks is a graceful, early-nineteenth-century mansion set in a 16-acre park on the edge of the Georgetown section of Washington. It had lately been given by its owners, Mr. and Mrs. Robert Woods Bliss, to Harvard University for use as a center for Byzantine studies. Its high-windowed music room, hung with elegant paintings and tapestries, was set aside as the main conference center for what was officially titled the "Dumbarton Oaks Conversations"; "conference" or even "meeting" was eschewed as suggesting more formality and definitiveness than Roosevelt, at least, felt was prudent at the current stage of progress. The principal participants were all of sub-Cabinet status—Edward R. Stettinius, U.S. Under Secretary of State; Sir Alexander Cadogan, British Permanent Under Secretary for Foreign Affairs; Andrei A. Gromyko, Soviet Ambassador to the United States; and V. K. Wellington Koo, Chinese Ambassador to London—and each was backed up by a small corps of aides and advisers totaling about 50 all told. The conferees were to seek no binding conclusions, only a "meeting of the minds" which they could take back to their respective governments as tentative elements of a UN charter, to be negotiated later. (Because of protocol difficulties previously mentioned, the Chinese and the Russians could not participate in the proceedings together. A second series of sessions was held which the Chinese attended and from which the Russians abstained.)

The conference planners insisted on absolute secrecy in the proceedings to enhance freedom of discussion. The site was patrolled by MPs and newsmen were barred. This last precaution proved ineffectual. An enterprising young reporter for the *New York Times,* James B. Reston, found an old London acquaintance on the staff of one of the visiting delegations and within a week had laid an exclusive and trustworthy pipeline that ran right through the conference room door. Thereafter, the *Times* carried almost daily reports, detailed and well-informed, on the progress of the discussions, illuminating the various tactical maneuvers of the diplomats and their areas of agreement and disagreement. The "leak," which went unplugged for the seven weeks the conference lasted, drove Stettinius nearly to distraction, and later won "Scotty" Reston his first Pulitzer award.

There is no evidence that this journalistic coup caused any impediment to the work of the statesmen at Dumbarton Oaks. From the start the talks were conducted in an atmosphere of sincerity and optimism quite unusual for an international gathering of its kind. The preparatory work which had gone on beforehand produced a considerable degree of similarity in the various position papers offered by the different delegations. With two exceptions, which remained unresolved when the conference adjourned, most of the discussions and arguments were over procedural and administrative details of the projected world organization that were, in the long run, relatively minor.

The conference wound up on October 7 with the issuance of a 5,000-word document in the name of the four powers represented and entitled, "Proposals for the Establishment of a General International Organization." Its broad purpose was summarized in the opening paragraphs as follows:

There should be established an international organization under the title of The United Nations, the Charter of which should contain provisions necessary to give effect to the proposals which follow.

The purpose of the organization should be:

1. To maintain international peace and security; and to that end to take effective collective measures for the prevention and removal of threats to the peace and the suppression of acts of aggression or other breaches of the peace, and to bring about by peaceful means adjustment or settlement of international disputes which may lead to a breach of the peace;

2. To develop friendly relations among nations and to take other appropriate measures to strengthen universal peace;

3. To achieve international cooperation in the solution of international economic, social and other humanitarian problems; and

4. To afford a center for harmonizing the actions of nations in the achievement of these common ends.

In greater detail, the paper went on to spell out the structure of the organization as built around a General Assembly, a Security Council, a Secretariat, an International Court of Justice, "and such subsidiary agencies as may be found necessary." Membership, it was stated, should be open to "all peace loving nations," and the dominance of the Big Four was assured by granting them permanent seats on the Security Council.

The two big unresolved questions were these: Should a permanent (Big Four) member of the Security Council have the privilege of vetoing a decision by the Council to take up a dispute to which that member was a party? Suppose, for example, that Guatemala wanted to air charges against the United States for infringement of its sovereignty, or that Egypt should demand return of the Suez Canal from Britain. Should the defendant in such a case be permitted to call off the trial simply because of his privileged status in the community? The United States and the United Kingdom held that such a veto should be applicable only on "substantive" issues, as where punitive action, either economic or military, might be the consequence. The Russians held out stubbornly for retention of the Big Four veto privilege on "procedural" as well as "substantive" matters; to deny consideration by the Council of any question or dispute which any one of the permanent members might find objectionable or embarrassing. Without admitting as much, they could foresee that future exercises in the particular brand of communist realpolitik could cause the other powers to gang up on them.

The other unsettled question concerned membership in the organization. The Russians demanded that all 16 constituent republics of the Soviet Union be admitted on an equal footing with all other peace-loving nations, citing the admission of the British Dominions as precedent. The Americans countered by saying if that were done then the 48 states of the Union would have to be admitted too, a obviously preposterous arrangement that could lead only to chaos. The Russians were neither chagrined nor persuaded by this rebuttal, and the issue was laid over for future settlement. The dilemma thus created was so acute that it was obscured in the official documents of the conference under the euphemistic designation of "the X matter."

These two deadlocks were glossed over in the final communique from Dumbarton Oaks (they would reemerge later in sharp and thorny relief) and the "conversation" was adjourned on a high note of international cordiality and optimism. Its output was a detailed and promising blueprint for a world organization designed to free mankind from its greatest scourge, war.[3]

VI

The Big Three conference at Yalta, held in February 1945, was a replay in capital letters of the script followed at Tehran 14 months earlier. It nailed down the final strategy for the defeat of the Axis powers in both Europe and Asia, which was to come sooner than any of the participants expected. And it built the UN edifice up to the roof line according to the plans drawn at Dumbarton Oaks, sealing in some structural defects in the process. It was an epochal occurrence in world history and it marked the climax of Franklin Roosevelt's career in world diplomacy. He would not live to see the ultimate fulfillment of his grand design in the perfecting of a United Nations Charter at San Francisco a few months later.

Roosevelt was in declining health that winter of 1944–1945. It was evident to many of those who gathered on the south lawn of the White House on that cold, blustery January 20, 1945, as the sixty-three-year-old President, hatless and without an overcoat, stood stiffly at the lectern to deliver his fourth inaugural address. His face was gray and more lined than usual, and his voice lacked some of that fine clarity and timbre that had so often brought reassurance (and sometimes angry frustration) to a whole generation of Americans. Some of his companions on the long sea voyage to Yalta that began a few days later were troubled by his appearance (aggravated at the time by a head cold) and by a certain apathy in his manner that was quite uncharacteristic of him on the eve of an important encounter. Unquestionably, Roosevelt was tired and slowing down: To the burdens of the war had been added, only a few months earlier, the demands of a difficult political campaign. But there is no substantial evidence to support later charges by his critics that his physical and mental energies were seriously impaired; that he was "the sick man of Yalta" over whom Stalin rode roughshod. On the contrary, the evidence is that he was an alert and aggressive bargainer at these sessions who gave up no more than he got back in the high-stakes give-and-take.

Yalta, an historic resort on the Black Sea in the Crimea, was Roosevelt's choice as a site for the conference once it became clear—again—that Stalin could not be induced to come to a more convenient location outside Soviet borders. Only within the last months had the region been cleared of Nazi despoilers, and the President was eager not only for a firsthand view of the battle scenes but to see a storied corner of the world which he had never visited before. He won only the grudging agreement of Churchill and many of his own aides to the site because of its distance and inaccessibility. The nearest airport was 60 miles away and the Navy's communications ship had to be anchored at Sevastapol, which was even more distant from the center of action. But the President was enchanted by the setting, and with the baroque Czarist palaces in which he and most of his numerous entourage were quartered. He had come by ship as far as the island of Malta and flown the last leg of the journey from there, bringing along, among others, his Chiefs of Staff, Harry Hopkins, and his new Secretary of State, Edward R. Stettinius. (Hull had resigned in November for reasons of health.)

There were compelling reasons for this get-together of the Big Three. Victory over Hitler's Germany was now clearly within reach. The Battle of the Bulge, to crush the Nazi's last great offensive in the west, had been won in January, and the Red Army was closing in slowly but implacably from the east along a great arc stretching from the Baltic Sea to the Balkans. Decisions on how to deal with a defeated Germany and its satellites were crucial; so was the perennial problem of Poland, now with a Soviet army of occupation in virtually full control of its territory as "liberators." Meanwhile in the Pacific, American and British sea and air power were sweeping relentlessly northward: MacArthur's forces recaptured Manila on February 6, just as the Yalta conferees were getting down to business. But invading and overpowering the Japanese home islands was something else again. The best military judgment in Washington and London was that this would take another year to 18 months and cost as much as a million Allied casualties, unless . . . the Russians moved in at the right moment with a massive infusion of ground troops. Then the timetable and the losses might be cut in half. Stalin had to be pinned down irrevocably on this, with numbers and a date certain. (The atomic bomb at this point was too dubious a proposition on which to count.) Finally, and to Roosevelt most important of all, the stumbling blocks left over from Dumbarton Oaks that lay in the path of a viable United Nations had to be removed. Principally this meant Soviet obstructions relating to the voting procedure in the Security Council and her demand for membership of all the 16 Soviet republics.

On most items of this agenda the American and British positions were reasonably close together. At the worst, differences between them could be worked out with only a tolerable residue of rancor and resentment. With the Russians it was different; after all the good fellowship of Tehran and a string of shared military successes, their mood in matters of diplomacy remained dogmatic, truculent, and suspicious. If this carried over into their postwar relations with their allies, it would blast any hope of effecting a unified organization for preserving world peace. Roosevelt, ever confident of his prowess as a persuader and conciliator, set as a main goal of his visit to Yalta a permanent breakthrough of this barrier of temperament; to win for good the confidence, possibly even the friendship, of "Uncle Joe" Stalin toward his western teammates.

The meeting at Yalta (officially the Crimea Conference) lasted eight days, from February fourth to eleventh, 1945. Its official records occupy several cubic feet of storage space in the government archives, and the literature about it, both learned and unlearned—books, articles, theses, speeches, polemical tracts—consume many inches of catalogue space in most large libraries. It had its moments of levity and of high drama. Roosevelt gleefully confided to one of his aides that he had discovered the secret of Stalin's capacity for downing endless glasses of vodka as toasts were being drunk without getting tipsy: The wily old Bolshevik surreptitiously watered his drinks each time amid the confusion of the standing and hand clapping. Churchill erupted at one point in a magnificent display of Tory dudgeon when he suspected that an American proposal regarding UN trusteeship for dependent territories was aimed at dismantling the British Empire.

"I absolutely disagree," he bellowed, rising to his feet in majestic wrath. "I will not have one scrap of British territory flung into that area. After we have done our best to fight in this war and have done no crime to anyone, I will have no suggestion that the British Empire be put into the dock and examined by everybody to see whether it is up to their standard."

Roosevelt calmed him down by explaining that the reference was not to British holdings but those of the Japanese Empire.

In spite of such diversions and digressions, however, the principal characters in the Yalta drama, as well as their military and technical subordinates, wrought mightily and fruitfully in this extraordinary arena of realpolitik. The catalogue of their agreements—or what seemed to be agreements—was impressive. Some, as will be noted later, were subjected to harsh reevaluation. The conclusions which concern us here were the following:

Far East. The Russians agreed to enter the war against Japan within three months after the final defeat of Germany, transferring a large part of their European forces to join the conflict. They also agreed to enter a treaty of friendship with Nationalist China and to respect Chinese hegemony over Manchuria. In exchange, the Russians were granted sovereignty over a portion of Japanese-owned Sakhalin and the Kurile Islands, certain rights in the Manchurian port of Dairen, and partial control of the Manchurian railway.

These agreements were made without the foreknowledge and consent of the Chinese. Chiang had not been invited to Yalta, nor could he be informed immediately of these decisions vitally affecting his government. The information had to be kept from the Japanese at all costs, it was reasoned (the Russians greatly feared a preventive attack on their unprotected Far Eastern frontier), and even coded communications to Peking were highly vulnerable. Roosevelt undertook the responsibility of sending a special emissary to the Chinese leader to tell him what commitments had been made in his name and to win his consent thereto.

All of this was omitted from the official communiques at Yalta, of course, thus concocting one of the "secret deals" which would inflame public controversy in the United States in later weeks.

Poland. After much hopeless debate, Roosevelt and Churchill conceded Stalin's take-it-or-leave-it claim to Polish territory up to the Curzon Line, the Poles to be compensated with a portion of East Prussia taken from Germany. In exchange, Stalin promised to broaden the puppet Lublin Polish government (which he controlled) by the inclusion of representatives from the more democratically oriented London group, and to permit the holding of free elections for a new Polish government. This agreement was stated in such ambiguous terms as to be virtually meaningless—which, in terms of practical results, it soon proved to be. Here, too, a "secret deal" was charged.

United Nations. Here, a secret deal *was* consummated. The Russians were persuaded to back down from their demand for across-the-board veto powers in the Security Council, accepting the British-American formula, in exchange for the admission of two—not 16—additional Soviet Republics to full UN membership. Roosevelt exacted in turn agreement to a compensating increase in voting power for the United States, but in actuality this bonus was never claimed by the Americans. This membership arrangement was also omitted from the official communiques. When it was exposed in the American press some weeks later, to Roosevelt's embarrassment, there was a sizable outburst of public indignation.

Beyond this, as respects the UN, the Yalta negotiators agreed that France, once she regained her political footing, should become a member of the power elite as a permanent member of the Security Council, and that a call should go out to all member nations to assemble in San Francisco on April 25 to participate in the writing of a United Nations charter.

In modern times, few meetings at the summit of world power have been more laden with promise than that at Yalta, and few have fallen later into more acrimony and distrust. Roosevelt was pounded by his enemies at home for being "duped" by Stalin and for having sold Poland down the river. Such charges echo down to the present. But the evidence of history seems to be that the President made the best deal possible under the circumstances that faced him. There were two unalterable imperatives that had to be met: Russia's entry into the Pacific war, and survival of the United Nations concept. Stalin held high cards in both of these but they fell to Roosevelt's trumps. As to Poland and the political fortunes of eastern Europe, the Russian army and Russian influence were already dominant in those areas and simply could not be dislodged. Hence, the only alternative to a rigid standoff was a compromise, to exact promises of the right of self-determination and free elections to ameliorate the condition of these "liberated" peoples.

"I didn't say it was good, Adolf," the President explained wearily to Assistant Secretary of State Adolf Berle after his return to Washington. "I said it was the best I could do."

Stalin, of course, did not keep his promises about free elections in Poland or anywhere else, and probably never intended to. If Roosevelt was culpable in respect to all of this the fault lay in his naive assumption that the Russians could be persuaded to act like a country and not a cause.[4]

VII

Roosevelt did not live to see the fruition of his grand design. He died suddenly on April 12 at Warm Springs, where he had gone in hopes of restoring his waning health. But he had unwittingly placed upon the nation and upon his successor, Vice-President Harry Truman, a firm injunction to carry out his great, consuming purpose. Looking gray and worn as he stood upon the south balcony of the White House to deliver his fourth inaugural address on that cold January 20, he spoke these memorable words:

We have learned that we cannot live alone at peace; that our own well-being is dependent on the well-being of other nations far away. We have learned that we must live as men, and not as ostriches, nor as dogs in the manger. We have learned to be citizens of the world, members of the human community.

Wilson had spoken thus nearly a quarter of a century earlier, summoning the nation to join the "human community" of the League of Nations. But the clamor of dissent drowned out his words. This time, the dissenters were all but mute. The brutal reality of a world war and the irrefutable logic of the "four freedoms" had brought an almost complete turnabout in the nation's awareness of both its vulnerability to and its responsibility for the tides of political change surging around the globe. Even such once-uncompromising isolationists as Senator Arthur Vandenberg had willingly been recruited to serve on the American delegation to frame a United Nations charter. The new President, Truman, made it in his first order of business to decree that the San Francisco conference would proceed on schedule irrespective of the overshadowing tragedy that had befallen its chief architect.

The conference convened on the afternoon of Wednesday, April 25, 1945. It was a raw, drizzly day in San Francisco, the towers of the majestic Golden Gate Bridge lost in the enveloping mists. But the mood of that beautiful city, suddenly become the focus of world attention, was electric. Its streets and public buildings were festooned with flags and bunting and thousands jammed the sidewalks around the Memorial Opera House to watch the arrival of what may have been the largest assembly ever of the world's leading diplomats. They numbered some 300 (not counting their staffs) and represented 46 nations from all the continents and all the races of man. Here and there amid the sartorial uniformity of their appearance were flashes of military scarlet and gold braid, of colorful turbans, of a flowing white burnoose or other exotic native garb suggestive of distant and romantic climes. Inside upon the vast stage of the Opera House the massed flags of the member nations were arrayed against a blue velvet backdrop, and in the foreground were four golden pillars symbolizing the Four Freedoms, the theme and the dream which had brought this historic assembly into being. Each country's delegation was assigned a block of seats in the orchestra; the press, outnumbering the official participants at least six to one, occupied the dress circle and lower balcony, and the public at large crowded into every available remaining space.

Promptly at 4:30 P.M. Secretary of State Edward Stettinius, an improbably handsome man with silvery hair, dark eyebrows, and imposing carriage, stepped to the rostrum.* As chief of the host delegation he opened the conference with three gentle taps of his gavel and asked the audience to join him in a moment of silent meditation. Then, by long distance circuits from Washington the voice of President Truman was piped over the hall's loud speakers. It was a flat and to most an unfamiliar voice but the new President's words conveyed a sense of confidence and personal warmth:

You members of this conference are to be the architects of a better world. . . . We hold a powerful mandate from our people. They believe we will fulfill this obligation. . . . If we do not want to die together in war, we must learn to live together in peace. . . . Justice remains the greatest power on earth. To that tremendous power alone will we submit.

The conference lasted a little over two months, a period highlighted and given an extra sense of urgency by the fiery collapse and surrender of Germany on May 8. Its deliberative course was smoother than many had anticipated, but even so there were tense intervals of dispute and acrimony during which it appeared that things might come apart. Comrade Molotov

---

* The U.S. delegation, in addition to Secretary Stettinius, was composed of former Secretary of State Cordell Hull (as senior adviser); Senators Arthur Vandenberg (R.–Mich.) and Tom Connally (D.–Texas); Representatives Sol Bloom (D.–N.Y.) and Charles A. Eaton (D.–N.J.); Dean Virginia Gildersleeve of Radcliffe College; Commander Harold Stassen, USN, former Republican Governor of Minnesota; and John Foster Dulles of New York, chief foreign policy adviser to Republican Governor Thomas E. Dewey. In the large corps of relatively anonymous aides serving the delegation, two were later to achieve unique notoriety in highly dissimilar fashions—Alger Hiss and Adlai E. Stevenson. Britain's delegation was headed by Anthony Eden, and the Soviet Union's by Viacheslav Molotov, their respective Foreign Ministers.

was frequently churlish and disruptive, alternating with occasional displays of disarming good-fellowship. Many of the smaller nations acted defensively against the inevitable domination by the big powers, threatening at times to coalesce into blocs that might have thwarted fulfillment of the basic design which had been hammered out at Dumbarton Oaks.

The most serious obstacle was, predictably, Poland. Britain and the United States flatly refused the Russians' demands that the Lublin regime as then-constituted be seated as an original member of the conference. They insisted that Stalin stand by his promise to dilute its all-Communist complexion by including a significant representation from among the so-called "Free Poles" based in London. In retaliation, the Soviets refused to seat Argentina which, in spite of that country's overt flirtation with the Axis powers during the war, the United States was under severe pressure from other Latin American governments to admit into the club. A shaky compromise was not effected until the final week of the conference. Sixteen of 20 Free Poles whom Stalin reluctantly invited to Moscow for consultation were promptly clapped into jail for "atrocities" against the Red army of occupation in Poland, but the remainder were given posts in the new government, including that of Deputy Premier. Roosevelt and Churchill recognized this gesture as considerably less than half a loaf but as better than no bread at all. They signaled their acceptance of the Provisional Government of Poland as a signatory of the United Nations Charter and the Soviets followed suit by withdrawing their blackball of Argentina.

In spite of such distractions and the unwieldiness of so large a multilingual body of participants the conference accomplished its main purpose with reasonable dispatch and in a general air of amity. The Dumbarton Oaks agreement provided the main script for deliberation but scores of amendments, resolutions, and compromises were threshed out in separate working committees and in formal plenary sessions. The end product was a unanimously approved document defining in 111 Articles the precise structure and functions of the United Nations Organization and the International Court of Justice, plus a separate "statute" for the Court consisting of 70 Articles. The number of member states had grown to 50 during the course of the conference, and the instruments were to become operative when ratified by 29 of their governments, including the five permanent members of the Security Council (to which France had been admitted along with the original Big Four).*

* The U.S. Senate approved the Charter on July 28 by the overwhelming vote of 89 to 2. (The dissenting votes were cast by Senators William Langer, North Dakota, and Henrik Shipstead, Minnesota, both Republicans, and firm isolationists.) The United States formally deposited its notice of ratification on August 8, being the first of the signatories to do so. The Soviet bloc, including Poland, deposited theirs on October 24, bringing to the requisite 29 the number of ratifications. Thereupon the Charter vas declared to be "a part of the law of nations."

The high ceremonial climax, the signing of the Charter by the respective chiefs of delegations, occurred on Tuesday, June 26. (It had to be postponed from Monday because of the inability of the printer to produce on time an official text in the five prescribed languages—English, Russian, French, Chinese, and Spanish.) The scene was the huge auditorium of San Francisco's Veterans Building, its stage resplendent with flags and bathed in brilliant lights to accommodate a host of photographers and newsreel cameramen. On a table in the center of the stage were two large volumes bound in gold-embossed blue leather, one containing the Charter and the other containing "interim arrangements" that would prevail until the Charter should become fully effective. Beginning at noon, the delegates came forward one by one in great solemnity to affix their signatures and, in most cases, to utter a few history-laden words into the battery of microphones for instant radio transmission to every corner of the world. Then came a final plenary session addressed by President Truman in person. He said, in part:

The Charter of the United Nations which you are now signing is a solid structure upon which we can build for a better world. History will honor you for it. Between the victory in Europe and the final victory in Japan, in this most destructive of all wars, you have won a victory against war itself.

It was the hope of such a charter that helped sustain the courage of stricken peoples throughout the darkest days of the war. For it is a declaration of great faith by the nations of the earth—faith that war is not inevitable, faith that the peace can be maintained.

If we had had this charter a few years ago—and above all the will to use it—millions now dead would be alive. If we should falter in the future in our will to use it, millions now living will surely die. . . .

The voice was the voice of Truman but the words unmistakably were the words of Franklin Roosevelt, coming as if from beyond the grave. (They were written for the President, in fact, by that same Sam Rosenman who had shaped so many of FDR's speeches. Thus, the ideal of the Four Freedoms, first enunciated four and one-half years earlier, was now afforded a practical and promising vehicle for fulfillment. The Grand Design was completed, the structure to preserve peace with justice "everywhere in the world" erected and in place.

How durable and efficient a structure it was would require the passage of decades to determine, and that assessment will not be attempted here. But to the world of the mid-forties the birth of the UN was an epochal event occurring in its own time and responding to its own deepest needs and aspirations. A sense of sober exultation was almost universal, as typically expressed in this editorial from the *Times:*

From every land that has felt the curse of this war, from every land which escaped this time but may not escape if another such war takes place, prayers must be going up today that June 26, 1945, will actually represent a turning point in human history. Whatever happens, this day will not be forgotten. As the ink dries this morning on the signatures of the new charter a great hope is born and a new and heavy responsibility lies on all those who have responsibility and influence in fifty nations, and particularly on the leadership of the Great Powers.

Field Marshal Smuts (Republic of South Africa) who had a great part in creating the League of Nations, has made an enlightened comparison between the Covenant of 1919, inspired by the "high idealism" of Woodrow Wilson and the new Charter with its mixture of "idealism with realism." The Charter is no dream. It demands no revision of human nature. At the back of every decision has been the question, Will it work? Obviously no decision can be made to work if all the Great Powers do not accept it. There must be, as Marshal Smuts says, "Great Power leadership" and "Great Power unity." There must be force. The League required absolute unity between all member nations, which was impossible. It did not provide force. Under the Charter we shall see the world controlled by the Great Powers but subject to numerous self-denying ordinances and subject also to world opinion which can be marshaled in an Assembly where each nation, big and little, has a vote. Big Power control is not new. It is the restrictions upon such control that are new and that constitute the gains made under the Charter.

The old Court of International Justice is reborn as the International Court of Justice. In time we may see compulsory jurisdiction accepted by all the member nations. The Economic and Social Council will bring together representatives of many countries in an effort to ease economic frictions and raise living standards. The new trustee system, operating through a Trusteeship Council, imposes more responsibility on colonial powers than was ever realized under the old mandate system. Great things may come out of these by-products of the central organization. Indeed, they surely will if the main objective of collective security is realized. If the trunk of the tree of peace stands, the branches will grow. . . .[5]

9

Year of Climax—1945

1

Official war maps for January 1, 1945, gave abundant proof that the tides of World War II had turned strongly in favor of the United States and our allies. A year earlier the shading on these maps had shown the Axis powers in control of some 20 million square miles of the earth's surface: all of western and central Europe from the Pyrenees (except for the bottom of the Italian boot) north to the Arctic and eastward to the Black Sea and the line of the Dnieper River; and in the Pacific, all of China north of the Yellow River and of a great arc southward that embraced Indochina up to the borders of India, the Philippines, the vast Malaysian archipelago, and the northern half of New Guinea.

Now, as 1945 began, the enemy's holdings had been cut to about 13.5 million square miles. The maps showed that Italy was in Allied hands up to the Apennines; so was all of France and Belgium, up to or within striking distance of the Rhine, and on the eastern front Russia's counteroffensive had thrown the Nazis back to a line running roughly from Warsaw through Belgrade and on to the Adriatic. Progress in the Pacific had been equally spectacular. Critical island chains had been secured from the Solomons to the Marianas, affording naval anchorages and air bases for long-range bombing, and General MacArthur, landing at Leyte Gulf in the Philippines in October 1944, had begun to fulfill the promise he had made two years before: "I shall return."

We had suffered our share of degradation in the early stages of this war, and for two years, as we slowly gathered our strength to confront a rampant enemy, the nation's mood fluctuated between hope and despair. We were still on the seesaw for much of 1944, but then on that historic D-Day —June 6—our spirits soared as the greatest amphibious invasion of all times stormed the beaches of Normandy. Against incredible odds of both weather and Nazi resistance, General Dwight D. Eisenhower, Supreme Allied Commander in Europe, put a quarter of a million men ashore in the first 24 hours of Operation Overlord, backing them up with 4,000 ships and 11,000 planes. There followed weeks of the bloodiest and costliest fighting of the entire war—fighting which the home front followed minutely through superb on-the-spot coverage by the press and radio—before General Omar Bradley's First Army achieved the first significant breakout at St. Lo in mid-July.

As these forces fanned out and hammered against German positions from the west, a fresh assault—Operation Anvil—was mounted against them from the south of France, while other American and British armies hacked their way past Rome into central and northern Italy. (Italy had been knocked out of the war a year earlier; its "defense" was now wholly in the hands of a strong German occupation force.) Meanwhile on the Eastern Front, the Red Army launched its promised summer offensive out of White Russia, thereby completing a vast pincers squeezing in on Hitler's domain from all directions. In addition, Allied bombing fleets kept up sustained and massive raids on German industrial sites and transportation facilities, leaving havoc in their wake.

By the end of that year it was clear that Germany was a beaten foe, sustained, like a doped fighter in the prize ring, only by the suicidal mania of Adolf Hitler. The war had come to the very borders of the Reich and she was virtually bereft of allies. Her economy was in chaos, her navy was bottled up, the Luftwaffe had been decimated. Only the Wehrmacht, in spite of heavy losses in men and material, remained an effective and disciplined force. In a desperate, last-ditch effort to regain the initiative (a gamble that was opposed by most of his Generals), Hitler sent 25 of his best divisions smashing against Allied lines in the Ardennes region of Belgium and Luxembourg. The attack, well planned in great secrecy, was launched on December 16. The 60-mile front he chose was the weakest segment in the Allied perimeter and it caught the defending VIII Corps by surprise. The Nazis scored some early successes and their forward elements penetrated some 40 miles toward the Meuse River before they were slowed down and dug themselves in. This was the famed Battle of the Bulge, and as the year 1945 dawned it still cast an ominous shadow over the prospects for an early Allied victory.

Success in the Pacific Theater had been no less marked than in Europe. Although the war against Japan suffered all through 1944 from a lower priority in men and weapons than that against Germany, Allied forces fought their way 2,500 miles nearer the Japanese homeland—and within bombing range—during the year. The Pacific Fleet under Admiral Chester W. Nimitz swept through and around strong Japanese positions in the Gilbert and Marshall Islands, and in some of the most furious fighting of the war took Saipan, Tinian, and Guam in the Marianas during June and July, all the while administering crushing blows upon the enemy's sea and air power. General MacArthur's command meanwhile pushed its way north and westward from bases in New Guinea from one island stronghold to another, making its first landing in the Philippines in October. In November B-29s from his command—the newest, biggest, and deadliest bomber in the skies at the time—made the first of many daylight attacks on Tokyo from bases more than 1,000 miles away on the island of Saipan. Japanese naval and air power had been seriously crippled during the year and the home islands were now within target range of American armor. But Japan's huge, well equipped, and fanatically courageous army deployed in China and in the homeland was believed to be relatively untouched. It was this grim fact that gave pause to Allied war planners as they contemplated the ultimate subjugation of the Land of the Rising Sun.

It was with a mood of cautious optimism, then, that we welcomed the new year, 1945. There was confidence in the ultimate victory of Allied arms, but misgivings about how painful and costly the final stages of that victory might be.[1]

II

There was little doubt in anyone's mind, except perhaps his own, that President Roosevelt would seek a fourth term in 1944. It is easy to believe that his purely personal preference was to lay down the heavy burdens of an office he had held for nearly 12 years and retire to the life of elder statesman at his lovely ancestral home on the Hudson. He said as much to his intimates frequently. But vanity and his public obligation ruled out that choice. The war was far from won and the role of Commander-in-Chief could not lightly be transferred in mid-battle. Nor could another, however adept, easily pick up the threads of his intimate, complex relationship with the two other great Allied leaders, Churchill and Stalin. Neither could he be sure that another would pursue with his own zeal and purpose the perfection of his grand design for a United Nations. So there was as much truth as poetry in his words when he told Democratic Chairman Robert Hannegan early in June that if the people so commanded, he would, "like a good soldier," serve.

Determining upon a Vice-Presidential candidate to run with him was a far more difficult business. Roosevelt was warmly attached to Henry A. Wallace, who had been elected with him in 1940, and in the beginning he insisted that Wallace should again be his running mate in 1944. But the moody and enigmatic Iowan, a prime target of conservatives throughout the New Deal years, had become anathema to powerful segments of the Democratic Party. The Southern wing in particular detested him and his standing with congressional Democrats was uniformly low. Also, Roosevelt was getting along in years. He was now 62; his hair had thinned, his face was lined and occasionally haggard, and some of the familiar old bounce and vitality had drained away. Though the world had long become accustomed to his confinement to a wheelchair, that device was a constant, subtle reminder to all that he, too, was mortal and perhaps more vulnerable than most. To many who pursued this line of speculation it was unthinkable that, if the worst should happen, the Presidency would fall to a man as erratic and unknowable as Henry Wallace. It was with the greatest difficulty that Hannegan and other party leaders finally persuaded the President that Wallace would be a drag on the ticket, that his presence might seriously jeopardize the chances of victory.

This was the sort of dilemma that Roosevelt hated: Any breach of loyalty or affront to a friend, however necessitous, paralyzed his will. He delegated to the faithful Sam Rosenman the unpalatable task of telling Wallace that he had been dumped—and then backed off half-way when Wallace, himself, confronted him demanding confirmation. Meanwhile, he ducked and weaved with petulant indecisiveness as Hannegan and others tried to pin him down on the choice of a successor. None of half a dozen names they presented to him struck more than a feeble spark of interest, and he allowed at least two other self-appointed candidates—War Mobilizer James F. Byrnes and Senate Majority Leader Alben Barkley— to believe that they had won, if not his affirmative approval, at least his implied assent to their intentions.

Chairman Hannegan and a few other powerful party leaders had their hearts set on Senator Harry S. Truman of Missouri. He had a good New Deal voting record, he had won favorable notice around the country through his chairmanship of the War Investigating Committee, and he was at least acceptable to, if not wildly favored by, both the Southern conservatives and the powerful liberal-labor contingent represented by the Political Action Committee (PAC) of the CIO. If, by the rule book, Truman had barely enough going for him, he had very little going against him. One can't ask for much more than that in a tough political choice.

At last, with the convention only a week away, the party men brought the President around, part way at least, to their way of thinking. He gave Hannegan a letter, to be used with proper discretion in huddles with the delegates, saying that he would be content to have *either* Supreme Court Justice William O. Douglas *or* Senator Harry Truman on the ticket with him. And then, to protect his flank and/or to further muddy the waters, he sent another letter to Senator Samuel D. Jackson, permanent chairman of the convention, stating that if he, Roosevelt, were a delegate to the convention he would vote for Wallace's renomination (Wallace having decided meanwhile to make a fight for it on his own). "At the same time," the President added, "I do not wish to appear in any way as dictating to the convention. Obviously the convention must do the deciding."

A typical Democratic mess!

Truman was unaware of the lengths to which his friend Hannegan had gone in trying to nail down the nomination for him. He had told the Chairman earlier he did not want the job, and there is good reason to believe he meant it. Two days before the convention was to open he received a call at his home in Independence from Byrnes in Washington, saying that the President had just given him "the go sign" and asking if Truman would put his name in nomination. The Senator said he would be happy to do so, and set off for Chicago determined to do all he could for his friend from South Carolina. (He also received a similar request that same day from Barkley but turned it down because of his commitment to Byrnes. How many "go signs" had the President scattered around?)

Since Roosevelt's nomination for the Number One spot was a foregone conclusion, all interest at Chicago centered on the Vice-Presidential race, for which there was a full field—Wallace, Byrnes, Barkley, Indiana's Paul McNutt, a clutch of "favorite son" Governors, and of course the reluctant Truman. Since the President had not made a public and unequivocal choice of his own, the Jackson letter notwithstanding, the job seemed to be up for grabs—and the grabbing was furious. Sidney Hillman of the PAC was in Wallace's corner, Truman was shilling with all his might for Byrnes, and Hannegan was quietly cutting the ground from under these and all the other contestants in favor of Truman—to Truman's intense indignation, once he discovered the full scope of the conspiracy swirling around him. Forty-eight hours before the balloting was to begin, he and Hannegan had a heated hotel room confrontation. Hannegan told Truman he "had" to run because the President wanted him, and showed him for the first time the "Douglas or Truman" letter, now amended to read "Truman or Douglas." *

"Tell him to go to hell," the Missourian snapped. "I'm for Jimmy Byrnes."

A few hours later the determined Hannegan put through a call to the

* As the convention was getting under way the President, on his way to the West Coast, stopped briefly and secretly at Chicago at Hannegan's earnest request. He begged the President for a forthright endorsement of Truman as the only way of avoiding a disruptive head-on collision between Wallace and Byrnes. The President refused, having promised Wallace as a consolation not to put any such impediment in his path. But he did agree finally to a reversal of the order of names in the letter he had given Hannegan earlier, for whatever advantage his now-desperate Chairman might derive.

As he handed over the retyped letter, Roosevelt is supposed to have said, "Clear it with Sidney [Hillman]." This admonishment, real or imaginary, somehow reached the ears of the press and was expanded into "Clear everything with Sidney." Thus was born one of the most effective Republican slogans of the campaign, for the PAC which Hillman headed as an unofficial arm of the Democratic organization, was widely suspected of having a Communist taint.

President, who was then at San Diego en route to a meeting with his Pacific commanders in Hawaii. Truman sat beside him on the bed so that he could overhear the ensuing conversation, which apparently had been previously rehearsed.

Roosevelt: Bob, have you got that fellow lined up yet?

Hannegan: No, Mr. President. He is the contrariest Missouri mule I've ever dealt with.

Roosevelt: Well, you tell him for me that if he wants to break up the Democratic Party in the middle of a war, that's his responsibility.

Truman (dazed and mumbling): My God!

That did it. Truman was caught on a gold hook with steel barbs (and he never really regretted it afterwards). Hannegan immediately gave out the word, "it's Truman," and gave the President's letter to the newspapers. Justice Douglas, meanwhile, had affirmed his unavailability for the honor. Truman tried to make his peace with Byrnes. The hot tempered Southerner was furious and stayed that way the rest of his life, but he withdrew from the race. Wallace was angry, too, but he refused to step aside. When the showdown came on the final day of the convention, he outpolled Truman on the first ballot, 420½ to 319½. On the next ballot Hannegan threw in his reserves, the votes of the big city machines which had promised a courtesy vote to Wallace plus those of a handful of one-shot favorite sons. The final tally was overwhelming—Truman 1,031, Wallace 105.

Looking back upon these hectic five days of July 1944, Jonathan Daniels, aide to Roosevelt's press secretary, wrote:

As time passed, it became increasingly clear that this was not only an important convention in American history but one which qualifies as almost the cream of the American political jest. Truman was nominated by men speculating beyond the death of Roosevelt who knew what they wanted but did not know what they were getting.

The Republican convention, held a month earlier, also in Chicago, was by comparison a quiet tame affair. At no time did it promise enough excitement to fill the 20,000 seats of the steaming old Chicago Stadium, where it was staged. From the outset the proceedings were under the firm, disciplined control of the managers for the forty-two-year-old New York Governor, Thomas E. Dewey. Wendell Willkie, hoping to make a comeback, had sallied forth gallantly into the bellwether Wisconsin primary back in April. He got only a broken spear and deep humiliation for his trouble and withdrew. The same fate befell General Douglas MacArthur, represented in absentia by a small band of devout ultraconservatives. Dewey remained aloof from the primaries, refused even to acknowledge his candidacy, maneuvering for a "draft." By the time the convention opened only the gregarious, silver-haired, third-term Governor of Ohio,

John W. Bricker ("He looks like an honest Harding," the acidulous Alice Roosevelt Longworth said of him) remained in serious contention, and he was bought off with a promise of the Number Two spot on the ticket. Dewey's draft strategy worked without a flaw. He was nominated on the first ballot, unanimously save for a single die-hard vote for MacArthur.

In spite of his comparative youth Dewey had already become a prominent feature of the political landscape. During the late 1930s he won renown as a special prosecutor in New York by breaking up some of the more notorious rackets in that city and sending a score of their crime lords off to prison. Running for Governor in 1938 he came within an eyelash (64,000 votes) of unseating the immensely popular Herbert W. Lehman, a close ally of FDR. In the 1940 Presidential tryouts he, like all the other contenders at Philadelphia, was swept into the wings by the onrushing Willkie bandwagon. But he came back in the 1942 gubernatorial race to win by a smashing margin of 648,000 votes. It was this shining victory, along with some other wins of governorships and gains in congressional representation, that led many Republican leaders to believe that their party had emerged at last out of the New Deal eclipse, and that 1944 would be the year of their final deliverance from exile. And who better than Dewey to carry the flag?

That was a debatable question at best among many leaders of the GOP. Dewey had the knock, the charisma, and indeed the record of a successful vote-getter. But he was a hard man to know or to like. He was small of stature, meticulous in dress and manner, possessed of a manifestly superior mind sharpened to a keen forensic edge (his speaking voice, a rich baritone, was one of the best in the business)—and with an indelible air of arrogance about him. He seemed to many what a Republican leader of a later generation would call "an effete Eastern snob." Ideologically he seemed to fit somewhere to the right of the liberal-internationalist Willkie and somewhere to the left of his conservative-pseudoisolationist running mate, Governor Bricker. But he had a talent for sensing where the middle of the road was, for keeping out of the potholes and off the soft shoulders. Moreover, he was a superb organizer and tactician, and he could put the finger on the moneymen needed to finance an inevitably expensive campaign. Above everything, he was "regular," and to the party's ruling Old Guard still smarting from the effrontery of the Willkie uprising four years earlier, that was conclusive. Like him or not, Dewey was a good bet.

It was, on the whole, rather a lusterless campaign, such highlights as there were being clustered mainly in the closing two or three weeks. Reporters combing the country for clues at the grassroots found more apathy than interest in politics. There were many other things to absorb the public's attention. The war had reached a new pitch of intensity in

France and in the islands of the Pacific. The monetary conference at Bretton Woods got under way in the early summer; Dumbarton Oaks convened in August. Rationing and the shortages in consumer goods were beginning to pinch worse than ever, and there was fear of a serious fuel shortage during the coming winter. There were angry flare-ups on the labor front over the wage strictures of the Little Steel formula, and manpower shortages in some defense industries were becoming acute. In August the President went off to Ottawa for another high-level strategy conference with Churchill. These and similar events dominating the front pages day after day made it tough for politicians to stir up partisan excitement among the voters.

This created a special dilemma for the Republican candidate. Roosevelt had said in the beginning that he would not campaign "in the usual way" because of the press of his official duties. And indeed he scarcely needed to: Those official duties kept him constantly in the center of the stage, doing in fact what his opponent could only promise to do. Conduct of the war was scarcely a debatable issue and by tacit agreement between the two sides it was understood that "politics ends at the water's edge." This confined Dewey very largely to domestic affairs, both current and those to come with postwar readjustment, and with the philosophy and the capacity of "the tired group of men" who had been in power for over a decade to deal with those problems. (If one tried, a likeness of the ageing Roosevelt could be discerned in this metaphor.)

This was rather sterile grist for a politician's mill in the midst of the nation's intense preoccupations with other matters, but Dewey did the best with it he could. In his swings across and around the country, beginning in early September, his major speeches were constructive, well-thought-out and flawlessly delivered. He acknowledged the inevitability of most New Deal reforms of the past but sharply criticized their execution. He was basically in accord with Roosevelt's plan for a United Nations but raised valid questions about the obligations that adherence to the pact would entail. It was a "high-level campaign" and reporters covering the Republican candidate gave him high marks for effort. But it was difficult to escape the impression that Dewey was punching the air; that what he needed was a visible, viable target who would punch back. Unhappily, of course, his exalted adversary was conspicuously engaged in other pursuits of higher import.

Two main concerns haunted the Democratic campaign managers. One was that overconfidence within their constituency would result in a small turnout on election day and thus jeopardize the prospect of victory. To counter this they mounted a massive registration and get-out-the-vote drive spearheaded by the CIO-PAC through its hundreds of local affiliates. Their second concern had to do with the candidate, himself; to get his fighting blood up and put him on display as the high-spirited scrapper of old. This would not only inspire the troops but it would take the sting out of the "tired old men" analogy and check the whispering campaign about the state of the President's health, now beginning to circulate openly. An opening for this ploy soon presented itself.

The President had agreed to make a speech to the national convention of the Teamsters Union in Washington on the night of Saturday, September 23. A few weeks earlier some anonymous Republican propagandist had floated a story to the effect that on a recent inspection trip to Alaska, the President's pet Scotty, Fala, had inadvertently been left behind when the party departed, and that a Navy destroyer had, at great cost to the taxpayers, been sent back to retrieve him. This was a fable but it was picked up half seriously by a number of columnists and commentators. Roosevelt decided to make it the piece de resistance of his Teamsters speech.

That speech will never be expunged from the anthologies of political satire. This was an art form in which Roosevelt excelled and on this night he was at his best. His audience was, of course, sympathetic and responsive. He put them into a laughing, foot-stomping mood at the outset by confessing that, yes, he was four years older than he was when last they met—"which is a fact which seems to annoy some people." And he and a lot of other Americans, he went on, "are more than 11 years older than when we started to clean up the mess that was dumped in our laps in 1933." And on he went to poke fun at the Republicans for discovering their great love and concern for labor every four years when they wrote their platforms; how the Old Guard at election time always tried to pass itself off as a better New Deal than the original; how the party of isolationism now asserted its qualifications for making the peace—"Why [they say], just turn it over to us. We'll do it so skillfully that we won't lose a single isolationist vote or a single isolationist campaign contribution." The crowd roared with laughter and applauded lustily.

Then, in an abrupt change of pace, in total deadpan, and in measured tones of righteous indignation, he said:

> These Republican leaders have not been content with attacks on me, or my wife, or my sons. No, not content with that they now include my little dog Fala. Well, of course I don't resent attacks, and my family doesn't resent attacks, but Fala *does* resent them. You know, Fala is Scotch, and being Scotch, as soon as he learned that the Republican fiction writers had concocted a story that I had left him behind on the Aleutian Islands and sent a destroyer back to find him—at a cost to the taxpayers of two or three or eight or maybe 20 million dollars—his Scotch soul was furious. He has not been the same dog since. I am accustomed to hearing malicious falsehood about myself. But I think I have a right to resent, to object to libelous statements about my dog.

This sally just about broke up the meeting. Hundreds in the audience jumped to their feet howling, whistling, and applauding in delight, and their enthusiasm spilled over to the millions listening by radio. It was pure Roosevelt; no ghost writer had prepared those lines for him, and he delivered them with the fine nuances of manner and inflection of the polished actor. Here was *V*irtue outraged—with a mischievous twinkle in its eye. It was the old gambit of "Martin, Barton, and Fish" all over again, the devastating thrust of ridicule for which there is no parry. Fala was suddenly a national celebrity, and at almost any public appearance of the Republican candidate some heckler was likely to call out, "What's Fala been up to?"

Stung by these jibes, Dewey put a sharper edge on his attack. "They asked for it," he told an audience in Oklahoma City, "and we're going to let them have it." He bore down harder on the "group of tired men" theme; embroidered the "Clear everything with Sidney" slogan to imply that the Democratic Party was about to be taken over by the Communists; accused the President of having failed adequately to prepare the nation for war and of "starving" General MacArthur's forces in the Pacific. This last thrust backfired embarrassingly, when, a week or so after it was uttered, the General led his troops ashore at Leyte in one of the major victories of the Pacific campaign. But the total effect of the new tactic was salutary and by late October the public opinion polls, which had consistently shown Dewey several points below the winning line, began to flutter encouragingly.

Roosevelt, deciding that he had gotten about all the useful mileage out of giving his opponent the silent treatment, now stepped up the tempo of his own attack. He scheduled four major speeches in the closing weeks of the campaign, at New York, Philadelphia, Chicago, and Boston, with whistle stops along the way, and spiced his twice-weekly press conferences with lively and quotable partisan commentary. At last, it appeared to those around him, the old pro had gotten a whiff of resin in his nostrils and was panting to climb back into the ring.

His New York appearance was clearly the highlight of this stage of the campaign, as brilliant a tour de force in its way as his Fala speech. He was scheduled to address the Foreign Policy Association on the evening of October 21, preceding which he planned an extensive see-and-be-seen tour through four of the city's five boroughs. He and his party arrived from Washington that morning in a downpour of driving, chilling rain. The President's doctor and members of his staff urged him to abandon the tour. But he would not hear of it: He would not even consent to the use of a closed car, but, bundled in his cape and an old felt hat, rode in a convertible with the top down completely exposed to the elements. Within minutes he was drenched to the skin, and he remained that way throughout the four-hour, 50-mile procession.

Hundreds of thousands of sodden citizens lined the streets along the route, cheering and waving as he went by. Near Times Square a couple of theater orchestras abandoned their pits, reassembled under the marquees of their playhouses, and serenaded the Presidential party as it passed. Roosevelt, seemingly unfazed by the weather, grinned his famous grin and waved back happily to one and all. And that night, full of vigor and good humor, he gave one of his most trenchant speeches on the problems of postwar diplomacy, which was a political theme whether so labeled or not.

The whole episode was a ringing rebuttal to the allegations that he was too old, worn, and sick to be entrusted with another four years in the White House. To the millions who saw him in the flesh, in the newsreels, in pictures in the newspapers with the rain dripping from his bared head, he looked pretty much like the FDR of old. The talk about his poor health subsided noticeably.

The campaign came down to the finish line with the opinion polls showing Dewey climbing moderately in the closing weeks but still trailing by anywhere from one-half to three percentage points. The final vote tally on the day after election (which fell on November 6) gave Roosevelt 24.7 million, Dewey a shade over 22 million. This was a quite respectable share of the popular vote for the loser, but the spread in electoral votes was far more pronounced: Roosevelt 432, Dewey 99. Even so, Dewey carried more states—12—than had any Republican candidate since Herbert Hoover in 1928. The Democrats picked up two new governorships and 24 seats in the House of Representatives but lost two from their abundant margin in the Senate. Among the congressional casualties were some of FDR's bitterest enemies: Senators Robert R. Reynolds of North Carolina, Ellison D. "Cotton Ed" Smith of South Carolina, Gerald P. Nye of South Dakota, and Representatives Hamilton Fish of New York and Joe Starnes of Alabama.

At no time had Roosevelt been concerned over the outcome but he had developed a biting contempt for Governor Dewey. Late on election night after the loser had conceded, he muttered to Bill Hassett, one of his secretaries: "I still think he's an s.o.b." [2]

III

The weeks that followed the election were intensely busy ones for the President. Congress came back in a lame duck session to wrestle over taxes, social security, price controls, and manpower shortages, with the obstructionist Republican-Southern conservative coalition seemingly unchastened by the results at the polls. There were problems for the President about arranging for the big power conference soon to be held at Yalta, with Churchill in a particularly truculent mood over matters involving Greece and the Balkans, and with Stalin relentlessly pushing his advantage in Poland. There was work to be done on the new budget and a critical State of the Union message to be prepared. In addition to everything else, the President had to keep abreast of fast-moving events in a two-front war. Bone tired, and showing it in his face and manner, he took off for a vacation at Warm Springs early in December, returning to the White House a few days before Christmas.

The President's annual message to Congress on the State of the Union —his twelfth—was not delivered in person but read to that body on January 6, 1945. It was his longest, running to some 8,000 words, and it was pitched to a deeper note of crisis than any which had preceded it. Its central theme was that while military victory was assured, its timing and its cost in lives and suffering were not. His aim was to dispel the euphoric notion that the worst was over and that the nation could begin to wind down and take life easy. To drive home the point, he called for a national service law that would put upon every able-bodied male in the population the requirement to "work or fight"; for inclusion of women nurses in the military draft; for universal military training in the postwar period. And beyond the immediate goal of victory on the battlefield, he reminded the nation, lay the immensely difficult task of creating the will and the machinery to ban forever the scourge of war.

"We Americans of today," he said, "together with our allies, are making history—and I hope it will be better history than ever has been made before. We pray that we may be worthy of the unlimited opportunities God has given us."

Two weeks later the President stood on the south portico of the White House for one of the briefest and most somber inaugural ceremonies on record—and only the third to be held while the nation was at war.* There were no parades, no balls, no crush of beribboned dignitaries from the provinces. The day, January 20, was raw and overcast, and a thin dusting of snow lay upon the White House lawn and the ellipse and the monument grounds beyond the tall iron fence. During the late morning hours some 7,000 pass holders, including 50 wounded veterans from nearby hospitals, were admitted into the area below the portico where they were serenaded briefly by the red-jacketed Marine Corps Band. Some 2,000 of the more favored visitors also held invitations to the Inaugural Luncheon to be held inside the White House later—an appropriately Spartan feast of chicken salad, rolls sans butter, and cakes sans icing.

Some two score members of the official party and their families sat huddled in heavy wraps on the White House balcony. At a few minutes past noon the band struck up "Hail to the Chief" and then the National Anthem. A prayer was said, the oath was administered to the President

* The two other wartime inaugurals were Madison's in 1813 and Lincoln's in 1865.

and the Vice-President by Chief Justice Harlan Fiske Stone, and the President, walking stiffly on his steel braces and assisted by his son, James, moved to the lectern and its wicket of microphones. He wore neither hat nor overcoat against the biting weather. And many in the audience who were seeing him for the first time in many weeks were shocked by the grayness and haggardness of his features. "He looked so badly I was frightened," Henry Wallace's wife confided that evening to Labor Secretary Frances Perkins. "Are you sure he is well?" Miss Perkins put her finger to her lips in mild remonstrance. It was not something to be talked about. But in spite of his physical appearance Roosevelt's voice came over the loudspeakers strong and vibrant and reassuring.

It was the shortest inaugural address on record, only 551 words long; and it was less a speech in the usual sense than a kind of litany, an invocation of the power of courage, patience, and determination to carry the nation and the world through the remaining ordeals of war and its aftermath:

We have learned lessons at a fearful cost, and we shall profit by them. We have learned that we cannot live alone, at peace; that our well-being is dependent on the well-being of other nations, far away. We have learned to be citizens of the world, members of the human community. . . .

The Almighty God has blessed our land in many ways. He has given our people stout hearts and strong arms with which to strike mighty blows for freedom and truth. He has given our country a faith which has become the hope of all peoples in an anguished world. We pray now to Him for the vision to see our way clearly—to see the way that leads to a better life for ourselves and for all our fellow men—to the achievement of His will for peace on earth.

To listen to these words was a deeply moving experience. To Sam Rosenman it seemed to be a prayer—"A prayer, on the eve of his departure for Yalta, that all the peoples of the world, and their leaders, be endowed with the patience and faith that could abolish war."

The President departed two days later for his historic meeting in the Crimea with Churchill and Stalin, the details of which we have already reviewed. He returned at the end of February refreshed in spirit—he believed the conference had been a great success—but showing evidence of physical strain and weariness. His report to Congress was made from his wheelchair rolled into the well of the House of Representatives—an indulgence he had never permitted himself before—and his delivery was halting and imprecise. Already, talk had begun to revive about the state of his health and this performance gave new impetus to these morbid speculations. There was no hard evidence to back up the guesswork, and for the next several weeks the President held to a rigid routine of hard work and daily appointments. But to reporters at the White House who saw him frequently, and to members of his family and staff, Roosevelt's failure to "snap back" from the ordeal of the political campaign and his trip to Yalta was a source of growing concern and even of alarm. The dark circles remained under his eyes, the pallor of his complexion was unchanging, his hands trembled when he lighted a cigarette or signed a letter, there were times when he seemed listless and depressed. He complained to his doctor of poor appetite and of sleeplessness.

He was persuaded at last to go off to Warm Springs for a long rest. He would need it to set him up for the strain of the upcoming United Nations conference. He left Washington on March 29 and never returned.

How ill was Roosevelt during those last 12 gruelling months in office? This was a question which, for years after his death, was debated with deep and even partisan intensity: It was inevitably a question with marked political overtones. The simple answer is that he was a good deal sicker than he and his associates and most of the public realized, but not nearly so sick or incapacitated as his enemies and some well-disposed alarmists sought to depict him. In layman's terms he had serious heart trouble and high blood pressure along with frequent bouts of respiratory distress, but he never suffered a disabling heart attack nor a series of small strokes, nor was there any evidence of syphilis, cancer, epilepsy, or the other ailments so often alleged in the rumors about him. The immediate cause of death was a massive cerebral hemorrhage.

That assessment has lately been confirmed and documented by Dr. Howard G. Bruenn who, as a Navy cardiologist, first examined President Roosevelt at the Bethesda Naval Hospital in March 1944, and was thereafter constantly in attendance upon him, in Washington and abroad, until his death on April 12, 1945. Dr. Bruenn's report, the first detailed clinical analysis of the state of the President's health during his final year, was published in the April 1970, issue of the *Annals of Internal Medicine,* an official organ of the American College of Physicians.

Roosevelt had gone to the hospital on that initial visit because of the aftereffects of an attack of influenza; he had been unable to throw off the weakness, the bodily aches, and the persistent cough of that seizure. Dr. Bruenn, called in for a routine check of the patient's heart, was alarmed by what he found, particularly when he compared the current data with earlier charts in the hospital's files. The President was suffering from progressive enlargement of the heart and steadily rising blood pressure, the reading at the time being 186/108. The official diagnosis was of hypertension, hypertensive heart disease, cardiac failure (left ventricular), and acute bronchitis. After consultation among the hospital staff and with outside specialists, a regime of complete rest, improved diet, and regular dosages of digitalis was prescribed. It was also recommended that Lieutenant Commander Bruenn be detailed to maintain a regular watch on the patient's progress. (The regular White House physician, Admiral Ross T. McIntire, was not a heart specialist.) The President accepted the doctors' advice with no show of alarm or complaint. He went off for an extended stay at "Hobcaw," the South Carolina plantation of his friend Bernard Baruch; took his medicine, cut down on his smoking, got a lot of rest and sunshine, and within a week had regained much of his spirit and vitality.

During most of the remaining months of his life, according to Dr. Bruenn, there was no substantial worsening of the President's condition. His blood pressure continued to fluctuate abnormally but within tolerable limits; he had a single, brief experience of anginal pain that left no measurable aftereffects, and he encountered occasional periods of exhaustion and lowered vitality. These setbacks were attributed to the effects of tension and overexertion when the President, under the pressure of his duties, would ignore the regimen of rest and medication which had been prescribed for him. But his recuperative powers were great: Within a week or so he would be back at his normal level of vigor and well-being. Even at Yalta, where the demands upon his reserves were most severe, he suffered no impairment of his physical and mental resources, although Dr. Bruenn found it necessary there to impose on him a rigid rest schedule. (The conference sessions customarily began in the late afternoon and ran well into the night, a period when Roosevelt's vitality was usually on the decline.)

What accounted for most of the public concern about the President's health, Dr. Bruenn asserts, was his loss of weight, which gave a lined, haggard look to his face and made him appear to have shrunken so that his clothes no longer fitted his once-robust torso. During that last year Roosevelt lost approximately 20 pounds due in part to medical restrictions on his diet and in part to his own determination to "get rid of some fat." The effects showed up strikingly—especially in photographs and to those who saw the President only at infrequent intervals. Robert Sherwood, called back from Europe in October after an eight months absence to help out with campaign speech writing, recorded his impression thus:

When I first went in to see the President . . . I was shocked by his appearance. I had heard that he had lost a lot of weight, but I was not prepared for the almost ravaged appearance of his face. He had his coat off and his shirt collar seemed several sizes too large for his emaciated neck. But I soon began to suspect that the fears expressed by Hopkins, Watson, and the others were groundless. He seemed to me more full of good humor and of fight than ever.

Dr. Bruenn records the final weeks and moments of President Roosevelt's life in these words:

During the two weeks after his return from Yalta, the President again began to ignore his rest regimen. In addition to a heavy schedule during the day, he began to work much too late in the evenings. His appetite had become poor, and, although he had not been weighed, it appeared that he had lost more weight. He complained of not being able to taste his food. There was no nausea. Because of his anorexia, digitalis was withheld for several days although no digitalis toxicity was discernible in the electrocardiogram. There was no cough or cardiac symptoms. Heart size was unchanged. The sounds were clear and of good quality. The rhythm was regular, and the apical systolic murmur had not changed. Blood pressure values were somewhat lower. Despite the withdrawal of digitalis, he was still troubled with his lack of appetite. Otherwise, he insisted that he felt well. Digitalis therapy was resumed.

Last Days at Warm Springs

By the end of March he began to look bad. His color was poor, and he appeared to be very tired, although he continued to sleep well. Heart and lungs were unchanged. A period of total rest was urged. Accordingly, on March 29 the President left Washington for Warm Springs, Georgia. The weather there was ideal, and within a week there was a decided and obvious improvement in his appearance and sense of well-being. He had begun to eat with appetite, rested beautifully, and was in excellent spirits. He began to go out every afternoon for short motor trips, which he clearly enjoyed. He had given up the eggnogs in favor of a gruel between meals. The physical examination was unchanged except for the blood pressure, the level of which had become extremely wide, ranging from 170/88 and 240/130 mm Hg. There was no apparent cause and effect. By April 10 improvement had continued. His color was much better, and his appetite was very good; he asked for double helpings of food. Although he had not been weighed, it was apparent that he had begun to gain a little weight. He had been resting very well, and he began to increase his activities. He was in excellent spirits and began to plan a weekend, involving a barbecue and attendance at a minstrel show.

On April 12 I saw the President at 9:20 A.M., a few minutes after he had awakened. He had slept well but complained of a slight headache and some stiffness of the neck. He ascribed this to a soreness of the muscles, and relief was experienced with slight massage.

He had a very good morning, and his guests commented on how well he looked. He was occupied during the morning going over State papers and, while doing so, was sitting in a chair, as the subject of some sketches that were being made by an artist. He suddenly complained of a terrific occipital headache. He became unconscious a minute or two later.

1:30 to 2:30 P.M.: When I saw him 15 minutes later, he was pale, cold, and sweating profusely. He was totally unconscious with fairly frequent generalized tetanic contractions of mild degree. Pupils of the eyes were at first equal, but in a few minutes the right pupil became widely dilated. The lungs were clear, but he was breathing stertorously but regularly. Heart sounds were excellent, heart rate was 96/min. Systolic blood pressure was well over 300 mm Hg; diastolic pressure was 190 mm Hg. He had voided involuntarily.

Warmth in the form of hot water bottles and blankets was applied, and papavarine, 1 grain, was administered intravenously. Amylnitrite was also given to relieve the apparent intense vasoconstriction. Reflexes were unobtainable in the legs; right elbow was. . . .

It was apparent that the President had suffered a massive cerebral hemorrhage. I immediately called Washington on the private telephone line and contacted Dr. McIntire and informed him of the catastrophe. He told me that he would call Dr. Paullin in Atlanta immediately.

2:45 P.M.: Color was much improved. Breathing was a little irregular and stertorous, but deep. Blood pressure had fallen to 240/120 mm Hg. Heart sounds were good—rate, 90/min.

3:15 P.M.: Blood pressure was 210/110 mm Hg; heart rate, 96/min; right pupil, still widely dilated, but the left pupil, from moderate constriction, had become moderately dilated. Occasional spasm of rigidity with marked slowing of respiration was noted. During latter phases, he had become cyanotic.

3:30 P.M.: Pupils were approximately equal. Breathing had become irregular but of good amplitude.

3:31 P.M.: Breathing suddenly stopped and was replaced by occasional gasps. Heart sounds were not audible. Artificial respiration was begun and caffeine sodium benzoate given intramuscularly. At this moment Dr. Paullin arrived from Atlanta. Adrenalin was administered into the heart muscle.

3:35 P.M.: I pronounced him dead.

The news of the President's death, coming late on that Thursday afternoon, hit the nation with the same jolting impact as those first stuttering bulletins about Pearl Harbor. There was an instant of stunned disbelief when one first got the word, then a gradual, anguished realization, as the word was reiterated, that it must be true. One first heard it in varying ways—a breathless announcement breaking into the bland routine of a radio program; a telephone call at one's home or office from a friend asking incredulously, "Have you heard the news?"; a snatch of conversation picked up on the street, in a bar, in a homeward-bound trolley or subway, "The President is dead! . . . Roosevelt just died! . . ."; the peremptory ringing of the alarm bell on wire service tickers in hundreds of news rooms all across the country as the keys clacked out their dire tidings: "Bulletin . . . Bulletin . . . Early announces President died Warm Springs 3:55 this afternoon . . . Stand by . . ." At New York's Stage Door Canteen a lively musical program with actress Beatrice Lillie in the cast was abruptly halted in mid-song when the director walked onto the stage, held up his hand and said: "I have a terrible announcement to make. Out of respect to the memory of the President of the United States, this show cannot go on." The message left only puzzlement on the faces of the several hundred service men in the audience. "I mean," the speaker said falteringly, "the President has just died."

The effect of this news intruding so unexpectedly upon a sunny spring afternoon in 1945 was no less stunning than that which exploded on the afternoon of December 7, 1941. But there was a difference in the emotional response. Pearl Harbor had induced anger, frustration, a boiling over of the primitive impulse for revenge and retribution. Roosevelt's sudden death played a different kind of havoc with people's emotions—one of sorrow, of personal bereavement, of loneliness in the realization that a face and symbol so long familiar was never to be seen again. Many wept quietly and unashamedly, and many prayed. As dusk fell in Washington, pedestrians found their way to Lafayette Square, across Pennsylvania Avenue from the White House, and stood there, singly and in small clusters, silently or in hushed conversation, gazing reverently toward the tall white portico, the dimly lighted windows, the flag hanging limply at half staff. A reporter leaving the press room a little after midnight observed that there were still 300–400 in this mute congregation. And across the Square in the opposite direction, the doors to St. John's Church remained open through the night and occasional passersby drifted in to sit or kneel briefly in silent communion with their various dieties, and then went on their way.

This somber mood pervaded the entire country, and indeed much of the civilized world. For Franklin Roosevelt had become in his lifetime a towering symbol of strength and hope, a leader who seemed able to surmount the usual human frailties of both the body and the spirit, a seer whose gaze swept past the horizons that limited the vision of lesser men. To millions of his countrymen he could do no wrong. Their allegiance to him was bound in unquestioning faith and affection. And even those other millions who disavowed any such allegiance—who marked him as cunning, devious, unscrupulous, even dishonest—had perforce to acknowledge the magnitude of his personality and the immense forcefulness of his leadership. For 12 years he had so dominated the life of this country, so shaped its fortunes and its attitudes, that his image seemed almost to have become inscribed upon the nation's crest. Whether one loved or despised him, one could not demean his enormous hold upon the public imagination, nor contemplate without some tremors of uncertainty the disruptive impact of his sudden passing. What will happen now? one asked, and groped for answers.

One thing that did happen, almost immediately, in fulfillment of the Constitutional mandate, was that another man became President in Roosevelt's stead. And that was far from reassuring to many, friend and foe alike of the departed chieftain. David Lilienthal, hurrying to Washington from his base in the Tennessee Valley that night, scribbled in his diary: "Complete disbelief. That was first. Then a sick, hapless feeling. Then consternation at the thought of that Throttlebottom, Truman. The country and the world doesn't deserve to be left this way, with Truman at the head of the country at such a time."

The special train bearing Roosevelt's body from Warm Springs arrived at Washington's Union Station at 10 o'clock on Saturday morning. Thousands packed the station plaza to pay silent tribute to him on this last home-coming, and an estimated half million others lined the sidewalks of the mile-long route down Pennsylvania Avenue to the White House. The casket was borne on a caisson drawn by six white horses and accompanied by a military procession representing all the branches of the service, including the Army and Naval academies. The bands were muted and their drums muffled and draped in black. Mrs. Roosevelt and other members of the immediate family, President and Mrs. Truman, and members of the Cabinet followed in black limousines. To the onlooker the scene had the quality of a tragic, ritualistic pantomime; a vast, nearly immobile quietude but with a palpable emanation of choked emotion that was almost overpowering. This sense of grief was inadvertently underlined for the millions who followed the procession by radio, when newscaster Arthur Godfrey, stationed near the White House gate, broke down in sobs as the caisson rolled slowly past him.

"Now," he said, his voice husky and tremulous, ". . . now just coming past the Treasury I can see . . . I can see the horses drawing the caisson . . . And behind it . . . behind it is the car bearing the man on whose shoulders now falls . . . now falls the terrific burden and responsibilities . . . that were handled so well by the man to whose body we are paying our last respects now . . . God . . . *God bless him, President Truman!*" And then, in a losing effort to fight down the sob in his throat, he blurted out: "We now return you to the studio."

The dead President's body did not lie in state. Instead, a few score friends and officials were permitted to visit the bier where it stood in the flower-banked East Room. In the late afternoon a brief memorial service was held there presided over by Bishop Angus Dun of the Washington Cathedral. That night the body was returned to the train for the trip to Hyde Park and the funeral on Sunday morning.

Not since the death of President Lincoln, 80 years earlier almost to the day, had the collective heart of the nation been more severely wrenched than now. It may be historically useful, therefore, to provide an eyewitness account of the final rites for one of the most illustrious figures of the century after Lincoln.

Hyde Park, N.Y., April 15.—It must have been on just such a day as this that Franklin D. Roosevelt hoped to come home to Hyde Park, free of the labors and responsibilities of state, to live out his years in quiet contentment in the company of his family and neighbors. . . .

Today one can understand the deep yearning that must have been in his heart. For he must have visualized then such a day as this at Hyde Park: The crisp, brilliant, sun-drenched atmosphere of early spring: the sparkling Hudson between low rolling hills painted with the tender green of new foliage; the ancient elms, poplars, and sycamores burgeoning anew with life; the bright yellow forsythias and jonquils, and the apple trees of his orchard in snowy white bloom. . . .

Funeral Pure Drama.

The funeral services were impressive as only pure drama can be. They were held in the semi-formal rose garden, an L-shaped park about an acre in extent, lying between the manse and the library. It is completely shut off from the rest of the grounds by a 15-foot hedge of clipped hemlock, and shielded from without by towering elms and cedars.

Formal beds of roses, peonies, and iris surround a large central mall carpeted in velvety grass. Near its southern end the grave was dug, its head toward the east. . . .

By 9:45 some 300 people had entered the garden. They were there by special invitation only; members of the cabinet and their wives; the justices of the Supreme Court and their wives; the Earl of Athlone and the Canadian Prime Minister W.L. Mackenzie King; General Marshall, the chief of staff, and Admirals King and Leahy; 15 members each from the two houses of Congress, headed by Majority Leader Alben Barkley and Speaker Sam Rayburn; Bernard Baruch, friend and counselor of the late President; Jim Farley, his political mentor through the greater part of his political career; Mrs. Louis Howe, widow of his closest friend and confidante; former Governor Lehman of New York; Mayor Kelly of Chicago, former Justice James Byrnes, former Secretary of the Navy Josephus Daniels, and numerous others of prominence. . . .

The special train bearing the President's body had stopped on a spur track at one end of the estate. There the flag-draped casket was lowered to a black artillery caisson drawn by six black horses and accompanied by eight body bearers representing each branch of the armed services.

Escort From West Point.

The procession was led by the band from the U.S. military academy at West Point and a battalion of cadets in full dress uniform. Immediately behind the caisson a riderless horse, hooded in crepe and with empty boots and a saber at the saddle, was led by a Negro soldier. In three following limousines rode the immediate members of the funeral party.

At exactly five minutes to ten, the officer in charge of the guard of honor issued a subdued command. Three hundred rifles snapped at "present arms." A short distance away a cannon boomed. Its echo rolled across the still countryside. At 20 second intervals it repeated until all 21 guns in the presidential salute had been fired.

As the last echo died away, a distant flourish of trumpets was heard signifying the start of the procession from the siding a quarter of a mile away. For five minutes or more there was no sound whatever in the garden, save for the flight of a fleet of bombers overhead.

Then there emerged from the distance the muted notes of Chopin's Funeral March. Very slowly the volume grew, cadenced to a slow funeral pace, magnificent in its solemn grandeur.

Every head was bowed, every breast was choked with emotion as the sad, sonorous dirge pulsated through the morning air. Many of the congregation wept quietly or betrayed their grief in saddened, contorted faces.

The band and then the cadet battalion marched slowly into the enclosure at 20 minutes after 10, and halted near the grave. The caisson and limousines stopped outside a natural arch in the hedge giving access to the garden.

Rector Leads Way.

As the band played softly a few bars from "Nearer My God to Thee," a white surpliced figure bearing a gold crucifix entered through the arch and walked slowly to the left of the grave. He was followed by the Reverend George W. Anthony, patriarchal rector of St. James Episcopal Church, where the Roosevelt family has worshiped for generations. Following him, the body bearers brought the heavy casket and rested it gently on the framework over the grave.

Mrs. Roosevelt, dressed in heavy black but with her widow's veil thrown back, looked more pale and worn than she has at any time during the last three days' ordeal. She was accompanied to the graveside by the only two of her children who were present, Elliott on her left, Anna on her right.

They stood about 10 feet in front of the grave.

Immediately to the rear were the four Roosevelt daughters-in-law and Colonel John Boettiger, husband of Anna. At the back of the group were President and Mrs. Truman, their daughter, Mary Margaret, and the President's military aide, Colonel Harry Vaughn.

The services, conducted entirely by the rector, opened with the moving invocation from the Book of Common Prayer. In ten minutes they were concluded with the benediction:

"Father, in thy gracious keeping leave we now thy servant sleeping. Grant him, O Lord, eternal rest."

As the benediction was pronounced, a squad of cadets moved to the rear of the grave and fired the traditional salute to the dead of three volleys. There was a muffled roll of drums. A trumpeter stepped forward and sounded taps. The body bearers at the grave-side lifted the flag from the casket, folded it ceremoniously, and one of their number delivered it into the hands of Mrs. Roosevelt.

At 10:47 the family turned and left the enclosure.[3]

IV

"If you fellows know how to pray, pray for me now."

So spoke in all solemnity the thirty-second President of the United States to a group of reporters he encountered in the Capitol on his first full day in office. The remark was symptomatic not only of the emotional shock that Fate had dealt him, but of the humility he felt under the staggering weight of the responsibility which had fallen so suddenly upon him.

Few men have entered upon the Presidency with fewer of the visible qualifications for the job than Harry Truman, and no one sensed the deficiency more keenly than he. But it is also true that few men have brought to it a greater measure of courage, determination, honesty, and plain, unpretentious common sense. His tenure was one of the most torturous of any President in history. It spanned the chasm between what the present older generation means by "The Past" and "Modern Times" —the era of the atom, the cold war, world leadership, and the infinite ramifications of the "affluent society." It was a tenure also marked by intense and sometimes paralyzing political strife, by personal denigration such as no President since Andrew Johnson has had to endure. Truman did not surmount all these challenges and obstacles in triumph, but he survived their buffetings with a high score for achievement and spirit. And when he departed from office after seven and three-quarters years he left the unmistakable imprint of greatness on the Presidency and upon the history of his time.*

Truman's genius lay in his ability to do the best he could with what he had and not to despair over what he did not have. He was a quite ordinary man who had to make do without any special endowments of learning, intellect, or presence. He never suffered the illusion that he was another Roosevelt or Churchill, and neither did he agonize over whether he was their inferior. He simply applied what talents he had according to the old Biblical prescription, "Whatsoever thy hand findeth to do, do it with all thy might." That rule had been drilled into him as a boy, and he practiced it all his life. It gave him the will to face up squarely to the toughest decisions and never to shirk a responsibility. It led him to respect such strength and wisdom as the Lord had given him and not to lament what the Lord had withheld. He was a great President not because he had brilliance—which he did not—but because he had courage. There was more than caprice in the little sign he kept on his White House desk for many years—THE BUCK STOPS HERE.

"Who is this Truman?"

People asked that question in honest puzzlement and with a touch of scorn when he was nominated for the Vice-Presidency. They asked it again, and with an overtone of concern, when he was inducted into the

---

* This is, of course, a highly subjective judgment but it is shared by many competent authorities. Professor Clinton Rossiter, the country's leading scholar on the Presidency, wrote in 1956: "I am ready to hazard an opinion, to which I did not come easily or lightly, that Harry Truman will eventually win a place as President, if not as a hero, alongside Jefferson and Theodore Roosevelt." And Harvard historian Arthur M. Schlesinger published the result of a poll of 75 historians in 1962 in which Truman was ranked ninth among all occupants of the White House. Schlesinger thus put him in the category of "near great" rather than "great," but a number of those in the poll rated Truman among the top five.

Presidency at a hasty, impromptu ceremony at the White House in the early evening of April 12, 1945.

He was not, of course, a total stranger. His name had often cropped up in the newspapers in connection with the Senate War Investigating Committee of which he was Chairman. And he had made stump speeches around the country as Roosevelt's surrogate in the last campaign. But the impression he had left on many was indistinct, in small dimension. He seemed to be a cardboard cutout; a dapper, Prairie-state politician in a bow tie and double-breasted suit who spoke flippantly in a twangy, earthy vernacular that contrasted gratingly with the cultured elegance of FDR. But when one tried to place him more precisely it could be recalled that he had done a pretty good job with his War Investigating Committee, turning up many instances of fraud and inefficiency. If he was a product of the Pendergast machine, no taint of its corruption had yet soiled his name. And his 10-year Senate record, so far as it was visible, indicated that he had faithfully voted the New Deal line without ever identifying himself with the extreme liberals and left-wingers. So the uneasy consensus about him was, "Wait and see, and hope for the best."

Who *was* this man Truman?

His roots went back to the rustic, egalitarian society of the middle western frontier. His grandparents on both sides had emigrated from Virginia and Kentucky to the Missouri country early in the decade of the 1840s. His father, John Anderson Truman, was born in Jackson County in 1851 and pursued variously the life of a farmer and livestock trader. In 1881 he married Martha Ellen Young, the twenty-nine-year-old daughter of Solomon Young, a neighbor in the little farming community of Hickman's Mill. The young couple settled into a small white cottage in the village of Lamar and there on May 8, 1884, the first of their three children was born. They named the boy Harry and gave him a middle initial "S", but never agreed on what the letter stood for.

John Truman found it hard to stay put anywhere for very long, and over the next several years he moved his family a number of times, to Belton, to Grand View where the Youngs lived, to Kansas City very briefly, and finally to the little Jackson county seat of Independence. This became "home" to Harry, his brother, and his sister and they grew up there in its bucolic surroundings and attended the local schools. A long bout with diphtheria when he was ten left the boy with permanently impaired eyesight, for which he had to wear glasses ever after. This eliminated him from the rough-and-tumble play of his peers and he turned to books as the principal source of his amusement. History fascinated him particularly and he began to devour everything in the little town's library, getting to know the heroes of Plutarch and Carlyle as intimately as those of the Civil War. It was an addiction from which he was to profit greatly in later life. Music was also a serious preoccupation and at the age of thirteen he began to take piano lessons from a professional teacher in Independence.

Martha Truman was small and vivacious, but where John Truman tended to be footloose and had a streak of the gambler in his makeup, she had the iron will and sense of duty that went with her Baptist faith. Her influence on Harry Truman's character was profound. There was in her the tough-fibered, resolute qualities of the women of the frontier from whom she was immediately descended. Duty was sacred and its performance inescapable. Waste and sloth were not only wicked but repugnant as well. Truth was less an adornment of the soul than an imperative of one's daily conduct. One said what was in one's mind without devious evasions. One lived by the eternal verities of good and evil, heaven and hell, as set forth in the Bible, and went regularly to church because it was a natural part of life.

But one need not be a bluenose about these things: Righteousness was not a cross to be borne in pain. Martha Ellen described herself as a "lightfoot Baptist," which meant that she did not regard dancing and other worldly diversions with the pious horror that was prevalent among many of that faith. Thus, gaiety and discipline, fun and duty, love and forbearance blended harmoniously in the household in which Harry Truman grew to young manhood. And on this experience the kernel of his character was formed: to do what has to be done the best one can and without hesitancy or self-pity.

"I never take a problem to bed with me at night," he once said after becoming President. "When I've made a decision I know it's the best decision I can make under the circumstances, and I stop worrying about it."

Harry Truman graduated from the high school in Independence well up in his class but he did not, like several of his friends, go on to college: The family finances were not equal to it. For the next several years he held a variety of jobs, including that of bank clerk in Kansas City, and in 1906 he settled down to becoming a farmer, operating with his father the Young farm at Grandview which they had inherited. There were some moderately prosperous times between 1909 and 1914 and young Harry celebrated by buying one of the first automobiles to be seen in that part of Jackson County—a four-cylinder Stafford with gleaming brass trim and a pair of headlights as big as a locomotive's. With so much status and mobility he was able to step up his attentions to that blue-eyed blonde in Independence, Bess Wallace, whom he had been courting since high school days; to go regularly to meetings of the Masonic Lodge which he had joined in nearby Belson; and to keep up with the weekly drills of the National Guard company in Kansas City of which he had become a member.

When war was declared in 1917 Harry Truman's National Guard

outfit was mustered into service as Battery D, 129th Field Artillery, 35th Division. When they went into training at Fort Sill, Oklahoma, he had his First Lieutenant's silver bar, and when they shipped out for France nine months later he bore the rank of Captain. The company had a substantial taste of frontline action under fire and acquitted itself well if not conspicuously. Truman's war experience made two important contributions to his character. It obliterated forever the gnawing sense of physical inadequacy that he had carried over from childhood, and it gave him a confident sense of command.

He was discharged from the Army on May 6, 1919, and on June 28 he and Elizabeth Virginia Wallace were married in Trinity Episcopal Church, in Independence. After a short honeymoon they settled down in the spacious white clapboard Wallace house at 219 North Delaware Street, which always remained home to them, the White House notwithstanding. Their only child, Margaret, was born there February 17, 1924.

Harry Truman was thirty-five years old when he came home from the war, acquired a wife, and began to cast around for a suitable niche in the civilian world. He had been a tolerably good farmer and a tolerably good bank clerk, but neither of these occupations appealed to him now. Moreover, he could afford to be a bit choosy; he estimated his net work in cash and farmlands at about $15,000, with no strings attached. The postwar boom was in full swing; it was a period of easy money and high expectations. So guided, he and a wartime buddy, Eddie Jacobson, pooled everything they owned and could borrow to set themselves up in the haberdashery business, selecting a choice Kansas City location across the street from the then-new Muehlebach Hotel.

Things went swimmingly for the new enterprise for a year: There was a brisk market for such luxuries as $12 silk shirts and high-button shoes with suede tops at $20 a pair. But the boom collapsed, the bottom fell out of the wheat market, and the firm of Truman & Jacobson went under. The two partners did their best to pay off their obligations. Jacobson ultimately was forced into bankruptcy. Truman managed to avoid this dread expedient, but when he came to the Senate in 1934 there was still an unsatisfied judgment of $8,994 outstanding against him in favor of a Kansas City bank. In time, however, all the firm's obligations were paid off in a manner that left little tarnish on the partners' reputations.

There was one important dividend for Truman out of the haberdashery episode. The shop on Main Street, during its brief existence, became a popular rendezvous for many of his wartime colleagues and Truman's circle of friends and acquaintances in the city widened greatly. One afternoon shortly before the crash, Mike Pendergast, brother of Boss Tom of the ruling Democratic faction in the county and known to

Truman only by sight and reputation, strolled in, leaned casually on the counter, and quietly put a surprising question to him.

"How'd you like to be county judge?"

"Gosh, I don't know," the startled Truman answered.

"Well, think it over," said Mike. "If you want it you can have it." And he turned and walked out.

As Harry Truman's formal entry into politics has been reconstructed by local observers, the consensus is that the Pendergasts needed him about as badly as he needed them. Truman at that time—the summer of 1922—badly needed a secure income, it is true, but there were other avenues open to him beside the public payroll. (The judgeship, incidentally, is an administrative and not a judicial position.) On the other hand, Boss Pendergast badly needed a presentable and winning candidate from the Eastern District of Jackson County, in which both Independence and Kansas City are located. He was at war with two rival Democratic factions and at stake in that year's election was not only control of the patronage-rich county government but control of the Democratic organization as well. The Pendergasts were not then openly involved in the criminal activities that cut them down later, but they were a rough, tough lot and the target of much suspicion. In the circumstances, no ordinary hack wearing the Pendergast colors would be likely to win against the relatively respectable candidates whom the other factions had put into the field.

Truman, for his part, was strictly a political nobody (which may have been more of a help than a hindrance at the time), but he had a good reputation, he was popular, he was a leader in veteran's organizations, he was a Baptist and a Mason, and he had relatives and family friends scattered in nearly every precinct in the county. What was more, he was willing. He soon accepted the Pendergast offer, went bouncing about the county's back ways in an old Dodge roadster to shake every hand he could find, and won the primary contest in a narrow three-way split. The election that followed was a walkaway, and Harry Truman's political star was in orbit.

The evidence is that Truman made a good county judge, that he was industrious and conscientious in looking after the county's affairs, and that he was scrupulously honest in the handling of contract awards and public expenditures. He was defeated for reelection in 1924—the only electoral defeat he ever suffered—but came back strong two years later. By all accounts his relations with the Pendergasts were proper and aboveboard: He gave them his loyalty and they gave him their trust, and neither sought to impose his scruples upon the other. As William M. Redding, an on-the-spot observer of Kansas City politics of the period, puts it, Truman:

. . . wore the boss's collar more lightly than any important figure identified with the machine. The collar didn't chafe very often for the two good reasons that the Independence man had a strong mind of his own together with a highly developed sense of party regularity, and Tom Pendergast was able to see and appreciate the rare quality of this combination.

One of the most fascinating anomalies of Harry Truman's career is that he, a man of such impeccable honesty and political integrity, could have maintained so close a relationship and dependence upon the Pendergast organization without being corrupted by it. For the organization was in time shown to be one of the most brazen and corrupt in the whole glittering history of American bossism. But Truman's political enemies, as well as more objective students, have combed through the records time after time and not found one substantial clue of Truman's complicity in any of its myriad misdeeds. Until 1934 County Judge Truman was too small a cog in the Pendergast operation to affect its course one way or the other, even if he had tried. So he did what many another smart political comer has done: He rode the machine as far as it would take him but kept his hands clean along the way. That is a pragmatic rather than a moralistic philosophy, but under the rules of the game it is what pays off.

"I controlled the Democratic party in eastern Jackson County when I was County Judge," Truman told Jonathan Daniels. "Mike [Pendergast] turned it over to me. In any election I could deliver eleven thousand votes and not steal a one. It was not necessary. The vote stealing in Kansas City was silly."

Harry Truman carried his belief in organization politics right into the White House, which accounted in no small measure for his success as President.

Truman was picked to run for the Senate in 1934 by much the same combination of political factors that led to his choice for County Judge 12 years earlier: The Pendergasts badly needed a "clean" candidate to insure their control of the statewide Democratic organization in a particularly difficult contest. Truman had been passed over (to his keen disappointment) in selections a couple of years earlier for the Governorship and a newly created congressional district for Jackson County. But the Senate race in 1934 presented the machine with a different set of problems. The Republican incumbent was not one of those problems: He could be knocked over without difficulty by any Democrat. The choice of that Democrat was what was crucial to Big Tom—whether the new Senator would be "his" man or anothers'.

By Missouri tradition, one Senator had always come from the western half of the state, around Kansas City, and was therefore a

Pendergast man, and the other from the eastern half, based on St. Louis, and thus beholden to its current satrap. Pendergast's man had lost out to Republican Roscoe Patterson in 1928, whose seat was now on the block. Currently, the "eastern" Senator was Democrat Bennett C. Clark, elected in 1932. Now, Clark was backing the candidacy of another "easterner," Jacob L. "Tuck" Milligan, for the Democratic nomination to oppose Senator Patterson in the statewide election. If Milligan should win, Clark would thus be in a position to challenge Pendergast's claim to being boss of the Democratic Party in all of Missouri, an intolerable thought to Big Tom. An added complication was that Pendergast, as a staunch anti-Roosevelt man, had been getting short shrift on the favors and patronage of the New Deal, while Senator Clark, who was only slightly less adamant in his opposition to FDR, was being sedulously courted by the powers in Washington. Big Tom thus needed his own man in Washington—first, to preserve his balance of power in Missouri, and second, to direct into the proper Missouri channels the flood of jobs and relief money now flowing from the federal spigot.

After some hemming and hawing, the choice finally came down to County Judge Truman as the man to make the race. He was clean, he had a good public record, and he had shown a happy facility for tapping the New Deal pipeline in behalf of Jackson County. Truman made support of the New Deal a principal prop of his campaign, in fact, since the other candidates arrayed against him were conservative, old-line Democrats who viewed the goings-on in Washington with suspicion. His candid, folksy manner, meanwhile, allayed suspicions that he was merely a tool of the Pendergast organization and built a strong following for him in the rural districts of the state. He won the primary with a comfortable 40,000-vote plurality over the runner-up, and went on to win in the general election by a landslide margin over his Republican opponent, Patterson.

Harry Truman was fifty years old when he was sworn into the Senate on January 3, 1935. He was one of a freshman class of 13, but something a bit special attached to him: He stood out from the rest, according to one columnist, as "the Senator from Pendergast." Truman was aware of this shadow clouding his status; he was also conscious of a feeling of self-doubt and insecurity at finding himself mingling in the exalted company of the United States Senate. He confessed his ignorance to, and sought the guidance of many, and resolved to take night courses in a local law school to make up for his deficiencies (which he never did).

"There is hardly a record or a memory of that time," Jonathan Daniels has written, "which does not reflect a humility which went beyond modesty almost to apology."

Truman managed in time to overcome his want of confidence and

Across from the White House crowds gathered through the night, following the announcement of Roosevelt's death. (UPI)

The Roosevelt funeral at Hyde Park. (UPI)

Harry S. Truman at the White House, April 12, 1945, taking the oath of President from Chief Justice Harlan F. Stone, immediately after it was learned in Washington that President Roosevelt was dead. Mrs. Truman and daughter Margaret stand behind him. (UPI)

In San Francisco for the United Nations Conference on International Organization, the foreign ministers of the "Big Four" read a message of the collapse of Western Germany. Left to right: Anthony Eden, Britain; Edward Stettinius, U.S.; V. M. Molotov, U.S.S.R.; and Dr. T. V. Soong, China, May 1945. (UPI)

Faced with the deployment of three million troops from the European theater
of war to the Pacific in 1945, the Office of Defense Transportation appealed to
the American public to save gas. (Wide World Photos)

General Eisenhower holds pens used to sign the German surrender documents at Reims, May 7, 1945. (UPI)

Albert Einstein, with his daughter, taking the oath of allegiance. (UPI)

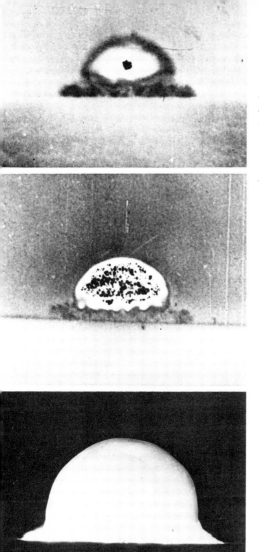

The atomic bomb explosion at Alamagordo, New Mexico, July 16, 1945. These photos were made at a range of six miles with an automatic movie camera. At the top: the start of the explosion. Middle: The cloud is growing bigger and taking an egg shape. The black areas in the middle were said by witnesses to be brighter than the sun. Bottom: The cloud rose to a height of 40,000 feet. (UPI)

Air view of Hiroshima shortly after the bomb dropped on August 6, 1945. (UPI)

"Little Boy," the type of atomic bomb detonated over Hiroshima. (UPI)

The "Big Three" at Potsdam, Germany: British Prime Minister Clement Attlee, President Truman, and Soviet Marshal Josef Stalin, August 1945. (UPI)

Japanese Foreign Minister Mamoru Shigemitsu signs the documents of Japanese surrender aboard the U.S.S. Missouri in Tokyo Bay, September 1 (?), 1945. General MacArthur, back to camera at right, watches. (UPI)

General MacArthur receiving Japanese Emperor Hirohito at the United States Embassy in Tokyo, September 1945. (UPI)

VJ-Day on Okinawa, the 1st Marine Division Cemetery. (UPI)

Crowds jam Times Square, New York City, waiting for the announcement that the war with Japan was over, August 14, 1945. (UPI)

Mao Tse-tung and Chiang Kai-shek toast each other at a welcoming party for Mao, Chungking, China, 1946. (UPI)

J. Robert Oppenheimer testifying before the Special Senate Committee on Atomic Energy, December 1945. (UPI)

The "Big Three" union leaders of the CIO: Albert Fitzgerald, United Electrical Workers (left); Philip Murray, President of the CIO; and Walter Reuther, United Auto Workers. (UPI)

United Mine Workers President John L. Lewis shakes hands with President Truman as the soft coal strike was settled, May 29, 1946. (UPI)

Senate Atomic Energy Committee meets on March 3, 1947, to consider the appointment of David E. Lilienthal (right, foreground) as Chairman of the AEC. At far left, Senator Kenneth McKellar. (UPI)

George F. Kennan. (UPI)

Bernard Baruch with Mrs. Eleanor Roosevelt, July 1947. (UPI)

Americans build a 5,000 foot airstrip inside bombed-out Berlin, large enough to handle the B-29 transport planes that would airlift supplies into the occupied city, July 1948. (UPI)

Governor Thomas E. Dewey opening his presidential campaign in Des Moines, Iowa, September 1948. (UPI)

Henry Wallace (right) with his running mate Senator Glen Taylor of Idaho, third party candidates. (UPI)

Harry Truman, with Margaret, and "the Boss," on 1948 campaign train. (UPI)

Truman holds an early edition of the Chicago Daily Tribune *for November 4, 1948. (UPI)*

Japanese war leaders before the eleven-nation international military tribunal in Tokyo, November 1948. Former Premier Hideki Tojo (fifth from left in the prisoner's dock) and six others were sentenced to death by hanging. (UPI)

Secretary of Defense James V. Forrestal, with President Truman. (UPI)

Dean Acheson (right) replaces
George Marshall as Secretary
of State, January 20, 1949.
(UPI)

President Truman signing the North Atlantic Pact at the White House. Left to right: Senators Henry Cabot Lodge, Jr. and Walter George; Secretary of Defense Louis Johnson; Senators Scott Lucas, Tom Connally, and J. William Fulbright; Secretary of State Dean Acheson; Senator Claude Pepper; Vice President Alben Barkley; Representative John W. McCormack; Senator Arthur Vandenberg. July 1949. (UPI)

Dr. Ralph Bunche, with U.S. delegates John Ross (left) and Philip Jessup (right), in Paris for UN meetings on the Palestine issue, October 1948. (UPI)

Alger Hiss (standing left) and Whittaker Chambers (standing right) at the public hearing of the House Committee on Un-American Activities, August 1948. (UPI)

Chairman of the AEC David Lilienthal, General Eisenhower, Senator Brien McMahon, Secretary of State Dean Acheson, and Secretary of Defense Louis Johnson, before meeting to discuss atomic relations with Great Britain and Canada, July 1949. (UPI)

to throw off substantially at least, the onus of his Pendergast background. He was fortunate in his major committee assignments, being named to Appropriations and to Interstate and Foreign Commerce. He was a studious and conscientious committeeman and soon won respect for his ability to plow into and to grasp complex legislative problems. He did what he could to satisfy the demands of his constituents, including the Pendergast organization, but found himself embarrassingly hampered in matters of patronage and preference by the deference shown his senior colleague, Senator Clark. Though the New Dealers from the White House down tended to ignore him, he faithfully voted the New Deal line—on one important occasion, at least, directly contrary to the expressed wish of Boss Tom. He made friends easily. Vice-President "Cactus Jack" Garner admitted him into the select circle of his cronies who assembled in the Vice-President's office at the end of the day to partake of bourbon and branch water and philosophical discourse. His intimacy with Burt Wheeler of Montana, the populist dragon slayer, served to crystallize in Truman's mind some of the hazy liberal folklore he had brought from the Middle West about the evils of Wall Street and the great monopolists of steel, rails, and oil. But throughout the six years of his first term Truman remained essentially an obscure backbencher—a dependable Senate workhorse, undistinguished and unrenowned.

Truman was strongly of a mind to give up his Senate career as the end of his first term approached in 1940. He had paid off all of his debts but he was flat broke, unable even to prevent the foreclosure of a mortgage on his mother's farm at Grandview. The base of his political power in Kansas City lay in ruins, with Tom Pendergast packed off to prison for bribery and income tax evasion. He would be opposed for the nomination not only by Governor Lloyd Stark, who had strong White House backing, but also by Maurice Milligan, brother of "Tuck," who, as United States Attorney, had led the spectacular assault on the Pendergast empire. It was a bleak prospect. If he ran he probably would be beaten; if he dropped out he would be a quitter. His dilemma in 1940 was almost a scale model of what it would be in 1948—and so was his solution. He would do anything rather than be a quitter.

It was a ramshackle campaign that he and a dozen friends put together, financed on a frayed shoestring of small donations and promissory notes. Radio time, billboards, and big rallies were out of the question. The candidate had to go to the people instead of the people being brought to him, and over a period of two months he showed up smiling and full of bounce in just about every courthouse and town square, every union hall and Masonic lodge in the state. Toward the end of this arduous trail he got help from some of his friends in the Senate, who showed up on the platform with him, and especially from Burt Wheeler. Wheeler stood high with the powerful Railway Brotherhoods. He told them a friend of theirs' was in trouble down in Missouri and they had better give him a hand. They did, extravagantly. "Truman Clubs" sprang up almost overnight in every railroad terminal and roundhouse in the state, and the infection quickly spread to neighboring strongholds of the AFL and the CIO. Suddenly there was money for billboards and radio time, and a few days before election half a million mailboxes across the state were stuffed with complimentary copies of a special "Truman Edition" of *Labor,* the Brotherhoods' weekly newspaper.

In a final, clinching ploy in his strategy, Truman worked out a deal with Robert E. Hannegan, the Democratic leader in St. Louis, whereby Hannegan would throw his powerful, last-minute support to Truman in the three-cornered senatorial race, in exchange for Truman's endorsement of Hannegan's candidate for Governor. This was a vital stroke, for it gave the man from Jackson County the leverage he so desperately needed in the eastern section of the state, traditionally "enemy territory."

In spite of all these stratagems and maneuverings, the primary election on August 6 came down to a photo finish. Truman won renomination but by a statewide plurality of only 7,476 votes, with the slender winning margin coming from the St. Louis precincts. In the general election that followed, Truman beat his Republican rival with a more comfortable edge of 50,000, but his coattails were not wide enough to carry Hannegan's man (who also had won in the Democratic primary) into the Governorship.

The 1940 campaign was Truman's toughest, and in many ways his most valuable. First, it established him beyond any question as a Senator who had won election in his own right. He was nobody's man but his own, and when he got back to Washington he was to have a new measure of respect and admiration, not only from his fellows in the Senate, but from the New Deal hierarchy downtown. Second, it was a seasoning experience which gave a hard new sophistication to his political craftsmanship. Now he understood at first hand, as he never had before, the nature and employment of partisan political power, the secrets and subtle nuances of the public mind, the uses of "the art of the possible"—compromise and accommodation—to surmount political obstacles. And on a more practical level, he had forged a political bond with organized labor that would serve him through many vicissitudes to come.

Truman's second Senate term was a glowing political and public relations success compared to the drab anonymity of his first. Within weeks after the new Congress assembled in January 1941, he proposed to the Senate and won agreement for the creation of a Special Committee to Investigate the Defense Program, and in the usual order of such things was named its chairman. He began modestly enough, with a staff of two investigators and a budget of $15,000, but in a matter of months he had a dozen people working for him and an appropriation of $100,000. He knew what he was after, and he was not long in striking pay dirt. His own observations at a dozen new Army camps which he visited told him that a great deal of waste was being tolerated through shoddy construction and payroll padding. His work on the Appropriations Committee had revealed similar patterns of extravagance and duplication in dizzily expanding defense industries. The control of these activities seemed nowhere to be centralized or adequately monitored, with the military and civilian agencies in Washington often working competitively and at cross-purposes among themselves. The result was a gross waste not only of public funds but of production efficiency.

It was typical of the way Truman went about things that, as his committee was getting under way, he borrowed from the Library of Congress its only copy of the hearings of the Committee on the Conduct of the War, which had operated in the time of the Civil War. He studied its yellowed pages closely and resolved that his committee would not visit upon Roosevelt the humiliation, the obstacles, and the presumptuous meddling that a hostile Congress had visited upon Lincoln from 1863 to 1865 with nearly disastrous results. He remembered from his own reading of history what Lee had said of that committee: that it was worth two divisions to the Confederate cause. The Truman Committee would stick strictly to the issue of how the business of supporting the defense effort was being conducted; how contracts were awarded and fulfilled; how the economic and manpower resources of the nation were being utilized. He would not tell the war agencies how to do their job nor tell the President and the generals how to run the war.

It was a sound formula and it worked well. For the next three and one-half years Truman's committee was a model of probity, thoroughness, and conscientious fact-finding. It called before it in public and private hearings scores of manufacturers, raw materials suppliers, contractors, labor chieftains, military procurement officers, and assorted government officials to unravel bureaucratic red tape, break bottlenecks and monopolies, and to expose inefficiency and fraud. A congressional committee, bound by no rules of procedure save the chairman's whim, has a flexibility (often abused) in getting results in an adversary proceeding not possessed either by the courts or the Executive. It is exposure, the extorted public confession, the implication of guilt. Truman used all these tools, but generally with circumspection. By the summer of 1944 the committee had issued 44 frequently illuminating studies and reports and, according to the proud boast of its chairman, saved the government $15 billion. It also provided a convenient stepping stone for Senator Truman into the Vice-Presidency.

Vice-President Harry S. Truman, natty as always in a double-breasted gray suit, white shirt, and blue polka-dot tie, sat in the big leather chair on the dais as the presiding officer of the United States Senate late on the afternoon of Thursday, April 12, 1945. A dozen Senators nodded in their chairs or fiddled with papers on their desks as one of their colleagues droned through a dull discourse on a pending water treaty with Mexico. Neither was the Vice-President paying much attention. Instead, he was writing a dutiful and chatty letter to his mother and sister back home.

Dear Mamma and Mary—I am trying to write you a letter from the desk of the President of the Senate while a windy Senator is making a speech on a subject with which he is in no way familiar. . . . Hope you are having a nice spell of weather. . . . Turn on the radio tomorrow night at 9:30 your time, and you'll hear Harry make a Jefferson Day address to the nation. I think I'll be on all the networks. . . . Hope you are both well and stay that way. Love to you both. Write when you can.

Harry

As he finished he looked up at the big clock on the facing wall—it was getting on toward five—caught the eye of Majority Leader Alben Barkley with a knowing glance, and signaled the adjournment of business for the day. In the ornate, chandeliered lobby behind the chamber he chatted briefly with a couple of Senators, handed the letter to his administrative assistant to be mailed, and set off at a brisk pace across the Capitol, through the fading light of the rotunda, and down a narrow, twisting corridor to the suite of his good companion, Speaker of the House Sam Rayburn. There he would find a refreshing draught of "bourbon and branch" and the cheery fellowship of Mr. Sam's "Board of Education."

This had become pretty much the pattern of his days. There was no sweat in being Vice-President for Harry Truman; the obligations of the job were far from onerous and the President often seemed almost to have forgotten his existence. He had never had it so good.

As he pushed through the big mahogany door of the Speaker's office, Rayburn said to him: "Harry, Steve Early called you just a minute ago. He wants you to call him at the White House right away."

The call was put through. Early's voice was oddly strained. "Please come over right away, Harry," he said, "and come to the residence, through the main Pennsylvania Avenue entrance."

Truman's face hardened as he put down the phone. "I have to go to the White House at once, and as quietly as possible," he said. He had no knowledge of what this summons was about, but he sensed its urgency. He left without another word, located his chauffeur and was driven off.

In his memoirs Mr. Truman described what happened during the ensuing 20 minutes in these words:

I reached the White House about 5:25 P.M. and was immediately taken in the elevator to the second floor and ushered into Mrs. Roosevelt's study. Mrs. Roosevelt herself, together with Colonel John and Mrs. Anna Roosevelt Boettiger and Mr. Early [the President's press secretary], were in the room when I entered, and I knew at once that something unusual had taken place. Mrs. Roosevelt seemed calm in her characteristic, graceful dignity. She stepped forward and gently placed her arm about my shoulder.

"Harry," she said quietly, "the President is dead."

For a moment I could not bring myself to speak.

The last news we had had from Warm Springs was that Mr. Roosevelt was recuperating nicely. In fact, he apparently was doing so well that no member of his immediate family, and not even his personal physician, was with him. All this flashed through my mind before I found my voice.

"Is there anything I can do for you?" I asked at last.

I shall never forget her deeply understanding reply.

"Is there anything *we* can do for *you?*" she asked. "For you are the one in trouble now."

Now that the Vice-President had been notified, Early got representatives of the three press associations on a simultaneous telephone hookup and made the first official announcement of President Roosevelt's death. It spread instantly to every part of the nation and the world. Mr. Truman called Mrs. Truman at their Connecticut Avenue apartment, told her the tragic news and asked her to come with their daughter Margaret to the White House at once. He then called Chief Justice Harlan Fiske Stone and asked that he come as soon as possible to conduct the swearing in of the new President. Meanwhile, Early and his aide, Jonathan Daniels, summoned members of the Cabinet and the congressional leaders. Some, who had heard the first bulletins on the radio, rushed to the White House of their own accord.

The center of activity was now the large Cabinet Room, uncomfortably crowded with officials and with scores of reporters and White House staff members standing in the doorways and adjacent corridors. There was a low murmur of voices as people tried desperately to find something to say to relieve the almost intolerable tension, and here and there a Cabinet Secretary or a White House clerk gave way quietly to tears.

At a few minutes after seven Justice Stone arrived. He and Mr. Truman took their places at one end of the room under a portrait of Woodrow Wilson. Mrs. Truman stood at her husband's right, dabbing repeatedly at her eyes with a wet handkerchief. As the clock's hands showed 7:09, Harry Truman, standing erect and grim-faced, his eyes unnaturally magnified behind the thick lenses of his glasses, repeated the simple oath, ". . . and will to the best of my ability preserve, protect, and defend the Constitution of the United States. So help me God." As he completed the words, the thirty-second President of the United States took the Bible in both hands and revently put it to his lips.[4]

V

Just as the first Roosevelt administration had its memorable "hundred days," so did the first Truman administration have its "hundred days," give or take a few. But they were of a vastly different order. The New Deal was born between March and June 1933, in a heroic legislative operation that salvaged a tottering economic and political system here at home. Between mid-April and mid-August 1945, history's greatest war ended with wholesale disruption of the world power balance, and the cosmic force of atomic energy was unleashed. In consequence of these events, civilization was flung into an epoch of social and technological upheaval whose tremors are still being felt. It is hard to disagree with Irving Kristol, who wrote in the *New York Times Magazine* 20 years after Hiroshima: "The twentieth century began in 1945."

And there sitting uneasily in the driver's seat was President Harry S. Truman.

Even as the new Commander-in-Chief assumed his duties, the Nazi warlords were within the shadow of their götterdämmerung. The banner headline in the *Times* on that crucial April 12 told the story succinctly: U.S. NINTH AT ELBE 63 MILES FROM BERLIN.

Day after day the bells ever more insistently tolled Germany's doom. On May 1 it was learned that Hitler had committed suicide in his concrete bunker beneath the Reich Chancellery; command passed to Grand Admiral Karl Doenitz. On May 2 Berlin fell to the Red Army * and a million Nazi soldiers in Italy surrendered to Allied Field Marshal Sir Harold Alexander. On May 3 the Nazi north front around Hamburg collapsed and Admiral Doenitz flew to Copenhagen to try, for the third time, to engineer a separate surrender to the Americans and the British. On May 4 half a million Nazi troops in Holland and Denmark gave up the fight. On May 5 the remnants of Wehrmacht holding out defiantly in Bavaria and western Austria laid down their arms.

Sometime after midnight on the morning of Monday, May 7,

---

* Here was a pivot of history. Had the western allies agreed to a separate surrender, leaving the German army free to engage the Russians on the eastern front, Berlin in all probability would have fallen to the American Ninth Army and Russian influence in the postwar control of Germany, and of eastern Europe, would have been greatly reduced. But unconditional surrender to all allied forces simultaneously, as well as the partitioning of Germany into zones of occupation, had been agreed upon at Yalta, and President Truman, upon the recommendation of General Marshall, refused to alter this arrangement. Had he done otherwise, some aspects of the cold war which ensued might have been mitigated. But at what price in honor?

Colonel General Alfred Jodl, Chief of the German General Staff, walked stiffly and grim-faced into the auditorium of a red brick trade school in Reims, France, headquarters of Supreme Headquarters, Allied Expeditionary Force (SHAEF). He was accompanied by Admiral Friedeburg, head of the German Navy. They were coldly received by Lieutenant General Walter Bedell Smith, chief of staff to General Eisenhower, and by Generals Ivan Susloparov of the Russian Army and Francois Savez of the French. The protocol of this encounter was rigidly formal; there were no handshakes or polite conversation. Lying on the table was a document bearing the title, "Act of Military Surrender." At precisely 2:41 A.M. Jodl, muttering "I can see no alternative—signature or chaos," stepped up to the table, affixed his name to the document, turned and walked from the room. The war with Germany was over. The new Reich which Hitler had said would "live for a thousand years" had died in less than five.

The news of the surrender was flashed to the United States in an Associated Press bulletin at 9:30 A.M., New York time, that day. There was a spontaneous outburst of joyful celebration that filled Times Square, Wall Street, and the garment district with thousands of shouting, singing demonstrators and cascades of torn paper fluttering from skyscraper windows. The news and the excitement spread to other cities in the eastern and central time zones—and then began to peter out: There was something fishy about it. Other news services were hours late confirming the AP bulletin, and then did so with cumbersome qualifications. And there was no confirmation of this biggest news story since Pearl Harbor from any official source, the White House saying only that it would have a statement "tomorrow." Was this a repetition of the "false armistice" that had sent the nation on a brief emotional binge back in 1918, only to be followed by days of disappointment? Many suspected that it was and went about their business.

The news in that first AP bulletin was valid enough, but its timing was off. It had been filed by the AP's chief correspondent at SHAEF, Edward Kennedy, in violation of an embargo subscribed to by all the other correspondents accredited there, who had been apprised of the postmidnight ceremony in the little schoolhouse at Reims. The embargo had been imposed at General Eisenhower's instruction in order that a duplicate German surrender could be enacted some hours later at the Russian command post near Berlin, the news then to be released simultaneously in each of the allied capitals. This probably was an over-ambitious feat of bureaucratic news management, but Kennedy's breaking of the deadline infuriated not only his colleagues in the press corps but the brass at SHAEF. The AP's filing privileges within the theater were suspended for 24 hours and Kennedy's credentials were permanently withdrawn.

When official confirmation did come its effect was largely anticlimatic. President Truman addressed the nation by radio the next morning (Tuesday) in these somber words:

This is a solemn but glorious day. I only wish that Franklin D. Roosevelt had lived to witness this day. General Eisenhower informs me that the forces of Germany have surrendered to the United Nations. The flags of freedom fly all over Europe. . . . We must work to finish the war. Our victory is but half won. . . . When the last Japanese division has surrendered unconditionally, then only will our fighting job be done. . . . I call upon every American to stick to his post until the last battle is won. . . .

VE-Day and VJ-Day were three months and a world apart. Even before the collapse of Hitler in May, allied men and weapons were being moved out of Europe to the Pacific theater of operations in one of the greatest military-naval concentrations in history. Joint command of the final assault on Japan was vested in General Douglas MacArthur and Fleet Admiral Chester W. Nimitz. It included British naval forces under Lord Louis Mountbatten. As recently as March, the Combined Chiefs of Staff in Washington had estimated that as much as a year to a year and a half would be required to bring the Japanese empire to heel, particularly if, as seemed evident at the time, the job would have to be done in a mile-by-mile invasion of the home islands. (The A-bomb was still a scientific uncertainty and it could not be included in strategic planning.) The cost of such an operation, from beachhead to the heart of Tokyo, was reckoned at a million American casualties and perhaps half as many British.

Allied forces had come a long way back since the humiliating retreat from Bataan in the winter of 1941. In the spring and early summer of 1945 they were safely reestablished in the Philippines, and the scarred and blood-soaked beaches of Okinawa and Iwo Jima were theirs. Guam fell in June after an 82-day siege that cost 45,000 American and 94,000 Japanese casualties. From air bases in these outlying islands, American war planes by the hundreds flew around-the-clock missions against targets in the homeland, deluging them with incendiaries and explosives with virtually no opposition except from generally ineffective antiaircraft fire. "We are sending Japan back to the Stone Age," said General Curtis LeMay, the Air Corps Commander.

American and British warships shelled the coasts almost at will, and mined the sea approaches so thoroughly as to create a virtually impenetrable blockade. Japan's great cities and once-powerful industrial complexes had been ruined or crippled; the production of weapons had fallen to a trickle; fuel and raw material supplies had dwindled almost to the vanishing point; eight million of her people were homeless; and the daily ration of rice and other essential foods had been reduced to 1,500 calories. The offensive power of her Navy and Air Force had been all but extinguished.

But the Japanese Army was still relatively intact, relatively well fed, and relatively well armed, with some three million men in Japan proper and another 1.5 to 2 million in Manchuria and the China mainland. It was being held in reserve to meet the expected invasion, and upon it rested the hopes and the stubborn defiance of those in the Emperor's war council who scorned surrender and demanded resistance to the bitter, suicidal end.

The war was only half won, President Truman had said on VE-Day. And it was upon such considerations as these about Japan's residual capacities that he shaped his view about the second half of the job as, early in July, he set off for his first meeting with Churchill and Stalin at Potsdam. Such a meeting had become crucial: He needed not only to establish a personal relationship with these leaders, but there were urgent problems to be settled between them concerning control of Hitler's shattered empire and intensification of the war in the Pacific. But Truman had barely arrived in Germany when he was handed a crudely coded cable from his Secretary of War reading, "Operated on this morning. Diagnosis not yet complete but results seem satisfactory and already exceed expectations." The President needed no code book to translate this; it meant that on that day the A-bomb had passed its qualifying test in an historic blast in the New Mexico desert.

Suddenly, a whole new strategy had emerged for crushing Japan. Churchill had been informed at the same time of the scientific victory, but he and Truman kept the secret from Stalin save for guarded hints about the development of "a powerful new weapon." The Russians had already begun a large-scale massing of troops on the Manchurian border and a formal declaration of war had been scheduled. It was too late—and still too risky—to try to cut the Soviets out of the script now, as desirable from the Western viewpoint as that was beginning to seem.

What could be, and was, done was to frame a new and dire ultimatum to the Japanese people warning them that the only alternative to complete destruction, such as had been visited upon Germany, was prompt and unconditional surrender. This message was beamed to Japan for 24 hours by the powerful transmitters of the Office of War Information, beginning on July 26. This was followed by a rain of millions of leaflets, carrying substantially the same message, dropped on the homeland by Flying Fortresses. There was no hint of an atomic bomb, but 11 prominent cities were listed of which at least four would be picked for total destruction from the air. We know now that this ultimatum created violent dissension within the Emperor's war cabinet, but that a slender majority, holding out for resistance to the end, won. On July 29 the Japanese radio broadcast the news that Premier Suzuki had rejected the declaration as containing "nothing of important value."

So the hinge of fate snapped shut. President Truman thereupon initialed the extraordinary flight orders of the 509th Composite Group, 20th Air Force, to "deliver its first special bomb as soon as weather will permit visual bombing after 3 August 1945, on one of the targets: Hiroshima, Kokura, Niigata, and Nagasaki. . . . Additional bombs will be delivered on the above targets as soon as made ready by the project staff. . . ."

Just as the actual surrender of Germany came as anticlimax in the wake of stirring preliminaries, so was Japan's ultimate capitulation unerringly foretold for days, like the closing scenes of a tragic opera. Here are the relevant headlines from the Times for that momentous second week of August 1945: *

Tuesday, August 7
> FIRST ATOMIC BOMB DROPPED ON JAPAN;
> MISSILE IS EQUAL TO 20,000 TONS OF TNT:
> TRUMAN WARNS FOE OF A "RAIN OF RUIN"

Wednesday, August 8
> ATOMIC BOMB WIPED OUT 60% OF HIROSHIMA;
> SHOCK AWED FLIERS; TOKYO CABINET MEETS;
> CARRIER PLANES STRIKE NEAR CHINA COAST

Thursday, August 9
> SOVIET DECLARES WAR ON JAPAN;
> ATTACKS MANCHURIA, TOKYO SAYS:
> ATOM BOMB LOOSED ON NAGASAKI

Friday, August 10
> TRUMAN WARNS JAPAN: QUIT OR BE DESTROYED;
> SAYS WE WILL HOLD MILITARY BASES WE NEED;
> SOVIET PINCERS DRIVE 14 MILES INTO MANCHURIA

Saturday, August 11
> JAPAN OFFERS TO SURRENDER;
> U.S. MAY LET EMPEROR REMAIN

It was not until the early afternoon of Tuesday, August 14, that Japan formally acknowledged her acceptance of the surrender terms and that President Truman could proclaim that the war had ended. The nation and the world, by that time, had so exhausted its emotional energies that there was little left for mass displays of jubilation. But the

---

* The dates here given are those of publication. The events themselves occurred a day earlier.

usual crowd assembled in Lafayette Square across from the White House when the word was first spread that afternoon, and rushed pell-mell up to the tall iron fence shouting and cheering when the President and Mrs. Truman showed up on the White House portico to wave to them. To the consternation of the Secret Service, and to the delight of the multitude, a grinning, jubilant President came across the lawn and shook hundreds of hands thrust through the wickets toward him. But no parades or demonstrations were necessary to testify to the nation's deep sense of thanksgiving that night that the world's costliest and most destructive war had been won and was over.

No natural catastrophe—earthquake, volcano, tidal wave—has ever equaled the instant devastation of the man-made cataclysm that struck the city of Hiroshima at 9:15 on the morning of Monday, August 6, 1945. Hiroshima was an important port and industrial center lying in a wide valley surrounded by low hills and bisected by a meandering river. Its normal population was about 265,000. In a fragment of time too brief to be measured by any clock, one blinding, shattering blast detonated 1,000 feet above its center killed 78,150 people instantly, mortally wounded some 20,000 more, and incinerated virtually every building, tree, and morsel of living tissue within a three-mile radius. Aerial photographs of the scene a day later showed nothing but a flat, ash-strewn landscape with here and there the tortured remnants of a wall or smokestack standing in surrealistic loneliness.

The agent of its destruction was a specially adapted B-29 with the euphemistic legend *Enola Gay* stenciled on her nose. She had taken off from the island of Tinian, a bit of coral in the Pacific 1,500 miles to the southeast, at 2:45 that morning. At the controls was Colonel Paul W. Tibbits, Jr., a very senior pilot of the secrecy-shrouded 509th Composite Group: He and other members of his crew were not told until their postmidnight final briefing precisely what their mission was. The navigator of the *Enola Gay* was Captain Theodore Van Kirk and the bombardier was Major Thomas W. Ferebee. A nonmember of the crew on board that night was Navy Captain William S. Parsons, but his function was superior to that of the regular crew. Trained at Alamagordo, his assignment was to climb down into the cavernous bomb bay of the *Enola Gay* once she was safely in flight and to fuse the black, 2,000-pound metallic monster cradled there. About the size and shape of a baby whale, this was "Thin Boy," the first operational atomic bomb in the world. That is, it was *hoped* that "Thin Boy" was operational. No one could be sure that it would go off at all, or if it did that it wouldn't blow the plane and crew to bits in the process. Two other B-29's took off from Tinian at the same time, to accompany the *Enola Gay* as observers—at a safe distance of more than a mile.

The brief log of this historic flight indicates that everything went according to schedule. The weather was clear, visibility unlimited, interception zero. Right on the nose at 8:50 A.M. the shoreline of Honshu, the main Japanese island, swept past 25,000 feet below. At 9:11 the navigator signaled they had reached the "initial point" for a straight run directly over the target. At 9:15 Major Ferebee fixed "target zero" in his bomb sight and "Thin Boy" plunged from the belly of the plane.

What was it like, that apocalyptic blast of atomic fire? A million words and pictures have been evoked describing it, but few survived who had a firsthand experience of it. Among them was the crew of the *Enola Gay*. Their debriefing immediately upon their return to Tinian that morning was condensed for cabling to Washington in this almost laconic fashion:

[Initial report by radio from plane.] Results clear-cut, successful in all respects. Visible effects greater than New Mexico tests. Conditions normal in airplane following delivery.

Following additional information furnished by Parsons, crews, and observers on return to Tinian at 060500Z . . .

Sound—None appreciable observed.

Flash—Not so blinding as New Mexico test because of bright sunlight. First there was a ball of fire changing in a few seconds to purple clouds and flames boiling and swirling upward. Flash observed just after airplane rolled out of turn. All agreed light was intensely bright and white cloud rose faster than New Mexico test, reaching thirty thousand feet in minutes; it was one-third greater diameter.

It mushroomed at the top, broke away from the column and the column mushroomed again. Cloud was most turbulent. It went at least to forty thousand feet, flattening across its top at this level. It was observed from combat airplane three hundred sixty-five miles away with airplane at twenty-five thousand feet. Observation was then limited by haze, not curvature of earth.

Blast—There were two distinct shocks felt in combat airplane similar in intensity to close flack bursts. Entire city except outermost ends of dock area was covered with a dark gray dust layer which joined the cloud column. It was extremely turbulent with flashes of fire visible in the dust. Estimate diameter of this dust layer is at least three miles. One observer said it looked as though whole town was being torn apart with columns of dust rising out of valleys approaching the town. Due to dust visual observation of structural damage could not be made.

Parsons and other observers felt this strike was tremendous and awesome even in comparison with New Mexico test. Its effects may be attributed by the Japanese to a huge meteor.

An eyewitness whose experience of the bomb was more personal and terrifying was Dr. Terefumi Sasaki, a surgeon on the staff of the Red Cross Hospital in Hiroshima. His account of that cataclysmic instant and its immediate aftermath was one of six John Hersey carefully chronicled which *The New Yorker* devoted its entire issue of August 31, 1946. It was later published in book form by Alfred A. Knopf under the title, *Hiroshima.*

Dr. Sasaki took the train from his suburban home into Hiroshima early that morning as he customarily did, Hersey relates, continuing:

At the terminus he caught a streetcar at once. . . . He arrived at the hospital at seven-forty and reported to the chief surgeon. A few minutes later he went to a room on the first floor and drew blood from the arm of a man in order to perform a Wassermann test. The laboratory containing the incubators for the test was on the third floor. With the blood specimen in his left hand, walking in a kind of distraction he had felt all morning . . . he started along the main corridor on his way to the stairs. He was one step beyond an open window when the light of the bomb was reflected, like a gigantic photographic flash, in the corridor. He ducked down on one knee and said to himself, as only a Japanese would, "Sasaki, *gambare!* Be brave!" Just then (the building was 1,650 yards from the center) the blast ripped through the hospital. The glasses he was wearing flew off his face; the bottle of blood crashed against one wall; his Japanese slippers zipped out from under his feet—but otherwise, thanks to where he stood, he was untouched.

Dr. Sasaki shouted the name of the chief surgeon and rushed around to the man's office and found him terribly cut by glass. The hospital was in horrible confusion: heavy partitions and ceilings had fallen on patients, beds had overturned, windows had blown in and cut people, blood was spattered on the walls and floors, instruments were everywhere, many of the patients were running about screaming, many more lay dead. (A colleague working in the laboratory to which Dr. Sasaki had been walking was dead; Dr. Sasaki's patient, whom he had just left and who a few moments before had been dreadfully afraid of syphilis, was also dead.) Dr. Sasaki found himself the only doctor in the hospital who was unhurt.

Dr. Sasaki, who believed the enemy had hit only the building he was in, got bandages and began to bind the wounds of those inside the hospital; while outside, all over Hiroshima, maimed and dying citizens turned their unsteady steps toward the Red Cross Hospital to begin an invasion that was to make Dr. Sasaki forget his private nightmare for a long, long time.

Two days later an even more powerful bomb shattered the city of Nagasaki. Before a third bomb could be made ready, Japan had surrendered and the war was over.

The debate over the moral implications of the A-bomb began before the bomb itself was perfected, and it continues to this day. A group of scientists involved on the project headed by Dr. Szilard protested formally and vigorously as early as April 1945, against the employment of this great scientific discovery for destructive purposes. Shortly after President Truman assumed office he had a long, searching session with Secretary of War Stimson, whom President Roosevelt had designated as his chief civilian liaison with MED, to explore the enormous ramifications of the capture of atomic energy. The Secretary, whose record of distinguished statesmanship spanned three decades, dwelt at this session less on the weaponry aspects of the atom than on the larger questions of its place in broad military and political strategy and the moral implications of America's monopoly of it. There was first, he said, the question of whether such a terrifying weapon should be used at all. Beyond this was the question of our obligation to humanity as the custodians of this secret cosmic force, and how that custodianship was to be exercised in a postwar world full of tensions and jealousies. He urged the President to look beyond the immediate prospect of the first man-made atomic blast to the frightening long-range ramifications of its use that would begin immediately to ensue. At the Secretary's suggestion, Mr. Truman agreed to the prompt creation of a special committee of knowledgeable civilians to study and to advise him on the whole range of moral and political questions presented by the emergence of this totally new component of civilization.

There have been few government committees of higher caliber than the so-called Interim Committee which resulted from this talk. Mr. Stimson was its chairman, and on its roster were such names as James F. Byrnes, former Senator, Supreme Court Justice and now Director of War Mobilization; Ralph A. Bard, Assistant Secretary of the Navy; Vannevar Bush, director of the Office of Scientific Research and Development; and James B. Conant, who left the presidency of Harvard to become Chairman of the National Defense Research Committee. Serving in an advisory capacity were several of the brightest luminaries from the new science of nuclear physics, such as J. Robert Oppenheimer, Enrico Fermi, and Arthur H. Compton, each of whom had had a commanding role in the capture of atomic energy.

There were, in effect, two basic items on the committee's agenda: first, how this new source of energy was to be controlled internationally, particularly with respect to Russia (Great Britain was, of course, privy to the secret as a collaborator); and second, how the bomb was to be used in the war against Japan.

On the first proposition the committee was unable to arrive at a clear-cut consensus. Opinions varied all the way from the argument that it should be jealously hoarded as an American monopoly, with this country assuming the Messianic role of enforcer of the world's peace, to the opposite extreme where we would immediately take the Russians into our confidence and, with them, deliver control into the hands of an international commission under the United Nations.

The divergencies on the second point were equally wide at the beginning but they gradually narrowed. There were those who held out for no military use of the bomb whatever. Others argued for a nonlethal demonstration at sea or over an uninhabited Pacific island, but near enough to the Japanese homeland to frighten its rulers into submission. This position was ruled out on the grounds, first, that there was no guarantee that the fanatical Japanese would so respond, and second, that if the advertised fireworks display proved to be a dud—a contingency which could not then be ignored—more harm than good to the allied cause would have been done. On the other hand, if the bomb were used on an important military target, and if its destructive power came even close to its calculated potential, there was at least a near-certainty that the war could be brought quickly to an end. That would save not only American lives, but in the long run Japanese lives as well.

In mid-June, after two weeks of arduous labor and soul-searching, the Interim Committee delivered its report to the President. Its essence is contained in the following paragraph:

The opinions of our scientific colleagues on the initial use of these weapons are not unanimous: they range from the proposal of a purely technical demonstration to that of the military application best designed to induce surrender. Those who advocate a purely technical demonstration would wish to outlaw the use of atomic weapons, and have feared that if we use the weapon now our position in future negotiations will be prejudiced. Others emphasize the opportunity of saving American lives by immediate military use, and believe that such use will improve the international prospects, in that they are more concerned with the prevention of war than with the elimination of this special weapon. We find ourselves closer to these latter views; we can propose no technical demonstration likely to bring an end to the war; we see no alternative to direct military use.

Such was the warrant upon which President Truman sent the *Enola Gay* on her historic mission. "The final decision of when and where to use the bomb was up to me," he said later. "Let there be no mistake about it. I regarded the bomb as a military weapon and never had any doubt it should be used."

The bomb was, of course, vastly more than a military weapon. It signaled the arrival of a new age of man—an age in which the promise of infinite bounty and the threat of ultimate holocaust seem irrevocably tied together and destined to hang in precarious balance.[4]

10

The Dilemmas of Peace

THE TRANSITION FROM WAR to peace was as convulsive an experience for American society as the transition from peace to war had been four years earlier. Then, the bitter task of girding for war had been concealed partially at least in a euphoria of patriotism and high purpose. There were slogans and banners and marching bands; the casualty reports had not begun to pile up and the pinch of personal sacrifice was but a distant threat. Now, in late 1945 and the years immediately following, war was perceived as a fresh and aching wound on the national consciousness, a nightmare to be expunged with all its trappings and reminders as quickly and as heedlessly as possible. "Bring the boys back home," the people cried, and with it went a clamorous demand for more meat and cigarettes and tires, for a boost in wages and dividends and profits, for an end to rationing and production controls and all the other irksome disciplines of wartime regimentation. It was an obsessive mood of impatience to be done with the past and to get on with the now—a now about which there was a deceptive sheen of opulence and freedom and promise.

But no amount of wishing could make so gaudy a dream real. The American economy had become a gigantic engine of war charging ahead under undreamed-of momentum. To stop it in its tracks, turn it about and direct its energies into peaceful channels, could not be done without the risk of shattering consequences. The whole edifice of war production, from mine to production line to bureaucratic bookkeeping, would have to be restructured with care to avoid collapse. Overhanging this imperative was the specter of some 10 million soon-to-be veterans changing from uniforms to work clothes and demanding jobs. The memory of the Great Depression with its armies of jobless was still fresh in most minds, and even the most optimistic projections of the reconversion curve predicted heavy unemployment as one of the inevitable by-products of peace.

And peace itself, in those first postwar years, was less than a riveted certainty. Treaties, reparations, the control and political reordering of the former enemy states involved delicate and explosive manipulations among the victors. A plague of hunger and social unrest had swept over most of Europe and Asia in the wake of the plague of war, threatening new eruptions of violence. The United States, the only major power of the world still rich and powerful, could not, as she had done in 1918, turn and walk away leaving others to clean up the wreckage.

The dilemmas of peace, though of a different order, were to prove as hard to deal with as the dilemmas of war. For it was not a simple case of picking up the familiar patterns of life where we had left off five years earlier. We in the United States, and the world at large, were, in the popular phrase, faced with a whole new ball game.

I

In five years of war these things had happened to the American economy:

It had sunk more than $300 billion into guns, airplanes, warships, atomic bombs, soldiers' and sailors' pay, and the countless other appurtenances of warfare for itself and its allies.

The gross national product had risen from an annual rate of $101.4 billion in 1940 to $215.2 billion in 1945. (It would exceed $285 billion by 1950.)

We were geared to make guns, not butter. In 1944 factory production lines turned out 95,272 military aircraft as against only 70,000 passenger automobiles. Five years before the ratio had been the reverse: 3,700,000 autos, 6,000 airplanes.

Farmers harvested 813,000,000 bushels of wheat the year the war began; in its last year their yield was 1,123,000,000 bushels.

A total of 16,353,000 men had been drawn out of jobs and schools and put into uniforms. On VJ-Day there were still 12,123,000 in the armed forces, and the civilian labor force was at an all-time high of 53,140,000. The federal bureaucracy alone had more than tripled, reaching a peak in 1945 of 3,526,000 employees.

Average weekly earnings in manufacturing had almost doubled in five years (from $24.20 to $44.39) and the 48-hour work week was standard. Scarcities plus price controls had kept a lid of sorts on living costs with the result that, at war's end, there was a huge nest egg of $136.4 billion of personal savings in banks and government bonds itching to be spent.

And therein lay the fuse of a disastrous inflation—too much money bidding for too few houses, refrigerators, automobiles, overcoats, nylon stockings, sirloin steaks, steel girders, plumbing fixtures, and just about everything else. Abundant dollars chasing scarce commodities inevitably leads to boom and bust.

Such was the warning contained in a lengthy report placed on President Truman's desk in September 1945, by John W. Snyder, director of the Office of War Mobilization and Reconversion. "There should be no mincing of words," the report said. "The sudden termination of the major portion of war contracts will cause an immediate and large-scale dislocation in our economy. . . . Unemployment will rise to five million or more within three months, perhaps to eight million or more by next spring."

The report went on to lay out a carefully detailed blueprint for easing the national economy down from a wartime peak to a peacetime plateau. There would be some slippages and landslides in the process, but by careful management the damage could be held within tolerable limits. The steps consisted essentially of a *rapid* military demobilization and termination of war contracts, and a *gradual* relaxation of controls over production, wages, and prices until supply and demand in the starved consumers' marketplace could be brought into reasonable balance. The estimated time required was 18 months.

The Snyder report was issued amid a cacophony of demands for an immediate ending of all wartime controls. Labor, freed of its no-strike pledge by the ending of hostilities, was clamoring noisily for wage boosts to catch up with the rise in the cost of living. Strikes proliferated wildly. Manufacturers and suppliers were clamoring with equal intensity to be freed from onerous restrictions on prices and production. Essential goods were held off the market to force the government's hand. Consumers, with money burning their pockets, wanted all their pent up needs gratified at once, blaming "bureaucrats" and "red tape" for their denial. Politicians, with their own fish to fry—a midterm election was coming up in less than a year—fanned the flames of discontent. Congress, in special session late in the year, gave grudging consent to a six-months reprieve for the principal control mechanisms—they would have expired automatically at the end of the year—but promised to renew the battle for their extinction in the session beginning in 1946.

In his state of the union message in January of that year the President laid out a staggering 21-point program that, along with a number of unrelated reforms and programs, called emphatically for a full year's extension of price control and similar legislation to effectuate an orderly reconversion of the economy. The contest over this soon degenerated into a political brawl such as had not been witnessed since the fading years of the New Deal.

The principal target was the OPA, the price control mechanism which was the keystone of the reconversion arch. Some of the opposition to extending the life of OPA was undoubtedly based on honest conviction: That if the "natural laws" of supply and demand were given free play they would in time achieve a tolerable balance, just as the classical theorems said they would. But the essential heat to raise this controversy to the boiling point was political. President Truman, still unsteady at the helm of government, generally was held in low esteem. Even to liberals and loyal Democrats he seemed a poor substitute in the White House for the dynamic presence of FDR. To most Republicans, as well as to a growing segment of dissident Southern Democrats, he appeared an agent for the revival and perpetuation of the New Deal, of which a peacetime OPA was manifestly a tool. Now, in 1946, with a congressional election in the immediate offing and a general election but two years away, was the time to undermine these impious pretensions and pave the way for a return to "sane" government—conservative certainly, Republican probably. They gathered their forces for a showdown battle on Capitol Hill to scuttle the OPA once and for all.

Joining happily in the fray were the massed business interests of the country as represented by such powerful agencies as the Chamber of Commerce of the United States and the National Association of Manufacturers. They provided a steady parade of prestigious industrialists and bankers to give public testimony before the legislative committees, denouncing the OPA as a "socialistic" bottleneck that was strangling production and employment and, in fact, "holding a dagger at the very heart of the free enterprise system." Away from Washington, they sponsored scores of business conventions and trade association meetings that deluged Congress with resolutions protesting OPA. Housewives, doctors, teachers, and ministers were proselytized through elaborate "educational campaigns" to do the same thing. Millions were spent on newspaper, magazine, and radio advertisements urging people to write their Congressmen to vote to "strike the shackles from American business." It was the most massive lobbying campaign of the sort since the assault on the National Recovery Administration (NRA) 10 years earlier.

The other side of the controversy was less well organized but scarcely less strident in defending the cause of OPA. As cattlemen held back livestock from the slaughtering pens and the black market prices of scores of commodities soared out of sight, consumers sent up an angry roar of protest against "artificial scarcities" they believed to be engineered by the embattled producers. "Housewives strikes" and boycotts erupted in hundreds of communities; there were rallies and protest meetings and letter-writing campaigns directed to the newspapers and to Congress. Officials of women's clubs and labor unions demanded to be heard by the legislative committees. In April there was a "March of the Housewives" on Washington, bringing hundreds of angry protesters to the Capital to badger members of Congress and to confront them with yards-long petitions from their constituents demanding a full-scale restoration of OPA.

"As the battle has grown," the *New York Times* commented, "each side has become progressively more voluble, they have started calling each other names, and a few blows have been struck below the belt. Those who have watched the fight from the ringside have become convinced that reasoned conviction ceased to be a factor after the first couple of rounds."

But the victory, an ambiguous one at that, went to the anti-OPA forces. Under the skilled leadership of Republican Senator Robert A. Taft, a thoroughly mangled version of the price control bill was enacted late in June, only days before the existing legislation was due to expire. It did continue the life of OPA for a year, as the administration had asked, but with so many limitations and exemptions that any effective control over prices was nullified. Its effect was to give the President a mandate to control prices but to deny him the authority with which to do it. Mr. Truman vetoed the bill and went on the radio the following night to deliver a tart rebuke to its architects. "In the end," he said, "this bill would lead to disaster." And he was not far off the mark.

In the month that followed—July 1946—the cost of living made the biggest jump ever recorded in any 30-day period. The Labor Department's index of retail prices, for example, which had gained only about 30 points during all the five war years, leaped 20 points in that month alone, from 145.6 to 165.7. Shoppers in New York City saw milk go from 16¢ to 19¢ a quart, butter from 68¢ to 79¢ a pound, veal cutlets from 50¢ to 95¢, and so on across the board. Before the end of the year the index had gained another 20 points, and it was destined to keep right on climbing through 1947 and 1948 toward a peak of 200 in 1949.

The outcry that followed the dismantling of OPA was so intense that Congress was persuaded to make a halfhearted attempt to backtrack. In August it enacted a new short-term price control bill, but it, too, was so burdened with restrictions as to be virtually inoperable as an effective weapon against inflation. The President let it stand, however, as a grim public reminder of how right he and how wrong Congress had been. It would serve his political needs in later days. Thus ended in defeat a principal phase of the postwar battle against inflation.[1]

II

Organized labor did its bit—a very substantial bit—to fan the inflationary fires. While joining sporadically in the fight to save price controls, it threw the bulk of its weight into a determined campaign to raise wages, to gain new "fringe" benefits and to expand its power at the bargaining table. Its success was substantial but uneven in each of these areas but its gains were won at an enormous cost in industrial strife and in public support for the unions. The year 1946 saw the greatest eruption of strikes in the nation's history—the loss of 116 million man-days of work—that literally crippled entire segments of the nation's industry for weeks and months at a time. There were violence and bloodshed and incidents of near-anarchy that triggered an angry public and political reaction. What unionists were long to call the "slave labor act," the Taft-Hartley Act (which is still in force at this writing) was a direct outgrowth of the unparalleled turmoil in the labor-management front during 1946.

Although it did not materialize, the specter of massive unemployment contributed strongly to the anxiety over reconversion. The huge wartime military establishment was being dismantled at a headlong pace, returning veterans to civilian ranks at the rate of 200,000 to 300,000 each month. The rapid cancellation of war contracts was dislodging tens of thousands of workers from their jobs at the same time. The government's economic planners foresaw unemployment totals reaching toward 10 million before the end of 1946. In actuality the total did not go above three million. What the planners had failed to take into account was, first, that the domestic labor force had more cushion to it than they knew: It contained millions of women and school-age youths who, once the war was over, dropped out of the job-seeking category; and second, the enormous demand for civilian goods would keep the wheels of industry spinning with little more than a hiccough due to canceled war contracts.

There was a firm consensus among management chieftains that if ever the time was at hand to roll back the vast political and economic power which labor had achieved under the New Deal, and which had been held in only temporary abatement during the war, it was now. And that goal would be immeasurably advanced as unemployment created a plentiful and dependent labor market. They proceeded on that assumption in their early post-war confrontations at the bargaining table.

But the leaders of organized labor were not as beguiled by this specter of unemployment as were the employers. They were determined to hold on to and expand their power base and, moreover, to get back all they believed had been denied them in wages and other emoluments during the war years. They argued with a good deal of justification that the wage increases granted them under the "little steel formula" had failed substantially to keep up with the rising cost of living; that in spite of price ceilings and other restrictions industry had accumulated vast wartime profits and tax benefits. They could show that with the abandonment of overtime pay and the long work week that average weekly earnings had slipped from $47.50 in January 1945, to $41.15 in January 1946, while the consumer price index maintained a steady (though marginal) upward climb. They wanted not only more money but union security, pension funds, and other fringe benefits. And with the no-strike agreement a dead letter they set out to get them.

The first big showdown of the reconversion period came late in November 1945, when 180,000 members of the United Auto Workers (CIO) walked quietly and simultaneously off the job, closing down every production facility of the giant General Motors Corporation in 20 states.

In many respects this was a landmark event, for it signalized the advent of a new style of labor militancy, a style which enabled the workers to confront the employers on a basis of intellectual and managerial parity. The picket line and the bludgeon were still there to be called upon when needed, but in the initial rounds at least of a bargaining match the union men employed a sophisticated brand of economic, political, and public relations savvy that promptly threw their antagonists on the defensive.

Walter P. Reuther, the aggressive, forty-year-old president of the UAW, was the prototype of this new breed of union negotiator. He had grown up on the assembly lines of Detroit and in the liberal wing of the labor movement, but he made it his business to learn—and, as a union official, to surround himself with experts who knew—about the corporate intricacies and the boardroom mentality of the auto industry as a whole. He was not easily put down by the slide-rule logic or the economic semantics of a vice-president in charge of Labor Relations. He had arrows just like them in his own quiver.

The choice of General Motors as the first target on the list in labor's broad-scale reconversion strategy was, in itself, a calculated ploy in this new style of economic squeeze play. GM not only was dominant as a maker and seller of automobiles but also bought from and sold huge quantities of parts to other auto makers and consumed up to 60 percent of the output of hundreds of independent suppliers. Hence, a break in this pipeline would quickly reverberate to the very fringes of the auto industry. The industry as a whole, in turn, was a linchpin of the nation's entire economic structure: It consumed three-quarters of the total output of rubber and plate glass, two-thirds of all upholstery leather, one-fifth of all steel. Autos were steel's biggest customer; steel was the biggest customer for coal; coal was the biggest customer for the railroads—ergo: If Detroit got a cold a lot of other places like Pittsburgh and Appalachia and Chicago sneezed. If GM could be forced to capitulate to labor's demands, Ford, Chrysler, and the other auto makers would be forced to follow suit, and at the least a pattern would be set for other major elements of American industry. It was the classic strategy of divide and conquer.

Negotiations on the GM contract had begun in August. The basic demand was for a 30-percent increase in wages—from $1.12 to $1.46

an hour—that would yield for a 40-hour peacetime week approximately the same take-home pay that had prevailed for a 48-hour week in wartime. Under the relaxed government regulations then in effect, any wage increase was permissible that did not result in a corresponding price increase. Predictably, General Motors said it could not grant such a pay boost without raising the price of new automobiles. The best it could do, it said, was offer a 10 percent increase for a 45-hour week. Reuther and his men had prepared well for such a stalemate. They had assembled impressive economic data on the wartime experience of GM, its earnings, dividends, and tax shelters, and on projected operations and earnings at the proposed new pay levels. They produced charts and statistics to show that the company could grant the increase without raising prices and still better the profits it earned in prewar years. These arguments were widely proclaimed in a carefully planned publicity program during the weeks of autumn; it was a form of psychological warfare for which the company was ill-prepared. To the public, GM seemed simply to have dug in its heels, determined to wait out the storm in glum silence.

Early in November Reuther put his big ace on the table. The union was willing, he said, to scale down its demand if GM could prove, by opening its books to inspection, that the pay raise could not be granted without an increase in prices. Correspondingly, if this disclosure of financial data turned out to warrant it, the pay raise should be made retroactive to August. Furthermore, the union insisted, the whole bargaining process should be conducted in the open with press and public present. What he was proposing, in effect, was the right to hitch wages to profits, to the ability to pay, with a new role for public opinion as arbitrator in this and future negotiations. Business leaders around the country reacted to this bold gambit with anger and alarm, charging that the "labor bosses" were attempting to "usurp the prerogatives of management"—which in a traditional sense, they were. To GM Vice-President Harry W. Anderson this was a demand "not to arbitrate but to abdicate" and, as everyone expected, he turned the proposition down.

Reuther and his men had won a telling psychological advantage —there was an insistent plausibility to their proposal and even President Truman gave it his offhand endorsement (which he later withdrew)— and they wisely determined to preserve it. When the strike deadline came on Wednesday, November 21, 180,000 men in over 100 GM installations around the country walked off the job as quietly and peaceably as if it were a routine change in shifts. This was not time, the locals had been told, for horseplay or rioting, and there was none. The picket lines went up, but there were no bricks through the windows, no cops with tommy guns at the ready, nor, as the *New York Times* reported, "blood on the cobblestones." But the shutdown was total; the nation's largest corporate empire had been brought to an instant standstill. For the time being at least the labor wars were being fought to a new beat of the drums.

The impasse at General Motors snapped the tether against which other unions had been straining. Over the next several weeks scores of major bargaining sessions broke up in deadlock. Before Christmas 700,000 steel workers banked their furnaces around Pittsburgh, Cleveland, and Birmingham and went out on strike. They were followed by 200,000 electrical workers; 50,000 communications workers; 263,000 packinghouse workers; and by tens of thousands of others in assorted industries all across the country. For two desperate weeks late in January New York City faced the threat of severe food and fuel shortages as dock workers tied up the port. At the same time tens of thousands of cliff dwellers in that high-rise metropolis were either stranded on their balconies or forced to sleep in apartment house lobbies as unionized building employees shut off elevator service. Pittsburgh was immobilized by a strike of transit workers and was forced to revert to evening "brownouts" when the local power company was shut down. At the end of January 1946, it was estimated that some 1,650,000 union workers were on the picket lines strung out from coast to coast, and that at least twice that number had been rendered jobless as secondary casualties of this massive conflict. By then the gloves had come off: Strikers battled police before the Chicago stockyards; overturned and burned the autos of white collar workers trying to get to their offices in General Motors plants at Flint; hurled stones through the windows of an electrical supply manufacturer in St. Louis.

Never had the country been faced with a labor-management crisis of such proportions. Editorialists warned that the free enterprise system was in danger of collapse. Business leaders charged labor with attempting to "sovietize" American industry, and union leaders countercharged by asserting there was a conspiracy within big business "to crush the labor movement." Congress rang with impassioned oratory aimed mainly at the strikers, and the legislative hoppers were clogged with bills designed to curb the unions' power. President Truman meanwhile convened repeated conferences with union and management leaders at the White House seeking formulas for peace, experimented with fact-finding boards, voluntary arbitration, and other panaceas. His core problem, of course, was to try to keep a lid on the seething cauldron of inflation; to give labor some wage relief but not enough to wreck the controls over prices.

In mid-February a shaky compromise was reached. Steel by this time had become the number one problem area. Weeks of idleness in the steel mills had spread a creeping paralysis over the whole spectrum of the nation's industry. Until that was relieved the wider malaise could not be cured. In consequence, reconversion chief John Snyder (after a stormy bureaucratic hassle) evolved a formula for increasing both wages and prices moderately on a compensatory basis calculated according to their prewar levels. In the case of steel this meant a basic wage rise of 18.5¢ an hour (the union had demanded 25¢ originally) and a rise in the price of steel of $5 a ton. This solution wholly pleased neither side in the dispute but it was accepted on the half-a-loaf principle and the steel strike was over. The same formula was used to end the General Motors strike (and to avert strikes at Ford and Chrysler), to put the meatpackers back to work, and to bring a period of relative calm to several other major industrial war fronts.

The tension had been eased but it was far from dissipated. Two other sore spots, in coal and in rails, had festered meanwhile into cancers.

In mid-April, 20 railroad brotherhoods, after long months of negotiations, turned down a proposed arbitration settlement that would have given them a little more than half the wage increase they sought and that put off for a year important changes in work rules. President Truman intervened in the dispute at this point and won from 18 of the brotherhoods an agreement to continue peaceful negotiations. However, two of the most powerful unions, the Engineers and the Trainmen, refused this compromise and called a strike of their members 30 days thence—for May 18. A walkout by this minority would, of course, be indistinguishable from a wholesale walkout by the majority: Not a wheel would turn on any railroad in the land.

In the ensuing weeks official anxiety and public anger toward the unions rose to a high pitch. For in addition to the impending transportation crisis—the first general shutdown of the railroads in almost 50 years—400,000 coal miners had walked off the job on April 1. As coal stocks above ground dwindled, many cities reinstituted the wartime "brownouts," hundreds of factories either closed down or went on half-time with consequent cuts in jobs and pay, and thousands of householders in northern cities were left to shiver miserably for lack of fuel. It was plain to the simplest citizen that if the rail strike became a reality, shutting off shipments of food and other necessities, his individual woes would multiply grievously. As the White House struggled desperately to find workable solutions for these twin crises, public indignation boiled over in a flood of demands upon the President and Congress that they "*do* something."

The resultant pressure of public opinion and the fear of repressive legislation caused a partial break in the rail dispute. A week before the May 18 strike deadline set by the engineers and the trainmen, officials of the other 18 affected brotherhoods announced their willingness to accept the earlier arbitration decision with a few minor modifications. But spokesmen for the two big operating unions defiantly held out: They wanted the full ticket of their demands honored or they would walk out, and without the 78,000 engineers and the 215,000 trainmen aboard no trains would move over the nation's 228,000-mile rail network.

By now President Truman had taken the dispute into his own hands. Time after time he sat with the two belligerent union leaders across from his desk in the Oval Office and by turns cajoled, pleaded with, and threatened them. Once they had been his political allies—they had bailed him out in his difficult Senate campaign of 1940—but now the issue ran deeper than politics. Heels were dug in on both sides.

The President now rolled out his big guns. Two days before the strike deadline he issued an executive order seizing the railroads in the name of the government: If the workers wouldn't operate the trains, the Army would. The workers would not, and at the designated hour the trains stopped running. Truman gave the union leaders 48 hours to change their minds and sent his top labor mediator, John Steelman, to sit with them around the clock until the zero hour should come. The next night he went on a nationwide radio hookup and lashed out at the two recalcitrant union bosses, Alvanly Johnston and A. F. Whitney, as men of greed and traitorous instinct. The next day, a Saturday, he summoned Congress to meet in joint session with him at four o'clock, when the 48-hour deadline would be reached. Grim-faced and tight-lipped he asked the legislators for the most drastic antistrike law ever enacted—the right, when a national emergency threatened, whether in peace or war, to draft strikers into the armed forces irrespective of age or other considerations.

The President had barely launched his attack when a Senate aide scurried up to the podium and laid a scribbled note before him. Truman looked at it briefly, a grin crossed his face, and he said: "Gentlemen, the strike has been settled!" Steelman had just telephoned frantically from downtown that Johnston and Whitney, suddenly discovering the kind of weapon they had put in the President's hand, had caved in.

It was a rousing climax to a cliffhanger that had built up in the most approved Hollywood fashion. The announcement was greeted with boisterous cheers and applause from the packed House chamber. The President went on, however, to lay out his tough strike-breaking proposal and asked for its immediate enactment as necessary to head off other threatened crises. The House accommodated him that same evening by a whopping vote of 306 to 13. The Senate, however, in its more sedate and deliberate fashion, refused to be panicked. It put the bill aside for future consideration, and there, unmourned at the last even by its chief sponsor, Harry Truman, it ultimately expired.

As the crisis on the railroads subsided the crisis in the coal mines worsened, although it took a considerably longer time to reach its ultimate climax. The central issue here was a novel one. The miners were demanding not only improved pay and working conditions but also that for every ton of coal mined the operators pay ten cents into a pension fund for aged and disabled miners. This was virtually an unheard-of demand in an industrial bargaining session and when it was laid on the table back in January the operators threw up their hands in pained disbelief and refused even to consider it. The mine workers union had a fixed tradition of "no contract, no work," and when their existing contract ran out on March 30, they walked out of the coal pits en masse.

It scarcely needs saying that coal mining in the mid-forties, as today, was one of the most hazardous and physically exhausting occupations by which men seek a livelihood. For as long as one can remember, the very epitome of destitution and social degradation in America has been reflected in the hundreds of dilapidated little coal company towns tucked into the isolated hollows or perched precariously on the hillsides of Appalachia and wherever else coal is dug. Mixed with the slag and other debris around every coal tipple are the ambulant shells of men who have spent a lifetime in the pits, their scrawny women and grimy children, locked into a life-style of ignorance and want and seemingly impenetrable hopelessness. Miners live constantly with danger, either of sudden death or of crippling disaster. In 1946 there was no financial protection for the aged, the infirm, or the widowed family beyond the uncertain pittances that might come from workmen's compensation insurance or social security.

This was the dismal pattern of dependency for nearly half a million families that John Llewellyn Lewis, president of the United Mine Workers of America, sought to break at the bargaining table with the mine owners in 1946. Lewis possessed enormous power and enormous presence. Then in his mid-sixties, he was a big, beefy man with broad shoulders and wide girth who moved with the deliberate purposefulness of a bull elephant. He wore a resplendent crown of iron gray hair that fell almost to the collar line and his eyes glared like probing searchlights from beneath black brows of an incredible lushness. He habitually wore an expression of sullen belligerence, rarely smiling, and when he spoke it was in the cavernous tones and measured cadence of the old time pulpit. Often his language was laced with Scriptural allusions and orotund rhetoric. "Good day, gentlemen," he told the coal operators in April, rising in majestic finality from the bargaining session. "We trust that time, as its shrinks your purse, may modify your niggardly and antisocial propensities."

John L. Lewis, like most other miners of his generation, was the son of a coal miner and went to work himself in the mines of his native Southern Illinois as a boy of twelve. He gravitated naturally into the union movement during the skull-cracking days before the First World War, and in 1920 was elected president of the then-struggling UMW. He was tough, determined, and ruthless, but he won many important gains for the miners, along with their fanatical loyalty. Over the next 20 years he built up the union in both membership and prestige to the point where he stood unchallenged as the most powerful labor leader in the country —and the most feared. He fathered the split within organized labor that gave birth to the CIO, whose policies he dominated for the next decade. He was a maverick in politics as in most other things. He had been an early supporter of the New Deal but later broke with Roosevelt and had nothing but scorn for President Truman. His attitude toward public opinion was one of arrogant disdain, and even during the war years he did not hesitate to shut down or to interrupt the vital flow of coal whenever it suited his purpose. Now, in the heat of reconversion effort, he did so again.

As President Truman fended off the railroad brotherhoods with one hand during those spring weeks of 1946, he sparred with the miners' union with the other. Lewis and the operators had become hopelessly deadlocked, yielding neither to White House entreaties nor to their own immediate economic necessities. For 40 days scarcely a ton of coal had moved from the pit heads and smoke was disappearing from factory chimneys and power plants all over the country when, on May 21, the President by executive order seized the mines and put them under the control of his Secretary of the Interior, Julius A. Krug. Negotiations were immediately reopened, with the government occupying the seat lately held by the operators' representatives. A week later Krug signed a new contract with the UMW that gave the miners just about what they had asked for, including a five-cent—instead of a ten-cent—royalty on each ton of coal to underwrite their ambitious welfare program. The mine owners, as well as most of their business allies, were, of course, outraged: A "dangerous" precedent had been set that welded the concept of social responsibility into the industrial wage structure. "Where will it all end?" they asked. It was not hard to see where it would end, but meanwhile coal began to pour out of the hills to the cities and another industrial crisis had been reached and passed.

The peace that settled over the coal fields, however, was a deceptive one. John L. Lewis was a man of towering ambition and his combative instinct was not fully appeased by having the government take over as surrogate for his old adversary, the operators. In October he announced his dissatisfaction with a relatively minor clause in his new contract, one having to do with vacation pay, and requested that it be reopened for fresh negotiations. When Secretary Krug refused, Lewis said Very well, the miners would cancel it themselves, setting a deadline 30 days away, November 20. And, of course, "no contract, no work."

This was a harsh dilemma for the government, and one in which public opinion took a lively and self-centered interest: The prospect of winter without coal was, indeed, a chilling one. What if the miners refused the government's order to stay on the job, heeding their union chieftain instead of their titular employer? In the case of the railroads it was probable that the military transportation services might, under government seizure, have maintained a semblance of rail traffic. But, as Lewis was prompt to proclaim, "You can't dig coal with bayonets," and everybody from the President down knew he was right. Nor, since Congress had refused to enact the "draft-the-strikers" bill, which the President had asked for six months earlier, was it possible to impose military discipline on the miners to make them do what they did not want to do. As the weeks of official indecision went by and the day of reckoning drew nearer the air of public suspense became almost palpable.

The government's decision at the last was to seek an injunction in the courts prohibiting the UMW from abrogating its contract. It was a dubious decision at best, but about the only one available. For more than 50 years the "yellow dog" injunction had been the most feared and hated weapon in the antilabor arsenal, aligning the power of the courts on the side of management in countless labor disputes. It had been outlawed at last in the Norris-LaGuardia Act of 1932 and the ban had been further strengthened in the Wagner Act three years later. But in 1946 White House lawyers discovered an apparent loophole: The law forbade the use of injunctions as between a *private employer* and a union but it was silent as to circumstances when the *government* was the employer. The issue had never been raised and whether such an assumption of the law's validity would stand up in court was a wide open question.

And if it did not, what then? It would mean, in all probability, that President John L. Lewis had put down President Harry S. Truman in a most embarrassing and far-reaching power struggle.

There was a good deal of fanfare by the press and public in and around Justice T. Alan Goldsborough's court in the Federal District Court building in Washington on Monday, November 18, as the contest opened. Attorney General Tom C. Clark, appearing in person as the government's counsel, sought as a first step a temporary restraining order prohibiting the union from carrying out its strike threat two days thence. After cursory arguments, the judge issued the order that day pending a full hearing on the larger issue a week later. The order was duly served on officials at the UMW national headquarters a dozen blocks away. But already, in one bleak, soot-covered mining camp after another throughout Pennsylvania, West Virginia, and Kentucky, miners by the tens, fifties, and hundreds had failed to report in for their shifts as if in anticipation of their leader's purpose. No contrary orders reached them from Washington. By the Wednesday midnight deadline the ritualistic phrase, "no contract, no work," had penetrated along the farthest hollow and railroad spur in the Appalachian coal fields. By morning virtually every soft coal mine in the country was shut down. Justice Goldsborough promptly cited

Lewis and the union for contempt of court but the order was ignored and the mines remained closed.

Now began a brief but historic sequence of legal maneuvers. Before a packed courtroom and amid an atmosphere of national tension, hearings on the primary issue, that of the injunction against voiding of the contract, opened on Monday, November 25. It was a highly legalistic debate between the opposing lawyers on interpretations of the Norris-LaGuardia Act that lacked the anticipated fireworks. On Friday the court rendered its opinion, finding in favor of the government across the board. The union's lawyers announced their intention of an immediate appeal to the Supreme Court.

The first two rounds had gone to the government. Now came the crucial third round. Lewis and his legal battery came again into court the following Monday to stand trial on charges of contempt for permitting the strike to occur in defiance of the restraining order. This was a more emotional issue than the previous one and it gave off some verbal sparks. After three days of testimony the judge handed down his decision: Lewis and the UMW "have committed and continue to commit a civil [and criminal] contempt of this court." He assessed fines of $3,500,000 against the union and $10,000 against Lewis personally, the stiffest penalties ever imposed in a labor contempt case. Lewis, rage showing in every feature, rose to protest. The judge warned him against compounding his guilt. "Sir," the old thespian boomed, "I have already been adjudged in contempt of your court." And, as if to underline the greatness of his contempt, he turned and strode majestically from the courtroom, his hat clamped down squarely to his glowering eyes.

This was not the end of the story. Goldsborough's verdict was delivered on a Wednesday and it, too, was promptly appealed to the Supreme Court. But no word issued from the UMW headquarters in downtown Washington to the hundreds of Coaltowns, U.S.A., to get the coal cars moving again. The strike was still on. John L. Lewis had defied both the Executive and the Judicial branches of the government. Now what? Where did that leave the *other* president?

The ball was squarely in Truman's court. He fell back on the only play left to him. It was announced from the White House on Saturday morning that the President would go on national radio that night in a last ditch appeal to the miners over Lewis' head; he would ask them as patriots and in the national interest to go back to work. It was a desperate gamble with the majesty of the government and the prestige of the Presidency at stake—but it never reached a final showdown. Late that afternoon Lewis summoned reporters to his paneled office in the old City Club building on 15th Street and with all the dignity and Olympian scorn he could command, capitulated. He capitulated not to the President nor to the alleged demands of the public interest but, he said, to "the dignity of this high tribunal" (the Supreme Court) where the issue of "the government's 'yellow dog' injunction" then rested. Accordingly, he said, all members of the union were being directed to return to work forthwith under contract terms as they existed prior to the strike.

With this climactic scene the curtain was rung down on the most bruising, strife-torn year in the history of American labor relations. (The Supreme Court ultimately upheld the government in every particular against the UMW but reduced the fine levied on the union to $750,000.) As the dust settled some important bench marks could be discerned. An immediate loser was the administration's program to combat postwar inflation; as labor won one wage concession after another the battle to hold the line on prices was weakened and the cost of living spurted upward. Big business learned that big labor was a fact of life and here to stay. Labor, for its part, had won not only new stature as a determinative force in the shaping of national corporate policy but it had staked out some important gains in terms of its own social and economic prerogatives, its right to a fuller share of the affluent society it had helped to create. Pensions and other fringe benefits were soon to become as important in many bargaining sessions as wages and hours.

Inevitably, these gains carried a price tag. To most people outside organized labor the unprecedented number of strikes that year, the many pitched battles between pickets and police, the crippling jurisdictional disputes between rival unions, the "extravagance" of some union demands, seemed in their cumulative impact to be an irresponsible assault upon the national welfare. To some alarmists the turmoil contained the seeds of anarchy and communist plotting: Some of the CIO unions were, in fact, conducting a painful purge of Communists from their ranks. For all these reasons public opinion became heavily weighted against labor, a fact that was promptly translated into political reprisal.[2]

III

The political climate grew hot and stormy as the midterm elections of 1946 approached. The unparalleled strife on the labor front was a dominant cause, but not the only one. The fight over price controls had split the nation into warring ideological camps, with Republicans and the business community generally lined up anti, Democrats and consumers generally lined up pro. But regardless of which side one was on in this argument, just about everyone was bedeviled by high prices, by rent gougers, by the scarcity of meat and nylon stockings and new cars and decent housing, and by the flourishing black markets thus spawned. Their ire targeted naturally on Washington, picking out the hapless figure of President Truman for the bulls-eye. It was easy to picture him as rattling around in a job that was too big for him; as a small-bore politician from the Middle West surrounded by "cronies" and other incompetents. "Among the members of his own party," the *New York Times* reported late in 1946, "the prevailing attitude toward the President is one of simple despair and futility. Most seem to think he has done the best he could, but that his best simply was not good enough." The Republicans, with inspiration, compressed this mood of national discontent into two words—"Had Enough?"—It was one of the most devastating campaign slogans of all time.

And, indeed, a substantial majority of the electorate concluded that they *had* "had enough." In the biggest turnout for a midterm election in almost a decade they wrote finis to 16 years of unbroken Democratic control of Congress. Republicans picked up 11 seats in the Senate and 54 in the House for a comfortable working majority in both chambers. At the same time they won enough state contests to give them 25 governorships to the Democrats' 23, erasing virtually every regional advantage the Democrats had held outside the South.

The election was an unmistakable repudiation both of President Truman and of his party. Anticipating a period of national paralysis, Senator J. William Fulbright of Arkansas, an immature first-termer in those days, seriously suggested that Mr. Truman should step aside and let a Republican successor take over. But the man from Missouri was not easily put down. He brushed off the suggestion by denominating the Arkansan as "Senator Halfbright." But no wisecracks could conceal the fact that the Truman administration—and the country at large—faced mountainous new obstacles in the years immediately ahead.

The Republicans were jubilant as they returned to Washington in January 1947, for the opening of the Eightieth Congress. For the first time since the lamented days of Herbert Hoover, their party was in undisputed control of the legislative branch of government—and a Presidential election glimmered invitingly on the horizon just two years away. Among the many "mandates" they felt had been handed them by the electorate none had a higher priority than laws "to curb the power of the labor barons." Or, as defined in more politic language, "to redress the balance in labor-management relations" which, it was argued with some justice, had been out of balance since the passage of the Wagner Labor Relations Act 10 years earlier.

A number of state legislatures already had enacted such laws of their own, many of them clearly punitive in intent and of doubtful constitutionality. The Governor of Virginia had drafted striking electric utility workers into the state militia and other governors stood ready to follow his lead. In the preceding summer Congress had passed a tough and comprehensive labor control measure, the Case bill, only to have it vetoed by

President Truman. That veto was sustained by a slender margin of only five votes in the House of Representatives, reflecting, no doubt, a residual sensitivity to political realities in an election year. But the election was over, labor had a bad odor to the victors and much of the public, and in the opening days of the New Congress both the House and the Senate were flooded with bills aimed at putting a legislative halter on the unions' power.

The President himself, in his state of the union message, had advanced a relatively moderate proposal that would have outlawed boycotts and jurisdictional strikes, but this received only glancing attention from the lawmakers. In the process of winnowing out the many pending bills attention soon focused on two that were roughly similar and were modeled on the Case bill of the preceding year. One was sponsored in the House by Representative Fred J. Hartley of New Jersey, and the other in the Senate by Senator Robert A. Taft of Ohio, both Republicans. The thrust of each was, without proscribing labor's right to its ultimate weapon, the strike, to surround its use on an interstate basis with certain legal restraints, most importantly a mandatory "cooling off" period.

The refinement and evolution of the steps necessary to this goal took weeks of committee hearings throughout the late winter and spring—and endless expenditures of emotional energy. The leaders of organized labor unanimously opposed virtually every facet of the two bills, condemning them as "union busting" tactics designed to deliver the workers into the hands of their "exploiters." The defenders from the world of industry and finance were equally vehement. Both sides marshaled their forces in public demonstrations of one kind or another; debated loudly on the floors of Congress, at conventions, and at rallies; clogged the news channels with their charges and countercharges. The Truman administration remained rather aloof from the fray. Most of its high ranking officials were known to favor the bill, or at least something like it, while the President confined himself to mild reiterations of the proposal he had advanced in his state of the union message. There was no doubt, however, that Mr. Truman was concerned as much with repairing his damaged political relations with organized labor as with legislation to curb its troublemaking propensities. As the battle neared the showdown stage he made his opposition to the bill emphatic.

At last, early in June, the combined Taft-Hartley bill won resounding approval in both houses of Congress. On final passage, only 66 Democrats in the House and 15 in the Senate supported the President with a "nay" vote. There was an anguished outcry from labor and its liberal supporters. The President took to the radio to add his voice to their chorus, while Senator Taft was granted equal time the following night "to put the record straight." Two days later, against the earnest entreaties of his legislative leaders, President Truman sent the bill back to Congress with his veto.

That same day the House voted to override, 320 to 79, and the Senate followed suit within a couple of days, 68 to 25. In the two chambers there were 25 more votes to override the veto than there had been to pass the bill in the first instance, and the Labor-Management Relations Act of 1947 became the law of the land.

Here, in substance, is what the new law was designed to do: (1) It banned the closed shop and restricted applicability of the so-called union shop. (2) It imposed a 60-day "cooling off" period before a strike or a lockout could be ordered. (3) It made unions liable for damage suits arising out of jurisdictional strikes, secondary boycotts, and violations of contracts. (4) It authorized the use of injunctions against certain union practices and against strikes "imperiling the national health and safety." (5) It banned members of the Communist Party from holding national office in a union. (6) It placed enforcement of the act in a strengthened and enlarged National Labor Relations Board.

This was far and away the most sweeping labor legislation ever enacted in one package, and it imposed some restrictions on the unions from which they hitherto had been immune. Their leaders promptly tagged it "the slave labor act" and promised unyielding defiance. But it really was not as bad as all that, and when the partisan rhetoric cooled down even many people of moderate prolabor persuasion found much of merit in the new law. Over the years it has withstood every major assault on it in the courts, and the frequent application of its terms in industrial disputes no longer sends labor buffs into a rage.

The political climate of the early postwar years seemed hardly conducive to constructive legislative action. Yet, in spite of the partisan friction and stresses in which public affairs were embroiled, some historic advances in national policy were registered during those years.

One such landmark was the Employment Act of 1946, which President Truman signed into law in February of that year. This bill, with strong liberal backing, had been the focus of bitter controversy in Congress for over a year. The aim of its sponsors was to establish federal responsibility for maintaining a state of economic health that would ensure a job at decent wages for every citizen able and willing to work. The motivation came, naturally, from the searing experience of the Great Depression, and fresh impetus was provided by the dread prospect of a massive new wave of unemployment following demobilization. Conservatives and liberals alike acknowledged the need of heading off another such disaster, but they were divided over how to go about it. The backers of the legislation had initially labeled it the Full Employment Act, and that raised the red flag of danger to the conservatives. They foresaw a subtle attempt to have the central government become the *guarantor* of jobs for all through some such device as the revival of a permanent WPA. At the least, they feared an intrusion by the heavy hand of bureaucracy in the most intimate details of corporate wage and labor policy, inflicting thereby irremedial harm to the system of free enterprise.

In its long journey through the legislative mills the more inflammatory features of the bill were ground off, to the still somewhat guarded satisfaction of the conservatives. "Full" was dropped from its title and the operative language in respect to jobs was reduced to an ambiguous statement that it should be the continuing policy of government "to use all practical means for the purpose of creating and maintaining conditions under which there will be afforded useful employment opportunities for those able, willing, and seeking work." To the disappointment of many, this fell considerably short of a commitment to provide jobs for the jobless, but the omission did not seriously diminish the overriding importance of the new law.

What it achieved, in effect, was to establish at the very summit of government—at the President's right hand, so to speak—an economic general staff which, like its military counterpart, was charged with detecting and averting trouble within its area of command before the trouble got out of hand. There had been nothing like it before. Such economic wisdom and policy guidance as was available to the government came from hither, yon, and everywhere—haphazard, conflicting, and often out of focus. The instrument of this new centralized function was the Council of Economic Advisers (CEA), a small and highly professional bureaucracy attached to the Office of the President. Its duty was to keep a stethoscope on the nation's economic heartbeat and to advise the President and Congress in the formulation of national economic policy, with the primary objective of maintaining a "full employment economy." From a shaky start—the whole concept suffered from a lack of public understanding and acceptance—the Council and its function have become indispensable components of the national policy-making process. The President's annual economic message rates in importance along with his state of the union and budget messages, and the Joint Economic Committee (chief congressional client of the CEA) is one of the most influential legislative committees on Capitol Hill.

The Employment Act of 1946 has never produced "full employment" nor has it always charted a clear course through the shoals of economic upset. But without it, we almost certainly would have been in much deeper trouble than we were during many times of stress in the last 25 years.

Another legislative event of equal and possibly even greater importance was the creation of the Atomic Energy Commission and the writing into law of a total governmental monopoly on the production and use of fissionable materials. This event, too, was surrounded by intense and long drawn-out controversy, a controversy that involved not only a critical issue of foreign relations but a high degree of personal drama as well.

Even as the atomic dust was settling over Hiroshima in August 1945, an earnest debate began over how this awesome new power source was to be regulated for the benefit of mankind rather than of his extinction. The notion that this cosmic "trade secret" could be locked away in American laboratories and arsenals had already begun to lose ground. The theory of splitting the atom was known to scientists in a dozen countries; only the hardware for so doing, and for the making of bombs, was an American monopoly, and a transient one at best. The debate revolved principally around the twin questions of national versus international control agencies and, within those agencies, of military versus civilian dominance. There were still some holdouts, however, for preserving the American "secret of the atom" at all costs.

In October 1945, the Truman administration sent to Congress a bill for the creation of a domestic atomic agency and at the same time formally proposed to the United Nations the creation of a special agency within that body to look into the question of international control. The Truman bill leaned heavily toward the idea of putting civilians in full charge of all atomic activity, including weapons production, but on Capitol Hill it ran into conflict with another measure, already well advanced, the May–Johnson bill, that favored strong military control.

There was a sharp ideological cleavage here. On the one side were the "hawks," mostly Generals and Admirals (with strong conservative backing within the political community) who regarded atomic energy primarily as the ultimate weapon—who wanted the military not only to have first say in its production and use here at home but also to guard its "secret" from falling into foreign hands, meaning chiefly, of course, the Russians. On the other side were the "doves," their ranks led by a suddenly aroused and militant scientific community—the Federation of Atomic Scientists sprang almost spontaneously into being in November of that year—who demanded not only that the military should keep hands off but that ultimate control of atomic energy should be placed within an international body such as the UN. They contended further that all military uses of it be barred. The intensity of this debate was underlined when the Truman bill was prompty engulfed in a jurisdictional dispute over which committees of Congress should handle it, Military Affairs or Foreign Relations. This argument rocked along noisily for a couple of weeks before a compromise was reached. A special Joint Committee on Atomic Energy was created to take jurisdiction in the field, with Democratic Senator Brien McMahon of Connecticut as its chairman. Hearings were begun promptly.

Meanwhile, the infant UN organization, meeting in London, agreed to the setting up of an atomic energy agency of its own and invited proposals from all interested member nations on the scope and operations of such a body. This meant primarily the United States, Britain, and Canada, who had shared a partnership in the initial taming of the atom; but it also meant the Soviet Union, which was darkly suspected of knowing a good deal more about the subject than it had let on. President Truman named elder statesman Bernard Baruch as this country's delegate to the UN atomic body, and he also appointed a high-level group of consultants to prepare a detailed U.S. position paper defining the authority and functions of an international atomic agency for Mr. Baruch's guidance. Included in this working group were some of the nation's leading scientists and industrialists, the Under Secretary of State, Dean G. Acheson, and the chairman of the Tennessee Valley Authority, David E. Lilienthal. Lilienthal, a quiet, scholarly man in his forties with a distinguished career in public service behind him, was named chairman—an event, as it turned out, laden with personal destiny.

The legislation for setting up a domestic Atomic Energy Commission, now designated as the McMahon bill, had a stormy passage through Congress during the late winter and spring of 1946. Not only did it provide for an airtight monopoly by the government over the raw materials and all manufacturing processes involved in atomic fission, it denied the military any role beyond an advisory one at the top administrative level of the proposed agency. Advocates for a higher military prerogative lobbied stubbornly for their viewpoint, recalling the tragedy of the nation's unpreparedness at Pearl Harbor and citing the ongoing truculence of Communist Russia as the dark harbinger of dangers yet to be faced. They were backed up by less bellicose spokesmen who abhorred the thought of a government monopoly over so promising a source of industrial energy. These and similar arguments against the measure were bolstered by the suspicion that, irrespective of what happened to the bill at hand, the administration was conspiring to "give away" the nation's advantage to some yet-to-be-defined international authority.

Proponents of the McMahon bill were not to be outdone in the lobbying or the application of pressure. Led by an imposing body of scientists, scholars, clergymen, and other public figures they mounted a kind of holy crusade against what they characterized as an impending "modern barbarism," a world terrified by atomic holocaust. And, fortuitously, compelling documentation was at hand. Two massive demonstrations of the shattering power of an atomic explosion were conducted at Bikini Atoll in the South Pacific during the spring and early summer. Full coverage by the news media brought home to the American public forceful testimony of the hideous nature of man's most recent triumph over nature.

The debate raged on well into the summer but in the end the

McMahon bill, only slightly modified to appease the disappointed "hawks," was passed by both houses of Congress. It was signed by the President on July 27. It called for the establishment of an all-civilian, five-man Atomic Energy Commission (AEC), to be named by the President and confirmed by the Senate, to take over the functions, assets, and personnel of the pioneering Manhattan Engineer District as of January 1, 1947. The legislative intent focused clearly on the doctrine of "atoms for peace" but as a practical matter the development and stockpiling of weapons was to remain the top priority of the AEC for a number of years.

Shortly after signing the McMahon bill President Truman sent to the Senate his nominations for the five commissioners of the new agency. They were a reasonably distinguished lot, and to no one's surprise the President designated David Lilienthal for the critical post of chairman. The so-called Acheson–Lilienthal report which the UN was currently—and warmly—debating, had attracted a highly favorable response both in the United States and among the Western powers generally, and Lilienthal was credited with being its principal architect. Given his temperament and his background as the chief executive of the giant TVA enterprise, his choice to head the AEC seemed to most observers a highly propitious one. In the context of the times, the early morning of the Atomic Age, it was a job of unparalleled responsibility.

But the best of men are to be judged by the enemies they make as well as by the friends. And along the pathway of his career Lilienthal had picked up an enemy whose formidability was now to come close to doing him in. He was Kenneth G. McKellar, the senior Democratic Senator from Tennessee, an aging, cranky relic of the old school of Southern political despotism. The headquarters of the TVA at Knoxville, and the area of some of its most conspicuous conservation success, lay within Senator McKellar's constituency. Like most Tennesseeans—as well as other residents of the sprawling "TVA Empire"—he had no fault to find with the vast stores of economic wealth which the TVA had recovered and uncovered along the blighted river valleys and mountain slopes of its domain. But for a dozen years his personal political prerogatives, his ordained privilege of patronage—to have a creek dammed here, a generating plant located there, to hire this man and to fire that one—had been blunted against the gentle but implacable apolitical rectitude of David Lilienthal. Now this impudent Puritan was about to fall heir to another imposing resource in Tennessee, the atomic city of Oak Ridge, and McKellar decided that this was more than he could bear. He would destroy Lilienthal once and for all.

In mid-January 1947, the five nominees for the AEC appeared before the Senate wing of the Joint Committee for their confirmation hearings. The composition of the committee had been slightly altered by the recent election; the Republicans were now in the majority and Republican Senator Bourke B. Hickenlooper of Iowa held the chairman's seat. This seemed to presage no difficulty for the AEC nominees since the appointments were generally regarded as nonpolitical. But such reckoning failed to take into account the inflexible will of Kenneth McKellar. Exercising one of the traditional privileges of the Senate "Club" (his seniority was impressive) he took a seat at the committee table on the opening day as a "guest inquisitor," not being a regular member of the panel. Like the fictional "man who came to dinner," he stayed on and on and on, monopolizing the proceedings, wearing out his welcome, exhausting the patience of his hosts, the press, most of the public, and, by the relentless, repetitive pressure of his vituperation, driving the defenseless Lilienthal toward the brink of nervous collapse.

McKellar's strategy, which was about as subtle as a knock on the head, was to depict Lilienthal as a Communist or at the least a confirmed and dangerous fellow traveler. This was an inviting approach, for a renewed "Red scare" was rapidly building up in the postwar public mind, and Lilienthal, a Harvard law graduate who got his political indoctrination in the LaFollette Progressive movement in Wisconsin, had come to maturity steeped in the liberal tradition of the New Deal. Add to this the fact that he was Jewish and there was enough grist here to set a bigot's mill to grinding.

A witness before a congressional committee has few of the immunities available to a defendant in a court of law, and by the same token the inquisitor is unrestrained by any rules of relevance or imputation in his line of questioning. Senator McKellar was thus free to forage as he pleased through the manifold complexities of the TVA's administration over the past decade; to nitpick over obscure executive decisions and to try to pry out incriminating philosophical and ideological rationales that lay behind those decisions. And always the questioning led back, with the deadening monotony of a third-degree grilling, to the implication that Communist loyalties had guided Lilienthal's hand.

This relentless inquisition went on for nearly two weeks and Lilienthal, a sensitive and introspective man, began to show signs of emotional strain. (His published diaries confirm that the stress had become almost intolerable.) He had repeated his denials with patient firmness over and over again but they had no effect on his dogged adversary. At last, a crack appeared in the dam of his reserve and then his outrage poured forth in a torrent.

With poorly concealed malice, McKellar had asked him, for the fourth or fifth time during the proceedings, where in Austria his (Jewish) parents had come from. The answer was the same as before: "from near Pressburg." Then he asked why the TVA, some time before, had authorized a minor change in the price of ammonium nitrate fertilizer. Lilienthal answered that was not the sort of information "I carry in my head," but offered to procure it from the files. The Senator, seeming to have arrived at his target at last by clumsy locutions, said: "I think it is very important what your views are on Communist doctrine. What about them?"

Lilienthal seemed transfixed in silence for a moment. Then he swung his chair around to face McKellar squarely where he sat near the end of the raised committee dais. There was no tremor or anger in his tone as he spoke, nor did he raise his voice, but it conveyed a quiet intensity that, for about 10 unbroken minutes, held the packed hearing room silently in its grip.

This I *do* carry in my head, Senator. And I will do my best to make it clear.

My convictions are not so much concerned with what I am against as what I am for—and that excludes a lot of things automatically.

Traditionally, democracy has been an affirmative doctrine rather than merely a negative one.

I believe in—and I conceive the Constitution of the United States to rest, as does religion, upon—the fundamental propositon of the integrity of the individual; and that all government and all private institutions must be designed to promote and protect and defend the integrity and dignity of the individual; that that is the essential meaning of the Constitution and the Bill of Rights, as it is essentially the meaning of religion.

Any form of government, therefore, and any other institutions, which make men means rather than ends in themselves, which exalt the state or any other institution above the importance of men, which place arbitrary power over men as a fundamental tenet of government, are contrary to this conception; and therefore I am deeply opposed to them.

Lilienthal held neither manuscript nor notes in his hand. The words came spontaneously, uninterruptedly, from some deep well of conviction within him. Communist philosophy, he went on, fell within this proscribed category, holding that the state is an end in itself, and "that I deeply disbelieve." It is very easy, he said, to assert that one is against communism, but it is even more important that one have a strong faith in the positive alternative that is democracy. And among the basic tenets of democracy which he cherished were a belief in the integrity of the individual—"that all men are the children of God and their personalities are therefore sacred"—and a repugnance for those who, by innuendo or insinuation, would falsely injure another's character. For to do so, he said, even under the guise of protecting democracy, is to traduce the very spirit of democracy itself. He concluded:

I deeply believe in the capacity of democracy to surmount any trials that may lie ahead provided only we practice it in our daily lives. . . .

I want also to add that part of my conviction is based upon my training as an Anglo-American common lawyer. It is the very basis of the great heritage of the English people to this country . . . that strictest rules of credibility of witnesses and of the avoidance of hearsay and gossip shall be excluded in courts of justice. . . .

And whether by administrative agencies acting arbitrarily against business organizations, or whether by investigative activities of the legislative branches, whenever those principles fail, those principles of the protection of an individual and his good name against besmirchment by gossip, hearsay, and the statement of witnesses who are not subject to cross-examination: then, too, we have failed in carrying forward our ideals in respect to democracy.

This I deeply believe.

As Lilienthal stopped speaking no one else spoke or moved for half a moment. Then there was a reflective shuffling of feet and papers. People straightened up in their chairs, looked about mildly dazed as if seeking the open window though which a fresh breeze had come. "That was the statement of a very real American," Senator McMahon said in a barely audible voice, more to himself than to the assemblage. Then the spell was broken: Senator McKellar "harumphed" nervously, fiddled with his glasses, and in a dry, gravelly voice, continued his interrogation—"Mr. Lilienthal, while you were the head of TVA, did you have any Communists in your employ?"

Lilienthal's profession of faith was deeply moving to most of those who heard it. When the hearing adjourned a few moments later several Senators came over to shake his hand and to congratulate him, and dozens of reporters and spectators swarmed about the witness table where he sat, somewhat limp and dismayed, to shower him with praise. The next morning's *Washington Post* carried the full text of his statement with a few paragraphs of explanatory matter in a long two-column box on its front page. By evening the 2,000 reprints which the *Post* offered its readers had been snapped up, and another 5,000 copies were exhausted before the end of the week. Lilienthal, himself, was swamped by hundreds of congratulatory letters and telegrams in the next few days as radio commentators and newspaper all across the country recounted his remarkable tour de force.

Lilienthal's troubles were not over but they were greatly ameliorated and his dialectical feat had restored his self-confidence. Senator McKellar withdrew from the scene after another desultory week of questioning, but Republican Senators Taft and Wherry picked up approximately where the Tennessean had left off, accusing the nominee of being not a Communist but a New Dealer. At long last they, too, ran out of ammunition and in April—84 days after the hearings began—Lilienthal and his four colleagues were confirmed by substantial votes in the Senate and the Atomic Energy Commission was in business. Its UN counterpart never came to fruition, the move being blocked by a Russian veto in the Security Council after nearly two years of contention.[3]

IV

The dilemmas of peace were not all entirely homegrown. They poured in upon us from across two oceans. In their stubborn complexity they seemed to set at naught much of the idealism, much of the geopolitical sanity, for which this nation had fought. As they demanded new exactions of leadership and succor by the United States, they exacerbated the frictions and mutual suspicions of our domestic political life. We were sucked into the role of the Free World's almoner and its Big Brother (later to be known to some as "Uncle Shylock").

In respect to Europe this dilemma took the shape of a cold war that overflowed from and then superseded the hot war. On this hard anvil the one-world myth was hammered into a bipolar reality. Only the United States and the Soviet Union emerged from World War II as viable international political powers. It was foreordained, and soon became patently evident, that their goals worldwide were deeply contradictory and mutually antagonistic. The genesis of this historic conflict might well be written as an international folk drama centering about a cast composed of Stalin the Cynic, Churchill the Pragmatist, and Roosevelt the Altruist.

Stalin never made any serious pretensions that he had committed his country to the war against Hitlerism for any abstract principles of freedom and human dignity, but rather for hardheaded considerations of national security. Like the Czars who preceded him, he was obsessed with distrust and fear of the West, Germany in particular. He wanted Germany destroyed, and beyond that he wanted a safe barrier of friendly states— which in his terms could only be Communist states—shielding Russia against the mendacity and corruption of the rest of Europe. With ruthless determination he achieved his goal, from the Baltic to the Aegean.

Churchill was imbued, naturally, with the Anglo-Saxon tradition of freedom, but he was an old-style imperialist as well, skilled in the arts of realpolitick. For the post-Hitler era, he had less faith in the platitudes of one-world unity than in the practical applications of an advantageous balance of power. He early perceived the thrust of Stalin's intentions; foresaw that unless he was checked in his headlong political absorption of Poland and the satellite states of East and Central Europe, that a balance of power would result heavily disadvantageous to Western interests. Repeatedly before, during, and after the Yalta conference Churchill warned Roosevelt of this inexorable drift, urged him to take steps to reverse it— as, for example, the launching of a subsidiary offensive through "the soft underbelly of Europe" that would have given the Western allies a military-political foothold in the Balkans ahead of or jointly with the Red Army. The President would have none of it. He refused to mix his military and political objectives.

Roosevelt has been called naive by some. With the special acuity of hindsight some basis for this charge can be discerned. But it is more accurate to say that he was possessed by a great ideal, the ideal of a world family of nations living in perpetual amity. This was the ideal for which his mentor, Woodrow Wilson, had struggled futilely, but in Roosevelt's mind that goal was now within the reach of his own hands. Stalin's ruthlessness disturbed him, as did Churchill's stubborn penchant for power politics, but he saw his own role as that of arbiter who would lead the doubters and dissidents at last to fulfillment under the True Grace. If trusts were fully extended, he believed, it would be fully reciprocated: This he *had* to believe if his goal was to have any viability at all. So he refused as long as the war was going on to accede to any anti-Russian strategies, to destroy Stalin's trust by preclusive political arrangements for a postwar Europe. He insisted that everyone should come to the UN peace table with clean hands. It did not, of course, work out that way.

So the hot war ended with the Russian presence, military and political, firmly implanted from the shores of the Baltic through half of Germany and all of the Balkans to the portals of Asia Minor. It was, in overwhelming measure, an unwelcome presence to those whom it engulfed and a frightening menace to those who lived within its long shadow, which meant most of the rest of Europe. Russian communism was a dynamic, aggressive political force and the chaotic conditions that prevailed in the wake of the war were conducive to its spread, even where the democratic tradition had taken root. The cold war sprang inevitably from the fierce clash of ideologies for the soul of Europe. It has persisted for more than a quarter of a century virtually to monopolize the diplomacy of the Western world, to shape its pattern of thought and its political processes.*

The war against Germany had barely been won before the structure of allied unity began to fall apart—and with it the hope that Roosevelt's dream could ever be truly fulfilled. The scene was the Big Three meeting at Potsdam in July–August 1945, which had been called for the purpose of welding into practical and usable shape the peacemaking principles which had been designed at Yalta the winter before. There, it will be recalled, Stalin, Churchill, and Roosevelt had wound up their historic session in a mood of self-congratulatory optimism and good-fellowship. They had blueprinted—with some conspicuous gaps and deferred details—a brave

---

* The intensity of the cold war had abated substantially by 1974 due in large measure to the detente achieved by President Nixon and Communist Party Chief Leonid I. Brezhnev of the U.S.S.R. How durable it might be was anyone's guess.

new world of peace and harmony to be erected on the ashes of the old once the detritus of war was swept away. Its principal adornment was the United Nations, for which at least the facade was now in place. Now the time had come for the brickwork on its broad foundation—peace treaties and the fashioning of democratic societies for Germany and its Axis satellites and, of course, for Poland. (A similar settlement in the Pacific would come later, now that both Russian collaboration in that affair and the atomic bomb were assured.)

President Truman now occupied the seat formerly held by the late President Roosevelt. It was his first head-on experience with high-level diplomacy, and inevitably he was the prisoner of Roosevelt's philosophy and that of the advisers whom he had inherited along with the Presidency. He was immediately charmed by Churchill's grandeur and by Stalin's sly amiability, but he was quick to assess the stubborn self-interest as bargainers that underlay their pleasant meins. He was a wiser politician when he left Potsdam 17 days later even if he brought away no trophies.

The Potsdam conference resolved itself into an almost unbroken series of stalemates that found Truman and Churchill often divided or uncertain about the ends and means they were seeking while Stalin seemed to know precisely what he wanted and in many cases, by virtue of the presence of the Red Army, to have it in hand. The unresolved issue of Poland was typical. At Yalta, Poland's new western border was vaguely defined as the Oder river, involving a considerable cession of existing German territory. And its postwar government was to be determined by "free democratic elections." By the time of the Potsdam meeting the Russian occupying forces had pushed even farther westward to the Neisse river, absorbing in Poland's name some of Germany's most productive agricultural lands, and had put in control a provisional Polish government handpicked by and completely subservient to Moscow. Stalin simply presented his American and British conferees at Potsdam with a fait accompli and refused to be budged. Poland was permanently enclosed behind the Iron Curtain.

Much the same pattern evolved in the overrun countries of Central Europe—Czechoslovakia, where in the closing days of the war American forces had actually turned back from Prague to allow a triumphal entry by Red Army "liberators"; Austria, where in the early postwar weeks British and American members of the tripartite Allied Control Commission were forbidden entry into the country by Russian military commanders until a makeshift Communist provisional government could be put in place; the Balkan states, where Churchill preferred not to oppose the Russians' on-the-spot dominance in the region in exchange for their promise to keep hands off Greece. In each instance the Potsdam conferees managed to hack and scratch their way toward agreement on peace treaties and political regimes for these onetime Axis satellites (most of these agreements would be consummated a year later), but almost invariably on Stalin's harsh terms. The Iron Curtain now hung across all of east Europe.

Germany was the principal magnet that had drawn the allied leaders to Potsdam. There it lay, at the very heartland of Europe, utterly prostrate. Before there could be a peace treaty with Germany there had to be a German state and before that could come about some plan for its social and economic rebirth had to be devised and set in motion. It had been agreed at Yalta that the four occupying powers (France had been admitted into the company of Big Powers for this purpose) would each serve as an interim government within its respective zone of occupation, but—and this was to be spelled out in detail at Potsdam—in a cooperative fashion that would permit the gradual, cautious rehabilitation of Germany as a political entity. Her war-making potential was to be forever denied and the Nazi spirit expunged from the German character, but meanwhile, under the benign tutelage of her conquerors, she was to be allowed to regain a measured economic self-sufficiency and to restructure her society along peaceful, democratic lines.

Fair enough, but things were not to work out that way, as became painfully evident at Potsdam. The Russians had no interest in a restructured Germany: A political vacuum would have suited their purpose better. Presenting a $10 billion due bill for reparations (largely justifiable in a military sense), they regarded Germany primarily as a supply depot for the rebuilding of the Soviet economy. The shooting had barely stopped before they began stripping their zone of foodstuffs, minerals, and rolling stock, and dismantling entire factories for shipment to Russia. The French were only a little less interested in a restored German economy, hoping to replace the Reich as Europe's industrial powerhouse, but they stopped short of excessive reparations demands. The British concern, with a wary eye on Communist imperialism, was aimed primarily at avoiding the political vacuum of a permanently impotent German state. Beyond that, they made common cause with the Americans in trying to see to it that Germany, though made to pay dearly for its sins, did not remain totally helpless and thus dependent on the charity and nursing care which only the United States and Britain could and would supply.

Thus was THE GERMAN QUESTION framed at Potsdam in the summer of 1945. It has continued to be spelled in capital letters in all the diplomatic history since; to remain the most stubborn, unyielding salient of the Cold War. Nor did anything else of substance come out of the Potsdam conference. All the principal issues were papered over with brave ambiguities, but the problems themselves were bucked along to a new instrumentality, the Council of Foreign Ministers. Over the next several years that body did negotiate peace treaties for the former satellites and for Italy but it made no progress whatever in respect to Germany and Poland. Nor, in Western terms, has there been much progress since.[4]

V

The desolation that pervaded Europe in the years immediately following the war is almost impossible to imagine two decades and more afterward. Scores of its cities and towns had been blasted into heaps of rubble. Factories, mines, port facilities, power stations, transportation, and communication systems had been crippled. Thousands of families lived in tents, shacks, the patched remnants of bombed-out buildings. A searing drought in the summer of 1946 destroyed half of the anticipated wheat crop and ruined a proportionately large share of other farm produce. The hot summer led into one of the most devastating winters on record with blizzards and prolonged periods of subfreezing temperatures such as the continent had seldom known. Governments, including that of Great Britain, were literally bankrupt and in France and Italy surging Communist parties, numbering as much as a third of the electorates, threatened the delicate balance of democratic control. Hunger and destitution were acute and a spirit of bitter hopelessness overhung the region from the North Sea to the Mediterranean, in the lands of victor and vanquished alike.

These facts were well known to the American public: They were among the more agonizing of the dilemmas of peace. The United States had contributed more than three billion dollars to various rescue operations, including that of the United Nations Relief and Rehabilitation Administration (UNRRA). The public had joined wholeheartedly in food conservation programs in order that surpluses might be sent to Europe. Columnist Drew Pearson's "Freedom Train" (there were several) rolled across the country picking up boxcar-loads of food and medical supplies for dispatch abroad, and CARE packages by the tens of thousands were sent by American citizens to relatives and friends, or to anonymous sufferers, in England and on the continent. It was a typically generous and emotional response, but the implications of the problem went too deep to be cured by charity. Anne O'Hare McCormick pinpointed this truth in a dispatch to the *New York Times* in February 1947, in which she said:

The crises in Britain and France [point up] a truth the United States knows but shrinks from facing. They are primarily economic crises, signs of the difficulty of treating post-war breakdown by democratic means. They reveal how battered and shaken are the old strongholds of democracy in Europe, and how few these strongholds are. Most of all, they throw the ball to us, giving notice that if freedom as we understand it is to survive, it's up to the United States to save it. . . .

Everywhere the pressures to give up the fight for freedom are almost irresistible. The fight for survival is so primitive, the submergence of the middle class so general, the individual so helpless, the senses of human dignity so blunted by inhuman transfers of people, the desire for change, and the feeling that any change must be for the better so overwhelming, that it is harder to stand fast than to follow the easier path—toward a Communist dictatorship or reaction. It cannot be said too often that the greatest danger to democracy . . . is the weariness and faltering spirit of democrats. . . .

The extent to which democratic government survives on that continent depends on how far this country is willing to help it survive.

This country was willing to help democracy survive and it did so in a fashion unparalleled in the history of international relations. The impetus was both humanitarian and pragmatic. The sequence of its fulfillment falls into three main stages.

The first stage was intellectual, a preparation of the official mind—the government planning apparatus—with a rationale for doing what had to be done. At the war's end and for months afterwards President Truman and most of his advisers were still in the thrall of Roosevelt's doctrine that the partnership with Russia must be preserved at all costs; that once their Slavic suspicions were allayed Stalin and company would bend to the task of helping to build a democratic world. Not precisely according to Western patterns, of course, but close enough to be compatible and harmonious. Since VE-Day, however, this faith had been subjected to many harsh tests and each encounter left it a bit more weakened and wavering than before. By the beginning of 1946 official confidence in Stalin's good intentions had all but evaporated but there was no consensus on a contrary doctrine to take its place.

This deficiency was soon remedied. In February Stalin made a speech to a huge party gathering in Moscow that was, in effect, an ultimatum to the non-Communist world. In blunt and forthright terms he said there could be no long-term collaboration between the young, dynamic world of socialism and the dying, corrupt world of capitalism; that the Soviet Union was now launched upon huge development programs that would soon give it mastery, military and economic, over the combined forces of its enemies in the West. The analysis of this ominous manifesto, which reached Washington a few days later, was prepared by our Counselor of Embassy in Moscow, George F. Kennan, a brilliant student of Russian history and psychology. This was no routine bit of bureaucratic communication. Rather, it was a profound and scholarly dissertation running to some 8,000 words that reached far back into the history and culture of the Russian nation to explain and interpret its contemporary posture in world affairs.

This document, destined soon to become a cornerstone of American diplomacy, has been exhaustively analyzed and dissected by experts. A very brief summary, however, will serve our purpose here. What Kennan said in substance was that Russian political philosophy was not a rational system based on Western concepts, but a religion full of dogmas and demonology with strongly Oriental overtones. The Russian revolution of 1916, the overthrow of the existing order by the proletariat, was a preordained stage in the evolution of man's destiny. But the complete fulfillment of that destiny remained to be secured, both at home and in the world at large. And that task required continued austerity, sacrifice, and belligerency, fortified by the unchanging image of a hostile outside world intent upon the destruction of communism. This means, Kennan wrote:

there can never be on Moscow's side any sincere assumption of a community of aims between the Soviet Union and powers which are regarded as capitalist. It must be invariably assumed in Moscow that the aims of the capitalist world are antagonistic to the Soviet regime. . . . [From this] flow many of the phenomena which we find disturbing in the Kremlin's conduct of foreign policy: the secretiveness, the wary suspiciousness, the duplicity, and the basic unfriendliness of purpose. These phenomena are there to stay for the foreseeable future. . . .

The Soviets' political action, he went on, "is a fluid stream which moves constantly wherever it is permitted to move toward a given goal . . . [to fill] every nook and cranny available to it in the basin of world power." The United States cannot expect in the foreseeable future "to enjoy political intimacy with the Soviet regime. It must continue to regard the Soviet Union as a rival, not a partner, in the political arena. . . ."

And then coming to the heart of his argument, Kennan wrote:

In the light of the above it will be clearly seen that the Soviet pressure against the free institutions of the western world is something that can be contained by the adroit and vigilant application of counterforce at a series of constantly shifting geographical and political points corresponding to the shifts and maneuvers of Soviet strategy . . . *a policy of firm containment* [italics added] designed to confront the Russians with unalterable counterforce at every point where they show signs of encroaching upon the interests of a peaceful and stable world. . . .*

The containment doctrine quickly gained credence in the policy-making levels of American diplomacy. It provided the rationale, if not the direct motivation, for the next two major steps in postwar foreign policy which followed shortly. Its influence, indeed, remained dominant for more than two decades and underlay this country's interventions in Korea and Vietnam.

---

* This resume is based on "The Sources of Soviet Conduct," an article written by Mr. Kennan under the pseudonym "X" and published in the July 1947 issue of *Foreign Affairs*. The article is a paraphrase and condensation of the memorandum Mr. Kennan wrote for the State Department and, for the public at large, its first introduction to the containment doctrine. In recent years Mr. Kennan has modified somewhat the rigid tenets on which he based his thesis and speaks more hopefully of the possibilities of coexistence. (See his *On Dealing with the Communist World*, Harper & Row, 1963).

The second stage in the fulfillment of this country's determination to help preserve democracy in the world saw the emergence of something we all have since become familiar with as "foreign aid." This was an innovation of great daring and magnitude that paid off handsomely in the dividends of peace, of human welfare, and—to a substantial degree at least—of political stability within those nations it touched. It evolved through two separate but related phases, the Truman Doctrine (as embodied in the Greek-Turkish Aid Program) and the Marshall Plan.

By agreement stemming back to the last weeks of the war in Europe, Britain and the United States had shared a mutual responsibility to preserve the political integrity of Greece and Turkey. Britain's side of the bargain, by far the preponderant one, was chiefly military, while the United States had an almost wholly economic role. But constant and massive Communist pressure on the two Mediterranean powers soon began to threaten both with collapse. Each, weakened by the war, was highly vulnerable. If Greece fell, Turkey would be drawn under with her; and if Turkey fell the fate of Greece was automatically sealed. And once Communist power broke through these slender political barricades into the Mediterranean, all of the Middle East, India, North Africa, and even Italy would be in jeopardy —and so also would the concept of a free-world counterforce to Communist aggression. Such was the conventional wisdom of the day.

By late 1945 the Soviets had begun to put pressure on the Turks to "share" with them joint control and defense of the Dardanelles, the narrow strait through which the Black Sea empties into the Mediterranean. The pressure was stepped up in mid-1946 and coupled with a claim that several thousand square miles of territory in eastern Turkey bordering the U.S.S.R. actually belonged to and should be returned to Russia. This was by now a familiar gambit of Communist aggression, the preliminary to a designed takeover of Turkish sovereignty. Turkey was no jewel, certainly, in democracy's diadem, but its authoritarian regime had brought a new measure of freedom to its people and was striving genuinely for still higher attainments. At all events its preservation was of sufficient importance to Britain and the United States late in 1946 for those powers to tell Moscow unequivocally to keep "hands off." To underscore the language the U.S. Mediterranean Fleet began a long series of "training maneuvers" in Turkish waters.

This brought a standoff in the threat to Turkey but of what permanency no one could guess. As our Ambassador in Ankara warned President Truman at the time: "Turkey will not be able to maintain indefinitely a defensive posture against the Soviet Union. The burden [of maintaining a 600,000-man army] is too great for the nation's economy to carry much longer."

Unlike Turkey, Greece had been plundered and ravaged by Nazi occupation during the war. King George had fled to London to set up a paper government-in-exile. British and American agents had infiltrated the peninsula and helped to organize thousands of natives into roving bands of guerrillas to fight the invaders, and Communist agents flowed across the borders from Albania and Bulgaria to lend a hand. But long before the Germans began to withdraw in 1944 the native irregulars had splintered into mutually hostile ideological groups and began fighting among themselves for political control of the country when liberation should come. The dominant band was the Communist-oriented ELAS (People's National Army of Liberation), with an army estimated at about 20,000 men. It was strongly backed with weapons and manpower by Communist governments to the north and by the loud support of the Soviet Union in the UN and in its organs of worldwide propaganda. The opposing forces were scattered and poorly organized. Britain had moved some of its forces into Greece behind the retreating Germans in the hope of averting a disastrous civil war until such time as the Greek King could be returned to his throne. But the monarchy, which had been plagued in the past by corruption and reaction, was not a popular symbol and warfare between the partisan bands and the tottering provisional government in Athens raged on with stubborn, exhausting violence. The regime was prevented from total collapse and thus dropping into Moscow's hands only by the presence of British soldiers and large infusions of money and food from UNRRA and the United States. The American Ambassador cabled Washington in January 1947, that he doubted the Greek government as it stood could last beyond another two weeks without an immediate and massive grant of more aid.

This was the state of affairs late in February 1947, when Lord Inverchapel, the British Ambassador in Washington, walked into the office of Secretary of State George Marshall and told him somberly that His Majesty's Government, already teetering on the edge of financial insolvency, had reached the end of its rope in Greece and Turkey; that it was pulling out all of its forces and relinquishing all of its responsibilities there in exactly 30 days. If the stopper was to be kept in the bottle there —if a Communist breakthrough into the eastern Mediterranean and beyond was to be averted—the United States would have to shoulder the whole burden itself.

This eventuality was not wholly unexpected: Britain had been badly buffeted, her internal condition was precarious, her empire was withering away. But it came with such suddenness and such finality as to produce a shock in the White House and the Department of State. However the first response from these quarters was prompt and affirmative: Yes, the United States would assume alone the entire burden of salvaging Greece and Turkey, of *containing* communism at this break in freedom's dike.

It was a momentous decision and its rapid implementation showed something heartening about the adaptability of the American political system. For a hostile Congress and a disenchanted public opinion were disposed to give only the backs of their hands to President Truman in whatever he proposed to do around this time.

But this sentiment crumbled as the urgency of the crisis was made plain. After many days of intensive staff work a bold plan of action was formulated. It called for the prompt appropriation of $400 million for both military and economic aid to be divided between Greece and Turkey and for the stationing of United States missions in those countries to oversee—to direct, actually—the rebuilding of their armed forces and their economies. Then, congressional leaders were brought to the White House for an intensive briefing that won important allies for the project just prior to its public disclosure. The successful recruitment in the cause of Senator Arthur Vandenberg of Michigan, the onetime isolationist Republican chairman of the Foreign Relations Committee, was the crucial achievement of this session.

Two days later, on March 12, President Truman went before a joint session of Congress to lay out the problem and to ask for the necessary legislation. In candid but unemotional terms he described the desperate plight of Greece and Turkey as threatened outposts of the free world and delineated the consequences of their subjugation by communism. Not only in Greece and Turkey, he said, but in many other parts of the world people were being forced to choose between alternative life styles, between freedom and totalitarianism. Whenever the choice was imposed upon them, whenever free institutions were suppressed by alien aggressors, then were the goals for which this country had sacrificed so much debased and destroyed. He set out certain principles which he said should henceforth guide this country's foreign policy, principles which came to be known as the Truman Doctrine:

I believe that it must be the policy of the United States to support free peoples who are resisting attempted subjugation by armed minorities or by outside pressures.

I believe that we must assist free peoples to work out their own destinies in their own way.

I believe that our help should be primarily through economic and financial aid which is essential to economic stability and orderly political processes.

The world is not static, and the status quo is not sacred. But we cannot allow changes in the status quo in violation of the charter of the United Nations by such methods as coercion or by such subterfuges as political infiltration. . . .

Should we fail to aid Greece and Turkey in this fateful hour, the effect will be far-reaching to the West as well as to the East.

Congress responded generously to the President's appeal; so also, in preponderant measure, did public opinion. Within a matter of weeks the Greek-Turkish aid program was operating in high gear. If democracy never achieved a full flowering in those turbulent states, they won at the least a lasting reprieve from mass starvation, from incipient anarchy, and from foreign subjugation. The tide of Communist conquest, so dire a threat in that distant time, was halted at their borders and has remained so since.

But even as the rescue of Greece and Turkey was being formulated in the early months of 1947 a larger plan was taking shape to meet the still larger threat to freedom in western Europe. The warning contained in Anne O'Hare McCormick's dispatch to the *Times,* referred to above, was by no means unique. There were many others like it, especially in official reports to the White House and the State Department. Hunger and destitution were endemic all the way from the British Isles to the toe of the Italian boot. Agricultural and industrial production were limping, causing acute shortages in food, fuel, electric power, and essential consumer goods of every kind. Treasuries were bankrupt and purchasing power sagged under the mounting weight of inflation.

In the wake of this almost universal distress came political chaos. This was true especially on the Continent, in the Low Countries, in France, and in Italy. Existing governments seemed powerless to halt the deepening tide of human misery. Their desperate citizens were ready to grasp at any straw, to try any political panacea, that promised relief. In this climate indigenous Communist parties flourished, aided and abetted by a rising volume of propaganda and direct assistance from Moscow. In the 1947 elections in France Communists cast nearly one-third of the total vote and the Ramadier government was obliged to take prominent Marxists into the Cabinet. The situation in Italy and, to a lesser degree, in Belgium and Denmark was almost as extreme. A wave of strikes, riots, and sabotage spread across Western Europe clearly designed to topple existing regimes—and in the process, democracy itself. It was the Greek-Turkish syndrome projected on a far larger and more ominous scale.

The United States had striven mightily to arrest this deadly erosion. In the two years following Hitler's defeat it had poured some $6 billion in cash and goods into a variety of European relief projects, not all of them in the West. Its effort was largely on a piecemeal, problem-by-problem basis; a bucket-brigade approach aimed at damping down each crisis as it flared into the open. Now, in the early months of 1947, it had become apparent that this haphazard attack offered no permanent solutions at all. It was an extravagant use of bandaids to treat what obviously was a cancer. What Europe needed was rehabilitation, not emergency relief; a restoration of her economic vitality—production, transportation, currency stabilization, trade—without which self-sufficiency and political stability would never come. It would cost a great deal of money and take a long time. It was a very large order, indeed.

One man whose influence was preeminent in shaping much of American foreign policy during the middle and late forties was Dean Gooderham Acheson, who in every respect seemed to be the very archetype of the polished, aristocratic Foreign Minister. He was tall, well-proportioned, impeccable in dress and carriage. He was austerely handsome, with a strong, Nordic profile, crisp, graying hair, and a bold mustache defiantly uptilted at the ends. The eyes under his dark, shaggy brows were clear, confident, commanding. His speech was tailored to the image: unhurried, self-assured, precise in syntax and meaning. The dimension of his intellect was manifest. The sum of these attributes was an aura of arrogance, an impression which Acheson was at no particular pains to dispel. But it was a natural, uncontrived arrogance—a built-in defense against bores and inconsequential demands upon his attention. Beneath that formidable facade, however, there was a reservoir of warmth and geniality and wit, of personal affection and loyalty, even occasional traces of sentimentality. And when the gates of that reservoir were lifted the stern lines about the eyes and the mouth dissolved in an expression of regal merriment or of simple compassion, as the occasion might warrant, making the beholder feel that he was being favored by some special sort of dispensation.

He was, indeed, well-born; reared in a cultivated New England home (his father was the Episcopal Bishop of Connecticut); schooled at Groton, Yale, and Harvard; law clerk for a year to Supreme Court Justice Louis D. Brandeis; senior partner (ultimately) of Washington's most prestigious law firm, Covington, Burling. He joined Roosevelt's sub-Cabinet in the mid-thirties as an Assistant Secretary of the Treasury; broke with the President after a few months in a disagreement over gold policy; returned in 1941 as an Assistant Secretary of State. With a year-and-a-half lapse between 1947 and 1949 he remained at the Department of State through the remainder of Roosevelt's tenure and all of Truman's, becoming successively Under Secretary and Secretary in a period of the most revolutionary change in foreign policy in the country's history. He was "present at the creation" (which is the apt title of one volume of his memoirs) of most of these great innovations, from lend-lease to the Marshall Plan to the Korean "intervention" of 1950. Yet, paradoxically, he tended toward the Churchillian, nineteenth-century concept of the efficacy of power in world politics; was mildly contemptuous of such idealistic schemes as the United Nations, and harbored an abiding distrust of communism and of its Comrade-in-Chief, Stalin. This obvious fact, however, did not shield him from unmatched abuse by more visceral anti-Communists during the long night of McCarthyism.

There was, inevitably, no uniform consensus about Dean Acheson in the Washington of his day. Depending upon the sociopolitical plane from which one viewed him, he was either a pretentious snob, a Machiavelli, or a diplomat of rare genius. These contrasting attributes were heaped upon him throughout his public career. But none could deny the enormous reach of his influence on national and world affairs during the 10 years of his ascendancy. President Truman rated him a "great" Secretary of State, and most objective historians of the period concur in that assessment.

The gestative process from which the Marshall Plan emerged proceeded in considerable secrecy even as the Greek-Turkish Aid Program was coming to fruition. One of the core problems that had to be faced was political—how to make an undertaking of such magnitude and of such a revolutionary character acceptable to the American people. Their mood, aggravated by inflation and endless contentions over domestic problems, was restless. There was growing cynicism over the fruits of military victory, so recently won at so great a cost. And their confidence in the Truman administration to lead them into a better day was at a low ebb. True, aid to Greece and Turkey had gone down the national gullet relatively painlessly. But might not this big morsel have sated the public appetite for such grandiose eleemosynary fare?

There was an odds-on chance that this was the case, and the risks of failure would have to be minimized wherever possible.

The softening-up process was adroitly managed. It began with a speech by Under Secretary Acheson in Mississippi in May, laying the philosophical groundwork for a radical change in approach to treating the problems of Europe. The speech did not receive much coverage in the press but it alerted key persons in Congress and a handful of journalists here and abroad that something significant was afoot. Speculation mounted with willing assists from "sources" in the White House and State Department.

The formal unveiling of the idea fell to Secretary Marshall, since his prestige at the time outshone that of the President. In a brief commencement address at Harvard on June 5 he defined in broad outline what had to be done if freedom was to be preserved in Europe. "The remedy," he said, "lies in breaking the vicious circle and restoring the confidence of the European people in the economic future of their own countries and of Europe as a whole." And it is logical, he went on, "that the United States should do whatever it is able to do to assist in the return of normal economic health in the world, without which there can be no political stability and no assured peace."

Marshall ventured no cost figures, no timetable, no operational blueprint. The initiative in the whole enterprise, he said, should come from those governments most needful and desirous of help. That door seemed to be wide open, for, the Secretary explained, the plan should not take the form of a fight *against* any political system (read communism) but a fight *for* economic recovery and freedom. And finally, it should not be regarded as a palliative for recurrent illnesses but as a sustained course of curative treatment.

Acheson, who of course had a leading hand in formulating and advancing the whole scheme, also at this point doubled as publicity "flack." The day prior to Marshall's speech he prompted a handful of leading U.S. and European correspondents to be on the alert for it; that beneath the cautious prose there lurked an innovation of vast import in world affairs. The effort paid off well. The speech was widely reported here at home—the *Times* carried the story under a three-column banner on its front page—and in many European papers it was treated as a sensation. A London editor awoke Foreign Minister Ernest Bevin in the middle of the night to read him the full text, according to one report (more of Acheson's handiwork), leaving that doughty old Laborite so excited he could not go back to bed. Before lunchtime he had his opposite number in Paris on long-distance telephone laying the groundwork for the conference of European leaders which the Marshall proposal obviously called for.

Now a critical dilemma emerged. Secretary Marshall's invitation could be read as open to all comers—designedly but warily so. But what if the Soviets and their string of satellites, with their bottomless needs and copious appetite, *did* come in? They probably would drain the well before anyone else could lower a bucket, and at worst they might even dynamite the wellhead because of its capitalist contamination. It looked for a time as though this was exactly what was going to happen. Czechoslovakia (still clinging to the remnants of a democratic regime under the scowling surveillance of Red commissars) quickly indicated its eagerness to participate; so did Poland and Hungary. And when the European leaders sat down in Paris for their first conference on implementing the Marshall Plan, there was Comrade Molotov from Moscow at his contumacious, doggedly suspicious best. The outlook was dark indeed. Then suddenly on the fifth day, branding the whole scheme a capitalist plot, he walked out of the conference for good taking other members of the Soviet bloc with him. The Plan, by now named the European Recovery Program (ERP), was saved.

What the Paris conferees—they represented 16 nations, including Greece and Turkey, after the Communist walkout—were expected to do was to prepare, singly and collectively, a realistic inventory of their needs and a modus operandi for putting their economies back in working order. Once this was done, the United States would see what it could do to supply the money and material to set the recovery program in motion.

As this planning proceeded during the summer and fall, a great deal of preparatory work was going on here, as well. A special government commission was set up to study the impact of a years-long multibillion-dollar outflow on the domestic economy. (The report was favorable.) With the issue of rescuing Europe out in the open, public interest and controversy over both ends and means became lively. There appeared to be a majority consensus for doing whatever had to be done and at whatever cost to keep democratic institutions alive wherever they were threatened. But there was skepticism and opposition, as well. From such voices on the Left as that of Henry Wallace (now gearing himself for a third-party run for the Presidency) came the charge that the proposed ERP was a wedge deliberately contrived to isolate and humiliate the Soviet Union. From the Right came cries of dismay over such a wholesale involvement in European affairs and over the enormity of the cost: Senator Taft derided the scheme as "a global WPA." President Truman and his aides sought ceaselessly to guide public opinion toward full acceptance of the obligation, whatever it might entail, and lobbied effectively with such leaders of the political opposition as Senator Vandenberg. The President's major coup in this strategy was to induce a bipartisan group of 16 members of Congress to make an on-the-spot inspection of Europe's plight and prospects late in the fall. Though a few were hard-core isolationists, they returned fully convinced advocates of the Marshall Plan.

As the end of the year approached a comprehensive blueprint for the ERP had been perfected. It was, for the times, a staggering construction: It called for the expenditure of $17 billion of U.S. tax money to finance a program for the benefit of Europeans that would run for four years and maybe longer. The President presented it to a special session of Congress on December 19, reminding the lawmakers, "Our deepest concern with European recovery . . . is that it is essential to the maintenance of the civilization in which the American way of life is rooted." His appeal for enabling legislation met with a generally favorable response. Even so, it was April before the bill was passed, by overwhelming margins in both houses. A prominent Republican, Paul G. Hoffman, was called from the presidency of Studebaker Motors to take charge, and the European Recovery Program—called by Winston Churchill "the most unsordid act in history"—swung into action on a gigantic scale.

The Marshall Plan cost the United States less than was expected. The total through 1951, when ERP as such expired (it has had an unbroken line of collateral descendants), came to $12.5 billion. It did not, as latter-day critics of foreign aid correctly contend, buy for us the friendship and affection of the world. But it *did* save free and independent governments in Western Europe; it *did* contain Communist expansion on the Continent behind the frontiers it had reached in 1947; it *did* make impossible the convulsive explosion of a hot war out of a cold war; and it *did* put Europe on the road to economic salvation (and ultimately, to prosperity). That last achievement, which was at the very eye of the target, can be measured quite accurately by statistics published by the Brookings Institution in 1955 in a study entitled *American Foreign Assistance*. Using 1938 as a base of 100, the index of industrial production for the principal beneficiaries of ERP showed the following growth in the period 1947–1951:

	1947	*1949*	*1951*	% increase *1947–51*
All participating countries	87	112	135	55
United Kingdom	110	129	145	32
France	99	122	138	39
Italy	93	109	143	54
Greece	69	90	130	88
West Germany	34	72	106	312

States are not without a sense of gratitude, nor history without its glowing postscripts. The following news story appeared on the front page of the *New York Times* for June 6, 1972:

Cambridge, Mass., June 5—Chancellor Brandt [of the Federal Republic of Germany] came today to Harvard where the Marshall Plan was offered 25 years ago and announced that West Germany would donate $47 million to the United States in gratitude for the plan's heavy contribution to Western Europe's economic recovery.

He told a Harvard convocation that 150 million West German marks would be given in equal installments over the next 15 years for the establishment and operation in this country of an independent, American-run educational foundation specializing in European problems. It is to be known as the German Marshall Fund of the United States—a memorial to the Marshall Plan. . . .

Mr. Brandt said of the Marshall Plan:

"History does not too often give us occasion to speak of fortunate events. But here in this place a quarter of a century ago an event took place which could rightly be termed one of the strokes of providence of this century, a century which has not very often been illuminated by the light of reason. . . ."

The ERP was destined to go a long way toward containing communism by erecting economic check dams wherever it threatened to spill over into Western Europe. But it was soon realized that economic fortifications could be highly vulnerable to a hostile neighbor—could, indeed, be conducive to raiding and conquest—without the military means to protect them. In a particularly brutal coup d'etat in February 1948, the Red Army snuffed out the last vestige of democratic freedom in Czechoslovakia, turned down the screws in Hungary and Austria, increased the tempo of its belligerent propaganda against the West.

Intelligence sources in London and Washington warned of the possibility of the outbreak of armed aggression at weak defensive points along the perimeters of Soviet dominance.

And as if to emphasize that threat the Russians clamped down a blockade on Berlin in June. The former German capital lay 100 miles inside the Soviet zone of occupation, a small international enclave under joint administration of the four allied powers. Without explanation, the Red Army suddenly sealed off the highways and rail lines leading from the other zones into Berlin, declared the city off limits to American, British, and French personnel, and banned the shipment of food and other supplies. (The move was in obvious protest against a plan by the other three powers to set up, after repeated failures to reunify all of Germany: a semiautonomous West German Republic.) The response in Western capitals was outrage and there was talk of blasting a way through the barricades with tanks and troops. Instead, a monster airlift was instituted. Fleets of American and British bombers hastily converted to freighters delivered an average of 2,000 tons of supplies daily—food, clothing, medical supplies, even coal in duffle bags—to keep West Berlin's 2.4 million residents alive and out of Moscow's clutches. The Berlin airlift was one of the most dramatic exploits of the postwar period, and one of the most harrowing. It was the sort of exercise in which, on any day, an "incident" might flare up into open combat. It was maintained for almost a year before the Russians called off their blockade in May 1949.

These mounting fears of Communist belligerence drew Britain, France, and the Benelux countries into a mutual defense compact—the Western Union—in the spring of 1948. This was a brave but meaningless gesture, for their combined military power was grossly outmatched by that of the Soviets. To redress that dangerous imbalance President Truman proposed broadening the alliance to include all the free nations bordering the North Atlantic, including Canada and the United States (and ultimately Italy, Greece, and Turkey in the northern Mediterranean). The glue to such a union would be an agreement that an attack upon any would be regarded as an attack upon all and to be resisted accordingly. The "how" and "with what" of that resistance was deliberately left vague in the President's proposal: It would be enough just to get the idea of such a treaty accepted here at home—the first genuinely "entangling alliance" to be perfected since George Washington had denounced the idea a century and a half ago—without getting into the stickier details of its cost and implementation.

Again, all the administration's resources of persuasion and propaganda were called into play. It was not too difficult to defend the thesis that American security depended upon the security of Western Europe, that such a defensive pact was but a logical extension of the Marshall Plan. But there were worrisome implications voiced from both the Left and

Right: a calculated affront to Stalin; a deliberate incitement of World War III; an undercutting of the United Nations; an open-ended commitment that led no man knew where, or at what cost. Why not a simple extension of the Monroe Doctrine? And what about the guns and planes and manpower needed to make this thing effective?

But the arms issue was sidestepped, for the time being at least. The North Atlantic Treaty was formally promulgated at elaborate ceremonies in Washington on April 4, 1949, with 12 nations as disparate geographically and culturally as Iceland and Italy as the initial signatories. Meanwhile, the Senate took up the question of ratification by the United States. The prolonged debate ran its expected course, with the great prestige of Senator Vandenberg steadily tipping the scales toward approval. This was consummated on July 21 when, by a one-sided vote of 82 to 13, the Senate gave its "advice and consent" that the treaty be ratified. One month and three days later the North Atlantic Treaty Organization (NATO) became a reality.

But the battle was not quite over. Two days after the ratification vote President Truman sent to Congress a bill titled "Mutual Defense Assistance Act of 1949." He asked an appropriation of $1.45 billion to provide military assistance to "nations which have joined with the United States in collective defense . . . and to other nations whose increased ability to defend themselves against aggression is important to the national interests of the United States." The "other nations," he indicated, were Greece and Turkey (not then within the NATO fold) and Iran, and, on the other side of the world, the Philippines, South Korea, and "the general area of China."

The bulk of the aid, naturally, was for Western Europe, $1.09 billion of it. The size of the request shocked even the treaty's most ardent supporters, including Vandenberg and John Foster Dulles, who was to become Secretary of State in a few years. They protested that the bipartisanship which had made collaboration on the NATO treaty so successful had been breached by the administration in formulating its arms program. Their disenchantment gave courage to the other dissenters, not only in the Senate but in the House, which would have an equal say this time since legislation rather than treaty ratification was involved.

Acheson (who had succeeded Marshall as Secretary of State) was again the administration's chief ball-carrier. He found himself in the anomalous position of now pleading the urgency of a cause which only weeks earlier he had attempted to minimize. In his marathon testimony before the congressional committees he called to his support the nation's chief military authorities and its leading Europe-based diplomats. The running dialogue was, in most respects, a repetition of the arguments that had preceded the treaty ratification, with the exception that the critics found themselves with stronger support. At one point only a tie vote in the

House Armed Services Committee averted a 50 percent slash in the money authorization for the program.

It was Moscow, however, which supplied the decisive argument in support of the Mutual Defense Assistance Program (MDAP). On September 23 President Truman shocked the nation with this brief news bulletin: "We have evidence that within recent weeks an atomic explosion occurred in the Soviet Union."

America's A-bomb monopoly was over. The shadow of communism's aggressive imperialism spread not only across Europe but across the rest of the world as well. Four days later, with heavy majorities in both houses of Congress, the military assistance bill became law with a first-year appropriation of $1.3 billion, only $100 million less than the President's request. NATO was not only a political reality; it was a going concern.

So now the policy of containment, first broached in 1946, had come to full maturity in late 1949. It continued for more than two decades to be the strategic core of this nation's foreign policy, just as NATO was to become its chief structural member.[5]

VI

While U.S. foreign policy in Europe was marked by brilliant initiatives and substantial successes, that in most of the Far East was marred by ineptitude and failure. This stricture does not apply to our efforts in Japan. The Japanese, fanatical in war, turned out to be docile in peace. In spite of the existence of an 11-power Far Eastern Advisory Commission, the United States, which had borne almost the entire brunt of the war in the Pacific, assumed virtually unitary control of the nation after the surrender. Under the stern dictatorial rule of General Douglas MacArthur, the war makers in the old hierarchy were rooted out and many were imprisoned. The Emperor was stripped of his sacred status but left as titular head of the government and a new constitution embodying many democratic principles that were quite strange to the ancient Japanese culture was written and imposed upon the nation. Most of the trappings of empire, including many outlying territorial possessions, were also stripped away, and a course was charted whereby Japan would be reconstituted as only a second-class economic power in the Far East. This was in deference to the dogma, still dubiously adhered to in Washington, that China would be the great power in Asia and the eastern anchor of the free world consortium.

To all of this the Japanese submitted, if not meekly at least without violent resistance. Industrious and intensely loyal to their cultural traditions, they made the best of a hard bargain; rebuilt their shattered cities and factories, bound up the wounds of their humiliating defeat. And as Nationalist China sank ever more deeply into eclipse as a Great Power, and as Communist influence spread on the Asian mainland, the restraints on Japan's development and independence were progressively lessened. Within comparatively few years it was clear that Japan was preempting the role of the free world's industrial and political anchor in the Far East. And that she has remained with both profit and prestige.

But China was the focus of America's postwar strategy and aspirations, and there the record was one of unrelieved failure. It failed not because of any Machiavellian conniving by the Soviets but because of the stubborn incompetence of the Nationalist Chinese government and the bungling of its American ally. And there ensued from this one of the most bruising and prolonged conflicts ever to darken the domestic political scene in the United States. Of all the dilemmas of peace none was more vexing than the China tangle—the inquisitorial search for a culprit for "the loss of China." It was an ordeal that lasted for more than a decade and left in its wake the bleached bones of many innocent victims.

The story of how things went awry in China between 1942 and 1950—from the apotheosis of Chiang Kai-shek to the triumph of Mao Tse-tung—is a long and confused one that has generated a literature of its own. In its barest outlines the record is this:

China had been in the grip of a social revolution since the beginning of the century. This was intensified in 1927 by the first open break—between a strong leftist minority led by Mao, a disciple of Lenin, and the dominant Kuomintang Party, which had been bequeathed by China's "liberator," Sun Yat-sen, to his brilliant son-in-law, Chiang. The history of China from that date onward became one of almost continual civil war, interrupted (but never stilled) first by the Japanese aggression of 1937, which sliced away the whole of Manchuria, and then by World War Two.

In spite of massive support in money, weapons, and supplies from the United States, China proved to be an ineffectual ally in the war against Japan. The Nationalist government was shot through with corruption and dominated by the warlord mentality of many of its leading ministers and generals. Chiang, though a man of high aspirations and great patriotism, was never able to impose his ideals on his subordinates nor to win political authority over the Communist followers of Mao Tse-tung. There were, in effect, two hostile Chinese military and political commands toward the end of the war, and their effectiveness against the Japanese was largely dissipated as they carried out guerrilla raids and reprisals against each other. When Japan capitulated in August 1945, there was a disorderly scramble between detachments of Nationalist and Communist forces to effectuate the surrender of the nearly two million

Japanese troops on Chinese soil. Where the Communists succeeded they gained great stores of weapons and materiel, plus sizable defections to their ranks from units of the Nationalist army whom they confronted. (The Russians, who had infiltrated heavily into Manchuria, conducted themselves in this situation with admirable restraint. They adhered to the promise made at Yalta to recognize the Nationalists as the responsible government of all China and gave but a civil nod to Mao, whose Leninist ideology they distrusted.)

In his campaign against the Japanese, Chiang Kai-shek had been pushed far to the southwest with his capital resting at Chungking. Mao's forces were widely dispersed through North China and parts of Manchuria, holding many key points where they exercised effectual political control. With Japan out of the picture, the civil war between these two intensified. The problem for the United States, committed to the proposition of a China dominant in Asia, now became the urgent one of finding a cohesive Chinese government with which to deal. Chiang remained the favorite in these considerations, but he was becoming progressively a more slender staff upon which to lean. Mao was steadily overpowering him both militarily and politically. With the economy of China in almost total collapse, its social and political fabric torn asunder, Chiang diverted virtually all of the substantial financial assistance flowing to him from Washington to his military adventures, none to the rebuilding of his government or the nation. He was obsessed with the notion that communism could be exterminated by force alone. He ignored the guidance of his American advisers, as well as the massive corruption within his own bureaucracy, and demanded ever more extravagant outlays of help from the United States.

A succession of high-level emissaries sent out from Washington during the closing phases of the war and afterward reported back with uniform discouragement on their efforts to stiffen Chiang's resolve and to set him on a more constructive course in pulling his country together. It was emphasized repeatedly that, in spite of his superiority in manpower and weapons, his chances of beating Mao into submission were poor and steadily worsening: His troops lacked the will and dedication of the enemy, for one thing, and so did much of the populace. His only prospect of achieving a united China, Chiang was told, lay in reaching some sort of detente with the Communists. All such warnings he dismissed impatiently. Meanwhile, millions of dollars in U.S. aid were going down the drain; were being skimmed off for the enrichment of corrupt officials and generals, or, in the case of weapons and military supplies, were being captured in brigade-sized lots by the Maoists. Washington policy planners wallowed in a sea of confusion. Like a distressed lover, they could not live with Chiang nor, it seemed, could they live without him.

In January 1946, President Truman sent General Marshall, just retired as Chief of Staff, to China as his personal emissary to try his talented hand at unraveling the tangle. The General's mission was to attempt to bring the opposing sides in the civil war together in a coalition government but with Chiang as the dominant partner. The inducement offered was a continuation and even an enlargement of economic aid if the plan succeeded, an ultimate cutoff if it did not. Marshall's early efforts met with considerable success. He arranged a series of cease-fires monitored by tripartite teams of observers—Nationalist, Communist, and American. He also arranged for the convening of a National Assembly to write a new constitution for China and for the establishment meanwhile of a provisional government with substantial Communist representation. Plans were laid, too, for a consolidated army of 60 divisions, only 10 of them under Communist control, to disarm and expel the Japanese, to maintain the peace and to back up the civilian government. For a few months at least it looked as though peace and tranquility were about to come once again to the land of the lotus.

That cheerful prospect began to fall apart in April. In spite of the truce teams, fighting erupted all over again in one key area after another. The National Assembly, convening in May, was soon disrupted as each side raised the ante for its cooperation. The Nationalists now reverted to their earlier policy of trying to exterminate the Communists before considering political reforms, and demanded for that purpose heavy increases in United States military support, including troops and air power. The Communists reacted in kind and threatened to invoke the aid of Russia. Both sides launched a heavy barrage of anti-American propaganda and Marshall found himself stalemated at every turn.

In January 1947, the General requested that he be recalled from China, acknowledging that his mission had failed. At the same time President Truman made good his threat to cut the flow of American aid to that country and withdrew all but a token rear-guard of our sizable civilian and military missions there, including some 50,000 Marines. China was to be left to work out her own destiny.

That decision heaped fresh fuel on a domestic political issue that had already begun to flame and was destined to rage out of control for years—"Communists in government" and its malevolent offshoot, McCarthyism.

Early in the postwar period there had emerged a loose confederation of interests that became known as the China Lobby. With no formal organization, it was made up principally of businessmen who had once had or hoped to have a stake in trade with China, and of moderate to extreme right-wingers who opposed any concessions to "Godless communism" at home or abroad, but most particularly in Asia. All along they had clamored for ever more money and arms for the Nationalists in the war against the Communists, and in their propaganda had apotheosized Chiang and Mao as the incarnations of Good and Evil. Now, with the government's decision to pull out of China, their imprecations reached a higher level of stridency and virulence. Chiang, they said, had been "sold out" by Communists and other subversives within our own government, working hand in hand with Mao and the Kremlin. They named names within the Foreign Service and the State Department and adduced "evidence" of a highly inflammatory but dubious quality. This proved in the end to be a lot of mischievous nonsense, but the administration's fumbling efforts to find a workable policy for China gave some surface plausibility to the charges. Nor could they categorically and convincingly be refuted.

The uproar over "the sellout of China" grew in volume and breadth and was eagerly seized upon by Republicans in and out of Congress as a clout to belabor the Truman administration. Even Truman's surprising victory at the polls the next year, 1948, brought only a temporary cessation in the assault. The pillorying of suspected culprits for the China debacle was to continue well into the next decade, destroying careers and reputations and leaving an ineradicable scar on the nation's political conscience. No culprit as such, of course, was ever found.

Left to his own devices, Chiang mounted a series of ambitious attacks upon his Communist foe but with diminishing success. Over the next year and a half he was pushed farther and farther to the south, establishing a temporary capital at last at Canton, and leaving virtually the whole of China north of the Yangtze River under Communist control. Entire divisions of the American-equipped Nationalist army were swallowed up by, or defected to, the Maoist conquerors. Major General David Barr, whom Truman sent over for a recheck of Chiang's situation late in 1948, reported back to Washington:

I am convinced that the military situation has deteriorated to the point where only the active participation of United States troops could effect a remedy. . . . No battle has been lost since my arrival for lack of ammunition or equipment. Their military debacles, in my opinion, can all be attributed to the world's worst leadership and many other morale-destroying factors that led to a complete loss of will to fight.

Late in April 1949, a million-man Red army under General Chu-Teh swarmed across the Yangtze on a front hundreds of miles long, encountering only half-hearted resistance from scattered Nationalist forces. Chiang, pushed to the wall, deployed what was left of his navy and air force and some 200,000 of his best troops to the island of Formosa (Taiwan). Early in May he fled there himself along with his principal ministers and hundreds of stout chests containing the assets of the national treasury. He proclaimed Taipei the capital of the Republic of China and promised that in time he would return to the mainland to "liberate" it from its Communist oppressors. He never got there.

Of all the dilemmas of peace deriving from the Second World War this was the most intractable. It engendered a schism in this country's political life of almost unparalleled virulence and persistence. And for more than two decades American foreign policy was forced to walk awkwardly across the international stage, on the one hand hobbled by exaggerated bonds of guilt and loyalty to the anachronism of the Republic of China on Formosa, and on the other prevented by pride and political timidity from acknowledging the reality of the Communist government that controlled all of mainland China.

Of the personal political fortunes affected by this schism none profited more richly than that of a then-obscure young first-term Republican Congressman from California, Richard M. Nixon. He was to fashion a spectacular political career out of the national obsession with "Communists in government." And yet, ironically, it was he who, as President on an historic pilgrimage to Peking in 1972, first sat down with Chairman Mao in an effort to bridge this gap of pretense and unreason between the two nations. In the process, Chiang Kai-shek was again cast adrift by his American protectors (evoking an echo of protest from the China Lobby), this time apparently for good.[6]

11

The Great Upset—1948

No Presidential election campaign held so far in this century has equaled that of 1948 for drama, suspense, and the shock effect of its wildly improbable climax. Not since David and Goliath squared off in the Biblical arena had two such mismatched foes faced one another in high public combat as did Harry S. Truman and Thomas E. Dewey. An incumbent seeking reelection is supposed to have an edge in the contest, it is true, but, as far as the most perceptive eye could tell, that was all that Truman had going for him that year. His popularity in the polls was dragging bottom; the leaders of his own party did their best to deny him nomination, and two renegade candidates from within Democratic ranks sniped at him from left and right determined to deny him victory at the ballot box. Governor Dewey, on the other hand, was riding high on a wave of popular acclaim; the Republican Party was solidly behind him and comfortably financed, and on the hustings he displayed an image of calm and competent self-assurance that persuaded virtually every political expert in the land that he was just what the country needed —and what it would get.

They were wrong, every one of them. In a finale that outstripped the best cliffhanger ever devised by Hollywood, Truman came from behind in the agonizingly drawn-out vote count to upset the laws of probability, to whip the challenger as well as the experts, and to walk off with a decisive victory in his hands. It was the greatest political upset the country had ever seen.

Just when and why President Truman made his final decision to seek a full term is not clear from any extant record. That he was in a state of doubt during the closing months of 1947 seems certain; he, himself, toyed with the prevalent idea of handing the Democratic nomination to General Eisenhower, then sitting above the strife in the president's chair at Columbia University. There is every reason to believe that he felt

324

discouraged over his White House tenure so far, that he was battle-weary from his relentless conflicts with Congress and the mounting frustrations of his foreign policy by the intransigent Russians. But the alternatives of handing over the Presidency to untried hands were equally disturbing. He had set goals which he believed to be supremely important to the nation and to the world and he felt compelled to continue leading the fight for them. And there was another consideration of equal force: It was repugnant to his nature and his pride to back away from a challenge when he thought he was in the right. He had always been a scrapper and it was an article of faith with him that even defeat was supportable if one went down fighting.

One circumstance stands out that clearly helped him to make up his mind to take the plunge. Late in 1947 his trusted White House Counsel, Clark M. Clifford, prepared for him a lengthy and detailed study outlining "a course of political conduct for the administration extending from November 1947 to November 1948." This was a cogent and penetrating analysis of the current state of the Democratic party and of the disparate elements of the electorate upon which it relied. It asserted, in effect, that the old New Deal coalition of labor, minorities, big-city bosses, and the solid South was still viable, and that the fealty of much of the Midwest farm vote, which Roosevelt had released from its Republican moorings, probably could be counted on as long as the current wave of farm prosperity continued. However much it might appear that this coalition had come unstuck, Clifford argued, it was a dead certainty that it had not regrouped around the banner of the GOP. And it was equally certain, he said, that it was not enchanted with the conservative, obstructionist record of the Republican-controlled Eightieth Congress. Therefore, the Democratic candidate should shape his appeal to the liberal New Deal instincts of this proven majority with the Republican Eightieth Congress as the villain of record.

The analysis went wrong, as events were to prove, in assuming that the South would remain solidly Democratic. But it correctly foresaw that the left-wing group around former Vice-President Henry Wallace would grow and mount a campaign of its own that would draw off substantial liberal and labor support from the Democratic ticket, particularly in the big industrial centers. The only antidote to this threat was to bear down on the strong Communist influence behind the Wallace movement and to isolate it from the more orthodox liberal majority.

The Clifford study did not promise Mr. Truman that he could win. What it did do was to cut down to size some of the mountainous imponderables in his situation and to suggest that he did not have to lose. It must have been persuasive, for in his State of the Union address and subsequent messages to Congress early in 1948 the President withdrew not one step from the boldly liberal program he had been defiantly espousing all along, a program that was to be embodied virtually unchanged in the Democratic party platform later that year.

Mr. Truman's formal announcement early in March that he would "accept the Democratic nomination if offered" was received with unconcealed despair by virtually all of his party's hierarchy. As the *New York Times* noted during that same week, "The barometer of Mr. Truman's popularity, which has registered some extreme fluctuations in the past, seems at the moment to be in a particularly depressed state." His civil rights proposals had sent Southern governors and lawmakers into open revolt, with threats—later fulfilled—to field a candidate of their own if he should get the Democratic nomination. The Virginia and Alabama legislatures contrived changes in their election laws that would keep his name off the ballot in their states. His frustrations with Congress multiplied. His veto of a tax bill which he had condemned as "a rich man's bill" was swiftly overridden, with only 10 Democratic Senators standing by him. A concerted "Dump Truman" effort got under way with high-level party backing, and two sons of FDR, Elliott and Franklin, Jr., publicly proclaimed their support of a movement to draft General Eisenhower. In April the Gallup poll reported that in its survey of voters of all parties Truman rated only a fraction of a point above Dewey and, among independent voters only, his popularity registered six points below that of former Governor Harold Stassen of Minnesota, then a comer in the Republican trial heats. "At this time," Arthur Krock wrote during that month, "the President's influence is weaker than any President's has been in modern history."

By contrast, Republican prospects were brighter than they had been in 20 years, when they had last elected a President. They had an attractive field of candidates. In addition to Dewey there were Senator Robert A. Taft of Ohio, who eloquently bespoke the strong conservative reaction which had set in in many parts of the country since the end of the war; the thirty-nine-year-old Governor Stassen, who appeared to represent a reviving Republican Populism; California's progressive and photogenic Governor Earl Warren; Senator Arthur Vandenberg of Michigan, the party's leading internationalist; and, briefly, the messianic figure of General Douglas MacArthur, who consented to his candidacy from his headquarters in far-off Tokyo. There were a few other entries further away from the starting gate, but of the whole field Dewey, with his national reputation as a gang buster and effective two-term Governor of New York (as well as his having been the GOP candidate four years earlier), was early in the lead.

All of these GOP contenders showed promisingly in the diminishing glow of Mr. Truman's public image. He was widely caricatured now as a misfit who had stumbled into a job that was too big for him. So the time for a change was at hand; it was time to stop dependence on worn out New Deal liberalism, time to stop coddling the labor bosses, time to bring some hard-headed business sense into government, time, it was said, for new leadership that would pull the country together, restore its confidence, and set it on a course for permanent prosperity. The Republicans had won control of Congress for the first time in 16 years in 1946. Now they had every reason to be confident of taking the White House in 1948. The most troublesome question in the spring and summer of that year was which in their stable of champions should claim the privilege.

The campaign began to assume definite shape in the spring. First off, General MacArthur was brusquely eliminated from the Republican list in the only primary in which he had been entered, that of Wisconsin, which he claimed as his native heath. Running in absentia but with a passionate band of promoters touting his virtues, he won only eight delegates while Stassen made a clean sweep on the remaining 19. The General bowed out. For a time the broad shouldered young Minnesotan looked like the man to beat: He moved on to three or four other bright primary victories in the farm belt; had the effrontery (and the bad luck) to challenge and lose to Taft in Ohio. But then, in May, came a humiliating put-down by Dewey in a nationally broadcast radio debate in Oregon. Their topic, a hotly controversial issue at the moment, was "Should the Communist Party Be Outlawed?" From the outset, the sharp-witted former New York prosecutor had his adversary floundering in a sea of constitutional legalisms and a confused, unintended defense of communism. The debate was a disaster for Stassen and his campaign lost steam from then on. Taft's shadow still lay across Dewey's path, but it was never a very long shadow.

While the Democratic high command—or most of it—wrestled itself into a state of bitter impotence during these weeks, Candidate Truman decided to test the political waters on his own by the formula he understood best—direct contact with the voters. Late in May he set out on a proclaimed "nonpolitical" tour to the West Coast and back. It was nonpolitical only in the sense that there was a fragily legitimate excuse for charging the journey up to his White House expense account: He had been invited to make the commencement address and to receive an honorary degree from the University of California at Berkeley, and the Democratic party treasury was too broke to underwrite such an excursion. Not a man to be blocked by trifles, President Truman put a half-dozen of his personal political aides to work scheduling the first "whistle stop" campaign in American history—or at least the first such campaign to be so named.* It was a 17-day junket by special train with a complement of more than 100 reporters and photographers aboard that ambled at a leisurely pace across the northern tier of states and back via the southwest, and that called for full dress speeches in five major cities and scores of brief stopovers and impromptu rear platform appearances. He addressed himself to the large problems of statecraft in most of these talks but always, it seemed, as a polite preface to what was uppermost in his and his audiences' mind: plain old-fashioned politicking.

And here Truman excelled. Crowds responded warmly and enthusiastically to his homespun manner and his earthy, unpretentious prose. The Republican-dominated Congress was the eye of his target and he poured upon it full blame for high prices, inflation, and all the other assorted ills from which the populace was suffering.

"You've got the worst Congress you ever had," he said over and over, "and if you send another Republican Congress back to Washington you are a bigger bunch of suckers than I think you are!"

The people loved it. "Give 'em hell, Harry," they shouted; "Pour it on!" And pour it on he did, to ever larger and more enthusiastic crowds that turned out to see him as he "whistle-stopped" across Ohio, Illinois, and the Dakotas, into Oregon, and down into California. At the Berkeley campus, where he altered his tone to make a serious address on foreign policy that won praise from even hostile newspapers, the biggest crowd ever to attend a commencement exercise there piled into the stadium to see and applaud the embattled President. And in Los Angeles two days later, back in his sprightliest politician's role, a million cheering spectators lined his parade route through the city and turned his visit into a day-long gala.

It was a triumphant tour and it reassured Harry Truman's gut instinct about his prospects: that in spite of what all the pollsters and the pundits said about his being a "dead duck," he had the people with him. If he could get out to see enough of them face to face between then and November, he could be elected.

That assurance did not get through, however, to the cabal of Democratic politicos who were intent on dumping Mr. Truman before or at

---

* The phrase was coined, innocently enough, by Senator Taft. In a talk before the Union League Club of Philadelphia while Truman was en route, he complained petulantly about the spectacle of a President "blackguarding Congress at whistlestops all across the country." Chairman Howard McGrath of the Democratic National Committee and his publicity man, Jack Redding, pounced gleefully on the Senator's semantic blunder. They wired the Mayors of 35 cities and towns through which the President had passed and asked if they agreed with Taft's derogation of their community as a "whistlestop." Most of the replies were tartly negative and inevitably, of course, made their way into countless newspaper columns and radio commentaries. Whereupon the word became firmly implanted in the political vocabulary.

the party's national convention, which was scheduled for mid-July. Their eyes were fixed in a glazed, hypnotic stare upon the shining image of General Eisenhower. He had already turned down Republican inducements to run as their candidate and had made it as clear as he could that he felt the same way about the Democrats. This seemed to matter not at all to several score of the party's most prominent wheelhorses—the Mayors of New York, Jersey City, and Chicago, among others; a dozen of the most powerful state chairmen of traditionally Democratic states; an even larger number of Democratic Senators and Congressmen; a whole phalanx of New Deal stalwarts with high political clout; a handful of important labor leaders; and most symbolically of all, James and Elliot Roosevelt, sons of the late President. With undisguised intensity, they made known their disaffection with President Truman and, as the weeks of summer lengthened toward convention time, openly conspired at means to impose the nomination on the reluctant Ike even, it appeared, if he had to be brought before the convention in chains. Seldom had there been a more visible and shoddily conceived intraparty rebellion than this one of 1948, and it was not until the very eve of the convention itself that the plotters were convinced of the futility of their scheme—an unequivocal repudiation thereof by Eisenhower—and gave up.

While these defections were going on at the center of Candidate Truman's base, there were guerrilla attacks simultaneously on his right and left flanks. In May the so-called Dixiecrat party was born in a noisy and undisciplined rump convention of several hundred Southern Democrats at Jackson, Mississippi. Its central figures were Governors Strom Thurmond and Fielding Wright of South Carolina and Mississippi, respectively. Their pledge was to field a presidential slate of their own should the Democratic National Convention nominate Truman, or any other "civil rights candidate." Meanwhile, Harry Wallace's "Gideon's Army" was reaching the peak of its crusade to become the champion of the downtrodden masses. The earnest and harried former Vice-President had been barnstorming the hustings since winter, his rhetoric and his entourage becoming steadily more recognizably pink. However dim his electoral prospects might be—and not even his own backers took them seriously—he had managed by late June to qualify his Progressive party for balloting in 44 states. Some pollsters guessed he might draw as many as three million votes, most of them in the ghettoes and working-class districts of the large cities—and all of them at the expense of Candidate Truman.

To even the most obdurate Democratic optimists it was clear that even if Truman should manage to nose out Dewey in the November balloting, the Progressive and Dixiecrat defections would combine to deny him the necessary majority of electoral votes. Thus, for the second time in history, the decision could be thrown into the House of Representatives, where Truman loyalists were in very short supply and Southern Democrats held the balance of power. It was in this context that Representative Clare Booth Luce of Connecticut, a lady widely known for her sharp wit and sharper tongue, wrote off Harry Truman as "a gone goose." There weren't many around to disagree with her.

The Republican convention opened on Monday, June 21 in Philadelphia's Municipal Auditorium in a mood of cheerful confidence, a confidence born of the virtual certainty that whoever they chose for candidate would be the next President of the United States. But there was no dead certainty at the outset on whom that choice would fall. Tom Dewey had a commanding lead in pledged delegates—331 to 219 for the runner-up, Taft, with 548 needed to lock up the prize. He also had an edge in organizational strength and in experience: He had been around this track twice before, as a contender in 1940 and as the party's nominee in 1944.

But the GOP, as so often in its history, was badly split internally along ideological lines: bedrock conservatives versus "progressives" (liberal was a bad word in their lexicon), and nationalists (read neo-isolationists) versus internationalists. With many local variations these cleavages also ran geographically across the Republican domain in patterns that obscured and confused measurements of their relative strength. In broad terms, Taft was the dour darling of the conservative-nationalist wing, and Vandenberg of the conservative-internationalists; Stassen, a largely unknown quantity, seemed to have an uncertain foot in both camps; while Dewey, in eloquent ambiguity, managed to project himself as a progressive-internationalist from whom the conservative-nationalists—or any other faction—had nothing whatever to fear. Accurately reflecting these ambivalent notions, the platform agreed upon in the first days of the convention managed to straddle just about every conflicting issue that arose. It asserted the party's devotion to a wide catalogue of liberal-international objectives, but promised that their fulfillment would have to be governed by sound conservative doctrine. Aside from the usual platitudes of political rhetoric there were few positive commitments to action on anything. Typically, it was a platform "made to run on, not to stand on," one designed to meet the lowest common denominator of dissent.

On the surface the proceedings at Philadelphia ran smoothly and reassuringly: This was the first political convention to be broadcast nationally on the new television networks and the managers wanted it to look good. Behind the scenes there was a flurry of infighting, however, as candidates and their lieutenants sought to woo the uncommitted delegations and to build up their second-ballot commitments. Inevitably, a "stop Dewey" movement emerged from the Taft and Stassen camps but it fell apart when neither of the two contenders would agree to take second place on a combined ticket. Their scheme was further confounded when they learned on the night before the balloting was to begin that half the Pennsylvania delegation and the entire delegation from Indiana had loosed their favorite son moorings and promised their votes to Dewey. Thus, when the first poll was taken on Wednesday afternoon, the New Yorker was far out front with 434, followed by Taft with 224, and Stassen with 157, the remaining 276 votes scattered. On the second ballot, Dewey picked up 81 additional votes for a near-winning total of 515, Taft gained 50 and Stassen lost eight. That put the seal of finality on the Dewey drive, and on the next roll call the other contenders conceded and made his choice unanimous.

The next day California's Governor Earl Warren was chosen for the Vice-Presidential spot by acclamation. It was a strong, attractive ticket and it won praise all across the country. "Barring a political miracle," *Time* magazine observed, "it was the kind of ticket that could not fail to sweep the Republican party back into power."

The Democrats were scheduled to meet in the same Philadelphia hall three weeks later, on July 12. As that date approached it became pretty clear that, in spite of all the "dump Truman" maneuvers, the President was still the only visible candidate the party had and that by the inexorable workings of machine politics he had enough delegates committed to him to sew up the nomination on the first ballot. Ten days before the opening gavel was to fall the draft-Eisenhower managers decided upon a last, desperate ploy to upset this design. First, they sent telegrams to all of the 1,592 convention delegates urging them to attend a special caucus in Philadelphia on the Saturday preceding the opening of the convention. The purpose: "to pick the strongest and ablest man available" for the nomination, which, without saying so, meant Eisenhower. Second, having failed repeatedly to get a personal emissary past the barricades to the General's office at Columbia, 10 of the most prominent members of the strategy group put their names to a telegram informing him that, with or without his permission, they were determined to place his name in nomination before the convention. In the conjunction of these two maneuvers the conspirators foresaw the happy fruition of their scheme, a stampede to their man. Provided Ike didn't let them down.

But Ike did let them down, with a resounding thump. He responded to the committee's telegram in terms as closely approximating those of General Sherman as any latter-day politician has used: "I would refuse to accept the nomination under any conditions, terms, or premises." And that ended the Eisenhower boom of 1948. It also ended the grand conspiracy to freeze Mr. Truman out of his party's nomination.

The weather in Philadelphia that week in mid-July was hot, humid, and depressing, which was matched exactly by the mood of the more than 3,000 delegates, alternates, political handymen, and reporters who crowded into convention hall. The whole proceeding seemed anticlimactic, an empty ritual devoid of meaning. "None of us," Clark Clifford said later, "really felt at that time that the nomination meant very much. Our aim was just to get the President nominated, to spare him the humiliation of being rejected."

But as the opening day ceremonies droned on before a restless and inattentive audience—the spectator galleries were half empty—drama was building offstage. This involved a fight within the 104-man resolutions (platform) committee over the wording of the civil rights plank. A determined band of "Young Turks," led by the bouncy, thirty-seven-year-old Mayor of Minneapolis, Hubert H. Humphrey, demanded that the platform spell out in detail just what the party stood for—equal voting rights for blacks, a federal anti-lynching law, a law to end racial discrimination in hiring, an increase in the minimum wage, national health insurance, a program of public housing—as the President had enunciated it in his message to Congress back in February. Opposed to them was a group of party "regulars" who wanted to water down this flammable issue in the hope of appeasing the angry Southern bloc; they favored the safely ambiguous language that had appeared in the platform four years earlier. After a day and night of tumultuous bickering the committee found itself deadlocked and the issue had to be laid before the open convention.

Meanwhile, however, a number of big-city leaders had been won over to the "Young Turks" cause, not for ideological or moral reasons but for the pragmatic political ones. The Democrats were going to lose the Presidency in any event, they reasoned, so it mattered little to New York or Detroit or Cook County whether the South defected or not. But a strong stand on civil rights would help local Democratic candidates in the industrial centers up North where black votes were crucial. And that was what counted with the big city "bosses" now: holding their own political domains together.

The question of a strong versus a weak civil rights plank was put before the convention on Wednesday. After three hours of noisy wrangling the vote was finally completed—651½ for the strong plank, 582½ against. The "Young Turks," and inferentially Mr. Truman, had won. And amid a rising din of cheers and boos 35 delegates representing the full Mississippi contingent and half of that from Alabama formed ranks in the center aisle and marched stolidly off the floor and out of the convention for good. Their gesture fell a little short of expectations as a majority of their Southern confederates stayed glumly in their seats. But there was no mistaking the symbolism of their action: The Dixiecrat revolt had come to pass.

As further evidence of that fact, the only name offered in opposition to President Truman's at the "call of the states" that night was that of Senator Richard B. Russell of Georgia. It was not a serious bid but rather an additional—an impromptu—token of the South's unyielding stance. It was followed by the ritualistic floor demonstration and seconding speeches, all acted out under the pall of cynical boredom that hung like a fog in the steaming convention hall.

The scene was not much livelier when, close on to midnight, Governor Donelly of Missouri rose to put the President's name in nomination. It was a tough and challenging speech that sought to call this convention to its senses. He emphasized as no other speaker had done the positive accomplishments of the Truman administration and its kinship to the New Deal. It was an effective elixir for jaded spirits and it seemed to find its mark. The demonstration that followed—the familiar snake dance by the sweating delegates up and down the aisles, whooping and hollering above the din of the huge pipe organ—had about it a more genuine note of spontaneity than reporters in the press box had detected before. Had some latent spark of enthusiasm been struck at last?

The balloting went pretty much according to expectations. Senator Russell garnered all the votes of the old Confederacy save those of North Carolina for a total 263. President Truman swept up all the rest—948— for a decisive first ballot victory. The convention managers wisely decided to forego the usual request to make the vote unanimous, knowing it could not be achieved. But when Senator Alben Barkley's name was offered for the Vice-Presidential nomination it was approved by acclamation.

Now the withering pall of apathy began to drop away. This was the climax of an ancient and happy ritual that called for a boisterous response. Whether they liked Truman or deplored him, the delegates almost to a man admired him for the underdog fight he had waged to gain this moment. When the beaming President stepped out on the rostrum at 1:45 in the morning (he had been secluded for hours in a steaming anteroom just behind the stage), crisp and cocky in a white linen suit, he was greeted with a roar of cheers such as had not been heard in that hall all week. And his opening words sent another roar rocketing to the rafters: "Senator Barkley and I will win this election and make those Republicans like it— don't you forget that!"

In the space of minutes, what had been written off as a political wake was transformed into a rousing political rally. As the *New York Times* was to report later that morning, "President Truman set the Democratic convention on fire with his acceptance speech." Speaking from notes instead of from a script, chopping the air with quick, awkward gestures of his hand, Truman recited the accomplishments of his administration in the hallowed tradition of FDR and the New Deal: gains for the farmers, for the working man, for the poor and underprivileged. He excoriated the Republicans and their representatives in Congress who had thwarted his best efforts "for the common everyday man." He noted that at their recent convention in this same hall they had adopted a platform promising to do many of the things—price controls, medical care, aid to education, better housing—which, as the party controlling Congress, they had prevented his administration from doing. Then he let go with a well-concealed Sunday punch:

On the twenty-sixth day of July, which out in Missouri we call "Turnip Day," I am going to call that Congress back in session, and I am going to ask them to pass some of those laws they say they are for in their platform.

Now, my friends, if there is any reality behind that Republican platform, we ought to get some action from a short session of the Eightieth Congress. They can do this job in 15 days if they want to do it, and they will still have time to go out and run for office. . . . What that "worst" Eightieth Congress does in this special session will be the test of whether they mean what they say.

This bold challenge was flung amid such a din of cheers that Truman had to shout into the microphone to make himself heard. Suddenly a fighting spirit, a wild and reckless partisanship, had displaced the gloom and apathy in which this gathering had been sunk for days. A discredited leader had come roaring back tall in the saddle and the troops loved it. Truman told them they could win the big battle ahead. How many really believed him is not certain, but as they left Philadelphia for home the next day many of the delegates were now ready and eager to put their backs into the effort.

Truman's call for a special session of Congress (it convened on July 26 and ran for 12 days) undoubtedly was a gross abuse of the Presidential prerogative, and it was denounced in appropriate terms of outrage by every Republican who could make himself heard and by most newspapers as well. But it was a stroke of political genius. Predictably, the legislative results were negligible, but it focused the nation's attention squarely on the target the President had selected for his campaign, "the do-nothing Eightieth Congress."

The Dixiecrats held a one-day convention in Birmingham immediately following the adjournment of the Democrats at Philadelphia. On the surface it was a rousing affair with some 6,000 Southern patriots on hand waving Confederate flags, marching to spirited cadence of "Dixie," and shouting slogans for "states rights" and of defiance to their "betrayers" up North. But it was notably short on politicians of stature from the region: Russell of Georgia and Byrd of Virginia were among the scores of Senators and Governors who prudently stayed away, reluctant, perhaps, to commit such an act of political heresy in broad public view. The nominations thus went, more or less by default, to the two principal organizers of the split: South Carolina's Governor Thurmond for President and Mississippi's Governor Wright for Vice-President. It was obvious that some of the steam had leaked out of the Dixiecrat boiler but it was equally obvious that the movement still threatened a serious weakening of the regular Democratic party's hold on the solid South.

The Progressive party moved into Philadelphia a week behind the Democrats for the formality of confirming their already-stated choice of Henry A. Wallace for President and Senator Glen H. Taylor, a virtually unknown first-term Democrat from Idaho, for Vice-President. By now the Communists and fellow travelers had become conspicuous in the organization and the party platform closely paralleled that of the Communist Party of America. It contained all the liberal slogans of the far Left but its principal emphasis lay in a denunciation of the administration's foreign policy. It demanded an all-out accommodation to Russia's political and territorial aspirations in Europe and the United Nations and especially the termination of the Marshall Plan, which the Soviets regarded as an economic conspiracy aimed at them. Wallace went out of his way at Philadelphia to welcome Communist support, telling a press conference, "They support me because I say we can have peace with the Russians." Political writers had by now substantially reduced their estimates of Wallace's vote-getting potential, but they still credited the new party with the power to hurt, and possibly to kill, Truman's narrow victory prospects in such big cities as New York, Chicago, and Los Angeles.

Both campaigns were slow getting off the ground. Newspapers across the country reported a pervasive apathy among the voters, a disinterest which they attributed to the fact that the element of suspense was lacking in the contest, that its outcome had long been foretold. Elmo Roper, a leading public opinion sampler, published a poll on September 9 showing Dewey leading Truman by an unbeatable 44 to 31 percent. He said that since there was little prospect that this margin of 13 points could be altered that he would conduct no more such polls for the remainder of the campaign. Republicans found the slow pace much to their liking. Their strategy called for a relaxed, low-keyed campaign in any event; to ignore Truman and whatever concrete issues he raised and to concentrate instead on defining the policies and objectives of a Dewey administration that would certainly be in control after January 1949. For its part, the Democratic high command was in a desperate struggle to raise money—its treasury was bankrupt—and to revitalize a party structure that in many places had virtually fallen apart. The big opening gun of the Truman campaign, his Labor Day speech in Detroit, came within an eyelash of being cut off the air by the radio network, which demanded its $50,000 fee in cash on the line before it would plug in its microphones. With only hours to spare, this disaster was averted by Governor Roy Turner of Oklahoma, a millionaire oilman and a loyal Truman Democrat. Similar crises were to haunt the Truman party all through the next two months.

Crises of any sort were mild and infrequent in the Dewey entourage. The young Governor himself was a remarkably disciplined, well-engineered person, impeccable in speech and manner, a cautious calculator of the gambler's odds. His enemies said he had "a computer where his heart ought to be." He was an experienced campaigner and had built up an efficient and dedicated personal staff. Money was not a serious problem; it rarely is for a candidate who looks like a winner. If some segments of the GOP looked upon him with misgivings—to the Taft people he was suspected of harboring certain New Deal heresies—he nevertheless enjoyed the full support of his party's organization. In his campaign against Roosevelt in 1944, and even in the primary battles of 1948, Dewey had employed the slashing offensive of the trained prosecutor, carrying the fight to his opponent. But in this campaign against Truman he opted for "the high road"; for an aloof, disdainful manner toward his opponent that enabled him to concentrate in his speeches on the broad problems of statecraft and to ignore the jibes and challenges of the other side.

Typical of this strategy was Dewey's response to Truman's Detroit speech. There in "labor's capital" the President had had a warm and enthusiastic reception. More than half a million auto workers and their families packed into Cadillac Square to hear and cheer him as he lambasted the Taft-Hartley Act and the Republican Congress that had passed it over his veto. If the same forces are allowed to stay in power after this election, he said, labor could expect to be hit by another series of body blows, adding: "And if you stay at home as you did in 1946, and keep these reactionaries in power, you will deserve every blow you get." This was a major theme in the Democrats' handbook and one on which the Republicans were vulnerable in every labor center in the country. But Candidate Dewey chose to ignore it himself, sending Governor Stassen instead as his surrogate a few days later to make a dignified defense of Taft-Hartley before a small audience of Detroit business executives. That, pretty much, was the pattern to be followed over the next two months.

As the campaign moved into high gear the Democrats' effort gained some much needed underpinning. The CIO Political Action Committee voted to throw its full support—money and manpower—behind Truman. Some other independent unions followed suit. An intensive organizing campaign resulted in a scattering of "Truman-Barkley Clubs" springing into existence across the country. Here and there badly fractured state and local Democratic organizations were revived with splints and bandages— and promises. Vigorous arm-twisting, and more promises, opened up a few hitherto resistant pocketbooks. Things indeed looked better in mid-September than they had in mid-July. But crises of cash and confidence were still to shadow the creaking Truman bandwagon wherever it went.

The course that bandwagon followed was a bruising one. It encompassed two rambling "whistle-stop" tours across the continent and back, each of 10 to 12 days' duration, and four briefer forays into the Northeast, the Middle West, and some of the Border States: It did not venture into the Deep South. Mr. Truman covered more than 25,000 miles in these travels, made some 250 speeches (few of which were broadcast because of a lack of money), and estimated that he had been "seen in the flesh" by six million of his constituents. The vehicle for this odyssey was the "Truman Special," a 16-car train of sleeping and dining coaches, including a work car for the 80 to 100 newsmen who were usually aboard, another for the President's staff, a communications car for the Secret Service and Western Union, and, at the end, the *Ferdinand Magellan,* a Pullman specially adapted for Presidential use in the days of FDR. This provided commodious living and working quarters for the President and his family, and at the back end there was an oversized platform with a striped canopy and a public address system from which the serious business of "whistle-stopping" could be conducted.

The pattern of these days on the road varied but little. As the "Truman Special" rolled to its first stop in a state, usually between six and eight o'clock in the morning, it would be boarded by a delegation of local politicians: the Governor, Senators, a Congressman or two if they happened to be Democrats, or the Democratic candidates for these and other major offices. There would be welcomes and picture-taking, a brief back-platform appearance to greet the local citizenry who had come to the depot to witness this rare spectacle, and then the train would take off for the next stop down the line. Usually the leading statewide candidates would stay aboard for the remainder of the day to gain what advantage they could, in their own bid for votes, by being seen at the various stops in the President's presence or by introducing him to the local audiences.

On most such days there would be one or two outdoor rallies at a ball park or the town square, or even a major speech, to which the Presidential party would be whirled in a motorcade with screaming police sirens. Afterward there would be another traffic-curdling dash to the schedule-bound train. As the train rolled across the countryside it would pause at station after station where crowds had gathered. Men, women, and children would spill out on the tracks at the rear of the train or climb nearby roofs and signal towers for a better view. As the local band struggled through "Hail to the Chief," the "Missouri Waltz" (a Truman trademark), or the state anthem, the President and half a dozen others would step out onto the back platform to be met by cheers and applause—sometimes merely perfunctory but more often spontaneous and voluble. One of the accompanying guests would introduce the President, rarely omitting a plug for his own political interests. Then the President, bareheaded and beaming with a bright smile, would take the microphone and say:

Every time I come out this way I feel again the tremendous vitality of the West [or of New England or Ohio or Texas]. This is straight-from-the-shoulder country and it has produced a great breed of fighting men. . . . I am going to call on your fighting qualities. For you and I have a fight on our hands, a fight for the future of the country and for the welfare of the people of the United States.

This was pure corn, of course, but it was a natural and not a contrived sort of corn. Truman's words reflected the way he thought and felt, and they sounded right in his flat, unpolished Missouri accent. And because they sounded right, people were moved to yell approvingly, "Give 'em hell, Harry," to this plain, unpretentious man who was their President.

There might follow a brief allusion to a nearby dam or conservation project or other federal benefaction from which the locality had gained, and a reminder that this and most other blessings carried a Democratic label. Then, a note of indignation coming into his voice, Truman would close in on his main target:

Republicans in Washington have a habit of becoming curiously deaf to the voice of the people. But they have no trouble at all in hearing what Wall Street is saying. They are able to catch the slightest hint from Big Business.

When I talk to you here today about Republicans, I am talking to you about the party that gets most of its campaign funds from Wall Street and Big Business. I am talking to you about the party that gave us the phony Wall Street boom of the nineteen-twenties and the Hoover depression that followed. I am talking to you about the party [and here he spaced his words for emphasis] that gave us *that no-account, do-nothing Republican Eightieth Congress. . . .*

There would follow a brief but sizzling catalogue of what Congress had and had not done that was inimical to the interests, not only of the country at large, "but of you good folks right here in Calabash County!" Flogging Congress is a safe ploy in almost any political setting. As Mr. Truman did it, it was nearly always good for fresh outbursts of whoops and yells from the crowd. "Give 'em hell, Harry!"

"And now," he would say at the end, "I want you to meet the Boss." Turning proudly he would reach into the door of the car and lead Mrs. Truman out by the hand. Plump and matronly, she would acknowledge the applause with a smile and a wave.

"And here's the one who bosses her," the President would say as daughter Margaret, young, radiant, and usually with an armful of roses, stepped onto the scene. Her appearance always set off the loudest response of all, liberally spiced with wolf whistles from the boys and young men.

As Margaret tossed a rose or two into the crowd, the President would bend down over the railing to grasp a few of the scores of hands thrust toward him and to swap good-natured jibes with whoever could make himself heard over the uproar. The local band would strike up another tune, the engineer would give a warning toot on his whistle, the reporters and staff men would scamper down the platform toward their cars, and the

"Truman Special" would begin to pull slowly away. The whole episode would not have lasted more than 15 or 20 minutes. But Fence Post, Nebraska, would have a red-letter day to talk about and to mark down in its memory book, and Harry Truman would have done again the one thing he knew best how to do, personal politicking. The same routine would be repeated 50 miles down the line, and again and again until midnight or exhaustion put an end to the day.

Governor Dewey's performance was considerably less frenetic. The "Dewey Victory Special" covered only about half the mileage and the candidate made far fewer public appearances than did the competing road show. Reporters who covered both candidates noted with approval the cool competence and efficiency aboard the Dewey train—the rigorous scheduling, the careful advance planning, the superior press facilities available to them at major stops—as contrasted with the atmosphere of good-natured but exasperating confusion that reigned in the Truman camp. "Whistlestops" were less frequent but they were better organized and they invariably turned out large, responsive crowds. Candidate Dewey put far more emphasis than did Truman on formal addresses to large evening audiences, most of which were broadcast over either regional or national networks to widen their impact. This was a costly luxury in which the Democrats could indulge only infrequently.

The lofty tone of the Dewey campaign and the candidate's refusal to be drawn into rhetorical brawls with his free-swinging opponent drew the nearly unanimous approval of the nation's editors and commentators. He spoke much of "America's destiny," of the nation's vast potential for growth and prosperity, of the need for "unity" under a Republican administration to "insure peace in the world and our own well-being at home." When he addressed himself to issues of current concern—inflation, tax policy, labor legislation, civil rights—it was usually in general terms lacking specific goals or remedies. "I pledge you," he told a midwestern farm audience, "that your next administration will cooperate with the farmers of the country to protect all people from the tragedy of another dust bowl." (There were far more immediate concerns to the farmer than the dust bowl, about which no one had worried much for a decade.) And in the Far West he said, "I propose that we develop a national policy that will really save our forests through federal, state, and local cooperation."

"Governor Dewey," the *New York Times* reported from California about midway in the campaign, "is acting like a man who has already been elected and is merely marking time, waiting to take office. In his speeches and in his manner there is an attitude that the election will be a mere formality to confirm a decision already made." At about the same time the *Herald-Tribune* observed approvingly that the Dewey campaign "has lacked fireworks because the advocacy of unity and the sober, efficient management of public concerns are not causes which lend themselves to oratorical pyrotechnics. The public reaction to the campaign has been calm, on the whole, because Mr. Dewey represents the viewpoint of the majority." And *Newsweek* magazine in mid-October polled 50 of the nation's leading political writers and found them *unanimous* in the opinion that Dewey would sweep to an easy, one-sided victory.

About the only person aboard the "Truman Special" who seemed not to share the forebodings of failure was Mr. Truman himself. Through one grueling 18-hour, 20-speech day after another, his spirits and good nature —and as far as any one could tell, his confidence—remained undiminished. This transmitted itself inevitably to the people around him, his staff, and the reporters and the visiting politicos, but they tended to discount it as a kind of hopeless gallantry; as a manifestation of that "never say die" ethic that had guided so much of Harry Truman's life.

However, as the weeks wore on and Election Day drew near, spirits aboard the "Truman Special" began to lift. It was a subtle but exhilarating change. No one was quite sure what it was, but the motion and hubbub on the Truman train began to acquire a sense of purpose. The most tangible factor was that the crowds were getting larger, friendlier, noisier. On a swing through bedrock Republican Indiana, 25,000 people turned out to greet the President at Kokomo, 20,000 at Hammond, and more than 12,000 at Logansport. Dewey had been over the same route a week earlier and had not done so well. Five thousand people waited beside the tracks in a downpour of rain in Albany, New York, to greet the President's train when it rolled in at eight o'clock one late October morning. On the night before, 6,000 people filled every seat in the armory at Springfield, Illinois, and other hundreds gathered outside in this citadel of Republicanism to hear the Democratic candidate lambaste his opponent for not having spelled out a farm program. In St. Paul, Truman filled the 15,000-seat civic auditorium and three adjacent halls and drew applause 42 times with his excoriation of the "do-nothing Eightieth Congress." Dewey drew only 7,000 in the same auditorium. At the traditional Democratic "Friday night before election rally" in the Brooklyn Academy of Music (some of its organizers had been prominent in the "dump Truman" drive before the convention) the crowd gave the President a 12 minute ovation when he rose to speak.

Something was in the air, all right: the biggest political upset in history. "We felt it but we just couldn't believe it," a chief staff man confessed later. So did many of the reporters who had followed the campaign closely. Some began cautiously to hedge their predictions, but they could not trust their eyes above their judgment—or at least above the collective judgment of their peers. They were trapped by professional timidity into going along with the consensus that Dewey was going to win, and win big. That was what the politicians in the various states had told them; that was what they told one another in endless bull sessions in the press car; that was what all the polls told them.

Everyone had it cold, apparently, except Truman himself and Howard McGrath, his campaign manager. On the Sunday before election McGrath and his publicity man, Jack Redding, sitting alone amidst the debris and overflowing ashtrays in their New York headquarters, telephoned a score of top Democratic state leaders across the country to get their last-minute estimates of the outcome. One after another they gave almost identical replies: "Things have been looking up the last couple of weeks. We'll certainly carry the state for the Senator (or Governor or the congressional delegation), but the President probably won't make it."

When the roundup was completed McGrath looked at Redding and said: "You can't win all the things they say we are going to win and not elect a President, too. After all, he's at the top of the ticket.

"We're either going to lose everything—every senatorial race, every congressional race, every courthouse—or we'll elect a President. I think we'll elect Truman."

Tuesday, November 2, 1948—Election Day—was, by some reckonings, the longest day on record. For thousands of incredulous, bleary-eyed election-watchers across the nation, glued to their radios, it stretched past midnight into the daylight hours of Wednesday. (Not for Candidate Truman: He went to bed at his accustomed hour of 11 P.M. at a hideaway in Excelsior Springs, Missouri.) From the time the first scattered returns began to filter in around the dinner hour, Truman held a narrow and fluctuating lead. The commentators said confidently this was to be expected; this was the city vote, but wait until the rural precincts are heard from. But a little before midnight Iowa—Iowa, the heartland of midwestern Republicanism—dropped irretrievably into the Democratic column. The commentators were not so sure anymore and they noted in troubled tones that nowhere across the map had the expected signs of a Dewey landslide appeared. Stunned and electrified, voters of every persuasion across the country turned up their radios, opened another beer, and changed their minds about going to bed.

As Truman's popular vote lead held steady, the electoral vote seesawed back and forth agonizingly as the hours ticked on. At 4:30 Wednesday morning, Jim Hagerty, Dewey's press man, broke a long and ominous silence to tell reporters, "We're still in there fighting." Then came the shocking news that Illinois had conceded—Democratic. At six o'clock Truman had a commanding lead in both popular and electoral votes but still not enough to win. His electoral score was 227 to 176 for Dewey. But some key states were still out, including Ohio and California, and the experts had all agreed that Ohio, the Taft domain, was a shoo-in for the Republicans and that Governor Warren could hardly be expected to lose his home state. There was still a long, thin chance for Dewey.

Then at 9:30 came the climax, a tension-snapping end to one of the most exhausting political cliff-hangers of all time. As idling teletypes in a hundred newsrooms across the country suddenly began to chatter, red-eyed radio announcers grabbed their microphones to proclaim almost hysterically: "Ohio has gone Democratic! This puts Truman over the top with 270 electoral votes.

"Ladies and gentlemen, President Truman has won the election!"

What happened? How did this greatest of political miracles come to pass?

It was the closest Presidential election since 1916, yet far from a "squeaker." Truman's popular vote margin over Dewey was 2,148,125—49.5 percent to 45.1 percent. The spread in electoral votes was substantially greater: Truman 304 (28 states), Dewey 189 (16 states), with 38 electoral votes from four southern states going to Thurmond. Wallace drew 1.1 million popular votes but no electoral votes, although it seems certain he deprived Truman of electoral wins in both New York and New Jersey. In a general way, each of the leading candidates lost where he assumed he was strongest, and won where his prospects seemed thinnest. Dewey swept all of the industrial Northeast, from Maryland through Maine, except for Massachusetts and Rhode Island. This was traditional Democratic territory. Truman captured many of the important farm states, most notably Wisconsin, Iowa, and Colorado, which were traditionally Republican. In addition he swept the whole tier of 11 western states (excluding Oregon) in which, though they often voted Democratic, the Republicans had confidently expected to make important gains. And to double-rivet their Presidential victory, the Democrats dumped the Republicans out of control of Congress, picking up 9 seats in the Senate and 75 in the House for a safe working majority in both chambers.

What were the factors in this upset?

There were many, but in this writer's view the controlling one was this: Truman had formulated, in the November 1947 memorandum by Clifford and his political strategy team, a basic campaign plan that was unique to his needs and to his capacities, and he stuck with it. It was a strategy of go-for-broke; of recognizing that he was the underdog and that he had little to lose and much to gain; of seizing the initiative and pressing it with every weapon and against all risks. His banner was the New Deal, his targets were familiar and well-defined, and the obstacles were starkly portrayed. He did not deviate importantly from his master plan throughout the campaign. The result was that he knew what he was doing every step of the way.

Another major factor was the contrast in campaign techniques and in the motivational appeals to the voters. The Truman campaign was positive, hard-hitting, and directed to the gut interests of the voters. He named names and places and gave chapter and verse (with whatever injury to the cause of accuracy) when he criticized something. And for every wrong and every fear he had palpable villains—the Eightieth Congress and, by easy inference, Republican candidates and Republican officeholders in general. He gave the voters something to be "agin," which is a powerful motivator in voter behavior.

By contrast, both Dewey's campaign and his personality on the stump were arid. He avoided direct controversy with his opponent. He was seldom specific or convincing when he elucidated the issues. Intellectually, his campaign was on a higher level than Truman's, just as it was in the matter of decorum. By the same token it was overlaid with a tinge of superciliousness that turned off many thoughtful voters and drew bitter criticism from some Republican leaders in their postmortems.

In fact, the demerits of the Dewey campaign may have bulked as large in shaping the outcome as did the merits of the Truman technique. Jules Abels, in *Out of the Jaws of Victory,* pointed to what may have been a decisive and fatal factor in the Dewey operation in these words:

The election was not thrown away by indifference or lack of effort. Preparation and more preparation had always been the distinguishing characteristic of Dewey and his team throughout his career. . . . The truth is that the type of campaign was the result not of carelessness, but of too careful and painstaking calculation. The Dewey campaign line was frozen into inertia not because it had been underthought, but because it had been overthought.

The consequence of this, as Abels and others have pointed out, was that when the first turbulence of a Truman tide began to appear late in October, the Dewey crew, geared for smooth water only, was unable to trim sails in order to meet the rising seas.

Among the lesser casualties of this debacle were the public opinion pollers and the news media. Their mea culpas spilled out in a torrent in the days immediately after the election. Elmo Roper, who had ceased his poll-taking back in September thinking nothing was likely to change, protested helplessly: "I could not have been more wrong. The thing that bothers me most at this moment is that I don't know why I was wrong." Columnist Marquis Childs, seeming to pass the buck, lamented, "[Our] fatal flaw was reliance on the public opinion polls." James Reston of the *Times,* on the other hand, put the burden squarely on the reporters' shoulders, saying:

Neither on the [campaign] train nor in the [state] capitals do we spend much time walking around and talking to the people. We tend to assume that somebody else is doing the original reporting in that area, and if the assumptions of the political managers, or the other reporters, or the polls are wrong (as they were in this campaign), then our reports are wrong. . . . We were wrong not only on the election, but what's worse, on the whole political direction of our time.

At all events, Harry Truman was now President in his own right, his record vindicated and his leadership open to no man's challenge. "You just have to take off your hat," the *New York Sun* (which rarely had said anything kind about him before) editorialized the day after election, "to a beaten man who refuses to stay licked! . . . The next few days will produce many long and labored explanations of what happened. To us of the *Sun* there is no great mystery about it. Mr. Truman won because this is still a land that loves a scrapper, in which intestinal fortitude is still respected."

The President took all such accolades with becoming modesty. He set off for a rest in Key West, and within a week had summoned his aides to begin work on a new budget and State of the Union message.[1]

12

Fair Deal—and Foul

As THE DECADE OF THE FORTIES wound down the national mood was one of perplexity and fretfulness; a dissatisfaction with things as they were and no clear image of what they ought to be. The certainties and the moral imperatives of the war years were gone. Old cultural relationships had been set askew—child to parent, worker to boss, downtown to uptown, country bumpkin to city slicker. The postwar years had brought a tumult of shifting values, of new crises and alarms, of extravagant expectations and unfulfilled hopes. A wave of technological innovation had spilled out of war plants and laboratories to engulf the consumer market and alter popular tastes—television, speedier automobiles with automatic transmission and tubeless tires, a new generation of plastics and synthetic fibers, home air-conditioners and electric refrigerators, frozen foods and concentrates, DDT, vitamin capsules, a host of miracle-working antibiotics. The promise of all this was glittering; the reality was something else again. In many basic categories—housing, for example, and automobiles, and meat—there wasn't enough to go around, and prices all along the line were "sky-high."

The persistent gap between the fact and the potential of postwar life was especially galling to those hundreds of thousands of families whom the great wave of wartime prosperity had deposited on the shores of middle-class affluence and respectability. The lesser class lines had been all but obliterated in the upheaval; even Jews and Italians and others of immigrant stock had improved their standing in the white social structure. Only the blacks remained unaffected and largely unnoticed in their ordained confinement at the bottom of the heap. But status alone was an empty prize. The middle class is the true barometer of a nation's disenchantment and discontent. And there was plenty of both in the sovereign middle class of those closing years of the forties decade.

Nineteen forty-eight, 1949 . . . these were the years that sealed off the first half of the twentieth century, or more accurately, that opened the highway into what we now call Modern Times. It was a rough passage.

I

The political orchestration of those years was woven in and about two antiphonal themes, the Fair Deal and the Red Menace. These two embroiled the nation in sustained and bitter controversy.

The Fair Deal was the banner President Truman unfurled in his bid to capture the liberal dynamism of FDR for his second administration. He sought to apply it not only to the "unfinished business" of the New Deal but to move forward with it in application to social and economic problems arising out of the war. He signaled this trend clearly in his election campaign of 1948 beginning with his State of the Union message in January of that year, and confidently reaffirmed it in various messages to Congress a year later. It was a bold thrust aimed at the mood of reaction that seems always to afflict the body politic in postwar years. That mood moved toward a crest in 1948–1949, Truman's stunning electoral victory notwithstanding.

Like its predecessor, the Fair Deal was not a tidy catalogue of postulates and programs but rather a shopping list that swelled and dwindled according to the fluctuations in the political marketplace. There were all told some 30 propositions for reform through governmental action advanced at one time or another. They were about evenly mixed between pragmatism and idealism, between expedient and enduring goals. But common to most of them was the ideal of a broader, more responsive democracy—a wider sharing of the fruits and opportunities of a life-style that was shaking itself free of the inhibitions of the old economics of scarcity. "Socialism!" some cried in dismay. But more accurately it was the harbinger of the "welfare state," a category of hazy dimensions which other critics found equally dismaying.

The Fair Deal legislative program fell into several major groupings as follows.

Civil Rights. Here were included a variety of measures to eradicate political, economic, and to some extent social discrimination against blacks: elimination of the poll tax and other barriers to full voting privileges; making lynching a crime punishable under federal law; establishment of a permanent Fair Employment Practices Commission (a wartime phenomenon) to combat job discrimination on account of race; elimination of "Jim Crow" segregation in education and in hotels, restaurants, theaters, etc.; creation of a governmental Civil Rights Commission to monitor progress in the field; and setting up within the Department of Justice of a full-fledged Civil Rights Division for enforcement of the civil rights statutes. (Such federal statutes as existed at the time—most of them dating from the time of Reconstruction—were so vague and so circumscribed by adverse Supreme Court decisions that prosecutions were rare and seldom successful.)

This cluster of civil rights proposals soon came to epitomize the Fair Deal and to generate the most rancorous partisan opposition to it.

Social Welfare. The most prominent and controversial proposal here was for a program of national health insurance, making prepaid medical care available to all citizens at little or no direct cost. This proposition brought forth an apoplectic—and highly efficacious—reaction from the American Medical Association. Also proposed was an extension of social security coverage to some three million workers then exempted, an upgrading of benefits, and substantial improvement of the system of unemployment insurance. A further recommendation in this category was for a solid program of federal aid to education which, up to that time, had been on a meager and narrowly selective basis.

Housing. Home building came virtually to a halt during the war, and in the postwar years the shortage of low- and moderate-cost housing was one of the most aggravating afflictions the public had to endure. President Truman pushed persistently for a program of federal loans and grants to construct a million new housing units over a six-year period, to provide rent supplements for the poorer tenants of such units, and to underwrite municipal slum clearance projects. (Repairing the housing shortage was not exclusively a concern of the Fair Deal. Republican Senator Robert A. Taft, for example, was deeply committed to the idea, differing with the President only as to scope and method.)

Labor. Truman persisted in his opposition to the Taft-Hartley Act (mainly for political reasons it appeared), called for its repeal. He also pressed for an increase in the minimum wage from 40¢ to 75¢ an hour.

Other planks in the Fair Deal platform that were stressed from time to time included extension of the TVA conservation concept to other major river basins in the country; reform of the agricultural price support program to even out the inequitable distribution of benefits between big farmers and little farmers (the so-called Brannan Plan); a standby battery of wage, price, credit, and other economic controls with which to subdue a rapidly spiraling inflation; and tax reforms designed to shift more of the fiscal burden onto corporations (enjoying unparalleled profits in 1948–1949) and off the back of "the little man." A brief but high-voltage shocker was tacked onto the Fair Deal platform in the President's 1949 State of the Union message. This was a suggestion that if private producers of such basic commodities as steel could not overcome the critical shortages that had persisted ever since the war's end, the government would step in to build production facilities on its own! The sparks from this ignited boardrooms all the way from Wall Street to

Chicago's Loop but subsided harmlessly as it became apparent the administration harbored no serious intention of trying to nationalize the steel mills.

The Fair Deal was an aggressively liberal program, one that, in the words of its critics, sought to "out-deal the New Deal." Its civil rights package was the most comprehensive put forward since the early days of Reconstruction and was aimed at specific targets of racial discrimination—at customs and attitudes deeply imbedded in the WASP ethos, Northern as well as Southern—which the New Dealers had largely ignored. The national health insurance proposal was equally innovative. It had been on the agenda of liberal intellectuals for many years, a sort of Utopian dream, but Truman was the first President to invest the idea with serious political clout. Public housing was not a new concept; it had begun haltingly as far back as 1935 and had been pursued on a strictly emergency basis during the early war years. What the Fair Deal offered was a crash program on the order of $1.5 billion to break a severe housing bottleneck for the primary benefit of low- and middle-income families, providing subsidies for them on a grand new scale. Similarly, federal aid to education had a long but quite narrow history, beginning in the 1880s with the land grant colleges and encompassing the 1944 "GI Bill of Rights" which gave educational subsidies to war veterans. President Truman proposed a $300 million program designed primarily —and for the first time—to raise the educational level of public schools generally, but especially in the poorer states, where the facilities and performance of the schools were far below the national mean.

The Fair Dealers proceeded on the premise that the 1948 election had given them a mandate to push forward with a liberal program. It is possible that such a consensus did exist among the population at large—the *New* Deal was a cherished memory to most ordinary citizens—but its pervasiveness would be hard to ratify on the basis of the election returns. And that skepticism prevailed where it counted most, in the Eighty-first Congress newly assembled in the Capitol in January 1949. It was again a Democratic Congress, the slender Republican margins won in 1946 having been wiped out in the latest election. But it was anything but a "Truman" Congress (except on major items of foreign policy) and the balance of power rested easily in the hands of a coalition of Southern Democrats and conservative Republicans. These blocs were adamantly opposed to a return of the New Deal philosophy of government, and they were fortified in this by the widening furor over Communist subversion. Elizabeth Bentley and Whittaker Chambers had already put a match to this dry tinder and now it was blowing up into a firestorm. Virtually every plank in the Fair Deal platform, accordingly, was denounced at one time or another as "socialistic" or "communistic" and a great many people were perplexed by it. Even moderates on the health insurance issue, for example, fell innocently into the habit of calling it "socialized medicine," which was a tribute to the skillful lobbying campaign of the AMA.

Central to the whole Fair Deal controversy was the fight over civil rights. Some significant progress in this area had been made since the end of the war without recourse to legislation. Chiefly as a result of long-drawn-out litigation by the National Association for the Advancement of Colored People (NAACP), the Supreme Court had banned "lily white" primary elections which, in the South, effectively disfranchised the black; it had ruled as unconstitutional racial covenants in real estate transactions that barred blacks from obtaining homes in white neighborhoods; it had ruled similarly against "Jim Crow" accommodations on interstate trains and buses, and, by the end of 1949, was moving close to its first direct assault on statutory segregation in education. (This came the following June when the Universities of Texas and Oklahoma were directed to admit qualified black students and to give them identical opportunities enjoyed by whites.) In the same period President Truman issued executive orders calling for full integration of the races in the armed services (which proceeded with a good deal of foot-dragging by the Generals and Admirals), and for the opening up of federal civil employment on a nondiscriminatory basis at all job and salary levels. Independently meanwhile, Jackie Robinson had made an historic break-through into the ranks of big-league baseball; Ralph Bunche had distinguished himself as an official of the United Nations; Duke Ellington and Louis Armstrong were preeminent in the world of popular music; a handful of black writers were beginning to gain a recognition that ignored the color line; and more than 90,000 black students were enrolled in colleges and universities—most, however, in all-black institutions generally of inferior quality.

As salutary as these developments were, however, there still remained gaping voids in the national fabric of equality of treatment for all citizens. The war itself had exacerbated racial animosities, spread their poisons far beyond the confines of the old Confederacy. As blacks by the tens of thousands migrated north and west to cash in on abundant war jobs, cities like New York, Chicago, Los Angeles, and many in between, suddenly discovered themselves confronted with a "Negro problem." The emigres cluttered the already-crowded ghettoes, clogged the schools and health and other public services, flooded the labor market in many low-paid occupations. The low order of literacy and casual life-style that many brought with them from their poverty-stricken backgrounds affronted their scarcely more cultivated white neighbors, and racial tensions grew in the slums where they lived and in the factories where they worked.

Violent race riots erupted in Detroit and the Harlem district of New York a few weeks apart during the summer of 1943, with a combined toll of over 40 dead, hundreds injured, and property damage running into the millions of dollars. There were lesser flare-ups of the same sort in a dozen other cities across the nation during the decade, and in the South 31 blacks died at the hands of lynch mobs between 1940 and 1950. Local juries rarely punished the guilty in these outrages and efforts to make lynching a federal offense were regularly defeated by Southern "patriots" in the Congress.

A new dimension was added to these frustrations for the million or more blacks who went into uniform during the war. Almost without exception they were put into segregated units, given the most menial tasks, denied combat roles, and virtually barred from promotion to the middle and upper echelons of the commissioned officer class. There was no disparity in the quality of sacrifice the white and the black soldier might be called upon to make for the preservation of democracy in the world. But when the black GI came home he knew that the democracy to which he had returned was of the same fraudulent variety he had always known. Even the nation's capital, now a symbol of freedom the world over, was a "Jim Crow" city where blacks were as rigidly segregated as in Mississippi.

By inflexible custom and often by law, the vast majority of blacks in the United States were condemned to a life of second-class citizenship. In spite of court rulings to the contrary, the bulk of Southern blacks dared not exercise their right to vote for fear of reprisal, physical or economic. In six of those states they were further inhibited by the poll tax, which often was applied cumulatively, and in most other states by complex registration and literacy requirements. In 17 states public school systems were segregated by law, and in 20, state laws and municipal ordinances either forbade or limited service to blacks in theaters, restaurants, hotels, rest rooms, and other places of public accommodation. In most fields of employment, North as well as South, there was one pay scale for blacks and another for whites. Blacks were denied admission to most labor unions, or accepted grudgingly at best. And invariably when hard times came the black man was "the last to be hired, the first to be fired." In 1948, the first "full employment" year since the end of the war, the unemployment rate among blacks was approximately twice that of whites, and the median annual income of black workers—$1,210— was just half that of the white worker.

In spite of these glaring injustices there was no organized militancy by the black minority. The quest for reform was conducted through legal and peaceful channels by such conventional bodies as the NAACP and the National Urban League, and by a few influential white liberals and intellectuals. The Communist party had, by the end of 1949, about given up any hope of stirring up a proletarian revolt, or even enrolling many members, among the depressed black masses in the United States.

It was on President Truman's initiative that the decision was made for a frontal attack on this deeply ingrained social evil. Late in 1946 he set up the Presidential Commission on Civil Rights, with a distinguished and influential membership, and directed it to examine the whole area of rights assumed and guaranteed under the Constitution and to recommend how those rights could be implemented and protected under federal law. The Commission's report, submitted the following October, proved to be a landmark in the literature on this subject and became, of course, the foundation on which the President's legislative program was built.

The Truman civil rights package was presented to Congress in a special message in February 1948. Southern politicians from sheriffs to Governors to members of Congress reacted in nearly unanimous outrage. They described it variously as a scheme "to mongrelize the South," a plot to destroy the hallowed doctrine of states' rights, a device to enforce social equality—maybe even mixed marriages—on Southern gentility, and much more. Four thousand irate party members from the old Confederacy attended a rump convention in Jackson, Mississippi, during the spring to sound a new call for secession—this time from the Yankee-dominated Democratic party. That call was echoed by scores of stump speakers across the Southland, by writers of editorials and letters to the editor, even from some pulpits. And as was noted in the preceding chapter, there was indeed a substantial walkout of Southern delegates from the party's national convention that summer after a full civil rights plank was nailed into the platform, resulting in the creation of the Dixiecrat party with its own slate of candidates. Republicans took full advantage of this disruption in the ranks of the foe: They piously endorsed most of the civil rights measures Truman had advanced but gave him scant help in Congress to get them written into law. That goal, they confidently assured themselves, could be deferred for a few months until their own man was in the White House.

There was, inevitably, no legislative action on civil rights during the political turmoil of 1948. But in the invigorating afterglow of their great electoral upset in November, the Fair Dealers returned to the fray, as the new Congress assembled in January 1949, with a fresh surge of determination and hope. Here a new strategy was decided upon: to spike the enemy's biggest gun before the first shot was fired.

That big gun was the filibuster, the unique parliamentary device in the Senate that permits unlimited debate; a frequently used stratagem by which a small minority can "talk a bill to death" and thus prevent its coming to a showdown vote. In theory it was devised to protect a minority of Senators from being regularly trampled into submission by the majority. But in practical application, particularly over the preceding dozen years, its effect had been just the reverse: A minority had used it time and again to thwart the will of the majority. And during that period its chief practitioners had been Southern conservatives using it to block legislation they considered inimical to their personal and regional interests.

Although the filibuster was a privilege that was often, and sometimes flagrantly abused, the Senate had always been reluctant to tamper with it. This stemmed in part from that body's institutional sense of tradition and in part from the members' cautionary self-interest—regardless of his ideological stripe, a Senator could never tell when the time might come that he would want to seek shelter behind a filibuster himself. Only once had a qualification been imposed on this ancient prerogative. This was in 1917 at a critical juncture in the First World War. To break the strangulating grip of a small cadre of war protesters in its midst, the Senate added to its official manual of procedures Rule XXII which provided that, upon the affirmative vote of two-thirds of its membership, debate could be cut off—"cloture" applied, in parliamentary jargon—so that the body could proceed to consideration and a vote on the measure at hand. But in all the years from 1917 to 1949, though it was attempted many times, cloture had been successfully invoked on only four occasions, which was compelling testimony of the efficacy of the filibuster as a weapon in the hands of a determined minority. And this was a fact of political warfare to which the Truman administration had been frequently and painfully subjected.

The new stratagem was to amend Rule XXII to permit cloture by a simple *majority* of Senators "present and voting," which could be as few as 25 (a quorum in that day was 49), instead of *two-thirds* of the entire membership—64—as currently required. That arithmetic had great appeal for the Fair Dealers. To the cadre of Truman "loyalists" already on hand they felt they could add support from the dozen new Democrats who had won seats in the 1948 upset, thus giving the administration muscle to win a showdown on almost any filibuster. The immediate problem was to round up enough votes—a simple majority—to change the Senate rules, and that seemed on the face of it not too difficult.

But there was a catch, wired to a finespun interpretation of still another Senate rule. Thus, when Majority Leader Scott Lucas arose on March 1 to move consideration of his resolution to change Rule XXII, Senator Richard B. Russell of Georgia, field marshal of the Southern dissidents, arose right behind him to oppose even the motion to take up the rule change. He and his colleagues, Russell said with that splendid courtliness that was a part of his offensive armor, were prepared to talk on this subject "at some length." Thus a filibuster was mounted, not against a substantive *measure* pending before the Senate, but against a *motion to take up* a measure. This was a semantic twister likely to confuse any but the most dedicated Senate buffs, which it assuredly did.

Now the question was, could cloture be invoked on a "motion to take up" as well as on a "measure"? Rule XXII was not specific on the question and there was the rub. The only answer could come from a ruling of the chair. That question in almost identical form had come up the year before, and Republican Senator Vandenberg, then officiating as president pro tem, had ruled in the negative. This time the chair was occupied by the Democratic Vice-President, Barkley, and there was no doubt in anyone's mind that, when the time came, he would reverse Vandenberg's dictum and rule that a "motion to take up" *was* subject to cloture. Once past that hurdle, the administration's forces figured, they had enough votes—by a narrow margin—both to shut off the current filibuster and to amend Rule XXII.

Lucas decided not to try to force the issue at once. In order "to sweeten the pot," as he expressed it, he let the southern objectors talk on to their heart's content—Senator Allen Ellender of Louisiana held the floor one day for 12 hours and 21 minutes, a near-record for one man—knowing that the longer this parliamentary burlesque persisted the more votes he would win to his side. At last, after 10 days of unbroken southern oratory, he put the crucial question to the chair: Could cloture be applied to a "motion to take up"? And as expected, Barkley solemnly and lengthily opined that it could.

But Senator Lucas's nose count was not as reliable as it should have been. A ruling of the Senate's presiding officer can be upset by a simple majority vote. Such a test was now demanded by Senator Russell. Word of this critical confrontation between pro- and antiadministration forces spread quickly through the Capitol, bringing absent Senators on the run and a rush for seats in the press and spectators' galleries. As the clerk slowly called the roll, tension mounted as the balance between "yeas" and "nays" shifted back and forth.

At last it was over: The "nays" had won 46 to 41. The ruling of the chair had been rejected. For the conservative coalition, it was perhaps its finest hour. Twenty-three southern Senators—only three fewer than the total from that region—were joined by an exactly equal number of Republicans, mostly from the Middle West, to preserve the narrow interpretation of Rule XXII, and thus the integrity of the filibuster. This meant simply that, for the remainder of the current session of Congress, the door had been slammed not only against civil rights legislation but against most other domestic planks in the Fair Deal platform as well. The only survivor of the bold program which President Truman had first laid out in 1948 was a public housing bill—a quite substantial one which he signed into law in July 1949.

Like most reform movements when they are first broached, the Fair Deal was ahead of its time. The nation's mood in the late forties was dominated by other concerns than social welfare and civil rights. In spite of inflation and high prices, the economy was booming, jobs were relatively plentiful, and the areas where want and injustice did prevail were conveniently outside most people's line of vision. The crises that did alarm them were of foreign rather than domestic origin. President Truman, for all his courage and other attractive qualities, lacked the charismatic spark of leadership. He was incapable of endowing the Fair Deal with that emotional magnetism that Roosevelt had imparted to the New Deal. No quitter, he would pursue his goals to the end of his term in 1952, but it would fall to other Presidents in years yet to come to transmute the social vision of the Fair Deal into legislative reality.[1]

II

One of the more notable side attractions of the political playbill during those years was known variously as "The Battle of the Pentagon" and "The Revolt of the Admirals." While such labels tended to reduce the conflict to the level of satire, the events themselves were played out in an aura of intense emotion and deep personal involvement. And the central issue at stake, the unification of the armed services, was one of crucial significance.

The crushing lesson drawn from the disaster of Pearl Harbor was the utter inadequacy of a defense establishment in which control was divided between two autonomous and mutually suspicious military services, the Army and the Navy. The extent of that disaster can be traced, in large part at least, to the failure of the two Pacific commands to know what the other was doing or to react in consistent fashion to the warnings sent from Washington and to the last-minute alerts of their own intelligence units. From the very beginning the War and Navy Departments had been separate and independent governmental entities, each with its own Secretary sitting in the Cabinet, each with its own concept of roles and mission, each with its own budget and managerial apparatus, each with its own committees and constituencies in Congress. From top to bottom throughout the whole defense structure an old-school rivalry had long since frozen into an institutional posture, and only the exigencies of actual warfare could bring them together in common purpose—a hazardous contingency at best. As a congressional committee investigating the Pearl Harbor debacle observed, "The evidence . . . reveals the complete inadequacy of command by *mutual cooperation* where decisive action is of the essence."

Moreover, the enormous growth in the size and complexity of the military establishment, and the emergence of its air arm into a status of equal importance with the ground and sea forces, made it clear that, in peacetime as well as in war, unified control had become necessary in terms of both political logic and national security.

Unification had been debated on and off ever since the Spanish-American War. Harry Truman had become a strong advocate of it during World War Two from his privileged position as chairman of the Senate War Investigating Committee. He gave it high priority as President when, on December 19, 1945, he urged Congress to give the idea legislative sanction. At the same time, he put a high-level committee of Generals and Admirals to work threshing out the myriad technicalities involved and to come up with a workable compromise of all the competing prejudices and prerogatives of the two services.

This was no small task, and the pride and tradition of the Navy proved to be a major obstacle. The Army people were generally agreeable to unification. Both sides agreed in principle that the air arm should be elevated to coequal status. But the Navy stubbornly resisted any diminution of its autonomy, of its historic role in national defense strategy, and most especially of the expanding scope of its own air power. The men in blue soon found themselves on the defensive, convinced that the Army and Air Force advocates had ganged up against them. They sensed a plot to nibble away at the whole concept of sea power, to do away with the Marine Corps, to reduce naval aviation to the innocuous routine of coastal and antisubmarine patrols. The resultant debates grew rancorous and noisy, and soon spilled out of the confines of formal committee sessions to create a public clamor of vast dimensions. It resounded angrily in the press, in Congress, among the civilian constituencies of the various services, and the brass on both sides hurled intemperate accusations and countercharges at one another.

By the beginning of 1947, however, the President's committee had managed to patch together a basic unification blueprint. It was shot through with ambiguities and makeshift compromises, many of which were concessions to the Navy's fear of being downgraded. But it did incorporate such fundamental innovations as the creation of a Department of the Air Force of coequal status with the Army and Navy, and of a National Defense Establishment presided over by a Secretary of Defense. Only the Secretary of Defense would have Cabinet rank, but the three departmental secretaries would have direct access to the President and administrative autonomy within their respective departments. The plan also called for a Joint Chiefs of Staff, consisting of three officials representing the services (and a nonvoting fourth representing the President), concerned mainly with strategy and logistics, but subject to the authority of the Secretary of Defense. Also included in the proposal was the creation of several ancillary organizations answerable directly to the President, such as the National Security Council and the Central Intelligence

Agency. The Navy was specifically empowered in these recommendations to preserve the Marine Corps and both its land-based and carrier-based aviation.

This was an agreement in principle only, a distillation of what the nation's military chieftains found tolerable and attainable in so monumental a reshaping of their domain. But the President accepted their report with relief and turned to Congress for the legislation to make unification a reality. This was a difficult and complicated process, and in the weeks of public hearings which followed many of the old suspicions and interservice rivalries surfaced again. There were objections that the nation's fighting men would be hobbled by civilian "do-gooders"; that too much administrative power was being placed in the hands of the Secretary of Defense; and the Marine Corps demanded that guarantees of its status be written explicitly into the new law. After five months of wrangling, however, the National Security Act of 1947, incorporating most of the features previously agreed upon by the President's committee, was signed into law on July 26. The next day President Truman sent to the Senate his nomination of James V. Forrestal, then Secretary of the Navy, to become the nation's first Secretary of Defense.

Forrestal, a Navy flier in the First World War and later a successful New York investment banker, entered public service in the late years of the Roosevelt administration and was named Secretary of the Navy in 1944. He was tall and spare with an attitude of pugnacity (enhanced by a broken nose suffered in a college boxing match) and a tense, brittle manner that betokened great efficiency if not much patience. He was a late convert to the gospel of unification and it may have been for this reason that Truman, as a placatory gesture to the Navy, chose him for the crucial assignment as Secretary of Defense.

Whatever his misgivings may have been, Forrestal pursued his task with vigor and determination. The legislation gave him two years in which to effect this massive organizational transformation; to devise and establish a new bureaucracy called the National Defense Establishment (later to be named the Department of Defense) and to superimpose it effectively upon two existing and tradition-bound bureaucracies, the Army and the Navy, plus a new one, the Air Force, which was struggling mightily to obtain a proper birthright. The complications of the assignment were staggering, for it laid bare and demanded final yes-or-no resolution of most of the superheated conflicts of principle and of prejudice in which the unification issue had been embroiled from the start. Deadlocks developed among the service Secretaries, among the Chiefs of Staff, and among their subordinates down the line which only the Secretary of Defense, often with the affirmative backing of the President, could break. Agreements and compromises hammered out in this environment left most of the old scars unhealed and added some new ones.

In January 1949, Forrestal reported to the President that the process of unification had gone as far as it could under the existing statute; that its full scope could not be achieved without, among other things, more power in the hands of the Secretary of Defense to knock heads together to get things done. The President agreed and asked Congress for prompt and substantial amendments to the unification law.

At this point—on March 28—Forrestal resigned, physically and mentally broken. He entered Bethesda Naval Hospital for intense psychiatric treatment. Six weeks later he ended his life by leaping from a window high in the hospital tower—"as much a casualty of the war," President Truman said of him, "as if he had died on the firing line."

Forrestal's successor was Louis A. Johnson, a big-framed, dynamic, no-nonsense businessman whose financial exertions in behalf of Mr. Truman in the 1948 election campaign had been rewarded with his appointment as Secretary of the Army. In that post he had been generally cooperative with Defense Secretary Forrestal in the interorganizational battles, but in a brusque, hard-nosed fashion that won him few friends among the Generals and none at all among the Admirals.

The Navy's low opinion of Johnson was riveted firmly into place when, soon after taking office, he gave the Air Force a go-ahead for a costly expansion of its strategic bombing program and at the same time ordered cancellation of contracts for a supercarrier, the *United States*. To the Admirals this was a mortal blow, a confirmation of their darkest suspicions. All their hopes for preserving a major offensive role for the Navy were concentrated on the *United States,* the first carrier designed to deliver heavy bomber strikes on enemy targets from a safe sanctuary hundreds of miles at sea. Now this bold innovation was washed out even as the Air Force was being groomed for bigger things.

The Navy people refused to take this lying down. As congressional hearings on the amendments to the unification law proceeded into the spring, they concentrated their fire not on organizational questions but on a corollary development: a decision by Secretary Johnson, backed by a divided Joint Chiefs of Staff, to put primary emphasis for the nation's defense on land-based bombers, specifically the B-36, an aerial monster of unprecedented size and cost supposedly capable of delivering the A-bomb on targets half a world away. This could only mean a secondary role for the Navy's big warships and carriers in any future war, and the end, perhaps, of the unique function of the Marines.

When this decision was made in the early months of 1949 the B-36 was barely out of the experimental stage, but it had won the confidence of every leading spokesman for the Air Force. This did not impress Navy partisans. At first they alleged that chicanery had dictated the choice of the B-36, pointing out that both Defense Secretary Johnson and Air Force Secretary Stuart Symington had at one time had financial connections with Consolidated Vultee, designers and manufacturers of the plane. They then broadened their indictment to charge that the B-36 was untested and unproven under simulated battle conditions, and that it was incapable of fulfilling the global mission planned for it.

So angry and vehement was the Navy's protest, and so defiant the response by the Air Force, that the Congress decided that only a full inquiry of its own into the B-36 could settle the controversy. Accordingly, in late summer the House Armed Service Committee opened a long series of public and executive hearings into this latest phase of the "Battle of the Pentagon." And now in a great marble chamber of the House Office Building, playing daily to packed audiences largely dominated by wearers of khaki and blue, and with a full complement of reporters and cameramen on hand, the "Revolt of the Admirals" erupted in full and acrimonious splendor. One after another, more than a dozen of the Navy's most senior officers, led by the most senior of them all, Admiral Louis E. Denfeld, Chief of Naval Operations, took the stand to affirm publicly their opposition—to many facets of the unification law; to the authority of Defense Secretary Johnson, and the submissive role played under him by Navy Secretary Francis P. Matthews; to the new strategic concept that put air power ahead of sea power; and most particularly to the concentration of strategic might—and of the money for armaments—in the "vulnerable" and "untried" B-36.

The Admirals were answered with almost equal vehemence by their civilian chiefs and by such military equals as General Omar N. Bradley, just named to the newly created post of Chairman of the Joint Chiefs of Staff, General Eisenhower, and General Hoyt S. Vandenberg, Chief of Staff for the Air Force. General Bradley drew blood at one point in his testimony when he icily remarked, "This is no time for Fancy Dans who won't hit the line with all they have on every play unless they can call the signals." Navy partisans were stunned and angry. At another stage in the proceedings Navy Captain John G. Crommelin let it be known that he was responsible for having made the charges (later shown to be false) of criminal conflict of interest in the award of the B-36 contract to Consolidated Vultee, and that his continuing vendetta against unification had been endorsed by a number of top ranking Admirals. He was publicly reprimanded and threatened with court martial by Secretary Matthews. And the Secretary was so offended at parts of Admiral Denfeld's testimony—they conspicuously snubbed one another outside the hearing room—that he persuaded the President to "fire" him as Chief of Naval Operations.

Never before had the Army and the Navy of the United States engaged publicly in such a political brawl; and never, except on the football field on the Saturday after Thanksgiving, had the ancient rivalry between them been displayed with such primitive ferocity. The Navy was the loser, but not by much, and in the process it acquired a new pantheon of undecorated heroes: a score of "martyrs" who laid their careers on the line fighting for the Navy's status and tradition. The congressional hearing ended late in October without reaching any definitive conclusions, but it had served to let off an explosive head of steam and to leave combatants on both sides with the satisfaction of knowing they had had their day in court. The new budget which the President presented in January gave the Air Force its B-36 (though fewer than it hoped for), but it also gave the Navy back its big carrier and more planes to arm it with. So, the tensions of the "Battle of the Pentagon" wound down during the early months of 1950, to be dissipated completely with the onset of the Korean crisis that summer.

Meanwhile, the amendments to the National Security Act were written into law—and virtually lost to public view—during the height of the squabble over the B-36. Just as Secretary Forrestal had recommended, these strengthened the authority of the Department of Defense and its Secretary vis-à-vis the three military departments and their Secretaries, and created the new post of Chairman of the Joint Chiefs of Staff answerable directly to the President. Although a number of modifications were yet to come, the essential framework of a unified defense establishment such as we have since known was put in place.[2]

III

One day in February 1946, President Truman sent an urgent summons to his Attorney General Tom C. Clark, and his Secretary of the Treasury, Fred M. Vinson, to meet with him forthwith in the White House Oval Office. When they arrived the grim-faced President laid before them a 15-page memorandum he had received that morning from FBI Director J. Edgar Hoover. The memo asserted that the G-Men had learned of an extensive Communist espionage ring centered in New York with strong connections in Washington that reached into the very upper echelons of the government. The report was based on revelations made by two admitted former members of the ring, Elizabeth Bentley and Whittaker Chambers, who were currently telling their full stories to a New York grand jury. While the memo was hazy as to details of the espionage operation, it was emphatic in listing some 37 Washington "contacts" from whom or through whom the spies said they frequently received secret documents and other confidential information for transmittal to Moscow.

Of a dozen of these alleged contacts who then occupied positions of responsibility in the government, the most important by far—and the most shocking to the men grouped about the President's desk—was Harry Dexter White, Assistant Secretary of the Treasury in charge of international

monetary affairs. An urbane man in his early fifties, White was a professional economist of wide distinction. He had served in the Treasury in a
number of capacities throughout the war years, was one of the principal
architects of the Bretton Woods Agreement, and only days before the
arrival of the Hoover memorandum at the White House, the President
had nominated him for the post of United States Director of the International Monetary Fund. The nomination was even then awaiting confirmation by the Senate, a formality to which no objections were anticipated.

The Hoover report in its overall dimensions was alarming enough,
but its greatest impact by far on the President and his visitors was the
impeachment of Harry Dexter White. It was incredible that a public
servant of his stature, a man whom each of them knew and respected,
should be leading a double life as a traitor. True, the allegation against
him was unspecific, lacking in detail or proof; his name was simply
listed with others as "one who." But in the tense climate of those times
no tale of Communist wickedness seemed too fanciful for credence. And
in Ottawa at that very moment a Royal Commission was unraveling
a spy plot of its own that appeared to be reaching high into the Canadian
government. It *could* happen here, yes. But with Harry Dexter White at
its center. . . ?

Truman and his two Cabinet chiefs found that possibility too hard
to believe but too worrisome to be dismissed. They decided to wait and
see; to keep quiet; to let White's nomination and appointment go through,
but to have the FBI keep him under constant surveillance.*

Meanwhile, Hoover was ordered to mount an immediate and massive
investigation into the whole field of Communist subversion and espionage;
to double and triple his present exertions in that direction, sparing neither
money nor manpower. He was to make regular reports of his progress
directly to the President.

This episode was neither the beginning nor the end but rather a
significant upsurge in the fever chart of a virulent distemper that afflicted

---

* This was not the end of the White affair. He served for more than a year as
this country's chief officer at the International Monetary Fund. When he resigned
in April 1947, to enter private business he received a cordial letter from President
Truman praising his services to the government. The following year White was
called before the House Un-American Activities Committee to be grilled in public
about his alleged Communist connections. He firmly denied all the allegations made
against him, just as, he reminded the Committee, he had done before the New York
grand jury previously. Two days after testifying he died of a heart attack. Nor was
this the end of the affair. In 1953 Eisenhower's Attorney General Herbert Brownell
described White as a "known Communist spy" whom President Truman, in full
knowledge of the facts, had elevated to a high government post. Brownell produced
no evidence of the charge, nor has anyone else come forward with proof that
Harry Dexter White was a Communist, a fellow traveler, or disloyal to his country.

the reason and deformed the political life of this country for more than a decade after the Second World War. The fear of Communist subversion in those years became a national neurosis. At least half the population, it seemed, from Senators and board chairmen to clerks and housewives, were gripped by a dogmatic conviction that Communists and fellow travelers, under the evil aegis of the Kremlin, were "boring from within" to destroy the American way of life. These malevolent spirits were not spies and bomb throwers in the traditional sense; rather they were seen as zealots of a secret and sinister cult who affected the disguise of quite ordinary and peaceable citizens—like Harry White, for instance. Their aim was not so much revolution (although this was not ruled out!) as dissolution: the steady, relentless erosion of the nation's moral and civic fiber to the point where a Communist state would arise out of the debris. It was firmly believed, moreover—and documentation was adduced claiming to prove it—that all of this was a calculated, well engineered plot moving forward on an inexorable timetable.

As for the other half of the population, many shared these fears but with lesser conviction, a more cautious credulity. One couldn't be sure about such things, what with the state the world was in, they reasoned. Nor need one risk rebuke for his doubts in the face of so much certitude. Things *did* happen from time to time, and were reported in the newspapers or cropped up in local gossip, that gave at least the color of substance to such fears. The where-there's-smoke-there's-fire syndrome had a facile plausibility.

And at the far end of this spectrum of opinion—the left end naturally—there was a minority who regarded the whole issue as morbidly dangerous nonsense. Certainly communism was opposed to capitalism, and Russia was hostile to the United States, but the day of reckoning between them was not at hand and probably would not be within a lifetime, if ever. To pretend otherwise with so much vehemence was to invite trouble of another kind.

The voicing of such a viewpoint, naturally, made one suspect in the eyes of the majority: What about *that* fellow's loyalty? That was a question freighted with peril.

The fact was, of course, that a glimmer of truth was reflected from both ends of that spectrum of opinion. An international Communist conspiracy *did* exist, and its paid agents and its voluntary disciples *did* pursue their goals in the United States. It cannot be questioned that Elizabeth Bentley and Whittaker Chambers and Klaus Fuchs and a handful of others like them were genuine spies; that the Communist Party, U.S.A. and some of its organizational spin-offs were creatures of the Comintern; that some unions of the fledgling CIO, the directorate of Henry Wallace's Progressive party, a number of "peace" and cultural associations, for example, were influenced in greater or lesser degree by

Communist doctrine. The roots of this apostasy went back, in most instances, to the suffering and anxiety of the Great Depression when it was not hard to believe that the Capitalist system faced collapse. The Communists who hoped to scuttle the system outright, however, were a tiny minority compared to the more orthodox reformers who wanted only to repair it and bring it up to date, although their rhetoric was sometimes confusingly similar. From the perspective of 30 years we know that hardcore communism never had either the numerical weight or the ideological clout in this country to threaten its security seriously. This was more patently true in the mid-forties than in the mid-thirties, but it suited the design of demagogues—always in abundant supply—to pretend otherwise. And they came on strong in the postwar years.

It was out of this miasma of fear and suspicion that the national preoccupation over subversion grew. This was not an occasional or isolated phenomenon; not just the sporadic bawlings of crackpots and alarmists and knee-jerk patriots. This was a mania, a mass neurosis, that infected in some degree every part of the country and every level of society; that intruded into the churches, the schools and universities, the arts and sciences, into business and social relationships. Most conspicuously of all, the political processes of the nation, from the county courthouse to the national capitol, were poisoned by it. From the mid-forties through the mid-fifties the obsession with communism and disloyalty persisted as a bleak and pervasive disfigurement of the American spirit.

There were a variety of focal points from which this infection spread. The American Legion was one, the Daughters of the American Revolution another; some elements in the hierarchy of the Catholic Church as well as some among the more conservative Protestant sects, the Hearst and the McCormick newspapers, and an array of individual and organizational sentinels who elected themselves to stand guard against the encroachments of ideological heresy. But the most powerful and proficient by far was the Un-American Activities Committee of the House of Representatives (HUAC). Armed with the authority of the United States Congress, with a stage for its performances of unmatched dimensions and visibility, and with most of the powers and few of the restraints of a court of law, HUAC became the nation's main tribunal for the exposure and punishment of subversion.

HUAC was set up in 1938 as a "special" (temporary) committee of the House at the behest of and under the chairmanship of Martin Dies, a bellicose, rough-and-tumble, small-town Congressman from eastern Texas. The national mood was ripe for Dies' style of evangelism at the time: Europe was convulsed by the preliminaries for World War Two. Fascist storm troopers on the one hand and Communist guerrillas on the other were harassing the cities of Central and Southern Europe and ravaging its political and industrial life. The reverberations of this convulsion leaped the Atlantic, spreading consternation across much of the United States. The country was predominantly isolationist, and in many quarters it had begun to turn against the liberal, leftward thrust of the New Deal. It wanted no part of Europe's troubles and no contamination from its "alien" ideologies. Political profit can be made in exacerbating such fears and Martin Dies had the raw talent and the native instinct to do just that. He quickly became the nation's Number One Dragon Slayer, slashing out at "un-American" influences wherever he suspected they might be, and he gained a large and fanatical following.

His first target was the German-American Bund and he asserted that there were no less than half a million Nazis and Nazi-sympathizers in the United States ready to do the Fuehrer's bidding. But he soon found Communists and Communist-sympathizers to be a wider and more inviting target. From then on he (and other chairmen who succeeded him after 1944) concentrated the Committee's fire on whatever liberal and left-wing groups and individuals they suspected might bear a Marxist taint. As the Committee's membership was overwhelmingly conservative and anti-New Deal, they used their license to go gunning at will through the Washington bureaucracy. One of their earliest trophies was the WPA Writers Project, which unquestionably had a sprinkling of Communists and fellow travelers on its rolls, as did numerous other federal agencies. What dangerous subversion they were carrying on was never conclusively shown but Dies and his cohorts raised such a furor over the case that Congress was persuaded to cut the Writers Project out of the 1940 appropriation act.

This was only one of scores of targets of convenience against which the Committee directed its fire, within and outside the government. Labor unions, particularly those of the newly-formed CIO (which was itself waging an internal struggle against Communist influence), were a favorite prey. So also, in the early years, were groups or individuals supporting the Loyalists in the Spanish civil war; those sponsoring U.S.–Soviet friendship; peace and antiwar advocates of all varieties; movements aimed at extending civil rights or social and cultural reform; writers, producers, and others in the creative arts whose expressions ventured beyond the banal and conventional.

No lead was so fragile, it seemed, no facade of innocence so persuasive, as to discourage the Committee from looking under the unlikeliest beds and into the remotest corners for the harborers of "un-American" beliefs. Its investigators, armed with subpoenas, indiscriminately scooped up membership lists, letterheads, and correspondence files and dumped them into the Committee's hungry maw. Volunteer witnesses were encouraged to appear either privately or in public hearings to make accusations, supported or otherwise. Hundreds of persons were summoned, like defendants in a trial, to be quizzed on their beliefs, their associations, their guilt or innocence of subversive tendencies. Subversiveness and un-Americanism were, of course, what the Committee said they were, and guilt-by-inference—as, for example, one's name on the mailing list of a left-wing periodical—was freely dispensed.

In 1944 the Committee published a bulky report listing the names of approximately 22,000 persons and organizations whom it adjudged to be subversive. Some unquestionably were insofar as membership in or strong sympathy for communism was an acceptable criterion. But for the vast majority guilt consisted of nothing more substantial than advocacy of liberal or unorthodox causes; the presence of their name, by consent or otherwise, on a mailing list or letterhead; or the misfortune of being identified as subversive by one of the Committee's array of witnesses and informants. Only a relative handful of those whose reputations and loyalty were thus impugned were ever given an opportunity to deny the charges or to face their accusers. To have been "cited" by the HUAC as a person of dubious patriotic virtue was, for the Committee and its widening army of supporters, prima facie evidence of guilt. While this massive "Red Index" was technically withdrawn a few months after publication, hundreds of copies remained in circulation and a number of digests and extracts from it were printed and published under private labels. And for well over a decade it was used as a sort of standard litmus test for the civic purity and the employability of thousands of government workers, school teachers, entertainers, and even Hollywood script writers.

The Committee went into partial eclipse during the height of the war. Communist Russia was an ally, and other agencies like the FBI held prime responsibility for guarding the nation against such subversives as spies and saboteurs. But with peace, HUAC came roaring back to life, strengthened with new status as a "standing" rather than a "special" committee and with generous allocations of congressional funds. From 1946 onward its aggressiveness and its influence ballooned. For a few years it wielded more hard political clout than any committee of Congress. The Russians were suddenly our mortal enemies again, threatening war, spreading Communist "poison" across the globe. Here at home we were beset with turmoil and strife of alarming virulence and it was easy to believe that that same Communist "poison" had entered our national bloodstream. A vast and chilling conspiracy could be envisioned, if you were so minded, that spread downward from disciples of the New Deal still in power in the Washington bureaucracy and outward to embrace great patches of society from organized labor to organized religion and no telling how many unattached "dupes and fellow travelers." And then in 1947 came Whittaker Chambers and Elizabeth Bentley in a prolonged and agonized public confessional to put the seal of probability on these dark forebodings. Belief in the Red Menace became an article of faith for millions of Americans, and they acclaimed HUAC as its most fearless exorcist.

This obsession with Communist subversion spread far and wide. A number of state governments set up their own "little HUACs" to guard the purity of their statehouse establishments. In scores of communities public or private inquisitors set out to purge school books and public libraries of "un-American doctrines." School boards and university regents hired and fired teachers on the basis of their professions of anti-Communist zeal. Hollywood and the radio industry blacklisted writers and actors whose affiliations—real or alleged—made them "controversial." Liberal spokesmen in many fields were locally harassed and sometimes ostracized. Federal agencies like the Department of State and the Department of Labor nervously and secretly dropped from their payrolls dozens of employees whose continued presence, they feared, might invite the wrath of the HUAC and its powerful political alliance. The exposure of this practice by a prominent Washington newspaperman, Bert Andrews, in a book called *Washington Witch Hunt* proved to be a double-barreled sensation: It drew cries of protest from civil libertarians, and demands for even sterner vigilance from the Right.

When President Truman sought to damp down this spreading hysteria he and his administration were accused of being "soft on Communism." That theme dominated the Republican campaign in the midterm elections of 1946. They promised that a Republican Congress would "clean house" in Washington and pass tough laws not only to keep Communists and other disloyal elements out of the government but possibly to put them in prison as well. The Republicans did win control of Congress that year, for the first time since 1931, leaving no doubt they intended to fulfill their pledge when the new session began in January 1947.*

The President moved to head off this threat shortly after the election and while Congress was in recess. He set up a Presidential Commission on Employee Loyalty to review the existing and generally haphazard procedures that had been installed in most government departments during wartime and to devise a new, uniform system that would protect individual rights as well as the national security. The Commission's report was submitted in March 1947, and the President promptly issued an executive order based upon it creating a permanent Federal Employee

---

* An obscure winner that year, destined to become more notable later on, was Richard M. Nixon. Just out of naval uniform, he ran for Congress from the 12th District of California (Los Angeles), defeating fifth-term Democrat Jerry Voorhis by a comfortable margin. Voorhis was one of the few liberals on HUAC, where his dissent was totally ineffectual, and Nixon succeeded to his Committee seat but not to his dissenter's role.

Loyalty Program. This was a milestone of sorts in the life of the nation, almost certainly an inevitable one, but it is not one upon which many will look back today with pride or satisfaction. In many instances it gave legal sanction to what was, indeed, a witch hunt.

The loyalty program was vast in magnitude and complex in execution. It called for the FBI to make a "name check" on each of the more than two million persons already on the federal payroll, from letter carriers to Cabinet officers, and of the approximately 500,000 who would apply for jobs each year. Wherever any "derogatory information" (a term steeped in ambiguity) about the loyalty of an individual was found, a "full field investigation" was to be conducted, which meant probing into his past life and associations sometimes even further back than high school. The substance of these investigations was then transmitted to the loyalty board in the agency where the individual worked or sought a job. The board's discretion was sufficient to throw out the charges or call the accused before it for a hearing. If the board's verdict after such a hearing was adverse (job applicants were rarely accorded a hearing, they just weren't hired if any question had been raised about them), the employee could appeal first to a regional loyalty board and finally to the Loyalty Review Board in Washington. This was the court of ultimate jurisdiction, and if it said the employee had to go, that was the end of it.

For all its structured safeguards the system contained some very hazardous boobytraps. The criterion for an adverse finding was the semantically vulnerable phrase, "reasonable grounds exist for belief that [the person involved] is disloyal." * This was a reverse of the accepted legal concept wherein "reasonable doubt" supports the *innocence* of an accused person rather than his *guilt*. The effect in a loyalty proceeding, therefore, was to put the burden of proof on the defendant rather than upon the prosecutor. The "court" proceeded from a presumption of guilt and required that the accused disprove its bias.

An even more difficult obstacle to justice for the accused in these proceedings was that rarely was he permitted to confront and cross-examine those who had given evidence against him. In almost every instance this evidence was second-hand and hearsay, supplied to the loyalty boards in the form of memoranda and documents by the FBI. The informants were anonymous and unsworn, their reliability untested beyond the verbal warranty of the FBI.

A not untypical case was that of Dorothy Bailey, forty-one years old and a graduate of the University of Minnesota and Bryn Mawr, who in March 1948, was branded as disloyal to the United States and fired from

---

* This language was altered in 1951 to "reasonable doubt as to the loyalty of . . . etc.", which was a measurable improvement.

her job in the United States Employment Service where she had worked for nearly 15 years. She was dismissed on the basis of anonymous reports to the Civil Service Commission that she was, or had been, a member of the Communist party and had "associated on numerous occasions with known Communist party members." Her case was heard by the regional Loyalty Board for the District of Columbia, which questioned her not only about the formal accusations but about her activities as president of her local of the United Public Workers of America, a labor union. She was confronted with no evidence beyond a summary of the reports of the anonymous informants, nor did any witnesses appear against her. She denied the charges of Communist affiliation and produced a number of character witnesses in her own behalf. The regional Loyalty Board, nevertheless, confirmed her dismissal and she appealed to the Loyalty Review Board, the ultimate tribunal in such cases.

When her case came before this board, Miss Bailey's counsel, Paul A. Porter, argued that the charges must have originated out of malicious gossip arising from an interunion power struggle in which his client had been involved. The board chairman, Seth Richardson, replied that "five or six of the reports come from informants certified to us by the Federal Bureau of Investigation as experienced and entirely reliable." He refused to identify them further, saying: "I haven't the slightest knowledge as to who they are or how active they have been in anything."

Further along in the inquiry this colloquy occurred between members of the board and Miss Bailey and her counsel:

Board Member: Then another one says it first came to the informant's attention about 1936, at which time [you were] a known member of the so-called "closed group" of the Communist party operating in the District of Columbia.

Miss Bailey: First of all, I don't know, or didn't know that there is a "closed group." The terminology is unfamiliar to me. I can say under oath and with the strongest conviction that I was not then and have never been a member of the Communist party.

Board Member: Here is another that says you were a member of the Communist party, and he bases his statement on his knowledge of your association with known Communists for the past seven or eight years. That is part of the evidence submitted to us.

Mr. Porter: It is part of the allegations. I don't think that can be considered evidence.

Chairman: It is evidence.

Mr. Porter: We renew our request, although we recognize the futility of it, that some identification of this malicious gossip be given this respondent or her counsel.

Chairman: Of course, that doesn't help us a bit. If this testimony is true, it is neither gossip nor malicious. We are under the difficulty of not being able to disclose this.

Mr. Porter: Is it under oath?

Chairman: I don't think so.

Board Member: It is a person of known responsibility who has proffered information concerning Communist activity in the District of Columbia.

Miss Bailey: You see, that point in it worries me, because if I am convicted here that will make this person who has made these charges a reliable witness; and they are not because the charges are not true, and whatever is said here should not add to their reliability.

Dorothy Bailey took her case to the Supreme Court, contending that she had been deprived of her good name and livelihood without due process of law. The Loyalty Board's verdict against her was sustained on April 30, 1951, in a tortured, inconclusive four-to-four per curiam opinion of the Court which Justice Robert H. Jackson bitterly described as "justice turned bottom side up."

For a full decade after 1947 the loyalty program was a conspicuous feature of the political landscape. It was under almost continuous attack from both the right and the left, alternately denounced and defended in countless editorials, speeches, and congressional debates. Its own security system was regularly breached and its supposedly secret interrogations and findings leaked freely to the outside world and to Capitol Hill in particular. It spread a pall of fear through the ranks of the federal bureaucracy, from file clerks to bureau chiefs. For one never knew what his loyalty board "had" on him, or who among his colleagues might be an informer. Merely to have been questioned by a security officer was enough, in many instances, to put a person under suspicion and to have his neighbors shun him. Scores of reputations were shattered.

By the end of 1952, when the Truman program was superseded by a harsher one devised by the incoming Eisenhower administration, over 4,750,000 persons had had their loyalty scrutinized by "name checks." Of these, 26,236 were referred for consideration by loyalty boards. And of these, 560 were either dismissed or denied employment because of "adverse findings," as in the case of Dorothy Bailey. How grave a risk were these 560—a fractional percentage of the whole—to the national security? Chairman Richardson suggested the answer when he told a Senate Committee in 1950: "Not one single case or evidence directing toward a case of espionage has been disclosed in the record."

But as the decade of the forties ended the national mania over subversion and disloyalty was gathering, not less, but stronger impetus.[3]

IV

The agitation over subversion during the decade came to a climax in 1949 in the Alger Hiss affair. In the perspective of 25 years it can safely be said that no conflict in this century over one man's veracity, no probing into the dark labyrinths of treason and espionage, has so roiled the emotions of the populace as this. On and off for the better part of a year the unfolding story decorated the news and editorial columns of the nation's press; it was an inescapable topic of disputation at country clubs and neighborhood taverns; it split up old friendships and forged new ones. It was an intensely personal drama, set against a backdrop of international intrigue, and orchestrated in almost perfect counterpoint to the nation's prevailing mood of anxiety and suspicion. It bore many resemblances to the case of Captain Alfred Dreyfus which had rocked France and much of the western world around the turn of the century; and like that case, the final resolution of the Hiss affair would leave a bitterly partisan after-taste for many years to come.

Alger Hiss was a most implausible character to be cast in the role of a traitor. Born of a genteel family in Baltimore, he was a Phi Beta Kappa graduate of Johns Hopkins and had a law degree from Harvard, class of 1929. There he had been a protege of Professor Felix Frankfurter. Later he was a law clerk of Supreme Court Justice Oliver Wendell Holmes, and then joined a distinguished New York law firm. He entered the State Department in a minor capacity in 1936 but rose through the ranks to become an adviser to President Roosevelt at Yalta, executive secretary for the Dumbarton Oaks conference, and a top-level functionary of the U.S. delegation at the United Nations Charter Conference in San Francisco. In 1946 he left government to accept the prestigious post of president of the Carnegie Endowment for International Peace. He was forty-four years old in 1949.

Alger Hiss was tall and spare, with intense gray eyes and crinkly dark hair. His manner was cool, restrained, and markedly self-assured. He was the archetype of the well-born Ivy Leaguer who knows where he is and where he's going. He and his wife, Priscilla, and their young son lived comfortably but modestly in Georgetown, attended the Episcopal church, were listed in the Washington *Social Register,* and were accorded the friendly deference that went with his standing as one of the more prominent "bright young men" of the New Deal. In almost every respect he was a symbol of the liberal-intellectual establishment that had achieved eminence during the Roosevelt era.

Hiss' name was among those along with Harry Dexter White's made known to President Truman by the FBI in early 1947. He was one of more than a score of current and former employees of the government whom Elizabeth Bentley and Whittaker Chambers charged before the New York grand jury with aiding them in their espionage operation. It was not until August of the following year, however, that his name surfaced publicly at an open hearing of HUAC, with Chambers on the stand.

Whittaker Chambers was a short, plump, disheveled man of forty-seven, hesitant in speech and manner. He was a Philadelphia Quaker by birth, had studied journalism at Columbia, joined the Communist party in 1924, and become for a time editor of the *Daily Worker,* the official party newspaper. From about 1930 to 1938, he told the Committee, he had engaged in underground work for the Party, principally in Washington. In the latter year, however, in great anguish of spirit and deadly fear of physical harm, he broke with the Communists and sought to make a new life for himself. A few years later he joined the staff of *Time* magazine and became one of its stable of senior editors.

Chambers and Miss Bentley, it turned out, had not known one another in the Communist underground although their missions had run parallel. His service covered the prewar years only, hers extended into the war years, after which she, too, broke away from the Party. Their joint testimony before the Committee was given over a number of days in the late summer of 1948 before a packed, expectant audience in a large hearing room of the old House Office Building. Though their stories were often rambling and inconclusive, the impact of their disclosures was sensational. For here at last, it seemed, was evidence at first hand that a Communist "fifth column" had, indeed, penetrated the government and probably was still lodged there. Each of them, they said, had manipulated separate, well-insulated "cells" in Washington from which they collected documents and other intelligence data to be turned over to their Russian "controls" in New York. And the identities of their contacts—John Abt of the Agricultural Adjustment Administration; Lee Pressman and Nathan Witt of the National Labor Relations Board; Gregory Silvermaster of Treasury; William Remington of the Commerce Department; Lauchlin Curry of the State Department; Harry Dexter White, and others—were written boldly into the public record and displayed in the press.

It was at an open hearing of the Committee on August 3 that Chambers made his first public accusation against Hiss. Sitting hunched at the witness table he droned through a recitation of his career and ultimate break with the Communist party. "For a number of years," he said, "I had myself served in the underground, chiefly in Washington, D.C. . . . I knew it at its top level, a group of seven or so men. . . . A member of this group was Alger Hiss." He went on to say that the immediate aim of this group was "infiltration" of the government at its upper levels but that espionage was an "ultimate objective." Hiss, he said, was an active participant in all these operations.

Most of the two dozen or more persons named in the Bentley–Chambers testimony chose initially, either through caution or contempt, to ignore the allegations. Hiss did not. From his office at the Carnegie Foundation in New York he sent off an angry telegram to the Committee the next day demanding an opportunity to appear "formally and under oath" to refute the charge Chambers had made against him. Two days later he was on the witness stand, coldly indignant but self-possessed.

"I am not and have never been a member of the Communist party," he said with measured emphasis. "I do not and have not adhered to the tenets of the Communist party. . . . To the best of my knowledge I never heard of Whittaker Chambers until 1947, when two representatives of the Federal Bureau of Investigation asked me if I knew him. . . . So far as I know I have never laid eyes on him, and I should like to have the opportunity to do so."

In the fortnight following, Hiss appeared at two other Committee sessions; both were "closed" but their substance, as usual, was promptly leaked to the press. The questioning, lead chiefly by Representative Richard M. Nixon, was aimed at weakening Hiss' denial that he had known Chambers a dozen or so years earlier. They pressed him with scraps of intimate information about himself and about the Hiss household, which Chambers claimed to have acquired during what he described as a fairly intimate relationship running from 1934 to 1938. He had lived briefly in the Hiss' Georgetown house, he said; had subleased an apartment from them; had been given a decrepit old Model T Ford when the family bought a new car; knew the nicknames by which they called one another; and much more in similar vein.

Hiss' rebuttal was that possibly Chambers was a man whom he had known during the depression years as George Crosley. This Crosley, he said, was a destitute free-lance writer whom he had briefly befriended and tried to help prepare a series of magazine articles on the work of a Senate investigating committee with which he, Hiss, was then connected. If Crosley was also a Communist agent, Hiss said he was never aware of it. He did become aware that Crosley was a deadbeat and a nuisance and soon broke off the relationship. But of none of this, he insisted to his interrogators, could he be certain unless he could confront Crosley/Chambers in person. And again he demanded such a confrontation.

That demand was granted in dramatic fashion a few days later. Mr. Nixon and two other members of the Committee invoked a secret evening session of HUAC in a guarded suite of the Commodore Hotel in New York City. Hiss was brought in, and then Chambers.

"Have you ever known this man before?" the chairman asked Hiss.

Hiss studied the face for a moment and then said, "May I ask him to speak?"

"My name is Whittaker Chambers. I am a senior editor of *Time* magazine."

"I think this is George Crosley," Hiss responded, "but I would like to hear him talk a little longer."

There followed a brief colloquy in which Chambers repeated some of the allegations that he had previously laid before the Committee. Hiss, his anger showing, said he was now certain that this was the man he had known as George Crosley. Rising, with a menacing gesture toward his antagonist, he said:

"May I say for the record at this point that I would like to invite Mr. Whittaker Chambers to make those same statements out of the presence of this Committee without its being privileged against suit for libel? I challenge you to do it, and I hope you will do it damned quickly."

That was a fatal blunder for Alger Hiss, as will shortly be shown. The confrontation at the Commodore, from the Committee's viewpoint, had been disappointing. Now they concluded that they could not make a valid case of espionage against Hiss or any of the others whose names had been tossed up in the Bentley–Chambers revelations. The steam had gone out of their highly touted exposé and, in resignation, they prepared to turn their files over to the Department of Justice where the matter faced almost certain interment and oblivion.

But Hiss, by his impulsive challenge to Chambers, had pushed his luck too far. On Sunday, August 30, Whittaker Chambers was interviewed on "Meet the Press," a nationwide radio program. In response to a question from one of the panelists, he said in a low but firm voice: "Alger Hiss was a Communist and may still be one." Hiss promptly brought suit for slander against him, asking $75,000 damages.

And now, for the first time, hard evidence that espionage had been involved at some point in this murky drama came to light. At a pretrial hearing in Baltimore in November Chambers produced a faded manila envelope stuffed with cables and memoranda unequivocally drawn from State Department files which he swore Hiss had turned over to him for transmission to the Russians in 1937 and 1938. A few days later he led investigators to a kitchen garden behind his Maryland farm home and there extracted from a hollowed-out pumpkin three rolls of undeveloped microfilm on which still more official documents were recorded.

These disclosures caused not only a newspaper sensation; they caused the New York grand jury, which had originally questioned Hiss back in 1947, to reopen its inquiry in respect to his testimony. With the Chambers documents before them, the grand jurors on December 16, 1948, indicted Alger Hiss on two charges of perjury: (1) denying that he had passed State Department papers to Chambers, and (2) denying that he had seen or had any contact with Chambers after 1937. Espionage was not mentioned in the indictment: The three-year statute of limitations on such an offense had long since run out.* But the *implication* of espionage, of treasonous duplicity, was stridently clear.

---

* It is worth noting that none of those implicated in the Bentley–Chambers testimony before the grand jury in 1946 and 1947 were indicated either for espionage or any lesser offense. While the statute of limitations in respect to espionage was applicable to all of those named by Chambers, Hiss included, it did not apply to many of those named by Miss Bentley. Espionage in wartime, which was the period

Dismay over this startling development reverberated across the country. Was Alger Hiss a Communist spy, the visible link in an invisible web of subversion that spread through the government? Or was he the victim of a plot born in a diseased and malevolent mind?

People tended to answer those questions according to some inner social and moral orientation; according to what they most wanted to believe. The evidence of guilt was formidable. But the evidence wasn't all in yet.

Liberals and intellectuals in general rallied to Hiss' defense: He was one of their own. President Truman had branded the Committee hearings at which Hiss was first accused as "a red herring"—not once but twice. Dean Acheson, the Secretary of State, said solemnly after the indictment, "I will not turn my back on Alger Hiss." Prominent members of the academic community and many editorialists and columnists expressed their confidence in him outright, or did it obliquely through denigration of the forces aligned against him. Among the score of character witnesses who volunteered to testify in his behalf, and who did so at his trial later, were Justices Frankfurter and Stanley Reed of the Supreme Court; Charles Fahey, former U.S. Solicitor General; Governor Adlai Stevenson of Illinois, and Rear Admiral A. J. Hepburn. A man of Alger Hiss' intelligence, background and public stature, many people reasoned, simply *couldn't* be a traitor to his country.

But there were others, a great many more indeed, who thought he could be and probably was all that the HUAC and Whittaker Chambers said he was. For three years all that they read in their newspapers had conditioned them to believe the worst of the Russians, to regard the worldwide Communist conspiracy as a clear and present danger to the peace of the world. The Red tide was ravaging the political underpinnings of wartorn Europe, encircled Berlin was being kept alive by an American airlift, and in China the Communists were pushing Chiang Kai-shek into the sea. And just as clearly, it was reasoned, the Communists were at work right here at home, "boring from within" to pull down the government of the United States. Even as the Hiss scandal moved toward a climax, 12 leaders of the American Communist party went on trial in New York charged with conspiracy to overthrow the government; Judith Coplan, a minor official of the Justice Department, allegedly was caught by the FBI handing over secret documents to a Russian agent; powerful unions of the CIO were locked in a highly publicized struggle to free themselves of Communist control; and almost daily there were fresh symptoms of treachery

---

covered in her testimony, is not protected under the three-year limit. The failure of the grand jury to bring indictments, or adverse findings of any kind, after so long an inquiry, led many persons to conclude that the evidence offered by Miss Bentley and Mr. Chambers was weak and possibly tainted by neurotic motivations. Both appeared to have disturbed, unstable personalities.

emanating from the loyalty boards, HUAC, and other like sources. "Spy jitters," the *New York Times* noted in an editorial in the summer of 1949, afflicted the entire nation to an extent not matched since the aftermath of the First World War. During a single week in June, it added, "spy stories" of one sort of another occupied 32 percent of the combined front page space of the New York dailies. And in September there would come the stunning disclosure that the Russians had perfected an A-bomb of their own.

In this widespread mood of anxiety and doubt it was not hard to prejudge the guilt of Alger Hiss—or of anyone else at whom the finger of suspicion might be pointed.

There was a strong political connotation in all of this in which the Hiss case acted as a sort of constant in an ideological equation. How you felt about Hiss determined, in a relative sense, where you stood in the political spectrum, and you gave and took your lumps accordingly in the endless and often heated arguments over the issue. Conservative partisans, Republicans and Democrats alike, found it useful by extrapolation to extend Hiss' culpability to liberals in general and to New Dealers in particular, to detect subversive intent—or dangerous gullibility at the least—in any deviation from right wing orthodoxy. Republican politicians for their part, still smarting from the humiliating defeat handed them by Truman Democrats in 1948, cultivated this schism assiduously in the reasonable belief that it would make a winning issue for them in the midterm elections of 1950 and the Presidential election two years beyond that. They would, they promised, turn back the whole liberal-leftward-Communistic drift that had endured from Roosevelt's days to Truman's and now had reached flood stage.

Thus, Alger Hiss became more than just a solitary supplicant standing at the bar of justice: He was the symbol of an intense ideological and political conflict that divided the nation.

Hiss went on trial in U.S. District Court in New York City on May 31, 1949, Judge Samuel H. Kaufman presiding. His chief defense counsel was Lloyd Paul Stryker, an imposing figure with closely cropped gray hair, florid complexion, a bagful of dramatic mannerisms, and a reputation as one of the city's most effective trial lawyers. Thomas F. Murphy, the Assistant U.S. District Attorney who led the prosecution team, was in many visible respects Stryker's opposite. He was more than six feet tall and massively built, wore a heavy black mustache, and was sedate in manner but with the relentless, unflappable perseverance of a determined tortoise. The paneled courtroom was of modest dimensions with only 60 seats for the several hundred spectators who clamored and jostled each day to gain admittance, and the 50-odd reporters who showed up daily were jammed elbow-to-elbow at two long press tables. The jury was a fair cross-section of the working men and women of Manhattan, including a couple of housewives. A focal point of interest to many in this crowded setting was Priscilla Hiss, a prim, sad-eyed little woman, who occupied a chair next to her husband's throughout the proceedings.

It required almost two weeks for Murphy to lay out his case for the state. He led Chambers through his now familiar narrative of his relations with Hiss, but buttressed it strongly with the introduction of actual documents and memoranda from State Department files—47 items in all—which he said came to him from Hiss and bearing dates as late at 1938. He recounted conversations and incidents involving Communist activities with the Hisses, and told of an anguished, tearful parting in the spring of 1938 when he pled with them to follow his example and break with the party. Murphy called some 30 witnesses to corroborate various facets of Chambers' testimony, most of it to authenticate the genuineness of the exhibits offered but some of it supporting his contention that Hiss was a Communist—if not by membership, at least by conviction.

Stryker took an equal amount of time to lead Hiss through his rebuttal of this testimony. In substance it was what he had said earlier about his relationship with "George Crosley," but in greater detail. He did not deny that the exhibits offered by the prosecution were genuine originals or copies of State Department papers; some of the scribbled memoranda were even in his own handwriting, he said. But he insisted that he had never given or shown them to Chambers; that Chambers must have obtained them from someone else. Most of the papers in evidence, he pointed out, were of the noncritical sort that circulated fairly widely within the Department, but he had no idea where along the line the leak might have been—perhaps some clerk or surreptitious visitor. It furthermore would have been impossible, he said, for him to have given his accuser anything dated in 1937 or 1938, for he had had no contact with the man after the end of 1936. He denied emphatically, of course, that he had ever been either a Communist or a sympathizer, and some two score witnesses gave impressive testimony of their faith in the good character and truthfulness of Alger Hiss.

Cross-examination and other courtroom maneuvers occupied another fortnight and it was during this phase of the the trial that public interest in this real-life drama reached new heights of suspense and fascination. Stryker and Murphy played out their contrasting roles with theatrical finesse, but neither succeeded markedly in shaking the testimony of the two principals. Of these two, Hiss appeared to observers to be making the more favorable impression on the impassive jurors. His manner on the witness stand was alert, self-assured, positive, and the presence of his demure wife at his side evoked a sympathetic response. Chambers, on the other hand, was lethargic and sullen and was described by one reporter as resembling "a person acting under hypnosis." Both men held doggedly, however, to the essentials of their wildly conflicting stories and avoided the legalistic and semantic snares laid for them by the lawyers. For days during this period many large newspapers around the country carried columns of verbatim "Q" and "A" text as it was fed to them from the courtroom, so intense was the public appetite for any shred of news about this epic spectacle.

The end came at last, a deflated, inconclusive climax that left all the main questions unanswered. After six weeks of testimony and impassioned argument, of such sustained tension as had rarely been engendered in a court of law, the case went to the jury on the afternoon of Wednesday, July 6. Two days later, after 29 hours of exhausting and often angry deliberation, the jurors informed the judge that they could not reach a verdict. The last concession had been made, the last doubt among them resolved. They were split eight to four for conviction. The case of *The United States vs Alger Hiss* would have to be retried.

Partisans on neither side of this controversy appeared in the end to have been shaken in their preconceived notions of where truth and justice rested. They were back where they started when the trial began. The nearest thing to a public consensus arising out of the six-week ordeal was: "One or the other of these men—Hiss or Chambers—is a monumental liar."

The second trial got under way on November 17. There were a few changes in the cast of characters—Judge Henry W. Goddard was now on the bench and Claude B. Cross had replaced Lloyd Stryker as defense counsel—but the script was largely repetitious of what had gone before. There were few fresh faces and few new exhibits to be displayed. Public interest in the case subsided from the emotional peak it had reached in the summer, only to be revived momentarily when the trial reached its conclusion on January 21, 1950.

There was no hung jury this time. Hiss was found guilty on both charges of perjury in the indictment and sentenced by Judge Goddard to five years imprisonment and a fine of $10,000. Hiss' lawyers made the expected appeal to the Supreme Court but that body decided unanimously (Justices Frankfurter, Reed, and Clark abstaining) not to intervene in the lower court's decision. On March 22 Alger Hiss, visibly aged and wasted by his long ordeal, entered the federal prison at Lewisburg, Pennsylvania.

The faith of many of the thousands who had believed in Hiss' innocence was unshaken by the verdict against him: The most generous explanation they could come up with was that somehow, somewhere, there had been a deplorable miscarriage of justice. For a few, at least, this belief translated itself into a quiet crusade to dredge up, from whatever source, conclusive proof of his innocence.* But a projected reopening of the case in 1951 with some "new evidence" of uncertain merit never got off the ground. The dubious mantle of martyrdom was about the only benefaction these faithful ones could bestow upon their hero.

If there was jubilation over the outcome by the other side it was kept within discreet bounds. *Time* magazine, which had steadfastly supported the position of its former senior editor, observed: "A brilliant but weak man had proved unworthy of the trust placed in him. A fine talent had been put out to doing evil. . . . A man who, once having served an alien master, lacked the courage to retract his past."

Cheers would have been superfluous in any event: The Right had won a resounding ideological and political victory the appearance of which, if not its substance, could not be denied. Communists threatened the government, the American way of life, wearing the deceptive garb of liberalism. The proof was in: On with the purge! . . . Now, for a generation to come, the name of Alger Hiss would be synonymous with treason.[4]

---

* This was one of the most written-about trials of the mid-century with at least a dozen book titles either pro or con appearing over a span of five years. Nor was interest in the case confined to this country. Many foreign journals covered the case closely and two noteworthy books about it, generally favorable to Hiss, were written by Englishmen: *The Strange Case of Alger Hiss,* by Lord Jowitt, a former Lord Chancellor and Attorney General of Great Britain, and *A Generation on Trial* by Alistair Cooke, a prominent British journalist. As evidence of the lingering concern over Hiss' fate, this writer (who had touched on the case in a previous book) was the recipient as late as 1970 of several letters from a lady in London who apparently had dedicated herself to the task of running down every lead that might yield evidence of Hiss' innocence. (I don't know how she came out.)

13

Epilogue: Never the Same Again

THE FORTIES: DECADE OF TRIUMPH AND TROUBLE. Yes, certainly. But perhaps a more accurate label would be "the transition decade." Because this was the period in which we bridged the gap between a remembered past and the historical present; between "old" times and "modern" times. Obviously each surveyor uses his own calculus to measure such distances: there are no firm benchmarks to go by. But it can be argued, I believe, that in the nineteen-seventies we are living in a well-defined continuum that grew directly out of the social and economic upheaval of World War II, and that what went before is obsolete and irrelevant.

The "old order" drew its substance and flavor from the victorian-capitalistic-nationalistic concepts of the first third of this century. These began to crumble under the economic and intellectual impact of the Great Depression. Their destruction was completed in part by the war itself and in part by the social and technological revolution that erupted from it. By the end of the war decade we had acquired a totally new concept of our national stance in the world and a greatly enlarged concept of the individual's place in society—of his independence, of his prerogatives, of his material expectations. The old dieties, the old values, the old pecking order went into the discard, and new ones—whether for good or ill—took their place. Thus the "new order" was shaped in a more pragmatic, more democratic mould that imparts a distinctive coloration to today's pattern of life.

During the forties the nation grew in almost every dimension. The population in 1950 was 150.6 million, an increase of 14.5 percent over 1940. Historically it was a modest increase that reflected the sharp drop in the birth rate that occurred during the depression years of the 1930s and early 1940s. But that trend was abruptly reversed as the war drew to an end. There was a bumper crop of "war babies" during the latter part of the decade, and we—and the rest of the world—were on the way to what we have since called the population explosion. There was a

378

dramatic and lasting shift in population as well, mainly a tidal surge westward. The lure of the war industries that mushroomed along the Pacific coast and the incantations of its chambers of commerce and real estate developers drew emigrants by the hundreds of thousands from inland America. The eleven states of the western region registered a growth of over 40 percent between 1940 and 1950, more than three times that of the rest of the country. And California, the inevitable bellwether in such matters, more than doubled its population and leaped into second rank among all the states. It now ranks first. Meanwhile, the long-time trend from country to city living was intensified all across the map with the 174 "standard metropolitan areas" of the Census Bureau showing an unprecedented gain of 22 percent during the period. Most cities that were jammed to the gates during the war-time boom pretty much stayed that way in the post-war boom—Dallas from 399,000 in 1940 to 615,000 in 1950; Denver from 408,000 to 564,000; Newport News–Hampton, Va., from 85,000 to 143,000; Los Angeles–Long Beach from 2.9 million to 4.3 million; Phoenix, Arizona, from 186,000 to 332,000; Washington, D.C., from 968,000 to 1.4 million, and more in like manner. Here was the tinder that, in due course, would fuel a massive flight to the suburbs and lead eventually to the now-familiar disease of urban decay.

Statistics of the period afford almost endless examples of the phenomenal rate of growth during the decade. The gross national product—GNP, a handy measure of the nation's total economic clout—went from a bare $100 billion in 1940 to $285 billion in 1950 to $391 billion in 1955 and has not since slackened in its march toward the trillion dollar level. The size and cost of government has kept pace: The federal bureaucracy had just over a million civilian employees in 1940 with a payroll of $1.8 billion; in 1950 there were just over two million workers and a payroll of $6.9 billion. That trend has not slacked off either. War costs boosted the national debt virtually out of sight for the average viewer, from $42.9 billion in 1940 to $257.3 billion in 1950, and it has hovered in and above that astronomical range ever since. Footing the bill—or a good part of it— were 14.5 million individuals paying $1.4 billion in personal income taxes in 1940 as compared with 52.6 million individuals paying $18.3 billion in 1950. Nor has that trend slackened: the per capita share of *all* Federal taxes collected in 1940 was just under $50, in 1970 it was close to $950. All of this was accompanied by a vast burgeoning of industrial activity, its momentum only minimally affected by the switch from a war-time to a peace-time footing. Electrical energy production, for example, went from 180 million kilowatt hours in 1940 to 389 million in 1950 to 629 million in 1955 and onward in perpetuity. In the 1970s we measure that output in *trillions* of kilowatt hours. Similarly, automobile registrations (in spite of a virtual shutdown in production during the war years) jumped 50 percent between 1940 and 1950 and doubled by 1955. Only a decade later, the vast proliferation of automobiles was to be condemned as a national health hazard by poisoning the atmosphere with their exhaust emissions.

We call our present epoch (among other less flattering terms) the "age of affluence." Practically, if not theoretically, it can be said to have begun in or around the year 1950. Before, our national concern was how to produce all we could consume; since, it is how to consume all we can produce. The old "economy of scarcity" has been replaced by the new "economy of abundance." But don't be misled by such simplistic definitions. The implications of this historic turn-about on the social and political climate of our times is enormous and it constantly engages the best brains among scholars and statesmen. It will have to suffice here, however, to deal with only a few of its more obvious manifestations.

Probably the most important cause-effect element in this syndrome is what is popularly called the technological explosion. (That word "explosion," by the way, seems to have replaced such gentler terms as "evolution" and "mutation" to describe the processes of change. There must be a reason.) The preeminent example in this category is, of course, the harnessing of atomic energy, an event of such magnitude that it fully warrants designation as an "age" all by itself. Its ramifications have spread into virtually every facet of our national life, cultural, scientific, political.

Of more widespread, everyday concern, however, has been the simultaneous eruption in the field of electronics. The science of electronics is, in a sense, making a small volume of electrical energy behave in a highly efficient and disciplined fashion. It is not a new science: Lee De Forest employed its principles in his radio experiments as far back as 1907. But its practical application in later decades was discouraged by the sheer bulk and complexity of the necessary equipment. (Do you remember what the guts of a 1940 "superheterodyne" parlor radio looked like? A dense cubic foot of machinery weighing around fifty pounds!) The breakthrough came in 1948 when (in a war-related contract at Bell Laboratories) the transistor was perfected which substituted coin-sized wafers for vacuum tubes and yards or miles of copper wire circuitry. From that point on electronics took off like a rocket—quite literally—and caused a quantum leap in the design and control of the pioneer ballistic missiles with which the Army was experimenting. It brought television out of the laboratories into the marketplace and ultimately into every living room in the land. It spawned a brand new industry that would grow in a couple of decades into the multi-billion-dollar bracket and flood the consumer market with a bewildering array of gadgetry and the industrial market with such miracles as automation and computers.

The world's first practical electronic high-speed computer was unveiled at the University of Pennsylvania on February 14, 1946. It was built almost from scratch by the engineering school under contract with the Army Ordnance Corps, which was faced with insuperable mathematical problems in plotting the trajectories of modern bombs and missiles. It was called ENIAC, which stood for Electronic Numerical Integrator and Calculator. Its 32 separate units stood nine feet high, occupied 1,800 square feet of floor space, weighed over 30 tons, and cost $487,000. Its miles of wiring and 18,000 vacuum tubes generated so much heat that special refrigerating machinery had to be installed to keep it from melting. But it could perform a wide range of mathematical functions a thousand times faster than any other calculator, human or mechanical, in existence (including the roughly similar Mark I introduced at Harvard a few months earlier). It was an instant marvel, a "mechanical brain" that some excited prophets said would push its biological counterpart into the discard. It never quite did that, of course, but it had a momentous and lasting impact in such fields as engineering, business, and education. The second generation of computers which came along in the early fifties, slimmed down and vastly improved in performance, were the forerunners of the now-commonplace contraptions that have taken over thousands of human functions from controlling the flow of hot gasses in oil refineries to preparing your monthly bank statement.

The editors of *Fortune* magazine, sensing the early rumblings of the technological revolution, wrote about it with prophetic foresight back in 1951. They said:

> But clearly foreshadowed in modern technology—as clearly as almost all of today's basic inventions were foreseen in the great awakening of science in seventeenth and eighteenth centuries—is an entirely new level of controls and energy. In the new high speed electronic calculating machines, industrial television, magnetic tape recorders and other components, are the means of achieving the completely automatic production or assembly line, as well as even more revolutionary automatic machines for taking over all the dull, routine tasks of government and business offices. Few minds have begun to apply themselves yet to the problems in such upheavals.

If "few minds" had begun to tackle the implications of automation in 1951, it was not long before they got around to it. So pervasive did this transformation become that, twenty years later, workers in some automobile plants were striking against the de-humanizing effects of the automated assembly line that reduced them to the status of robots.

Nor are automation and computerization the only end-products of the technological revolution. The war years saw the greatest conjunction of scientific energy and government money in all history. The Office of Scientific Research and Development corraled some 30,000 scientists and engineers and, with half a billion dollars to spend and the facilities of virtually every laboratory in the country at its disposal, gave them free rein. The primary emphasis, of course, was on war-related projects—aerodynamics, ballistics, telemetry, explosives, radar, the proximity fuse, etc. But out of that cornucopia of applied knowledge there also came an infinite variety of discoveries and techniques and adaptations that affected the way people lived rather than the way they died—medicines, disinfectants, plastics, synthetics, electronics, a whole catalogue of innovations great and small whose novelty has long since become commonplace. The war-time conjunction of science and government has persevered as a partnership of science and industry—as very big business indeed—and there probably are ten times as many scientists today in industrial jobs as there are in the universities. We live on such intimate terms with technology today that it has lost its power to surprise us.

Technology = Abundance = Affluence, or so at least goes one homespun formulation of the case. In any event we do live today in an "affluent society," as John Kenneth Galbraith has so ably demonstrated, and this is, he adds, an historically unique circumstance for any substantial segment of the human race. Today, he writes, "the ordinary individual (in the U.S.A. and most of Western Europe) has access to amenities—food, entertainment, personal transportation, plumbing—in which not even the rich rejoiced a century ago. So great has been the change that many of the desires of the individual are no longer even evident to him. They become so only as they are synthesized, elaborated, and nurtured by advertising and salesmanship, and these, in turn, have become among our most important and talented professions. Few people at the beginning of the nineteenth century needed an adman to tell them what they wanted."

Another eminent scholar, Andrew Hacker, states the case in a more relevant time frame, thus: "The span of a single generation [since World War II] has witnessed the emergence of a new American people. Lofted to new eminences by an exploding technology and stirred by the democratic spirit to new attitudes, tens of millions of quite ordinary individuals have undergone a transformation more profound than any the world has hitherto known. America is the first nation in history to have succeeded in bestowing material comfort and moral equality throughout that majority of a population."

Such heady pronouncements do not mean that Utopia has been reached or that poverty has vanished. What they do mean, and there is substantial evidence to back them up, is that in terms of relative well-being—relative to a generation ago, and relative class to class—the vast majority of people today enjoy a higher level of material gratification and of social participation than they have ever known before. There are still the very rich and the very poor at either end of the spectrum, but in between there is an enormously expanded and expanding middle class that is accustomed to living well beyond the reach of poverty—from "decently situated" to "comfortably well-off" might be the appropriate code words to define their condition.

From the onset of the Second World War and almost continuously since, this country has experienced an unparalleled rate of economic growth, a seemingly self-generating boom—rising employment, rising income, rising production, rising consumption. It has faltered and wavered occasionally, but its onward thrust has not seriously abated, and it has spewed money around with a profligate hand. The income of an average city family rose 32 percent between 1940 and 1955—from $3,663 to $4,826—but the rise for those in the lowest one-fifth of the income tables was almost double that rate, or 59 percent. The rich may be getting richer in this age of affluence (they are, in fact), but it doesn't follow that the poor are getting poorer. A number of years back government economists defined "poverty" as the status of a family of four living on an income of $2,000 or less (a level that has been raised several times to compensate for inflation). In 1960, when the yardstick was first used, it was determined that about 24 percent of all families were living below the "poverty line"; in 1970 that proportion had dropped to 15 percent. Looked at from a higher level on the scale, the $10,000 to $15,000 income bracket—which is a long way from "poor" but also a very long way from "rich"—the picture of a widening prosperity is strongly reinforced. Thus, in 1950 less than one-half of one percent of taxpayers fitted into that enviable bracket; ten years later the proportion had risen to 6 percent, and in another ten years—1970—it had reached almost 20 percent. About one in five of the working population today, then, can be said to be "comfortably well-off," which is a phenomenon that must baffle the ghosts of the old theoreticians from Adam Smith to Karl Marx to the latter-day prophets of the New Deal.

What has happened in this country in the last generation is that we have had a redistribution of wealth on a scale never witnessed before. Poverty remains a shameful blight on the most opulent society in the world, but there is some small satisfaction in knowing that it is diminishing rather than growing.

Generalizing from such data as this is a hazardous occupation, even for the experts. But I am persuaded that the most significant consequence in human terms of the changes we have been considering, is the democratization of American society, and that it is this quality that sets this present generation apart from all its predecessors; makes it, in fact, unique. Democratization is not used in a political or ideological sense but rather in the context of sharing on more or less equal terms in the common wealth and of a common acceptance of the ideal of individual dignity and independence. Today's dominant middle class, unlike that of the past, is not relegated to the periphery of power and influence; it sits at the center, or close enough to it not to feel disenfranchised. Nor does it look with servile and hopeless envy upon the perquisites of the upper class, the rich. The visible class lines have shrunk and become obscure, and they are transgressed with increasing frequency. A car, good clothes, comfortable housing, money enough for recreation and a few luxuries, maybe even for college—these are the common lot of the many today, not just of the few. All of which is a very far cry indeed from the world of the forties.

Does this mean, then, that we have won our way at last to the best of all possible worlds? In a material sense it does: Everybody has more of everything than they ever had before, most of us a great deal more. But in a spiritual and moral sense the answer is something else again: We seem to be beset with as many discontents and anxieties as ever, although their shape and content have changed. This is not the happiest of all possible worlds. Andrew Hacker (among a few other scholars) concludes, in fact, that American society is now approaching the brink of extinction; that it has run its ordained course of greatness and has exhausted its powers of regeneration. Such gloomy predictions can neither be proved or disproved nor can the comfortable assumption that somehow we will always find a way out of our troubles. But our record over the last third of a century is conducive more toward hope than despair.

Notes

CHAPTER 1—THE WAY IT WAS

1. This is a largely subjective rendering of what the year 1940 was like, and poets and historians alike will quarrel with its highlights and nuances. Be that as it may, my impressions and recollections have been abundantly supplemented from the files of the *New York Times* and a dozen other contemporary periodicals, and by samplings from a number of published memoirs, treatises, and other exegetical works touching on the period. Of particular value (in this and in several subsequent chapters as well) in recapturing the political and bureaucratic climate of the times was *The United States at War: Historical Reports on War Administration* (Government Printing Office, 1946). Prepared by the Bureau of the Budget, it is an abridgement and surprisingly candid critique of the final reports of most of the agencies involved and is intended as a guide to mobilization planners in a future emergency. A purview of the gathering world diplomatic crisis is provided (in part) in *Foreign Relations of the United States, 1940–1945,* prepared by the Department of State. Figures on the state of the national economy are from *Statistical Abstract of the United States, 1944–1945* (Dept. of Commerce, Washington).

CHAPTER 2—POLITICS NOT AS USUAL

In addition to contemporary news accounts of the 1940 election campaign, I have drawn substantially on the following books: *Roosevelt and Willkie,* by Warren Moscow (Prentice-Hall, 1968); *Jim Farley's Story,* by James A. Farley (McGraw Hill, 1948); *Willkie,* by Joseph Barnes (Simon and Schuster, 1952); *This I Remember,* by Eleanor Roosevelt (Harper & Row, 1949); *Working With Roosevelt,* by Samuel I. Rosenman (Harper & Row, 1952); *Roosevelt and Hopkins,* by Robert E. Sherwood (Harper & Row, 1948); *The United States in World Affairs—1940,* by the Foreign Policy Association.

1. The biographical material on Willkie and the build-up of his campaign for the nomination is drawn principally from the books by Moscow and Barnes, op. cit., and from articles by Dorothy D. Bromley in *Harper's* (October 1940),

and by Janet Flanner in *The New Yorker* (October 12, 1940). The observation by Arthur Krock is from his *Memoirs* (Funk and Wagnalls, 1968), p. 194.

2. This account of the Republican convention is based principally on contemporary press accounts, mainly from the *New York Times;* on relevant chapters in Moscow and Barnes, and on several interviews with my colleague, Arthur Krock. I did not attend either convention in 1940.

3. Historians and pundits of great eminence, including those listed above, have picked at the riddle of FDR's decision to seek a third term with conclusions no more profound than those I offer here. The quotations are from Farley, op. cit., p. 186, and Roosevelt, op. cit., p. 212. Mr. Corcoran's views were given the writer in an interview.

4. Press accounts of the Democratic convention, while important, are less illuminating than those of the Republican convention, since so much of the strategy at Chicago was hidden from view. Many of the details cited here have been pieced together from the retrospective accounts of Moscow, Rosenman, Sherwood, and Farley, cited above, and the personal recollections of Arthur Krock—who was as close as any newsman to what went on behind the scenes.

5. The Willkie and Roosevelt election campaigns are reconstructed here almost exclusively from such contemporary sources as the *New York Times,* the *New York Herald-Tribune, Time,* and *The New Republic,* with backup material from Moscow and Barnes, op. cit. The original of the "Martin, Barton, and Fish" incident cited is described in Rosenman, op cit., p. 240, and Willkie's reaction to it is from Sherwood, op. cit., p. 189.

CHAPTER 3—DAY OF INFAMY

As noted in the text, the account of the attack on Pearl Harbor with which this chapter begins is based on an article by the author published in the *New York Times Magazine,* 12/2/51, marking the tenth anniversary of the event. For the background of diplomatic and other events leading up to the rupture of relations between the United States and Japan, I have relied principally on Herbert Feis, *The Road to Pearl Harbor* (Princeton University Press, 1950); Walter Millis, *This Is Pearl* (Morrow, 1947); Cordell Hull, *Memoirs,* Vol. II (Macmillan, 1948); Harold U. Faulkner, *American Political and Social History* (Appleton-Century-Crofts, 1952). For the military and political impact of the event my principal sources, aside from the *New York Times,* have been Robert E. Sherwood, *Roosevelt and Hopkins* (Harper & Row, 1948); Winston S. Churchill, *The Grand Alliance* (Houghton Mifflin, 1951); John Toland, *But Not in Shame* (Random House, 1961). As indicated in the text, I have received valuable guidance at several points from Hanson W. Baldwin, former military editor of the *Times.*

1. The quote by Hull is from his *Memoirs,* pp. 1,069–70. The text of the Japanese cable is so quoted in Feis, p. 229, and the cabled warning to American commanders is from Millis, p. 350.

2. The excerpt from the Roberts report is from the *Times,* 1/28/42. The quote by Roosevelt is from Churchill, p. 593.

3. Excerpt from the President's address to Congress is from the *Times,*

12/9/41. The Sherwood quote is from Samuel I. Rosenman, *Working With Roosevelt* (Harper & Row, 1952), p. 310.

4. This summary of the war and the national mood in the immediate wake of Pearl Harbor is based principally on contemporary press reports and on "World War II—A Chronology," prepared by the College and School Service of the *New York Times* and published on July 12, 1950. The quote from Churchill is from Churchill, op. cit., p. 669.

CHAPTER 4—MOBILIZATION

A basic text for the study of civilian mobilization during the Second World War is *The United States at War: Historical Reports on War Administration,* prepared by the Bureau of the Budget and published by the Government Printing Office in 1946. It is an extended abridgement and critique (surprisingly candid in some respects) of the final reports of the major emergency war agencies. Its principal deficiency as a research tool is that it concentrates largely on the development and analysis of administrative procedures, and treats only sketchily the operational and political aspects of those agencies. To round out the picture of what went on and who did what, other sources, and particularly the contemporary news media, have been consulted, as indicated below.

1. *The United States at War*, op. cit., and contemporary files of the *New York Times*. Legislative history and background of the Selective Service Act is drawn mainly from *Editorial Research Reports* (Washington, D.C.), 1940, vol. II, p. 247 ff.

2. *The United States at War*, op. cit., chaps. 2–5; Eliot Janeway, *The Struggle for Survival: A Chronical of Economic Mobilization in World War II* (Yale University Press, 1951), chaps. III and IV; Bruce Catton, *War Lords of Washington* (Harcourt Brace, 1948), chaps. 2–4 and 9. For legislative and related actions see *Editorial Research Reports* (Washington, D.C.), 1941 vol. II, 1942 vols. I and II, under relevant headings in tables of contents. The Roosevelt press conference quote is from *The United States at War*, op. cit., p. 54.

3. Chapter 9 of *The United States at War*, op. cit., deals specifically with price controls, but there are many other references throughout the book relating to the fight against inflation. See also, Harvey C. Mansfield et al., *A Short History of OPA* (U.S. Government Printing Office [GPO], 1948). The excerpt from the Bureau of the Budget memorandum is from *U.S. at War*, op. cit., p. 250. Leon Henderson, during his brief tenure as OPA chief, was one of the most witten-about of contemporary Washington luminaries; see especially *New York Times Magazine*, 4/27/41; *Time*, 5/12/41; and *Reader's Digest*, 12/1942.

4. *The United States at War*, op. cit., chap. 7 and 14; John J. Corson, *Manpower For Victory* (Farrar and Rinehart, 1943); "A Short History of the War Manpower Commission" (mimeographed, U.S. Employment Service, 1948), on file in the library of the U.S. Dept. of Labor; Frances Perkins, *The Roosevelt I Knew* (Viking, 1946), chapter XXVII.

5. *The United States at War*. op. cit., chap. 8; Elmer Davis and Byron Price, *War Information and Censorship* (American Council and Public Affairs, 1943), a brief exposition of the function and aims of the authors' respective

agencies. Details of the personalities and issues involved in government information policy are woven throughout Bruce Catton's *War Lords of Washington,*
op. cit. The excerpt quoted on p. 96 is from an article by Walter Davenport in
Collier's magazine, 6/6/44. The quotation on p. 97 is from *The United States
at War,* p. 220, and those on pp. 102 and 103 from relevant issues of the *New
York Times.* The Library of Congress has a large selection of publications
and program outlines produced by OWI such as those mentioned on p. 103
and elsewhere in the text.

6. Figures on war production are drawn mainly from the concluding chapter
of *Industrial Mobilization for War, A History of the War Production Board
1940–1945* (GPO, 1947). Figures on income and savings are from *Statistical
Abstract of the U.S.—1950* (GPO).

Chapter 5—Enemies Within the Gates

Among the basic texts consulted in the preparation of this chapter were:
Annual Report of the Attorney General for the years 1942–1946 (U.S. Dept.
of Justice, Washington); *The Craft of Intelligence,* by Allen W. Dulles (Harper
& Row, 1963); *Central Intelligence and National Security,* by Harry Howe
Ransom (Harvard University Press, 1959); "Intelligence and Security Activities
of the Government," report to the President of the Bureau of the Budget, Aug.
20, 1945 (mimeograph copy in National Archives); *Soviet Espionage,* by David
J. Dallin (Yale University Press, 1955); *The Traitors,* by Alan Moorehead
(Scribners, 1952); *In Brief Authority,* By Francis Biddle (Doubleday, 1962);
The FBI Story, by Don Whitehead (Random House, 1956). Also contemporary
files of the *New York Times, Time* and *Newsweek* magazines and, for legislative developments, relevant volumes of *Editorial Research Reports* (Washington, D.C.).

From 1942 to 1944 the author served as a Press Information Officer for the
Department of Justice which gave him a slightly privileged vantage point from
which to observe many of the developments recorded in this chapter.

1. Amid all the turmoil and distractions of the early months of the war, the
press and the public—elsewhere than on the West Coast at least—gave little
attention to the mass evacuation of the Japanese in California or to the problems of enemy aliens in general. Contemporary comments on these developments are therefore relatively meager. Some documentary information is to
be had from the annual reports of the Attorney General, cited above, and related material in the DOJ Library. Two official, but uncommonly vivid and
detailed, reports on the movement of the Japanese population on the West
Coast are, *Impounded People: Japanese-Americans in the Relocation Centers,*
and *Wartime Handling of Evacuee Property,* both published in 1946 (for the
War Relocation Authority) by the U.S. Department of the Interior, Washington.
The Eisenhower quote is from *Impounded People,* op cit., at p. 35. The quote
by Attorney General Biddle is from *In Brief Authority,* op. cit., at p. 226.
The quote by Gov. Warren and that by Gen. DeWitt are from pp. 105 and
108, respectively, of *Warren: The Man, The Court, The Era,* by John D.
Weaver (Little, Brown, 1967). The long excerpt on p. 111 is from *Wartime*

Handling of Evacuee Property, op. cit., at p. 38. The excerpt on pp. 112–3 is from *Impounded People,* op. cit., at p. 98.

2. Unlike the enemy aliens, the seditionists—real and putative—were a conspicuous feature of the landscape particularly during the period immediately preceding our entry into the war. For this reason, plus the fact that legal proceedings against them did not get seriously under way until 1944, there was extensive coverage of their activities in the daily and periodical press from which much of this account is derived. The propaganda materials of the more important groups are on file in the Library of Congress, and the indictments and court records are available for public inspection. Biddle devotes a rueful chapter in his book to the subject, and O. John Rogge, the government prosecutor in the case, published many years later, *The Official German Report: Nazi Penetration 1924–1942* (Youselof, 1961), which purports to be a confirmation of the charges in the case based on captured German documents.

3. This account of Nazi espionage activity (Sebold et. al.) is based principally on extensive summaries supplied the author by the Federal Bureau of Investigation and on relevant chapters in the books by Biddle and Whitehead, cited above. The story of the Nazi saboteurs ("Operation Pastorious") is drawn from a special report by the Attorney General dated Nov. 7, 1945, and from *They Came to Kill* by Eugene Rachlis (Random, 1961), a dramatic and painstaking reconstruction of this bizarre episode.

4. Many details of wartime atomic espionage came out during the trials of Fuchs and the Rosenbergs. A more documented account is contained in the Moorehead and Dallin volumes, cited above, and in *Soviet Atomic Espionage,* a report by the Joint Committee on Atomic Energy, U.S. Congress (Government Printing Office 1951).

Chapter 6—Arsenal of Democracy

The program of industrial production during World War Two was an undertaking of such magnitude that, to the best of my knowledge, no succinct and coherent history of it has ever been produced in usable form for the nonexpert. In the preparation of this chapter I have delved to varying depths (and with variable results) into more than 50 books, official reports, and contemporary newspaper and magazine accounts, of which the following have been the most useful:

Donald M. Nelson, *Arsenal of Democracy* (Harcourt Brace, 1946), the personal memoir of the man who was director of the program for nearly all of the war years; Bruce Catton, *War Lords of Washington* (Harcourt, Brace, 1948); *The United States at War,* op. cit; *Industrial Mobilization for War— History of the WPB and Predecessor Agencies,* Civilian Production Administration (GPO, 1947, and reprinted by Greenwood Press, 1969), hereafter referred to as *Ind. Mob.; Wartime Production Achievements and the Reconversion Outlook,* Report of the Chairman, WPB, Julius Krug (GPO, 1945), hereafter referred to as *Krug Report;* several vols. as noted later from *The United States Army in World War II,* Office of the Chief of Military History, Department of the Army (GPO, various years), hereafter referred to as *Army Historical* coupled with the title of the appropriate volume; *Men and Planes,* vol. VI of

The Army Air Force in World War II, USAF Historical Division (University of Chicago Press, 1955), hereafter referred to as *USAF Historical* coupled with the appropriate title; various reports of "The Special Committee Investigating the National Defense Program," U.S. Senate, 77th and 78th Congresses (GPO, 1943–1945), hereafter referred to as *Truman Committee;* various printed and typescript documents from "Historical Reports of the War Production Board" deposited in the National Archives, Washington, hereinafter referred to as *Archives,* coupled with appropriate designation of the document.

1. The quote by General Marshall is from "Annual Report of the Secretary of War, 1941" (GPO), p. 48. The production data is from *Krug Report,* pp. 1–10 and 106–110, and from *Army Historical—Planning Munitions for War,* pp. 6–12.

2. Nelson, chaps. 5–9; Catton, chaps. 2, 3, and 6; *The United States at War,* chaps. 3–4; contemporary accounts from files of the *Times.*

3. This profile of Nelson is based principally on articles about him in the *New York Times Magazine,* 2/22/42, and in the *New Yorker,* 3/28/42. Catton, who worked closely with Nelson at WPB, provides many illuminating insights into his character, and a quite candid appraisal of him as an administrator is contained in *Ind. Mob.,* pp. 208–211.

4. The description of WPB organization and operations, which was constantly shifting, is drawn in bits and pieces principally from *Ind. Mob., The United States at War,* Nelson, and Catton. Details of the Eberstadt incident come from contemporary press accounts and from Nelson and Catton. The conversation quoted on p. 150 is from Catton, p. 206, and that on p. 151 from Nelson, p. 389. The statement by the Truman Committee is found in *Truman Committee* Report No. 10, Part 4, p. 3.

5. The rubber program is treated at several places in *Ind Mob.;* in *Krug Report,* pp. 90–95; in Nelson, chap. 15. An extended summary is provided in Archives, "Brief Survey No. 11," from which the Baruch quote is taken. The Truman Committee held a number of hearings on the subject and the most relevant of these are contained in its "Second Annual Report," issued 5/26/42, pp. 22–78. The "rubber mess" was abundantly covered in the daily and periodical press during 1941–1943.

6. The aircraft program and the conversion of the automobile industry to large-scale aircraft production are chronicled with limited detail in *Archives,* "Brief Survey No. 1" (aircraft, typescript), and "Brief Survey No. 2" (automotive, typescript); also in *USAF Historical, Men and Planes,* chaps. 6–10; Nelson, chaps. 3 and 11; *Truman Committee,* "Third Annual Report," Part 10, pp. 347–372, and Part 16, pp. 97–111. The quotation on p. 158 is from Nelson, p. 212, and the examples of industry cooperation are culled from an article by Frank J. Taylor in the *Saturday Evening Post,* 11/22/42. There was an intense popular fascination with airplanes throughout the war years that is reflected abundantly in the newspapers and magazines of the period.

7. The story of the A-bomb has been told by many writers and participants in its development. I have relied here chiefly on William L. Laurence, *Men and Atoms* (Simon and Schuster, 1959) and *Dawn Over Zero* (Knopf, 1947), for reasons explained in the footnote on p. 165. Details concerning the letter from Professor Einstein to President Roosevelt are from an article by Ralph E.

Lapp in the *New York Times Magazine,* 8/2/64. Wider pictures of wartime scientific development, particularly as related to the OSRD, are contained in Vannevar Bush, *Modern Arms and Free Men* (Simon and Schuster, 1949), and James Phinney Baxter 3d, *Scientists Against Time* (Little, Brown, 1946).

8. Figures on corporate profits are from *Statistical Abstracts of the United States—1950* (GPO), p. 329; on recoveries through contract renegotiation from *Army Historical, The Army and Economic Mobilization,* p. 69. A summary of the operations of the Department of Justice War Frauds Unit is contained in the "Annual Report of the Attorney General," 1946. Data on strikes are from "Handbook of Labor Statistics—1967" (U.S. Dept. of Labor), p. 301. Overall production statistics are from *Ind. Mob.,* p. 962.

CHAPTER 7—WAR ON THE HOME FRONT

This chapter is a melange of things remembered and things read. The year 1943 was chosen for the sample because it represented a sort of plateau in the noncombatant's wartime experience. The initial shock of being at war had diminished but the promise of victory was far off, and the people had settled into coping with a state of emergency as an inevitable way of life. But there was little that was routine about "the war on the homefront." It was full of challenges, riddles, contradictions, endless aggravations, and even some suffering. These facets of wartime living can be abundantly recreated by thumbing through the newspapers and popular magazines of the period, and for purposes of short-range perspective, the relevant yearbooks of the *Americana* and *Britannica* encyclopedias, *The World Almanac,* etc. Two excellent books contributing to the overall picture are *The Big Change,* by Frederick Lewis Allen (Harper & Row, 1952), and *While You Were Gone,* a symposium edited by Jack Goodman (Simon and Schuster, 1946).

1. The quote from Dr. Poling is from the *New York Times,* 7/5/43.

2. The ration guide is from the *Times* of 6/6/43.

3. The data on juvenile delinquency is from the FBI's "Uniform Crime Reports" for 1943. The quote from *Time* magazine on vacations is from the issue of 7/15/43. Lewis Nichol's observations on the theater are from the *Times* of 12/26/43.

4. The only available source of official information on the OCD is from "Inventory of Records of Office of Civilian Defense," on file in the National Archives, Washington, D.C.

CHAPTER 8—THE GRAND DESIGN

An exhaustive and authoritative account of the formation of the UN, including the full text of most of the relevant documents, is contained in Ruth B. Russell et al., *A History of the United Nations Charter* (Brookings Institution, 1958). I have drawn heavily on this excellent work throughout this chapter. For informed commentary and eyewitness accounts of many of the incidents covered here I have relied principally on the following: Winston S. Churchill, *The Grand Alliance* and *Closing the Ring* (Houghton Mifflin, 1951); Robert E. Sherwood, *Roosevelt and Hopkins* (Harper & Row, 1948); Sumner Welles,

Where Are We Heading? and *The Time for Decision* (Harper & Row, 1946); Samuel I. Rosenman, *Working With Roosevelt* (Harper & Row, 1952); and Edward R. Stettinius, Jr., *Roosevelt and the Russians: The Yalta Conference* (Doubleday, 1949). Other works that have proved useful either for background or historical narrative include James MacGregor Burns, *Roosevelt: The Soldier of Freedom* (Harcourt Brace Jovanovich, 1970); Allan Nevins, *The New Deal and World Affairs* (Yale University Press, 1950); Richard C. Snyder and Edgar S. Furniss, Jr., *American Foreign Policy* (Holt Rinehart, 1954); and Walter Lippmann, *U.S. Foreign Policy: Shield of the Republic* (Little, Brown, 1943). Contemporary files of the *New York Times* were invaluable in setting the context and the popular reaction to the events here recorded at the time they occurred. Where these works are cited below they are indicated by the name of the author.

1. The framing of the Atlantic Charter is covered in documentary fashion in Russell, chaps. 1 and 2, and in more intimate detail in Churchill, vol. 3, Book Two, chap. 4; in Sherwood, chapter XX; and in Burns, pp. 125–131. The Churchill quote on p. 202 is from his vol. 3, p. 432. The full text of the Atlantic Charter, which I have paraphrased, is contained in Russell, p. 975. Justice Frankfurter's letter is from Max Freedman, *Roosevelt and Frankfurter: Their Correspondence* (Little, Brown, 1967), p. 612. The bedroom confrontation between Churchill and Roosevelt is drawn from Sherwood, p. 442. Churchill alludes to this amusing incident (vol. 3, p. 442) in somewhat less colorful fashion. Text of the UN Declaration is from Russell, p. 976.

2. Developments leading up to the Cairo-Tehran conference, and details of the conferences themselves, are covered in Russell, chaps. 6 and 7; Churchill, vol. 5, Book Two, chaps. 1–6; Sherwood, chaps. XXIX and XXX; Cordell Hull, *Memoirs* (Macmillan, 1948), vol. 2, chap. 93; Rosenman, chap. XIX, and Burns, chap. XIII. The Churchill quote on p. 216 is from his vol. 5, p. 387.

3. Procedural and documentary aspects of the Dumbarton Oaks conference are treated in great detail in Russell, chaps. 17–20. Full text of the Dumbarton Oaks Proposal, here summarized, is in Russell, p. 1019. Contemporary files of the *New York Times* and some other leading periodicals contain a wealth of informed speculation and commentary on the proceedings.

4. The Yalta Conference, because of its long-range diplomatic and political implications, produced an extensive literature, much of it retrospective and critical. The principal sources consulted here have been Russell, chaps. 20 and 21; Churchill, vol. 6, Book Two, chaps. 1–4; Sherwood, chap. XXXIII; Stettinius, chaps. 1–14; Burns, pp. 654–580; Rosenman, chap. XXVII; and James Byrnes, *Speaking Frankly* (Harper & Row, 1947), chaps. 1 and 2. The Churchill outburst cited is from Byrnes, p. x (preface). The Roosevelt quote on p. 226 is from Burns, p. 580. The summary of agreements reached at Yalta is a synthesis derived from various sources cited above. A more detailed discussion of these points is contained in Russell, pp. 526–544, and in Stettinius, chap. 15.

5. The proceedings of the San Francisco conference are treated in minute detail in Russell, chaps. 25–35. Some of the sidelights included here are from Cabell Phillips, *The Truman Presidency* (Macmillan, 1966), chap. 4, and from the voluminous on-the-scene reporting in contemporary issues of the *Times*.

Notes

CHAPTER 9—YEAR OF CLIMAX–1945

Substantial portions of this chapter are derived from my earlier book, *The Truman Presidency* (Macmillan, 1966). Source references, which included material from the Truman Memorial Library, are given there in great detail but are repeated here only as they bear special relevance to the current text. As with other chapters in this book, extensive use had been made of contemporary press reports, especially those of the *New York Times*. It should be added, perhaps, that the author was an on-the-scene observer to many of the events recorded here as a member of the Washington press corps.

1. This summary of the closing year of the war is based on contemporary news reports with documentation from *American Military History: World War II* (Office of the Army Historian, Washington).

2. The strategies and exertions by which Harry S. Truman was chosen for the Vice-Presidential nomination at the Democratic National Convention of 1944, as well as details of the election campaign itself, are exhaustively covered in Phillips, op. cit., ch. 2, from which the present account is adapted. The quote by Jonathan Daniels on p. 236 is from Daniels, *The Man of Independence* (Lippincott, 1950), p. 234. Roosevelt's demeaning comment on Dewey's parentage is from William D. Hassett, *Off the Record With FDR* (Rutgers University Press), p. 294.

3. This account of Roosevelt's final weeks and death is derived from many sources including principally Hassett, op cit.; Robert E. Sherwood, *Roosevelt and Hopkins* (Harper & Row, 1946); Samuel I. Rosenman, *Working With Roosevelt* (Harper & Row, 1952); Grace Tully, *FDR My Boss* (Scribners, 1949), and James MacGregor Burns, *Roosevelt: The Soldier of Freedom* (Harcourt Brace Jovanovich, 1970). Permission to reprint portions of Dr. Bruenn's clinical report on President Roosevelt's terminal illness was granted by Edward J. Huth, M.D., Editor, "Annals of Internal Medicine," Philadelphia. The comment by Mrs. Henry Wallace on FDR's appearance is from Frances Perkins, *The Roosevelt I Knew* (Viking, 1946). The quote by Judge Rosenman on p. 243 is from Rosenman, op. cit., p. 517. David Lilienthal's dismay over Truman's accession is from Vol. 1, p. 690, of his *Journals* (Harper & Row, 1964). (For the benefit of latecomers, the "Throttlebottom" here alluded to is the inept, stumbling character of the Vice President in an hilarious Broadway musical of the period, "Of Thee I Sing.") The excerpt from Arthur Godfrey's broadcast of the funeral procession in Washington is lifted from the phonograph album, "I Can Hear It Now" (Columbia, MM800). The account of the funeral services at Hyde Park appeared under this writer's by-line in the Chicago *Herald-Examiner,* which he then served as Washington correspondent.

4. This profile of President Truman is based principally on Chap. 2 of Phillips, op. cit., the chief sources for which included *Memoirs* by Harry S. Truman, Vol. 1 (Doubleday, 1955); Daniels, op. cit., and *Tom's Town: Kansas City and the Pendergast Legend* by William M. Reddig (Lippincott, 1947). Truman's relationship to the Pendergast organization as described is from Reddig, op. cit., p. 265. The Truman quote on vote stealing is from Daniels, op. cit., p. 152, and Daniel's quote on Truman's humility is from the same

source, p. 177. The text of Truman's letter home is from *Memoirs,* op cit., vol. 1, p. 6, and the account of his visit to the White House is from the same source, p. 5.

5. The concluding days of the war in Europe are reconstructed from contemporary press reports and from *U.S. Military History,* op. cit. The bombing of Hiroshima and the conclusion of the war in the Pacific are based principally on *Japan Subdued* by Herbert Feis (Princeton University Press, 1961); *Dawn Over Zero* by William L. Laurence (Knopf, 1947); *On Active Service in War and Peace* by Henry L. Stimson (Harper & Row, 1948), and on Phillips, op. cit., chapter 3. The eyewitness reports on the bombing of Hiroshima are from *Now It Can Be Told: The Story of the Manhattan Project* by Maj. Gen. Leslie R. Groves (Harper, 1962), pp. 322–3, and from *Hiroshima* by John Hersey (Knopf, 1946), pp. 19–21. The quote from the report of the Interim Committee is from Stimson, op. cit., p. 617, and that by President Truman is from *Memoirs,* op. cit., vol. 1, p. 419.

CHAPTER 10—THE DILEMMAS OF PEACE

The material in this chapter is drawn mainly from two principal sources, contemporary editions of the *New York Times* and the original research files for an earlier book by the author, *The Truman Presidency* (Macmillan, 1966). Chapters 4, 5, 7, and 10 from that work are particularly relevant to this chapter on "The Dilemmas of Peace." The research covered not only standard reference works but included a number of personal interviews with and access to oral history recordings by a number of former officials of the Truman adminstration. The source notes in the earlier work are quite extensive but they will not be duplicated here except as individual entries happen to be particularly pertinent to some portion of this chapter. Where sources additional to the foregoing have been consulted they are appropriately identified below.

1. The statistical material on p. 275 is from *Statistical Abstract of the United States: 1958* (GPO). The Snyder memorandum mentioned is a mimeographed document titled "From War to Peace" on file at the Truman Memorial Library, Independence, Mo.

2. Further details on labor strife during this period are in *Truman Presidency* (op. cit.), pp. 111–127, and Harry S. Truman, *Memoirs* (Doubleday, 1955), vol. 1, chap. 32.

3. This section on legislative development is reconstructed almost entirely from contemporary press accounts. However, see *The Journals of David E. Lilienthal,* vol. 2 (Harper & Row, 1964), under relevant date headings, for more on his participation in the creation of the AEC, and especially his reaction to the Senate confirmation hearings. The partial text of his "profession of faith" is from the *Washington Post,* 2/5/47, p. 1.

4. A great deal has been written on the genesis and the nature of the cold war of which only a brief resume is included here. The principal sources from which this is derived include *The Truman Presidency* (op. cit.), chaps. 4 and 10; John Lukacs, *A History of the Cold War* (Doubleday, 1961); William Reitzel et al., *United States Foreign Policy: 1945–1955* (Brookings In-

stitution, 1956), various chaps. in Parts One and Two; Dean G. Acheson, *Present at the Creation* (Norton, 1969), especially chap. 22. It is particularly rewarding in this connection to read chaps. 8 and 10 (Book Two) of the concluding volume of Winston Churchill's great memoir, *Triumph and Tragedy* (Houghton Mifflin, 1953), and, for illuminating counterpoint, Nikita Khrushchev's memoir (ed. by Edward Crankshaw), *Khrushchev Remembers* (Little, Brown, 1970), pp. 219–226.

5. This discussion of major foreign policy developments from 1946 to 1949 is based largely on chaps. 7 and 10 of *The Truman Presidency* (op. cit.), with special indebtedness to Joseph M. Jones, *Fifteen Weeks* (Viking, 1955), for inception of the Greek-Turkish aid program; to *Present at the Creation* (op. cit.), for inception of the Marshall Plan, and to vol. 2 of the Truman *Memoirs* for general discussion of these and related subjects. The full text of the Kennan statement excerpted on p. 306 will be found in *Foreign Affairs* for July 1947, under the title, "The Sources of Soviet Conduct."

6. One of the best studies of this disastrous episode is the work of historian Herbert Feis, *The China Tangle* (Princeton University Press, 1953). A detailed chronology of the event is contained in *China White Paper* (State Dept. publication no. 3573, 1949), the factual accuracy of which is generally recognized although its conclusions in some instances are self-serving. *Present at the Creation* (op. cit.) contains much information of value from the privileged viewpoint of Mr. Acheson, who was Under-Secretary and later Secretary of State. The quotation from General Barr is from *Military Situation in the Far East,* Joint Committee on Armed Services and Foreign Relations (U.S. Senate, 82nd Congress, 1951, p. 1856). The intense political agitation over the course of events in China is heavily documented in the daily and periodical press of the period.

CHAPTER 11—THE GREAT UPSET–1948

1. This account of the 1948 election is adapted in large part from chaps. 8 and 9 of the author's *The Truman Presidency* (Macmillan, 1966). As indicated therein, the principal sources were his own experiences as a reporter covering that campaign; contemporary files of the *New York Times* and other newspapers and periodicals; and extensive interviews with other newsmen and with various officials of the Truman and Dewey campaign organizations. Among published sources consulted at that time were *Inside the Democratic Party,* by Jack Redding (Bobbs-Merrill, 1958); *Out of The Jaws of Victory,* by Jules Abels (Holt Rinehart, 1959); *Henry A. Wallace: Quixotic Crusade, 1948,* by Karl M. Schmidt (Syracuse University Press, 1960); *Southern Politics,* by V. O. Key, Jr. (Knopf, 1950); and *The Voter Decides,* by the Survey Research Center (University of Michigan Press, 1954). Subsequently, I have had recourse to such recently published works as *The Loneliest Campaign,* by Irwin Ross (New American Library, 1968), and *Harry S. Truman,* by Margaret Truman (Morrow, 1973). The little tableau in Chairman McGrath's office on election eve is from Redding, op. cit., p. 290.

Chapter 12—Fair Deal—and Foul

1. The author as a Washington reporter was a witness to most of the events and developments recorded in this chapter. His recollections have been reinforced and documented by extensive reference to contemporary issues of the *New York Times* and other periodicals, to *Congressional Quarterly* and the *Congressional Record*. In the section on civil rights beginning on p. 349, much use was made of *Freedom to the Free*, a report by the U.S. Commission on Civil Rights (GPO, 1963).

2. This account of the "Battle of the Pentagon" has been woven from the voluminous reports in the *Times* and elsewhere, and from Harry S. Truman, *Memoirs* (Doubleday, 1956), chap. 4, vol. II.

3. Portions of this account of the national concern over communism and the federal loyalty program are adapted from the author's *The Truman Presidency*, chap. 13. This was based on original research and personal interviews and on such published sources as *The Federal Loyalty Security Program* by Eleanor Bontecou (Cornell University Press, 1953); *The Fear of Freedom* by former Attorney General Francis Biddle (Doubleday, 1952); *Communist Espionage in the U.S. Government*, Hearings of the House Un-American Activities Committee, 80th Congress (GPO, 1948), and *The Loyalty of Free Men* by Alan Barth (Viking, 1951). Much of the background on HUAC is drawn from *The Dies Committee: A Study of the Special House Committee for the Investigation of Un-American Activities, 1938–44*, by August Raymond Ogden (Catholic University Press, Washington, 1945). The colloquy between Dorothy Bailey and members of the Loyalty Review Board is from Barth, op. cit., p. 111.

4. In addition to sources cited above substantial use was made of *Witness*, by Whittaker Chambers (Random House, 1952); *In The Court of Public Opinion*, by Alger Hiss (Knopf, 1957), and *The Strange Case of Alger Hiss*, by Earl Jowitt (Doubleday, 1953).

Chapter 13—Epilogue: Never the Same Again

1. The mid-point of a century is a great occasion for literary reflection and prophecy, and this was notably true of the years around 1950. Out of the profusion of books of this genre in the libraries, I have found the following to be most useful: *The Big Change*, by Frederick Lewis Allen (Harper & Row, 1952); *U.S.A.: The Permanent Revolution*, by The Editors of *Fortune* Magazine (Prentice-Hall, 1951); *The Great Leap: The Past Twenty-five Years in America*, by John Brooks (Harper & Row, 1966); *The End of the American Era*, by Andrew Hacker (Atheneum, 1970); *American Society Since 1945*, edited by William L. O'Neill (Quadrangle, 1969); *Social Profile: U.S.A. Today*, extracts from the *New York Times*, edited by Amitai Etzioni (Van Nostrand Reinhold, 1970); *Encyclopedia Britannica*, Year Books for 1949, 1950, 1951. The statistical data used throughout this chapter is from *Statistical Abstract of the United States*, volumes for 1950, 1958, 1971; U.S. Department of Commerce (Government Printing Office).

Notes

The quotation on p. 381 is from *U.S.A.: The Permanent Revolution,* op. cit., pp. 185–6. The quotation on p. 382 is from *The Affluent Society,* by John Kenneth Galbraith (Houghton Mifflin, 1958), p. 2. The quotation on p. 382 is from Hacker, op. cit., p. 9.

Index